MARIOLOGY

Contributors

EAMON R. CARROLL, O.CARM., S.T.D.

ERIC MAY, O.F.M.CAP., S.T.D., S.S.L.

MICHAEL J. GRUENTHANER, S.J.

WALTER J. BURGHARDT, S.J.

ALFRED C. RUSH, C.SS.R., S.T.D.

VERY REV. CUTHBERT GUMBINGER, O.F.M.CAP., S.T.D.

SIMEON DALY, O.S.B.

GEORGE W. SHEA, S.T.D.

AIDAN CARR, O.F.M.CONV., S.T.D.

GERMAIN WILLIAMS, O.F.M.CONV., S.T.D.

SALVATORE BONANO, C.M.F.

RICHARD KUGELMAN, C.P., S.T.L., S.S.L.

Mariology

VOLUME 1

Edited by
Juniper B. Carol, O.F.M.

MEDIATRIX PRESS
MMXVIII

NIHIL OBSTAT:
John M. A. Fearns, S.T.D. Censor librorum

IMPRIMATUR:
✠ Francis Cardinal Spellman Archbishop of New York
July 21, 1954

ISBN: 978-1-953746-22-1

©Mediatrix Press, 2018

To His Excellency
THE MOST REVEREND JOHN J. WRIGHT, D.D.
Bishop of Worcester
Episcopal Chairman of
The Mariological Society of America
Outstanding Promoter of Marian Studies
This Mariology Set Is Dedicated
With Sentiments of Profound Gratitude

THE Marian Year proclaimed by Pope Pius XII has seen widespread and intense increase of devotion to the Blessed Mother of Christ. Programs at home and pilgrimages abroad have focused the attention of millions on the resplendent figure of her who is our life, our sweetness, and our hope in a sense which every Catholic Christian understands.

The deepening and development of our understanding of the dogmas respecting the Blessed Mother must necessarily be a principal accomplishment of the Marian Year if its fruits are to endure and its purpose is to be achieved. Catholic devotion does not spring from poetry, but from that love which is born of knowledge. *Nil amatum nisi prius cognitum* applies also to the objects of our piety and religious cult. Neither is devotion nourished, substantially at least, by sentiment or emotion; it is made strong by theological science and by the strict truth which the scholar unfolds for the admiration and the profit of even the saints, those actual and those to be.

That is why we may properly hail the publication of the present collection as a major event of the Marian Year, a praiseworthy and enduring contribution to the observance of the hundredth anniversary of the first of the solemn pronouncements of the Church concerning Mary in these modern times which seem destined to be dedicated in a special way to her.

The credit for this work, its conception and execution, belongs in more than usual degree with the editor, Father Juniper Carol. Father Juniper brings unique qualifications of spirit and skill to a work of editing so ambitious. By ancestry he is heir to the blood of Spain and therefore lightens his labor with that ardent love for the Queen of Heaven which has warmed the songs of Spain and fired the speculations of her great theologians. By spiritual genealogy he is a son of the Franciscan family, a kinsman of those friars who, in every age and land, have preached love of Mary together with love for her Son. Out of the blend of these temperamental and spiritual influences there has come the predilection for reflection on and study of the mysteries surrounding Mary which has dominated his priestly work.

It is, however, on the scholarly and scientific side that Father Juniper pre-eminently qualifies for the work of research and orderly presentation reflected in this ponderous work. First president of the Mariological Society of America, he has long and energetically sought to rear solid dogmatic bastions for the growing devotion to Mary. A specialist in the extensive bibliography and current development of Mariology, he makes available to other scholars by lecture and by writing the results of his own painstaking and patient studies as he now furnishes them with the collection of the work of many. His theological training featured Mariological branches and his citation in 1952 for the Award of the Mariological Society was universally approved and applauded.

It is, then, with grateful admiration for the editor and for all who have had a part in the work he has compiled and organized that I accept the honor of presenting this Mariological anthology. May it give scholars outside the household of the faith some idea of the learning behind our love for Mary and add to Our Lady's convinced clients new reasons for the faith that is in us!

✠ John Wright
Episcopal Chairman
The Mariological Society of America

THE present Mariology traces its origin to a series of informal conversations held between the Editor and several Marian scholars in the Eternal City as early as the year 1938. One of the topics of these discussions was briefly this: the definite need of a comprehensive symposium, in the vernacular, covering the entire theological tract relative to Our Blessed Lady. As a result of these preliminary deliberations, the Editor undertook to elaborate a suitable program to meet this deficiency as far as the English-speaking public was concerned. While the global conflagration which followed in 1939 virtually shattered any hopes of immediate action in this respect, nevertheless the original idea continued its process of development during the war years until it reached the desired maturity. The establishment of the Mariological Society of America in 1949 may be credited with having contributed considerably toward carrying the original plans into effect. By stimulating interest in Mariology and, at the same time, co-ordinating the efforts and talents of its members, this national organization soon furnished the most important element in an undertaking such as this, namely, willing and able contributors. Finally, the approaching one hundredth anniversary of the dogmatic definition of Our Lady's Immaculate Conception seemed to the Editor a most propitious opportunity to launch the publication of at least the first volume of the contemplated trilogy and thus pay a humble tribute to Our Blessed Lady as patroness of these United States.

That there is at present a growing demand for a work of this nature, has been evidenced in recent years by the enthusiastic reception accorded in other lands to similar projects, such as the *Katholische Marienkunde*, edited by Paul Sträter, S.J.;[1] *Maria. Études sur la Sainte Vierge*, edited by H. du Manoir, S.J.;[2] and *La Madonna*

---

[1] A set in three volumes published in 1947-1951 by F. Schöningh, Paderborn, Germany.

[2] Two volumes published by Beauchesne, Paris, in 1949 and 1952, respectively. A third volume is now in preparation.

secondo la fede e la teologia, written by G. M. Roschini, O.S.M.[3] English-speaking Catholics should be—actually are—just as eager to broaden their knowledge concerning the Mother of God as their brethren in continental Europe. Hence we feel that they, too, will welcome the publication of a work containing up-to-date, solid, and authoritative information on the entire field of Marian theology and cult.

The theological tract known as "Mariology" is vast and complex indeed, as the reader will gather from a mere perusal of this symposium. The rich Marian patrimony bequeathed to us as part of the faith of our fathers, and integrated by not a few biblical texts and countless patristic, papal, and liturgical documents, constitutes a varied and almost inexhaustible fund of knowledge. The patient culling of the Mariological data scattered throughout these "sources" is the task undertaken in the first volume of the present set. It is here that both the research-loving scholar and the devout client of Mary will discover abundant, and perhaps even unsuspected, material for study and meditation. Once this necessary foundation has been laid, the systematic treatment of Our Lady's singular prerogatives will be attempted in a forthcoming volume. And since an adequate appraisal of Mary's position in the scheme of salvation has ever prompted her children to express outwardly their inner sentiments of gratitude and dependence, our project would be incomplete if it failed to gather in a third volume the multiple manifestations of Marian cult and devotion as found in the various spheres of Catholic life. Against the rich background furnished by this vast panorama, the alluring figure of Our Heavenly Mother will stand in all its splendor and beauty, giving us an idea, however faint, of the exalted mission assigned to her by the Almighty.

So much concerning the appropriateness of this publication and its contents in general. As to the contributors selected for the various papers, the Editor feels that they need no special introduction. Most of them are seasoned writers in the various

---

[3] Three volumes so far, published this year (1953) by the *Libreria Editrice F. Ferrari*, Rome, Italy. A fourth volume has been announced for the near future. This is by far the best, most complete, and most up-to-date set of systematic Mariology written by a single author.

branches of the sacred sciences and all have shown sufficient familiarity with contemporary Mariological problems and with the solutions to meet these problems. The criteria adhered to in the preparation of their papers have been determined with a view to reaching the widest possible circle of readers. For this reason, while the contributions are written according to accepted standards of scientific methodology, their style of presentation is never abstruse or excessively technical.

The symposium, then, is offered, first of all, to the members of the Catholic clergy, who will find in it not only a refreshing and stimulating review of their previous theological studies, but likewise a clear and accurate exposé of more recent currents of thought in the field of Mariology. Second, to the lay members of religious orders and congregations, to our seminarians, and to the large group among our Catholic laity, always eager to broaden and deepen their knowledge of Marian doctrines. Finally, to non-Catholic groups earnestly seeking the justification for our teaching relative to Our Blessed Lady. It should prove rather revealing to them, especially when brought into comparison with the offensive caricatures of Marian doctrines drawn at times by some of their less enlightened coreligionists. It should serve as a timely antidote against the recriminations of such pseudo critics as Dr. Karl Barth who contends that Catholic Mariology is, in fact, "a pathological conception of theological thought," a cancerous growth which ought to be immediately excised.[4] May we note, with a feeling of relief, that not all our separated brethren share the distorted views of this misguided theologian. Indeed, it is consoling to observe in this connection that among contemporary Protestant scholars there are not a few engaged in an honest and sincere endeavor to re-evaluate their former position and reconstruct a "non-Roman" Mariology on a more orthodox basis. Witness, for example, the commendable work of Dr. Hans Asmussen in Germany,[5] the

---

[4] K. Barth, *Die kirkliche Dogmatik*, I, 2, Zollikon, 1939, pp. 151-160. Reference taken from Hugo Rahner, S.J., *Die Marienkunde in der lateinischen Patristik, in Katholische Marienkunde* (ed. P. Sträter, S.J.), Vol. 1, Paderborn, 1947, p. 138.

[5] *Maria, die Mutter Gottes*, published by Evangelisches Verlagswerk, Stuttgart, Germany, 1950.

Dialogue sur la Vierge, compiled by Paul Couturier in France,[6] and the symposium *The Mother of God*, edited by E. L. Mascall in England.[7] While the net result gathered from these essays of rapprochement is not as yet totally satisfactory, nevertheless, the very effort which inspired them represents a significant step in the right direction and hence deserving of our praise. May the pages that follow be of some help to these and many other sincere non-Catholics in their search for the fullness of God's revelation concerning His Immaculate Mother.

On the appearance of this first volume the Editor takes occasion to express his heartfelt gratitude to all who have in any way assisted him in this difficult enterprise. He is particularly thankful to His Excellency, the Most Reverend John J. Wright, Bishop of Worcester, for having enhanced the prestige of this publication by writing its preface; to the various contributors for their erudite and highly informative dissertations; and to the publishers for their valuable co-operation and many courtesies.

Rev. Dr. J. B. Carol, O.F.M.
Editor
New York
December 8, 1953

---

[6] Published by E. Vitte, Paris, 1951.

[7] Published by Dacre Press, Westminster, England, 1949.

It has been over 70 years since the initial publication of *Mariology*, and yet it remains perhaps the best and most exhaustive treatise of the subject in English, even in our own times.

The confusion following the close of the Second Vatican Council has given rise to many false teachings in regard to the Blessed Virgin which arise both among the clergy and among Catholic laity. In many places, these errors have arisen not so much on account of malice, but ignorance of the sources of Mariology in both the Church Fathers, and the Scholastics and Baroque theology. The republication of these volumes seems essential to provide an antidote, as it were, to the confusion that reigns at present on a number of points even among Catholics who might otherwise be described as faithful.

We wish to especially acknowledge the work of Ben Douglass, whose editing of the scan for retypesetting has proven invaluable to producing a text in conformity with the original in all points. Moreover, at his suggestion, we have integrated certain essays in the order which Fr. Carol originally intended but was prevented from due to time constraints.

We offer these volumes again to the English speaking public for the glory of Almighty God, and the Word Incarnate, Jesus Christ, Who took flesh from the Ark of the New Covenant, the incomparable Virgin Mary. May it be profitable to all Catholics to reconnect with the fruits of the whole tradition in praise of God's Virgin Mother.

Post Falls, ID
Winter, 2018

Mariology

MARY IN THE DOCUMENTS OF THE MAGISTERIUM

By EAMON R. CARROLL, O.Carm., S.T.D.

ALL these with one mind continued steadfastly in prayer with the women and Mary, the mother of Jesus, and with his brethren" (Acts 1:14). Our Lady's last appearance in the historical books of the New Testament shows her at the very heart of the apostolic band. "She it was," Pope Pius XII writes, "who through her powerful prayers obtained the grace that the Spirit of Our Divine Redeemer, already given to the Church on the Cross, should be bestowed through miraculous gifts on the newly founded Hierarchy on Pentecost."[1] Before Our Lord ascended into heaven He had promised, "The Advocate, the Holy Spirit, whom the Father will send in my name, he will teach you all things, and bring to your mind whatever I have said to you" (Jn. 14:26).

The prayerful preparation in the Cenacle for the coming of the Advocate was not the first time Our Lady had awaited His coming. The Holy Spirit had come upon her in the mystery of the Incarnation when the Son of God was made man in her virginal womb. She well knew the Spirit of truth; under His influence the Blessed Virgin's brilliant mind manifested itself in the *Magnificat*. The many mysteries she pondered in her heart were truths that she would confide to the Church's care.

The presence of Mary in the Gospels is a sign of Christ's presence—at the Crib, in Cana, on Calvay. Her presence before Pentecost was a sign that the Holy Spirit was at hand. Our Lady's presence through the history of the Church is still the guarantee that her divine Son is there. Nowhere is this better exemplified than in the history of Catholic doctrine. The body of Catholic truth is a unified whole. If the divine personality of Christ is attacked, then His Mother is no longer the Mother of God. If the full humanity of the God-Man is denied, the true and perfect motherhood of Mary is

---

[1] *Mystici Corporis*, in A.A.S., Vol. 35, 1943, pp. 247-248; English translation of the N.C.W.C., No. 107.

its defense. When Our Lady's God-given privileges are rejected and ridiculed, how sadly history shows that her Son soon fares no better.

A. The magisterium

Mary in the Documents of the magisterium is a gathering of the principal teachings of the Church about the Blessed Mother of God.[2] Christ was not only Priest and King, He was also the divine Teacher. He conferred all three powers on His Church. The term *magisterium* means the right and office of teaching truths revealed by God with that supreme authority to which all must assent. The word *magisterium* is used in two ways: first, for the power of teaching; second, for the persons themselves who possess the teaching authority.

In the present article, only what the *Papal magisterium* has taught about Mary will be examined; this will include the decisions of ecumenical councils, i.e., general assemblies to which all the bishops of the world are invited, with the Pope calling or at least approving the assembly.

Another necessary distinction is between *solemn magisterium* and *ordinary magisterium. Solemn magisterium* refers to definitions given by General Councils in union with the Pope, or also by the

---

[2] The principal sources used have been the following: H. Denzinger et C. Bannwart, *Enchiridion symbolorum, definitionum et declarationum de rebus fidei et morum*, ed. 27 augmentata a J. B. Umberg (Barcelona, 1951); Paul Palmer, S.J., *Mary in the Documents of the Church* (Westminster, Md., 1952), with grateful acknowledgment for many useful ideas and translations; G. Roschini, O.S.M., *Mariologia*, 2a ed. (Romae, 1947-1948), particularly Vol. 1, pp. 33-50 on the Marian Doctrine of the Roman Pontiffs; *idem, La Madonna nel pensiero e nell'insegnamento di Pio XI, in Marianum*, Vol. 1, 1939, pp. 121-172; D. Bertetto, S.D.B., *Maria nel domma cattolico* (Torino, 1950), pp. 261-323 on the popes of the past hundred years; J. Bittremieux, *Doctrina Mariana Leonis XIII* (Brugis, 1928); idem, *Ex doctrina Mariana Pii XI, in Ephemerides Theologicae Lovanienses*, Vol. 11, 1934, pp. 95-101. Besides the *Acta Apostolicae Sedis* (1909-   ), *Le Encicliche Mariane*, ed. A. Tondini (Roma, 1950) (from the time of Pius IX to the present) has been useful; it will be referred to as Tondini. G. Filograssi, S.I., *La dottrina Mariana dei Papi* (da Pio IX a Pio XII), in *La Civiltà Cattolica*, Vol. 103, 1952, iii, pp. 347-364, is a commentary on Tondini. The English translations have been taken from many sources, sometimes with slight adaptations. For Pope Leo XIII, the translations are usually from *The Rosary of Mary*, ed. by William R. Lawler, O.P. (Paterson, N. J., 1944), cited simply as Lawler.

Pope alone when he speaks *ex cathedra*. The Holy Father speaks *ex cathedra* (Latin for "from the chair," i.e., from St. Peter's Chair, as his successor) when as the supreme shepherd and teacher of all Christians he proposes by his supreme apostolic authority a doctrine of faith or morals to be believed by the universal Church.[3]

The *ordinary magisterium* includes the teaching of the Papal encyclicals, of the ordinary documents of the Congregations (*e.g.*, the Congregation of the Holy Office in Rome), and of the body of bishops. *Humani generis*, encyclical letter of August 12, 1950, thus explains the authority of the ordinary *magisterium*:

> Nor must it be thought that what is expounded in Encyclical Letters does not of itself demand consent, since in writing such Letters the Popes do not exercise the supreme power of their Teaching Authority. For these matters are taught with the ordinary teaching authority, of which it is true to say: "He who heareth you, heareth Me" (Lk. 10:16); and generally what is expounded and inculcated in Encyclical Letters already for other reasons appertains to Catholic doctrine. But if the Supreme Pontiffs in their official documents purposely pass judgment on a matter up to that time under dispute, it is obvious that that matter, according to the mind and will of the same Pontiffs, cannot be any longer considered a question open to discussion among theologians.[4]

If the Holy Father declares by the extraordinary exercise of his teaching authority that a certain doctrine is a revealed truth, as occurred, for example, in 1950 about the Assumption, the truth is technically known thereafter as a *dogma*, and the Pope's action recalled as a dogmatic definition. In such *ex cathedra* definitions he is infallible; the Holy Ghost protects him from error.

But even before any solemn definition, it may be clear from the ordinary *magisterium* that a doctrine is a truth revealed by God and

---

[3] *D.B.*, 1839. *On the magisterium*, see M. Cordovani, O.P., in the article "Chiesa", in *Enciclopedia Cattolica*, Vol. 3, cols. 1455-1456 (Città del Vaticano, 1950).

[4] *A.A.S.*, Vol. 42, 1950, p. 568; authorized Vatican translation. On the authority of the encyclicals, cf. J. C. Fenton, *The Religious Assent due to the Teachings of Papal Encyclicals*, in *The American Ecclesiastical Review*, Vol. 123, 1950, pp. 59-67; *The Doctrinal Authority of Papal Encyclicals*, ibid., Vol. 121, pp. 136-150, 210-220; *The Lesson of Humani Generis*, ibid., Vol. 123, 1950, pp. 359-378.

forming part of the Deposit of the Faith. Thus, the Assumption was already a matter of faith before the definition of November 1, 1950. But the Church's proposal of the doctrine, by dogmatic definition, puts it beyond doubt and discussion. According to *Munificentissimus Deus*:

> From the universal agreement of the Church's ordinary teaching authority we have a certain and firm proof, demonstrating that the Blessed Virgin Mary's bodily Assumption into heaven—which surely no faculty of the human mind could know by its own natural powers, as far as the heavenly glorification of the virginal body of the revered Mother of God is concerned—is a truth that has been revealed by God and consequently something that must be firmly and faithfully believed by all the children of the Church.[5]

The popes issue many kinds of documents: some are Apostolic Constitutions (*Munificentissimus Deus*, for example), some are encyclicals addressed to the universal Church, some are radio messages to particular places or to the whole world. Still others are letters to bishops and superiors of religious orders. Modern communications bring the Pope's words, even short addresses to small groups of pilgrims, to the whole world. Particular or local pronouncements frequently explain more general documents.

B. Deposit of the Faith

The phrase "Deposit of the Faith" (*depositum fidei*), or simply the Deposit, means public Revelation, intended by God for all men, complete and entire, such as it is contained in Holy Scripture and in divine and apostolic tradition. This Deposit of the Faith was closed with the death of the last Apostle, so that the whole content of truths revealed by God was entrusted to the Church before St. John died. Some of them were written in Scripture, many others were passed on by word of mouth to subsequent generations. The Church, called by St. Paul "the pillar and mainstay of the truth" (1 Tim. 3:15), is the custodian of the Deposit of the Faith. As custodian, it neither adds to nor alters the truths revealed once for all in the Deposit. "The Church," declares Pius XI, "never adds anything to

---

[5] *A.A.S.*, Vol. 42, 1950, p. 756; English of the N.C.W.C. translation by Fr. Fenton, No. 12. *D.B.*, 1792, says "sive solemni iudicio sive ordinario et universali magisterio."

the sum of truths which are contained at least implicitly in the revealed deposit which it has received from God."[6]

But the Church is a living dynamic thing, the Mystical Body of Christ. And so the unchanging conservation of the Deposit does not prevent a real progress in the understanding of the contents of the Deposit by individuals and by the whole Church. This progress is known as the development of doctrine. It is a gradual flowering under the guidance of the Holy Spirit, whereby doctrines that were but dimly perceived in early times are now seen as part of the harmonious pattern of revealed truth. As Newman describes it, "What the Church once had she never has lost. ... She has not changed possessions, but accumulated them." In the course of time, both the teaching and the taught Church discover, by prayer and study, a doctrine that has been there beneath the surface all along. In Newman's words: "Even centuries might pass without the formal expression of a truth which had been all along the secret life of millions of souls." At length the Church, infallible interpreter of Revelation, may judge a doctrine to be part of revealed truth, and by dogmatic definition or by the ordinary *magisterium* so declare it.[7]

In the Gospels Our Lord speaks of the householder who brings forth from his storeroom things old and new (Mt. 13:51-52). In like manner the Church is forever producing from its treasure of revealed wisdom truths old and new; the treasury is of inexhaustible

---

[6] A.A.S., Vol. 20, 1928, p. 14. Cf. Giacinto Ameri, O.F.M., *Deposito della Fede, in Enciclopedia Cattolica*, Vol. 4, cols. 1442-1443 (Città del Vaticano, 1950); C. Vagaggini, Dogma, ibid., cols. 1799-1804, on the evolution of dogma.

[7] On Cardinal Newman's Mariology, and his *Essay on the Development of Christian Doctrine*, 1845, which he began as an Anglican and finished as a Catholic, see Francis J. Friedel, S.M., *The Mariology of Cardinal Newman* (New York, 1928), especially pp. 50-87. Newman applied his principles on development in the famous Letter to Pusey, 1865, in defense of the Immaculate Conception. His own summary of his views on development with the comments of Fr. Perrone, S.J., are given in "The Newman-Perrone Paper on Development," ed. Rev. T. Lynch, in *Gregorianum*, Vol. 16, 1935, pp. 402-447. E. Druwé, S.J., uses Newman's theories in La Médiation Universelle de Marie, in Maria. *Études sur la Sainte Vierge*, ed. H. du Manoir, Vol. 1 (Paris, 1949), e.g., pp. 459, 477, 478, 496, 516. B. Capelle, O.S.B., finds the great Cardinal's ideas vindicated in the Assumption in Théologie de l'Assomption d'après la bulle "Munificentissimus Deus," in *Nouvelle revue théologique*, Vol. 72, 1950, pp. 1009-1027, esp. p. 1024 ff.

richness, a reflection of the substantial truth of the Divine Word.[8] There is no better example of this development than to survey the Church's teachings on the Virgin Mary from her divine motherhood to her coronation as Queen of heaven.

I. MOTHER OF GOD

A. Creeds

After the New Testament, no form of early Christian literature is more ancient than the primitive Creeds. By these early symbols catechumens committed to memory a brief summary of the principal doctrines of Christianity. The teaching Church, under the guidance of its bishops and Supreme Pastor, presented to the believing faithful a compendium of theology in the succinct form of a set of articles of belief. Although our present Apostles' Creed is not earlier than the sixth century, an ancient Roman Creed appears at the end of the second century, and in its essential content comes from the age of the Apostles. Hippolytus' *Apostolic Tradition*, c. 215, quotes this question from the Roman Rite of Baptism: "Dost thou believe in Christ Jesus, the Son of God, who was born by the Holy Spirit from the Virgin Mary ... ?"[9]

The Virgin Mary's true motherhood of the Son of God is set forth as the Church's teaching in these first formulas of faith. Our Lady appears in the first pages of the Gospel as the Mother of Jesus; with the same right and clarity her maternal office is mentioned in the earliest Creeds of the Church. The first symbol listed in the *Enchiridion Symbolorum*, that of Rufinus, the old Roman Creed form, has: "I believe in God the Father Almighty, and in Christ Jesus His only Son, Our Lord, who was born from the Holy Spirit and the Virgin Mary, who was crucified under Pontius Pilate. ..."[10]

The Nicean Symbol, 325, does not directly refer to the Virgin Mary, although it says that Our Lord Jesus Christ, the Son of God "for us men and for our salvation came down and was made flesh,

---

[8] Cordovani, *loc. cit.*

[9] Palmer, *Mary in the Documents of the Church*, p. 4. On the early Creeds, see J. Quasten, *Patrology*, Vol. 1 (Westminster, Md., 1951), pp. 23-27; he notes that the West tended more than the East to stress the birth from the Virgin Mary in the early symbols.

[10] D.B., 2, Palmer, p. 4.

and became man, suffered, and rose on the third day. ..."[11] In defending the divinity of the Second Person of the Blessed Trinity, the Council of Nicea was implicitly protecting Mary's privilege as Mother of God.

B. Council of Ephesus

The Nicean Symbol was called forth by the need to defend the divinity of the Son of God. The first Council of Constantinople, 381, affirmed the existence of the human soul in Christ, against Apollinaris, who said that the Word took the place of the soul. Its Creed said that the Son of God "was made flesh by the Holy Ghost of the Virgin Mary."[12] Neither at Nicea nor at Constantinople was there a direct attack on the Virgin Mary. But the error of Nestorius revealed itself precisely in relation to Mary as the Mother of God. The controversy that raged between Nestorius, Patriarch of Constantinople, and St. Cyril, Bishop of Alexandria, centered on the term *Theotokos* (Mother of God). Nestorius at an earlier date had himself used this term indifferently with *Christotokos* (Mother of Christ). But the battle lines were clearly drawn when a follower of his openly denied the title *Theotokos* to the Virgin Mary. It was no mere quarrel about words. "Mother of God" was refused to the Virgin Mary on the basis that there were two distinct persons in Christ—one God the Word, the other Jesus—and that they were united only by a moral union. Mary was said to be the mother of the *man* Jesus, but not of the other Person, God.

Cyril openly challenged Nestorius in 429, and informed Pope St. Celestine of his action. At the Ecumenical Council of Ephesus, 431, convened with the Pope's permission, Cyril presided. Nestorius was condemned, and Cyril's second letter to Nestorius, 430, read out and approved:

> Nor was He first born of the holy Virgin as an ordinary man, in such a way that the Word only afterwards descended upon Him; rather was He united [with flesh] in the womb itself, and thus is said to have undergone birth according to the flesh, inasmuch as He makes

---

[11] *D.B.*, 54, Palmer, p. 7.

[12] *D.B.*, 86, where the Latin has "incarnatus est de Spiritu Sancto ex Maria Virgine." The Greek has: "from the Holy Spirit and the Virgin Mary." The same difference is true of the Roman Creed of note 11.

His own the birth of His own flesh. ... For this reason [the holy Fathers] have boldly proclaimed the holy Virgin Theotokos.[13]

Pope Celestine sent two delegates with orders to put into effect his decision that Cyril's interpretations, including *Theotokos*, were the true faith of Nicea and binding on all. The Papal legates arrived two weeks after the Council had already condemned Nestorius. A second meeting was called, and the delegates confirmed the decision already taken. The voice of Rome had been heard: the matter was now settled for all Christianity and for all time. The cornerstone had been placed by this definition of dogma for the subsequent development of Mariology. The intimate bond between the *Theotokos* and the God-Man was indicative of the trend the developing Mariology would take. The belief embodied in the term *Theotokos* was at once the glory of Mary's divine Maternity and the affirmation that God Himself became man, the son of Mary, took to Himself a human nature without prejudice to the unity of His divine person. The Church in ages to come would discover the deeper treasures of the divine Maternity, for in the words of Pius XII, "from this sublime office of the Mother of God seem to flow, as it were from a most limpid hidden source, all the privileges and graces with which her soul and life were adorned in such extraordinary manner and measure."[14]

Ephesus also showed clearly the Roman Primacy. In word and act the Papal participation in the Council called by the Emperor was the intervention of the Supreme Pastor. Cyril, even when he convened the Council, June 22, 431, before many of the bishops and

---

[13] *D.B.*, 111 a, Palmer, p. 10. The Latin reads: "Non enim primo vulgaris quispiam homo ex Virgine ortus est, in quem Dei Verbum deinde se demiserit; sed in ipso utero carni unitum secundum carnem progenitum dicitur, utpote suae carnis generationem sibi ut propriam vindicans. ... Ita [scl. sancti Patres] non dubitaverunt sacram virginem Deiparam appellare." On the history of Ephesus, see G. Bardy, *Les débuts du Nestorianisme* (428-433), in *Histoire de l'Église*, ed. Fliche et Martin, Vol. 4 (Paris, 1945), pp. 163-186; G. Jouassard, *Marie à travers la Patristique: Maternité divine, Virginité, Sainteté, in Maria. Études sur la Sainte Vierge*, ed. by H. du Manoir, S.J., Vol. 1, 1949 (Paris), pp. 69-157; M. Jugie, A.A., *Efeso, Concilio di*, in *Enciclopedia Cattolica*, Vol. 5, cols. 114-119 (Città del Vaticano, 1950); Philip Hughes, *A History of the Church*, Vol. 1 (New York, 1935), pp. 292-306.

[14] *Fulgens Corona*, A.A.S., Vol. 45, 1953, p. 580.

the Roman delegates arrived, did so as "holding the place of the Bishop of the Church of Rome." The legates on their arrival demanded and received without question a complete review in a new assembly of the bishops. Philip the Priest addressed them in words that have become a classic expression of the primacy of authority of Peter's successor.[15] The Mariology of Ephesus can be said to come directly from the Supreme *magisterium* of the Church. Here again a pattern has been set: in the subsequent development of doctrine about Our Lady, the decision will ever rest with Rome. For Philip stated that the Council had been reunited to carry out the decisions made by Rome. The members of the Church are joined to the head, and the blessed Apostle Peter is the head of the faith and the head of the Apostles.[16]

C. After Ephesus

Many popes and councils in the centuries immediately after Ephesus reaffirmed the divine maternity. The Council of Chalcedon (fourth ecumenical), 451, made its own the word *Theotokos*: "as regards His Godhead, He was begotten of the Father before the ages, and as regards His manhood He was for us and for our salvation born in these last days of the Virgin Mary, the Mother of God."[17]

The second Council of Constantinople (fifth ecumenical), 553, defended the word *Theotokos* against false interpretation. It also accepted and thereby conferred dogmatic value on St. Cyril's anathemas against Nestorius. There is no evidence that these anathemas were read and approved at the Council of Ephesus itself. The first anathema concerns the divine Maternity: "If anyone does not confess that Emmanuel is in truth God, and that the holy Virgin is, in consequence, Theotokos (Mother of God), since she brought forth according to the flesh the Word of God who has become flesh, let him be anathema."[18]

---

[15] Philip's words are in *D.B.*, 112, and were incorporated verbatim at the fourth session of the Vatican Council, 1870, D.B., 1824.

[16] G. Bardy, *art. cit.*, p. 184, n. 4.

[17] *D.B.*, 148.

[18] *D.B.*, 113, Palmer, p. 11. D.B. and Palmer both note that this anathema was probably not read at Ephesus, on the basis of Fr. Galtier's research, reported in *Recherches de science religieuse*, Vol. 23, 1933, p. 45 ff. Also Nilus a S.

D. *Lux veritatis*

The outstanding document of modern times on the divine motherhood is Pius XI's encyclical commemorating the anniversary of Ephesus, *Lux veritatis*, December 25, 1931.[19] *Lux veritatis* reviews the history of the Nestorian heresy and the events at Ephesus, considering both the defense of the traditional faith, and the authoritative position of the Roman Primacy recognized on that occasion. The central dogma of the Incarnation—that Christ is true God and true man, the divine and human natures existing unconfused in the hypostatic union (the union of the one divine Person with the human nature)—is explained. The divine Maternity is shown as the corollary of Christological doctrine. From this truth the Pope derives also the belief that Mary is our spiritual Mother. He concludes by a double gesture to commemorate the Ephesian anniversary: the restoration of the mosaic in St. Mary Major of the *Theotokos*, first placed there after the triumph of Ephesus by Pope St. Sixtus III in 432; and the extension to the universal Church of the feast of the Divine Maternity on November 21.

II. EVER VIRGIN

The early Creeds not only affirm with St. Paul that Christ was "born of a woman" (Gal. 4:4); they specify "born of the Virgin Mary." And the Council of Ephesus used St. Cyril's words to state that the holy Virgin was truly *Theokotos*, Mother of God. The challenge to the divine Maternity had sprung from Nestorianism, an Eastern heresy. The West was less disturbed by speculative errors. Its more practical bent manifested itself in a vigorous defense of Mary's perpetual virginity. Some have asserted that Mary's perpetual virginity was *invented* as a spur to asceticism, but such an

---

Brocardo, O.C.D., *De maternitate divina B. Mariae semper Virginis* (Romae, 1944), p. 45, n. (60). According to Jouassard, *art. cit.*, p. 135, nos. (56-57), the divine Maternity strictly speaking was not defined at Ephesus; nonetheless, the conciliar decisions were the equivalent of a definition, even before the approval of the anathema at the Fifth Ecumenical Council.

[19] *A.A.S.*, Vol. 23, 1931, pp. 493-517; in Tondini, pp. 369-406. Cf. A. Luis, C.SS.R., *San Cirilo y Nestorio. Encíclica "Lux veritatis," in Estudios Marianos* (Asamblea del año 1948), Vol. 8 (Madrid, 1949), pp. 325-344; the whole volume treats the divine Maternity.

opinion is contradicted by the Creeds accepted in the East and the West, and is contrary to the Gospels themselves.[20] Asceticism, e.g., the respect for clerical celibacy, did play a part in the acknowledgment of Mary's perpetual virginity, but it was not the leading role. It was rather the part of an agent, working effectively to present to the teaching Church an adequate formula to state its doctrine precisely. The *Ecclesia docens*, the teaching Church, made the final decision.[21]

Pope St. Siricius (384-399), on the occasion of a dispute about Our Lady's perpetual virginity, intervened in 392 with a letter to Anysius, Bishop of Thessalonica. The Bishop had taken Bonosus, a bishop in Illyria, to task for saying Our Lady had other children.

> ... you had good reason to be horrified at the thought that another birth might issue from the same virginal womb from which Christ was born according to the flesh. For the Lord Jesus would never have chosen to be born of a virgin if He had ever judged that she would be so incontinent as to contaminate with the seed of human intercourse the birthplace of the Lord's body, that court of the Eternal King. To assert such a view is to do nothing less than to accept as a basis that Jewish falsehood which holds that He could not have been born of a virgin.[22]

The attack on Mary's virginity—especially on her virginity after the birth of Christ—was motivated by practical rather than by dogmatic reasons. Helvidius wished to show that the state of virginity was no better than marriage, and proposed Mary as an

---

[20] On the value of the Creeds concerning Mary's virginity, cf. A. Janssens, *De Heerlijkheden van het goddelijk moederschap, tweede herziene druk* (2nd edit.), Brussel, 1939, p. 111 ff. On the Gospels, cf. C. C. Martindale, S.J., *Christ's Virgin Birth and the Gospel of the Infancy* (London: Catholic Truth Society, 1948).

[21] Cf. O. Faller, *De priorum saeculorum silentio circa Assumptionem B. Mariae Virginis* (Romae, 1946), pp. 74-75; Jouassard, *art. cit.*, p. 120.

[22] *D.B.*, 91, Palmer, p. 28. On these controversies, cf. Jouassard, art. cit., p. 106 ff.; Hugh Pope, O.P., The Perpetual Virginity of Our Blessed Lady, in *Our Blessed Lady* (*Cambridge Summer School Lectures for 1933*) (London, 1934), pp. 121-141; J.-R. Palanque, *Les métropoles ecclésiastiques à la fin du IVe siècle*, in *Histoire de l'Église*, ed. Fliche et Martin, Vol. 3 (Paris), p. 476 ff.; Hugh Rahner, *Die Marienkunde in der lateinischen Patristik*, in *Katholische Marienkunde*, ed. Paul Sträter, S.J., Vol. 1 (Paderborn, 1947), p. 146 ff.

example of both states—of virginity until Christ's birth, of the motherhood of a large family in later life. At Rome Christian asceticism was emphasizing the superiority of virginity. The young St. Jerome wrote his vigorous *Adversus Helvidium* (Against Helvidius) in 383, demonstrating from Scripture and tradition that Mary was ever a virgin. That was under Pope Damasus, who died in 384. The enemies of asceticism reformed their ranks under the ex-monk Jovinian. Pope Siricius had his clergy examine and condemn their propositions and excommunicate Jovinian.

When Jovinian fled to the safety of the court at Milan, Pope Siricius advised the Bishop, St. Ambrose, of the attempt Jovinian might make to misrepresent true asceticism as Priscillianism, a kind of Manichaeism with its teaching that the body comes from Satan, and its condemnation of marriage as evil. St. Ambrose, by a clever counterstroke, obtained the expulsion of the Jovinian party by the civil authorities, on the charge of Manichaeism. Jovinian's denial of Our Lady's virginity in the actual bringing forth of the Christ Child was answered by Ambrose.

The Bonosus case next occupied Ambrose's attention. About 390, this Illyrian bishop, living in an area of Asia Minor where earlier in the same century even prominent and orthodox preachers had not considered Mary's virginity after Christ's birth a matter of faith, said Mary had other children.[23] His neighboring bishops condemned him. Ambrose, appealed to from both sides, suggested to the Council of Bishops of Illyria the norms by which they might defend Mary's perpetual virginity, the greatest argument being the demands of the divine Maternity. The episcopate of Illyria, under Anysius, to whom Pope Siricius had written, reaffirmed the condemnation of Bonosus.

Fifty years later, Monophysitism under Eutyches taught that the divine and human natures blended so perfectly in Christ that He had only a single nature (hence the name: *Mono-phusis* or "single-nature"). Against this denial of the true and perfect humanity of Christ, Pope St. Leo I (440-461) wrote the Archbishop of Constantinople, Flavian, in 449,24 after the following series of events: Eutyches concealed his teaching under the mask of

---

[23] Jouassard, *art. cit.*, pp. 88-90, 111-112.

opposition to Nestorianism, and even wrote to Pope Leo I in 448. The Pope replied in praise of Eutyches' zeal, but said he was not well enough informed about the Eastern controversy. The same year Eutyches was hailed before an episcopal council under Flavian and, refusing to retract his teaching, was condemned as heretical. Eutyches appealed to Rome, and accompanied his appeal with a letter from Emperor Theodosius. Pope Leo wrote back that he was still not well informed on events. But when the case was laid before him in full he confirmed the judgment against Eutyches.

Meantime the Emperor convened another council at Constantinople and the Pope sent three delegates to it, one of them the deacon Hilary, later to become pope himself. Among the letters they brought, dated June, 449,[24] was one to Archbishop Flavian, containing a complete résumé of Leo's doctrinal position, since famous as the "Tome of Pope St. Leo I." The document reaffirms the truth of two natures in the one Person of Christ, each with its proper faculties. In the same tone Our Lady's perpetual virginity — before Christ's birth, in childbirth, afterward (ante partum, in partu, post partum) — is presented as the Church's doctrine:

> Unquestionably, therefore, He was conceived of the Holy Spirit within the womb of His Virgin Mother. She brought Him forth without the loss of virginity, even as she conceived Him without its loss. ...
>
> The Son of God, therefore, came down from His heavenly throne without relinquishing the glory of His Father, and entered this lower world by way of a new order and a new mode of birth. ... By way of a new mode of birth, insofar as virginity inviolate which knew not the desire of the flesh supplied the material of flesh. From His Mother the Lord took nature, not sin. Jesus Christ was born from a virgin's womb, by a miraculous birth. And yet His nature is not on that account unlike to ours, for He that is true God is also true Man.[25]

---

[24] *D.B.*, 143-144, Palmer, pp. 29-31, where Flavian is mistakenly called Emperor rather than Archbishop. Background history in G. Bardy, Le Brigandage d' Éphèse de le Concile de Chalcedoine, in Histoire de l'Église, ed. Fliche et Martin, Vol. 4 (Paris, 1945), pp. 211-240.

[25] *D.B.*, 143-144, Palmer, pp. 30-31. Fr. Palmer gives more of the tome than *D.B.* Leo I is quoted in the encyclical *Sempiternus Rex*, in *A.A.S.*, Vol. 43, 1951, p. 634, on the occasion of the 1500th anniversary of Chalcedon: "de ea Virgine de qua est natus." Chalcedon's own Creed, D.B., 148, is also quoted,

The council met at Constantinople in 449. From the first assembly it was evident that the meeting had been arranged with the connivance of the Emperor for the advantage of Eutyches alone. It well earned the title Pope Leo later gave it — *latrocinium*, den of thieves. The Pope's letters were ignored, his legates protesting in vain. Eutyches was restored, Flavian charged with heresy and jailed. Emperor Theodosius died in 450 and was succeeded by Empress Pulcheria. Both she and her consort, Marcian, favored the Faith.

The truly universal council that Pope Leo desired was summoned, and met at Chalcedon, October, 451, with over five hundred bishops present. First the Nicean Creed and St. Cyril's letters to Nestorius were read, then Pope Leo's tome. When the tome was read, the assembly accepted it unconditionally and enthusiastically: "Behold the faith of the Fathers! the faith of the Apostles! So do we too, all of us, believe, all who are orthodox believe the same! Anathema to whoever believes otherwise! Thus through Leo has Peter spoken!"[26]

It remained for the first Lateran Council, held in 649 under Pope St. Martin I, to give the dogmatic definition of the perpetual virginity of Mary. The occasion was the condemnation of Monothelism, still another attack on the full reality of Christ's humanity. The heresy held there was only one will (*mono-thelema*) in Christ, namely the divine will.

> If anyone does not in accord with the Holy Fathers acknowledge the holy and ever virgin and immaculate Mary as really and truly the Mother of God, inasmuch as she, in the fulness of time, and without seed, conceived by the Holy Spirit God the Word Himself, who before all time was born of God the Father, and without loss of integrity brought Him forth, and after His birth preserved her virginity inviolate, let him be condemned.[27]

---

loc. cit., p. 635. Rouët de Journel, S.J., *Enchiridion Patristicum*, ed. 14a (Friburgi Brisgoviae, 1947), Nos. 2182-2183, quotes more from the tome.

[26] Hughes, *op. cit.*, Vol. I, p. 316.

[27] *D.B.*, 256, Palmer, pp. 31-32. The Latin is: "Can. 3. Si quis secundum sanctos Patres non confitetur proprie et secundum veritatem Dei genitricem sanctam semperque Virginem et immaculatam Mariam, utpote ipsum Deum Verbum specialiter et veraciter, qui a Deo Patre ante omnia saecula natus est, in ultimis saeculorum absque semine concepisse ex Spiritu Sancto, et incorruptibiliter eam [eum?] genuisse, indissolubili permanente et post

The Lateran canon just quoted expressed the belief of East and West alike; and although the council was not ecumenical, the canon embodies a true dogma. In 681, the Sixth Ecumenical Council, the third to be held at Constantinople, accepted the canon of the Lateran on Our Lady's virginity without question.

Professions of faith and symbols formulated by later popes contain the same doctrine: among them, Leo III's profession of faith of Nicephorus, Patriarch of Constantinople, 811;[28] Innocent III's profession of faith prescribed for the Waldensians, 1208;[29] the formula for the union of the Greeks of the second Council of Lyons (fourteenth ecumenical) under Gregory X;[30] and the Council of Florence in the Decree for the Jacobites, 1441.[31]

Paul IV in 1555 thus answered the Unitarians, who denied the Trinity, the Incarnation, and the virginity of Mary:

> In a spirit of paternal severity we are anxious to admonish each and everyone who has heretofore asserted, taught or believed ... that the same most Blessed Virgin Mary is not truly the Mother of God or that she did not always retain the integrity of her virginity, that is, before birth, during birth, and continuously after birth. ...[32]

III. FULL OF GRACE

Once the divine Maternity and the perpetual virginity of Mary had been proposed by the Church's teaching authority as true Catholic doctrine, the way was open for further development. Chalcedon was a stimulant to progress in Mariology. The doctrinal defense of the true flesh, the full humanity of Christ, emphasized more than ever the importance of the glorious Virgin Mother. Similarly, Christian writers were inspired to develop the theme of the tender love the Mother of God had for the Son truly born of her

---

partum eiusdem virginitate, condemnatus sit." (The square brackets are in *D.B.*)

[28] *D.B.*, 314 a, n. (3).

[29] *Ibid.*, 422.

[30] *Ibid.*, 462.

[31] *Ibid.*, 708 ff.

[32] *Ibid.*, 993, Palmer, pp. 77-78.

very substance.[33]

For the East the decisions of Ephesus seem to have consecrated the notion of "ever Virgin" along with "Mother of God." And by the time of St. Augustine's death in 431, the perpetual virginity was also a pacific possession in the West. The Tome of Pope St. Leo expressed the common belief about it; and finally the Lateran Council, under Pope Martin I, defined the perpetual virginity. In the light of these two truths, under the guidance of the Holy Ghost, the Church would now penetrate into the mystery of Mary's sanctity. First, we will consider freedom from personal sin through fullness of grace, leaving to the next section freedom from original sin.

Belief in Mary's virginity led to emphasis on her holiness. The experience of the ascetics first showed the connection between a life of perpetual virginity and holiness. But still deeper reflection was needed to appreciate the full treasure of Mary's sanctity, and this came through reflection on the divine Maternity. From the divine motherhood had come the awareness of perfect virginity; now Christian thought saw that God would make His Mother all-perfect, by gifts of grace beyond compare.

In his controversy with Pelagius, who denied original sin and held the natural perfectibility of man even without supernatural aid, St. Augustine emphasized the universality of sin. Yet he exempted Our Lady from the universal law:

> Now with the exception of the holy Virgin Mary in regard to whom, out of respect for the Lord, I do not propose to have a single question raised on the subject of sin — after all, how do we know what greater degree of grace for a complete victory over sin was conferred on her who merited to conceive and bring forth Him who all admit was without sin — to repeat then: with the exception of this Virgin, if we

---

[33] On Chalcedon's influence on subsequent Mariology, cf. the articles of H. Weisweiler, S.J., in *Scholastik*, Vol. 28, 1953: *Das frühe Marienbild der Westkirche unter dem Einfluss des Dogmas von Chalcedon — Die vertiefte Schau der Virgo-Mater Gloriosa*, pp. 321-360, and *Die verstärkte Einzeichnung des Zuges der zärtlich liebenden Mutter*, pp. 504-525.

On Mary's sanctity, cf. Jouassard, art. cit., pp. 114-116, 136-155; E. Dublanchy, Marie, in D.T.C., Vol. 9, cols. 2413-2428; P. G. M. Rhodes, Our Lady's Endowments, in Our Blessed Lady (Cambridge Summer School Lectures, *1933*) (London, 1934), pp. 174-179; J. I. Cartmell, Our Lady in Tradition and the Fathers, ibid., pp. 80-84.

could bring together into one place all those holy men and women, while they lived here, and ask them whether they were without sin, what are we to suppose that they would have replied?[34]

St. Augustine's opinion is the real attitude of Christian antiquity. There were occasional Fathers, even after Ephesus, who said Mary was guilty of the venial sin of vainglory, misinterpreting the Gospel incidents of her charitable request to Christ at Cana (Jn. 2:1-12), and her presence with those relatives of Our Lord who interrupted a sermon in order to speak to Him (Mt. 12:47). Newman says of the harshest of these, St. John Chrysostom, "his whole passage is as much at variance with what we hold, as it is solitary and singular in the writings of antiquity."[35]

The *magisterium* did not speak on Mary's holiness, her freedom from even venial sin, until the Council of Trent. Direct attacks on Our Lady were not among the many points the theologians of Trent felt pressed to refute. Yet Trent, in its teaching on justification, 1547, under Paul III, refers to Our Lady's freedom from sin as an exception to the general rule:

> If anyone shall say that a man once justified ... can through the whole of life avoid all sins, even though they be venial, except by a special privilege of God, as the Church holds to have been the case with the Blessed Virgin, let him be anathema.[36]

St. Pius V safeguarded this teaching in his condemnation of an error of Baius in 1567:

> Error 73: No one, with the exception of Christ, is without original sin. Therefore, the Blessed Virgin died because of the sin contracted from Adam, and all her afflictions in this life, no less than those of the rest

---

[34] Palmer, pp. 33-34; Rouët de Journel, *Enchiridion Patristicum*, No. 1794.

[35] J. H. Newman, *The New Eve*, with introduction by P. Radcliffe (Oxford: Newman Bookshop, 1952), p. 57.

[36] *D.B.*, 833, Palmer, pp. 76-77. The Latin concerning Our Lady is: "Can. 23. Si quis hominem semel justificatum dixerit ... posse in tota vita peccata omnia etiam venialia vitare, nisi ex speciali Dei privilegio, quemadmodum de beata Virgine tenet Ecclesia: A.S." On the value of Trent in reference to Mary's privileges, cf. Ernst Böminghaus, S.J., *Geschichte der Marienverehrung seit dem Tridentinum, in Katholische Marienkunde*, ed. Paul Sträter, Vol. 1 (Paderborn, 1947), pp. 333-337.

of the just, were the punishment of actual or original sin.[37]

Mary's holiness was protected again under Alexander VIII in 1690 by the condemnation of the Jansenist opinion that Mary's purification in the temple showed she needed it:

> Error 24: The offering which the Blessed Virgin Mary made in the temple on the day of her purification with two young turtledoves, one as a holocaust, the other as a sin offering, is sufficient evidence that she needed purification, and that Her Son, who was presented, was also marked with the stain of His Mother, according to the words of the Law.[38]

It is noteworthy that here again the honor of Mother and Son are a common cause.

The recent popes say much in praise of Our Lady's sanctity. Pius IX will serve as a good example:

> He [God], therefore, filled her, far more than all the angelic spirits and all the saints, with an abundance of all heavenly gifts from the treasury of His divinity, in such a wonderful manner that she would always be free from absolutely every stain of sin, and that, all beautiful and perfect, she might display such fullness of innocence and holiness that under God none greater is known, and which, God excepted, no one can attain even in thought.[39]

Our Lady's freedom from personal sin has never been defined, as has her lifelong virginity and her freedom from original sin, but it is nevertheless an article of faith, as Trent states — "as the Church holds."[40] It is a step further to say that Mary could not sin — that she was confirmed in grace and impeccable (unable to sin). This is an opinion defended by many theologians, again on the grounds of her divine motherhood.

---

[37] *D.B.*, 1073, Palmer, p. 78.

[38] *D.B.*, 1314, Palmer, pp. 78-79.

[39] *Ineffabilis Deus*, Tondini, p. 30. The English translation is from Mary Immaculate, by D. Unger, O.F.M.Cap. (Paterson, N. J., 1946), p. 2.

[40] Cf. Roschini, *Mariologia*, 2a ed., Vol. 3, p. 110 ff., for different opinions of the theologians on the dogmatic value of Trent's words. Also J. A. de Aldama, S.J., *El valor dogmático de la doctrina sobre la inmunidad de pecado venial en Nuestra Señora, in Archivo Teológico Granadino*, Vol. 9, 1946, pp. 53-67.

IV. IMMACULATE

A. *The Beginnings*

If the fact that St. Augustine did "not propose to have a single question raised on the subject of sin in regard to the holy Virgin Mary out of respect for the Lord" virtually settled the question of Mary's freedom from personal sin, the same author's insistence on the universality of original sin proved a deterrent to the development of belief in Mary's Immaculate Conception.[41] Although some writings of Pope Leo the Great and Pope Gregory the Great would seem to exempt Mary from original sin, many more centuries of thought and prayer were required before the Church would realize that the Immaculate Conception was among the gifts God provided for His Mother. And still more centuries would elapse before the supreme *magisterium* would solemnly declare the doctrine of Mary's freedom from original sin to be a revealed truth, i.e., contained in the original Deposit confided to the Apostles.

The doctrine of the Immaculate Conception is a classic example of the development of doctrine.[42] Theologians distinguish three stages in the progressive awareness of a revealed truth not explicitly contained in the sources of revelation. The first stage is implicit

---

[41] Jouassard, *art. cit.*, p. 151.

[42] Cf. F. J. Connell, C.SS.R., *Historical Development of the Dogma of the Immaculate Conception*, in *The American Ecclesiastical Review*, Vol. 114, 1946, p. 340 ff., and the same article in *Studies in Praise of Our Blessed Mother*, ed. J. C. Fenton and E. D. Benard (Washington, D. C., 1952), pp. 93-99; T. E. Flynn, *The Immaculate Conception of Our Lady*, in *Our Blessed Lady* (*Cambridge Summer School Lectures*, 1933) (London, 1934), pp. 93-120; X. Le Bachelet, *Immaculée Conception*, in *D.T.C.*, Vol. 7, cols. 979-1218; E. Druwé, S.J., *Kerkleer omtrent de Onbevlekte Ontvangenis in Middeleeuwen en Moderne Tijden*, in *Verslagboek der zevende Mariale Dagen*, 1937 (Tongerloo, 1938), pp. 111-131 (the whole Volume 7 of *Mariale Dagen* is on the Immaculate Conception); B. A. McKenna, *The Dogma of the Immaculate Conception* (Washington, D. C., 1929); M. Cabrera, E. Schoenstein, C. Mondor, *The Immaculate Conception*, in *Priestly Studies* (Santa Barbara, Calif.), condensed in Our Lady's Digest, Vol. 6, 1951, pp. 301-320 (subtitle: *A Franciscan Study*); J. Duhr, S.J., *L'évolution du dogme de l'Immaculée Conception*, in *Nouvelle revue théologique*, Vol. 73, 1951, pp. 1013-1032; Friedel, *op. cit.*, pp. 294-311; A. Wolter, O.F.M., *The Theology of the Immaculate Conception in the Light of "Ineffabilis Deus,"* in *Marian Studies*, Vol. 5, 1954, pp. 19-72.

acceptance, the period of tranquil possession. The second stage in the development of a dogma is the period of discussion and controversy, during which the precise meaning of the doctrine is clarified, as well as its relationship to Revelation and to other doctrines. In the third stage, the doctrine is received by the entire Church, is the common teaching of the ordinary *magisterium*, or finally even solemnly defined.

In the present case, the first stage was the tranquil acceptance of the unique graces and privileges of Mary, which, as we now know, imply the Immaculate Conception. The early Christians accepted Mary's singular position as Mother of God, as ever a virgin, as all-holy, as the New Eve. Thereby they implicitly accepted the Immaculate Conception, which is implied by the divine motherhood. During the first period of undisputed acceptance, the first liturgical evidences appear: feasts of the "Conception of St. Anne," hymns, homilies.

B. Period of Discussion

The second phase, that of controversy, began with St. Bernard's (d. 1153) opposition to the spread of the feast of the Conception of Mary. The controversy raged through the age of Scholasticism, dividing into two camps the greatest doctors of theology, some of them saints and all of them loyal to Our Lady.

Many thought it impossible to reconcile freedom from original sin with the fact that Mary was born of human parents through natural generation. Some were against a feast of the conception of Mary, because they misunderstood it to refer to the active conception, namely to the generation of Mary by her parents Joachim and Anne. In reality, the feast concerned the passive conception of Our Lady, the union of her soul and body in her mother's womb. This confusion of active and passive conception still occurs, just as even Catholics sometimes confuse Mary's Immaculate Conception with Christ's Virgin Birth. Other opponents considered an immaculate conception incompatible with the universality of the Redemption of Christ. The Scholastic Doctors of the twelfth and thirteenth centuries, e.g., St. Thomas Aquinas, St. Albert, St. Bonaventure, were more commonly against the belief in a sinless conception. The Franciscan John Duns Scotus (d. 1308), perhaps under the influence of his confrere, William of Ware (d. 1300), showed that a preservation from original sin by the merits of Christ would be an even more perfect form of Redemption than to be rescued from already contracted sin. By the mid-fifteenth century the greater number of theologians were in favor of the Immaculate Conception, and the liturgical celebrations had widely spread. But still there had been no approval on the part of the *magisterium.*

A dogmatic decision on Mary's freedom from original sin was proposed at the Council of Basel, but the definition of 1439 was invalid because the Council had fallen under the excommunication of Pope Eugene IV.

C. Decisions From Rome

Pope Sixtus IV (1471-1484), a Franciscan (Conventual), was the first officially to encourage the doctrine.[43] His constitution Cum praecelsa of 1477[44] approved and indulgenced the feast of the Conception of the Immaculate Virgin:

> When, with that deep insight that comes of devout contemplation, we search and discover the sublime proofs of those merits which cause the Queen of heaven, the glorious Virgin Mother of God, raised upon her heavenly throne, to outshine like the morning star all other Constellations ... We deem it fitting, and even our duty, to invite by means of indulgences and the remission of sins all the faithful of Christ to offer thanks and praise to God ... for the wondrous Conception of this same Immaculate Virgin, and to celebrate or to be present at Masses and at other divine functions which have been instituted for this purpose.[45]

During Sixtus' reign, the long-standing controversy between the Dominicans, on one side, and the Franciscans, Carmelites, and Servites, on the other, flared anew when Bandelli, later General of the Dominicans, wrote two books against the Immaculate Conception, implying in the second that the Pope had not truly intended to make the object of the feast Our Lady's conception, but

---

[43] C. Sericoli, O.F.M., *Immaculata B. M. Virginis Conceptio juxta Xysti IV constitutiones* (Sibenici et Romae, 1945).

[44] Sericoli defends the date of February 27, 1477; see op. cit., pp. 31, 33, note 22. The constitution is also known as *Cum praeexcelsa.*

[45] D.B., 734, Palmer, p. 74; full text in Sericoli, op. cit., pp. 153-154.

rather her sanctification (like St. John the Baptist).

Two Bulls, both titled *Grave Nimis*, appeared in reply, one in 1481, directed to Lombardy where Bandelli was preaching: it specified that Mary's conception, not merely sanctification, was the object of the feast. The second, of September 4, 1483, was directed to the entire Church. It forbade either side to call the other heretical; but the adversaries of the belief were threatened with excommunication not only if they called the defenders heretics, but even if they charged the defenders with error and falsity.[46] Yet, in spite of such signs of favor to the belief, the Pope concludes by saying "since the matter has not yet been decided by the Roman Church and Apostolic See."[47]

Sixtus IV's successors continued to favor the feast. Many contented themselves with simply repeating his constitutions, as Leo X (in 1502 and 1515). So also Julius II (1503-1513), Pius IV (1559-1565), and Sixtus V (1585-1590). The question was discussed at the Council of Trent, but the determined opposition of a small group defeated definite decision on it. Nevertheless, the Council declared in the session on original sin (fifth session, June 17, 1546, under Pope Paul III):

> This same holy Synod declares that it is not its intention to include in this decree, where there is question of original sin, the blessed and immaculate Virgin Mary, Mother of God. Rather, the constitutions of Sixtus of happy memory are to be followed. ...[48]

Pius IX interprets the action of Trent as follows:

> Indeed, considering the times and circumstances, the Fathers of Trent sufficiently insinuated by this declaration that the Blessed Virgin Mary was free from the original stain; and thus they clearly signified that nothing could be reasonably cited from the Sacred Writings,

---

[46] Cf. Sericoli, op. cit., p. 40 ff.; D.B., 735, Palmer, p. 75, give part of the second *Grave Nimis*.

[47] D.B., 735. Cf. A Robichaud, S.M., The Immaculate Conception in the *magisterium* of the Church prior to 1854, in Marian Studies, Vol. 5, 1954, pp. 99-103.

[48] D.B., 792, Palmer, p. 77; cf. M. Tognetti, O.S.M., L'Immacolata al Concilio Tridentino, in Marianum, Vol. 15, 1953, pp. 304-374 — to be continued in a later number.

which would in any way be opposed to so great a prerogative of the Virgin.[49]

Trent also indirectly advanced the eventual acceptance of the belief by clarifying the notions of original sin, of grace, and of the supernatural life.

Pope St. Pius V (1566-1572) included the feast of the Conception in the reformed Missal, 1568, for the whole Latin Church, and likewise condemned the error of Baius which stated, "No one, with the exception of Christ, is without original sin. Therefore the Blessed Virgin died because of the sin contracted from Adam. ..."[50] He likewise forbade debates before the public on the subject. Paul V renewed this prohibition in 1617. In 1622 Gregory XV further forbade, except among the Dominicans themselves, even private writings and sermons against the Immaculate Conception. The celebration of the feast was enjoined on all, with a warning against replacing the word "Conception," by any other word, as "Sanctification."

Controversy continued nonetheless. Pope Alexander VII (1655-1657), appealed to for an authentic statement of the true object of the feast, issued his constitution, *Sollicitudo*, December 8, 1661. The document determines the object of the feast as understood by the common sentiment of the Church, pastors and faithful alike.

Ancient is the piety of the Christian faithful toward our Blessed Mother, the Virgin Mary. They believe that her soul, in the first moment of creation and infusion into her body, was, by a special grace and privilege of God, and in consideration of the merits of Jesus Christ her Son, the Redeemer of the human race, preserved free from the stain of original sin. And it is in this sense that the faithful cherish and celebrate with solemn rites the feast of her Conception... [Alexander VII then renews the decrees of Sixtus IV, Paul V and Gregory XV] ... in favor of the doctrine asserting that the soul of the Blessed Virgin, at its creation and infusion into the body, was endowed with the grace of the Holy Spirit and preserved from original sin. ...[51]

---

[49] *Ineffabilis Deus*; in Unger, *op. cit.*, p. 9.

[50] *D.B.*, 1073, Palmer, p. 78.

[51] *D.B.*, 1100, Palmer, p. 78.

D. Definition by Pius IX

It remained for Pius IX to take the final step. Crowned pope in 1846, he personally signed the decree of the Sacred Congregation of Rites of September 30, 1847, authorizing a new Mass and Office of the feast, extending it on February 2, 1849, to the whole world. Our present Mass and Office is from 1863, also by order of Pius IX. In 1848 a commission of theologians was named to study two questions: Can the Immaculate Conception be defined as a dogma? and: Is such a definition opportune? On February 2, 1849, the encyclical *Ubi primum* was sent to the bishops of the world, seeking their views on the definability.

The replies from the bishops were better than nine tenths (546 out of 603) favorable. Some did not consider the definition then opportune because of attacks on the Church; only four or five were quite against any dogmatic definition. Another commission was appointed to draw up the Bull of definition; they worked over a year on it. The document was not only to promulgate the dogma, but also to include arguments in its favor. It was then submitted to the cardinals and finally to members of the hierarchy assembled in Rome from the whole world. The result of the long process was a precisely phrased presentation of the belief of all Catholicism, the Church learning (*Ecclesia discens*) as well as the teaching Church (*Ecclesia docens*).

On December 8, 1854, in the presence of 200 cardinals, archbishops, and bishops, the Holy Father invoked the Holy Spirit, and then read the words that settled forever all dispute about Our Lady's privilege:

... To the honor of the holy and undivided Trinity, to the glory and adornment of the Virgin Mother of God, to the exaltation of the Catholic faith, and the increase of the Catholic religion, We, by the authority of Jesus Christ our Lord, of the Blessed Apostles, Peter and Paul, and by Our Own, declare, pronounce, and define that the doctrine which holds that the Blessed Virgin Mary, at the first instant of her Conception, by a singular privilege and grace of the omnipotent God, in consideration of the merits of Jesus Christ, the Savior of mankind, was preserved free from all stain of original sin, has been revealed by God, and therefore is to be firmly and constantly believed by all the faithful.[52]

In these words of the dogmatic definition, the Pope is speaking *ex cathedra*, that is, by his supreme infallible authority as Vicar of Christ. The terms are similar to Alexander VII's, yet so carefully chosen that it is clearly Mary's person, body and soul, that is the subject of the privilege. From the very first moment of union of soul and body, in view of the merits of Christ, Mary was kept free from original sin by the grace of God — a unique exception to the common lot of mankind. Moreover, this doctrine is revealed by God; therefore it belongs to the original Deposit of the Faith. And so the Catholic's "I believe" now extends to the privilege of the Immaculate Conception just as truly as it does to the divine motherhood — on the authority of God Himself, who cannot deceive.

The rest of *Ineffabilis Deus*, the document of the definition, makes a worthy setting for the dogmatic definition. The various arguments in the development of belief in the sinless conception of Mary are cited; the traditional interpretation of Sacred Scripture, especially of the *Protoevangelium* (Gen. 3:15), and of the greetings of Gabriel and Elizabeth (Lk. 1:28, 42); the evidence of the liturgy; and finally the proximate preparation when with one voice clergy and faithful entreated the Pope to define with his supreme judgment the Immaculate Conception. The bishops had been heard, indeed their advice had been first sought, but the final act was the Pope's

---

[52] *D.B.*, 1641, Palmer, pp. 86-87, Tondini, p. 54. The Latin is: "… Ad honorem Sanctae et Individuae Trinitatis, ad decus et ornamentum Virginis Deiparae, ad exaltationem fidei catholicae et christianae religionis augmentum, auctoritate Domini nostri Iesu Christi, beatorum Apostolorum Petri et Pauli ac Nostra declaramus, pronuntiamus et definimus, doctrinam, quae tenet, beatissimam Virginem Mariam in primo instanti suae conceptionis fuisse singulari omnipotentis Dei gratia et privilegio, intuitu meritorum Christi Iesu Salvatoris humani generis, ab omni originalis culpae labe praeservatam immunem, esse a Deo revelatam atque idcirco ab omnibus fidelibus firmiter constanterque credendam." Cf. R. Aubert, *La proclamation de l'Immaculée Conception en 1854, in Collectanea Mechliniensia*, Vol. 36, 1951, pp. 594-597; G. Geenen, O.P., *La Bulle "Ineffabilis Deus" in Marie*, Vol. 7, Nov.-Dec., 1953, pp. 41-43.

alone.[53]

Pius IX mentions in *Ineffabilis Deus* some benefits hoped for from the definition: that the "most powerful mediatrix and conciliatrix of the whole world" win peace for the Church, "pardon for the sinner, health for the sick, strength of heart for the weak, consolation for the afflicted, help for those in danger."[54] The century of development in Marian doctrine and devotion is the evidence of how graciously Our Lady accepted Pius IX's prayers.

Inspired by the fiftieth anniversary of the definition, Blessed Pius X gave the world the encyclical *Ad diem illum*, about Our Lady's part in the restoration of all things to Christ (Eph. 1:10) which the saintly Pope made the rule of his pontificate. According to Blessed Pius X, these were the lessons of the Immaculate Conception definition:

> Let the nations believe and profess that the Virgin Mary, in the first moment of her conception was free from all stain, and they must admit original sin, the redemption of mankind by Christ, the Gospel, the Church and even the law of suffering. ... This plague [the rejection of all authority] which is equally destructive of civil and Christian society, is destroyed by the dogma of the Immaculate Conception of the Mother of God. For by it we are all constrained to recognize in the Church a power to which one must submit not only the will but also the intellect, since it is through this subjection of the reason that the Christian people sing to the Mother of God: "Thou art all fair, O Mary, and there is no original stain in thee." So again we conclude that the Church rightly attributes to the august Virgin this that she by herself destroyed all the heresies in the whole world.[55]

V. ASSUMED INTO HEAVEN

A. *Present State of Belief*

"Studies were undertaken with new enthusiasm, which gave due prominence to the dignity and sanctity of the Mother of God."[56]

---

[53] R. Aubert, *Le pontificat de Pie IX (1846-1878)*, in *Histoire de l'Église*, ed. Fliche et Martin, Vol. 21 (Paris, 1952), pp. 278-280.

[54] Unger, *op. cit.*, p. 23, Palmer, p. 88, Tondini, p. 56.

[55] Tondini, p. 320; English from D. Unger, *Mary Mediatrix* (Paterson, N. J., 1948) p. 6.

[56] *A.A.S.*, Vol. 45, 1953, p. 578.

These words from the Marian Year encyclical, Fulgens Corona, describe one of the results produced by the definition of the Immaculate Conception. The Pontiff also recalls that it was his privilege to define,

> ... that the Mother of God was assumed body and soul into heaven; and thus to satisfy the wishes of the faithful, which had been more urgently expressed after the solemn definition of the Immaculate Conception. For then, as We Ourselves wrote in the Apostolic Letter *Munificentissimus Deus*, "the faithful were moved by a certain more ardent hope that the Dogma also of the corporal Assumption of the Virgin Mary into heaven should be defined as soon as possible by the Supreme *magisterium* of the Church."[57]

What the belief of the faithful and the studies of the scholars had held and hoped for became a reality on November 1, 1950, when the Holy Father, Pope Pius XII, in his office as supreme teacher of the universal Church solemnly defined:

> For which reason, after we have poured forth prayers of supplication again and again to God, and have called upon the Spirit of Truth, for the glory of Almighty God who has lavished His special affection upon the Virgin Mary, for the honor of her Son, the immortal King of the ages and the Victor over sin and death, for the increase of the glory of that same august Mother, and for the joy and exultation of the entire Church; by the authority of Our Lord Jesus Christ, of the Blessed Apostles Peter and Paul, and by Our own authority, We pronounce, declare, and define it to be a divinely revealed dogma: that the Immaculate Mother of God, the ever Virgin Mary, having completed the course of her earthly life, was assumed body and soul into heavenly glory.[58]

Munificentissimus Deus does not neglect the past history of Papal favor to the Assumption, but the theological principle invoked to justify the proclamation of the dogma is the present uniform faith of the whole Church. The Holy Father appeals, first of all, to the "concordant teaching of the Church's ordinary doctrinal authority

---

[57] *Ibid.*, p. 583.

[58] *Ibid.*, Vol. 42, 1950, p. 769. The Latin is: "... divinitus revelatum dogma esse: Immaculatam Deiparam semper Virginem Mariam, expleto terrestris vitae cursu, fuisse corpore et anima ad caelestem gloriam assumptam." English of the N.C.W.C. translation, No. 44; also in Palmer, p. 113.

and the concordant faith of the Christian people which the same doctrinal authority sustains and directs" as manifesting the bodily Assumption to be a revealed truth.[59]

B. The Assumption in History

The documents of the *magisterium* before the reign of Pius XII do not exhibit any official Papal statement clearly stating Our Lady's bodily Assumption. There has never been any doubt that her soul is in heaven. For example, Benedict XII authoritatively declared in 1336 that the souls of the saints enjoy the beatific vision.[60] Pope Pius XII's first express mention of Our Lady's presence, body and soul, in heaven is in the encyclical on the Mystical Body, 1943. Yet, as *Munificentissimus Deus* relates, "Various testimonies, indications and signs of this common belief of the Church are evident from remote times down through the course of the centuries."[61]

What are some of these signs? How have the popes shown their approval of belief in the Assumption in the history of the Church? Munificentissimus Deus looks first to the law of prayer (*lex orandi*), saying that the sacred liturgy "because it is the profession, subject to the supreme teaching authority within the Church, of heavenly truths, can supply proofs and testimonies of no small value for deciding any individual point of Catholic doctrine."[62] *Lex orandi, lex credendi* (the law of praying is the law of believing) is an old motto, based on the close connection between sound doctrine and true devotion. The Church's care of cult is not a merely disciplinary matter; in approving its liturgy the Church acts infallibly. The official prayers of the Church, particularly the Mass and Divine

---

[59] A.A.S., Vol. 42, 1950, p. 756; N.C.W.C. translation, No. 12. Cf. Bishop Wright, *The Dogma of the Assumption*, in *The American Ecclesiastical Review*, Vol. 124, 1951, pp. 81-96, and the same article in Studies in Praise of Our Blessed Mother, ed. J. C. Fenton and E. D. Benard (Washington, D. C., 1952), pp. 215-230; P. Parente, *La giustificazione teologica della definizione dommatica dell'Assunzione*, in *Euntes Docete*, Vol. 4, 1951, pp. 257-274; G. Filograssi, S.J., *Constitutio Apostolica "Munificentissimus Deus" de Assumptione beatae Mariae Virginis*, in *Gregorianum*, Vol. 31, 1950, pp. 323-360.

[60] D.B., 530.

[61] A.A.S., Vol. 42, 1950, p. 757; N.C.W.C. translation, No. 13.

[62] A.A.S., Vol. 42, 1950, p. 758; N.C.W.C. translation, No. 16.

Office, are a practical school of Christian doctrine. The Apostolic See has used its authority to encourage the feast of the Assumption and to explain its true sense. Nor does the Pope neglect the Rosary in the attitude of the faithful, for he adds, "Nor can we pass over in silence the fact that in the Rosary of Mary, the recitation of which this Apostolic See so urgently recommends, there is one mystery proposed for pious meditation which, as all know, deals with the Blessed Virgin's Assumption into heaven."[63]

Pope St. Sergius I (687-701) prescribed the litany or stational procession to be held on the four Marian feasts: the Nativity, Annunciation, Purification, and Dormition.[64] Under Pope St. Adrian I (772-795) appears for the first time in the West the title "Assumption" for the feast earlier called the "Dormition" or "Falling Asleep" of Our Lady. The Pope sent Charlemagne the Gregorian Sacramentary, a liturgical book containing the prayer Veneranda, in which occur the words, "this day on which the holy Mother of God suffered temporal death, but still could not be kept down by the bonds of death, who has begotten Thy Son Our Lord incarnate from herself."[65]

Pope St. Leo IV (847-855), again according to Munificentissimus Deus, "saw to it that the feast, which was already being celebrated under the title of the Assumption of the Blessed Mother of God, should be observed in even a more solemn way when he ordered a vigil to be held on the day before it and afterwards prescribed prayers on the octave day. When this had been done, he decided to take part himself in the celebration. ..."[66]

Pope Innocent IV (1243-1254) counted the Assumption an opinion that could be held or not held, for the Church had not yet

---

[63] *A.A.S.*, Vol. 42, 1950, p. 758; N.C.W.C. translation, No. 15.

[64] *A.A.S.*, Vol. 42, 1950, p. 760; N.C.W.C. translation, No. 19.

[65] This prayer now occurs as a Collect in the Assumption Mass of the Dominican, Carmelite, and other rites. Cf. the articles of Dom B. Capelle, O.S.B., *L'Oraison "Veneranda" à la Messe de l'Assomption, in Ephemerides Theologicae Lovanienses*, Vol. 26, 1950, pp. 354-364; *Le témoignage de la Liturgie, in Études Mariales (Assomption de Marie, II)*, Vol. 7, 1949, pp. 35-62; and *L'Assunzione e la liturgia, in Marianum*, Vol. 15, 1953, pp. 241-276.

[66] *A.A.S.*, Vol. 42, 1950, p. 760; N.C.W.C. translation, No. 19.

decided.[67] Many theologians were strongly in favor of the doctrine, among them St. Albert the Great, St. Thomas Aquinas, St. Bonaventure, Scotus. The Assumption never met the strong scholastic opposition found in the case of the Immaculate Conception.

Between the twelfth and fifteenth centuries a series of gradual changes in the Mass for the Assumption and its vigil emphasized more and more the glorious resurrection of Mary; less emphasis was placed on her death. St. Pius V (1566-1572) removed from the second nocturn of Matins the lessons wrongly attributed to St. Jerome. These readings, in an excess of prudence against the apocryphal stories of Mary's death and resurrection, had counseled an attitude of reserve toward the bodily Assumption. Pius V put in their place lessons explaining the bodily Assumption.[68]

C. Pius IX to the Present

From Pius IX to Pius XII, the popes have spoken more often of Mary in heaven. They have at the same time received petitions and encouraged the movement for the dogmatic definition. May we not then see in their references to Our Lady in heaven an implicit affirmation of her bodily Assumption?

Pius IX (1846-1878), in *Ineffabilis Deus*, emphasized the close bond that linked the Mother of God with her Son Jesus Christ: "from all eternity joined in a hidden way with Jesus Christ in one and the same decree of predestination."[69] *Munificentissimus Deus* connects the sinless conception and anticipated resurrection as parts of the same victory over sin and its consequences. "[Mary] by an entirely

---

[67] Cf. G. Geenen, O.P., *L'Assomption et les Souverains Pontifes. Faits, documents et textes*, in *Angelicum*, Vol. 27, 1950, pp. 327-355; this reference, p. 334. Fr. Geenen has gathered his facts from M. Jugie, A.A., *La Mort et l'Assomption de la Sainte Vierge* (Città del Vaticano, 1944); and from G. Hentrich et R. G. de Moos, *Petitiones de Assumptione Corporea B. V. Mariae in caelum definienda*, 2 vols. (Typis Polyglottis Vaticanis, 1942). Cf. also, for the popes of that period, C. Piana, O.F.M., *Assumptio beatae Virginis Mariae apud scriptores saec. XIII* (Sibenici et Romae, 1942).

[68] Cf. William O'Shea, S.S., *The History of the Feast of the Assumption*, in *The Thomist*, Vol. 14, 1951, pp. 127-128.

[69] Quoted in *Munificentissimus Deus*, A.A.S., Vol. 42, 1950, p. 768; N.C.W.C. translation, No. 40.

unique privilege completely overcame sin by her Immaculate Conception, and as a result she was not subject to the law of remaining in the corruption of the grave, and she did not have to wait until the end of time for the redemption of her body."[70]

In 1864 Pius IX received a petition for the definition of the Assumption from Queen Isabella II of Spain. Although the Pope judged the time not yet opportune for the definition, he wrote in reply, "There is no doubt that the Assumption, in the sense commonly believed by the body of the faithful, follows from the Immaculate Conception."[71] A petition was presented in 1870 at the Vatican Council.[72]

Pope Leo XIII (1878-1903) gave his explicit approval to the program of studies of the International Marian Congress held at Fribourg, Switzerland, 1902. The topics included the dogmatic study of the Assumption. Among Leo XIII's many Marian documents, especially the Rosary encyclicals, some references seem to concern the Assumption, especially those treating of Our Lady as Queen. For example, *Iucunda semper* (1894) thus describes the glorious mysteries of the Rosary: "... We behold her taken up from this valley of tears into the heavenly Jerusalem, amid choirs of angels. And we honor her, glorified above all the saints, crowned with stars by her Divine Son, and seated at His side, the sovereign Queen of the universe."[73]

Blessed Pius X was already interested in the Assumption when he was Patriarch of Venice. He was one of the instigators of the petition sent to the Fribourg Congress. As Pope he encouraged the movement for the definition, sending congratulatory messages concerning the Congresses of 1906 at Einsiedeln, Switzerland, and Valencia, Spain. Both conventions submitted petitions for the

---

[70] *A.A.S.*, Vol. 42, 1950, p. 754; N.C.W.C. translation, No. 5. On the relationship between the Immaculate Conception and the Assumption, cf. Roschini, The Assumption and the Immaculate Conception, in The Thomist, Vol. 14, 1951, pp. 59-71, and K. Healy, O.Carm., The Assumption among Mary's Privileges, ibid., pp. 77-81.

[71] Geenen, *art. cit.*, pp. 337-338; Healy, *art. cit.*, p. 78.

[72] *A.A.S.*, Vol. 42, 1950, p. 755; N.C.W.C. translation. No. 7.

[73] Tondini, 158; Lawler, 116 (*The Rosary of Mary*, ed. Wm. Lawler, O.P.) (Paterson, N. J., 1944).

proclamation of the Assumption as a dogma. On another occasion, in 1908, he said, "There is still need for many studies, and for serious ones."[74] The same year he ordered the definability thoroughly studied.

Some consider that *Ad diem illum* of Blessed Pius X alludes to the Assumption in its interpretation of the Woman of the twelfth chapter of the Apocalypse. "A great sign appeared in heaven: a woman clothed with the sun, and the moon was under her feet, and upon her head a crown of twelve stars" (Apoc. 12:1). After quoting this text, Blessed Pius adds: "No one is ignorant that this woman signified the Virgin Mary, who remained inviolate when she brought forth our Head. ... So John saw the most holy Mother of God already enjoying happiness ..."[75]

Benedict XV, like his two predecessors, decreed that all the petitions for the Assumption be kept. During World War I he requested that the sending of petitions be deferred until peace came again.

Pius XI encouraged the movement for the definition. On March 2, 1922, he named Our Lady under her title of the Assumption principal Patroness of France; and on May 31, 1937, gave his approval to the third-centenary celebrations of Louis XIII's solemn consecration of the kingdom to Our Lady, a vow that was annually commemorated on the feast of the Assumption.

The pontificate of Pius XII is distinguished by a whole series of statements and writings about the Assumption, before as well as after the definition. To list or attempt to analyze them would require a book. A few selected examples must suffice here.

In *Mystici Corporis*, June 29, 1943, there is the first explicit mention in a Papal document of Our Lady's bodily Assumption into heaven:

> May she, then, most holy Mother of all Christ's members, to whose Immaculate Heart We have trustingly consecrated all men, her body and soul refulgent with the glory of heaven where she reigns with her Son — may she never cease to beg from Him that a continuous copious flow of graces may pass from its glorious Head into all the

---

[74] Geenen, *art. cit.*, p. 339.

[75] Unger, *Mary Mediatrix*, pp. 16-17.

members of the Mystical Body.[76]

Meantime, the Holy Father was taking active steps toward the definition. He issued special orders commanding more advanced inquiries into the matter, and likewise ordered the publication of the petitions since Pius IX's time.[77] Following the same procedure which Pius IX had used before defining the Immaculate Conception, by the letter *Deiparae Virginis Mariae*, May 1, 1946, the Pope asked all the bishops,

> ... to make known to Us how much devotion is manifested by the clergy and the faithful entrusted to your care toward the Assumption of the Most Blessed Virgin, in accordance with the faith and the piety of each. Above all, We desire to know if you, Venerable Brethren, in your outstanding wisdom and prudence, are of the opinion that the bodily Assumption of the Blessed Virgin can be proposed and defined as a dogma of faith, and if, with your clergy and people, you so desire.[78]

D. "Munificentissimus Deus"

The replies of the bishops showed the "outstanding agreement of the Catholic prelates and the faithful."[79] On November 1, 1950, in the fullest exercise of his supreme teaching authority, speaking infallibly as Vicar of Christ, the Holy Father defined the Assumption of the Blessed Virgin Mary, body and soul, into heavenly glory, as a truth revealed by God.

The dogmatic definition concerns the Assumption alone: "... a divinely revealed dogma: that the Immaculate Mother of God, the ever Virgin Mary, having completed the course of her earthly life, was assumed body and soul into heavenly glory."[80] In the precise

---

[76] *A.A.S.*, Vol. 35, 1943, pp. 247-248; English of the N.C.W.C. translation, No. 108. There is also a connection between the doctrine of the Immaculate Heart, to which the Pope here refers, and the bodily Assumption, for Our Lady's Most Pure Heart is her physical heart; cf. Remigius De Roo, *Regina in Coelum Assumpta*, in *Les Tracts Marials*, Nos. 37-38, Mars-Avril, 1953, pp. 49-50. There are many studies on Mystici Corporis, e.g., J. Dillersberger, *Das neue Wort über Maria*, (Salzburg, 1947).

[77] *A.A.S.*, Vol. 42, 1950, p. 756; N.C.W.C. translation, No. 10.

[78] *A.A.S.*, Vol. 42, 1950, pp. 782-783.

[79] *A.A.S.*, Vol. 42, 1950, p. 756; N.C.W.C. translation, No. 12.

[80] *A.A.S.*, Vol. 42, 1950, p. 769; cf. note 57 for the Latin text.

words of the definition are mentioned, in addition to the Assumption, only the three privileges of Our Lady defined as dogmas in earlier centuries: Mother of God, ever Virgin, Immaculate. Nothing is said of when or where or in *what manner* the Assumption occurred. Nor does the actual formula say anything about Mary's Mediation, her Queenship, or other privileges.

Munificentissimus Deus provides a rich background for the better understanding of the newly defined dogma. The theological principle of the universal consent of the Church is explained, and new light shed on the role of the supreme *magisterium*. A survey is given of the belief across the ages, both in the liturgy and in patristic and theological writings.

The marvelous harmony between Mary's gifts is described: "God ... put the plan of His providence into effect in such a way that all the privileges and prerogatives He had granted to her in His sovereign generosity were to shine forth in her in a kind of perfect harmony. ... The wonderful harmony and order of those privileges which the most provident God has lavished upon this revered associate of our Redeemer ..."[81] The Assumption is compared with the Immaculate Conception; with Mary's association in her Son's victory over the devil, sin, and death; with her virginity in the birth of Christ. The common fountainhead of all Mary's privileges is the divine motherhood. The scriptural foundations are examined in the light of traditional interpretation: especially the Protoevangelium — the Woman of Genesis 3:15; the "full of grace" of Luke 1:28; and "that Woman clothed with the Sun, whom John the Apostle contemplated on the island of Patmos" (Apoc. 12:1 ff.).[82]

At the close, the Holy Father expresses his confidence:

> ... That this solemn proclamation and definition of the Assumption will contribute in no small way to the advantage of human society, since it redounds to the glory of the Most Blessed Trinity, to which the Blessed Mother of God was bound by such singular bonds. It is to be hoped that all the faithful will be stirred up to a stronger piety toward their heavenly Mother, and that the souls of all those who glory in the Christian name may be moved by the desire of sharing in the unity of Christ's Mystical Body and of increasing their love for her

---

[81] *A.A.S.*, Vol. 42, 1950, pp. 754, 758; N.C.W.C. translation, Nos. 3, 14.

[82] *A.A.S.*, Vol. 42, 1950, p. 763; N.C.W.C. translation, No. 27.

who in all things shows her motherly heart to the members of this august Body. ... In this magnificent way all may see clearly to what a lofty goal our bodies and souls are destined. Finally it is our hope that belief in Mary's bodily Assumption into heaven will make our belief in our own resurrection stronger and render it more effective.[83]

VI. MEDIATRIX WITH THE MEDIATOR

A. Mediation in General

Cardinal Mercier of Belgium began the movement to petition the Holy See for the definition of the doctrine of Our Lady's Mediation of all graces. On January 12, 1921, Pope Benedict XV,[84] permitted a special Office and Mass in honor of Mary Mediatrix on May 31. In 1922, Pius XI organized three commissions of theologians (in Rome, Spain, and Belgium) to make a serious study of the question. There is in the writings of the recent Popes, especially the encyclicals from Pope Pius IX to the present day, a mine of material about Mary's role in the gaining and distribution of divine graces.

Today many theological writers hold that this belief is contained implicitly in divine revelation and could be defined as a dogma. There is no Catholic theologian who denies to Our Lady the title: Mediatrix of all graces. But since the term "mediation" has many shades of meaning, the sense in which the Mother of God is called Mediatrix must first be explained.

A mediator is a person who stands in the middle and unites individuals or groups which are opposed. Our blessed Lord, the God-Man, was uniquely fitted to be the Mediator between God and man. St. Paul says, "For there is one God, and one Mediator between God and man, himself man, Christ Jesus, who gave himself a ransom for all ..." (1 Tim. 2:5-6). By offering Himself, through His whole life and the sacrifice of the cross, Christ, our Mediator, destroyed the middle wall between God and ourselves, wiped out the handwriting against us, brought His human brothers back to full friendship with God the Father. The Lord fulfilled His mission of mediation by becoming our Redeemer or "Ransomer."

The Redemption or mediation Christ accomplished on earth did

---

[83] *A.A.S.*, Vol. 42, 1950, pp. 769-770; N.C.W.C. translation, No. 42.
[84] *A.A.S.*, Vol. 13, 1921, p. 345.

not end there. The divine grace won by the Redemption must be applied to individuals through the means determined by Christ, that is, through His Church, by faith, the Sacraments, etc. The first phase of Our Lord's mediation was the work of Redemption perfected on the cross; the second phase is the individual application of the fruits of this work.

Where, then, is there place for another Mediator? In what sense is the Mother of Christ associated with her Son in His work of mediation? Does her association extend to both phases of His redemptive work? What has the Church's *magisterium* said on these topics?

If there is only "one Mediator," as St. Paul writes, then any other Mediator can only be such in strict dependence and in a secondary sense. Pope Leo XIII quotes St. Thomas Aquinas on the possibility of other mediators:

> ... As the Angelic Doctor teaches, "there is no reason why certain others should not be called in a certain way mediators between God and man, that is to say, insofar as they co-operate by predisposing and ministering in the union of man with God." Such are the angels and saints, the prophets and priests of both Testaments; but especially has the Blessed Virgin a claim to the glory of this title. For no single individual can even be imagined who has ever contributed or ever will contribute so much toward reconciling man with God. She offered a Saviour to mankind, hastening to eternal ruin, at that moment when she received the announcement of the mystery of peace brought to this earth by the angel, with that admirable act of consent — and this, "in the name of the whole human race." She it is from whom Jesus is born; she is therefore truly His mother, and for this reason a worthy and acceptable "Mediatrix to the Mediator."[85]

St. Thomas Aquinas' phrase "in the name of the whole human race" recalls what is the oldest idea about Mary found in Christian literature after the New Testament itself. By representing all humanity in consenting to the Incarnation and in offering the Victim on Calvary, Our Lady, like a new Eve, repaired the harm in which the first Eve was involved. Some writers claim the parallel between the first Eve and the second Eve goes back to the Apostles

---

[85] *Fidentem piumque*, Tondini, pp. 248-250; Lawler, pp. 150-151; *D.B.*, 1940 a.

themselves.[86]

Cardinal Newman showed in the writings of St. Justin (d. 165), St. Irenaeus (d. 200), and Tertullian (d. 240), Mary's association with Christ the new Adam. Adam called his helpmate and wife "Eve," meaning Mother of the living. Adam's fall introduced original sin into the world, but Eve had an intimate personal share in "that awful transaction" (Newman's phrase). Yet even in the hour of punishment God promised a Redeemer, and warned the serpent, "I will put enmity between thee and the woman and between thy seed and her seed" (Gen. 3:15). The woman who would crush the serpent's head was the obedient Virgin, Mother of the Redeemer.

Newman concluded from his investigations: "St. Justin, St. Irenaeus, and others, had distinctly laid it down, that she [Mary] not only had an office [i.e., of motherhood], but bore a part, and was a voluntary agent in the actual process of redemption, as Eve had been instrumental and responsible in Adam's fall.[87] St. Irenaeus' idea of the "Virgin who regenerates us" shows the close parallel between Eve, mother of all the living, and Mary, the new Eve, mother of those born again through Christ's redemption. "By the time of St. Jerome (331-420), the contrast between Eve and Mary had almost passed into a proverb. He says, 'Death by Eve, life by Mary.'"[88]

In the order of history the belief of the faithful and the writings of the Church's theologians were expressly directed to Our Lady's share in Christ's work of mediation even before such doctrines as the Immaculate Conception and the Assumption were explicitly held.[89] Newman saw the doctrine of the Immaculate Conception as "an immediate inference from the primitive doctrine that Mary is the second Eve."[90]

---

[86] Cf. R. Garrigou-Lagrange, O.P., *The Mother of the Saviour and Our Interior Life* (Dublin, 1948), p. 184; for this point and for many others, see E. Druwé, S.J., La médiation universelle de Marie, in Maria. Études sur la Sainte Vierge, ed. H. du Manoir, Vol. 1 (Paris, 1949), pp. 417-572.

[87] Cardinal Newman, An Essay in the Development of Christian Doctrine (London, 1845), p. 384 — reference from L. Riley, Historical Conspectus of the Doctrine of Mary's Co-Redemption, in Marian Studies, Vol. 2, 1951, p. 84, n. (229).

[88] Cf. Cardinal Newman, *The New Eve* (Oxford, 1952), p. 19.

[89] Cf. Druwé, *art. cit.*, p. 478.

[90] Newman, op. cit., p. 25.

A common term to describe Mary's participation in Christ's redemptive work is "Coredemptrix." By it is meant the association of the Mother of Christ in the properly redemptive work which Our Lord performed on earth, principally through His Passion and death. In the second phase of Our Lord's mediation Our Lady is called the "dispensatrix of all graces" or often simply "mediatrix." Some writers divide the two phases of mediation into the objective Redemption and the *subjective* Redemption.

Our consideration of the teaching of the popes on both Coredemptrix and Dispensatrix will be restricted to the past century, from Pius IX to the present. Earlier evidences do exist of Papal statements on Mary as mediatrix, but the many Marian writings and discourses of the recent Popes are more than sufficient expression of the ordinary *magisterium* of the Church. We say "ordinary" *magisterium* because up to the present the Church has not yet used its teaching authority to give a dogmatic definition of Mary's Mediation.

B. Coredemptrix

In interpreting statements of recent popes concerning the Coredemption, the advice of Bittremieux is opportune. Namely, we should presume that the popes have followed a consistent line in their teaching, the more so when they quote their predecessors, even though a predecessor may not have taken so clear a stand as his successor. This was the case in the history of the Immaculate Conception. The Coredemption seems to enjoy a similar development, with successive popes speaking ever more favorably.[91]

---

[91] J. Bittremieux, *Il movimento mariologico dell'anno* 1938-1939, in *Marianum*, Vol. 2, 1940, p. 12; Druwé, *art. cit.*, p. 458. On the Coredemption: J. B. Carol, O.F.M., *De Corredemptione B. Virginis Mariae* (Civitas Vaticana, 1950); H. Seiler, S.J., *Corredemptrix, Theologische Studie zur Lehre der Letzen Päpste über die Miterlöserschaft Mariens*, Rom, 1939; *Marian Studies*, Vol. 2, 1951, on the theme of the Coredemption. Studies in Praise of Our Blessed Mother, ed. J. C. Fenton and E. D. Benard (Washington, D. C., 1952), contains the following articles on this topic; after the pagination in studies is given in parentheses the volume, year and pages of *The American Ecclesiastical Review*, where these studies first appeared: T. U. Mullaney, O.P., *The Meaning of Mary's Compassion*, pp. 100-127 (Vol. 125, 1951, pp. 1-6, 120-129, 196-207); A. Michel, *Mary's Co-Redemption*, pp. 137-146 (Vol. 122, 1950, pp. 183-192); C.

What, then, do the popes tell us about Mary's share in her Son's redemptive work?

The title "*Coredemptrix*" first received Papal sanction under Pope Pius X, by his approval of its use in a decree of the Congregation of Rites concerning the feast of the Seven Dolors.[92] Pius XI used the term on several occasions, for example, in the radio address to Lourdes, 1935, which will be quoted later.[93] The word Coredemptrix is now accepted almost universally, for its use by Pius XI and by theologians has shown that Coredemption is still only a subordinate, secondary, dependent collaboration in Christ's all-perfect, self-sufficient work of salvation.

Pius IX in *Ineffabilis Deus* wrote of the association of Mary with her Son:

> ... Just as Christ, the Mediator between God and man, assumed human nature, blotted out the handwriting of the decree that stood against us, and fastened it triumphantly to the Cross (Col. 2, 14), so the Most Holy Virgin, united with Him by a most intimate and indissoluble bond, was, with Him and through Him, eternally at enmity with that poisonous serpent, and most completely triumphed over him, and thus crushed his head with her immaculate foot.[94]

Pius XI extends this union of Mother and Son to the Redemption: "The most blessed Virgin, conceived without original sin, was chosen to be the Mother of God so that she might be made an associate in the Redemption of mankind."[95] Our Lady's acceptance of the Annunciation was her consent to become Mother of the Redeemer. From this standpoint alone Mary had at least a remote part in the Redemption. Whether she had a proximate, immediate, direct share in the actual Redemption is a disputed question among Catholic scholars. Those who defend the Coredemption in the strict sense appeal to the following Papal

---

Boyer, S.J., *Thoughts on Mary's Co-Redemption*, pp. 147-161 (Vol. 122, 1950, pp. 401-415); J. Carol, O.F.M., *Mary's Co-Redemption in the Teaching of Pope Pius XII*, pp. 162-170 (Vol. 121, 1949, pp. 353-361).

[92] *A.A.S.*, Vol. 41, 1908, p. 409.

[93] Cf. Roschini, *Mariologia*, 2a ed., Vol. 2, p. 389; R. Laurentin, *Le titre de Corédemptrice. Étude historique, in Marianum*, Vol. 13, 1951, pp. 396-452.

[94] Tondini, p. 42; Unger, *Mary Immaculate*, p. 11.

[95] *A.A.S.*, Vol. 25, 1933, p. 80 (Epistola ad Card. Binet).

statements about Mary's role in Calvary; the adversaries (a small but strong minority) interpret the same documents differently.[96]

Pius X in *Ad diem illum* stated:

> ... The most holy Mother of God had not only the honor of "having given the substance of her flesh to the only begotten Son of God, who was to be born of the human race," whereby a victim was prepared for man's salvation, but she was also entrusted with the task of tending and nourishing this Victim and even of offering it on the altar at the appointed time.[97]

Leo XIII wrote that Mary was a "co-worker with Christ in His expiation for mankind," and that on Calvary "she offered up her Son to the divine justice dying with Him in her heart."[98]

Benedict XV said it more clearly: "Thus, she [Mary] suffered and all but died along with her Son suffering and dying; thus, for the salvation of men she abdicated the rights of a mother toward her Son, and insofar as it was hers to do, she immolated the Son to placate God's justice, so that she herself may justly be said to have redeemed together with Christ the human race."[99]

Pius XI in *Miserentissimus Redemptor*, 1928, wrote, "[Mary] by giving us Christ the Redeemer, and by rearing Him, and by offering Him at the foot of the Cross as Victim for our sins, by such intimate association with Christ, and by her own most singular grace, became and is affectionately known as Reparatrix."[100]

Pius XII has also spoken of Our Lady's part in the Redemption. The epilogue to *Mystici Corporis* tells us: "Free from all sin, original and personal, always most intimately united with her Son, as another Eve she offered Him on Golgotha to the Eternal Father for all the children of Adam sin-stained by his fall, and her mother's

---

[96] Cf. L. Riley, *Historical Conspectus of the Doctrine*, in *Marian Studies*, Vol. 2, 1951, p. 96 ff.

[97] Cf. Unger, *Mary Mediatrix*, p. 8; Palmer, p. 94; Tondini, p. 312.

[98] Tondini, pp. 204-206; Lawler, pp. 114-115. *Iucunda semper.*

[99] A.A.S., Vol. 10, 1918, p. 182; Palmer, p. 97; Carol, *De Corredemptione*, pp. 524-527.

[100] A.A.S., Vol. 20, 1928, p. 178; Palmer, p. 98.

rights and mother's love were included in the holocaust."[101]

Munificentissimus Deus shows the connection between the truths of the Assumption and the Coredemption, by stressing the close association between Mary and the Redeemer.[102] Our Lady is called the *alma socia Redemptoris*, "revered associate of our Redeemer."[103] The belief in the new Eve is recalled: the struggle and victory common to the Blessed Virgin and her Son. Finally Mary is again called "the noble associate of the divine Redeemer (*generosa Divini Redemptoris socia*) who has won a complete triumph over sin and its consequences."[104]

C. Dispensatrix

In *Doctor Mellifluus*, May 24, 1953, the encyclical on the 800th anniversary of St. Bernard's death, Pius XII repeats the great Marian writer's phrase on Our Lady's Mediation: "It is the will of God that we should have nothing which has not passed through the hands of Mary."[105]

St. Paul teaches that "... He [Christ] is able at all times to save those who come to God through Him, since He lives always to make intercession for them" (Hebr. 7:25). Mary's share in this second phase of Christ's mediation, namely the dispensing of the graces of the Redemption to individuals, has been believed in the Church from earliest times. The Gospels show Our Lady as the channel of divine grace, first of all through her divine motherhood, but also on other occasions. In the mystery of the Visitation, the unborn John was filled with grace through Mary's charitable visit. "Her only Son," says *Mystici Corporis*, "yielding to a mother's prayer in 'Cana of Galilee,' performed the miracle by which 'His disciples believed in him' (Jn. 2:11)."[106] *Iucunda semper* describes the scene in the

---

[101] *A.A.S.*, Vol. 35, 1943, pp. 247-248; N.C.W.C. translation, No. 107; Palmer, pp. 98-100.

[102] Cf. J. B. Carol, O.F.M., The Apostolic Constitution *"Munificentissimus Deus" and Our Blessed Lady's Coredemption*, in *The American Ecclesiastical Review*, Vol. 125, 1951, pp. 255-273.

[103] *A.A.S.*, Vol. 42, 1950, p. 758; N.C.W.C. translation, No. 14.

[104] *A.A.S.*, Vol. 42, 1950, p. 768; N.C.W.C. translation. No. 40.

[105] *A.A.S.*, Vol. 45, 1953, p. 382.

[106] *Ibid.*, Vol. 35, 1943, pp. 247-248; N.C.W.C. translation, No. 107.

Cenacle: "Mary is ... there, praying with the Apostles and entreating for them with sighs and tears, she hastens for the Church the coming of the Spirit, the Comforter, the supreme gift of Christ, the treasure that will never fail."[107]

Mary's office of dispensatrix of graces is the consequence of her part in the Redemption. *Adiutricem populi* says that after her Assumption

> she began, by God's decree, to watch over the Church, to assist and befriend us as our Mother; so that she who was intimately associated with the mystery of human salvation (*sacramenti humanae redemptionis*) is just as closely associated with the distribution of the graces which for all time will flow from the Redemption. The power thus put into her hands is all but unlimited.[108]

Pius XI spoke by radio to Lourdes, April 28, 1935, at the conclusion of the Jubilee Year of the Redemption. "O Mother of pity and mercy, who as Co-sufferer and Co-redemptrix (*compatiens et corredemptrix*) assisted thy most dear Son, as on the altar of the Cross He consummated the Redemption of mankind ... preserve in us and increase each day, we beg of thee, the precious fruits of the Redemption and of thy Compassion. ..."[109]

How great is Mary's power when she intercedes in our behalf? The popes set no limit on it; they speak of a truly universal Mediation — of all graces and for each individual, even for those who through forgetfulness or ignorance fail to ask her help. For Pius IX, "with her Son, the Only-begotten, she is the most powerful Mediatrix and Conciliatrix of the whole world."[110] Leo XIII in encyclical after encyclical on the Rosary extols Mary's Mediation; e.g., in *Magnae Dei Matris*: one of many similar passages reads:

> When we have recourse to Mary in prayer, we are having recourse to the Mother of mercy, who is so well disposed toward us that, whatever the necessity that presses upon us, especially in

---

[107] Tondini, p. 206; Lawler, p. 115.

[108] Tondini, p. 222; Lawler, p. 130.

[109] *L'Osservatore Romano*, April 29-30, 1935; English translation as in G. Shea, The Teaching of the *magisterium* on Mary's Spiritual Maternity, in Marian Studies, 3, 1952, p. 98. Bover, Shea, Carol, Seiler, and other Mariologists attach great doctrinal value to this message of the Pope.

[110] Tondini, p. 54; Unger, Mary Immaculate, p. 22; Palmer, p. 88.

attaining eternal life, she is instantly at our side of her own accord, even though she has not been invoked; and dispenses grace with a generous hand from that treasure with which from the beginning she was divinely endowed in fullest abundance that she might be worthy to be the Mother of God.[111]

Pius X: in *Ad diem illum* says:

By this community of pain and will between Christ and Mary "she merited to become in a most worthy manner the Reparatrix of the lost world," and consequently, the Dispenser of all the gifts that Jesus acquired for us by His Death and Blood. ... Who knew better than all others the secrets of His Heart, and who by maternal right distributes the treasures of His merits.[112]

After saying that Mary "may justly be said to have redeemed together with Christ the human race," Pope Benedict XV continues: "for this very reason, every grace we receive from the treasury of the Redemption is given to us as by the hands of the same sorrowing Virgin."[113]

Even the favors for which we thank the other saints come through the Queen of All Saints. Thus Pius XI in *Ingravescentibus Malis* (encyclical on the Rosary) mentions his gratitude for the recovery of his health: "This grace ... We attribute to the special intercession of the virgin of Lisieux, St. Therese of the Child Jesus, but we know nonetheless that all things are given to us by the great and Good God through the hands of His Mother."[114]

VII. SPIRITUAL MOTHER

Our Lady's Mediation is the proof of her motherly love for men. Pius XI wrote in *Lux veritatis*, "She, by the very fact that she brought forth the Redeemer of the human race, is also in a manner the most tender Mother of us all, whom Christ Our Lord deigned to

---

[111] Tondini, p. 158; Lawler, p. 79.

[112] Tondini, pp. 312-314; Unger, Mary Mediatrix, pp. 8-10; *D.B.*, 1978 a.

[113] *A.A.S.*, Vol. 10, 1918, p. 182.

[114] *Ibid.*, Vol. 29, 1937, p. 380; Tondini, p. 424.

have as His brothers (Rom. 8:29)."[115] The belief of Catholics that Mary is our spiritual Mother has never been solemnly proclaimed by the *magisterium* of the Church. Nor does the invocation of Mary as Our Mother occur in these words before the Middle Ages, but the spiritual motherhood was equivalently believed in the patristic phrases, "second Eve, new Eve, Mother of the living." The doctrine, as recent popes have told us, is implicit in the Gospels: in Mary's fiat at the Annunciation, and in Christ's legacy on Calvary "Behold thy mother" (Jn. 19:27). The popes by their ordinary teaching authority have been preaching Mary's spiritual motherhood with ever increasing emphasis. Papal statements on the "Mother of grace" are at least as old as Sixtus IV, who used this term in *Cum praecelsa*, 1477.[116]

Benedict XIV (1740-1758) wrote in approval of the Marian sodalities: "The Catholic Church, schooled by the Holy Ghost, has always most diligently professed, not only to venerate Mary most devoutly as the Mother of the Lord and Redeemer, the Queen of heaven and of earth, but also to honor her with filial affection as the most loving Mother who was left to her with the last words of her dying Spouse."[117]

Pius IX (1846-1878) frequently referred to Mary as Our Mother. The encyclical *Ubi primum*, February 2, 1849, asking the bishops' mind on the Immaculate Conception, speaks of "the most holy Mother of God, and the most loving Mother of us all, the Immaculate Virgin Mary."[118] *Ineffabilis Deus* calls Our Lady "the dearest Mother of mercy and of grace."[119] Addressing a group of

---

[115] Tondini, 400. These pages borrow heavily from the thorough treatment of Fr. George W. Shea, *The Teaching of the magisterium on Mary's Spiritual Maternity*, in *Marian Studies*, Vol. 3, 1952, pp. 35-110. The whole volume is devoted to the spiritual motherhood, with studies by W. Sebastian, O.F.M., William R. O'Connor, C. Vollert, S.J., etc. Cf. also C. Vollert, *Mother of Divine Grace*, in *Studies in Praise of Our Blessed Mother*, pp. 24-36, originally published in *The American Ecclesiastical Review*, Vol. 126, 1952, pp. 258-270. English translations for this section are Dr. Shea's.

[116] Shea, *art. cit.*, p. 42.

[117] Shea, *art. cit.*, p. 44, quoting *Benedicti XIV Opera Omnia*, Vol. 16 (Prati, 1846), p. 428. This was the Bull *Gloriosae Dominae*.

[118] Tondini, p. 2.

[119] Tondini, p. 56.

pilgrims September 17, 1876, Pius IX said, "There on Calvary, at the foot of the Cross, represented by St. John we were placed under the protection of Mary as our Mother. The last words of the testament which Jesus pronounced ... 'Woman, behold thy son.'"[120]

The ten Rosary encyclicals and the *Quamquam pluries* on the patronage of the Blessed Virgin and St. Joseph give us Pope Leo XIII's teaching. Mary "is our Mother not in a human way but through Christ."[121] She is "at one and the same time God's Mother and our Mother."[122] "Just as the most holy Virgin is the Mother of Jesus Christ, so she is the Mother of all Christians."[123] Indeed the "whole human race was entrusted" to her motherly care.[124]

Pope Leo's Marian doctrine pictures Mary's spiritual Maternity under a double aspect: first, because she is Mother of Christ; second, because of her association with the Redeemer even to Calvary.

By the very fact that she was chosen to be the Mother of Christ, Our Lord, Who is at the same time our brother, she was singularly endowed above all other mothers with the mission of manifesting and pouring out her mercy upon us. Moreover, if we are indebted to Christ in that He has shared with us in some way the right, peculiarly His own, of calling God our Father and possessing Him as such, to Christ's loving generosity we are similarly indebted for sharing in His right to call Mary Mother and to possess her as such.[125]

Just as the most holy Virgin is the Mother (*Genetrix*) of Jesus Christ, so she is the Mother of all Christians, whom indeed she bore (generavit) on Mt. Calvary amid the supreme throes of the Redeemer; also, Jesus Christ is as the first-born of all Christians, who by adoption and Redemption are His brothers.[126]

Blessed Pius X in *Ad diem illum* (1904) has a magnificent passage on Mary Our Mother. The reader is urged to consult the

---

[120] Shea, *art. cit.*, p. 54.

[121] Tondini, p. 160. Cf. J. Bittremieux, *Doctrina Mariana Leonis XIII* (Brugis, 1928), pp. 32-42, on the spiritual motherhood.

[122] *Adiutricem populi*, Tondini, p. 230.

[123] Tondini, p. 116 (*Quamquam pluries*).

[124] Tondini, p. 136 (Octobri mense): "universitatem humani generis, in Ioanne discipulo, curandam ei fovendamque commissit."

[125] *Magnae Dei Matris*, Tondini, 158; Shea, *art. cit.*, p. 59.

[126] *Quamquam pluries*, Tondini, p. 116; Shea, *art. cit.* p. 58.

whole encyclical:

> For is not Mary the Mother of Christ? She is therefore our Mother also ... as the God-Man He acquired a body composed like that of other men, but as the Saviour of our race He had a kind of spiritual and mystical Body, which is the society of those who believe in Christ. "We, the many, are one body in Christ" (Romans 12,5) ... Mary, bearing in her womb the Saviour, may be said to have borne also all those whose life was contained in the life of the Saviour. All of us, therefore, who are united with Christ and are, as the Apostle says, "Members of His body, made from His flesh and from His bones" (Ephesians 5,30), have come forth from the womb of Mary as a body united to its head. Hence, in a spiritual and mystical sense, we are called children of Mary, and she is the Mother of us all ... the Most Blessed Virgin is at once the Mother of God and of man. ...[127]

The final phrase in Latin is: "Dei simul atque hominum *parens* est." The word *parens* (parent), earlier used by Pius VII,[128] implied a genuine maternity. It is used by Pius XI, in his first encyclical, *Ubi arcano*, December 23, 1922: "The Virgin Mother of God and the most loving Mother of all of us."[129]

The new Code of Canon Law was promulgated under Pope Benedict XV. Canon 1276 tells us: "It is good and useful to suppliantly invoke the Saints of God, reigning together with Christ ... but above the others let all the faithful show the Most Blessed Virgin Mary *filial devotion*."[130] The letter *Inter Sodalicia* (to the Sodality of Our Lady of a Happy Death) contains these words:

> ... she, having been constituted by Jesus Christ as the Mother of all men, received them as bequeathed to her by a testament of infinite charity, and since with maternal tenderness she fulfills her office of protecting their spiritual life, the Sorrowful Virgin cannot but assist, more zealously than ever, her most dear sons by adoption at that moment when their eternal salvation is at stake.[131]

---

[127] Tondini, pp. 310-312; Shea, art. cit., pp. 72-73. Cf. Dillersberger, *Das neue Wort über Maria* (Salzburg, 1947), pp. 197-205; William G. Most, *Blessed Pius X and the Blessed Virgin Mary*, in *The Homiletic and Pastoral Review*, Vol. 52, 1952, pp. 311-314.

[128] Cf. Shea, art. cit., p. 48.

[129] *A.A.S.*, Vol. 14, 1922, p. 675.

[130] *Codex iuris canonici*, 1276; Shea, art. cit., p. 80.

[131] *A.A.S.*, Vol. 10, 1918, pp. 181-182; Shea, art. cit., pp. 81-84.

Pope Pius XI spoke or wrote of the spiritual Maternity on more than 50 occasions. Bertetto well calls him, "The Pope of the Spiritual Maternity and of the Rosary."[132] *Rerum ecclesiae*, the encyclical on the Propagation of the Faith, February 28, 1926, says: "... since on Calvary all men were commended to her motherly affection, she loves and cherishes no less those who do not know of their Redemption by Jesus Christ than those who happily enjoy the benefits of the Redemption."[133]

On the occasion of the jubilee year of the Redemption, Pope Pius XI made frequent references to the dying Saviour's words proclaiming His Mother as Mother of Men, for example, an allocution of August 19, 1933: "The nineteenth centenary of the Redemption ... is also ... the centenary of the universal Maternity of Mary, officially proclaimed by the Divine King from His throne, the Cross."[134]

On November 30, 1933, the Pope gave a discourse to pilgrims: "It is precisely under the cross, in the last moments of His life, that the Redeemer proclaimed her our Mother and universal Mother: 'Behold thy Son,' He said to St. John who represented us all; in the same Apostle we, all of us, received those other words: 'Behold thy Mother.'"[135]

The radio address to Lourdes, April 28, 1935, begins: "Let us all pray to our common Mother. ... Preserve in us and increase each day, we beg of thee, the precious fruits of the Redemption and of thy Compassion, and, thou who are the Mother of all, grant that ... we may finally enjoy untroubled the gifts of peace."[136]

Mystici Corporis of Pius XII, June 29, 1943, condenses in a few paragraphs of exact and beautiful phrases the Marian teachings of the Church. What recent popes have said about the spiritual Maternity is said here still more forcefully:

... She who corporally was the mother of our Head, through the added title of pain and glory became spiritually the mother of all His

---

[132] D. Bertetto, S.D.B., Maria nel Domma Cattolico (Torino, 1950), pp. 295-302.

[133] A.A.S., Vol. 18, 1926, p. 83.

[134] Shea, *art. cit.,* p. 92.

[135] *Ibid.,* p. 93.

[136] L'Osservatore Romano, April 29-30, 1935; Shea, *art.* cit., p. 98.

members. ... Bearing with courage and confidence the tremendous burden of her sorrows and desolation, truly the Queen of Martyrs, she more than all the faithful "filled up those things that are wanting of the suffering of Christ ... for His Body, which is the Church" (Col. 1,24); and she continued to show for the Mystical Body of Christ, born from the pierced Heart of the Saviour, the same mother's care and ardent love, with which she clasped the Infant Jesus to her warm and nourishing breast.[137]

The Latin term used for "Mother of all His members" is *genetrix* — the first time in a Papal document that this word is used for spiritual motherhood. It was previously used only in reference to the divine Maternity.[138]

Pius XII relates the mysteries of the Annunciation and of the Crucifixion to the spiritual motherhood:

But when the little maid of Nazareth uttered her fiat to the message of the Angel and the Word was made flesh in her womb she became not only the Mother of God in the physical order of nature, but also in the supernatural order of grace she became the Mother of all, who through the Holy Spirit would be made one under the Headship of her divine Son.[139]

(Mary) became our Mother when the Divine Saviour was accomplishing His sacrifice of Himself, and thus, under this title also, we are her children.[140]

In the homily delivered immediately after the solemn definition of the Assumption the Pope said: "We are all children of the same Mother, Mary, who lives in Heaven, the bond of union for the Mystical Body of Christ and new Eve, new Mother of the living, who wishes to lead all men to the truth and grace of her divine Son."[141]

---

[137] *A.A.S.*, Vol. 35, 1943, pp. 247-248; D.B., 2291; N.C.W.C. translation, No. 107; Palmer, pp. 99-100.

[138] Cf. G. Geenen, O.P., *Mother of the Mystical Body*, trans. Sister Mary Madonna, C.S.C., in Cross and Crown, Vol. 2, 1950, pp. 385-402; p. 391 on Genetrix.

[139] Tondini, p. 538: Radio message delivered in English to the National Marian Congress at Ottawa, June 19, 1947.

[140] *A.A.S.*, Vol. 39, 1947, p. 582. The encyclical, *Mediator Dei*, November 20, 1947.

[141] A.A.S., Vol. 42, 1950, p. 781.

The souls in purgatory still benefit from Mary's motherly care: "And certainly this most gentle Mother will not delay to open, as soon as possible, through her intercession with God, the gates of Heaven for Her children who are expiating their faults in Purgatory — a trust based on that Promise known as the Sabbatine Privilege."[142]

VIII. QUEEN

A. In Popes of the Past

For centuries, the Church has called Our Lady "Queen." Yet it comes as a surprise to many to discover that the *magisterium*, through the statements of the recent popes, and most of all through His Holiness, Pius XII, has presented a strikingly complete picture of Mary's Queenship in harmonious relationship with her other privileges.[143]

As early as Pope St. Martin I (d. 655) there are references to

---

[142] *Neminem profecto latet*, February 11, 1950, A.A.S., Vol. 43, 1950, p. 391.

[143] American Mariologists have been giving special attention to the Queenship. *Marian Studies*, Vol. 4, 1953, is entirely devoted to this theme; the present writer contributed Our Lady's Queenship in the *magisterium of the Church*, pp. 29-81. The United States section of the Mariological Congress held in Rome, October, 1950, treated the same question: cf. the Acts of the Congress, *Alma Socia Christi*, Vol. 3 (Romae, 1952), containing (in English) the episcopal addresses read at the meeting, by Cardinal Spellman, Archbishop Cushing, and Archbishop O'Boyle, and the studies on different aspects of the Queenship by J. C. Fenton, K. Moore, O.Carm., T. B. Falls, U. Mullaney, O.P., A. Rush, C.SS.R., F. Connell, C.SS.R.

Besides the many books and articles referred to in *Marian Studies*, Vol. 4, the following recent titles may be noted: Remigius J. De Roo, *Regina in coelum assumpta* (*Les rapports entre l'Assomption et la Royauté de Marie*), in *Les Tracts Marials*, Nos. 37-38, Mars-Avril, 1953, an excellent work, its Canadian author's doctorate thesis at the Angelicum University, Rome, 1952; Leone Jambois, *Regalità di Maria Santissima*, in *Enciclopedia Cattolica*, Vol. 10, cols. 635-638 (Città del Vaticano, 1953); G. Filograssi, S.J., *La dottrina mariana dei Papi (da Pio IX a Pio XII)*, in *La Civiltà Cattolica*, anno 103, 1952, Vol. 3, pp. 357-359. From the progress this belief in the Queenship has made, in the liturgy, the Papal teachings, among the theologians and the people, Filograssi calls it certain Catholic doctrine.

Mary as Queen and Empress.[144] Under Pope Adrian I (d. 795), the Seventh Ecumenical Council (second of Nicea) defended the use of sacred images, those of Our Lord (*Dominus*) God and Saviour Jesus Christ, and of our Immaculate Lady (*Domina* — a word with royal significance), the holy Mother of God.[145]

Boniface IX (1389-1404) calls Mary "perfect Queen, royal Virgin, Queen of the heavens."[146] Sixtus IV's *Cum praecelsa* of 1477 speaks of the glorious Virgin Mother of God as "Queen of heaven" and also of her tireless intercession with "the King whom she bore."[147] Benedict XIV in *Gloriosae Dominae*, September 27, 1748, not only recalls the long tradition in the Church of venerating Mary "as Mother of the Lord and Redeemer, Queen of heaven and of earth," and of honoring "her with filial affection as the most loving Mother," but also adds, "For this is the most beautiful Esther, whom the supreme King of Kings so loved that for the salvation of His people He seems to have given her not merely half his kingdom, but in some manner to have communicated to her His whole rule and power. This valiant woman is that Judith, whom the God of Israel permitted to gain victory over all the enemies of His people."[148]

Ineffabilis Deus[149] of Pius IX exalts Mary in these words, "... she has been appointed by God to be the Queen of heaven and earth, and is exalted above all the choirs of angels and classes of Saints." *"Queen conceived without original sin"* was placed in the Litany of Loreto after 1854.

Leo XIII frequently called Our Lady "Queen of the Most Holy Rosary."[150] The encyclical *Magnae Dei Matris* recalls Mary's continual association with her Son:

---

[144] Cf. P. Aubron, *De la Souveraineté de Maria, in Souveraineté de Marie, Congrès Marial de Boulogne S/Mer* (Paris, 1938), pp. 121-122.

[145] Cf. A. Luis, C.SS.R., *La Realeza de Maria* (Madrid, 1942), p. 80.

[146] *Ibid.*

[147] Carroll, art. cit., in *Marian Studies*, Vol. 4, p. 41.

[148] *Ibid.*, p. 43. The Epistle in the new Mass of the Assumption also recalls Judith's triumph (Judith 13:22-25; 15:10); cf. *A.A.S.*, Vol. 42, 1950, p. 793.

[149] Carroll, art. cit., p. 45.

[150] *Salutaris ille*, Tondini, p. 84, is the apostolic letter of December 24, 1883, commanding the insertion of "Queen of the Most Holy Rosary" in the Litany of Loreto.

It is thus that the crown of the kingdoms of heaven and of earth will await her because she will be the invincible Queen of martyrs; it is thus that she will be seated in the heavenly city of God by the side of her Son, crowned for all eternity, because she will drink with Him the cup overflowing with sorrow, faithfully through all her life, most faithfully on Calvary.[151]

Ad diem illum of Blessed Pius X mentions Mary's Queenship in the context of her association with Christ in the work of human salvation and in the ministration of graces. "Christ 'has taken His seat at the right hand of the Majesty on high' (Heb. 1:3), and Mary as Queen stands at His right hand. ..."[152] In a similar setting Mary is called "Queen of Martyrs": "With Mary present and witnessing it, that divine sacrifice was perfected by which we have been redeemed, and she shared in it to such an extent that the Queen of Martyrs both brought forth and nourished the most sacred Victim."[153]

Benedict XV's war-torn pontificate is full of his pleas to the "Queen of Peace." In adding the prayer "Queen of peace, pray for us" to the Litany of Loreto, the Pontiff said, "Will Mary, who is Queen not of wars and slaughter, but of the kingdom of peace, disappoint the trust and the prayers of her faithful children? ... Faith and history alike point to the one succor, to the omnipotence of prayer, to the Mediatrix, to Mary. In all security and trust we cry, *Regina pacis, ora pro nobis.*"[154]

Pius XI, in at least three encyclical letters, begs the Queen of the Apostles to grant unity to the Church, (1) In Ecclesiam Dei, November 2, 1923, on the third centenary of the martyrdom of St. Josaphat, Pius XI urges us — like St. Josaphat — to go to Our Lady, who is also loved by the schismatics. "Let us invoke this most kind Mother, especially with this title, Queen of the pastures, that the

---

[151] Tondini, p. 166; Lawler, p. 88. Note the connection between Coredemption and the Queenship.

[152] Tondini, pp. 312-314; Unger, pp. 9-10; Carroll, *art. cit.*, pp. 53-54.

[153] *A.A.S.*, Vol. 3, 1911, p. 266: a letter of April 30, 1911; cf. Seiler, *Corredemptrix*, p. 76; Druwé, *art. cit.*, p. 448.

[154] *È pur troppo vero*, Christmas Eve address to the cardinals, 1915, quoted from the translation in *Principles for Peace — Selections from Papal Documents, Leo XIII to Pius XII*, ed. by. H. C. Koenig (Washington, D. C., 1943), No. 425.

straying brothers may return to the life-giving pastures, where Peter, ever living in his successors and Vicar of the Eternal Shepherd, feeds and guides all the lambs and sheep of the Christian flock."[155] (2) *Rerum Ecclesiae*, February 28, 1926. "May Mary, the most Holy Queen of the Apostles, graciously second our common undertakings; Mary, who since she holds in her mother's heart all men who were committed to her on Calvary, cherishes and loves, not only those who happily enjoy the fruits of the Redemption, but those likewise who still do not know that they have been redeemed by Jesus Christ."[156] (3) *Lux veritatis*, December 25, 1931, in commemoration of Ephesus. "Under the auspices of the heavenly Queen, We desire all to beg for a special favor of the greatest importance, that she who is loved and venerated with such ardent piety by the people of the East, may not permit that they should be unhappily wandering and still kept apart from the unity of the Church and thus from her Son, Whose Vicar on earth We are."[157]

B. Pius XII on the Queenship

Pius XII, the Pope of the Assumption, the Pope of the consecration of the world to the Immaculate Heart of Mary, is also the Pope of Our Lady's Queenship. More than any of his predecessors, Pope Pius XII has brought into relief the fuller meaning of Our Lady's power as queen. Mary is Queen not alone in the sense of excelling all other creatures; she is Queen also in a *proper sense*, that is, with real power, with true association in her Son's kingdom of grace. The foundations of her Queenship are the divine Maternity and her cooperation in the work of the Redemption. Mary's kingdom is coextensive with Christ's; but the traditional title, Queen of Mercy, indicates the special sphere of her interest. About the exact nature of her Queenship theological writers are not agreed; some emphasize her Queenship as parallel (though subordinate and dependent) to Christ's kingship, through her conquest with Him; others insist on the feminine character of Mary's rule — through her mother's power over the heart of Christ.

---

[155] *A.A.S.*, Vol. 15, 1923, pp. 581-582.

[156] *Ibid.*, Vol. 18, 1926, p. 83; English from *The Global War for Christ* (New York, 1944).

[157] *A.A.S.*, Vol. 23, 1931, p. 513; Tondini, p. 402; N.C.W.C. translation.

From the abundance of Pius XII's documents on the Queenship we limit ourselves to a few selections. Addressing the world by radio on October 31, 1942, the twenty-fifth anniversary of Our Blessed Lady's apparitions at Fatima, Portugal, the Holy Father "in the role of representative of the whole human race" solemnly declared:

> As the Church and the entire human race were consecrated to the Sacred Heart of Jesus so that, in reposing all hope in Him, He might become for them the sign and pledge of victory and salvation: so We in like manner consecrate ourselves forever also to thee and thy Immaculate Heart, Our Mother and Queen, that thy love and patronage may hasten the triumph of the Kingdom of God.[158]

On Columbus Day, October 12, 1945, the Pontiff sent a radio message to the Mexican Marian Congress for the fiftieth anniversary of the crowning of the miraculous image of Our Lady of Guadalupe. The Pope addressed not alone the people of Mexico, recovering with Our Lady's help after the decades of persecution, but all America. His legate was Cardinal Villeneuve from Canada.

> The most holy Virgin was the providential instrument chosen by the designs of the heavenly Father to give to the world His beloved Son; to be the Mother and Queen of the Apostles who were to spread his doctrine to the whole world. ... [In conclusion the Pope speaks directly to Our Lady of Guadalupe.] ... We set again on your brow the crown, which places forever under your powerful patronage the purity and integrity of the holy faith in Mexico and in the whole American continent. For we are certain that as long as you are recognized as Queen and Mother, America and Mexico will be safe.[159]

On May 13, 1946, the Pope delivered what he has since called his *radio message on the Queenship* as his legate, Cardinal Masella, solemnly crowned the statue of Our Lady at Fatima.

---

[158] *A.A.S.*, Vol. 34, 1942, pp. 345-346; translation from Principles for Peace, No. 182. For other documents in connection with the consecration to the Immaculate Heart, and their bearing on the Queenship, cf. Carroll, *art. cit.*, pp. 162-166; K. Healy, O.Carm., *Theology of the Doctrine of the Immaculate Heart of Mary, in Proceedings of the Fourth Annual Meeting of the Catholic Theological Society of America* (Cincinnati, 1949), pp. 102-127.

[159] *A.A.S.*, Vol. 37, 1945, pp. 265-267; Tondini, p. 505 ff. The Pontiff alluded to the anniversary commemorated on October 12, without mentioning Columbus' name.

He, the Son of God, reflects on His heavenly Mother the glory, the majesty and the dominion of His kingship; for, having been associated to the King of martyrs in the ineffable work of human Redemption as Mother and co-operatrix, she remains forever associated to Him, with an almost unlimited power, in the distribution of the graces which flow from the Redemption. Jesus is King throughout all eternity by nature and by right of conquest; through Him, with Him and subordinate to Him, Mary is Queen by grace, by divine relationship, by right of conquest and by singular election. And her kingdom is as vast as that of her Son and God, since nothing is excluded from her dominion. And this queenship of hers is essentially maternal, exclusively beneficent.[160]

Space limitations preclude discussion of the queenly phrases in *Mystici Corporis:* "Queen of Martyrs" and "reigns in heaven with her Son."[161]

Munificentissimus Deus has several mentions of the Queenship in connection with the Assumption. In commemoration of the dogmatic definition another queenly title has been added to the Litany of Loreto: "Queen assumed into heaven."[162] From his study of this topic, Father De Roo concludes that the solemn proclamation of the bodily Assumption on November 1, 1950, has been an invitation given us by His Holiness, Pope Pius XII, the great Marian Pope of the twentieth century, to open a new chapter in Marian doctrine: Queen assumed into heaven![163]

Munificentissimus Deus contains a brilliant paragraph which is a striking summary of Marian doctrine:

The revered Mother of God, from all eternity joined in a hidden way

---

[160] *A.A.S.,* Vol. 38, 1946, p. 266; Tondini, pp. 518-519. This important message is sometimes titled *Bendito seja* from its opening words in Portuguese, other times called *Benedicite Deum.* Cf. Carroll, art. cit., pp. 66-69; J. B. Carol, O.F.M., *Mary's Co-redemption in the Teaching of Pope Pius XII,* in *The American Ecclesiastical Review,* Vol. 121, 1949, p. 359, and again in *Studies in Praise of Our Blessed Mother,* ed, J. C. Fenton and E. D. Benard (Washington, D. C., 1952), pp. 167-168; De Roo, op. cit.; Filograssi, art. cit.

[161] *A.A.S.,* Vol. 35, 1943, p. 248; cf. Carroll, art. cit., pp. 69-71. The Latin "unaque simul cum Filio suo regnat" for "reigns in heaven with her Son" is a very strong phrase, as the commentators note.

[162] *A.A.S.,* Vol. 42, 1950, p. 793.

[163] De Roo, *op. cit.,* p. 56.

with Jesus Christ in one and the same decree of predestination, immaculate in her conception, a most perfect virgin in her divine motherhood, the noble associate of the divine Redeemer who has won a complete triumph over sin and its consequences, was finally granted, as the supreme culmination of her privileges, that she should be preserved free from the corruption of the tomb and that, like her own Son, having overcome death, she might be taken up body and soul to the glory of heaven where, as Queen, she sits in splendor at the right hand of her Son, the immortal King of the ages.[164]

A CLOSING WORD

There are many more teachings which the popes have given us about Our Blessed Mother; for example, their recommendations of traditional Marian devotions like the Rosary and the Brown Scapular, or their praise of Marian saints, like St. Louis Marie Grignion de Montfort, St. Bernard, St. Ephraem, St. Simon Stock, St. Bernadette. In preaching the imitation of the holy Mother of God; in encouraging pilgrimages to her shrines, as Lourdes, Fatima, Loreto, La Salette; in extending consecration to her Immaculate Heart; or in approving any form of veneration of Our Lady, the *magisterium* at the same time reminds us that true devotion flows from sound doctrine. May the serious study of Mary, Seat of Wisdom, bring home to us the truth which our supreme Teacher underlines with these words: "Do not forget, Catholics of Mexico and of all America: true wisdom is that which she gives you, that which she teaches you, in the name of the Incarnate Wisdom!"[165]

---

[164] *A.A.S.*, Vol. 42, p. 768; N.C.W.C. translation. No. 40.
[165] *A.A.S.*, Vol. 37, 1945, pp. 265-267; Tondini, p. 511.

By ERIC MAY, O.F.M.Cap., S.T.D., S.S.L.

INTRODUCTION: "THE MOTHER OF JESUS WAS THERE"

 HEN Jesus Christ, King of Kings and Lord of Lords, came into the world, He was not very particular about the kind of place where He was to be cradled, or the clothes He would wear or the food He would eat. But on one point He was very definite. The woman who was to be His Mother had to be perfect. And perfect she was — sinless, stainless, Virgin as well as Mother.

We cannot doubt that the God-Man was very proud of His Mother Mary. And that fact, perhaps, emphasizes our astonishment at finding the Virgin Mary mentioned rather infrequently in the pages of Holy Writ. We do not know when or where she was born, for instance; we do not know when or where she finished the earthly course of her existence; and it is little enough that we read of her apart from St. Luke's infancy section. This comparative silence of Sacred Scripture concerning the Mother of God has teased the minds of men for centuries. We can always answer, as did St. Lawrence of Brindisi and Didacus Stella (concerning the Assumption), that divine mysteries are far above us, so that a holy silence and quiet admiration praise them more than fulsome words on tip of tongue or pen.[1] Ultimately, however, one must conclude that we know everything about Mary that God thought it good for us to know.

How much do we know? That is to say, in how many passages does the written Word of God speak to us of Mary? To satisfy this query, several prior questions must first be answered. The difficulty

---

[1] Laurentius de Brindisi, *Sermo II, In Assumptione*, in the *Mariale* (*Opera Omnia*, I) (Padua, 1928), pp. 590-591; Didacus Stella, *In sanctum Iesu Christi Evangelium*, Vol. 2 (Lugduni, 1583), p. 53. Fr. Anthony Cotter, S.J., has written a general article worthy of consideration: *The Obscurity of Scripture*, in *The Catholic Biblical Quarterly*, Vol. 9, 1947, pp. 453-464.

lies not so much with the New Testament where disputed Marian texts are few (e.g., the identity of the Woman in *Apoc.* 12), but rather with the Old Testament. Should we expect to find references to Mary scattered through the history of the Old Covenant? If so, they would have to be in the nature of a revelation and a prophecy. *A priori*, there is nothing against this inasmuch as the same holds true for Old Testament messianic passages regarding the Person of Christ. And one would almost expect to find the Messias and His Mother linked together in prophecy as in reality.

Granting the possibility of Marian passages in the Old Testament, in what manner do these texts refer to the Mother of God? Such a question draws one inevitably into a consideration of biblical hermeneutics and the various senses of Sacred Scripture. This ground has already been covered in scholarly fashion by other authors,[2] and since that is not our primary concern here, and because the terminology involved is still open to dispute, we merely summarize our position in the matter for our immediate needs. We accept, then, the customary pattern given in standard manuals of Introduction to Sacred Scripture.[3] We accept the literal sense as a strict biblical sense (whether this be properly literal, taking words or phrases in their obvious, etymological meaning; or improperly literal, understanding words in their transferred, figurative meaning; or literal in the fuller sense, i.e., taking words in their "developed" literal sense as known to God alone or those to whom He reveals it). The typical sense (the meaning in which persons, things or actions directly signified by a text, according to the intention of the Holy Spirit refer also to still other persons, things, or actions) is likewise a strict biblical sense. Besides these strict

---

[2] Outstanding is a recent article by Dominic Unger, O.F.M.Cap., *The Use of Sacred Scripture in Mariology*, in *Marian Studies*, Vol. 1, 1950, pp. 67-116. Cf. also S. Alameda, O.S.B., *La Mariología y las fuentes de la revelación*, in *Estudios Marianos*, Vol. 1, 1942, pp. 41-100; J. Coppens, *Les harmonies des deux Testaments*, in *Nouvelle Revue Théologique*, Vol. 70, 1948, pp. 799-810; Vol. 71, 1949, pp. 3-38, 337-366, 477-496; *Gabriel Roschini, O.S.M., La Madonna secondo la Fede e la Teologia*, Vol. 2 (Rome, 1953), pp. 49-147.

[3] E.g., H. Höpfl and B. Gut, O.S.B., *Introductio Generalis in Sacram Scripturam*, 5 ed. (Romae, 1950), p. 434 ff.; John Steinmueller, *A Companion to Scripture Studies*, Vol. 1 (New York, 1941), p. 226 ff.

scriptural senses[4] there is the so-called consequent sense (not strictly literal, but derived from words of Scripture by a reasoning process), and the accommodated sense (a meaning which one adapts to the words of Scripture, intended neither by the human nor the sacred Author). These, then, are the senses we take into consideration when investigating the Marian texts of the Old Testament.

Before proceeding to the Old Testament passages commonly considered as Marian, there are several points to bear in mind. Despite the tons of ink and paper devoted to Mariology in recent decades, agreement is still lacking on some fundamental concepts. Perhaps this is due mainly to a vague and conflicting terminology; perhaps not. But it is still possible to find authors who refuse outright, or at least hesitate to see literal references to Mary in the Old Testament because of a mistaken notion that in interpreting early and primitive texts one may not go beyond whatever the first readers could have understood.[5] Such an attitude surely exceeds the proper caution to be observed lest one read something into a text not intended by its divine and human coauthors. The attitude does less than justice to the strict scriptural senses, not excluding the fuller and the typical senses.

This fact leads logically to another consideration. It is frequently taken for granted that revelation, developing slowly as it did over the centuries before Christ, left those of the Old Dispensation (even the sages and prophets) helpless to understand the messianic message. Hence, some think a *direct* reference to the Mother of the Messias as early as the Protogospel (Gen. 3:15) is out of the

---

[4] According to another common division the biblical senses may be *explicit* (the meaning explicitly expressed in the words) or *implicit* (the meaning contained in the words either *formally* — making it equivalent to an explicit concept — or *virtually* — when the meaning is derived by a reasoning process). The "consequent sense" corresponds to the virtually implicit sense.

[5] Cf. D. Unger, *art. cit.*, pp. 107-108. As applied to Gen. 3:15, cf. bibliography in Eric May, O.F.M.Cap., *The Scriptural Basis for Mary's Spiritual Maternity*, in *Marian Studies*, Vol. 3, 1952, p. 114 ff. R. Galdós, S.J., *María en la Biblia*, in *Cultura Bíblica*, Vol. 3, 1946, pp. 113-115, contends that theologians of note limit Old Testament texts, which are applicable literally to Mary, to Isa. 7:14. He adds that "enthusiastic Marianophilists" (like Roschini) also try to bring forward texts like Gen. 3:15 and Jer. 31:22.

question. The same line of thinking governs their consideration of even the Virgin-Birth prophecy in Isa. 7:14. Too advanced a concept, they say; hence at best they grant a typical reference to the future Baby and His Virgin Mother.

Must we patiently breathe "Amen" to such a view? May we not probe deeper and perhaps come up with a different answer? Granted, that there is a gradual development of the messianic theme in the Old Testament.[6] Granted, that according to St. Augustine's famous dictum the New Testament lies hidden in the Old, and the Old Testament becomes manifest in the New.[7] Granted further, that nothing of a supernatural nature in the Old Dispensation could be learned apart from revelation. Is it not possible, however, that God may have revealed His mysteries more frequently than we have supposed? Could Moses have appreciated that it was of the Messias' Mother he was writing in that Woman-Seed prophecy of Gen. 3:15? Did Isaias understand what he was really saying when referring to the Virgin Mother (7:14) or the Suffering Servant (53)? The argument that Jewish contemporaries seemingly did not comprehend does not appear to be sufficient warrant to deny at least a possibility of knowledge to these men who stood in so intimate a relationship to God.[8]

Not yet has sufficient stress been placed on the fact that both Old and New Testaments had the same divine Author. Not yet has enough been written about oral tradition as a second source of revelation during the Old Dispensation. To give due consideration to this latter point, no doubt, will lead one to a position not too far removed from that of Father J. Arendzen. This author, in explaining Isaias' Virgin-Birth prophecy, remarks:

Does the exclusive stress of the prophecy [of *Isa.* 7:14] lie on the

---

[6] Cf. particularly E. F. Sutcliffe, S.J., The Meaning of the Old Testament, in A Catholic Commentary on Holy Scripture (henceforth: CCHS) (London, 1953), pp. 127-132; Augustin Bea, S.J., *Das Marienbild des Alten Bundes*, in *Katholische Marienkunde* (ed. P. Sträter), Vol. 1 (Paderborn, 1952), pp. 22-43.

[7] "In Vetere Testamento Novum latet, et in Novo Vetus patet," *Quaest.* in *Hept.*, II, 73; *PL*, 34, 623.

[8] Along similar lines cf. Eric May, O.F.M.Cap., *Ecce Agnus Dei* (Washington, D. C., 1947), pp. 100-108 and 123-129, for John the Baptist's advanced knowledge regarding the expiatory death of Christ.

miracle itself that it will be a *virgin* who will conceive and thus that God in one unique instance will give the crown of virginity and maternity to one person, making her mother and leaving her a maid? It would seem not. The miracle is indeed plainly and unmistakably foretold, but rather as a thing taken for granted, as a thing already known, something which needed not a repeated prophecy to bring it to the notice of Israel then living. Divine revelation in the Old Testament was no more limited to the Written Word, or the Bible, than it is in the New. It was then a living *progressive* revelation both by the spoken and the written Word, as it is now a living *completed* revelation contained both in Scripture and Tradition and maintained by the infallible Church. Hence there is no need to suppose or demand that Isaias then for the *first* time brought to the notice of Israel the glories of the Mother of the Messias. ... The prophets of Israel were living people who prophesied with the living voice. Some of their prophecies have by God's Will come down in writing, some of them have not. There is nothing to force us to say that the mystery of the Virgin birth must have been unknown to Elias or Eliseus, Amos, Osee or Joel because they preceded Isaias. Though the immediate purpose of Isaias' prophecy to Ahaz was the devastation of Palestine by the Assyrians within a few years, he states with utmost clarity that the Mother of the Messias is to be a Virgin as well as a Mother.[9]

With the increased interest in Mariology during recent years, an interest given greater impetus by the declaration of the dogma of the Assumption in 1950, authors are diligently re-examining Sacred Scripture in its bearing on this special branch of theology. As one writer has put it, "Mary is at the point of junction of the Old and the New Law, which means that one cannot realize the whole significance of her vocation without *replacing her in the Old Testament*; a thorough understanding of the passages in Matthew and Luke in their early chapters is impossible without this constant reference to the biblical atmosphere which we have in common with Israel."[10] We just cannot afford to study the biblical era as merely human history, or the Sacred Text solely in the light of literary criteria. To do so is to end up with what has been aptly

---

[9] J. Arendzen, *Our Lady in the Old Testament, in Our Blessed Lady (Cambridge Summer School Lectures for 1933)* (London, 1934), pp. 10-11.

[10] Charles Moeller, *The Virgin Mary in Contemporary Thought*, in *Lumen Vitae*, Vol. 8, 1953, p. 191.

called "minimum Mariology."

In recent Mariological research the trend has been toward an examination of biblical *themes* rather than of isolated texts. Thus, as C. Moeller explains in an article for prospective catechists, "the teacher should be aware of the general significance of the texts and, above all, of the Old Testament *themes* which are the foundation of the Marian revelation in the New Testament. Mary is placed at the turn of the old and new economy: on the one hand she is the supreme flowering of this *human* preparation (although realized through grace) of the 'cradle,' destined to receive the Messiah; on the other, after Jesus, Mary represents 'the consent and cooperation of the Church.'"[11] The theme motif is not always invoked in precisely the same way. The basic idea, however, is to consider the concatenation of Marian texts in both Old and New Testaments as bearing a unified message, one text helping to explain the other.[12] To our way of thinking, this is not only a justified approach — it is a necessity.

We have already seen that the Old Testament texts commonly recognized as Marian are relatively few in number. Of these texts, not all refer to Mary directly, or in the strict literal sense. It is disputed whether some refer to her at all. There are many Old Testament types which find their fulfillment in the Mother of God. There are innumerable other passages accommodated to Mary for

---

[11] Charles Moeller, *Doctrinal Aspects of Mariology*, in *Lumen Vitae*, Vol. 8, 1953, p. 227.

[12] The following are a few examples of how the biblical theme motif has been applied to Marian doctrine. A general article is that of Ermenegildo Florit, *Maria nell'Esegesi Biblica Contemporanea*, in *Studi Mariani*, Vol. 1, 1942-1943, pp. 87-90. In particular, for the universal Mediation of Mary, cf. Joseph Bover, S.J., *Universalis B. Virginis mediatio ex Proto-evangelio (Gen. 3:14-15) demonstrata*, in *Gregorianum*, Vol. 5, 1924, pp. 569-583; for the spiritual Maternity of Mary, cf. E. May, O.F.M.Cap., *The Scriptural Basis for Mary's Spiritual Maternity*, in *Marian Studies*, Vol. 3, 1952, pp. 111-141; for the Assumption, cf. Bonaventura Mariani, O.F.M., *L'Assunzione di Maria SS. nella Sacra Scrittura*, in *Atti del Congresso Nazionale Mariano dei Frati Minori d'Italia (Studia Mariana, 1)* (Roma, 1948), pp. 456-468; for Mary as Spouse of the Divine Word, cf. C. Moeller, *Doctrinal Aspects of Mariology*, pp. 236-238, and F.-M. Braun, Marie *Mère des fidèles. Essai de théologie johannique* (Paris, 1952). — Cf. also J. Levie, *Les limites de la preuve d'Ecriture Sainte en théologie*, in *Nouvelle Revue Théologique*, Vol. 71, 1949, pp. 1009-1029.

homiletic or liturgical purposes. It shall be our main concern to determine which Old Testament passages really refer immediately and formally to Mary. We shall discover that though the texts be few, the Old Testament has quite a bit to tell us about the Blessed Mother.

I. MARY IN PROPHECY

1. GEN. 3:15

Context. After the lamentable moral fall of Adam and Eve in the Garden of Eden (Gen. 3) they awaited their punishment. But before He punished Eve (v. 16) and Adam (vv. 17-19), almighty God meted out punishment to Satan who had seduced Eve under the guise of a serpent (v. 14). As part of Satan's punishment God addressed to him those momentous words which have come to be known as the Protogospel.

Text. "I will put enmity between you and the woman,
between your seed and her seed;
He shall crush your head
and you shall lie in wait for his heel."

The number of recent books and articles on this verse is simply phenomenal and offers perhaps the best indication of its importance to the study of Mariology.[13] Not that everyone agrees on the exact interpretation of the verse. In fact, some Catholics still find it difficult to see how Mary is concerned in the verse at all, except perhaps accommodatively.[14] How anyone can still question Mary's connection with Gen. 3:15 in a true scriptural sense, after the use

---

[13] For the purposes of bibliography in this treatise, we have been forced to select only the more noteworthy and pertinent books and articles. The most recent and most complete volume on the Protoevangelium is the study by Dominic J. Unger, O.F.M.Cap., *The First-Gospel, Genesis 3:15* (St. Bonaventure, N. Y., Franciscan Institute, 1954).

[14] E.g., Antonine De Guglielmo, O.F.M., *Mary in the Protoevangelium*, in *The Catholic Biblical Quarterly*, Vol. 14, 1952, pp. 104-115; Léon Leloir, *La Médiation Mariale dans la théologie contemporaine* (Bruges, 1933), pp. 87-90; B. Brodmann, O.F.M., *Quid doceat S.S. utriusque Testamenti de indole historica narrationis de paradiso et lapsu Gen. 2-3*, in *Antonianum*, Vol. 12, 1937, p. 355.

made of the verse by recent popes, is a mystery. Most recently, for example, in promulgating the Marian Year of 1954 His Holiness Pope Pius XII pointed out:

> In the first place, the foundation of this doctrine [the Immaculate Conception] is to be found in Sacred Scripture, where we are taught that God, Creator of all things, after the sad fall of Adam, addressed the serpent, the tempter and corrupter, in these words, which not a few Fathers, Doctors of the Church and many approved interpreters applied to the Virgin Mother of God: "I will put enmities between thee and the woman, and thy seed and her seed" (Gen. III, 15). Now, if at any time the Blessed Mary were destitute of Divine grace even for the briefest moment, because of contamination in her conception by the hereditary stain of sin, there would not have come between her and the serpent that perpetual enmity spoken of from earliest tradition down to the time of the solemn definition of the Immaculate Conception, but rather a certain subjection.[15]

However, interpretation of the verse remains an issue of dispute. Even those who agree that Gen. 3:15 is Marian, disagree on the precise scriptural sense involved. Thus, some explain the text as a reference first to Eve, then to Mary, and call it the typical sense.[16] In recent years more and more authors are seeing a literal reference to Mary in the Protogospel. Some explain it as the improper literal

---

[15] Fulgens Corona as translated in *The Catholic Mind*, Vol. 51, 1953, p. 739. (Is it possible that by the phrase "earliest tradition" His Holiness may have meant to go as far back as the primitive tradition of the Old Dispensation?) More than a few authors have stated in so many words that the Church is morally unanimous today in its Mariological interpretation of Gen. 3:15. On this point, cf. A. Bea, S.J., *Maria SS. nel Protoevangelo (Gen. 3, 15)*, in *Marianum*, Vol. 15, 1953, pp. 1-21; M. Peinador, C.M.F., *De argumento scripturistico* in *Mariologia, in Ephemerides Mariologicae*, Vol. 1, 1951, p. 337; V. Bertelli, *Il senso mariologico pieno e il senso letterale del Protoevangelo (Gen. 3, 15) dalla 'Ineffabilis Deus' al 1948*, in *Marianum*, Vol. 13, 1951, pp. 369-395. The latter concludes: "Abbiamo detto che si può dunque intendere mariologicamente il Protoevangelo. Ma oseremmo dire anche di più: che si deve interpretare in tal senso" (p. 395).

[16] E. Sutcliffe, S.J., *Protoevangelium, in* The Clergy Review, Vol. 2, 1931, pp. 155-159; G. Repetti, La tipologia mariana nel Protoevangelio, in Divus Thomas, Vol. 14, 1937, p. 289; J. Dougherty, The Fall and Its Consequences, in The *Catholic Biblical Quarterly, Vol. 3, 1941, pp. 230-231*; A. Robert, P.S.S., La Sainte Vierge dans l'Ancien Testament, in Du Manoir's Maria. Études sur la Sainte Vierge, Vol. 1 (Paris, 1949), p. 35.

sense.[17] Others prefer to see here a verification of the fuller sense.[18] Still others find a direct and properly literal reference to Mary in the verse,[19] and it is with this view that our sympathy lies — for exegetical as well as traditional reasons.

A scriptural passage is the work of God as well as of man; and while the exegete will first apply the principles of literary criticism to the text, he may not stop there. This is particularly true of a disputed text. It is most especially true of a text that has been used so frequently in connection with Marian dogma and Marian theology in general. Here the authentic interpretation of the Church as manifested by the authority of the Fathers, the analogy of faith, papal encyclicals, and the teaching *magisterium* must find place. Where *Gen. 3:15* is concerned, we believe that the teaching Church

---

[17] T. Gallus, S.J., sees the whole context as a continued metaphor. Mary is in the text figuratively or metaphorically, the so-called "allegorico-dogmatic" sense; Beata Virgo Maria Protoevangelio praesignata, in Alma Socia Christi, Vol. 11, 1953, pp. 58-67. This author has written extensively on the Protoevangelium. Cf. e.g.: Interpretatio mariologica Protoevangelii (Gen. 3, 15) tempore post-patristico usque ad Concilium Tridentinum (Romae, 1949); Observationes ad "Novam Protoevangelii mariologicam interpretationem," in Ephemerides Mariologicae, Vol. 2, 1952, pp. 425-437; Interpretatio mariologica Protoevangelii post-tridentina ... , *pars prior*: a Concilio Trid. usque ad annum 1660 (Romae, 1953). Cf. also J. R. García, C.M.F., Glosas crítico exegéticas. II, María en el Protoevangelio (Gen. 3:15), in Cultura Bíblica, Vol. 8, 1951, pp. 193-197.

[18] E.g., Teófilo de Orbiso, O.F.M.Cap., La Mujer del Protoevangelio, in *Estudios Bíblicos*, Vol. 1, 1941, pp. 187-207; J. Trinidad, S.J., Quomodo praenuntietur Maria in Gen *3:15?* in Verbum Domini, Vol. 19, 1939, p. 357; M. de Jonghe, *De Protoevangelio*, in Collationes Brugenses, Vol. 29, 1929, esp. p. 435; F. Ceuppens, O.P., Mariologia Biblica (Romae, 1951), p. 17.

[19] Cf. Francis X. Peirce, S.J., *Mary Alone is "the Woman" of Genesis 3, 15*, in *The Catholic Biblical Quarterly*, Vol. 2, 1940, pp. 245-252; idem, *The Woman of Genesis*, in *The Ecclesiastical Review*, Vol. 103, 1940, p. 94 ff.; idem, *The Protoevangelium*, in *The Catholic Biblical Quarterly*, Vol. 13, 1951, pp. 239-252; A. Vitti, S.J., *Maria negli splendori della Teologia Biblica*, in *La Civiltà Cattolica*, Vol. 3, 1942, pp. 193-201; Michael von Neukirch, O.F.M.Cap., *Kleine theologisch-praktische Mariologie* (Leipzig, 1925), pp. 19-20; G. Roschini, O.S.M., *La Madonna secondo la Fede e la Teologia*, Vol. 2 (Romae, 1953), p. 49 ff.; Theophilus ab Orbiso, O.F.M.Cap., *Sancti Laurentii Brundusini quaedam de theologica biblica quaestiones*, in *Collectanea Franciscana*, Vol. 22, 1952, pp. 251-280. A further elaborate bibliography will be found in Juniper Carol, O.F.M., *De Corredemptione B. V. Mariae* (Civitas Vaticana, 1950), pp. 86-91.

has said enough to provide a solid foundation for the directly literal Marian interpretation of the verse. And we believe that there are good exegetical reasons for saying the same.

Briefly, the two most cogent reasons for holding that Mary alone is the Woman mentioned in *Gen. 3:15* are: (1) the fact that the total and perpetual enmity placed between the Woman and Satan was verified in Mary alone; (2) the fact that the Woman's Seed, at total and perpetual enmity with Satan's seed, crushed Satan's head. Jesus Christ was the one who did this. He is the Woman's Seed; Mary is His Mother.

We proceed to positive proof. It was a complete and perpetual enmity predicted between the Woman and Satan. The Hebrew word for "enmity," *'êybâh*, means just that, as we can gather from its use elsewhere in the Old Testament (e.g., Num. 35:21 where it means a personal enmity that leads to murder; Ezech. 25:15 where it signifiesa national destructive enmity), as well as from the very nature of the passage. Which woman of history qualifies for such an enmity with the devil if not the Immaculate Mother of Jesus, who never for a moment fell beneath Satan's power? Eve surely does not. We know how Scripture speaks of her. She was the one who brought sin into the world (Ecclus. 25:33; 2 Cor. 11:3; 1 Tim. 2:14). Never was she said to be "full of grace." And even though Eve did repent of the original sin, are we really to suppose that never again for an instant did she yield to temptation until her dying breath?[20] Again, it will pay us to remember that Pope Pius IX had this perfect enmity in mind when defining the dogma of the Immaculate Conception.[21] The type of enmity predicted in *Gen. 3:15* is perhaps the strongest reason for rejecting the view that Eve, here, is a type of Mary.

It is the Woman's Seed who crushes Satan's power and is harmed somewhat in the crushing. Of whom is this perfect victory, the Redemption, verified if not of Jesus the Messias who brought salvation to the world by His bloody death on the cross? He and He

---

[20] Fr. Peirce, S.J., Protoevangelium, *loc. cit.*, p. 251, quite correctly ridicules the idea, as proposed (for example) by Fr. Ceuppens in his *Quaestiones selectae ex Historia primaeva* (Romae, 1947), p. 197.

[21] Cf. Dominic Unger, O.F.M.Cap., *Mary Immaculate, the Bull Ineffabilis Deus of Pope Pius IX* (Paterson, N. J., 1946), pp. 10-11 and note on p. 30.

alone brought about the objective Redemption (although Mary co-operated in a secondary capacity). Need this be proved? But if Christ is the individual to be identified through parallelism with the Woman's Seed, then surely the Woman herself can only be Mary His Mother.[22]

These reasons do not appeal to everyone, it is true. There are numerous objections, mainly on exegetical grounds. One widespread objection holds that Mary cannot be the Woman of *Gen. 3:15*, at least not primarily and directly, because the context is against it. Throughout Chapter 3 only one woman is mentioned: Eve. Therefore, the woman in verse 15 must also be Eve, according to the (literary) principle of hermeneutics that a word is determined by its context. This is more certain (say the objectors) in that the word for woman in Hebrew has the definite article (*hā'iššâ*), which by anaphoric usage refers to previously mentioned Eve. In reply, we may point out that there are very good reasons for identifying the Woman of verse 15 without reference to the *immediate* context. The surrounding verses, 14 and 16, are also prophetic it is true, but they are not messianic as is verse 15. And wherever else in the Old Testament the Woman appears in a messianic text (as we shall see), that Woman is Mary, Mother of the Messias. Therefore, considering *Gen. 3:15* in its *remote* context, i.e., the Old Testament — and indeed the entire Bible, we are to identify this Mother of the Perfect Victor with Mary. Then, too, the fact that the Hebrew word for Woman has the article does not by any means prove an anaphoric usage. There are many similar phrases in the Old Testament where use of the article is not anaphoric.[23] The reference here, then, is to a certain

---

[22] As is well known, the Vulgate reading of verse 15c is: "*Ipsa* conteret caput tuum" — "She shall crush your head." Philologically, this is an incorrect rendition of the Hebrew hû' ("he"). Theologically, though, as a strict traditional argument it has great value, linking the Blessed Mother with her divine Son in the perfect victory over Satan. Cf. E. Gallagher, S.J., *Evaluation of the Arguments in favor of Mary's Co-redemption*, in *Marian Studies*, Vol. 2, 1951, p. 109; L. Kösters, S.J., article *Maria*, in *Lexikon für Theologie und Kirche*, Vol. 6 (Freiburg i/Br., 1934), col. 887.

[23] "D'une façon générale on peut dire que l'emploi de l'article en hébreu est assez flottant. En poésie l'emploi de l'article est très libre. ..." Paul Joüon, S.J., *Grammaire de l'Hébreu Biblique* (Rome, 1947), p. 421. The author then goes on to show how the article can express perfect determination, lack of

Woman who with her Son will be victorious over Satan.

If this is true, what did the prophecy mean to Adam and Eve? So runs another line of objection. From the words of verse 15 alone, it is said, our first parents could not have understood a reference to a personal Messias (and His Mother). In answer, one may note in all justice that the time sequence of punishment was not necessarily immediately successive. There is nothing in the text to force us to believe that Adam and Eve even heard the original punishment of Satan.[24] True, at some time they must have learned of the prophecy. In any case, however, where is the necessity for Adam and Eve to have understood the prophecy in its fullness, inasmuch as even we of the twentieth century a.d. are not perfectly clear on all the messianic prophecies? For the rest, it is at least quite possible that Adam and Eve had had a revelation of the Incarnation prior to the fall, in which case there would have been no difficulty in recognizing the Woman and her Seed, regardless of when they learned of the Protogospel.[25]

Another objection looks to the precise meaning of the word "seed." Some argue thus. The seed of Satan in verse 15 is certainly a collective noun (because of scriptural passages which speak of Satan's offspring in the plural); but by parallelism the Seed of the Woman, then, is also a collective. But if it is collective, then we do not have here primarily a reference to the individual Messias, and consequently His Mother Mary is not primarily the Woman. However, it is not at all certain that Satan's seed is a collective noun. Why could it not very well be a metaphorical reference to the one thing the devil had spawned in Eden, and for which he was now being punished — original sin, which after all was that which necessitated the Redeemer?[26] Even granting, however, that the seed of Satan does refer to a collectivity, this does not demand that the

---

determination, or imperfect determination.

[24] Fr. Peirce, S.J., *Protoevangelium*, pp. 239-240.

[25] Cf. Dominic Unger, O.F.M.Cap., *Franciscan Christology, Absolute and Universal Primacy*, in *Franciscan Studies*, Vol. 2, 1942, pp. 454-458.

[26] As we have noted elsewhere (*Marian Studies*, Vol. 3, 1952, p. 121), we can see one real difficulty with a restriction of Satan's seed to the individual sense. In *Apoc.* 12:9 we find other devils associated with Satan, and this in a passage which evidently alludes to *Gen. 3:15*.

Woman's Seed equally refer to a collectivity. The parallelism in this part of the verse is already weakened, to the extent that a metaphorical generation is certainly indicated regarding Satan, true physical generation in the case of the Woman. The Woman's Seed is an individual, and parallelism seems equally well served by the generic idea of offspring against offspring.

In view of the solid arguments proving that Mary is certainly the Woman of *Gen. 3:15*, and even that she alone is the Woman directly intended by the Author and (through revelation) the coauthor of the verse, it is not surprising to see the fruitful use made of it in modern Mariology.[27]

2. Isa. 7:14-16

Context. In 734 b.c. the northern Jewish kingdom of Israel, and Damascus, were seeking to force the southern Jewish kingdom of Juda into an alliance against Assyria. To have a more pliable instrument at the helm of Juda, they plotted to replace King Ahaz with their own choice. In the face of this pressure Ahaz was assured by the prophet Isaias that all would go well, provided that the King of Juda spurned the human assistance of Assyria against Israel and Damascus and placed his entire trust in God. Then Isaias foretold the collapse of the Israel-Damascus project. King Ahaz was not to be afraid of their threats; their plan would fail (7:4-9). To help the King's faith Isaias offered him a sign, a miracle, as proof that he spoke in God's name (vv. 10-11). When King Ahaz refused to ask for a sign, on a flimsy pretext, Isaias gave him the providential and prophetic sign of the Virgin Birth.

---

[27] E.g., for the Immaculate Conception, cf. Jaime Lladó, *El Proto-Evangelio y la Inmaculada*, in *Cultura Bíblica*, Vol. 5, 1948, pp. 344-345; for the Coredemption, cf. J. Carol, O.F.M., *De Corredemptione B. V. Mariae* (Civitas Vaticana, 1950), pp. 86-91; N. García Garcés, C.M.F., *Mater Corredemptrix* (Romae, 1940), esp. pp. 30-33; for Mary's spiritual Maternity, cf. Eric May, O.F.M.Cap., *The Scriptural Basis for Mary's Spiritual Maternity*, in *Marian Studies*, Vol. 3, 1952, pp. 111-141; J. Bover, S.J., *Universalis B. Virginis mediatio ex Protoevangelio (Gen. 3, 15) demonstrata*, in *Gregorianum*, Vol. 5, 1924, pp. 271-272; for the Assumption, cf. F. S. Mueller, S.J., *Origo divino-apostolica doctrinae evectionis B. Virginis ad gloriam coelestem quoad corpus* (Oeniponte, 1930), esp. pp. 58-63; R. W. Gleason, *Studies on the Assumption: 3. The Assumption and Scripture*, in *Thought*, Vol. 26, 1951, pp. 533-539.

Text.   "Behold a Virgin [the Virgin] shall conceive and bear a son, and his name shall be called Emmanuel. He shall eat butter and honey, that he may know to refuse the evil and to choose the good. For before the child know to refuse the evil and to choose the good, the land which thou abhorrest shall be forsaken of the face of her two kings."

Again, as befits a text of this kind, very much has been written concerning it.[28] Unlike most Protestant authors,[29] Catholics are agreed that the prophecy refers to Jesus Christ the Messias. Pope Pius VI condemned the proposition that the prophecy does not refer to Christ in any way.[30] However, whether the words of Isaias are a literal or typical reference to the Messias (and to Mary His Mother) remains a point of disagreement among Catholic writers. How the Virgin Birth of Christ could be a sign to King Ahaz when it would only occur 700 years later remains the major difficulty to be explained. For our part, we believe that Isaias' momentous prophecy refers properly, directly, and exclusively to the Virgin Birth at Bethlehem; and this represents the much more common opinion among Catholic expositors.

The Hebrew prophecy reads literally: "Behold, the Virgin is pregnant and bearing a son, and she shall call his name 'God-with-us.'" The Hebrew word translated by "virgin" is ʿalmāh. Biblical

---

[28] Besides the standard commentaries on Isaias, a list of recent specialized sources would include: Hubert Vecchierello, O.F.M., *The Virgin Birth of Christ* (Paterson, N. J., 1932); Heinisch-Heidt, O.S.B., *Theology of the Old Testament* (Collegeville, Minn., 1950), pp. 305-307; C. C. Martindale, S.J., Mother in Israel, in The Mary Book (New York, 1950), pp. 10-11; T. E. Bird, Who is 'The Boy' in Isaias 7:16? in The Catholic Biblical Quarterly, Vol. 6, 1944, pp. 435-443; E. Power, S.J., The Emmanuel Prophecy of Isaias, in The Irish Ecclesiastical Record, Vol. 70, 1948, pp. 289-304; idem, Isaias, in CCHS, esp. pp. 546-548; A. Vaccari, S.J., De Signo Emmanuelis Is 7 in Verbum Domini, Vol. 17, 1937, pp. 45-49, 75-81; Schaefer-Brossart, The Mother of Jesus in Holy Scripture (New York, 1913), p. 18 ff.; Hipólito Arias, C.J.M., La Virgen Madre en Isaías, in Cathedra, Vol. 4, 1950, pp. 413-421.

[29] E.g., the Anglican L. S. Thornton, *The Mother of God in Holy Scripture*, in E. L. Mascall (ed.), *The Mother of God, a Symposium* (Westminster, 1949), p. 21.

[30] In his brief *Divina*, September 20, 1779; *Enchiridion Biblicum*, No. 59.

Hebrew had several words to designate a young woman. *Na'ărâh* was applied to a young lady, married or not. *B^ethûlāh* was used only for a virgin, young or old. *'Almāh*, in its etymology, implicitly although not necessarily, supposed the state of virginity (something like the German Jungfrau or the English "maiden"). In its usage, *'almāh* was quite similar to the more rigid Hebrew word *b^ethûlāh* and explicitly signified a young virgin of marriageable age.[31] In the light of the immediate scriptural context (the promise of an extraordinary sign) and the remote scriptural context (Mt. 1:23), the word *'almāh* in Isa. 7:14 must definitely be understood in the sense of "virgin." Confirmation of this is found in the Septuagint Greek translation, *parthenos* (virgin). It is noteworthy that the Jews were not scandalized at the translation *parthenos* until the Christians used it against them. The Messias, then, was to have a Virgin Mother.

Verses 15-16 of the prophecy are explained traditionally in this wise: the Child shall eat butter (or curds) and honey (i.e., shall be reduced to eating the natural products of the land, as an indication of His poverty —and this is confirmed by the subsequent verse 22); thus he was to learn from experience the exercise of virtue (refusing the evil life). For before that time (i.e., Christ's time, 700 years later) the land of Israel (Israel and Aram) was to be laid waste.

Fr. F. Peirce, S.J., reviewing an article by Feuillet on this question, has some enlightening remarks in modification of the "traditional" view.[32] It is a false supposition, he maintains, that in verse 16 there is an immediate time link between the two halves of the verse. All that the verse says is that at some time prior to the advent of the Child (whether this be sixty-five years or seven centuries) the Israel-Damascus combine will have ceased to be. It does not state that the Child is close at hand, or that He is a sign of an approaching liberation, much less that He will precede Juda's liberation. The Messianic Promise, when first given (Gen. 3:15) contained no reference to temporalities. Even when first given to

---

[31] C. Lattey, S.J., *The Term Almah in Isa. 7:14*, in *The Catholic Biblical Quarterly*, Vol. 9, 1947, pp. 89-95.

[32] Review of A. Feuillet, *Le Signe proposé à Achaz et l'Emmanuel* (Isaïe, 7, 10-25), in *Recherches de Science Religieuse* (April, 1940), pp. 129-151. Peirce's review appeared in *The American Ecclesiastical Review*, Vol. 104, 1941, pp. 80-84. Cf. also E. Power, Isaias, in CCHS, pp. 547-548.

Abraham (Gen. 12:3) it was without a temporal note and was absolute, independent of human wills. Later, because of Abraham's fidelity (Gen. 26:3-4) temporal prosperity was added to the picture. From then on the Messianic Promise held a twofold note, an absolute promise that Messias would come, and an additional promise of prosperity conditioned upon the obedience of the Chosen People. At the close of the patriarchal period, Jacob in his deathbed blessing (Gen. 49) conferred the Messianic Promise upon Juda (v. 10) and the blessing of special prosperity upon Joseph (vv. 25-26). In the days of David, who was king of all the Jews, this prosperity was stressed again (3 Kings 2:3-4). From King David on, fidelity and infidelity succeeded one another, so that at the time of King Ahaz infidelity loomed large in the history of the nation; and in God's designs the time had come for a definite stand. Ahaz and the House of David were put to the test: "If you will not believe, you will not continue" (Isa. 7:9). The sign is not merely (though it is primarily) the Virgin Birth, but the *Virgin Birth in poverty*; a sign therefore with a twofold aspect, one desirable and the other unpleasant. As verse 13 shows, the sign was directed not only to Ahaz but to the whole House of David. Since King Ahaz was out of favor with God, the unpleasant aspect of the sign was directed toward him. Though the Birth in poverty was still far in the future, within a short time the reasons for that poverty would begin to manifest themselves, in the gradual dissolution of the temporal power of David's House. Damascus and Israel would soon feel the power of Assyria; Juda herself would suffer, and all within the lifetime of Ahaz. And scion of the House of David as he was, although a faithless one, the King could not fail to recognize the sign of the divine displeasure in the constant incursion of enemy forces from the north and south into his borders, incursions far different from the hitherto sporadic attacks of small nations along its borders. This explanation of Fr. Peirce seems worthy of anyone's consideration; and it helps to set the marvel of the Virgin-Birth prophecy into its historical milieu.

It is hard to see how the typical sense could be verified in Isa. 7:14. Yet some Catholics imagine that Isaias was referring to his own wife and son as types of Mary and Jesus. The essential similarity necessary between a true type and its antitype is lacking here. No woman conceiving and bearing according to the normal laws of nature can represent the Mother of Emmanuel in that respect wherein the type and antitype should be really similar. Furthermore, the titles given to Emmanuel in Isa. 9:6, especially that of *'Ēl Gibbôr* — "Mighty God,"[33] cannot be applied metaphorically to any child other than the Messias.

Isa. 7:14-16, then, is Marian as well as messianic, and the reference to the Virgin Mother of the Saviour is at once directly and properly literal.

3. MICH. 5:2-3

Context. The prophet Micheas, like his contemporary Isaias, warned that Israel was to be reduced to a remnant before she could again be worthy of God's promised mercy. Not only would the Northern Kingdom of the Jews be taken into exile; Jerusalem itself was destined for destruction. But the final gathering together of the scattered people would be accomplished by a Mighty Ruler from a humble little town — a Ruler whose antecedents are mysteriously eternal, and who is born of a Woman.

Text. "And you, Bethlehem Ephrata, are a little one among the thousands of Juda: out of you shall he come forth unto me that is to be the ruler in Israel: and his going forth is from the beginning, from the days of eternity. Therefore will he give them up even till the time wherein she that travaileth shall bring forth: and the remnant of his brethren shall be converted to the children of Israel."

The exact relationship between the prophets Isaias and Micheas has not been fully determined,[34] but Catholics commonly agree that the Nativity prophecies of both refer as with one voice to Mary, the

---

[33] Cf. W. McClellan, S.J., *El Gibbor,* in *The Catholic Biblical Quarterly,* Vol. 6, 1944, pp. 276-288.

[34] Yet, according to C. P. Caspari, "Es möchte kaum zwei prophetische Schriften geben, die in allen Beziehungen in einer so starken Verwandtschaft mit einander stehen, als das Buch Micha's und das Jesaja's." *Über Micha den Morasthiten und seine Prophetische* Schrift (Christiana, 1852), p. 444.

Mother of Jesus.[35] We know that at Christ's time, Jews of all classes understood *Mich.* 5:2-3 in a messianic sense, the learned (Mt. 2:4-6) as well as the unlearned (cf. Jn. 7:40-42). Micheas foretold that a new Ruler was to emerge in Israel, i.e., was to be born in David's humble birthplace, Bethlehem. Yet this same Ruler to be born in Bethlehem was considered as having had existence from eternal days. Hence, a double origin: one eternal, one temporal. God would permit Israel's enemies to oppress her until "she that travaileth shall bring forth (the Saviour)." This mother, thus introduced suddenly as known and determined (Hebrew: *yôlēdāh, yālādāh*) but without mention of a husband, was to be understood in the same sense as the Virgin Mother of Isa. 7:14 who bears Emmanuel. This Ruler would gather together His brethren (the dispersed Jews) and form a blessed people at last secure from enemies, because He would be endowed with the majesty and authority of Yahweh.

Perhaps no one has brought out the Marian significance of this messianic passage better than Fr. K. Smyth, S.J. He writes:

Because it is God's plan to raise up a Saviour, not from royal Sion, but from Bethlehem, he will leave Israel at the mercy of her enemies, *till a Mother bears Child.* Then begin God's blessings, with the return of the Child's exiled brothers. Abrupt and succinct, this prophecy evidently supposes a great current of Messianic prophecy then familiar to all. It harmonizes perfectly with Isaias 7:14. There is the same sign of deliverance: the appearance of a Mother, the coming of the Child, then the return of the exiles; cf. Is 7:3 'A Remnant will Return.' Through the centuries which prophetic vision has to pierce, only figures gigantic in their import can be distinguished. But, however indistinctly perceived, a Woman looms large throughout the great prophecies of Redemption. In the Proto-Evangel, Gen 3, in Isaias and in Micheas salvation comes

---

[35] Cf. P. L. Suárez, *C.M.F., Un texto mariológico en Miqueas*, in *Cultura Bíblica*, Vol. 10, 1953, pp. 247-248; H. Arias, C.J.M., *La Virgen Madre en Isaías*, in *Cathedra*, Vol. 4, 1950, p. 419 (where he maintains that Mich. 5:2 is unintelligible apart from Isa. 7:14); Schaefer-Brossart, *The Mother of God* in *Holy Scripture*, pp. 56-58; Gaspare de Stéfani, *Maria Santissima nell'Antico Testamento, nella sua vita e nella vita della Chiesa* (Torino, [n.d.]), pp. 68-70; A. Vitti, S.J., *Maria negli splendori della Teologia Biblica*, in *La Civiltà Cattolica*, Vol. 3, 1942, pp. 193-201; E. Rosales, O.F.M., *La Realeza de Maria en las Sagradas Escrituras*, in *Actas del Congreso Asuncionista Franciscano de América Latina* (Buenos Aires, 1950), pp. 217-218; Heinisch-Heidt, *Theology of the Old Testament*, pp. 305-307.

through one who always associates with himself a Mother. Thus the Catholic Church follows out fundamental lines of revelation in the honour paid to the Virgin Mary, Mother of God, and in acknowledging her significance in the economy of Redemption.[36]

We agree with the view that Mich. 5:3 is a proper literal reference to Mary, the Mother of Christ, and another important part of the Marian picture in the Old Testament.

4. JER. 31:22

Context. Chapter 31 of Jeremias' prophecy holds out the hope of the restoration of the Jews (vv. 1-14). At present, Rachel (the mother of Joseph, i.e., Ephraim) is pictured in the prophet's imagination as watching from her tomb at Rama, and bemoaning the ruin of her children. But she need not grieve, says the prophet; Ephraim will yet repent (vv. 15-20), and both Ephraim and Juda will be restored together (vv. 21-30). In confirmation of this, a great sign is promised (v. 22).

Text. "How long wilt thou be dissolute in deliciousness, O wandering daughter? for the Lord hath created a new thing upon the earth: a woman shall encompass a man" (Douay Version).

As with the preceding texts, there seems little room for doubt that we are dealing here with a messianic text in a messianic context.[37] That raises once more the interesting question: Who is the Woman concerned in this messianic text? Could it be Mary? Is this in some way another Old Testament reference to the Virgin Birth? There is no unanimity among Catholics on the matter. Some say

---

[36] Kevin Smyth, S.J., *Micheas*, in *CCHS*, p. 675.

[37] F. Ceuppens, O.P., however, holds that Jer. 31:22 is to be considered messianic by reason of context, without any reference here to the Person of Messias, much less to His conception in Mary's virginal womb. The text, he says, concerns the conversion of the faithless Israelitic people (the spouse) to Yahweh her God in the messianic era, which will be truly "a new thing upon the earth." *De Prophetiis Messianicis*, pp. 428-433.

no;[38] some say yes;[39] the views of others are more or less in between.[40]

The exegetical arguments usually brought against a Marian interpretation of Jer. 31:22 are these. The Hebrew reads: *neqēbāh* (a female) *tesôbēb* (shall surround) *gāber* (a male). But (it is claimed) the word for "female" is never used in Sacred Scripture for a virgin; the word for "surround" is never found in the Bible in the sense of childbearing. As for the "traditional" interpretation of the text, say these authors, the Virgin-Birth analysis of the passage seems to have been something personal to St. Jerome.

The case in favor of the Marian character of the verse has been well stated by Fr. Cuthbert Lattey, S.J., as follows:

And then a great sign is promised, so great that it is even called a creation. The verb is in the perfect tense ("hath created"), but it is generally admitted that this is merely another example of the well-known idiom, the "prophetic perfect," a vivid manner of presenting a prophecy as already fulfilled. The present writer accepts Knabenbauer's explanation in CSS [*Cursus Sacrae Scripturae*] which he regards as far more plausible than any other, but of course it presupposes that miracle and prophecy are possible. Instead of the initiative being taken by the man, as is usual in human generation, the physical process on the purely human side will be set on foot by the woman, who will "*press round*" a man (a meaning given by BDB [Brown, Driver and Briggs] to the verb in this passage, but with a different implication). The miracle is emphasized by the word used for "woman" being an unusual one, which stresses the sexual character. The word for "man" (that found in *Gabri-el* "man of God") is also an unusual one, implying strength and power; a cognate word (a fact significant in the present context) is applied as a name to the Messias in Is 9:6 ("God the Mighty"), and directly to God Himself in Ps 23:8

---

[38] F. Ceuppens, O.P., *ibid.*; also in his *Mariologia Biblica* (Romae, 1951), pp. 48-54; A. Robert, P.S.S., *La Sainte Vierge dans l'Ancien Testament*, pp. 24-26; R. Galdós, S.J., *Maria en la Biblia*, in *Cultura Bíblica*, Vol. 3, 1946, pp. 113-115.

[39] C. Lattey, S.J., Jeremias, in *CCHS*, p. 584; Schaefer-Brossart, *The Mother of Jesus in Holy Scripture*, pp. 58-62; Anton Scholz, *Commentar zum Buche des Propheten Jeremias*, 1880, p. 368 ff.; M. Scheeben-T. Geukers, *Mariology*, Vol. I, (St. Louis, 1946), pp. 18-19.

[40] E.g., Fr. Closen, S.J., in an article in *Verbum Domini*, Vol. 16, 1936, pp. 295-304, translated the pertinent phrase "*mulier viro providet*" and found its ultimate verification in Mary.

(twice); Deut 10:17; etc. This explanation of the passage is confirmed by the fairly obvious reference which it contains to Is 7:14, which can reasonably be supposed to have been familiar to Jeremias' hearers and readers, as to those of Mic 5:3, immediately after the mention of Bethlehem. Like Isaias, Jeremias passes easily by a process of compenetration from the temporary deliverance to the full Messianic deliverance of which it is a type.[41]

It is very interesting to note that authors like Lattey, Smyth, Schaefer-Brossart, and Scholz do not hesitate to attribute a wide knowledge of previous Old Testament Marian texts to the contemporaries of Isaias and Jeremias. Scholz, for example, confesses that for him *Jer. 31:22* is a paraphrase and interpretation of *Isa. 7:14*; and he adds significantly: "Such explanations may be well assigned to the already existing knowledge in Scripture, down to the time of Jeremias, abused by pharisaism."[42]

True, one does not have quite the same confidence in referring this text literally to Mary as he would, say, the Proto-Gospel. But because of the striking similarity between this sign in Jeremias and the Virgin-Birth sign of Isaias; because, again, of the remote scriptural context, we see no serious reason to doubt that *Jer. 31:22* presents yet another high light in the over-all Marian picture in the Old Testament. We concur with Frs. Knabenbauer and Lattey.

5. CANTICLE OF CANTICLES

The *Canticle of Canticles* is a love song. It tells of an espousal. The interpretation of the book and the identification of the scriptural sense intended therein are well-known difficulties. Leaving aside for our present purpose all the ramifications found in biblical introductions to the book, we hold as the more probable view that the *Canticle* cannot be understood in a proper literal sense; that it embodies elements of both parable and allegory; that in God's intention it represents first in point of time the relationship between Yahweh and the Chosen People (cf. Osee 2:16-20; Isa. 54:6, 62:5; Jer. 2:2, 3:1 ff.; Ezech. 16:32-38), then the union of Christ with His Church (cf. Mt. 22:1 ff., 25:1ff.; Jn. 3:29; 2 Cor. 11:2; Eph. 5:23-32;

---

[41] C. Lattey, Jeremias, in *CCHS*, p. 584.

[42] Anton Scholz, *op. cit.*, p. 368.

Apoc. 21:9). Whether or not this last meaning is a verification of the fuller sense is a matter of opinion. The important further question that concerns us here is: did Almighty God also intend in the Canticle to refer to the close union between Christ and His Blessed Mother? Is this a Marian book in any sense?

From patristic times down to our own day there have been commentators who extended (if that is the correct word) the parabolico-allegoric understanding of the *Canticle* to an ascetico-mystical interpretation. Jesus is the Bridegroom, and the individual Christian soul is the bride. Since the Virgin Mary is the holiest of the Church's members; since her union with Christ is the most intimate imaginable; since after Christ she occupies the main position in the economy of salvation, in a special way Mary is the Bride discussed in the *Canticle*.[43] And for our part, we do believe that Mary was included in the mind and intention of God when He inspired the sacred author to write the *Canticle of Canticles*. Be this the "fuller" sense or the "fullest" sense (if you will), Mary's role as Sponsa Verbi is too evident within the remote context of both Testaments to cast serious doubt on a Mariological interpretation of the Canticle. Here we have one of those biblical themes mentioned earlier, a theme aptly indicated according to its general line of development by Charles Moeller when he writes:

> This first line of *explicit* biblical themes [i.e., espousals in the Old Testament; Church-Bride in the New] being thus recalled to mind, from *Genesis* to the *Apocalypse*, a second series can be discerned, renewing the former in its emphasis and revealing *Marian*

---

[43] Cf. D. Buzy, *Le Cantique des Cantiques* (Paris, 1949), p. 29 ff.; Juan G. Arintero, *Cantar de los Cantares* (Salamanca, 1926), Introducción; Pouget-Guitton-Lilly, *The Canticle of Canticles* (New York, 1948), pp. 144-145; P. P. Saydon, *The Canticle of Canticles*, in CCHS, pp. 497-498; Paschal Parente, *The Canticle of Canticles in Mystical Theology*, in *The Catholic Biblical Quarterly*, Vol. 6, 1944, pp. 142-158; Alfonso Rivera, *C.M.F.*, *Sentido Mariológico del Cantar de los Cantares?* in *Ephemerides Mariologicae*, Vol. 1, 1951, pp. 437-468; Vol. 2, 1952, pp. 25-42. Rivera gives as the conclusion to the first part of his article: "Admitimos como verdadero, junto con el sentido eclesiológico, el sentido mariano del Ct., con la probabilidad y fuerza que le da la interpretación tradicional y moralmente unánime de la exégesis cristiana, confirmada por el análisis interno y los criterios de analogía exegética del Ct." (p. 468).

implications. This second series of themes is to be found in the Johannine revelation, which, to our mind, together with the *Canticle of Canticles* for the Old Testament, represents the peak of the New. The Marian texts in St. John's Gospel (II, 1-11; XIX, 25-27) linked on the one hand to verse 13 of the prologue [*John 1*] and to Genesis III, 15 and on the other to *Apoc. XII*, sheds a flood of light on Mary the Bride of the Word, associated in the redemption, and the spiritual mother of the faithful. It is necessary to note that we are here using a *literal* exegesis founded on the secret connections placed by St. John himself between the different parts of his gospel and between that gospel and *Genesis* and the *Apocalypse.*[44]

The *Canticle of Canticles*, then, looked ahead in a fuller sense to the special relationship that would exist between the Word of God and His Bride, Mary — even though the author's contemporaries, perhaps, would not have plumbed the depths of the *Canticle's* meaning.

6. OTHER TEXTS

A passage from another of the major prophets is frequently mentioned in connection with the Virgin Birth. *Ezech.* 44:1-3 reads: "And he brought me back to the way of the gate of the outward sanctuary, which looked toward the east: and it was shut. And the Lord said to me: This gate shall be shut, it shall not be opened, and no man shall pass through it: because the Lord the God of Israel hath entered in by it, and it shall he shut for the prince. The prince himself shall sit in it. ..." The prophet refers to a prince who rules for Yahweh. Among his privileges is a special place for sacrificial meals, the eastern gate of the grand Temple in Jerusalem. This gate was never to be opened by another, inasmuch as Yahweh had entered through it. Now, it is true that a goodly number of the Church Fathers and writers and preachers have seen in this sealed gate a figure of Mary's perpetual virginity.[45] But was this merely by

---

[44] Charles Moeller, *Doctrinal Aspects of Mariology*, in *Lumen Vitae*, Vol. 8, 1953, pp. 236-238. D. Buzy calls the *Canticle of Canticles* "the fourth Gospel of the Old Testament"; ibid., p. 33.

[45] Cf. E. Power, S.J., *Ezechiel*, in *CCHS*, p. 619. Some patristic quotations are available in Schaefer-Brossart, *The Mother of Jesus in Holy Scripture*, p. 63 ff. Schaefer himself concludes: "This application [of Ezech. 44:2 to Mary] is

way of homiletic accommodation and not intended as the strict scriptural sense? We think so. There seems to be no good exegetical reason for thinking otherwise.

There are not wanting authors who imitate St. Jerome and see in *Isa.* 11:1 a reference to Mary along with her Messias Son.[46] But they do so without adequate foundation. The text reads: "And there shall come forth a rod out of the root of Jesse, and a flower shall rise up out of his root." Isaias contrasts the figure of a sprout from Jesse's root with the forest metaphor of the preceding verse. The forest (symbolizing Assyria) is utterly destroyed, but the stump of Jesse (the royal family of Juda) envisions a shoot springing up: the Messias. By parallelism the subjects of verse 1 "rod ... flower" both refer to the Messias — not one to Him, the other to His Mother.[47]

Still another passage is sometimes referred to Mary in a direct scriptural sense. It is the second half of Ps. 44 (45). This psalm, the nuptial song of the king, is certainly messianic. But (so the argument runs), if the first half of the psalm concerns the Messias, an individual, why should not the second half also refer to an individual Queen — Mary?[48] The more common view, however, seems to see in Ps. 44 either a reference to the espousals between Christ and the Church directly, or a literal reference to some royal wedding (Solomon's?) which is then a type of the messianic espousals (cf. Eph. 5:25-27). As for our opinion, we must confess to more than a little interest in the Marian interpretation through the fuller sense. We have here almost the same setup as in the *Canticle*

---

made in such a manner that the conviction becomes evident that such a reference to Mary was also intended by the Holy Ghost."

[46] E.g., Eduardo Rosales, O.F.M., *La Realeza de María en las Sagradas Escrituras*, in *Actas del Congreso Asuncionista Franciscano de América Latina* (Buenos Aires, 1950), pp. 216-217. He thinks the prophecy refers to the Messias in the literal, express sense, and to Mary in the implicit, literal sense

[47] Simon-Prado, *Praelectiones Biblicae. Vetus Testamentum,* Vol. 1 (Taurini, 1949), p. 463.

[48] Thus, Eduardo Rosales, O.F.M., *La Realeza de María,* pp. 218-220. E. C. Messenger, *Our Lady in the Scriptures,* in *CCHS,* p. 114, likewise thinks that the (primary) collective meaning of the Spouse does not exclude the "application" of the text to the King's Mother, Mary. However, Eustace Smith, O.F.M., doubts the Marian verification; *The Scriptural Basis for Mary's Queenship,* in *Marian Studies,* Vol. 4, 1953, p. 114.

of Canticles. When we note how consistently the Church and Mary are brought together in explanation of passages like Ps. 44, the *Canticle of Canticles*, and *Apoc.* 12, as by a kind of interrelationship, it seems difficult to restrict Mary's presence in Ps. 44 to one of mere accommodation.

II. MARY IN TYPE

Among the many beautiful things Monsignor Ronald Knox has written is a short article wherein he treats Esther of the Old Testament as a type of Mary. He asserts that "there is a mystical significance in the Old Testament everywhere; and that, above all, the history of the Jewish people foreshadows and typifies the glories of our Blessed Lady." Remarking that there is much that is violent and some things which are dull in the Old Testament, the distinguished author adds:

> But through this tangled skein runs a single golden thread; between these soiled pages lies, now and again, a pressed flower that has lost neither its colour nor its sweetness. That thread, that flower, is the mention, by type and analogue, of her whom all generations of Christendom have called blessed, the Virgin of Virgins, the Queen of Heaven, the holy Mother of God. It is not wonderful that it should be so. For our Lady is, after all, the culmination of that long process of selection, of choosing here and rejecting there a human instrument suited to his purpose, which is so characteristic of God's dealings with his ancient people.[49]

Many years ago His Holiness Pope Pius IX pointed out the same truth even more vividly in his incomparable Bull *Ineffabilis Deus*, wherein he solemnly defined the dogma of the Immaculate Conception. He took great pains to list many of the persons and objects in the Old Dispensation which, according to the Fathers, typified or prefigured the all-pure Mother of Christ. The pertinent passages read:

> This illustrious and singular triumph of the Virgin [mentioned in *Gen.* 3:15], together with her most excellent innocence, purity, holiness and

---

[49] Esther as a Type of Our Lady, in Sheed's *The Mary Book* (New York, 1950), pp. 15-16.

freedom from every stain of sin, as well as the unspeakable abundance and greatness of all heavenly graces, virtues and privileges — these the Fathers saw [typified] in that ark of Noe, which was built by divine command and escaped entirely safe and sound from the common shipwreck of the whole world (Gen. 6-9); also in that ladder which Jacob saw reaching from earth to heaven, by whose rungs the angels of God ascended and descended, and on whose top the Lord Himself leaned (Gen. 28:12-13); also in that bush which Moses saw in the holy place burning on all sides, but which was not only not consumed nor injured in any way but grew green and blossomed beautifully (Ex. 3:1-3); also in that impregnable tower before the enemy, from which hung a thousand bucklers and all the armor of the strong (Cant. 4:4); also in that garden enclosed on all sides, which cannot be violated nor corrupted by any deceitful plots (Cant. 4:12); also in that most august temple of God, which, radiant with divine splendors, is full of the glory of God (3 Kings 8:10-11); and in very many other types of this kind. By them the Fathers have handed down the tradition that exalted things have been signally predicted of the Mother of God and of her spotless innocence and holiness which was never subject to any blemish.[50]

The Holy Pontiff then goes on to demonstrate how the Fathers used the words of the Prophets of old to describe Mary's sinlessness and great gifts. Spotless dove, they called her (Cant. 6:8), and the Holy Jerusalem, the exalted throne of God, the ark and house of holiness which eternal wisdom built for herself (Prov. 9:1). They addressed Mary as that Queen who, full of delights and leaning on her Beloved (Cant. 8:5), came forth from the mouth of the Most High (Ecclus. 24:5), entirely perfect. And a little later in the encyclical the Pope brings together still further examples of how the Fathers appealed to Scripture in describing Mary's purity and holiness.

Hence, the Fathers have never ceased to call the Mother of God the lily among thorns, or the earth entirely intact, virginal, undefiled, immaculate, ever-blessed and free from all corruption of sin, from which was formed the New Adam; or the flawless, brightest and most pleasant paradise of innocence, immortality and delights planted by God Himself and protected against all snares of the poisonous

---

[50] *Mary Immaculate, The Bull Ineffabilis Deus of Pope Pius IX*, translated and annotated by Dominic Unger, O.F.M.Cap. (Paterson, N. J., 1946), pp. 11-12.

Serpent; or the incorruptible wood that the worm of sin had never corrupted; or the fountain ever clear and sealed by the power of the Holy Spirit; or the most divine temple; or the treasure of immortality; or the one and only daughter not of death but of life, the child not of anger but of grace, which by the singular providence of God has always blossomed, though it sprang from a corrupt and infected root, contrary to the ordinary and fixed laws.[51]

To the thorough list of His Holiness might be added other inanimate objects of the Old Dispensation which have been considered as types of Mary. Aaron's rod, for example (Num. 17:8). Only *Aaron's rod*, among many others, blossomed forth; so Mary is the one flower of innocence that sprang from our corrupt nature. *Gideon's fleece* is another example (Judges 6:36-40). At one time the fleece was wet with dew while the surrounding ground remained dry; then again the fleece remained untouched by dew though the earth around was soaked. Thus Mary was filled with God's grace from the first moment of her conception while all others remained deprived of it; she alone was preserved from sin while the whole world succumbed to it.

Nowhere is Marian typology more in evidence than with regard to certain Old Testament personages. Just a few pertinent examples.[52] Eve heads the list. She is the mother of all the living on the natural plane, Mary on the supernatural level. *Respha* the daughter of Aia, who mourned for her crucified sons (2 Sam. 21:8-10) and the *mother of the Machabean martyrs* who so generously offered up the martyrdom of her sons (2 Macc. 7), are types of Mary mourning for the death of her crucified Child after generously assisting Him in His sufferings. *Bethsabee* (3 Kings 2:19), seated on a throne at the right hand of her son Solomon, shared his glory and power. Mary, seated in heaven at the right hand of her Son Jesus, shares with Him our love and veneration. By her charms *Rachel* (Gen. 29) won the heart of Jacob; so Mary won the heart of God. Rachel's son Joseph, having been sold by his brethren, attained great

---

[51] *Ibid.*, p. 14.

[52] Cf. esp. Fr. Canice, O.F.M.Cap., *Mary, a Study of the Mother of God* (Dublin, 1950), Chap. 3; M. J. Scheeben, *Mariology*, Vol. 1 (St. Louis, 1946), p. 35 ff. For a fuller development of Eve as a type of Mary, cf. Francis Friedel, *The Mariology of Cardinal Newman* (New York, 1928), Chap. 2.

honor and saved his people. Mary's Son Jesus, sold by His brethren, saved the world and reached an infinite glory. *Esther, Judith, Debbora*, and *Jahel* were all types of Mary in that they were instrumental in the salvation of their people. More specifically, Esther who was of lowly birth won the favor of a most powerful king and became his spouse; so Mary, a poor and humble Jewess, won the heart of God and shares with Him the empire of the world. Esther alone was exempted from a law which bound everyone else; Mary alone was exempted from the law of original sin. As for *Judith*, whereas she saved her fellow Jews from harm by cutting off Holofemes' head, Mary played her grand role of Coredemptrix by crushing the head of the serpent. Judith's praises were on every tongue; so are the Blessed Mother's, as foretold in the *Magnificat*.

The question naturally arises whether these Old Testament persons, events, things are genuine scriptural types intended as such by Almighty God, or whether they fall into the class of mere accommodation. The question is very difficult to answer. Scripture itself seems to be silent on the matter (except for the generic reminder of St. Paul in 1 Cor. 10:6, 11 that the typology of the Old Testament was intended for us); and from the wording of the Fathers it is not always clear just how these Old Testament realities refer to Mary. Surely it places no strain on our credence to see in many of these types a deliberate anticipation on God's part of the tremendous role to be played by His Mother in the New Dispensation. The difficulty is where to draw the line between the strict biblical sense known as the typical, and mere accommodation.

Here, the relationship between Mary and the Wisdom literature calls for special consideration. Some remarks of Pope Pius IX in the Bull *Ineffabilis Deus* are pertinent. "From the beginning and before the ages," he says, "God chose and appointed a Mother for His Only-Begotten Son, from whom this Son would take His flesh and be born when the blessed fullness of time would arrive." A little later in the encyclical the Holy Father states that since the Church on the feast of the Immaculate Conception uses those passages of Sacred Scripture which speak of the origin of Eternal and Incarnate Wisdom, by that fact the Church implies that Mary's origin and conception was sacred and immaculate.[53] And the Holy Father concludes: "For her origin was preordained by one and the same decree with the Incarnation of divine Wisdom."

The Wisdom passages utilized in Church liturgy for the vigil of the Immaculate Conception are taken from Ecclus. 24:23-31 and Prov. 9:1. On the great feast day itself, the epistle is taken from Prov. 8:22-35 which reads (Douay Version):

I was set up from eternity, and of old before the earth was made.

The depths were not as yet, and I was already conceived, neither had the fountains of waters as yet sprung out:

The mountains with their huge bulk had not as yet been established: before the hills was I brought forth:

He had not yet made the earth, nor the rivers, nor the poles of the world.

When he prepared the heavens, I was present: when with a certain law and compass he enclosed the depths:

When he established the sky above, and poised the fountains of the waters;

When he compassed the sea with its bounds, and set a law to the waters that they should not pass their limits: when he balanced the foundations of the earth;

I was with him forming all things: and was delighted every day, playing before him at all times;

Playing in the world: and my delights were to be with the children of men.

Now therefore, ye children, hear me: Blessed are they that keep my ways.

Hear instruction and be wise, and refuse it not.

Blessed is the man that heareth me, and that watcheth daily at my gates, and waiteth at the posts of my doors.

He that shall find me, shall find life, and shall have salvation from the Lord.

Despite the aptness of the accommodation of these words to Mary, we believe that such passages are not Marian in a scriptural

---

[53] *Op. cit.*, pp. 1, 3. The Holy Father's words are: "For this reason the very words by which the Sacred Scriptures speak of Uncreated Wisdom, and by which they represent His eternal origin, the Church has been accustomed to use not only in the ecclesiastical offices but also in the Sacred Liturgy [the Eucharistic Sacrifice], applying them to this Virgin's origin."

sense. Not in the proper literal sense, inasmuch as the text refers to Hypostatic Wisdom;[54] not in the typical sense, because it would not be proper to make the more dignified (the Incarnate Word) a type of the less dignified (Mary).

For the rest, there are a multitude of Old Testament texts which the Church in her liturgy, and the Fathers in their homiletic works, have accommodated to Mary by extension or allusion. We have already mentioned some of these accommodations (e.g., the closed eastern gate of the Temple, Jesse's root, etc.). Pope Pius XII mentions more of them in his recent encyclical *Fulgens Corona*. There he notes that the Fathers, to support their belief in Mary's Immaculate Conception, claimed for her such titles as "Lily Among Thorns," "Land Wholly Intact," "Unfading Tree," "Fountain Ever Clear," and the like.[55] Other accommodations are contained in the Litany of Loreto, and in the Marian praises of medieval theologians and preachers.[56] Beautiful as such accommodations to Mary undoubtedly are, they were intended neither by the Holy Spirit nor by the human authors of Sacred Scripture. They do not constitute the biblical meaning of the text in any sense and hence may never be proposed as such; nor can they be used (as a scriptural proof) to prove Marian doctrine.

CONCLUSION

The scattered threads of our research have still to be tied together. As we have discovered, the Old Testament does not tell us all we would like to know about the Blessed Virgin, any more than does the New Testament; but it reveals a loving preparation on God's part for the advent of His Mother. In the key periods of Old

---

[54] Cf. Eric May, O.F.M.Cap., *The Logos in the Old Testament*, in *The Catholic Biblical Quarterly*, Vol. 8, 1946, esp. p. 442 ff.; also E. C. Messenger, *Our Lady in the Scriptures*, in *CCHS*, p. 114. In a rather unique way, Scheeben in his Mariology, Vol. 1, pp. 22-35, makes an attempt to reconcile the reference to both Eternal Wisdom and to Mary in this Wisdom literature.

[55] *Fulgens Corona*, as translated in *The Catholic Mind*, Vol. 51, 1953, p. 739.

[56] E.g., cf. Raphael Huber, O.F.M.Conv., *The Mariology of St. Anthony of Padua*, in *Studia Mariana*, 7 (Burlington, Wis., 1952), pp. 188-268. St. Anthony gave Mary affectionate titles like "Paradise of Humanity," "Rainbow in the Heavens," "Lily and Rose," "Door of Paradise," etc. — based on texts like Gen. 2:8 and 9:13; Ecclus. 50:8; Osee 14:6; 3 Kings 6:25.

Covenant history, beginning with the very dawn of revealed religion, the promise of the Mother as well as her Saviour Son is manifest — now in the bold tones of direct prophecy, now in the more subdued tones of type and figure.

Man's fall in paradise can indeed be called the *felix culpa,* bringing in its wake so grand a promise of salvation, a promise that associates Mary, "the woman," with her Messias Son in the redemption of mankind, a promise that implies her extraordinary purity and virtue. As time passed and the Holy Spirit in His great wisdom inspired more and more men to write the books of the Old Testament, He included many references to the Messias, His Kingdom, His Mother, in the form of minor incidents or major personages who served to prefigure the grand realities of a later century. These types no doubt were essentially obscure to the Jews of old and perhaps to the sacred writers themselves; by and large they achieve their full recognition and significance only in the light of the more complete New Testament revelation. But God did not rest content with type and figure. In the turbulent age of the prophets He saw to it that the men who spoke for Him would once again refer directly to His wonderful Mother. And He added a new, distinctive note. The Mother of the Messias was to be a Virgin Mother! Thus, the startling sign given the reluctant King Ahaz, entrusted to the lips and pen of Isaias. This news was fully confirmed by a contemporary, Micheas, and reasserted at a later date by the great Jeremias. In all of these major prophetical announcements the Woman concerned is Mary — Coredemptrix, Immaculate Virgin Mother of Jesus Christ. Not yet did these texts exhaust the Old Testament references to the Blessed Mother, for when the Holy Spirit inspired that intimate and beautiful composition known as the *Canticle of Canticles* which describes the vast bond of love and union between Yahweh and His Chosen People, Christ and His Church, likewise included in the meaning — and that by God's intent — was the ineffable bond of union between the God-Man and His Mother.

"The New Testament lies hidden in the Old, the Old Testament stands revealed in the New." How true those words are of Mary's presence within the pages of the Old Testament. Pope Pius XII makes a particularly practical observation in the middle of his encyclical *Fulgens Corona*. He says:

> Just as all mothers are deeply affected when they perceive that the countenance of their children reflects a peculiar likeness to their own, so also our Most Sweet Mother wishes for nothing more, never rejoices more than when she sees those whom, under the cross of her Son, she has adopted as children in his stead, portray the lineaments and ornaments of her own soul in thought, word and deed. ... The commemoration of the mystery of the Most Holy Virgin, conceived immaculate and immune from all stain of original sin, should, in the first place, urge us to that innocence and integrity of life which flees from and abhors even the slightest stain of sin.[57]

Sincere devotion to Mary, then, is a means of acquiring virtue. It is well to note again that the basic truths underlying devotion to Mary, though brought to fulfillment in the New Dispensation, were all prophesied with an astonishing degree of clarity already in the Old Testament. God could do no less for His Mother.

---

[57] *Fulgens Corona; loc. cit.*, p. 742.

Mary in the New Testament

By Michael J. Gruenthaner, S.J.

 INCE the Annunciation took place in Nazareth and most of Mary's relatives resided there, she was most probably born in that village. It is situated in the hill country of southern Galilee, bordering upon the great plain of Esdraelon. Though not a great religious, political or social center, it must not be conceived as an isolated settlement of a remote corner of northern Palestine. The great caravan routes to Egypt and the Mediterranean were within easy reach. Sepphoris, which Herod chose as the capital of Galilee from 4 b.c. to about 18 a.d., was a few miles north of Nazareth. The last stretch of the road from Jerusalem to Sepphoris passed through Nazareth. From the heights of Nazareth one could, looking southward, obtain a view of the scenes of not a few of Israel's exploits.

According to tradition, the house where Mary was born was located on the site where the Basilica of the Annunciation now stands. This is built over some caves or grottoes one of which is venerated as the scene of the Annunciation. Even in modern times Nazareth contains homes consisting of two parts: a small wooden flat-topped house fronting the street and an adjoining cave hollowed out by human hands or by nature. A home of this type may well have been the place of Mary's birth. This would be an additional proof that Mary's parents lived in modest circumstances, without being paupers.[1]

PARENTAGE

The Church venerates Mary's parents as Joachim and Anna. These names may be authentic but they are not guaranteed to be such, since they are derived from the apocryphal *Protoevangelium*

---

[1] Cf. J. M. Abel, *Géographie de la Palestine*, Vol. 2 (Paris, 1938), p. 395. Cf. also the standard guides to Palestine such as Meistermann, Bädeker, etc.

of James,[2] which goes back to the second century but embodies much that is pure fantasy. Nothing historically trustworthy is known about Joachim and Anna, but they must have been persons of superior sanctity, for they have been virtually canonized by the Church and we may rest assured that God must have chosen parents worthy to educate a child of such high destiny and singular holiness.

St. Paul emphasizes the fact that Christ is carnally descended from David. Writing to the Romans, he declares that Jesus is of the seed of David according to the flesh (Rom. 1:3). At Antioch, in Pisidia, he tells his audience that Jesus, the Saviour, was brought to Israel from the seed of David (Acts 13:23). He exhorts Timothy: "Remember Jesus Christ risen from the dead, of the seed of David according to my gospel" (2 Tim. 2:8). St. John calls Jesus "the root of David" (Apoc. 5:5) and represents Him as saying: "I am the root and the offspring of David" (Apoc. 22:16). There cannot be the least doubt, then, that Mary was of Davidic lineage, at least through Joachim, her father, and perhaps through Anna, her mother, as well. The bodily origin of the Messias from David had been predicted by Isaias (11:1), Jeremias (23:5; 33:15), and Zacharias (3:8; 6:12).

Joachim and Anna named their daughter *Miryam*, after the valiant sister of Moses (Exod. 15:20). In the Septuagint this was rendered *Mariam.* Hence Mary's name is occasionally given as *Mariam* in the Gospels, although the Greek form Maria is more frequent. This has been Anglicized into Mary.

Did Joachim and Anna have other children beside Mary? St. John tells us that "beside the cross of Jesus were standing His mother, and His mother's sister, Mary of Clopas, and Mary Magdalene" (Jn. 19:25). Since it would be quite unusual for two sisters to have the same name, we must probably distinguish four persons with the Syriac Peshitto, which clarifies the text by inserting the conjunction "and" before "Mary of Clopas." Who, then, was this anonymous sister of the Lord's Mother? St. Matthew, omitting the Mother of Jesus, names three women as witnessing the crucifixion: Mary Magdalene, Mary, the Mother of James and

---

[2] M. J. James, *The Apocryphal New Testament* (Oxford, 1926).

Joseph, and the mother of the sons of Zebedee (27:56). St. Mark mentions the same three with slight modifications: Mary Magdalene, Mary, the mother of James the Less and of Joses, Salome.

If we assume that the Johannine list enumerates four women, it follows from a comparison with the Synoptic list that Salome was the sister of the Mother of Jesus and that James and John, the sons of Zebedee, were His cousins. It is possible, however, that "sister" is employed by St. John in its broader Semitic sense of cousin or relative.

If, on the other hand, we suppose that St. John enumerates but three women, so that "His mother's sister" is the title of Mary of Clopas, we must conclude that she was the sister of Our Lord's Mother. According to Hegesippus[3] (c. 180), this Mary was the wife of Clopas, the brother of Joseph. Hence she was the sister of the Lord's Mother in the sense of being her sister-in-law. In addition, she may have been related to Mary by blood. Consequently, it is not clear that Mary had a sister in the proper sense of the word.

EDUCATION

While there were elementary and advanced schools for boys, there was no provision for the education of girls. The majority of the Jewish rabbis were hostile to female education, although this was endorsed by a few. Accordingly, if she acquired the arts of reading and writing, she did so at home under the guidance of her father or mother. That this was not impossible is shown by the fact that some Jewish women became distinguished scholars in the early centuries of the Christian era.[4]

Despite her lack of formal education, Mary must have acquired a familiarity with the history of the Chosen People and the messianic prophecies of which it was the recipient and custodian. This familiarity was assured by her attendance at the synagogue on the Sabbath and the Jewish festivals. In the morning and evening services held on these occasions selections from the Law and the Prophets were publicly read and translated into Aramaic, the

---

[3] As quoted by Eusebius, *Ecclesiastical History*, 3, 11, 2.

[4] J. Bonsirven, *Le Judaïsme palestinien*, Vol. 2 (Paris, 1935), p. 213.

current language of the common people. A discourse, also, was delivered on some text of Scripture. Certain psalms were chanted.[5] If, as seems likely, she accompanied her parents on pilgrimages to Jerusalem, she heard and learned the Psalms of Degrees sung by the pilgrims on their way to the holy city and listened to the chanting of the psalms in the liturgy of the Temple.[6]

Her spiritual life, also, was nurtured by private devotions. Every Jew was encouraged to pray often: he was expected to begin and end the day by lifting up his heart to God; grace was said before and after meals; certain psalms were recommended for private recitation; every contingency of life was to be met by suitable prayer. It seems reasonable to suppose that Mary even exceeded these high ideals and that she was, in fact, gifted with the highest forms of mystic prayer.

BETROTHAL[7]

We read in Mt. 1:18 that Mary was espoused to a man named Joseph and we glean from Lk. 1:27 and from the genealogies of the Gospels that he was a scion of David (Mt. 1:1-17; Lk. 3:23-38). But his illustrious origin did not imply social prominence. After the demise of Zorobabel (after 515 b.c.), the house of David seems to have declined steadily in wealth and influence. It is mentioned for the last time in the Old Testament in 1 Par. 3:1 f. So we find that Joseph was no more than a carpenter of Nazareth not famed for his erudition (Mt. 13:55; Mk. 6:3). This again is a sign that Mary's parents belonged to the artisan class, for, according to Jewish opinion, bride and bridegroom were supposed to be of the same social and economic status.[8]

---

[5] Cf. Bonsirven, *op. cit.*, Vol. 2, pp. 139, 141-143.

[6] Pss. 119-133 (120-134). Cf. Bonsirven, *op. cit.*, Vol. 2, pp. 119, 139, 147-148.

[7] Cf. P. Gächter, *The Chronology from Mary's Betrothal to the Birth of Christ*, in *Theological Studies*, Vol. 2, 1941, pp. 347-368; U. Holzmeister, *De nuptiis S. Joseph*, in *Verbum Domini*, Vol. 25, 1947, pp. 145-149; E. Neubert, *La chronologie depuis les fiançailles de Marie jusqu'à la naissance du Christ*, in *Marianum*, Vol. 4, 1942, pp. 10-20.

[8] Cf. Bonsirven, op. cit., Vol. 2, p. 209; W. L. Strack and P. L. Billerbeck, *Kommentar zum Neuen Testament aus Talmud und Midrash*, Vol. 2 (München, 1924), pp. 377-378.

That Joseph sought a wife does not surprise us, for marriage was obligatory for a Jew; an unmarried man was stigmatized by the rabbis as not a man and as devoid of joy, blessing, and well-being.[9] But that Mary, who was resolved to preserve perpetual virginity (Lk. 1:38), should consent to espousals seems strange. She may have yielded to pressure from her parents or guardian to conform to the prevailing custom, leaving it to Divine Providence to safeguard her resolution. Perhaps she disclosed her resolve to Joseph and persuaded him to consent to a virginal marriage. It is possible, also, that Joseph entertained the same ideals, so that he needed no persuasion to accept the kind of espousals contemplated by Mary.

A young man usually became betrothed between the ages of eighteen and twenty-four; a girl, between twelve years and one day and twelve years six months, the period when she was classified as a maiden (*na'arah*). The obligation to secure a husband for her was considered urgent when she became a *bogereth*, that is, when she reached the legal state of puberty, after the age of twelve and a half.

But these were standards set up by the rabbis; in practice, girls sometimes became betrothed at a more advanced age, although most probably not as late as twenty, as it was thought calamitous to postpone marriage so long.[10]

A great disparity in age between the bride and bridegroom was deprecated, but widowers sometimes were forced to marry young girls.[11] Hence Mary and Joseph were both youthful at the time of their betrothal, unless Joseph was a widower. Many of the apocryphal gospels and some Oriental writers believed that he was such and that the brothers and sisters of the Lord mentioned in the canonical gospels were Joseph's children by a first, deceased wife.[12] In the West, St. Jerome gave the deathblow to this opinion by asserting in his reply to Helvidius the perpetual virginity of Joseph.[13] This has been the unanimous belief of the Catholic Church ever since.

---

[9] Cf. Bonsirven, *op. cit.*, Vol. 2, p. 208.

[10] Cf. Strack-Billerbeck, *op. cit.*, p. 375; Bonsirven, *loc. cit.*

[11] Cf. Strack-Billerbeck, *op. cit.*, Vol. 2, p. 379.

[12] Carlo Cecchelli, *Mater Christi*, Vol. 2 (Romae, 1948), pp. 51-52.

[13] St. Jerome, *De virginitate perpetua B. Mariae adversus Helvidium. PL*, 23, 203AB, 213B.

Jewish nuptials consisted of two steps: betrothal and marriage proper. After certain financial arrangements concerning the bride had been signed, the bride and bridegroom were betrothed to one another in the house of the bride. The bridegroom gave her a small object having the value of a *peruta*, the smallest coin, in the presence of two witnesses, saying: "By this you are betrothed to me." Betrothal could also be accomplished by a written document and by intercourse with the expressed intention of betrothal.[14]

Betrothal was in every respect equivalent to our marriage. The betrothed girl was called the man's wife; she became a widow if her betrothed died; she was subject to levirate marriage; when widowed or divorced, she could claim the financial settlement accorded to a wife in the same circumstances; in case of infidelity she was liable to the same punishment as an adulterous wife; like a wife she could not be dismissed without a bill of divorcement. Marital relations were licit in Judea during betrothal. This does not seem to have been customary in Galilee.[15]

If the betrothed woman had not been married previously, she usually waited a year before the second step, the marriage proper, was taken. On the day set for the ceremony the bridegroom conducted his betrothed in solemn procession from her parental home to his own. Thereupon the wedding was celebrated for a week.[16]

ANNUNCIATION

Not long after her betrothal,[17] Mary received an epoch-making revelation while she was at prayer in her home. The angel Gabriel appeared to her, probably in visible form, as he had to Zachary in the Holy Place of the Temple (Lk. 1:11). He greeted her with the words: "Hail, full of grace, the Lord is with thee, blessed art thou among women" (Lk. 1:28). Some think that the Greek word for "hail" (*chaire*) represents the salutation *shalom*, meaning "peace," "prosperity," in common use among the Jews. But the literal sense

---

[14] Strack-Billerbeck, *op. cit.*, Vol. 2, pp. 384-394.

[15] Cf. *ibid.*, p. 393.

[16] *Ibid.*, Vol. 1, pp. 504-518, on Mt. 9:5; p. 879, on Mt. 22:2.

[17] Cf. D. Frangipane, *Utrum B. V. Maria ab angelo salutata jam in domo Joseph ut conjux fuerit, in Verbum Domini*, Vol. 25, 1947, pp. 99-111.

of chaire, "rejoice thou," may be intended. For this exhortation is repeatedly found in the Prophets and rendered chaire in the Septuagint (Soph. 3:14-17; Joel 2:21; Zach. 9:9; Lam. 4:21). In this supposition the very first word uttered by the angel suggests that he is a herald of spiritual happiness.[18]

"Full of grace" translates *kecharitomene*, the perfect passive participle of *charitoō*. It denotes one who has been and still is the object of divine benevolence, one who has been favored and continues to be favored by God, one who has been granted supernatural grace and remains in this state.[19] Verbs ending in *oō*, such as *haimatoō* (turn into blood), *thaumatoō* (fill with wonder), *spodoōmai* (burn to ashes) frequently express the full intensity of an action. Hence *kecharitōmĕnē* has been felicitously rendered "full of grace" by the Vulgate and the Peshitto. This rendering expresses the conviction of the Church that the divine favor was fully bestowed upon Mary, in the sense that she was ever immune from the least stain of sin and that she abounded in the graces of the supernatural life and in all the gifts and fruits of the Holy Spirit which flow from that life.

"The Lord is with thee"[20] continued the angel, enunciating the fact that she enjoyed the effective divine assistance in all her endeavors for God's glory, like Gedeon, to whom a similar declaration was made and who crushed the foes of Israel as one man (Judges 6:12, 16). Gabriel concludes his address with "blessed art thou among women," indicating that she occupied a unique position among the women of all nations and ages (Lk. 1:28, 29).

Mary was much perturbed by this salutation, far more than Zachary had been by the apparition of the angel in the Holy Place of the Temple.[21] The cause of her perturbation was not the eulogistic character of Gabriel's greeting, which her profound

---

[18] S. Lyonnet, *Chairē Kecharitōmĕne*, in *Biblica*, Vol. 20, 1939, pp. 131-141; cf. R. Bernard, *L'évangile de l'Annonciation*, in *La Sainte Vierge, figure de l'Eglise* (Paris, 1946), pp. 7-40.

[19] Cf. L. Cerfaux, *Gratia plena*, in *Mémoires et Rapports du Congrès Marial tenu à Bruxelles* (1921), Vol. 1 (Bruxelles, 1922), pp. 34-40.

[20] Cf. U. Holzmeister, *"Dominus tecum,"* in *Verbum Domini*, Vol. 23, 1943, pp. 257-262.

[21] Cf. the verbs in Lk. 1:12, 29.

humility must have borne with equanimity, but the intimation conveyed by his words that she was selected for some great task the difficulty of which she viewed with apprehension. While she was pondering on the possible import of the message, the angel reassured her, addressing her familiarly by her name, bidding her not to fear and reaffirming the fact that she had found favor in God's sight (Lk. 1:30). Then he recounted the nature of the grace conferred upon her: "And behold, thou shalt conceive in thy womb and give birth to a Son, and thou shalt call his name Jesus. He shall be great and shall be called the Son of the Most High. And the Lord God will give him the throne of David, his father. And he shall reign over the house of Jacob throughout the ages and his kingdom shall have no end" (Lk. 1:30-33).

This announcement of the dignity destined for Mary alludes to several messianic prophecies which she may have recollected from her attendance at the synagogue or from her private perusal of Scripture. First, there is a reference to the prediction of Isaias: "Behold, a virgin will conceive and bear a son, and she shall call his name Emmanuel" (7:14). Emmanuel (God is with us) is equivalent in meaning to Jesus (the Lord saves). "He shall be great" recalls the appellation *El Gibbor* (Strong God) bestowed upon the messianic Child by Isaias (9:6). "Son of the Most High" reminds us of the words of the Psalm: "Thou art my son; this day have I begotten thee" (Ps. 2:7). His Davidic descent explains why the Messias was termed "The Branch of David" (Jer. 23:5; 32:15) or simply "David" (Jer. 30:9; Ezech. 34:23; 37:24). His everlasting rule is a verification of the promise made to David (2 Sam. 7:13; Ps. 88:4).

At this point Mary asked the angel: "How shall this be since I know not man?" (Lk. 1:34.) If Mary had expected to have relations with her husband, the question would have been senseless. It only becomes intelligible if we assume that she was inalterably resolved never to have such relations. It is not unthinkable that she had taken a vow[22] of perpetual chastity even though we cannot find a similar instance among the holy men and women of the Old Law. Since her union with God was unparalleled among the saints of the

---

[22] Cf. J. J. Collins, *Our Lady's Vow of Virginity*, in *The Catholic Biblical Quarterly*, Vol. 5, 1943, pp. 371-381.

Old Testament, her mental attitude cannot be appraised by their standards. Her question was not prompted by incredulity, for she did not ask for a proof of the angel's words, nor is she charged with disbelief and punished as Zachary was in similar circumstances. As a matter of fact, she is praised by Elizabeth for her faith (Lk. 1:45). Her query did not spring from curiosity but from a legitimate desire to know what measures she must adopt to attain the realization of the angelic promise, since the use of the natural means of procreation were impossible to her.

Gabriel replied: "The Holy Spirit shall come upon thee and the power of the Most High shall overshadow thee; wherefore, the Holy One who shall be born of thee shall be called Son of God" (Lk. 1:35). The conception of the Child, therefore, will be due to a special intervention of God, which, being an outward act, was the work of the Most Holy Trinity but is appropriated to the Holy Spirit because it is a supreme expression of divine love and bears an analogy to His procession from the mutual love of the Father and the Son.

This act of divine omnipotence is compared to a cloud casting its beneficent shadow upon an object or covering and filling it with its presence.[23] The angel may be alluding to the miraculous cloud which filled the Tabernacle at Mount Sinai. It symbolized the presence of God dispensing benefits to His people (Exod. 40:34-38; Num. 9:22). Its action in filling the tabernacle is described by the verb episkiazein in the Septuagint version of Exod. 40:35, the very verb used by St. Luke in this passage and rendered "overshadow" in the English translation.

Gabriel closes his description of the coming Saviour with the words: "Wherefore the Holy One who shall be born of thee shall be called the Son of God." This cannot mean that He will be constituted Son of God in the proper sense of the term because of His virginal conception, for in this sense He is the Son of God by virtue of His eternal generation. Consequently, it must signify that His supernatural conception will be a sign or a proof enabling men to recognize Him as the Son of God.

The angel concludes his discourse to Mary by a reference to the

---

[23] Cf. H. Rongy, *La conception surnaturelle et virginale du Christ d'après Saint Luc, in Mémoires et Rapports du Congrès Marial tenu à Bruxelles* (1921), Vol. 1 (Bruxelles, 1922), pp. 21-33.

wonderful event which had befallen her kinswoman Elizabeth (Lk. 1:36-37). The relation of this event was designed, first, to gladden Mary: Elizabeth, advanced in years and sterile, unjustly suspected of being under a divine curse as all barren wives were among the Jews, was declared to be in the sixth month of her pregnancy. This marvel of divine goodness is said to be a proof that the incomparably greater prodigy of the Incarnation will be accomplished: "For with God nothing will be impossible" (Lk. 1:36). This was the second and more important reason for revealing the blessing bestowed upon Elizabeth to Mary.

Throughout her conversation with the angel, Mary displayed admirable virtues: simplicity, prudence, wisdom. When Gabriel finished speaking, Mary was confronted by the supreme test of her faith, obedience, and humility. Would she assent to the will of the Triune God, who did not wish to save the world without Mary,[24] to become the Mother of the Divine Word in His human nature? Would she satisfy the yearnings of mankind for salvation, the longing of the souls in Limbo for liberation, the hope of the angels for the redemption of man? Her answer to Gabriel was: "Behold the handmaid of the Lord! Be it done to me according to thy word" (Lk. 1:38). This shows that her faith in the angel's revelation was complete and unreserved, that her consent to be the Mother of God was not passive but active, unforced, absolutely free, that her humility was deep and her obedience wholehearted. At this moment the Incarnation took place, and the angel departed.

VISITATION[25]

After the Annunciation, Mary hastened to visit her kinswoman Elizabeth, who resided in an unnamed town in the hills of Judea, which is most probably to be identified with Ain Karim, about four miles west of Jerusalem. Various motives may be assigned for this

---

[24] Cf. H. Barré, *Le consentement à l'Incarnation rédemptrice*, in Marianum, Vol. 14, 1952, pp. 233-266; J. M. Bover, *Virginis consensus fuitne vera Corredemptio?* in *Alma Socia Christi*, Vol. 2 (Romae, 1952), pp. 164-176; A.-M. Malo, *Données de l'évangile de S. Luc pour la Corédemption de Marie, ibid.*, pp. 178-183.

[25] Cf. F. Ogara, *De doctrina mariana in visitationis mysterio contenta (Lk. 1:39-56)*, in *Verbum Domini*, Vol. 17, 1937, pp. 199-204, 225-233, 289-295.

visit, among which the resolve to aid her aging relative with her domestic duties was the least important. Above all, she must have desired to felicitate Elizabeth upon the extraordinary boon granted to her and to rejoice with her over the Incarnation, of which this gift was a guarantee, as she had been told by the angel Gabriel. She must, also, have been anxious to bring the blessing of the unborn Messias to Elizabeth, her child, and her husband. This is true all the more if Mary knew that Elizabeth's son was to be the precursor of Jesus.

Elizabeth had a supernatural experience when Mary entered her house and greeted her: the babe maturing within her womb leaped for joy (Lk. 1:41, 44). At the same time she was filled with the Holy Spirit, who led her to understand this phenomenon. The child's manifestation of joy was due to the pre-eminence of Mary and her Son. As she expressed it in the resounding tones of enthusiasm: "Blessed art thou among women and blessed is the fruit of thy womb" (Lk. 1:42). Elizabeth confessed herself quite unworthy to receive such distinguished guests: "Why this honor to me that the mother of my Lord should visit me?" (Lk. 1:43.)[26] Then she disclosed the cause which, under the guidance of the Holy Spirit, brought her to the recognition of this mystery: "For, lo! as the voice of thy salutation reached my ears the babe leapt in my womb for joy" (Lk. 1:44). Since the Incarnation was in part due to the faith of Mary, Elizabeth concluded by extolling this faith: "And blessed art thou who hast believed, for the message of the Lord to thee shall be fulfilled" (Lk. 1:45).

On this occasion Mary, too, was inspired by the Holy Spirit. She improvised the poem known to us as the *Magnificat*,[27] from the opening word of its Latin version. It is charged with reminiscences of the psalms and other writings of the Old Testament, showing that Mary's mind was steeped in Holy Writ. In the first strophe (Lk. 1:46-50), she meditates with restrained enthusiasm upon the mercy,

---

[26] R. Rábanos, *¿De donde a mi esto, que la Madre de mi Señor venga a mi?* (*Lk. 1:43*), in *Estudios Marianos*, Vol. 8, 1949, pp. 9-27.

[27] Cf. J. De Kaulenaer, *De Cantico "Magnificat,"* in *Collectanea Mechliniensia*, Vol. 8, 1934, pp. 542-547; G. Fregentino, *Il Magnificat nei commenti dei Santi Padri*, Siena, 1939; P. Luis Suárez, *Soteriología del Magnificat*, in *Ephemerides Mariologicae*, Vol. 3, 1953, pp. 447-466.

power, and holiness of God, who had chosen her for so great a dignity. She explains in the second strophe (vv. 51-53) that God is wont to exalt the weak and depose the proud. In the third strophe (vv. 54-55), she praises God's fidelity in fulfilling through His Son the promises made to Abraham and his posterity.

The Gospel informs us that Mary stayed about three months with Elizabeth (Lk. 1:56). She may, then, have assisted at the birth of John. Her name is not mentioned in connection with the remarkable happenings at John's circumcision. Hence she may have returned to Nazareth before this took place.

JOSEPH'S ORDEAL

St. Matthew relates the following crisis in the life of Joseph before he took Mary to his house: "When Mary, his mother, had been betrothed to Joseph, she was found to be with child from the Holy Spirit" (1:18). We are not told when this discovery was made; it certainly occurred after the Annunciation, and it may have happened before or after the Visitation. We are, also, left in ignorance of the person who made the discovery. Most probably it was Mary herself who informed Joseph about her miraculous conception. Why should she conceal so important a matter from her husband? Joseph's reaction to the discovery is described thus: "Joseph, her husband, being a just man and unwilling to expose her, was minded to give her a private release" (Mt. 1:19). The thought of being in such close proximity to the deity may have terrified Joseph and impelled him to divorce Mary. To make the divorce public would have exposed Mary to obloquy, since many of her acquaintances would not have readily believed in a conception wrought by the Holy Spirit. Being a just man and reluctant to inflict an injury upon anyone, especially upon a maiden of such sanctity, he was planning a secret divorce either by giving her a bill of divorcement or by leaving the city.[28]

While he was in this agonized state of mind, "an angel of the Lord appeared to him in a dream, saying, 'Joseph, son of David, fear not to take to thyself Mary, thy wife, for what is conceived in her is

---

[28] Cf. R. Bulbeck, *The Doubt of St. Joseph, in The Catholic Biblical Quarterly*, Vol. 10, 1948, pp. 296-309.

of the Holy Spirit. And she shall give birth to a Son, and thou shalt call his name Jesus, for he shall save his people from their sins'" (Mt. 1:20-21).

Thus Mary's statement about the origin of her child was confirmed by a special revelation. Joseph then completed the second and final stage of his marriage to Mary: he brought her to his dwelling, which may have been situated on the site of the ancient Church of the Nutrition, now pointed out as the workshop of St. Joseph. According to the Gospel, Joseph had no marital relations with Mary "until she gave birth to her firstborn Son" (Mt. 1:25). The "until" in the original does not signify that he knew her sexually afterward. It merely states what happened up to a certain point without affirming or negating anything about the subsequent period (cf. Is. 46:4 in the Septuagint; 1 Cor. 15:25; Ps. 71:7; 109:1).

In fact, the Church's belief in the perpetual virginity of Mary can be traced back to the second century.[29] It was impugned for the first time by Helvidius, an obscure heretic apparently residing in Rome, with an insignificant following. He was refuted by St. Jerome, whose treatise on the subject has become a classic of Catholic theology.[30] Nor does the appellation "firstborn" applied by the Evangelist to Jesus imply other children. It was a technical term, showing that the son in question was God's property and had to be redeemed (Exod. 34:20; Num. 3:41; 18:16). In addition, the first-born was especially esteemed because he was the first issue of a man's strength (Deut. 21:17). After the decease of his father he was entitled to the leadership of the family and to a double portion of the inheritance in case there were brothers (Deut. 21:15-17). Hence the brothers and sisters of Jesus repeatedly mentioned in the New Testament (Mt. 12:46; 13:55-56; Mk. 3:31-32; 6:3; Lk. 8:19; Jn. 2:12; Acts 1:14; 1 Cor. 9:5; Gal. 1:19) were cousins or kinsfolk of Jesus since the Hebrew and Aramaic words for brother and sister also have this broader sense.

St. Matthew stresses the fact that Mary's conception is a fulfillment of Isaias' prophecy: "Behold the virgin shall be with child

---

[29] Hegesippus; cf. Eusebius, *Ecclesiastical History*, 3, 11, 2; 4, 22, 4.

[30] St. Jerome, *De perpetua virginitate B. Mariae adversus Helvidium.* PL, 23, 185-206.

and give birth to a Son and they shall call his name Emmanuel" (Mt. 1:25). It seems probable that Mary and Joseph also adverted to the accomplishment of this prophecy at this time.

BETHLEHEM

As the time of Mary's pregnancy was drawing to a close, she and her husband were faced with a new problem. An edict of the Emperor Augustus was published ordering a census of all the inhabitants of Herod's kingdom. Similar enumerations had already been made in other provinces of the Roman empire or were then in progress, so that, popularly speaking, the whole world seemed to be in the process of enrollment (Lk. 2:1). This registration required each citizen to repair to the home of his clan. Since Joseph was of Davidic lineage, he had to go to Bethlehem, the birthplace of David and the center of his clan. The supervision of the census was entrusted to Quirinius, who was either governor of Syria at this time (11-8 b.c.) or acted as deputy of Saturninus, the governor of Syria in 7 b.c.[31]

The journey to Bethlehem from Nazareth covered about ninety to ninety-five miles and must have been arduous especially for an expectant mother. Mary accompanied Joseph either because women had to be enrolled also or because she owned taxable land in Bethlehem or because she wanted the companionship of Joseph in the hour of her destiny. Scripture does not enlighten us about the details of the journey. The character of the persons involved suggests that it was made without grumbling, with full trust in Divine Providence, and with complete submission to the will of God. Their thoughts, as they escorted the unborn Son of God, were too hallowed to be described here.

On their arrival, they met with a new bitter disappointment: they found that there was no place for them in the inn (Lk. 2:7). The inn is usually thought to have been a caravansary. But the Greek word translated "inn" does not necessarily have this meaning; it also denotes a lodging, a guest room. Joseph may have expected to find this in the house of a relative or friend, only to discover that all such rooms had already been taken by others. Somebody, perhaps the

---

[31] Cf. *Lexikon für Theologie und Kirche,* s.v.

intended host, then showed them a series of caves outside the city. Christian devotion has commemorated one of these caves as the birthplace of Christ by converting it into a shrine and building the Basilica of the Nativity over the site.

How long Mary resided here before Jesus was born is not known. His birth may have occurred on the very night of their arrival or after some days. When the time of her delivery came, Mary retired to the cave and gave birth to Jesus in utter solitude. It is an article of the Catholic faith that she did so without suffering the usual lesions of the tissues which occur in ordinary childbirth, so that she remained a virgin physically even in parturition. The passage of the child through her body has been compared to the transit of light through crystal. Like all mothers of Palestine in ancient and modern times, she wrapped her Babe in neat narrow bands of colorful material. Then she laid Him diagonally on a square cloth and folded the corners of the cloth over His hands and feet. Next she tied His hands to his sides with bandages, which in this case were plain, since only the rich could afford embroidered ones.[32] These bands together with the cloth and the bandages constituted the swaddling clothes to which St. Luke refers (Lk. 2:7).

The cave must at one time have been a shelter for animals, for, after swaddling the Babe, she laid Him in a manger, a stone eating trough for domestic beasts set conveniently low on the floor. Before placing the Child within it, she undoubtedly filled it with straw.[33] Thus the divine Infant did not lack the essentials of child care required in the Near East from time immemorial, although the articles used conformed in quality rather to the standards of a poor peasant than to those of the middle and upper classes. The census was probably held in late summer, after the harvest, not in winter, as is popularly supposed, when frequent rains and the cold make traveling extremely difficult. Hence the child was not exposed to the inclemency of the weather, although even in December the cave would have afforded some protection against wintry blasts.

While Mary and Joseph gazed in adoration, praise, thanksgiving,

---

[32] Cf. Madeleine S. Miller and J. Lane Miller, *Encyclopedia of Bible Life* (New York, 1944), p. 60.

[33] *Ibid.*, pp. 26, 248; Ill. 21.

and supplication upon the Incarnate Son of God, they must have reflected with some sadness upon the bitter poverty and dereliction of Israel's king. Their sorrow was mitigated by the sudden advent of the shepherds seeking to adore the Child wrapped in swaddling clothes and laid in a manger. From their enthusiastic story they learned that the birth of the Saviour was not without manifest splendor: a supernatural radiance illuminated the nocturnal sky; an angelic herald proclaimed the joyous tidings about Christ, the Lord, born in David's city; choirs of angels sang of peace and God's benevolence to men (Lk. 2:8-17). After leaving, the shepherds spread the news of Christ's nativity among their acquaintances, filling all their listeners with wonderment (Lk. 2:18-21). It would be odd, indeed, if at least some of these did not come to pay homage to the Child and His Mother. We are told that Mary kept all these things in her heart, pondering them (Lk. 2:19). She treasured them as precious testimonies to the dignity of her Son, compared them with previous revelations that she had received, and so penetrated even more deeply into the mystery of the Incarnation. The episode of the shepherds impressed upon her that wealth, learning, or any form of earthly honor were welcome to her Son only if accompanied by the strong faith and moral integrity of the shepherds.

At the end of eight days, she rejoiced over the rite of circumcision, which made Jesus a member of her own people (Lk. 2:21; Gen. 17:9-19). At the same time she may have reflected that this rite had lost its prophetic meaning: the promises made to Abraham and his posterity, of which it was a sign and a seal (Rom. 4:11), were realized in her Son. On this occasion, Mary and Joseph named the babe Jesus as they had been commanded (Mt. 1:21; Lk. 1:31). That the task of saving her people intimated by the name Jesus would be toilsome was suggested to Mary by the hardships of His infancy.

PRESENTATION AND PURIFICATION

The Mosaic Law decreed that a woman who had given birth to a male child should be ritually unclean for forty days (Lev. 12:1 f.). During this period, she was prohibited from touching anything hallowed and from entering the Temple. After the forty days she was obliged to go to the Temple and rid herself of her uncleanness by certain prescribed sacrifices: a lamb a year old for a holocaust and a young pigeon or a turtledove for a sin offering. In case she could not afford a lamb, she could substitute a young pigeon or a turtledove. If the male child was her first-born, she was also obliged to redeem him from the Lord, whose property he was, by the payment of five shekels to the priests (Exod. 13:13, 34:10; Num. 18:15, 16). Accordingly, Mary and Joseph, taking the Child, went up to the Temple in Jerusalem from Bethlehem and carried out the prescriptions of the Law, offering the sacrifices that were incumbent upon the poor (Lk. 2:22-24).

As they were proceeding to the gate of Nicanor, the eastern gate of the Court of the Women, where women to be purified were required to assemble,[34] they encountered a just and devout man named Simeon, to whom the Holy Spirit had revealed that he would not die before seeing the consolation of Israel, the Anointed of the Lord, the Messias. Under the influence of the Holy Spirit he recognized the long-awaited Saviour in Jesus. Attracted by his manifest piety and emotion, Mary acceded to his desire and allowed him to take Jesus in his arms. Swayed by prophetical inspiration, he exclaimed: "Now thou dost release thy servant, O Lord, according to thy word, in peace! Because my eyes have seen thy salvation, which thou hast prepared in the sight of all peoples — a light of revelation to the Gentiles and the glory of thy people Israel" (Lk. 2:29-32).

This prophecy filled the parents with admiration: it brought home to them the fact that the mission of Jesus would not be confined to the Chosen People but would extend to the other nations as well. This reminded them of the similar predictions of Isaias concerning the Servant of the Lord (42:6; 49:6).

That this mission would entail suffering not only for the Saviour but also for His Mother is evident from the words which Simeon addressed to her after blessing her and Joseph: "Behold, this child is set for the fall and rise of many in Israel and for a sign that shall be contradicted, and a sword shall pierce through thy soul also, that

---

[34] Cf. Strack-Billerbeck, op. cit., Vol. 2, p. 129, note b.

the thoughts may be laid bare in many hearts" (Lk. 2:34-35).[35] Jesus will cause the spiritual downfall of many in Israel and the rise of many others to a higher supernatural life. He will be a sign, a manifestation of the divinity which will be opposed by some. In consequence of this opposition, Mary, too, will suffer anguish so intense that a great sword will seem to pierce her soul. All this will bring to light the good or bad sentiments latent in many hearts.

Mary was distracted from her forebodings of evil engendered by this prophecy by the advent of Anna, a prophetess and a widow of venerable age, who worshiped day and night with fasts and prayer, never leaving the Temple. On this occasion, she praised the Lord for His salvation. After meeting the Saviour, she spoke about the Child repeatedly to those who looked forward to the deliverance of Jerusalem (Lk. 2:36-38).

THE MAGI

A year or perhaps a year and a half after the Presentation of the Child Jesus in the Temple, a stately caravan halted one evening at the humble home of the Holy Family in Bethlehem. This home is called a "house" by St. Matthew (2:11). Hence they may have exchanged the cave for a more suitable dwelling, built perhaps by the skill of Joseph. The leaders of the caravan explained that they were Magi, members of a priestly caste from far-distant Media, who had seen the newly created star of the Messias in the East and had been told by Herod that the prophet Micheas had predicted His birth in Bethlehem of Juda (5:1-3). They pointed to the star, which was sending down its rays upon the house of the Holy Family. After appearing to them in their native land, it had vanished as they traveled to Judea to adore the messianic King of the Jews. It had reappeared on their journey from Jerusalem to Bethlehem, filling them with exceeding great joy and guiding them to the goal of their longings, the house of the infant Saviour.

Their story revealed such palpable evidence of divine intervention and such extraordinary faith that their request to see

---

[35] Cf. J. Fernández, *El encuentro de Simeón y Ana con Jesús. Su testimonio*, in *Cultura Bíblica*, Vol. 5, 1948, pp. 338-343; C. De Koninck, *La prophétie de Siméon et la compassion de la Vierge Mere*, in *Alma Socia Christi*, Vol. 2 (Romae, 1952), pp. 184-191.

the Child and His Mother could not be denied. When they beheld Jesus in His Mother's arms, they prostrated themselves in silent adoration. Then they offered gifts indicative of their faith: gold, frankincense, and myrrh. These gifts suggest that they perceived in the Child more than merely a human Messias: they were the kind of offerings which men of that age presented to their gods. According to a common interpretation, the gold was a tribute to His kingship; the frankincense, to His divinity; the myrrh, to His humanity.

Mary and Joseph recalled the prediction of Simeon that Jesus would be a light of revelation to the Gentiles (Lk. 2:32) and the prophetic words of the Psalmist concerning the homage of the nations to the Messias: "The kings of Tarshish and of the isles will render tribute; the kings of Sheba and Seba will bring gifts; all kings will fall down before him, all nations serve him" (Ps. 71:10-11). They remembered also the parallel prophecy from Isaias: "All these from Sheba shall come; they shall bring gold and frankincense" (60:6).

THE FLIGHT INTO EGYPT

Mary and Joseph were not allowed to enjoy the triumph of the Son of God for long. Herod was determined to slay this Child, whom he falsely supposed to be an aspirant to his throne, and hoped to discover His whereabouts through the Magi, whom he had urged to return, simulating a pious desire to emulate their act of worship. Soon, therefore, after their arrival in Bethlehem, perhaps that very night, they were told in a dream not to return to Herod but to take another road back to their own country. Joseph, too, was warned in a dream about the murderous designs of Herod and bidden to take the Child and His Mother and flee to Egypt (Mt. 2:12, 13). He was to remain there until he was admonished to return. Joseph may have chosen the road which leads by way of Ascalon and Gaza along the sand dunes of the Mediterranean coast to Egypt. Or he may have taken the southern route by way of Hebron and Beersheba across the northern part of the Sinai peninsula to the seacoast and into the Delta. Either way was laborious, demanding about two weeks of exhausting travel. They were fortunate indeed if they owned a donkey or a camel upon which Mary and the Child could ride at least at intervals.

On reaching Egypt, they most probably settled in some Jewish colony. Their journey seems to have been without untoward incident, since nothing is recorded. But as they cast a retrospective glance upon their past experiences, they must have realized that the service of the messianic King could require heroic humility and obedience. If the news of the slaughter of the Innocents reached them in Egypt (Mt. 2:16-18), they perceived that martyrdom might even be exacted from guiltless children.

They were, no doubt, nauseated by the degrading idolatry of Egypt; it was a striking proof of man's crying need of a Saviour. Isaias had consoled Egypt with the words: "And the Lord will make himself known to the Egyptians and the Egyptians will know the Lord" (19:21). That this hour might be accelerated was undoubtedly the theme of Mary's prayer.

RETURN TO NAZARETH

When Herod I died in 4 b.c., an angel appeared in a dream to Joseph and bade him to return to the land of Israel with Mary and Jesus. In the course of his journey, he heard that Archelaus, Herod's older son by the Samaritan Malthace, had been appointed ethnarch of Judea; he hesitated about going back to Bethlehem, fearing that this monarch might persecute Jesus as ruthlessly as his father if he learned His identity. He was freed from all anxiety by another dream vision in which he was directed to go to Nazareth of Galilee, which was ruled by Herod Antipas as tetrarch, a full brother of Archelaus (Mt. 2:19-23). According to St. Matthew, who quotes Osee 11:1, the exodus of the Israelites from Egypt and their entrance into the Promised Land were a prophetic type of Jesus' return to Israel (2:15). The same Evangelist likewise notes that the Saviour took up His residence in Nazareth to fulfill the declaration of the prophets that He would be called a Nazarene (2:23). It is doubtful that these truths were apparent to Mary and Joseph.

THE HIDDEN LIFE

Two sentences summarize the retired life of Jesus in Nazareth, which endured until about His thirtieth year (Lk. 3:23). The first states that He rendered submission to His parents (Lk. 2:51). Since Mary and Joseph knew that He was the Son of God, they were no doubt filled with wonder and awe at the profundity of His abasement. The mainspring of His action was not the high esteem which He felt for Mary and Joseph on account of the perfect performance of their parental duties. His primary motive was the will of His Heavenly Father whenever and wherever it was manifest. Mary fully appreciated this motive since it governed her own demeanor toward Joseph as the head of the household.

The second sentence about the hidden life declares: "And Jesus increased in wisdom and in stature and in grace with God and men" (Lk. 2:52).[36] It is easy to understand how He increased in stature: this means simply that His physical development kept pace with His age. How He advanced in wisdom is more difficult to grasp. The knowledge which He possessed as the Divine Word was infinite and not susceptible to change. But His human nature, also, was gifted with knowledge, which was threefold in character: (1) intuitive, the continuous and immediate vision of the divine essence, (2) infused, comprising the species of objects and persons impressed upon His intellect by God, (3) experimental, acquired by the application of His senses and intellectual faculties. Obviously, the last named alone could increase, for the first two were perfect from the very first moment of His conception.

His advancement in knowledge, then, signifies that He gained and displayed an experimental knowledge which was proportionate to every stage of His age and growth. Since His senses were more acute and His intellect more keen than those of any boy that ever lived, His acquired knowledge must have surpassed that of any youth with comparable opportunities. This mental development unquestionably gave intense joy to Mary and Joseph; at the same time His humble obedience in concealing His talents in an obscure village like Nazareth must have aroused their unqualified admiration.

It is possible that He also revealed an ever increasing amount of His infused knowledge. The progressive manifestation of this knowledge could also be termed an advancement of knowledge, for so it would have appeared in the eyes of men. However, He seems to have given no evidence of this supernatural knowdedge during

---

[36] The Greek word translated "stature" means also "years," "age."

the hidden life at Nazareth, at least outside the family circle. For when He revisited Nazareth during His public life, its citizens were struck with astonishment and said: "Where did this man acquire this wisdom and these powers? Is He not the son of the carpenter?" (Mt. 13:54; Mk. 6:1-6; Lk. 4:14-30.)

Since Jesus was full of grace from the first instant of His conception, He could not increase in grace internally. As He advanced in years, He performed acts of virtue in harmony with each period of His life. Thus He progressed in grace with God, who was pleased with His actions and with men, who noted His outward progress with ever growing approval. The peerless beauty of Christ's demeanor, as it unfolded itself before them, must have been a source of inspiration and delight to His parents. They were rooted and grounded in the love of Jesus whose personality dominated their work, their recreation, their prayer, their mutual regard, and their attitude toward others.

THE CHILD JESUS IN THE TEMPLE

After completing his thirteenth year, every Jew was obliged to appear in the sanctuary at Jerusalem on three major festivals of the year: Passover, Pentecost, and Tabernacles. Women were not bound by this precept, although they could make these pilgrimages if they so desired. Devout parents introduced and habituated their sons to the observance of this law before the legally prescribed age. Hence we find Mary and Joseph taking Jesus to the Passover in His twelfth year. They may have done so on previous occasions, but this is the only instance commemorated in the Gospels (Lk. 2:41-50).[37]

Having fulfilled their religious duties at the Passover, Mary and Joseph joined one of the caravans returning to Galilee. At the first stopping place, after a day's journey, which may not have exceeded thirteen miles,[38] they noticed to their consternation that Jesus was not with the caravan. Fearing that some mishap might have befallen Him, they retraced their steps and combed the groups of acquaintances and friends going back to Galilee. On reaching Jerusalem, they searched all the localities where He might be

---

[37] Cf. Strack-Billerbeck, *op. cit.*, Vol. 2, pp. 141-149.

[38] *Ibid.*, p. 149.

tarrying. Finally they found Him on the third day in the Temple listening to the doctors of the Law and asking them questions. It was customary at this time for scholars to surround themselves with disciples and to encourage them to propose queries and to debate doctrinal and moral problems. The circle which Jesus joined was assembled either in one of the porticoes of the Temple or in the lecture hall of the synagogue attached to the Temple. All those in attendance were amazed by the intelligence of Jesus and by His responses.

When Mary saw Jesus thus occupied she, too, was astonished not so much by His intellectual brilliance as by the fact that He seemed oblivious of His parents and unconcerned about their anguish. Accordingly, she asked Him: "My child, why hast thou treated us so? Indeed, thy Father and I have been searching for thee in great distress." Jesus' reply indicates that their fears for His safety were unfounded: "Why did you search for me?" Then He proposes the motive of His seemingly unfilial conduct: "Did you not know that I must be in my Father's house?" (Lk. 2:49.) "But they did not comprehend what he said to them" (Lk. 2:50).[39] They knew indeed that He must be in His Father's house but they did not understand that His Father's call might involve the abandonment of family ties even in boyhood, without permission of the parents, without previous notification, and with the infliction of much sorrow. We need not be surprised that Mary did not grasp the mysteries of Christ's life at once. Just as she grew in love and grace, so could she increase in understanding. That she stored up this and other incidents of the hidden life in her memory for further meditation is expressed by St. Luke as follows: "And his mother kept all these incidents in her heart" (2:51).

CANA

We read nothing further about Mary until the beginning of Our Lord's public life. At that time Jesus, Mary, and some of His disciples were invited to the wedding festivities of a young couple in Cana of lower Galilee, situated, according to tradition, at Kefr

---

[39] Cf. J. M. Bover, *Una nueva interpretación de Lc. 2:50,* in *Estudios Bíblicos,* Vol. 10 (seg. ép.), 1951, pp. 205-215.

Kenna, three and a half miles northeast of Nazareth. Since nothing is said about Joseph on this occasion, it is reasonably assumed that he died during the hidden life at Nazareth (Jn. 2:1, 2).

The newly wedded couple were expected to provide food and drink for the invited guests, who streamed in from all sides in the course of the week. Owing to their poverty or to an unexpectedly large influx of visitors, the supply of wine intended for the entertainment of the guests became exhausted prematurely. Failure to provide this indispensable element of Jewish rejoicing would have exposed the bride and bridegroom to humiliation. Mary learned of their predicament and in the tactful kindness of her heart appealed to Jesus for alleviation. Having unbounded confidence in His resourcefulness, she merely stated the fact, without adding a plea: "They have no wine." "Woman," Jesus answered her, "what is there between me and thee?" (Jn. 2:3, 4.)

It is now recognized by scholars of all shades of thought that "woman" as a vocative does not imply any rebuke or reproach, that it may, in fact, denote the highest esteem.[40] Still it is puzzling that He chose this form of address in preference to the more affectionate "mother." Perhaps He wished to convey the idea that her maternal authority had ceased with the inception of the public life and that His regard for her was dominated primarily by her spiritual merits and not by the physical bonds of flesh and blood which united them.

The meaning of the question, "What is there between me and thee?" has been laboriously investigated by scholars,[41] but a solution satisfactory to all has not been attained. It is used to deny a petition (2 Sam. 16:10; 19:23) and to protest against a hostile measure (Judges 11:12; 1 Kings 17:18). It does not necessarily imply harshness of tone but may be friendly, as when David dissented from the opinion of Abisai, his most ardent supporter (2 Sam. 16:10).[42]

Jesus, then, seems to have rejected the petition of His Mother, giving as His reason: "My hour has not yet come." The expression

---

[40] Cf. Walter Bauer, *Wörterbuch zum Neuen Testament* (Berlin, 1952), s.v.

[41] See, for example, T. Gallus, *"Quid mihi et tibi, mulier? Nondum venit hora mea" (Jn. 2, 4): potestne intelligi tamquam allusio?* in *Verbum Domini*, Vol. 22, 1942, pp. 41-50.

[42] For an analysis of all the scriptural passages concerned, cf. Paul Gächter, *Maria im Erdenleben* (Innsbruck, 1953), pp. 171-177.

"my hour" is obscure and has been the subject of exegetical argument.[43] It seems to mean the time when He is to manifest His messianic mission in some conspicuous manner.

But if He rejected her request, how are we to explain her directions to the servants which denote consent: "Do whatever he bids you" (Jn. 2:5)? The explanation seems to be that He denied her prayer at first in order to afford her an opportunity to gain more merit and greater glory by making her petition more intense. This intensification of her supplication was not formulated in words but occurred in the secrecy of her heart, where Jesus alone could read it. She who knew her Son so perfectly read the affirmative answer in the expression of His face, in the light of His eyes, in the smile of His lips, perhaps even by the illumination of the Holy Spirit.

Thus her intercession resulted in a stupendous miracle, the transmutation of water into wine, possible only to the omnipotence of God. She also revealed the kindness of her heart, which intervened to save a relatively unimportant family of Galilee from a temporary social embarrassment.

THE PUBLIC LIFE

St. John relates that Mary and the brethren of Jesus accompanied Him and His disciples to Capharnaum (Jn. 2:12). This was for a time the center of His messianic ministry and the starting point for expeditions to other parts of Galilee. She may have settled down there and so may have listened to His discourses and witnessed some of His miracles. But she played no part in His public life. She is not mentioned among the women who ministered to Him and His Apostles in Galilee (Mk. 15:41). Only two incidents are recounted in which she is referred to. On the first occasion, Jesus was so besieged and importuned by a crowd of visitors in a house which was presumably in Capharnaum that He could not take necessary food. Then His brethren and His mother came to take Him away, for some people even accused Him of being beside Himself (Mk. 3:20). If His brethren shared this view, it cannot be attributed to His

---

[43] Cf., for example, F.-M. Braun, *La Mère de Jésus dans l'oeuvre de saint Jean*, in *Revue Thomiste*, Vol. 50, 1950, pp. 429-479; Vol. 51, 1951, pp. 5-68; J. Leal, *La hora de Jésus, la hora de su Madre (Jo. 2, 4)*, in *Estudios Eclesiásticos*, Vol. 26, 1952, pp. 147-168.

Mother, whose presence was motivated solely by solicitude for His welfare. When Jesus was informed that His Mother and brethren were without, He replied: "Who are my mother and my brethren?"[44] "Looking round on those who sat about him, he said: 'Behold my mother and my brethren! For whoever does the will of God, he is my brother, sister and mother'" (Mk. 3:33-38; Mt. 12:46). This reply does not imply a disparagement of His Mother; it merely exalts spiritual values above consanguinity.

The same doctrine was inculcated by Jesus on another occasion when a woman of His audience exclaimed enthusiastically: "Blessed is the womb that bore thee and the breasts which thou didst suck." Jesus answered: "Yes, indeed, blessed are they who listen to the Word of God and observe it" (Lk. 11:27-28). Mary's role, then, during the public life of Jesus was prayerful retirement. Jesus wished to avoid even the semblance of undue human attachment and to concentrate the attention of men upon Himself.

BENEATH THE CROSS

We do not encounter Mary again in the Gospels until we find her standing beneath the cross together with John, the beloved disciple, and the holy women (Jn. 19:25-27). Sorrow is in direct proportion to our comprehension and love of the person over whom we grieve. But Mary understood the prerogatives of Jesus and His relationship to herself more keenly than any other human being; the intensity of her love harmonized with this understanding. Hence she was truly the Queen of martyrs: every insult, every wound must have filled her with unparalleled anguish. She knew that the consciousness of her grief increased the agony of her Son. Still she suffered without flinching, in heroic silence, fully aware that the passion of her Son together with her own sorrow were necessary for the redemption of mankind.[45]

Amid the encircling gloom, which lasted from the sixth to the ninth hour (Mt. 27:45; Mk. 15:30; Lk. 23:44), the voice of Jesus was heard for the third time (Jn. 19:26-27). Addressing His Mother, He

---

[44] Cf. O. Rodriguez, *"Qui sunt fratres mei" (Mt. 12, 48)*, in *Verbum Domini*, Vol. 5, 1925, pp. 132-137.

[45] Cf. R. Rábanos, *La Corredención de María en la Sagrada Escritura*, in *Estudios Marianos*, Vol. 2, 1943, esp. pp. 51-59.

said: "Woman, behold thy son," thereby commending John to Mary's maternal solicitude. Then speaking to John in correlative terms, He conferred the privileges and duties of sonship upon him: "Behold thy mother." The beloved disciple understood the words in this sense. "From that hour," we read, "the disciple took her into his home" (v. 27).

Was John our representative on this occasion, so that Mary was proclaimed our Mother also? Various opinions have been expressed in this connection. Exegetes, in general, and a few theologians claim that the text under discussion does not furnish any *biblical* proof (either in the literal or the typical sense) for the doctrine of Mary's spiritual motherhood.[46] Their main argument seems to be that the Fathers of the Church do not interpret the text in this sense. However, the vast majority of theologians, and not a few exegetes, appealing principally to the teaching of recent pontiffs, consider the Johannine passage a valid *scriptural* argument in favor of that doctrine. Of this group, some do not specify what biblical sense they have in mind;[47] others show their preference for a *literal* sense (at least *plenior*),[48] while still others favor a Marian *typical* sense,

---

[46] Cf., among others: J. Corluy, *Commentarius in Evangelium Joannis* (Gandavi, 1889), p. 511; J. Knabenbauer, *Evangelium sec. Joannem* (Parisiis, 1898), pp. 546-547; A. Durand, *Evangile selon Saint Jean* (Paris, 1938), p. 493; W. Newton, *A Commentary on the New Testament* (Catholic Biblical Association of America, 1942), p. 357; F. Ceuppens, *De Mariologia Biblica*, ed. 2 (Taurini, 1951), pp. 199-202; H. Lennerz, *De Beata Virgine* (Romae, 1939), p. 127.

[47] Cf., for example, F. X. Maszl, *Erklärung der hl. Schriften des Neuen Testamentes*, Vol. 5 (Wien, 1841), pp. 433-435; Loch-Reischl, *Die Heiligen Schriften des N.T.*, Vol. 1 (Regensburg, 1899), p. 387; Lusseau-Collomb, *Manuel d'Etudes Bibliques*, Vol. 4 (Paris, 1932), p. 851.

[48] Cf. E. Legnani, *De theologica certitudine Maternitatis B. M. Virginis quoad fideles juxta Christi verba "Mulier, ecce filius tuus"* (Venetiis, 1899), p. 27; Hilary of St. Ahatha, *Beatissimae Virginis Maternitas universalis in verbis Jesu morientis: "Ecce filius tuus … ecce mater tua,"* in *Teresianum*, 1933, pp. 105-151; 1934, pp. 194-249; J. Prado, *Praelectiones Biblicarum Compendium*, Vol. 3 (Taurini, 1942), p. 446; R. Rábanos, *La maternidad espiritual de Maria en el Protoevangelio y San Juan,* in *Estudios Marianos*, Vol. 7, 1948, pp. 15-50; J. Leal, *Beata Virgo omnium spiritualis Mater ex Jn. 19, 26-27,* in *Verbum Domini*, Vol. 27, 1949, pp. 65-73; E. May, *The Scriptural Basis for Mary's Spiritual Maternity,* in *Marian Studies*, Vol. 3, 1952, pp. 125-130; G. M. Roschini, *La Madonna secondo la fede e la teologia*, Vol. 2 (Roma, 1953), pp.

expressed at times in equivalent terms.[49]

Our personal views on this matter may be summarized as follows: the doctrine of Mary's spiritual motherhood is not expressed in Jn. 19:26-27 according to the literal sense; the words themselves do not suggest it. However, it is not excluded by the literal sense, and certainly not by the typical or inclusive sense. If the declarations of the popes in this connection[50] are sufficient proof that this meaning is contained in Jn. 19:26-27, then, of course, it must be found there. But it would seem to us that the various Papal utterances relative to this point do not constitute true declarations of doctrine.[51]

Be that as it may, the truth of Mary's spiritual motherhood is deducible from other passages of the New Testament. Christ speaks of His disciples as His brothers (Mt. 28:10). St. Paul calls Him the first-born among many brethren (Rom. 7:22). Therefore, the teaching of tradition that Mary is our Mother, to which we must give credence, is not without scriptural foundation.

THE RISEN CHRIST

Scripture is silent about Mary's participation in the burial of Jesus. How she spent the days intervening before the Resurrection is likewise left to our imagination. She did not accompany the holy women who went to the tomb on Sunday morning to anoint Him. Being so absolutely convinced of His Resurrection, she considered this expedition useless. Great saints and scholars consider it almost self-evident that the Risen Christ appeared first to His Mother,

---

245-253.

[49] J. M. Bover, *Mulier, ecce filius tuus*, in *Verbum Domini*, Vol. 4, 1924, p. 340; D. Unger, in his review of *Katholische Marienkunde*, in *The American Ecclesiastical Review*, Vol. 125, 1951, pp. 239-240; P. Gächter, *Die geistige Mutterschaft Marias; ein Beitrag zur Erklärung* von Jo 19, 26f., in *Zeitschrift für katholische Theologie*, Vol. 47, 1923, pp. 391-429; T. Gallus, *"Mulier, ecce filius tuus,"* in *Verbum Domini*, Vol. 21, 1941, pp. 289-297.

[50] The various Papal references to this biblical passage may be found in the exhaustive dissertation of G. W. Shea, *The Teaching of the magisterium on Mary's Spiritual Maternity*, in *Marian Studies*, Vol. 3, 1952, pp. 35-110, esp. 68-69, 92-93.

[51] Others are of a different opinion. Cf., for example, Card. A. H. *Lépicier, Diatessaron*, Vol. 4 (Roma, 1927), p. 177.

although no apparition of this kind is narrated in the Gospels.[52] The forty days preceding the Ascension must have been a season of indescribable joy for other reasons also: Mary Magdalen, the Apostles, and others to whom Jesus appeared, must have given her glorious accounts of the glory of her Son. After the Ascension she is said to have been present in the upper room, persevering unitedly in prayer with the Apostles, the holy women, and the brethren of the Lord (Acts 1:13-14). Consequently, we may reasonably infer that she accompanied her Son to Mount Olivet and witnessed the glory of the Ascension. The great joy which filled the disciples on this occasion must have been hers also, even in greater measure (Lk. 24:52). Since she was united in prayer with the Apostles, she must have beheld the outpouring of the Holy Spirit on the day of Pentecost and the other stirring events inaugurating the promulgation of Christ's Church (Acts 2:1; 3:26). Nothing further is related about her in the Acts; the Epistles, too, are silent about her. Nevertheless, by her prestige as the Mother of the Lord, by her holy life, her prayers, and her encouragement, she must have exerted an inestimable influence upon the nascent Church. There is no direct allusion to her Assumption, which was the culmination of her privileges and the reward of her labors.

THE WOMAN OF THE APOCALYPSE

In the *Apocalypse* St. John describes a woman whom he saw in vision: she was clothed with the sun, the moon was beneath her feet, and upon her head was a crown of stars. "And she was with child and cried out in the pangs of birth and in pain to be delivered"

---

[52] On this interesting controversy cf. F. Tallachini, *Un silenzio nel Vangelo, in Palestra del Clero*, Vol. 19, 1940, p. 201; G. Gherardi, *Per un silenzio nel Vangelo, ibid.*, pp. 233-235; G. M. Roschini, *Intorno all'apparizione di Gesu risorto alla sua Ss. Madre, ibid.*, pp. 235-246; V. Buffon, *A proposito di una recente controversia mariologica, in Marianum*, Vol. 2, 1940, pp. 410-424; U. Holzmeister, *Num Christus post resurrectionem suae Ss. Matri apparuerit, in Verbum Domini*, Vol. 22, 1942, pp. 97-102; id., *Der Auferstandene und seine heiligste Mutter, in Klerusblatt*, Vol. 24, 1943, pp. 238-240; J. Blinzler, *Der Auferstandene und seine Mutter, ibid.*, pp. 113-116; id., *Nochmals zur Frage der Christophanie vor Maria, ibid.*, p. 240 ff.; A. M. Schuhmaier, *Controversia de Christophania B. M. Virgini die resurrectionis concessa, in Marianum*, Vol. 8, 1946, pp. 147-151.

(Apoc. 12:1, 2). The male Child to whom she gives birth on earth, who is the Son of God, is caught up to God and His throne (Apoc. 12:5). Then the dragon, or Satan, who was lying in wait to kill the Child pursues the woman into the desert and attempts to destroy her but she escapes with divine help and abides securely for three and a half years (Apoc. 12:6-9).

Now at Bethlehem Mary did not bring forth her divine Child in pain nor did she have to flee to the wilderness after the Ascension. Hence the woman before the birth of the Child, most probably represents the Israel of the Old Testament, whose heroes and heroines toiled to prepare the way for the Messias. After the birth of the Child and His Ascension into heaven, the woman symbolizes the Israel of the New Testament, the Church. Though periodically persecuted, she will always be secure under God's protection. Her persecution is said to last three and a half years to indicate that it will be relatively short when compared to the eternity of her duration.

But Mary is also included in the symbolism of the woman. She certainly is the most distinguished purely human person of the Old Testament: by her prerogatives, her prayers, her good works, her consent, she pre-eminently prepared the way for the Incarnation. Moreover, she physically gave birth to the Saviour, though without the pangs of childbirth. She is also the brightest ornament of the New Testament. If the sun, the moon, and the stars represent the glories of the Old and New Testaments, then her singular privileges and virtues must be included. Hence the woman of the Apocalypse designates Mary in an inclusive and pre-eminent sense.[53] Finally, the

---

[53] The various opinions on this may be grouped as follows: (A) Those who favor the exclusive ecclesiological interpretation, for example, J. Bonsirven, *L'Apocalypse de saint Jean,* in *Verbum Salutis,* Vol. 16, 1951, pp. 213-221; J. S. Considine, *A Commentary on the New Testament (Catholic Biblical Association of America,* 1942), p. 669; C. Rösch, Mulier, *draco et bestiae in Apoc. 12:13,* in *Verbum Domini,* Vol. 8, 1928, p. 271. (B) Those who claim that the "woman" is Mary alone, for example, J.-F. Bonnefoy, *Les interprétations ecclésiologiques du ch. XII de l'Ap.,* in *Marianum,* Vol. 9, 1947, pp. 208-222; id., *Le mystère de Marie selon le Protévangile et l'Apocalypse* (Paris, 1949); T. Gallus, *Scholion ad "mulierem" Apocalypseos (12, 1),* in *Verbum Domini,* Vol. 30, 1952, pp. 332-340. (C) Those who believe that the "woman" is both Our Lady and the Church in a literal sense, aliter atque aliter. For example: E. B.

woman's symbolism exhibits a feature which is borrowed from Mary's personality; she virginally conceives and bears, which reminds us of Isaias' celebrated prophecy about the virgin (7:14) and the similar prediction of Micheas about the woman in labor (5:3).

SUMMARY

The main elements upon which our devotion to Mary is based are contained in the New Testament: her fullness of grace, her unique position among women, her virginity, her co-operation in the Redemption, her divine motherhood, her power of intercession. She is rarely introduced as speaking but when she does speak, she charms us by her simplicity, her modesty, her prudence, her obedience, her love of God and Christ, her kindness to others. Despite the fact that she is kept in the background, it is easy to perceive that she shares in all the privations and triumphs of Christ's infancy and hidden life at Nazareth. Except at Cana, she is excluded from active participation in the public life of Our Lord. But she suffers with Him beneath the cross and tastes the joy of the Resurrection and Ascension. Her gifts and the virtues which she practiced are so extraordinary that they merit our most serious and loving study in the special branch of Theology called Mariology.[54]

Allo, *Saint Jean — L'Apocalypse*, ed. 3 (Paris, 1933), p. 194; G. Perrella, *Senso mariologico dell'Apocalisse XII*, in *Divus Thomas* (Pl.), Vol. 43, 1940, pp. 215-223; L. Di Fonzo, *Intorno al senso mariologico dell' Apocalisse, c. XII*, in *Marianum*, Vol. 3, 1941, pp. 248-268; E. May, *The Scriptural Basis for Mary's Spiritual Maternity*, in *Marian Studies*, Vol. 3, 1952, pp. 131-135; A. Rivera, *"Inimicitias ponas ..." — "Signum magnum apparuit ..."* (Gen. 3, 15; Apoc. 12, 1), in *Verbum Domini*, Vol. 21, 1941, pp. 113-122, 183-189; D. Unger, *Did St. John See the Virgin Mary in Glory?* in *The Catholic Biblical Quarterly*, Vol. 11, 1949, pp. 248-262, 392-405; Vol. 12, 1950, pp. 74-83, 155-161, 292-300, 405-415 (a complete review of the patristic exegesis of this passage); B. Le Frois, *The Woman Clothed with the Sun*, in *The American Ecclesiastical Review*, Vol. 126, March 1952, pp. 161-180. The author has recently published an exhaustive book on the same subject: *The Woman Clothed with the Sun* (Rome, 1954).

[54] For further study on Our Lady in the New Testament the following authors may be consulted with profit: Msgr. E. Florit, *Maria nell'esegesi biblica contemporanea*, in *Studi Mariani*, Vol. 1, 1943, pp. 83-132; G. Hilion, *La Sainte Vierge dans le Nouveau Testament*, in *Maria. Études sur la Ste. Vierge* (ed. H. du Manoir), Vol. 1 (Paris, 1949), pp. 43-68; R. Knox, *Our Lady in the New Testament*, in *Our Blessed Lady* (London: *Cambridge Summer School*

Lectures for 1933, 1934), pp. 48-67; C. Lattey, *Our Lady's Gospel, ibid.*, pp. 18-47; J. Leal, *La Virgen en et Evangelio*, in *Cultura Bíblica*, Vol. 9, 1952, pp. 115-116, 215-217; A. Merk, *Das Marienbild des Neuen Bundes*, in *Katholische Marienkunde* (ed. P. Sträter), Vol. 1 (Paderborn, 1947), pp. 44-84; M. Peinador, *La Sagrada Escritura en la Mariología durante los ultimos veinticinco años. Problemas suscitados y avances realizados*, in *Estudios Marianos*, Vol. 11, 1951, pp. 17-58; M. Sánchez del Villar, *María según el Evangelio ...* in *Crónica Oficial del Congreso Mariano Hispano-Americano de Sevilla* (Madrid, 1930), pp. 622-725; A Schäfer, *The Mother of Jesus in Holy Scripture* (New York, 1913).

Mary in Western Patristic Thought

By Walter J. Burghardt, S.J.

THE present essay is a theological enterprise. It is a theological enterprise realized in a precise way, which consists in exploring the data of one theological source, the Fathers of the Church, by availing ourselves of aids proper to the historical discipline.

The enterprise is theological; therefore it will not lose sight of the first principle of theological method, the achievement of truth in the light of revelation. The precise way in which the investigation is conducted does not violate this fundamental theological law, because the Church herself recognizes patristic consent as a valid expression of revealed truth.

And yet, though our precise approach does not fail to be theological, it nonetheless uses conscientiously the tools of the historiographer. The historian has as his first task the achievement of extant data in the highest degree of philologic purity. This we too attempt to do, and on this score the historian of any religious persuasion or of none is in a position to accept our findings. The historian's second task is to construct the data achieved according to some theory freely chosen. This the theologian is not free to do, for in his ultimate construction of the data he is led by the living *magisterium*, which does not conjecture but in faith claims to know the doctrine taught by patristic consent.

Individual Fathers are not patristic consent. They may, in principle, deviate from the consent. It is the function of philology to discover whether they did. In the theologian's use of philology, however, he supposes that the individual Father is thinking and writing in the atmosphere of patristic consent. This will not lead him to falsify the evidence, to put into a document what was never there; but he will be prone to hear in ambiguous or obscure statements a vague echo at least of the consent. Such an approach will not necessarily endear itself to the naturalistic historian, who does not share the theologian's supposition that patristic consent is directed in some fashion by the Holy Spirit; but the supposition is, for the theologian, basic.

The following pages will essay some initial insight into the thought of the Western Fathers and ecclesiastical writers of the first seven centuries on five prerogatives linked inseparably to Our Lady in contemporary Catholic theology: the Second Eve, Mary's perpetual virginity, her divine Maternity, her holiness, and the corporeal Assumption. In each instance the fundamental task will be to present the evidence in the light of philology; now and again, inevitably, a construction will be imperative in the light of revelation.

I

The primordial patristic insight with respect to the Mother of Christ is the vision of Mary as the New Eve. John Henry Newman framed the question at issue with his customary lucidity, then answered it with startling brevity, in the Letter to Pusey: "What is the great rudimental teaching of Antiquity from its earliest date concerning her? I mean the *primâ facie* view of her person and office, the broad outline laid down of her, the aspect under which she comes to us, in the writings of the Fathers. She is the Second Eve."[1]

The earliest patristic testimonies to the Eve-Mary parallelism stem from the West: from Rome, Lyons, and Carthage. The witnesses are the three most significant figures on the Western literary horizon in the latter half of the second century and at the dawning of the third: Justin, Irenaeus, and Tertullian.[2] The dean of second-century apologists, the martyr Justin († c. 165), composes a graphic overture to the Eve-Mary drama in his *Dialogue with Trypho*. In the course of a labyrinthine treatment of Isa. 7:14, he writes with respect to Christ, who proceeded from the Father before all creatures:

---

[1] J. H. Newman, *A Letter to the Rev. E. B. Pusey, D.D., on His Recent Eirenicon*, 3 ed. (London, 1866), pp. 33-34.

[2] For a brief treatment of the texts in question, cf. M. A. Nauwelaerts, *De Maria nova Heva doctrina patrum antenicaenorum*, in *Divus Thomas* (Piacenza), Vol. 34, 1931, pp. 480-491; E. Neubert, *Marie dans l'église anténicéenne* (Paris, 1908), pp. 240-254; also the literature cited below, footnotes 17 and 18. For background, and the atmosphere in which the usage of the Eve-Mary analogy developed, cf. W. Staerk, *Eva — Maria. Ein Beitrag zur Denk und Sprechweise der altkirchlichen Christologie*, in *Zeitschrift für die neutestamentliche Wissenschaft*, Vol. 33, 1934, pp. 97-104.

[The Son of God] became man through the Virgin, that the disobedience caused by the serpent might be destroyed in the same way in which it had originated. For Eve, while a virgin incorrupt, conceived the word which proceeded from the serpent, and brought forth disobedience and death. But the Virgin Mary was filled with faith and joy when the Angel Gabriel told her the glad tidings that the Spirit of the Lord would come upon her ... and she answered: "Be it done unto me according to thy word." And through her was He born ... by whom God destroys both the serpent and the angels and men who have become like the serpent, and delivers from death those who repent of their wickedness and believe in Him.[3]

Justin does little more than trumpet the parallelism. He tells us explicitly that, as designed by God, the pattern of man's redemption paralleled his fall: both were effected through the agency of a virgin. He leaves us to conclude that for the human race the consequences of Mary's co-operation with God contrasted sharply with the effects of Eve's seduction by Satan: Mary's issue, inferentially, is obedience and life. He makes no effort to penetrate the nature of her redemptive role; his gaze is fixed not on Mary but on Christ.

A score of years later, a pupil of Polycarp named Irenaeus († c. 202), perhaps the first theologian of the Virgin Mother, took hold of the analogy and integrated it with his theology. At the root of his Mariological thinking two principles lie. There is the principle termed *recapitulatio:* the human dilemma, the paradoxical imperative that fallen nature must be lifted to God by the nature that had fallen, is resolved in the Word made flesh, who identifies Himself with humanity by becoming its second head (caput).[4] And there is the complementary principle called *recirculatio:* the process of restoration is fated to correspond inversely to that of the fall, somewhat as a knot is untied — a complicated knot, fashioned of

---

[3] Justin, *Dialogus cum Tryphone,* cap. 100; PG, 6, 709-712.

[4] This is simply one aspect of Irenaeus' theology of recapitulation; cf. A. d'Alès, *La doctrine de la récapitulation en saint Irénée,* in *Recherches de science religieuse,* Vol. 6, 1916, pp. 185-211. For the Mariology of Irenaeus, cf. J. Garçon, *La mariologie de s. Irénée* (Lyon, 1932); B. Przybylski, *De mariologia s. Irenaei Lugdunensis* (Romae, 1937); N. F. Moholy, *Saint Irenaeus: The Father of Mariology,* in *Studia Mariana,* Vol. 7: First Franciscan National Marian Congress in Acclamation of the Dogma of the Assumption [1950] (Burlington, Wis., 1952), 129-187.

Eve's disobedience as well as the rebellion of Adam.[5] In the light of this latter principle, Irenaeus has left a provocative passage:

> Just as Eve, wife of Adam yes, yet still a virgin ... became by her disobedience the cause of death for herself and the whole human race, so Mary too, espoused yet a virgin, became by her obedience the cause of salvation for herself and the whole human race. And this is why the Law calls her who was espoused to a man the wife of him who had espoused her, though she was still a virgin: to show the cycle that goes back (*recirculationem*) from Mary to Eve. The point is, what is tied together cannot possibly be untied save by inversion of the process whereby the bonds of union have arisen, so that the original ties are loosed by the subsequent, and the subsequent set the original free. ... And so it was that the knot of Eve's disobedience was loosed by Mary's obedience. For what the virgin Eve bound fast by her refusal to believe, this the Virgin Mary unbound by her belief.[6]

This passage should be supplemented by another, equally impressive, where the Eve-Mary parallelism is set side by side with the Adam-Christ analogy:

> ... by the obedience that took place on a tree [the Lord] recapitulated the disobedience that took place on a tree; and, to the destruction of that seduction whereby the betrothed virgin Eve was evilly seduced, the glad tidings of truth were happily brought by an angel to Mary, virgin espoused. For, as Eve was seduced by the utterance of an angel to flee God after disobeying His word, so Mary by the utterance of an angel had the glad tidings brought to her, that she should bear God in obedience to His word. And whereas Eve had disobeyed God, Mary was persuaded to obey God, that the Virgin Mary might become patroness (*advocata*) of the virgin Eve. And as the human race was sentenced to death by means of a virgin, by means of a virgin is it delivered (*salvatur*). A virgin's disobedience is balanced by a virgin's obedience. For the sin of the first-formed was emended by the correction from the First-born; the guile of the serpent was overcome by the simplicity of the dove; and we were set free from those chains

---

[5] Cf. E. Druwé, *La médiation universelle de Marie*, in *Maria. Études sur la Sainte Vierge*, ed. H. du Manoir, Vol. 1 (Paris, 1949), p. 462.

[6] Irenaeus, *Adversus haereses*, lib. 3, cap. 32, 1 (Massuet 3, 22, 4); ed. W. W. Harvey (Cantabrigiae, 1857), Vol. 2, 123-124; PG, 7, 958-959.

by which we had been bound to death.[7]

In Irenaeus' eyes, Mary as the Second Eve has a distinctive function in God's design for man's redemption. The co-operation of the first Eve with Satan in effecting man's spiritual death is matched and outstripped by Mary's co-operation with God in effecting man's return to life. The co-operation in question is not a sheerly negative thing, as though the parallelism began and ended on the level of virginity. It is not an exclusively physical thing, as though Mary's role opened and closed with the bare fact of divine motherhood. Her co-operation involves activity of the moral order: she gave Gabriel and God a free consent. Her obedience was not compelled; with eyes open and will unfettered she placed herself at God's disposal for the accomplishment of His designs. That consent, moreover, has a soteriological character: its term was not simply an Incarnation, but an Incarnation recognized as redemptive. Mary knew as well as Joseph that she would call Him Jesus because He was to "save his people from their sins" (Mt. 1:21).[8]

The same essential ideas — virginity, disobedience, and death balanced by virginity, obedience, and life — are discoverable about the year 210 in the impetuous Carthaginian, Tertullian (✝ c. 220), who uses the Eve-Mary parallelism as a secondary argument in favor of the virginal conception of Christ, and emphasizes the act of faith involved in each instance. "For into Eve, as yet a virgin, had crept the devil's word, the framer of death. Equally into a virgin was to be introduced God's Word, the builder of life, to the end that what had been lost through one sex might by the same sex be restored and saved. Eve had believed the serpent, Mary believed Gabriel. The fault which the one committed by believing, the other

---

[7] *Ibid.*, lib. 5, cap. 19, 1; Harvey, 2, 375-376; PG, 7, 1175-1176. Essentially the same idea is present in Irenaeus' *Demonstratio apostolicae praedicationis*, cap. 33; Patrologia Orientalis, Vol. 12, 684-685; cf. the careful translation from the Armenian by J. P. Smith, in Ancient Christian Writers, Vol. 16 (Westminster, Md., 1952), 69. This is significant, because the *Demonstratio* is not a polemical but a catechetical work, which reveals how Christianity was presented to the people of Lyons at the end of the second century; cf. A. Harnack, in *Texte und Untersuchungen*, Vol. 31, n. 1 (Leipzig, 1907), pp. 65-66.

[8] Cf. J. B. Carol, O.F.M., *De Corredemptione beatae Virginis Mariae. Disquisitio positiva* (Civitas Vaticana, 1950), p. 38.

by believing emended. ... God, therefore, sent down into the Virgin's womb His Word, our good Brother, to blot out the memory of that evil brother."[9]

The insight of Justin, Tertullian, and especially Irenaeus will be repeated, if not significantly furthered, after Nicaea. Not only in the East,[10] but in the West as well. In the eyes of Ambrose († 397), "it was through a man and a woman that flesh was cast from paradise; it was through a virgin that flesh was linked to God." Little wonder that "Eve is called mother of the human race, but Mary mother of salvation."[11] Jerome († 420) is splendidly epigrammatic: "Death through Eve, life through Mary."[12] Augustine († 430) is impressed by "the profound mystery that, as death had befallen us through a woman, through a woman life should be born to us"; he muses that "the liberation of both sexes would not have been a proper punishment for the devil, were the liberation not effected by the agency of both."[13] Peter Chrysologus († c. 450) insists that the reason "why Christ wanted to be born is this: that, just as death came to all through Eve, so through Mary life might return to all."[14] And the poet Sedulius hymns the same theme in Latin dactyls:

> As the tender rose from sharp thorns grows,
> Knowing not how to wound, and fairer far than parent stem:
> So from the stem that was Eve the hallowed Mary bloomed,

---

[9] Tertullian, *De carne Christi*, cap. 17; C.S.E.L., 70, 233.

[10] Cf., e.g., *Ephraem, De diversis sermonibus, 3: De laudibus Dei genitricis Mariae; Opera omnia syr. et lat.*, Vol. 3 (Romae, 1743), 607; Cyril of Jerusalem, *Catecheses*, 12, 15; PG, 33, 741; Epiphanius, *Panarion*, haer. 78, n. 18; G.C.S., 37, 468-469; John Chrysostom, *Expositio in ps. 44, n. 7*; PG, 55, 193; John Damascene, *Hom. 1 in nativitatem beatae Virginis Mariae*, n. 7; PG, 96, 672.

[11] Ambrose, *Epist. 63, n. 33*; PL, 16, 1249-1250 (ed. 1866); *Serm. 45*, n. 4; PL, 17, 716 (ed. 1866); this latter text is taken from a sermon dubiously Ambrosian. For the Mariological teaching of Ambrose, cf. A. Pagnamenta, *La mariologia di S. Ambrogio* (Milano, 1932).

[12] Jerome, *Epist. 22, n. 21*; PL, 22, 408. For the Marian doctrine of Jerome, cf. J. Niessen, *Die Mariologie des hl. Hieronymus* (Münster, 1913).

[13] Augustine, *De agone christiano*, n. 22 [24]; C.S.E.L., 41, 125. For the Mariology of Augustine, cf. Ph. Friedrich, *Die Mariologie des hl. Augustinus* (Köln, 1907).

[14] Peter Chrysologus, *Serm. 99*; PL, 52, 479.

A spotless virgin new, to mend that ancient virgin's fault.[15]

Perhaps the most urgent theological problem which derives from the Eve-Mary parallelism is this: What role do the Fathers of the Church assign Mary in the redemptive task of her Son?[16] The majority of Catholic scholars insist that the contemporary doctrine of Coredemption, Mary's immediate co-operation in the objective Redemption, is inescapably affirmed in patristic literature.[17] A smaller group concludes, with comparable conviction, that the Fathers have nothing to say with respect to a genuinely coredemptive function; the germ, indeed, is there, in what they have to say; but the problem at issue had not presented itself, the Fathers consequently made no attempt to solve it, and it was to take centuries of doctrinal development before even the germ would be recognizable as such.[18]

---

[15] Sedulius, *Paschale carmen*, lib. 2, lines 28-31; C.S.E.L., 10. 46.

[16] The coredemptive function of Mary is by no means the only aspect of Marian theology which scholars have tried to trace to the Eve-Mary analogy of the Fathers; cf., e.g., J. M. Bover, *La mediación universal de la "Segunda Eva," en la tradición patristica*, in *Estudios eclesiásticos*, Vol. 2, 1923, pp. 321-350; also Bover's detailed treatment of Ambrose, *La mediación universal de María según S. Ambrosio*, in *Gregorianum*, Vol. 5, 1924, pp. 25-45. Nor is the Eve-Mary parallelism the sole patristic basis on which theologians rest the thesis of Coredemption. Among others, there are the texts which seem to ascribe to Mary various effects of the Redemption; cf. the classical, much-controverted passage from Ambrose on Mary's compassion beneath the cross: "Suscepit quidem [Christus] affectum parentis, sed non quaesivit alterius auxilium." Epist. 63, n. 110; *PL*, 16, 1271 (ed. 1866); cf. Pagnamenta, *op. cit.*, pp. 369-370; Carol, op. cit., pp. 142-144.

[17] Cf., e.g., J. Lebon, *L'apostolicité de la doctrine de la médiation mariale*, in *Recherches de théologie ancienne et médiévale*, Vol. 2, 1930, p. 143; id., *Comment je conçois, j'établie et je defends la doctrine de la médiation mariale*, in *Ephemerides Theologicae Lovanienses*, Vol. 16, 1939, pp. 655-744; G. M. Roschini, *De corredemptrice*, in *Marianum*, Vol. 1, 1939, pp. 365-367; F. Solá, *La corredención de María en la tradición patristica*, in *Estudios Marianos*, Vol. 2, 1943, p. 68.

[18] Cf., e.g., W. Goossens, *De cooperatione immediata Matris Redemptoris ad redemptionem obiectivam* (Parisiis, 1939), pp. 109-124; C. Dillenschneider, *Marie au service de notre rédemption* (Haguenau, 1947), pp. 268-288; J. Rivière, *Marie "corédemptrice"?* in *Revue des sciences religieuses.* Vol. 19, 1939, pp. 339-340; L. J. Riley, *Historical Conspectus of the Doctrine of Mary's Co-Redemption*, in *Marian Studies*, Vol. 2, 1951, pp. 46-47. Cf. the unqualified

The evidence of Irenaeus is a focal point in the controversy and may serve as a test case. The summary of his thought given above incorporates a minimal exegesis difficult to dispute: Irenaeus attributes to Mary, not technically but equivalently, a positive, moral co-operation in a specifically redemptive Incarnation. But this basic agreement leaves the heart of the matter untouched: In what sense is the Incarnation redemptive for Irenaeus?

As some scholars see it, Irenaeus does not limit Mary's co-operation in man's salvation to the production of the Redeemer, as to a preparatory stage in the story of Redemption; he associates her directly and immediately with the realization of the total effect. True, he stresses her obedience to the angel, but that stress stems from the fact that the Annunciation scene brings out so vividly the Eve-Mary analogy. The redemptive program is divinely designed to destroy a twin disobedience, Eve's and Adam's. Part of that program is the obedience of Mary, an obedience especially in evidence at the moment of the Incarnation. But, for Irenaeus, the Incarnation is intrinsically orientated to the cross, and the cross is the consummation of the Incarnation. Mary's fiat corresponds to her Son's *ecce venio* (cf. Hebr. 10:5 ff.); each finds its culmination on Calvary. Not that Irenaeus says this in so many words, but it seems a legitimate deduction from the direct, immediate fashion in which he links the efficacy of the Redemption to the obedience of Christ and of the Virgin. Briefly, in the architectonic of salvation and in its realization the role of Mary is attuned to the role of Christ in such wise that the total effect depends on a single total principle fashioned of Christ the Redeemer and Mary the Coredemptrix.[19]

Not quite true, others retort. For Irenaeus, the Incarnation is redemptive, of course. "The Lord readmitted us to His friendship by

---

rejection of any patristic basis by H. Lennerz, *De cooperatione b. Virginis in ipso opere redemptionis*, in *Gregorianum*, Vol. 29, 1948, p. 133.

[19] Cf. Druwé, *art. cit.*, pp. 464-465. Worth mentioning in this connection are the two passages in which Irenaeus speaks of Mary as the Virgin who "regenerates" us: *Adversus haereses*, lib. 4, cap. 52, 1 (Massuet, 4, 33, 4); lib. 4, cap. 55, 2 (Massuet, 4, 33, 11); Harvey, 2, 259, 266; *PG*, 7, 1074, 1080; cf. P. Galtier, *La vierge qui nous régénère*, in *Recherches de science religieuse*, Vol. 5, 1914, pp. 136-145.

His Incarnation."[20] It is redemptive, however, not in the sense that the hypostatic union and the objective redemption are coextensive concepts. The Incarnation is redemptive in the sense that it is the *beginning* of salvation. In taking our nature Christ "recapitulated" all men in Himself, became capable of effecting man's reconciliation by the theandric acts which followed in the wake of the Incarnation. "He reconciled us to God by His passion."[21] Inasmuch as Mary co-operated, wide-eyed and free, in an Incarnation integral to salvation, Irenaeus could justifiably speak of her as "cause of salvation."[22] But the further conclusion, that above and beyond this causality Mary was immediately associated with her Son in the remainder of His redemptive activity, specifically the Passion, goes beyond the thought of Irenaeus. The relationship between Adam and Christ, between Eve and Mary, is of concern to him; the redemptive relationship between Mary and Christ is not. To prolong his thought so as to see in them one total principle of Redemption is doubtless legitimate; but the prolongation is ours, not his; and the developed thesis is the fruit of a long, complicated doctrinal progression. The contemporary principle of redemptive co-operation may well be unassailable; but to find more than a germ of it, more than a basis for it, in the second century is to do violence to the texts.[23]

The conclusion of this latter band of scholars is confessedly modest; it is, I submit, justified by the texts. As a convincing demonstration of the thesis that Mary co-operated directly and immediately in the objective redemption, the extant evidence from the New Eve doctrine of the Fathers is somewhat inadequate. On the other hand, if we suppose the doctrine otherwise established, then a goodly number of patristic texts take on new meaning. We are justified in discovering therein indications, valuable elements,

---

[20] Irenaeus, *Adversus haereses*, lib. 5, cap. 17, 1; Harvey, 2, 369; *PG*, 7, 959.

[21] Irenaeus, *op. cit.*, lib. 3, cap. 17, 9 (Massuet, 3, 16, 9); Harvey, 2, 91; PG, 7, 959.

[22] Irenaeus, *op. cit.*, lib. 3, cap. 32, 1 (Massuet, 3, 22, 4); Harvey, 2, 123-124; PG, 7, 958.

[23] Two splendidly sober treatments of the patristic aspect of this problem, especially with reference to the thought of Irenaeus, are to be found in M. A. Genevois, *La maternité universelle de Marie selon saint Irénée*, in *Revue thomiste*, Vol. 41, 1936, 26-51; and Carol, *op. cit.*, pp. 128-150.

insights, which later ages would exploit and bring to a perfection unsuspected in the days of the Fathers. For, as Druwé has pointed out, from the death of Damascene in the middle of the eighth century the witnesses to the Eve-Mary parallelism follow one another in an endless wave, across the whole of the Latin Middle Ages, down to our own time, when Pius XII, in the moving epilogue to *Mystici corporis*, portrays the New Eve at the foot of the cross, offering her Son and herself to the Father for the sin-scarred children of Adam.[24]

II

If the Eve-Mary analogy is the first genuine insight of the patristic age with respect to Our Lady, the first problem that is clearly posed in her regard is Mary's virginity.[25] Not that the question springs up full-blown and unsuspected at a given point of time; it gives the impression rather of gradual growth, gradual awareness, from the first century to the fourth.

Historically, the investigation of her virginity has focused on three phases of Our Lady's life: the years before Bethlehem, the moment of childbearing in the cave, and the period subsequent to the birth of Jesus.[26] The crux of the first phase may be epitomized in two questions: Was Mary a virgin physically at the hour of Gabriel's visit? Was the conception of Christ a virginal conception, effected independently of intercourse with man? On this twin score there was no hesitation among the early Christians. There could hardly be; Scripture was all too clear. The primitive Eastern evidence

---

[24] Cf. Druwé, *art. cit.*, p. 468; Pope Pius XII, encyclical. *Mystici corporis*, June 29, 1943; *A.A.S.*, Vol. 35, 1943, pp. 247-248.

[25] Cf. [H. Rondet's] unsigned Preface to the eighth edition of J.-B. Terrien, *La Mère de Dieu et la Mère des hommes*, Part 2, Vol. 1 (Paris, 1950), (9). The Preface is a fine condensation of Marian theology, especially in its historical growth.

[26] Cf. E. Dublanchy, *Marie*, in *D.T.C.*, Vol. 9, Part 2, 2369-2382, for a brief presentation of the patristic texts. Precious insights on this and other aspects of early Western Mariology are given by H. Rahner, Die Marienkunde in der lateinischen Patristik, in Paul Sträter, ed., *Katholische Marienkunde*, Vol. 1, *Maria in der Offenbarung* (Paderborn, 1947), pp. 137-182.

offered by Ignatius of Antioch and Aristides of Athens[27] is supplemented in the West by Justin, Irenaeus, and Tertullian.

Justin is anxious to forestall misunderstanding of Isa. 7:14 from two quarters, pagan and Jewish. In the first place, he does not care to have the pagan turn against him the accusation flung by Christians against the poets, to the effect that Jupiter approached women with carnal lust in mind. "The words, 'Behold, a virgin shall conceive,' therefore mean that the virgin shall conceive without intercourse. For, if she had had intercourse with anyone at all, she was then no longer a virgin. The fact is, the power of God descending upon the virgin overshadowed her and caused her, while still a virgin, to conceive. ... And it was this Spirit who came upon the virgin, overshadowed her, and brought it about that she became pregnant, not by sexual intercourse, but by divine power."[28] Second, he accuses Trypho and his fellow Jews of an audacious distortion of the Septuagint; in their polemic preoccupation they have changed the original "virgin" ($\pi\alpha\rho\theta\acute\varepsilon\nu o\varsigma$) of Isa. 7:14 to "a young girl" ($\nu\varepsilon\tilde\alpha\nu\iota\varsigma$), "as though something of extraordinary importance was signified by a woman conceiving after sexual intercourse, as all young women, except the barren, can do."[29]

Irenaeus sounds like an echo of Justin or of a common tradition. He is aware that some, in the wake of Theodotion and Aquila, see in the Isaian prophecy merely "a young woman," and that the Ebionites insist that Jesus was begotten of Joseph.[30] He argues that Isaias was pointing to "something unexpected" with respect to the generation of Christ; he was pointing to a sign. But, "what great thing or what sign would there have been in a young woman bearing a child through conception from a man? That happens to all

---

[27] Cf. Ignatius, *Ad Ephesios,* n. 19, 1; ed. K. Bihlmeyer, p. 87; id., *Ad Smyrnaeos,* n. 1, 1; Bihlmeyer, p. 106; Aristides, *Apologia,* n. 2; *Texte und Untersuchungen,* Vol. 4, Part 3, p. 9.

[28] Justin, *Apologia* 1, cap. 33; *PG,* 6, 381; cf. tr. by T. B. Falls, in *The Fathers of the Church: Saint Justin Martyr* (New York, 1948), pp. 70-71. There is a rather detailed treatment of early Western thought on the virginal conception of Christ in E. Neubert, *op. cit.,* pp. 57-120.

[29] Justin, *Dialogus cum Tryphone,* cap. 84; *PG,* 6, 673-676; tr. Falls, op. cit., p. 282; cf. *Dial.,* cap. 100; PG, 6, 709-712.

[30] Cf. Irenaeus, *Adversus haereses,* lib. 3, cap. 23 (Massuet, 3, 21, 1); Harvey, 2, 110; *PG,* 7, 946.

women who bear a child. But because an unexpected salvation was to be initiated for men through God's help, an unexpected birth from a virgin was likewise accomplished. The sign was God-given; the effect was not man-made."[31]

Tertullian, too, asserts that the Word of God was brought down, of the Father's Spirit, "into the Virgin Mary, took flesh in her womb. ..."[32] As God fashioned Adam of virgin earth, unfurrowed, unsown, so the Second Adam was shaped by God "of a flesh not yet unsealed to human generation."[33]

Such is the personal belief of Justin, Irenaeus, and Tertullian. More significantly still, Irenaeus and Tertullian declare unequivocally that such is the belief of the Church. "The birth from a virgin," Irenaeus says, is a belief which, like the belief in God the Creator, in the Word made flesh, in the Holy Spirit, in the passion, resurrection, and ascension, the universal Church "has received from the apostles and their disciples."[34] In Tertullian's eyes, the virginal conception in a virgin's womb is part and parcel of "the rule of faith."[35] And this rule of faith Carthage has apparently received from Rome;[36] this rule of faith is common to the apostolic Churches.[37]

The unwavering belief of the West in the physical virginity of Mary before Bethlehem is summed up in the expression, "Virgin Mary," and is enshrined as early as the second century in the Roman form of the Creed, as we find it, for example, in Hippolytus: "I believe in God, the Father almighty, and in Christ Jesus, Son of God, who was born from the Holy Spirit of Mary the Virgin (*de Spiritu*

---

[31] *Ibid.*, lib. 3, cap. 26, 2 (Massuet, 3, 21, 6); Harvey, 2, 118; PG, 7, 953.

[32] Tertullian, *De praescriptione haereticorum*, cap. 13; C.S.E.L., 70, 17-18. A. d'Alès has a compendious section on Tertullian's Mariology in *La théologie de Tertullien*, 3 ed. (Paris, 1905), pp. 192-197.

[33] Tertullian, *De carne Christi*, cap. 17; C.S.E.L., 70, 232-233.

[34] Irenaeus, *Adversus haereses*, lib. 1, cap. 2 (Massuet, 1, 10, 1); Harvey, 1, 90-91; PG, 7, 549.

[35] Tertullian, *De praescriptione haereticorum*, cap. 13; C.S.E.L., 70, 17-18.

[36] Tertullian, *De praescriptione haereticorum*, cap. 36; C.S.E.L., 70, 45-46. 37 Cf.

[37] Tertullian, *De praescriptione haereticorum*, cap. 20-21; C.S.E.L., 70, 23-25. Tertullian proposes to prove that the rule of faith in question is derived from the tradition of the Apostles; cf. cap. 22; C.S.E.L., 70, 25.

sancto ex Maria virgine) ..."[38] The problem begins to take shape with the question: Did Mary remain a virgin while giving birth to Jesus? On this score the historical tradition is less clear and slower to solidify. Nor is this surprising. In the first place, the manner in which Jesus emerged from Mary's womb was not a likely topic for widespread Christian discussion. Second, it would not necessarily strike an early Christian as a problem in virginity. Third, some of those who did recognize the problem might well have been persuaded to silence with respect to the miraculous element in the actual birth of Jesus, for fear of giving aid and comfort to the Docetic enemy, to the heresy that Christ was only apparently born of Mary.[39]

It has been suggested that the very silence of the early authors is expressive, especially if reset within the aura of mystery and miracle which surrounds some contemporary accounts of Jesus' birth.[40] And it may well be that the unqualified title, "the Virgin," intimates that Our Lady's virginity remained unimpaired in childbearing.[41] In similar vein, the credal formula, "born of a virgin," of which the West was so fond,[42] perhaps involves the conclusion later drawn by Augustine: "And if only in His birth her virginity had been destroyed, from that moment He would not have been born of a virgin, and the whole Church would proclaim falsely,

---

[38] Cf. Hippolytus, *Traditio apostolica*, n. 73; ed. J. Quasten, *Florilegium patristicum*, Vol. 7 (Bonnae, 1935), p. 31. On the textual problem, cf. R. H. Connolly, *On the Text of the Baptismal Creed of Hippolytus*, in *Journal of Theological Studies*, Vol. 25, 1923-1924, pp. 131-139. Dom Connolly believed that the ex, whether due to translator or subsequent scribe, should be corrected to et; cf. p. 137.

[39] Cf. J. C. Plumpe, *Some Little-Known Early Witnesses to Mary's Virginitas in partu*, in *Theological Studies*, Vol. 9, 1948, p. 568. Some Docetists held that Christ had no genuine human body at all; others admitted a human body, but insisted that He came with this body from heaven, that He was not born *ex virgine* but simply passed *per virginem*.

[40] Cf., e.g., L. Kösters, *Maria, die Mutter Jesu*, in *Lexikon für Theologie und Kirche*, Vol. 6, 1934, p. 890; Plumpe, art. cit., p. 567.

[41] Cf., e.g., Justin, *Dialogus cum Tryphone*, cap. 100; PG, 6, 712; Irenaeus, *Adversus haereses*, lib. 3, cap. 32, 1 (Massuet, 3, 22, 4); Harvey, 2, 123; PG, 7, 958; Tertullian, *De praescriptione haereticorum*, cap. 13; C.S.E.L., 70, 17.

[42] Cf. J. Quasten, *Patrology*, Vol. 1 (Westminster, Md., 1950), p. 27.

which God forbid, that He was born of the Virgin Mary."[43]

But all this, though plausible, is still conjecture. The one Western author before Nicaea whose language on this score is unequivocal denies flatly that the virginity of Mary survived her childbearing. In his polemic against Docetists, Marcionites, and Valentinians, Tertullian presents the birth of Christ as quite normal. Revolting as parturition may be (and Tertullian takes a pathological delight in assembling the less attractive details), "birth will not be worse for Him than death. ... If Christ truly suffered all this, to be born was something less for Him."[44] In line with this brutal realism he applies to Christ the *primogenitus aperiens vulvam* of Exod. 13:2. "She did bear, because she produced offspring of her own flesh; she did not bear, because she produced Him not of a husband's seed. She was a virgin, so far as her husband was concerned; she was not a virgin, so far as her childbearing was concerned. ... She who gave birth, really gave birth; and if she was a virgin when she conceived, in her childbearing she was a wife. ... The Virgin's womb was especially opened, because it was especially closed. In fact, she ought rather to be called not a virgin than a virgin, becoming a mother at a leap, at it were, before being a wife."[45]

Tertullian is clear but vexing. He does not appeal for support to a tradition or current opinion; but neither is he conscious of contradicting official Church teaching. Is there an African tradition on Mary's virginity before Nicaea? Is this sheer polemics? Or Tertullian's pique? Neither Cyprian nor Arnobius nor Lactantius will help us settle that question. This much can be said: we are not justified in deriving from Tertullian the conclusion that we have here an echo of theological thought current in the Church of

---

[43] Augustine, *Enchiridion ad Laurentium*, cap. 34 [al. cap. 10, n. 34]; PL, 40, 249; tr. L. A. Arand, in *Ancient Christian Writers*, Vol. 3 (Westminster, Md., 1947), p. 42.

[44] Tertullian, *Adversus Marcionem*, lib. 3, cap. 11; C.S.E.L., 47, 394; cf. *Adversus Marcionem*, lib. 4, cap. 21; C.S.E.L., 47, 490-491.

[45] Tertullian, *De carne Christi*, cap. 23; C.S.E.L., 70, 246-247. A. d'Alès, *La théologie de Tertullien*, p. 197, note 5, says simply that the virginity in childbirth is "affirmed" in *De virginibus velandis*, cap. 6; PL, 2, 946 (ed. 1866). Tertullian's involved argumentation in this passage, however, does not seem to warrant d'Alés' conclusion.

Africa.[46]

With respect to Irenaeus, it can still be confidently urged, despite the research and reasoning of H. Koch,[47] that there is no text from his pen which clearly contradicts the virginity of Mary in Bethlehem. The well-known *adhuc virgo* texts — in which, for example, the birth of Christ from Mary, "who was as yet a virgin," is compared to the fashioning of Adam "from untilled and as yet virgin soil,"[48] or Mary's virginal obedience is contrasted with the disobedience of Eve "while still a virgin"[49] — reveal no interest on Irenaeus' part in any aspect of Mary's virginity save the virginal conception of Jesus. On the other hand, there may well be an indication of her virginity in childbirth in Irenaeus' paradoxical phrase, *purus pure puram aperiens vulvam* (the stainless Word of God opened His Mother's stainless womb stainlessly) — if indeed, as seems likely, it is the adverb and not the verb that merits the stress.[50] Even more strikingly, Irenaeus takes Isa. 66:7, where the prophet foretells a remarkable repopulation of Jerusalem through Mother Sion, and interprets it as messianic, as spoken of the Virgin Mary who gave birth to a man child in unique fashion, without birth pangs. "Also, concerning His birth, the same prophet [Isaias] says in another place: 'Before she who was in labour brought forth, and before the pains of labour came, there came forth delivered a man

---

[46] Cf. G. Jouassard, *Marie à travers la patristique: Maternité divine, virginité, sainteté*, in Maria. *Études sur la Sainte Vierge*, ed. H. du Manoir, Vol. 1 (Paris, 1949), pp. 77-78. This whole article, pp. 69-157, is crammed with information and is unusually rich in discernment; cf. the annotated bibliography, pp. 154-157.

[47] Cf. H. Koch, *Adhuc virgo* (Tübingen, 1929); id., *Virgo Eva — Virgo Maria* (Berlin und Leipzig, 1937). These two small volumes provoked spirited reaction from Catholic scholars; cf., e.g., O. Bardenhewer, *Zur Mariologie des hl. Irenäus, in Zeitschrift für katholische Theologie*, Vol. 55, 1931, pp. 600-604; J. Lebon, review in *Revue d'histoire ecclésiastique*, Vol. 34, 1938, pp. 336-345; B. Capelle, "Adhuc virgo" chez saint Irénée, in Recherches de théologie ancienne et médiévale, Vol. 2, 1930, pp. 388-395.

[48] Irenaeus, *Adversus haereses*, lib. 3, cap. 30 (Massuet, 3, 21, 10); Harvey, 2, 120; *PG*, 7, 954-955.

[49] Irenaeus, *Adversus haereses*, lib. 3, cap. 32, 1 (Massuet, 3, 22, 4); Harvey, 2, 123-124; *PG*, 7, 958-959.

[50] Irenaeus, *Adversus haereses*, lib. 4, cap. 55, 2 (Massuet, 4, 33, 11); Harvey, 2, 266; PG, 7, 1080; cf. Bardenhewer, art. cit., p. 604.

child'; he proclaimed His unlooked-for and extraordinary birth of the Virgin."[51] Irenaeus' language is not limpid, but it scarcely warrants the charge that he denied Mary a virginal childbearing.[52]

It is not until the second half of the fourth century that the extant patristic evidence indicates a general awareness of the problem in the West. Hilary of Poitiers († 367), whose exile in the East enriched his theology in general but not his Mariology, is explicit only on Mary's virginity before and after Bethlehem.[53] There are one or two texts which in isolation might well be judged unfavorable to the idea of a virginity in childbearing,[54] while the passages traditionally advanced to establish Hilary as a champion of the doctrine are not very convincing under analysis.[55] Not long after, Marius Victorinus, that remarkable old man whose conversion from Neoplatonism "stunned Rome and gladdened the Church,"[56]

---

[51] Irenaeus, *Demonstratio apostolicae praedicationis*, cap. 54; *Patrologia orientalis*, Vol. 12, 701; tr. J. P. Smith, op. cit., p. 83; cf. Plumpe, art. cit., pp. 569-570.

[52] It is regrettable that in the second or third century the West offers nothing comparable to the Eastern apocrypha: the *Protevangelium Iacobi*, with its graphic argument from sight and touch, and the suggestion that about 150 the question of Mary's virginity in childbearing was debated; the Ascensio Isaiae, with the clear testimony that Mary has conceived her Child as a virgin, has borne Him through a period of gestation as a virgin, and has given Him birth as a virgin; and the *Odes of Solomon*, where the odist's idea of Mary as Virgin Mother includes painless childbirth without need of midwife. Cf. Plumpe, *art. cit.*, pp. 570-577.

[53] On the virginity before childbirth, cf. Hilary, *De Trinitate*, lib. 3, n. 19; PL, 10, 87. For the virginity after childbirth, cf. *Commentarius in Matthaeum*, cap. 1, n. 3; PL, 9, 921-922.

[54] Cf. Hilary, *De Trinitate*, lib. 2, nn. 24-27; PL, 10, 66-68; *De Trinitate*, lib. 10, n. 47; PL, 10, 380.

[55] Cf. the well-known "perfectum ipsa de suis non imminuta generavit"; *De Trinitate*, lib. 3, n. 19; PL, 10, 87. Dublanchy insists that we have here an affirmation of the virginity in partu; cf. D.T.C., Vol. 9, Part 2, 2373. The passage is not utterly clear, however, and Druwé argues that it is in the light of the texts unfavorable to the doctrine (some of those he cites are not convincing) that we must conclude that this particular passage is dealing with the virginal conception alone; cf. *Marie à travers la patristique*, p. 102, note 7.

[56] Augustine, *Confessiones*, lib. 8, cap. 2; C.S.E.L., 33, 173.

seems little aware of the idea.[57] On the other hand, the unknown author of the *Consultationes Zacchaei* uses the Virgin Birth as a demonstration of Christ's divinity and insists that in His birth "He did not destroy the integrity of His Mother's body." Just as His fashioning by the Spirit was incorruptible, so too was His birth.[58] And in the north of Italy, Zeno, Bishop of Verona († c. 372), states emphatically that Mary "gave birth as a virgin."[59] She remained virgin after marriage, after conception, after childbearing.[60]

A high-water mark appears about 389-390 with the excommunication of Jovinian by Pope Siricius, specifically for unorthodox utterances on virginity and marriage. Siricius' letter, *Optarem*, to the Milanese Church proposed to acquaint Ambrose with the Jovinian problem and enlist his support.[61] Ambrose and the Synod of Milan (390) ratified the condemnation in their reply, *Recognovimus*, but pointed out what Siricius had omitted to mention: Jovinian and his followers denied the virginity of Mary, not indeed in her conception but in her childbearing. Milan is one in rejecting the thesis; and Milan argues from Scripture and tradition.

> If they do not believe the teaching of the priests, let them believe the words of Christ, let them believe the admonition of angels: 'For with God nothing is impossible' (Lk. 1:37). Let them believe the Symbol of

---

[57] Cf. Marius Victorinus, *In epist. Pauli ad Gal.*, lib. 2; PL, 8, 1176-1177. He does affirm the virginal conception; cf. *Adversus Arium*, lib. 4, n. 32; PL, 8, 1136.

[58] *Consultationes Zacchaei et Apollonii*, lib. 1, cap. 11; ed. G. Morin, *Florilegium patristicum*, Vol. 39 (Bonnae, 1935), p. 15. The virginal conception is likewise asserted; cf. ibid., lib. 1, cap. 10; ed. Morin, p. 14. Morin's ascription of the *Consultationes* to Julius Firmicus Maternus has not won acceptance; cf. B. Altaner, Patrologie, 3 ed. (Freiburg, 1951), p. 314. Altaner prefers to date the work about the beginning of the fifth century.

[59] Zeno, *Tractatus*, lib. 2, tr. 8, 2; PL, 11, 415.

[60] Cf. Zeno, *Tractatus*, lib. 1, tr. 5, 3; PL, 11, 303; *Tractatus*, lib. 2, tr. 9, 1; PL, 11, 417.

[61] Siricius, *Optarem*; ed. W. Haller, in *Texte und Untersuchungen*, Vol. 17, Part 2 (Leipzig, 1897), pp. 68-72. Haller reproduces the text of J. D. Mansi, *Sacrorum conciliorum nova et amplissima collectio*, Vol. 3 (Florentiae, 1759), 663-664, with the chapter division of Coustant. It is found twice in Migne: among the letters of Ambrose, PL, 16, 1169-1171 (ed. 1866); and with the letters of Siricius, PL, 13, 1168-1172.

the Apostles, which the Roman Church ever guards and keeps inviolate. ... This is the Virgin who conceived in the womb, this the Virgin who gave birth to a son. ... For [Isaias] did not say that a virgin would merely conceive; he said that a virgin would give birth as well. Now, what is that gate of the sanctuary, that outer gate looking to the East, which remains shut and no one, it says, shall pass through it save the God of Israel alone (Ez. 44:2)? ... This gate is blessed Mary; of her it is written: "the Lord shall pass through it," and it shall be closed after childbearing, because a virgin conceived and a virgin gave birth.[62]

This, Ambrose makes clear, is part and parcel of Catholic belief. Did ecclesiastical circles at Rome openly profess the same thing? In his answer to Siricius, Ambrose indicates that the pertinent article of the Symbol espoused at Rome was interpreted, or at least should be interpreted, not merely of a virginal conception but of a virginal childbearing as well. And yet, only seven years before, in Rome itself, Jerome had come to the defense of Mary's perpetual virginity against Helvidius, and had nonetheless expressed himself with reference to Christ's birth in terms that are a disconcerting echo of Tertullian. Retail all the horrors of childbirth, he challenges; you will produce nothing more outrageous than the cross.[63] And still he can add: "That God was born of a virgin we believe, because we read it; that Mary became a wife after childbearing we do not believe, because we do not read it."[64] A decade later, writing from Palestine against Jovinian, Jerome applies to Mary the words of the Canticle, "A garden enclosed is my sister, my bride, a fountain sealed" (4:12); but his language is so laconic that one wonders

---

[62] Ambrose, *Epist.* 42, n. 4; ed. Haller, op. cit., pp. 75-76. In Migne, PL, 16, 1174 (ed. 1866), the pertinent numbers are 5-6. Cf. also *De institutione virginis*, cap. 8, n. 52: "... virginali fusus est partu, et genitalia virginitatis claustra non solvit"; PL, 16, 334. Ambrose proposed the same doctrine to the people in his sermons; cf. *Expositio evangelii secundum Lucam*, lib. 2, n. 43; C.S.E.L., 32, Part 4, 66; *Expositio evangelii secundum Lucam*, lib. 2, n. 57; C.S.E.L., 32, Part 4, 73. This latter passage is not clear, and reveals the influence of Origen: "Hic ergo solus aperuit sibi vulvam ... hic est qui aperuit matris suae vulvam, ut immaculatus exiret."

[63] Cf. Jerome, *De perpetua virginitate adversus Helvidium*, n. 18; PL, 23, 212-213 (ed. 1865).

[64] Jerome, *De perpetua virginitate adversus Helvidium*, n. 19; PL, 23, 213.

whether or not he is being consciously ambiguous.[65] Shortly afterward, in a letter to the Roman senator, Pammachius, occasioned by the shabby reception given at Rome to his attitude toward marriage as expressed in *Adversus Iovinianum*, he remarks:

> Christ is a virgin, and the mother of our Virgin is herself ever a virgin; she is mother and virgin. Although the doors were shut, Jesus entered within; in the sepulchre that was Mary, which was new and hewn in hardest rock, no one was laid before or after. ... She is the eastern gate whereof Ezechiel speaks, always shut and full of light, which closing on itself brings forth from itself the Holy of Holies; whereby the Sun of Justice ... enters in and goes out. Let them tell me how Jesus entered [the Cenacle] when the doors were shut ... and I will tell them how holy Mary is both mother and virgin, virgin after childbirth and mother before marriage."[66]

Here we confront the same paradox which he will repeat in 415 against the Pelagians: "only Christ opened the closed gates of her virginal womb, and yet the gates remained unfailingly closed."[67] One is persuaded by the paradox to conclude that, in Jerome's eyes, Our Lord could somehow "open the womb" of Mary without violating her virginity.

But if Jerome is at times obscure on this score, Augustine, Peter Chrysologus, and Leo the Great are not. For Augustine, Mary is virgin before and during wedlock, virgin in her pregnancy, virgin in giving to Christ of her milk. In taking birth of her He did not steal virginity from her.[68] Tersely, "she conceives and is a virgin; she gives birth and is a virgin."[69] Peter Chrysologus sees Mary's integrity strengthened in childbirth;[70] it is the crown of her virginity;[71] Christ comes forth in such fashion that the virginal gate

---

[65] Cf. Jerome, *Adversus Iovinianum*, lib. 1, n. 31; PL, 23, 265.

[66] Jerome, *Epist. 49* [48], n. 21; C.S.E.L., 54, 386.

[67] Jerome, *Dialogus contra Pelagianos*, lib. 2, n. 4; PL, 23, 563. Cf. *Comm. in Isaiam*, lib. 3, cap. 7; PL, 24, 110 (ed. 1865); *Comm. in Ezechielem*, lib. 13, cap. 44; PL, 25, 449 (ed. 1865).

[68] Augustine, *Serm. 188*, n. 4; PL, 38, 1004 (ed. 1865).

[69] Augustine, *Serm. 189*, n. 2; PL, 38, 1005; cf. *Serm. 191*, n. 3-4; PL, 38, 1010-1011.

[70] Cf. Peter Chrysologus, *Serm. 142*; PL, 52, 581.

[71] Cf. Peter Chrysologus, *Serm. 175*; PL, 52, 658.

does not swing open, and so Our Lady realizes in Bethlehem the garden enclosed, the fountain sealed of the *Canticle*.[72] Leo declares that Mary's womb is a mother's womb, but the birth of Jesus is a virgin birth;[73] it is the incorruption of Christ that kept intact the integrity of Mary.[74] This is the tradition which will be ratified in 649 by the Lateran Council when it condemns anyone and everyone who "does not confess, in harmony with the holy Fathers, that ... Mary ... gave birth without corruption."[75]

A third phase of Mary's virginity concerns her life after Bethlehem. Did Mary have conjugal relations after the birth of Jesus? To point up the problem: Did Mary have any children besides Jesus? It is the age-old problem of "the brethren of the Lord."[76] What relationship to Christ did early Christianity see in these "brothers and sisters"? Were they perhaps children which Joseph had by Mary after her "first-born" Son? Or were they offspring of Joseph by a previous marriage? Or is the kinship a more distant thing?

If the extant evidence is typical, Western Christianity was slow to face the problem. Here again it is Tertullian alone whose language is unmistakable before Nicaea: and without hesitation Tertullian regards the Mother of Jesus as mother of other children as well. To begin with: "It was a virgin who gave birth to Christ and she was to marry only once, after she brought Him forth *(semel nuptura post partum)*. The reason for this was that both types of chastity might be exalted in the birth of Christ, born as He was of a mother who was at once virginal and monogamous."[77] After the

---

[72] Cf. Peter Chrysologus, *Serm. 145*; PL, 52, 589.

[73] Cf. Leo, *Serm. 24*, cap. 1; PL, 54, 204.

[74] Cf. Leo, *Serm. 22*, cap. 2; PL, 54, 196. Cf. *Epist. 28*, cap. 2; PL, 54, 759; Birth from a virgin is included among the truths of faith universally believed. "He was conceived of the Holy Spirit within the womb of a virgin mother; just as she conceived Him without loss of virginity, so without loss of virginity did she give Him birth."

[75] Cf. Mansi, Vol. 10, 1151.

[76] Cf. Mt. 13:55-56; Mk. 6:3; Jn. 2:12; 7:3, 10; Acts 1:14; 1 Cor. 9:5; Gal. 1:19.

[77] Tertullian, *De monogamia*, cap. 8; PL, 2, 989 (ed. 1866); tr. W. Le Saint, in *Ancient Christian Writers*, Vol. 13 (Westminster, Md., 1951), p. 86. A virginal marriage with Joseph would satisfy the words *semel nuptura post partum*, but only in the abstract; in other passages Tertullian supposes that Mary's monogamy was not virginal.

birth of Jesus he can speak of her as *virum passam*, one who has known a man, in explicit contrast to a virgin.[78] And when he deals with "the brethren of Jesus," he takes it for granted that they are sons and daughters of the same mother as He.[79]

And that is almost all the evidence we have before Nicaea.[80] It is a situation which calls, above all, for caution in deriving conclusions or fashioning reconstructions.[81] On the one hand, it will

---

[78] Tertullian, *De virginibus velandis*, cap. 6; *PL*, 2, 946.

[79] Cf. Tertullian, *Adversus Marcionem*, lib. 3, cap. 11; *C.S.E.L.*, 47, 393; *Adversus Marcionem*, lib. 4, cap. 19; *C.S.E.L.*, 47, 482-483; *De carne Christi*, cap. 7; *C.S.E.L.*, 70, 208-212.

[80] Helvidius later claimed as a witness against the virginity post partum not merely Tertullian but also Victorinus, bishop of the modern Pettau in Styria († 304). Jerome conceded Tertullian, but argued that Victorinus did no more than speak, like the Evangelists, of "the Lord's brethren"; he did not say they were Mary's children; cf. *Adversus Helvidium*, n. 17; *PL*, 23, 211. The pertinent texts of Victorinus are lost. Around the same time, an unidentified versifier from the region of Autun hinted at the perpetual virginity in certain Laudes Domini; PL, 19, 383:

> "Ne tamen insignem res nulla ostenderet ortum,
> Virgine concipieris: non sufficit esse pudicam,
> Nec quae nupta queat Domino conjungere fratrem,
> Ne procul ex utero contagio turpis abesset."

[81] For example, Hugo Koch, *op. cit.*, has reconstructed the evolution of the doctrine of Mary's virginity from what he considers the primitive and historically accurate belief to its ultimate, definitive forms in the fourth century. He distinguishes four stages. To begin with, Jesus was the eldest son of many children born to Mary and Joseph. Subsequently, the idea of a virginal conception was introduced; the brothers and sisters of Jesus were regarded as born of the later marriage of Mary and Joseph. Later still, the perpetual virginity of Mary being admitted, the brethren of Jesus became the fruits of a previous marriage of Joseph. A final stage was reached in the West alone: Joseph became a virgin in his turn, and the brethren of the Lord became merely cousins. Koch's unambiguous point of departure is Tertullian. In rejecting Mary's virginity in and after childbearing, he argues, Tertullian *cannot be* in opposition to a pre-existing tradition, because he would be the last so to act. He must have drawn his opinion from a good ecclesiastical source. This source can only be Irenaeus, on whom he depends for his Christology and Soteriology, and who is well suited to this role by reason of his Eve-Mary analogy. Tertullian and Irenaeus cannot have found a tradition favoring perpetual virginity in Justin, Theophilus, or Melito, whose writings, now lost, they read. The primitive tradition, therefore, had no room for perpetual virginity; it knew nothing of brethren improperly so

not do to dismiss Tertullian with the cavalier thrust of Jerome: "he was not a man of the Church."[82] For, as Neubert has observed, if the Catholic Tertullian had recognized the virginity of Mary after Bethlehem as defined doctrine, the Montanist Tertullian would hardly have rejected it.[83] On the other hand, Tertullian's rejection is scarcely indicative of a traditional or official rejection. We are not in a position to establish the source of his thesis, if any; we do not know to what extent he is playing the polemist. It is tempting to conjecture that Origen, who insisted between 226-229 that "no one whose mind on Mary is sound would claim that she had any child save Jesus,"[84] might well have found support for his view when he went to Rome about 212 and met men of the stature of Hippolytus. But conjecture is not evidence; the philological data at hand do not reveal that the Christian West at the dawn of the fourth century was conscious of an obligation to represent Mary as virgin save for the years before Bethlehem.[85]

A new phase in Marian theology opens in the West with the publication of Hilary of Poitiers' *Commentary on Matthew* before his exile in 356. Hilary knows of more than one (plures) adversary who believes that Mary had marital relations with Joseph after Jesus' birth; but these are "irreligious individuals, utterly divorced from spiritual teaching." He himself is aware that, whenever Scripture speaks of Mary and Joseph in the same breath, Mary "is called 'Mother of Christ,' because that is what she was; not 'wife of Joseph,' because she was not." He knows that there are people who insist that Jesus had many blood brothers; but these are "extremely wicked" men. The brethren of Jesus were children of Joseph by a former marriage; were that not so, Jesus would not have been

---

called, or of cousins of Jesus, etc. For this summary, and the weakness of individual links in Koch's chain, cf. J. Lebon, in *Revue d'histoire ecclésiastique*, Vol. 34, 1938, 341 ff.

[82] Jerome, *Adversus Helvidium*, n. 17; PL, 23, 211.

[83] E. Neubert, *Marie dans l'église anténicéenne*, p. 194. *De virginibus velandis, Adversus Marcionem*, and *De carne Christi* stem from Tertullian's semi-Montanist days; *De monogamia* is a product of the full-fledged Montanist.

[84] *Commentarius in Ioannem*, lib. 1, cap. 4, n. 6; G.C.S., Origenes, Vol. 4, 8.

[85] Cf. Jouassard, *Marie à travers la patristique*, pp. 83-84.

compelled to entrust His Mother to John from the cross.[86] Hilary's language is so strong that we are tempted to see in his adversaries recognized heretics; but the conclusion is not apodictic. At any rate, we find in Hilary, if not a convincing scriptural argument, a deep conviction with respect to the perpetual virginity of Mary that is rooted in her dignity as Mother of the Saviour.[87]

In the second half of the fourth century the fascinating unknown,[88] Ambrosiaster, is likewise aware of the opinion that Mary had other children besides Jesus. It is a thesis with which he has little patience. The Lord's brethren — specifically, James, "the Lord's brother" — are so called because their father is Joseph, and Joseph is called the father of Jesus. Those who claim that the brethren are genuine brethren of Jesus by birth from Mary are out of their minds and their affirmation is impious; they would logically have to regard Joseph as Jesus' real father.[89] Zeno of Verona offers a remarkable formula, apparently in the face of an adversary: "O marvelous mystery! Mary conceived as virgin incorrupt; after conception she gave birth as a virgin; after childbirth she remained a virgin."[90]

Perhaps the most significant documents appear in the decade between 383 and 392. The atmosphere, and the source of strife as well, is the ascetieal yearning of the age. It is the consecrated virgin who has succeeded the martyr as the witness without peer of the Church's holiness; and, understandably, the unequaled model of

---

[86] Cf. Hilary, *Commentarius in Matthaeum*, cap. 1, n. 3-4; PL, 9, 921-922.

[87] Cf. Jouassard, *art. cit.*, p. 101.

[88] The conclusion of C. Martini is that the author flourished at Rome during the pontificate of Damasus (366-384), though he apparendy had some connection with the Milanese Church and with Spain; cf. Ambrosiaster: *De auctore, operibus, theologia* (Romae, 1944), p. 160.

[89] Cf. Ambrosiaster, *In epist. Pauli ad Galatas*, cap. 1; PL, 17, 364 (ed. 1866). About the same time, Marius Victorinus does not combat the idea that James was Jesus' blood brother, though the opportunity knocks quite loudly; cf. *In epist. Pauli ad Galatas*, lib. 1; *PL*, 8, 1155-1166.

[90] Zeno, *Tractatus*, lib. 2, tr. 8, 2; PL, 11, 414-415; cf. *Tractatus*, lib. 1, tr. 5, 3; PL, 11, 303.

virgins is the Virgin Mary.[91] A reaction is inevitable, and the villains of the piece are primarily Helvidius and Bonosus.

The approach of Helvidius was attractive. He did not make the tactical blunder of affirming that virginity is inferior to marriage; he did not attack the Virgin Mary. He asserted that marriage and virginity are equal in honor, that Mary is doubly admirable for having been, in turn, virgin and mother of a family: virgin until the birth of Jesus, then mother of the brothers and sisters of Jesus spoken of in Scripture. The impression in Roman circles was profound; even the elect among the ascetics were disturbed; and the hierarchy did not intervene.

Jerome, lately come to Rome from Constantinople, reacted vigorously.

His pamphlet, *Adversus Helvidium* (383), develops the thesis that virginity is superior to marriage; his palmary proof is that Mary would never have dreamed of relations with any man, no matter who.[92] Tradition is summoned briefly to the stand: Ignatius, Polycarp, Irenaeus, Justin. But it is the scriptural difficulties, since become classical, which form the burden of his presentation: "before they came together" (Mt. 1:18); Joseph's "wife" (1:24); "he did not know her till she had brought forth" (1:25); "first-born" (1:25). The Lord's brethren are children not of Mary but of her sister. And there is a final touch: "You say that Mary did not remain a virgin. I claim still more; I claim that Joseph himself was a virgin for Mary's sake, so that from a virgin wedlock a virgin son might be born."[93]

The argumentation is not consistently convincing, but it is effective, linked as it is to a rare talent for the satirical. As Jouassard has pointed out, it quickly restored the fortunes of asceticism in Roman circles and accredited the virginity after childbirth to such an extent that there is no evidence of its ever being seriously contested there after that encounter.[94]

---

[91] For a brief insight into the ascetieal movement of the time, and the influence of Athanasius on Western asceticism, cf. Jouassard, *art. cit.*, p. 103 ff.

[92] Jerome, Adversus Helvidium; PL, 23, 193-216 (ed. 1865).

[93] Jerome, *Adversus Helvidium*, n. 19; *PL*, 23, 213; cf. n. 17; *PL*, 23, 211: the brethren are "fratres propinquitate, non natura."

[94] Cf. Jouassard, *art. cit.*, p. 107.

More bluntly, Bonosus, Bishop of Naissus (the modern Nish in Yugoslavia), submitted that Mary had had more than one child.[95] The most significant literary reaction stemmed from Ambrose, who cried sacrilege.[96] Not only does he deal with several Old Testament symbols of Mary's perpetual virginity (the "closed gate" of Ezechiel, the "enclosed garden" and "sealed fountain" of the Canticle); he explains the New Testament texts adduced by Bonosus (Mt. 1:18 ff.).[97] The brethren of Jesus are not children of Mary; they may have been Joseph's; in any event, the term "brother" need not be interpreted strictly.[98] It is the perfect, permanent virginity of Mary that Ambrose time and again proposes to virgins for their imitation.[99]

The condemnation of Bonosus by his fellow bishops of Illyricum was approved in a celebrated letter whose author may be Pope Siricius but is more probably Ambrose himself.[100] The writer assures Anysius, Bishop of Thessalonica, and through him the bishops of Illyricum: "Surely we cannot deny that Your Reverence was

---

[95] This happened about 390. Ambrose intimates that Bonosus was not alone in denying the permanence of Mary's virginity; the reason for interrupting his silence on this score is the presence of a bishop, Bonosus, in the enemy camp; cf. *De institutione virginis*, cap. 5, n. 35; *PL*, 16, 328 (ed. 1866).

[96] Cf. *ibid.*

[97] Cf. *De institutione virginis*, cap. 5, n. 36 ff,; PL, 16, 329 ff.

[98] Cf. *De institutione virginis*, cap. 6, n. 43; PL, 16, 331. Ambrose, too, argues from the fact that Christ entrusted Mary to John on Calvary; cf. *De institutione virginis*, cap. 7, nn. 46-48; *PL*, 16, 332-333.

[99] Cf. *De institutione virginis*, cap. 5, n. 35; PL, 16, 328; cap. 16, n. 97 ff.; PL, 16, 343 ff.; *De virginibus*, lib. 2, cap. 2, n. 7: ed. O. Faller, *Florilegium patristicum*, Vol. 31 (Bonnae, 1933), p. 47; *Exhortatio virginitatis*, cap. 5, n. 31; PL, 16, 360.

[100] *De Bonoso*; PL, 16, 1222-1224 (ed. 1866); also in PL, 13, 1176-1178, as Siricius, *Epist. 9, Ad Anysium Thessalonicensem aliosque Illyrici episcopos*. Cf. X. Le Bachelet, *Bonose*, in *D.T.C.*, Vol. 2, col. 1027 ff.; E. Amann, Sirice (saint), *ibid.*, Vol. 14, Part 1, 2173. The pertinent note in PL, 16 refuses to choose from among the authors suggested; the monitum in PL 13 ascribes the letter to Siricius. Jouassard assigns it to Ambrose; cf. *Le problème de la sainteté de Marie chez les Pères depuis les origines de la patristique jusqu'au concile d'Ephèse*, in *Etudes Mariales*, Bulletin de la Société française d'études mariales, 5e année, 1947, Sainteté de Marie (Paris, 1948), p. 23, note 31. F. Homes Dudden believes that "the style and the matter indicate Ambrosian authorship"; *The Life and Times of St. Ambrose* (Oxford, 1935), Vol. 2, p. 402, note 4.

perfectly justified in rebuking him [i.e., Bonosus] on the score of Mary's children, and that you had good reason to be horrified at the thought that another birth might issue from the same virginal womb from which Christ was born according to the flesh. For the Lord Jesus would never have chosen to be born of a virgin if He had ever judged that she would be so incontinent as to contaminate with the seed of human intercourse the birthplace of the Lord's body, that court of the Eternal King. To assert such a view is to do nothing less than to accept as a basis that Jewish falsehood which holds that He could not have been born of a virgin. And once the weight of episcopal authority is gained for the view that Mary gave issue to many children, they will strive with even greater zeal to attack the truth of faith."[101]

The condemnation of Bonosus and the unqualified rejection of his thesis by episcopal authority may well have influenced the Greek world; in the West it simply consolidated ground already won. As the fourth century draws to a close it is Ambrose and his thesis that emerge triumphant; it is his *De institutione virginis* that is the theological *chef d'oeuvre* of the time.[102] It is from this period that orthodoxy uncompromisingly involves belief in Mary's perpetual virginity, so much so that the manner of expression takes on a monotonous dogmatic ring. Augustine tells us over and over that Our Lady "conceived as a virgin, she gave birth as a virgin, she remained a virgin."[103] Peter Chrysologus and Leo the Great echo the phraseology of Augustine.[104] In the light of this development the definitive pronouncement of the Lateran Council (649) on Mary's "indissoluble virginity" will hardly come unawares on the West.[105]

---

[101] *De Bonoso*, n. 3; PL, 16, 1223-1224; 13, 1177.

[102] Cf. Jouassard, *Marie à travers la patristique*, p. 113. For the dating of *De institutione virginis*, whether in 392 with Palanque, or 393 at the earliest, cf. ibid., note 52.

[103] Augustine, *Serm. 190*, n. 2; PL, 38, 1008; cf. Serm. 196, n. 1: "Virgo concepit, miramini; virgo peperit, plus miramini; post partum, virgo permansit"; PL, 38, 1019.

[104] Cf. Peter Chrysologus, *Serm. 98*: "Virgo concipit, virgo parturit, virgo permanet"; PL, 52, 521. Cf. Leo, *Serm. 22*, cap. 2: "... divina potestate subnixum est, quod virgo conceperit, quod virgo pepererit, et virgo permanserit"; PL, 54, 195.

[105] Cf. Mansi, Vol. 10, 1151.

III

A third problem in patristic Mariology is Mary's Maternity. Strangely enough, what was first denied to Mary was not the prerogative, Mother of God, but what her contemporaries never dreamed of denying, that she was Mother of Jesus (cf. Mk. 6:1-3). The early crisis was Docetic — the affirmation that the Saviour simply did not have a genuinely human body, or at any rate, as Tertullian sums it up, that "He was born through a virgin, not of a virgin, and in a womb, not of a womb,"[106] without being fashioned of her substance. But there was a complementary denial. Where the Gnostics introduced a distinction between Jesus born of Mary and the Christ who descended into Jesus at baptism,[107] they denied implicitly that the Child of Mary was God.

The Christian reaction in the first three centuries is expressive. Not that Our Lady is categorically denominated Mother of God; there is no indisputable evidence for the title before the fourth century.[108] But, like Ignatius earlier in the East, Justin and Irenaeus and Tertullian have a two-edged answer for the Gnostic position.

---

[106] Tertullian, *De carne Christi*, cap. 20; C.S.E.L., 70, 238.

[107] Cf. Irenaeus, *Adversus haereses*, lib. 3, cap. 17, 1 (Massuet, 3, 16, 2); Harvey, 2, 83; PG, 7, 921.

[108] *On the antiquity of the title*, cf. V. Schweitzer, *Alter des Titels* Θεοτόκος, in *Der Katholik*, Vol. 83, 1903, pp. 97-103; Jouassard, *Marie à travers la patristique*, p. 86, note 2. Perhaps the most impressive modern advance in our knowledge on this point is the discovery of a papyrus leaf preserving scraps of our Sub tuum praesidium in Greek, with the word ΘΕΟΤΟΚΕ clearly written; cf. C. H. Roberts, ed., *Catalogue of the Greek and Latin Papyri in the John Rylands Library*, Vol. 3 (Cambridge, 1939), n. 470; F. Mercenier, *L'antienne mariale grecque la plus ancienne*, in *Muséon*, Vol. 52, 1939, pp. 229-233; id., *La plus ancienne prière à la sainte Vierge*, in *Questions liturgiques et paroissiales*. Vol. 25, 1940, pp. 33-36. The conservative dating of Roberts, not before the second half of the fourth century, has been disputed by G. Vannucci, who prefers the opinion of Lobel, based on sheerly paleographic grounds, that the document is not later than the third century; cf. La più antica preghiera alla Madre di Dio, in Marianum, Vol. 3, 1941, pp. 97-101. More recently, Otto Stegmüller has objected to Mercenier's restoration and substituted his own; paleographic, liturgical, patristic, and apocryphal data persuade Stegmüller that the prayer, so significant in the story of Marian veneration and invocation, ought not be dated before the end of the fourth century; cf. *Sub tuum praesidium: Bemerkungen zur ältesten Überlieferung*, in *Zeitschrift für katholische Theologie*, Vol. 74, 1952, pp. 76-82.

On the one hand, they use expressions that equivalently affirm the divine Maternity. On the other, they propound the twin premises for their conclusion: (*a*) Jesus was genuinely born of Mary; and (*b*) Jesus born of Mary is God.

Justin declares that the Word of God, who "is also God," the same God who appeared to Moses and the other prophets in the form of fire and the guise of an angel, "became man by a virgin"; He was actually "born" of her.[109]

What for Justin is sheer doctrinal affirmation, is in Irenaeus a thesis defended at length.[110] The New Testament (Mt. 1:20-23) reveals two things clearly: "that the Son of God was born of a virgin, and that He is Himself the Saviour Christ, whom the prophets proclaimed; not, as these men say, that Jesus is He who was born of Mary, while Christ is He who descended from above."[111] In the Old Testament the Holy Spirit points out in the Isaian prophecy (Isa. 7:10 ff.) "His birth, which is from a virgin, and His essence, that He is God."[112] In his argumentation Irenaeus employs several phrases strikingly indicative of the divine Maternity. Our Lord "is the Word of the Father and the Son of Man"; "Word that He is, He took birth of Mary"; the glad tidings were brought to Mary "that she should bear God."[113] Apart from Scripture, the proof of his predilection is drawn from the economy of Redemption. If man was to be saved, God had to become man, had to derive His human nature from the nature that had fallen. If His birth from Mary is unreal, our redemption is equally unreal.[114]

---

[109] Cf. Justin, *Apologia 1*, cap. 63; *PG*, 6, 425; *Apologia 2*, cap. 6; PG, 6, 453. Regrettably, Justin's work *Adversus Marcionem*, which Irenaeus used (cf. *Adv. haer.*, lib. 4, cap. 11, 2; Massuet, 4, 6, 2) and Eusebius mentions (Hist. eccl., lib. 4, cap. 11, 8 ff.), has been lost.

[110] Cf. E. Dublanchy, *Marie*, in *D.T.C.*, Vol. 9, Part 2, col. 2350.

[111] Irenaeus, *Adversus haereses*, lib. 3, cap. 17, 1 (Massuet, 3, 16, 2); Harvey, 2, 83; PG, 7, 921.

[112] Irenaeus, *Adversus haereses*, lib. 3, cap. 25, 2 (Massuet, 3, 21, 4); Harvey, 2, 116; PG, 7, 951.

[113] Irenaeus, *Adversus haereses*, lib. 3, cap. 20, 3 (Massuet, 3, 19, 3); Harvey, 2, 104; PG, 7, 941; lib. 3, cap. 30 (Massuet, 3, 21, 10); Harvey, 2, 120; PG, 7, 955; lib. 5, cap. 19, 1; Harvey, 2, 376; *PG*, 7, 1175.

[114] Cf. Irenaeus, *Adversus haereses*, lib. 3, cap. 31, 1 (Massuet, 3, 22, 1); Harvey, 2, 121; PG, 7, 956.

Tertullian, too, has Gnostics in view; he makes the same points as Irenaeus; and his belief with respect to Mary's motherhood does not change with his checkered career. In his Catholic days he has no doubt that the Son of God became flesh in Mary's womb; in His birth we find one who is "man and God united."[115] In fact, His being enfleshed in her womb and His birth of her is a truth which the rule of faith obliges us to believe.[116] The palpable model of divine patience is God's Son, who endured to be born in a mother's womb.[117] Dallying with Montanism does not prevent Tertullian from propounding an authentic Incarnation, e.g., in his works *On the Flesh of Christ* and *Against Marcion*. The novelty of Christ's birth does not lie in this (as the Gnostics claim), "that as the Word of God became flesh without a human father's seed, so there should be no flesh of the Virgin Mother"; it rests in this, "that His flesh, though not born of seed, still proceeded from flesh."[118] If Mary is not His Mother, then Scripture lies; if she is His Mother, He was in her womb. But "no flesh can speak of a mother's womb save that which is itself the offspring of that womb. ..."[119]

It has not been established incontrovertibly that Hippolytus, the first antipope, who died a martyr in 235, actually called Mary "Mother of God";[120] what is indisputable is that, for Hippolytus, Mary was literally pregnant with the Word of God, with God's

---

[115] Tertullian, *Apologeticum*, cap. 21, n. 13-14; C.S.E.L., 69, 55-56.

[116] Cf. Tertullian, *De praescriptione haereticorum*, cap. 13; C.S.E.L., 70, 17-18.

[117] Cf. Tertullian, *De patientia*, cap. 3; C.S.E.L., 47, 3.

[118] Tertullian, *De carne Christi*, cap. 21; C.S.E.L., 70, 241-242.

[119] Tertullian, *De carne Christi*, cap. 21; C.S.E.L., 70, 243.

[120] The crucial passage occurs in *De benedictionibus Iacob*, cap. 1; "... Joseph betroths Mary to himself and becomes a trustworthy witness to the Mother of God (Θεοτόκου)"; *Texte und Untersuchungen*, Vol. 38, Part 1 (Leipzig, 1911), p. 13. Unfortunately, there is nothing in the Georgian translation to correspond to it; only the Greek has it; cf. *Texte und Untersuchungen*, Vol. 26, Part 1 (Leipzig, 1904), p. 3. Hugo Rahner has made a laudable effort to accredit the Greek text, and concludes that Hippolytus, about 220, attests the title, Mother of God; cf. *Hippolyt von Rom als Zeuge für den Ausdruck Θεοτόκος*, in *Zeitschrift für katholische Theologie*, Vol. 59, 1935, pp. 73-81. Jouassard is not convinced; cf. *Marie à travers la patristique*, p. 86, note 2.

Son.[121] Another Roman priest, Novatian, who occupied a leading position among the clergy of Rome about 250 and later fell into schism, is subordinationist in his Logos doctrine, but emphatic on two points: Christ is born of Mary, and Christ is God and Man.[122] Cyprian, Bishop of Carthage († 258), in the second book of his *Testimonies*, written perhaps before 249 and "containing the mystery of Christ," includes the truth "that a sign of His birth would be this, that of a virgin He would be born man and God, Son of man and of God." His scriptural texts are Isa. 7:10 ff. and Gen. 3:14-15.[123]

With the fourth century the title "Mother of God" is quite common and its theological basis comes into view rather clearly. True, the development is more dramatic in the East — from the moment (c. 319) when Bishop Alexander of Alexandria, in announcing to his colleagues the deposition of Arius, made the first

---

[121] Cf. *De benedictionibus Iacob*, cap. 27; *Texte und Untersuchungen*, Vol. 38, Part 1, p. 41; *De antichristo*, cap. 45; G.C.S., Hippolytus, Vol. 1, Part 2, 28; *Contra Noetum*, cap. 4; PG, 10, 809. The last Christian author at Rome to express himself in Greek, Hippolytus may well have been a disciple of Irenaeus; at any rate, his Soteriology is Irenaean, revolving about the concept of recapitulation; cf. *Philosophumena*, lib. 10, cap. 33, 15; G.C.S., Hippolytus, Vol. 3, 291. His understanding of Mary's Maternity is unmistakable: "Let us therefore believe, brethren blessed, according to the tradition of the apostles, that God the Word came down from heaven into the holy Virgin Mary, with this in mind, that enfleshed of her, assuming a human (I mean rational) soul, become all that man is save for sin, He might save fallen man and offer immortality to those who believe in His name. ... As it was proclaimed, so was it done: He showed Himself in person of a virgin and the Holy Spirit, become a new man ... not by phantasy or alteration ... but man in all reality." *Contra Noetum*, cap. 17; PG, 10, 825-828; cf. *Contra Noetum*, cap. 15; PG, 10, 824-825.

[122] Cf. Novatian, *De Trinitate*, cap. 9 ff.; PL, 3, 927 ff. The expressions he uses in this second section (cap. 9-29) to show the unity of the two natures in Christ are significant for the divine Maternity and were of unusual influence on Latin theology; cf. H. Rahner, *Die Marienkunde in der lateinischen Patristik*, p. 144.

[123] Cyprian, *Ad Quirinum testimonia*, lib. 2, cap. 9; C.S.E.L., 3, 73; cf. *Ad Quirinum testimonia*, praef.; C.S.E.L., 3, 35. For the date, cf. J. Quasten, *Patrology*, Vol. 2 (Westminster, Md., 1953), p. 363.

indisputable use of *Theotókos*,[124] through Julian the Apostate's querulous charge against the Christians, "You never stop calling Mary Mother of God,"[125] to the celebrated anathema of Cyril and Ephesus: "If anyone does not confess that Emmanuel is God in truth, and that consequently the holy Virgin is Mother of God (for she gave birth after the flesh to the Word of God made flesh), let him be anathema!"[126] Nevertheless, the West, if more prosaic, is no less uncompromising.

Hilary of Poitiers may well speak for Gaul when he states so simply that Mary "was Mother of Our Lord according to the flesh";[127] He remains the God that He was, and is born of a virgin's womb.[128] Equally simple and precious is a hidden half sentence: Mary exercised, in regard of "the second man from heaven" (1 Cor. 15:47), the role of a mother; she gave Him, in His conception and birth, what any mother gives to the child of her womb.[129]

Ambrose uses the title "Mother of God" in several places with no hint of novelty or embarrassment.[130] In opening his defense of Mary's abiding virginity against Helvidius, Jerome invokes "God the Father, to show that the Mother of His Son was a virgin after childbirth, she who was mother before marriage."[131] Augustine does not use the title, but his mind is transparent. Though Elizabeth conceived a man, and Mary a man, still "Elizabeth conceived only a

---

[124] Cf. Alexander of Alexandria, *Epist. ad Alexandrum Constant.*, n. 12; PG, 18, 568. The offhand use of the term, with no apparent need to justify it, arouses the suspicion that Alexander is inspired by an established custom; cf. Dublanchy, *art. cit.*, col. 2351.

[125] Quoted by Cyril of Alexandria, *Contra Iulianum*, lib. 8; PG, 76, 901.

[126] Cyril of Alexandria, *Epist. 17*, n. 12; ed. E. Schwartz, *Acta conciliorum oecumenicorum*, Tom. 1, Vol. 1, Part 1 (Berolini et Lipsiae, 1927-1930), 40; PG, 77, 120.

[127] Hilary, *Tractatus in ps. 131*, n. 8; C.S.E.L., 22, 668.

[128] Cf. Hilary, *Tractatus in ps. 126*, n. 16; C.S.E.L., 22, 624.

[129] Hilary, *De Trinitate*, lib. 10, n. 17: "... quae officio usa materno, sexus sui naturam in conceptu et partu hominis exsecuta est"; PL, 10, 356.

[130] Cf. Ambrose, *De virginibus*, lib. 2, cap. 2, n. 7; ed. Faller, p. 47; *Exameron*, lib. 5, cap. 20, n. 65; C.S.E.L., 32, Part 1, 188-189; *Expositio evangelii secundum Lucam*, lib. 2, n. 26; C.S.E.L., 32, Part 4, 55.

[131] Jerome, *Adversus Helvidium*, n. 2; PL, 23, 194.

man, Mary God and man."[132] Christ was anointed with the spirit not at His baptism but "when the Word of God was made flesh, i.e., when human nature ... was linked to God the Word in the womb of a virgin, so as to form one person with Him. For this reason we confess Him born of the Holy Spirit and the Virgin Mary."[133] The Lord our God, he says, "without birth by woman is the only Son of the Father; without embrace of man His Mother bore Him as her only Son."[134]

Three years after Ephesus, Vincent of Lerins († 450) devoted a whole chapter of his *Commonitories* to Mary's divine motherhood.

It is by reason of the unicity of person in Christ that it is Catholic to believe, and godless to deny, that the Word of God, and not merely His flesh, was born of the Virgin. "God forbid, therefore, that anyone should try to cheat holy Mary of her privileges of divine grace and of her special glory. For by a unique favor of Him who is our Lord and God, but her Son, she is to be confessed *Theotókos* in the truest and most blessed way possible. But she is not *Theotókos* in the way a certain impious heresy supposes. To believe this heresy, she is to be called Mother of God in name only, because she gave birth to a human being who later became God – as we speak of the mother of a priest or the mother of a bishop; not that she gave birth to a priest or a bishop, but because she produced the human being who later became priest or bishop. Not thus, I say, is holy Mary *Theotókos*, but rather because ... in her sacred womb was accomplished this sacrosanct mystery, that by reason of a certain matchless, unique unity of person, even as the Word in flesh is flesh, so the Man in God is God."[135]

And that, in brief, is the Western tradition. Little wonder that Leo the Great, in his *Letter to Flavian*, observed that Eutyches might have learned what he was obliged to believe on the Incarnation, if he had "listened to that common and universal confession in which the whole body of the faithful acknowledges its belief in ... Jesus Christ, [God's] only-begotten Son, our Lord, who was born of the

---

[132] Augustine, *Serm. 289*, n. 2; PL, 38, 1308.

[133] Augustine, *De Trinitate*, lib. 15, cap. 26, n. 46; PL, 42, 1093-1094.

[134] Augustine, *Serm. 195*, n. 2; PL, 38, 1018.

[135] Vincent of Lerins, *Commonitorium* 1, cap. 15; PL, 50, 658.

Holy Spirit and the Virgin Mary. ...."[136]

IV

One of the most perplexing problems in patristic Mariology revolves about Mary's holiness. The issue becomes complex in that it involves an aspect of Mary's sanctity acute for the contemporary Christian: the state of Mary's soul at the moment of her conception. From the close of the Apostolic Age to the Council of Nicaea the literary heritage of Western Christianity contains so remarkably little on the theme of Our Lady's holiness that a pointed question is inevitable. Was the pre-Nicene West even conscious of the problem?

Several facts are not without significance. In the first place, Jewish and pagan circles in the second half of the second century, as a flanking attack on Christ, taxed His Mother with being a prostitute.[137] The reaction of the Christian West would make fascinating reading, but it is nowhere in evidence. It is not unreasonable, however, to conjecture that Christians who recognized in Mary the counterpart of Eve, whose rule of faith involved the virginity of Mary before Gabriel, must have reacted as strongly, if not as mordantly, as Tertullian was to do somewhat later.[138] This much will stand the test of criticism: for the orthodox Christian, Mary was not a woman of evil reputation.

Second, the Eve-Mary analogy is relevant here. Our Lady's consent to the redemptive program implicit in the Incarnation was recognized by Irenaeus as constituting an act not simply of singular significance but even of exceptional moral value; it was an act of obedience.[139] Regrettably, Irenaeus' insight into the Second Eve is

---

[136] Leo, *Epist. 28*, cap. 2; PL, 54, 757. Cf. *Serm. 24*, cap. 3: "... Creator ... electa sibi matre, quam fecerat, quae salva integritate virginea, corporeae esset tantum ministra substantiae ..."; PL, 54, 205.

[137] Cf. Tertullian, *De spectaculis*, cap. 30; C.S.E.L., 20, 29. The same story was peddled in the East by Celsus; cf. Origen, *Contra Celsum*, lib. 1, cap. 28 ff.; G.C.S., *Origenes*, Vol. 1, 79 ff.

[138] Tertullian, *De spectaculis*, cap. 30. Tertullian's reaction was prompted not so much by the insult to the Mother as by the assault on her Son.

[139] Cf. Irenaeus, *Adversus haereses*, lib. 3, cap. 32, 1 (Massuet, 3, 22, 4); Harvey, 2, 123-124; PG, 7, 958-959.

not paralleled by any conclusion in the texts with respect to the state of her soul prior to her *fiat*. Did the ante-Nicene Fathers glimpse a further consequence from the analogy, an indication of Mary's sanctity? Le Bachelet, for one, surrenders such investigation: "Who could possibly give a certain answer, one way or the other?"[140]

Third, the adjective "holy" is prefixed to "Virgin." Not often; still, it is used. Hippolytus, for example, states, without explanation, that "God the Word descended into the holy Virgin Mary."[141] The difficulty is, such a usage is ill-defined. The word sanctus or ἅγιος has not always been able to boast of a clearly delimited meaning in ecclesiastical use.[142] Does Hippolytus use ἅγιος as a rather vague laudatory epithet, or as a title of dignity, or to imply moral excellence, or to signify the respect reserved for one who is segregated from profane things and belongs to God by some sort of consecration? The answer must, in the state of the evidence, be a confession of ignorance.

Fourth, there is testimony which attaches more intimately to Mary's holiness. If we can trust a fragment on Ps. 22 attributed to Hippolytus, the Roman exegete wrote: "The ark which was made of incorruptible timber (cf. Exod. 15:10) was the Saviour. The ark symbolized the tabernacle of His body, which was impervious to decay and engendered no sinful corruption. ... The Lord was sinless, because in His humanity He was fashioned out of incorruptible wood, that is to say, out of the Virgin and the Holy Spirit, lined within and without as with the purest gold of the Word of God."[143]

---

[140] X. Le Bachelet, *Immaculée conception*, in *D.T.C.*, Vol. 27, col. 874; he grants, however, that the principles of solution are there. For Le Bachelet's treatment of the Western Fathers, cf. col. 872-893, 979-983. It is argued that, in Justin's description of Eve as "virgin incorrupt," there is question of Eve exempt from all corruption, and so the parallelism demands a similar exemption for Mary. The argumentation is not convincing. The seeds of future development with respect to Mary's sanctity are contained in the patristic Eve-Mary analogy; but they are seeds and not the full flower.

[141] Hippolytus, *Contra Noetum*, cap. 17; PG, 10, 825.

[142] Cf. H. Delehaye, *Sanctus*, in *Analecta Bollandiana*, Vol. 28, 1909, pp. 145-200.

[143] Hippolytus, In *ps. 22*; quoted by Theodoret, Dialogus 1; PG, 10, 610, 864-865.

The author's direct purpose is to reveal the sinlessness of Christ; but his reasoning shows that in his eyes the Virgin, incorruptible wood of which the humanity of Jesus was fashioned, is likewise all-pure, all-holy. The meaning is substantially clear; what fails to emerge is the precise nature of her purity, her incorruptibility.

The extant evidence, therefore, if meager, indicates sufficiently that for some of the ante-Nicene writers in the West the idea of holiness and purity did attach to the person of Mary. It does not justify us in concluding with certainty to the nature of this holiness, or in picturing them as carriers of an historical tradition, or in attributing to them a formal belief in an Immaculate Conception.

It is in this era that we confront a current of thought unfavorable to a thesis of Marian sinlessness. In its general form it is the principle that Christ alone is without sin, and it is unmistakably formulated by Tertullian. "Thus, some men are good, others, bad, yet their souls all belong to the same class. There is some good in the worst of us, and the best of us harbor some evil within us. God alone is without sin, and the only sinless man is Christ, since He is God."[144] In this general form there is no inescapable implicit which would rule out an utterly sinless existence for Mary. There is a sinlessness which is the fruit of nature; such sinlessness has always been, in orthodox Christian thinking, the exclusive prerogative of God. And there is a sinlessness which is the fruit of grace; it is theoretically compatible with human living. Did Tertullian deny such God-given sinlessness in the concrete order of things?

One phrase suggests it strongly: "the best of us harbor some evil within us."

However that may be, the stumbling block looms larger when specific defects are mentioned. If we credit Tertullian, Christ publicly denounced His Mother for her disbelief when He asked: "Who is my mother and who are my brethren?"[145] According to the

---

[144] Tertullian, *De anima*, cap. 41, n. 3; ed. J. Waszink (Amsterdam, 1947), p. 57; tr. E. A. Quain, in *Fathers of the Church*, Vol. 10 (New York, 1950), p. 273.

[145] Cf. Tertullian, De carne Christi, cap. 7; C.S.E.L., 70, 210-212. In the same chapter Tertullian adds another interpretation: "In the mother abjured there is a figure of the Synagogue, and in the disbelieving brethren a figure of the Jews." Cf. also Jesus' alleged indignation and His disavowal of mother and

Carthaginian, Mary apparently kept aloof from Jesus while Martha and others were in constant contact with Him. In standing outside she was guilty of disbelief *(incredulitas);* in calling Him away from His work she was importunate. And if we believe Irenaeus, whose Marian theology is otherwise so reverential, Jesus checked Mary's "untimely haste" at Cana, her yearning to quicken the miracle of the water made wine.[146]

The objection from Irenaeus is scarcely momentous. The Bishop of Lyons finds Mary's request inopportune, untimely; he does not hint that it was sinful. Tertullian, on the contrary, is harsh and unambiguous. And if his accusation is explicable in the light of his fiery polemic, so heedless of consequences, it remains nonetheless a candid accusation. Though he was flirting with Montanism at the moment, he still gives no indication that he is aware of a contrary belief or official teaching.[147] If it is unjustifiable to conclude that Tertullian is representative of a widespread tradition, it remains true that in Africa at the outset of the third century moral deficiencies were apparently not regarded as incompatible with the dignity of God's Mother.[148]

A significant turning point in the Mariological consciousness of the West does not occur until 377, with the publication of Ambrose's three books *On Virginity,* addressed to his sister, Marcellina. The inspiration for his portrait of Mary is not purely local, the contemporary aristocratic virgin vowed to Christian asceticism; it is more specifically Eastern, a work of Athanasius on virginity.[149]

---

brethren in *Adversus Marcionem,* lib. 4, cap. 19; C.S.E.L., 47, 483.

[146] Cf. Irenaeus, *Adversus haereses,* lib. 3, cap. 17, 7 (Massuet, 3, 16, 7); Harvey, 2, 88; PG, 7, 926.

[147] The problem becomes more acute when we reflect that in the East a score of years later Origen could preach to the people of Caesarea that the sword of sorrow is Mary's experience of scandal at the Passion of her Son, a sword of unbelief, of uncertainty. Even more startling is his theological reasoning: "If she did not experience scandal at the Lord's passion, Jesus did not die for her sins." *In Luc. hom. 17;* G.C.S., *Origenes,* Vol. 9, 116-118.

[148] Cf. Jouassard, *Le problème de la sainteté,* p. 18.

[149] It is reasonably certain that we have this important production in a Coptic translation discovered and edited by L. Th. Lefort, S. Athanase: Sur la virginité, in Muséon, Vol. 42, 1929, pp. 197-275. For the influence of this

The influence of Athanasius was fortunate, if only because the ideas of the fourth-century West on Mary's sanctity were so slender. In Gaul, for example, Hilary of Poitiers can somehow reconcile a profound reverence for Mary's virginity with a tortuous passage in which she seems destined to undergo the scrutiny of God's judgment.[150] He insists, too, that Our Lord alone is sinless, and this in virtue of His exceptional birth.[151] In Rome, Marius Victorinus extends specifically to Mary the imperfection which he attributes to the very idea of woman, while Ambrosiaster understands Simeon's sword of sorrow as Mary's doubting at the death of the Lord — a doubt removed only by the Resurrection.[152] In Africa, Bishop Optatus of Mileve († before 400) sees the flesh of Christ alone as sinless, because of His unique conception; only Christ is perfectly holy, the rest of us are "half perfect"; every man, even if of Christian parents, is born with an unclean spirit.[153] Near Granada in Spain, Bishop Gregory of Elvira seems to number Mary among the ancestors who would have transmitted to the Redeemer a body soiled and open to sin.[154]

And yet, the climate of thought and feeling promised the ideas of Ambrose an enthusiastic welcome, especially in his own North

---

work on Ambrose, cf. Lefort, Athanase, Ambroise et Chenoute "Sur la virginité," in Muséon, Vol. 48, 1935, pp. 55-73.

[150] Cf. Hilary, *Tractatus in ps. 118*, Gimel, n. 12; C.S.E.L., 22, 384. Jouassard believes there may be question here of faults that are slight; cf. *Marie à travers la patristique*, p. 102, note 6. The note in PL, 9, 523, recalls the marginal jotting of Erasmus: "Aliud sentiunt, qui liberant eam a peccato originis."

[151] Cf. Hilary, *op. cit.*, Vau, n. 6; C.S.E.L., 22, 414; ibid., Nun, n. 8; C.S.E.L., 22, 478; *De Trinitate*, lib. 10, cap. 25; PL, 10, 364-366. There is no insuperable problem in Hilary's belief that Mary was sanctified at the hour of the Annunciation, and that the Holy Spirit strengthened her (apparently bodily) weakness; cf. *De Trinitate*, lib. 2, cap. 26; PL, 10, 67-68.

[152] Cf. Marius Victorinus, *In epist. Pauli ad Galatas*, lib. 2; PL, 8, 1176-1177; Ambrosiaster, Quaestiones Veteris et Novi Testamenti, cap. 76, n. 2; C.S.E.L., 50, 131.

[153] Cf. Optatus, *Contra Parmenianum Donatistam*, lib. 1, cap. 8; C.S.E.L., 26, 9-10; ibid., lib. 4, cap. 7; C.S.E.L., 26, 112; Optatus, lib. 2, cap. 20; C.S.E.L., 26, 55-56; ibid., lib. 4, cap. 6; C.S.E.L., 26, 110.

[154] Cf. Gregory of Elvira, *Hom. in Cant. canticorum*; text established by D. Wilmart, in *Bulletin de littérature ecclésiastique*, Vol. 7, 1906, pp. 252-254.

Italy, where the influence of asceticism and the personal sojourn of Athanasius had paved the way. Thus, Zeno of Verona implies that Mary, like the virgins he is addressing, was "holy in body and spirit," and claims that she had "deserved" to carry the Saviour of souls.[155] But the attitude of Ambrose toward Mary is something novel in Latin literature. Mary was virgin not in body alone, but in mind as well. She is the unattainable model of all virtues; she has lived them to perfection. Not the slightest shadow mars his portrait of her, no smallest imperfection.[156] It is a vision of Mary which will inspire Ambrose all his days and lead him to still further insights. A decade later he can attribute to Mary a fullness of grace whose foundation is the divine Maternity: "For Mary alone was this greeting [full of grace] reserved; for she is well said to be alone full of grace, who alone obtained the grace which no one else had gained, to be filled with the Author of grace."[157] It may be that Ambrose is simply equating "full of grace" and "Mother of God"; the construction bears that exegesis. But about the same time, in a sermon on Ps. 118, he speaks of Mary as "a virgin free by grace from all stain of sin."[158] It is a text frequently invoked by defenders of the Immaculate Conception, who feel that to understand the phrase of actual or personal sins alone is to restrict arbitrarily the indefinite, unlimited assertion.[159] On the other hand, Ambrose does not seem aware of the implications in his phrase. In any event, the germ of future development is indisputably there, especially since, to his way of thinking, if you are to appreciate what Mary is, you must reckon with what is *fitting* in such a mother.[160]

---

[155] Zeno, *Tractatus*, lib. 1, tr. 5, 3; lib. 2, tr. 8, 2; PL, 11, 303, 414. In lib. 1, tr. 13, 10 Zeno seems to see in Mary moral faults which had to be cut away before the Incarnation, or simultaneously with it; PL, 11, 352.

[156] Cf. Ambrose, *De virginibus*, lib. 2, cap. 2, n. 6-18; ed. Faller, pp. 47-52. For a picture of fourth-century ascetical life and virginity, and Ambrose's place therein, cf. F. Homes Dudden, *op. cit.*, Vol. 1, pp. 144-159.

[157] Ambrose, *Expositio evangelii secundum Lucam*, lib. 3, n. 9; C.S.E.L., 32, Part 4, 45-46.

[158] Ambrose, *Expositio in ps. 118*, *Serm. 22*, n. 30; PL, 15, 1599 (ed. 1866).

[159] Cf. Le Bachelet, *art. cit.*, col. 882.

[160] Cf. Ambrose, *Epist. 63*, n. 110; PL, 16, 1270-1271. Jerome is rather vague on Mary's holiness. Mary is Ezechiel's gate to the East, a figure of her perpetual virginity; this gate is "always closed and full of light"; *Epist. 49*, n.

At the beginning of the fifth century the Spanish poet, Prudentius († after 405), alluding to Mary's role as New Eve, represents the serpent trampled beneath the feet of Our Lady, who has merited to become Mother of God and consequently has remained immune to all.[161] Once again, the text, as it stands, is susceptible of an interpretation excluding from Mary all possibility of sin from the initial moment of her existence. Once again, the sole lingering doubt is whether Prudentius had so comprehensive, so all-inclusive a concept of sin.

It is actually with Augustine and the Pelagians that the issues involved take on some measure of clarity. Here there are two significant moments. In the first (415) Augustine confronts Pelagius on the issue of Mary's personal holiness, her freedom from actual sin; in the second (c. 428) he confronts Julian of Eclanum on the score of her conception, her freedom from original sin.

Pelagius was not content to deny original sin; he ascribed to Adam's progeny the power to observe the whole moral law on their own, a native ability to live lives of justice. To bolster his belief, he cited a number of individuals — men and women, Old Law and New —who actually realized this program of sinlessness. The names range from Abel through Abraham to Joseph and John, from Debbora to Elizabeth, "and in fact the Mother of our Lord and Saviour too, whom piety must needs confess free from sin." Ambrose had found no imperfection in Mary; Pelagius asserted on principle that none *could* be found.

Augustine's response is a two-edged denial. Only Mary is free from sin, and her sinlessness is a triumph not of nature but of grace; its foundation is the divine Maternity. "With the exception, therefore, of the holy Virgin Mary, in whose case, out of respect for the Lord, I would have no question raised when there is talk of sin — for how do we know what further grace was conferred on her for absolute victory over sin, she who deserved to conceive and bear Him who obviously had no sin? — with the exception, then, of this Virgin, could we but gather together in their lifetime all those

---

21; C.S.E.L., 54, 386. The idea is taken up and accentuated elsewhere: Mary is a cloud that is never in darkness but "always in the light"; Hom. in psalmos; ed. G. Morin, *Anecdota Maredsolana*, Vol. 3, 65.
[161] Cf. Prudentius, *Liber cathemerinon*, 3, lines 146-155; C.S.E.L., 61, 18.

saints, men and women, and ask them whether they were free from sin, what in our opinion would have been their answer? ... No matter how remarkable their holiness in this body ... they would have cried out with one voice: 'If we should say that we have no sin, we deceive ourselves, and the truth is not in us' (1 Jn. 1:8)."[162]

It might be argued that Augustine simply prefers not to discuss the case of Mary. It is far more probable that his question is not really a question at all, that it conveys his own conviction of the incompatibility of actual sin with divine motherhood, that consequently it constitutes a landmark in the development of the Western Church's consciousness of Mary's sinlessness.[163]

Julian of Eclanum, a deposed bishop, lifted the discussion to the level of original sin. In his view, every man is born sinless; a unique proof of his position, he feels, is Mary. To attack the doctrine of original sin in its implications, he establishes a parallel between his enemy Augustine and the heresiarch Jovinian, to the advantage of the latter: "ille virginitatem Mariae partus conditione dissolvit; tu ipsam Mariam diabolo nascendi conditione transcribis."[164] Jovinian, says Julian, sacrificed Mary's virginity by submitting her to the usual circumstances of human childbearing; Augustine surrenders the very person of Mary to the devil by asserting that original sin is inseparable from human generation.

Augustine's retort ranks among the most passionately disputed sentences in Christian literature: "Non transcribimus diabolo Mariam conditione nascendi; sed ideo, quia ipsa conditio solvitur gratia renascendi."[165] The disagreements in detail among interpreters of this sentence are too many to be retailed here, but basically scholars divide into two camps. Both agree on one point:

---

[162] Augustine, *De natura et gratia,* cap. 36, n. 42; C.S.E.L., 60, 263-264

[163] Some theologians argue that the text indirectly or implicitly excludes original sin as well. In the context, they admit, Augustine is speaking of actual sin; but he asserts without reservation that she is free from all sin. The honor of Christ, on which his conclusion is based, is no less incompatible with the hypothesis of original sin than with the affirmation of actual sin; cf. Le Bachelet, *art. cit.,* col. 883.

[164] Augustine, *Opus imperfectum contra Iulianum,* lib. 4, cap. 122; *PL,* 45, 1417. Augustine quotes this objection from the fourth book of Julian's *Ad Florum,* written about 421, but no longer extant as such.

[165] Augustine, *Opus imperfectum contra Iulianum,* lib. 4, cap. 122; PL, 45, 1418.

Augustine denies that his doctrine of original sin surrenders Mary to the devil by the circumstances of her birth. But, for one group, no surrender is involved because the grace of regeneration subsequently annuls this condition by making it disappear. Conditio nascendi is synonymous with birth in original sin. Gratia renascendi necessarily involves a transition from sin to justification subsequent to birth, a spiritual rebirth unintelligible without a prior spiritual death. And Augustine's doctrine on the universality of original sin and on the method of its propagation precludes any exception in Mary's case.

This interpretation, unfavorable to an immaculate conception, was the accepted exegesis of Augustine for centuries; right or wrong, it exercised a vigorous influence on the West; even after *Ineffabilis Deus* it remains an exegesis championed by scholars of distinction.[166]

The opposing school denies that this interpretation is apodictic. For them, no surrender to the devil is involved because the grace of regeneration simply annuls the condition of birth (original sin) by preventing its realization in Mary. *Conditio nascendi* is not so much a fact as a law. *Gratia renascendi* does not necessarily involve, of itself or in Augustine, the removal of sin already contracted. Augustine's doctrine on original sin and the manner of its transmission is not an insuperable obstacle to a privilege in favor of God's Mother, because Mary's immunity from original sin is not to be regarded as of native right; it is sheer gift. In the other hypothesis, Augustine would actually have enslaved, surrendered Our Lady to the devil, despite his protestation to the contrary.[167]

---

[166] Cf. Ph. Friedrich, *Die Mariologie des hl. Augustinus*, pp. 183-233; L. Saltet, *Saint Augustin et l'Immaculée-Conception*, in *Bulletin de littérature ecclésiastique*, Vol. 11, 1910, pp. 161-166; B. Capelle, *La pensée de saint Augustin sur l'Immaculée Conception*, in *Recherches de théologie ancienne et médiévale*, Vol. 4, 1932, pp. 361-370; J. Götz, *Augustin und die Immaculata Conceptio*, in *Theologie und Glaube*, Vol. 25, 1933, pp. 739-744; A. Dufourcq, *Comment s'éveilla la foi à l'Immaculée-Conception et à l'Assomption aux Ve et VIe siècles* (Paris, 1946), pp. 12-15; Jouassard, *Le problème de la sainteté*, p. 25; B. Altaner, Patrologie, 3 ed. (Freiburg, 1951), p. 389.

[167] Cf. Le Bachelet, *art. cit.*, col. 884-885, 889-890. A more detailed defense of this interpretation is offered by F. S. Mueller, *Augustinus amicus an adversarius Immaculatae Conceptionis?* in *Miscellanea Agostiniana* (Romae,

Whatever the truth of the matter, Latin speculation on Mary's holiness derived a twofold orientation from Augustine. With respect to actual sins, the West would thereafter have little difficulty recognizing in Mary a perfection unblemished. On the score of her debt to Adam, it was to be centuries before the West could free itself from the myopia induced by anti-Pelagian concentration and by its interpretation of five individually intelligible words: *ipsa conditio solvitur gratia renascendi.*

Post-Augustinian patristic thought on the perfection of Mary reveals two conflicting currents. There is a negative, unfavorable trend rooted in Augustine's anti-Pelagianism; it accentuates the universality of original sin and articulates the connection between inherited sin and any conception consequent upon sinful concupiscence. The root idea is summed up by Leo the Great: "Alone therefore among the sons of men the Lord Jesus was born innocent, because alone conceived without the pollution of carnal concupiscence."[168] The same concept is discoverable in St. Fulgentius, Bishop of Ruspe in Africa († 533), the most significant theologian of his time; in Pope Gregory the Great († 604) at the end of the sixth century; and a century later in Venerable Bede, a scholar renowned throughout England.[169] At best, this manner of

---

1931), Vol. 2, pp. 885-914. Charles Boyer's answer to Capelle is typical and pointed: (a) Mary's flesh-of-sin demands only that she have an obligation of being conceived with sin unless God's grace intervenes; (b) the *excepta itaque Maria* text is directly concerned with actual sin, but the affirmation is so general and the reason given so fundamental that they outstrip the limited problem envisaged; (c) *the transcribimus* text involves Augustine unjustifiably in contradiction unless *gratia renascendi* signifies a preservative grace, only conceptually posterior to Mary's conception; cf. *Bulletin augustinien*, in *Gregorianum*, Vol. 14, 1933, pp. 93-96. Of some relevance is a sermon delivered by Augustine in 413 on the birth of the Baptist. He refuses to except John from the universality proclaimed in Rom. 5:12 ff., but it is his reasoning that is significant: "Invenisti plane praeter peccatum natum, quem invenis praeter Adam natum. ... Nam ille qui voluit ab ea [sententia] esse separatus, per virginem est venire dignatus"; *Serm. 223*, n. 12; PL, 38, 1335.

[168] Leo, *Serm. 25*, cap. 5; PL, 54, 211.

[169] Cf. Fulgentius, *De veritate praedestinationis et gratiae Dei*, lib. 2, cap. 2, n. 5; PL, 65, 605; Gregory, Moralia *in Iob*, lib. 18, cap. 52, n. 84; PL, 76, 89; Bede, *Hom. gen.*, lib. 1, hom. 2, *In festo annuntiationis*; PL, 94, 13. It is a concept

speaking is ambiguous; it opened the door to the grave controversies to come; and it was not of a nature to foster the development of belief in the Immaculate Conception.

Concurrently, however, there is a positive, more favorable current of thought. It is not simply that Mary is still the Second Eve, instrument of our salvation,[170] or that the merits she acquires lift her above the angels, to divinity's throne.[171] More pointedly, Peter Chrysologus declares that Our Lady was pledged to Christ in the womb at the moment of her fashioning, while Maximus of Turin, contemporary of Leo I, finds Mary a suitable lodging for Christ, apparently not so much because of her physical virginity as in virtue of some primal grace which he does not specify.[172] The poets, Sedulius and Venantius Fortunatus, sing of Mary in language which leaves no room for sin and is indefinite enough to provoke wonderment with respect to the state of her soul at conception.[173]

Historically, the strides taken by the West in advance of the East on the holiness of Mary — due primarily to Ambrose and Augustine — were slowed by the barrier which the West felt had been placed by Augustine in the way of an immaculate conception — a barrier not confronted by the East.

Theologically, we must face up to an evolution. From the extant philological data it does not seem that the personal sinlessness of Mary or her Immaculate Conception were explicitly taught as Catholic doctrine in the patristic West.[174] However, the work of

---

which leads to the thesis that Mary's flesh is a flesh-of-sin, because conceived in iniquity; cf. Fulgentius, Epist. 17, cap. 6, n. 13; PL, 65, 458. It leads likewise to the theory of a necessary purification of Mary at the hour of the Annunciation; cf. Leo, *Serm. 22*, cap. 3; PL, 54, 196; Bede, *op. cit.*; PL, 94, 12.

[170] Cf. Maximus of Turin, *Hom. 15*; PL, 57, 254.

[171] Cf. Gregory the Great, In 1 *Regum expositiones*, lib. 1, cap. 1, n. 5; PL, 79, 25.

[172] Cf. Peter Chrysologus, *Serm. 140*; PL, 52, 576; Maximus, Hom. 6; PL, 57, 235. On the argumentation of Dufourcq, *op. cit.*, from Maximus and some acta martyrum, cf. the critique of B. Capelle, in *Bulletin de théologie ancienne et médiévale*, Vol. 5, 1946-1947, pp. 255-256.

[173] Cf. Sedulius, *Paschale carmen*, lib. 2, lines 28-31; *C.S.E.L.*, 10, 46; Fortunatus, *Miscellanea*, lib. 8, cap. 7; PL, 88, 277, 281.

[174] Cf. Jouassard, *Le problème de la sainteté*, pp. 26-27.

elaboration evident in that era, certain fundamental and general principles baldly stated but scarcely fathomed, initial insights into the implications of divine Maternity and perfect virginity and Second Eve, all this will help legitimize the conclusion of a later theology that Mary's utter sinlessness from the first instant of her existence is a truth implicitly revealed by God and implicitly transmitted by the early Church.[175]

V

As with the first moment of Our Lady's earthly existence, so with the last, theology's quest of patristic data is initially hampered by the state of the evidence. For a discouragingly long period the problem is not that the Assumption is denied; it is rather that the final lot of Mary is apparently not discussed. In consequence, scholars have come to speak of the silence,[176] even the ignorance,[177] of the first three centuries with respect to Mary's end. In reaction, others have retorted that the silence is sheerly relative, a surface

---

[175] On the difficult problem of the patristic exegesis of Gen. 3:15, cf. L. Drewniak, *Die mariologische Deutung von Gen. III, 15 in der Väterzeit* (Breslau, 1934); also the controversy between H. Lennerz and G. M. Roschini, in *Gregorianum*, Vol. 24, 1943, pp. 347-366; Vol. 27, 1946, pp. 300-318; *Marianum*, Vol. 7, 1944, pp. 76-96; Vol. 8, 1946, pp. 293-299. Roschini's position is that there is a genuine patristic consent on a Mariological interpretation of the protoevangelium, and that Pius IX affirmed this consent in *Ineffabilis Deus*; Lennerz enters a denial on both counts. Cf. also Dominic J. Unger, O.F.M.Cap., *The First-Gospel, Genesis 3, 15* (St. Bonaventure, N. Y., 1954), pp. 90-235.

[176] M. Jugie, e.g., in his monumental *La mort et l'Assomption de la sainte Vierge* (Città del Vaticano, 1944), not only states that there is no patristic testimony on the Assumption before Nicaea, but insists that in the first five centuries there is no absolutely clear and explicit witness to the glorious Assumption as understood in Catholic theology today; cf. pp. 56, 101. This conclusion was approved by B. Altaner, *Zur Frage der Definibilität der Assumptio B.V.M.*, in *Theologische Revue*, Vol. 45, 1949, p. 135. Cf. also Enrico Recla, *Il silenzio e la dottrina dei Padri sull'Assunzione*, in *Atti del Congresso Nazionale Mariano [1947] dei Frati Minori d'Italia* (Roma, 1948), pp. 33-72.

[177] Cf. G. Jouassard, *L'Assomption corporelle de la sainte Vierge et la patristique*, in *Assomption de Marie: Bulletin de la Société française d'études mariales*, 1948 (publ. Paris, 1949), p. 102.

silence which was inevitable and is actually eloquent.177 [178]

In point of fact, both claims are justified. The early Church is silent on the destiny of Mary, in the sense that no extant document deals explicitly with that destiny until a half century after Nicaea. And if in the East we must wait until 377 before Epiphanius offers his three hypotheses on the manner of Mary's departure from this world,[179] the awakening of the West is a slower process still. Even when popular faith has been quickened, there is little evidence in the West of a theological movement to rival the homiletic productions of the East. If only because it is so surprisingly slender, the explicit witness of the West deserves to be detailed.

Explicit statements or conjectures on the final lot of Mary begin with the last quarter of the fourth century — contemporary, therefore, with Epiphanius. But the witnesses touch the problem ever so lightly, with evident uncertainty. Tychonius, a lay theologian among the Donatists, independent enough to be excommunicated by his own sect, seems to have identified Mary with the woman of Apoc. 12, and to have spoken of a "great mystery" in her regard.[180] Ambrose is more specific but equally unsatisfactory. Discussing Simeon's sword of sorrow, he dismisses the idea that Our Lady died a violent death; such a thesis has no warrant in Scripture or history.[181] But Ambrose does not tell us just how Mary did leave this life. In a remarkable passage he presents, as one hypothesis, the yearning of Mary to rise with Jesus in case she was fated to die with Him.[182] There may be an insinuation here

---

[178] Cf. O. Faller, *De priorum saeculorum silentio circa Assumptionem b. Mariae Virginis* (Romae, 1946), p. 129.

[179] Cf. Epiphanius, *Panarion*, haer. 78, cap. 23: "For either the holy Virgin died and was buried ... or she was killed ... or she remained alive ..."; *G.C.S.*, 37, 474. On the silence of Scripture, and the "extraordinary nature of the prodigy," cf. *Panarion*, haer. 78, cap. 10-11; G.C.S., 37, 461-462. For the problems involved in recapturing the thought of Epiphanius, cf. Jugie, *op. cit.*, pp. 77-81; Faller, op. cit., pp. 33-43; Altaner, in *Theologische Revue*, Vol. 44, 1948, pp. 131-133.

[180] Tychonius' view is transmitted by Cassiodorus, *Complexiones in Apocalypsin*, n. 16; *PL*, 70, 1411.

[181] Cf. Ambrose, *Expositio evangelii secundum Lucam*, lib. 2, n. 61; C.S.E.L., 32, Part 4, 74.

[182] Cf. Ambrose, *De institutione virginis*, cap. 7, n. 49; PL, 16, 333.

that the desire was not frustrated; against this conclusion is the flat statement elsewhere that Christ alone has risen once and for all.[183]

Paulinus, Bishop of Nola in Italy (✝ 431), is anxious to learn Augustine's mind on the exegesis of Simeon's prophecy; he himself, like Ambrose, is aware of no document reporting Mary's death by violence.[184] In his reply, Augustine mentions a previous letter of his own on the Lucan text; it is, regrettably, lost to us; but he does tell Paulinus that their views on the scriptural passage coincide.[185] Elsewhere, in several striking phrases, he makes it clear that Mary did die: she died after her Son; she died a virgin; she died, like Adam, in consequence of sin.[186]

Finally, however his silence may be explained, the fact remains that Jerome, who knew the local traditions of the Holy Land as well as Epiphanius, gives no indication that he is aware of any historical tradition with reference to the death of Our Lady, her grave, or an assumption.[187] Briefly, between Nicaea and Ephesus the allusions to Mary's destiny are rare and insignificant.

The first express witness in the West to a genuine assumption comes to us in an apocryphal Gospel, the *Transitus beatae Mariae* of Pseudo-Melito, which may stem from the middle of the sixth century.[188] This account is significant, in the first instance, because

---

[183] Cf. Ambrose, *De interpellatione Iob et David*, lib. 1, cap. 7, n. 25; C.S.E.L., 32, Part 2, 227.

[184] Cf. Paulinus, *Epist. 50*, n. 17-18; C.S.E.L., 29, 419-423. The same letter is contained among the letters of Augustine, *Epist.* 121, n. 17-18; C.S.E.L., 34, Part 2, 737-742.

[185] Cf. Augustine, *Epist.* 149, n. 33; C.S.E.L., 44, 378-379.

[186] Cf. Augustine, *In evangelium Ioannis*, tr. 8, n. 9; PL, 35, 1456; *De catechizandis rudibus*, cap. 22, n. 40; PL, 40, 339; *Enarratio in ps.* 34, Serm. 2, n. 3; PL, 36, 335.

[187] Cf. Altaner, in *Theologische Revue*, Vol. 44, 1948, pp. 133-134. The thesis of J. Niessen, *Die Mariologie des hl. Hieronymus* (Münster, 1913), that Jerome denies the anticipated resurrection of Mary in three passages (*Adv. Rufinum*, lib. 2, n. 5; PL, 23, 447; *Contra Ioannem Hieros.*, n. 31; PL, 23, 399; Epist. 75, n. 2; PL, 22, 687), is by no means convincing; cf. Jugie, op. cit., p. 65 and note 2.

[188] The *Transitus Mariae* literature attempts to fill up the lacunae of the canonical books on the life, death, and final lot of Mary. Perhaps the oldest is a fifth-century Syriac Transitus, which made its way into the West, probably in a Latin translation, and caused such scandal that it was listed in

it affirms unequivocally the death and burial of Mary, the reunion of her soul and body without delay, and her assumption into heaven in soul and body. It is significant, in the second place, for the developed Assumption theology which links this privilege causally with Mary's Maternity and virginity, and stresses the parallelism which ought to exist between Christ and His Mother in victory over death.[189] The account of Pseudo-Melito, like the rest of the Transitus literature, is admittedly valueless as history, as an historical report of Mary's death and corporeal assumption; under that aspect the historian is justified in dismissing it with a critical distaste. But the account is priceless nonetheless — historically and theologically. Historically, because it witnesses indisputably to the feeling of the faithful for Mary, a growing awareness of her dignity, even though we are unable to specify the full range of this awareness geographically or even to indicate its dawning. Theologically, because it postulates the Assumption on grounds that are valid not simply for piety but for scientific theology as well.

The next witness in the West is Gregory, Bishop of Tours in Gaul; the year, 590. Borrowing in all probability not from Pseudo-Melito but from a Syriac *Transitus* of the fifth century, Gregory states very artlessly:

> After this, the apostles scattered through different countries to preach the word of God. Subsequently blessed Mary finished the course of this life and was summoned from the world; and all the apostles were gathered together, each from his own area, at her home. On hearing that she was to be taken up (*assumenda*) from the world, they kept watch with her. All at once her Lord came with angels, took her soul,

---

the books proscribed by the Decretum Gelasianum at the beginning of the sixth century; cf. A. Thiel, *Epistolae Romanorum Pontificum genuinae*, Vol. 1 (Brunsbergae, 1868), p. 465. Pseudo-Melito, posing as a disciple of St. John, proposes to furnish an expurgated, decorous version; cf. A. C. Rush, *Assumption Theology* in the *Transitus Mariae*, in *The American Ecclesiastical Review*, Vol. 123, 1950, pp. 93-110, esp. 101. Jugie would date it about 550, while Faller argues for the fourth century. For the text, cf. C. Tischendorf, *Apocalypses apocryphae* (Leipzig, 1866), pp. 124-136; an English translation is given by M. R. James, *The Apocryphal New Testament* (Oxford, 1924), pp. 209-216.

[189] Cf. Pseudo-Melito, *Transitus beatae Mariae*, cap. 15, n. 2 ff.; Tischendorf, p. 134 ff.

delivered it to Michael the Archangel, and disappeared. At daybreak, however, the apostles lifted up the body together with the funeral-bed, placed it in a tomb, and kept watch over it, in readiness for the Lord's coming. And again, all at once the Lord stood by them and ordered the holy body taken up and carried on a cloud to paradise. There, reunited with the soul, it rejoices with His elect and enjoys eternity's blessings which will never end.[190]

In brief, Gregory affirms in sober fashion the death and burial of Our Lady, the assumption of her body into paradise with little delay, the reunion there of body with soul, and Mary's unending blessedness. He proposes no reasons for the privilege; the only inkling in that direction is the vague reference to the holiness of her body, and a later statement that she who was assumed into heaven was the Mother of Christ, virgin before and after His birth.[191] A formal connection, therefore, between Assumption and virginal motherhood is not made, but the suggestion seems to be there, especially if read in the light of similar apocryphal accounts. At any rate, Gregory's account influenced the development of popular belief in an anticipated resurrection of the Virgin, though it made little impression on the theologian because of the jaundiced eye which he cast on its apocryphal source. Jouassard is inclined to find Gregory's influence in some of the old Gallican Missals of the seventh and eighth centuries, e.g., the Bobbio Missal and especially the *Missale Gothicum.* Moreover, a friend of Gregory, St. Fortunatus, a native of Treviso who[192] became Bishop of Poitiers in Gaul about 595, celebrated Mary's queenship in verse; her triumph in glory is clear; not so her glorious Assumption in body as well as soul.[193]

---

[190] Gregory of Tours, *Lib. 1 miraculorum: In gloria martyrum*, cap. 4; PL, 71, 708. For the date, cf. W. C. McDermott, *Gregory of Tours: Selections from the Minor Works* (Philadelphia, 1949), p. 9. For the extant epilogue of the fifth-century Syriac *Transitus*, which Jugie regards as the oldest of the accounts, cf. W. Wright, Contributions to the Apocryphal Literature of the New Testament (London, 1865), p. 46 f. Jugie and Altaner both believe it likely that Gregory borrowed from this work, in an early Latin translation.

[191] Cf. Gregory, *op. cit.*, cap. 9; PL, 71, 713.

[192] Cf. Jouassard, *L'Assomption corporelle, pp. 111-112.*

[193] "Cuius honore sacro, genitrix, transcendis Olympum,
Et super astrigeros erigis ora polos.
Conderis in solio felix regina superbo,

In the seventh century, only Isidore, Archbishop of Seville in Spain († 636), breaks the silence, but simply to attest our profound ignorance on the way Mary left this earth. "Some affirm that she quit this life by suffering a cruel, violent death. Their reason is that Simeon ... said: 'And thy own soul a sword shall pierce.' As a matter of fact, we do not know whether he was speaking of a material sword or of God's word that is powerful and keener than any two-edged sword (Hebr. 4:12). The point is, however, that no narrative informs us that Mary was slain by the punishment of the sword, seeing that nowhere is there an account even of her death! Some do say, though, that her tomb is to be found in the Valley of Josaphat."[194] Isidore echoes Ambrose: we have no evidence that Mary died a martyr. He echoes Epiphanius too: we have no information at all about her death. We learn from Isidore that the thesis of Mary's martyrdom still persists; we learn, too, of the Jerusalem tradition on her tomb — a tradition which leaves him quite unmoved. We learn nothing about the Assumption.

A century later, the English Bede confesses his ignorance of the final disposition of Mary's body. He has read the account given by Adamnam, Iona's Abbot, of the pilgrimage undertaken by the French Bishop, Arculf, between 670 and 685.[195] He reproduces therefrom the data on the reputed death of Mary on Mt. Sion, and the empty tomb in the Valley of Josaphat, "in which holy Mary is said to have rested for a while; but who took her away, or when, we do not know."[196] Bede shows no awareness of an anticipated

---

Cingeris et niveis lactea virgo choris.
Nobile nobilior circumsistente senatu,
Consulibus celsis celsior ipsa sedes.
Sic iuxta genitum regem regina perennem,
Ornata ex partu, mater opima, tuo."
The lines are found in *Miscellanea*, lib. 3, cap. 7; PL, 88, 282; the poem belongs to the series of those written before 576; there is some doubt whether these lines were really composed by Fortunatus, but cf. H. Weisweiler, in Scholastik, Vol. 28, 1953, p. 520.

[194] Isidore, *De ortu et obitu patrum*, cap. 67, n. 112; *PL*, 83, 148-149. A later redaction presents the existence of the Jerusalem tomb as absolutely certain; cf. *PL*, 83, 1285-1286.

[195] Cf. Adamnan, *De locis sacris*, lib. 1, cap. 12; C.S.E.L., 39, 240-241.

[196] Cf. Bede, Liber de locis sanctis, cap. 2 and 5; C.S.E.L., 39, 306, 309-310.

resurrection. He may well have heard of it; after all, he was familiar with Pseudo-Melito. But he attacks this apocryphal work in sharp tones. Not, it is true, on the score of the Assumption; but his general criticism could hardly have encouraged in his readers any sort of confidence in Pseudo-Melito, even on the theological level.[197]

With this patristic background it will not be surprising to find the first orators of the feast of August 15 in the West — Paul the Deacon, for example — consistently wary of pronouncing on Mary's corporeal resurrection; a far cry from Pseudo-Modestus of Jerusalem, Germanus of Constantinople, Andrew of Crete, and John of Damascus.[198] It will not be surprising to find in Spain, at the close of the eighth century, some Asturians directly denying Mary's Assumption — the first to do so, as far as the evidence goes.[199] It will not be surprising to see develop in the ninth century, beside the tradition favorable to the Assumption represented by Pseudo-Augustine, another current of thought represented by Pseudo-Jerome and hostile, if not to the doctrine, at least to an unequivocal affirmation of the doctrine as somehow binding.[200] For the silence of the first three centuries has been broken in the West only by unambiguous affirmations which have the disadvantage of being tagged as apocryphal, or by genuinely patristic affirmations which reveal a regrettable indifference, uncertainty, or ignorance.

On the other hand, the silence is a relative thing and rather eloquent. Faller has undertaken to show that the early reticence is

---

[197] Cf. Bede, *Liber retractationis in Actus apostolorum*, cap. 8; PL, 92, 1014-1015. On the three Marian homilies falsely attributed to Bede, cf. Jugie, *op. cit.*, p. 272, note 2.

[198] Cf. Jugie, *op. cit.*, pp. 272-274.

[199] Cf. The correspondence between Bishop Ascarius and his friend, Tuscaredus; PL, 99, 1233, 1235. The Asturians in question insisted that Mary had died like anyone else, and that her body was still in the tomb awaiting the glorious resurrection. The thesis scandalized Ascarius; Tuscaredus replied that we have no evidence of a violent death, or of any death for that matter. It would seem that Tuscaredus believed in Mary's glorious immortality.

[200] Cf. Pseudo-Jerome, *Epist. 9: Ad Paulam et Eustochium de assumptione B.V.M.*, n. 2; PL, 30, 127-128; Pseudo-Augustine, *De assumptione B.V.M.*, n. 2-9; PL, 40, 1143-1148. On the problem of authorship, cf. Jugie, *op. cit.*, pp. 278, 290-291.

perfectly understandable, seeing that several more fundamental facets of Christian belief, such as the Trinity and Christology, had first to be confronted, before Mariology could claim attention.[201] Cayré, too, has indicated how the initial silence with respect to Mary is normal rather than surprising, for it goes back to her role in the early Church: "Her vocation was not to command, but to love and to pray, two functions that call for silence. ..."[202] The silence in question, theologians insist, does not reflect an absence of life; the life, the doctrine, is there in germ. The seed is discoverable in the patristic thesis of recapitulation, the Eve-Mary parallelism proposed by Justin, Irenaeus, Tertullian, and Ambrose, the analogy which associates the New Eve with the New Adam in a total triumph over Satan.[203] The seed is there in the twin privileges of divine motherhood and deathless virginity. Insight into these mysteries would lead to increasing reverence for the sacredness of the body which knew only God, to a realization that this body could not fittingly know corruption.[204]

These and other seeds of an Assumption doctrine are discoverable in Western patristic thought, but it would be sheer unsupported theorizing to suppose that the patristic West recognized the seeds for what they were. As the age of the Fathers draws to a close, the West is on the point of confronting the problem of Mary's destiny on theological grounds. On this score the task of theological elaboration has not kept pace with the Eastern development. What Jouassard has concluded of the patristic world as a whole, must surely be said of the West:

> In these conditions we shall not ask patristic thought — as some theologians still do today under one form or another — to transmit to us, with respect to the Assumption, a truth received as such in the beginning and faithfully communicated to subsequent ages. Such an

---

[201] Cf. Faller, *op. cit.*, pp. 69-76.

[202] Cf. F. Cayré, *L'Assomption aux quatre premiers siècles: Etat embryonnaire de la doctrine*, in *Studia Mariana*, Vol. 4: *Vers le dogme de l'Assomption* (Montréal, 1948), p. 135 ff.

[203] Cf. C. F. *De Vine, The Fathers of the Church and the Assumption*, in *Vers le dogme de l'Assomption*, pp. 408-410.

[204] Faller has developed these and other principles at length; cf. *op. cit.*, pp. 77-128.

attitude would not fit the facts. ... Patristic thought has not, in this instance, played the role of a sheer instrument of transmission; rather has it been the precious agent of a task that has enlisted the cooperation of all manner of people — authentic theologians, and individuals too who cannot claim that title. Both have played their part in harmony with the capacity of each; they will continue to play it in the years to come. ...[205]

* * *

Not a few aspects of Marian theology with seeds in the early Christian West have inevitably been omitted from these pages. There is, for example, the complex, intriguing problem of the relationship between Mary and the Church; here it is Justin and Irenaeus and Tertullian, Ambrose and Augustine, who have had the initial significant insights.[206] There is the lovely concept of Mary's Queenship, exercised not by jurisdiction but by intercession.[207] There is the idea of Mary's universal Mediation, rooted in her

---

[205] Jouassard, *L'Assomption corporelle*, pp. 115-116. A word of caution is not impertinent here. The investigation of patristic documents might well lead the historian to the conclusion: In the first seven or eight centuries no trustworthy historical tradition on Mary's corporeal Assumption is extant, especially in the West. The conclusion is legitimate; if the historian stops there, few theological nerves will be touched. The historian's mistake would come in adding: therefore no proof from tradition can be adduced. The historical method is not the theological method, nor is historical tradition synonymous with dogmatic tradition. Cf. W. J. Burghardt, *The Catholic Concept of Tradition in the Light of Modern Theological Thought*, in *Proceedings of the Sixth Annual Convention* (Catholic Theological Society of America, 1951), pp. 73-75. It is not true to say, with V. Bennett, that tradition "is but another name for the historical evidence of what the Church taught and believed in other ages"; *The Assumption: A Postscript*, in *Theology*, Vol. 54, 1951, p. 410.

[206] Cf. A. Müller, *Ecclesia-Maria: Die Einheit Marias und der Kirche* (Fribourg, 1951); G. Montague, *The Concept of Mary and the Church in the Fathers*, in *The American Ecclesiastical Review*, Vol. 123, 1950, pp. 331-337; K. Delehaye, *Maria, Typus der Kirche*, in *Wissenschaft und Weisheit*, Vol. 12, 1949, pp. 79-92.

[207] Cf. H. Barré, *La royauté de Marie pendant les neuf premiers siècles*, in *Recherches de science religieuse*, Vol. 29, 1939, 129-162, 303-334; A. Luis, *La realeza de María* (Madrid, 1942); M. J. Donnelly, *The Queenship of Mary during the Patristic Period*, in *Marian Studies*, Vol. 4, 1953, pp. 82-108.

function as Second Eve and suggested so vividly by Ambrose.[208] There is much more, but perhaps enough has been said in this study to insinuate that the treasures of patristic Mariology are not the legitimate plaything of aprioristic speculation, nor will they reveal themselves in their totality to unaided historical analysis. The thought of the Fathers on Our Lady will be mined in its purity only by theologians with a feeling for philology, and by philologists deeply rooted in theology.

---

[208] Cf. the articles of Bover cited in footnote 16.

Mary in Eastern Patristic Thought

By Walter J. Burghardt, S.J., S.T.D.

I. THE NEW EVE

N A recent study of Our Lady in early Western thought, it was suggested that the primordial patristic insight with respect to the Mother of Christ was the vision of Mary as the New Eve.[1] If we turn to the East, the same pregnant Eve-Mary parallelism reveals three stages of development: (*a*) the remote origins before Nicaea; (*b*) the startling enthusiasm of Ephraem; and (*c*) the full flowering of the patristic vision in the homiletic literature of the fifth century.

It is possible that the remote origins of the parallelism may be traced as far back as Papias, Bishop of Hierapolis in Asia Minor, at the turn of the first century.[2] Papias' use of an Eve-Mary analogy, however, is admittedly conjectural and its content is at best insignificant. The passage in question occurs in a fragment of Victorinus of Pettau,[3] which Dom Chapman recognized as "probably dependent on Papias, perhaps verbally."[4] The pertinent text, in a section where the seven days of creation are paralleled by seven days of redemptive activity, simply states that "the Angel Gabriel brought the good tidings to Mary on the day whereon the dragon seduced Eve."

If the passage derives from Papias, it may well be the inspiration for the more developed idea of Justin Martyr in Ephesus a half century later:

[The Son of God] became man through the Virgin, that the

---

[1] Cf. W. J. Burghardt, S.J., *Mary in Western Patristic Thought*, p. 122.

[2] On the evidence of Irenaeus and Eusebius, E. Gutwenger, *Papias: Eine chronologische Studie*, in *Zeitschrift für katholische Theologie*, Vol. 69, 1947, p. 416, dates Papias before 110, and his floruit while Clement of Rome was still alive.

[3] Victorinus of Pettau, *De fabrica mundi*, n. 9; C.S.E.L., 49, 8.

[4] J. Chapman, *Papias on the Age of Our Lord*, in *Journal of Theological Studies*, Vol. 9, 1907-1908, p. 42.

disobedience caused by the serpent might be destroyed in the same way in which it had originated. For Eve, while a virgin incorrupt, conceived the word which proceeded from the serpent, and brought forth disobedience and death. But the Virgin Mary was filled with faith and joy when the Angel Gabriel told her the glad tidings that the Spirit of the Lord would come upon her ... and she answered: "Be it done unto me according to thy word." And through her was He born ... by whom God destroys both the serpent and the angels and men who have become like the serpent, and delivers from death those who repent of their wickedness and believe in Him.[5]

Justin does little more than enunciate the parallelism. The pattern of man's redemption paralleled his fall: both were effected through the agency of a virgin. He leaves us to conclude that the consequences of Mary's co-operation with God contrasted sharply with the effects of Eve's seduction by Satan: Mary's issue, inferentially, is obedience and life. The nature of Our Lady's redemptive role is of no concern to him; his thought is focused not on Mary but on Christ.

It is in Irenaeus, who knew and used Papias' work and may have developed what he discovered in Justin,[6] that we find the Eve-Mary analogy integrated for the first time with a theology.

Just as Eve, wife of Adam yes, yet still a virgin ... became by her disobedience the cause of death for herself and the whole human race, so Mary too, espoused yet a virgin, became by her obedience the cause of salvation for herself and the whole human race. And this is why the Law calls her who was espoused to a man the wife of him who had

---

[5] Justin, *Dialogus cum Tryphone*, cap. 100; *PG*, 6, 709-712. I have already dealt with Justin in Mary in *Western Patristic Thought*, pp. 122-123, because the Dialogue was apparently composed in Rome. The two-day discussion, however (to the extent that it is historical), took place probably at Ephesus (cf. Eusebius, Hist. eccl., lib. 4, cap. 18, 6; *G.C.S.*, 9/1, 364) during the war of Bar-Cocheba (132-135), and so may be evidence of the Asia Minor aspect of the Eve-Mary tradition.

[6] As Chapman has observed, "Irenaeus may have elaborated what he found in Justin, or we may simply say that it was already a preacher's commonplace, or we may think that both used a common source"; art. cit., p. 51. I have treated Irenaeus at some length in Mary in Western Patristic Thought, p. 111 ff., because the passages in question stem from his literary activity in Lyons. There is no reason, however, for excluding an awareness of the Eve-Mary analogy from his earlier, Asia Minor period.

espoused her, though she was still a virgin: to show the cycle that goes back (recirculationem) from Mary to Eve. The point is, what is tied together cannot possibly be untied save by inversion of the process whereby the bonds of union have arisen, so that the original ties are loosed by the subsequent, and the subsequent set the original free. ... And so it was that the knot of Eve's disobedience was loosed by Mary's obedience. For what the virgin Eve bound fast by her refusal to believe, this the Virgin Mary unbound by her belief.[7]

In Irenaeus' theology, Mary as the Second Eve has a distinctive function in God's design for man's redemption. The co-operation of the first Eve with Satan in effecting man's spiritual death is matched and outstripped by Mary's co-operation with God in effecting man's return to life. The co-operation in question is not a sheerly negative thing, as though the parallelism began and ended on the level of virginity. It is not an exclusively physical thing, as though Mary's role opened and closed with the bare fact of divine motherhood. Her co-operation involves activity of the moral order: she gave Gabriel and God a free consent. Her obedience was not compelled; with eyes open and will unfettered she placed herself at God's disposal for the accomplishment of His designs. That consent, moreover, has a soteriological character: its term was not simply an Incarnation, but an Incarnation recognized as redemptive.

The evidence suggests that the Eve-Mary analogy, destined to be the leitmotif of later Byzantine Mariology, arose in Asia Minor, and that its chief center was the Christian community in and around Ephesus. For it was in Ephesus that Justin was educated, was converted, and debated with Tryphon; it was in Ephesus-centered circles that the young Irenaeus came in contact with Polycarp, the most significant influence on his theology.

Strangely enough, the Second Eve idea did not play a

---

[7] Irenaeus, *Adversus haereses*, lib. 3, cap. 32, 1 (Massuet, 3, 22, 4); ed. W. W. Harvey (Cantabrigiae, 1857), Vol. 2, 123-124; *PG*, 7, 958-959. Cf. also *ibid.*, lib. 5, cap. 19, 1; Harvey, 2, 375-376; *PG*, 7, 1175-1176. Essentially the same ideas are present in Irenaeus' *Demonstratio apostolicae praedicationis*, cap. 33; *Patrologia Orientalis*, Vol. 12, 684-685; cf. the careful translation from the Armenian by J. P. Smith, in Ancient Christian Writers, Vol. 16 (Westminster, Md., 1952), 69. For the underlying theory of recapitulation, cf. A. d'Alès, *La doctrine de la récapitulation en saint Irénée*, in *Recherches de Science Religieuse*, Vol. 6, 1916, pp. 185-211.

conspicuous role in the theology of the early Alexandrians.[8] After Irenaeus a century and a half was to elapse before Eastern Christianity would make capital of the analogy in the Syrian Church. In 337 the Persian Aphraates, who is theologically exciting if only because he is representative of a Christianity virtually uninfluenced by the Council of Nicaea, reminded his flock that it was through a woman that the devil won access to men, and continued:

> It was because of her that the curse of the law was decreed; it was because of her that the promise of death was made; for in sorrows she gives birth to children and gives them over to death. It was because of her that the earth was cursed, to bring forth thorns and thistles. From this time forth, however, through the coming of the blessed Mary's child, the thorns have been uprooted, ... the curse has been fixed on a cross, the sword's point has been removed from before the tree of

---

[8] There are three fragments in which Origen alludes to it: (1) In Lucam hom. 7; G.C.S., 35, 48: Origen seems to mean that Mary, in giving birth to Christ, restored to womankind the honor it had lost through Eve's sin; in this way woman "finds salvation in childbearing" (1 Tim. 2:15). (2) *In Lucam hom. 6*; G.C.S., 35, 40: the joy trumpeted by Gabriel to Mary ("the Lord is with thee") destroys the sentence of sorrow leveled by God against Eve ("in sorrow wilt thou bring forth"). (3) *In Lucam hom. 8*; G.C.S., 35, 54-55: Origen supposes the traditional idea of a parallelism between fall and redemption: "Just as sin began with the woman and then reached the man, so too the good tidings had their beginning with the women [Elizabeth and Mary]. ..." On this last text three points merit attention: (*a*) Jerome's translation, principium salutis (PG, 13, 1819), must be tempered by the simple τα αγαθά of the catena (*G.C.S.*, 35, 55) and the corresponding bona of Ambrose (C.S.E.L., 33, 56). (*b*) Origen is concerned not merely with Mary but with her cousin Elizabeth as well. It is misleading to say, as I. Ortiz de Urbina does in his article, *Lo sviluppo della Mariologia nella Patrologia Orientale*, in *Orientalia Christiana Periodica*, Vol. 6, 1940, p. 57, that for Origen salvation had its beginning "in una donna." The inaccuracy is repeated in his more recent *Die Marienkunde in der Patristik des Ostens*, in P. Sträter, ed., *Katholische Marienkunde, Vol. 1, Maria in der Offenbarung* (Paderborn, 1947), p. 100: "in einer Frau." (*c*) Origen does not attribute to Mary and Elizabeth the same active role in the economy of salvation which he assigns to Eve in the economy of sin; the "good things" in the context may be no more than the grace of prophecy given Mary and Elizabeth at the outset of the new order of things. On these texts and their authenticity, cf. C. Vagaggini, *Maria nelle opere di Origene* (Roma, 1942), pp. 110-113.

life, [which] is given as food to believers.[9]

But among the Eastern writers it is Ephraem, the most significant author of the Syrian Church, who is incomparably sensitive to the implications of the Eve-Mary analogy. As he sees it, the parallelism is at the root of man's dignity: man's "lovely and lovable glory was lost through Eve, was restored through Mary."[10] It is the crux of immortality; for, of the two historic virgins given to humankind, "one was cause of life, the other was cause of death. Through Eve death arose, and life by means of Mary."[11] Around it the problem of sin revolves; for it was reserved for Mary to pay Eve's debt to sin, the debt whereby her posterity was doomed to death.[12] Because Our Lady was blessed among women, it is through her, and specifically through her virginal childbearing, that the primordial curse against woman has been lifted.[13] She is the woman

---

[9] Aphraates, *Demonstratio 6: De monachis*, n. 6; *Patrologia Syriaca*, Part 1, Tom. 1, col. 265. The parallelism implies that it was through Mary that life found access to men; Aphraates, however, limits Our Lady's role to her childbearing. The ideas and language are similar to a sentence in Ephraem: "[Eve] saw him who trembled and was an exile because of the curse on the earth; [Mary] saw Him who removed the curse and fixed it with nails on the wood of a cross." *Explanatio evangelii concordantis*, cap. 2, n. 2; ed. L. Leloir, *C.S.C.O.*, Vol. 137, *Scriptores armeniaci*, Tom. 1 (Louvain, 1953), p. 24; Latin tr., Leloir, *C.S.C.O.*, Vol. 145, *Scr. arm.*, Tom. 2 (Louvain, 1954), p. 17.

[10] Ephraem, *Sermones exegetici; Opera omnia syriace et latine*, Vol. 2 (Romae, 1740), 318.

[11] Ephraem, *Hymni de beata Maria*, 2, n. 8; Lamy, Vol. 2, 525. Some doubt attaches to the authenticity of these hymns. Cf., in the same vein, the indisputably authentic Sermo de domino nostro, n. 3; Lamy, 1, 153, 155: Eve, mother of all the living, became the source of death for all the living; but something new sprouted, "Mary, a new plant, in place of Eve, the old vine, and in her dwelt the new Life" that is destructive of death. Cf. also De diversis sermonibus, 3: *De laudibus Dei genitricis Mariae; Opera omnia syriace et latine*, Vol. 3 (Romae, 1743), 607. The aspect of virginity is stressed again in *Hymni de instauratione ecclesiae*, 5, 23; Lamy, 3, 985: "Two virgins there were, but of these two quite different was the deed. One was the destruction of her husband, the other the support of her father. Through Eve man found a tomb; through Mary he was called to heaven."

[12] Cr. Ephraem, *Hymni de beata Maria*, 18, nn. 24-26; Lamy, Vol. 2, 611-613. Cf. also *Hymni de beata Maria*, 9, n. 4; Lamy, Vol. 2, 549.

[13] Cf. Ephraem, *Explanatio evangelii concordantis*, cap. 2, n. 6; *C.S.C.O.*, Vol. 137, 26-27 (Armenian); Vol. 145, 19-20 (Latin).

promised in paradise: "It was the serpent who struck the heel of Eve; it was the foot of Mary that trampled the serpent underfoot."[14] Although Ephraem's Mariology, bold and prolific as it was, exercised no perceptible influence on contemporary theology,[15] the Eve-Mary motif is discoverable in fourth century Jerusalem, Salamis, Nyssa, Iconium, and Antioch. In 348, for example, Cyril, Bishop of Jerusalem, preached the parallelism to his catechumens: "It was through the virgin Eve that death came; it was through a virgin, or rather from a virgin, that life had to come to light — that, just as a serpent deceived the former, so Gabriel might bring glad tidings to the latter."[16] Thirty years later Epiphanius, Bishop of Salamis, saw Mary signified in Eve: it is Our Lady who is "mother of the living" in its more profound meaning, because in obedience to grace she gave birth to Him who lives, to Life itself, the Lamb of whose glory, as of fleece, a garment of immortality has been fashioned for us. "Eve had become cause ($\pi\rho\acute{o}\varphi\alpha\sigma\iota\varsigma$) of death for men, for through her 'death came into the world' (Rom. 5:12); but Mary was cause ($\pi\rho\acute{o}\varphi\alpha\sigma\iota\varsigma$) of life: through her, life has been born to us."[17]

In a passage which may stem from Gregory, Bishop of Nyssa, Gabriel's greeting to Mary is found in striking contrast with God's primitive address to Eve. The Annunciation has transformed childbearing: "In Eve's case, birth's prelude was sorrow; with Mary, birth's midwife is joy."[18] More impressive still is the vision which

---

[14] Ephraem, *Explanatio ...*, cap. 10, n. 13; C.S.C.O., Vol. 137, 140 (Arm.); Vol. 145, 101 (Latin). Cf. also *Hymni de nativitate Christi in carne*, 2, n. 31; Lamy, Vol. 2, 457. Similar ideas are discoverable in the Syrian poet, Cyrillonas; ed. G. Bickell, in *Zeitschrift der Deutschen Morgenländischen Gesellschaft*, Vol. 27, 1873, pp. 591-592; Italian tr. by I. Ortiz de Urbina, *La mariologia nei Padri siriaci*, in *Orientalia Christiana Periodica*, Vol. 1, 1935, p. 111.

[15] Cf. L. Hammersberger, *Die Mariologie der ephremischen Schriften* (Wien, 1938), p. 87.

[16] Cyril of Jerusalem, *Catecheses*, 12, 15; PG, 33, 741.

[17] Epiphanius, *Panarion*, haer. 78, n. 18; G.C.S., 37, 468-469.

[18] *In diem natalem Christi*; PG, 46, 1140. Gregory's authorship is disputed; cf. summary of arguments pro and con in G. Söll, *Die Mariologie der Kappadozier im Licht der Dogmengeschichte*, in *Theologische Quartalschrift*, Vol. 131, 1951, pp. 185-188. Söll finds the style and content in harmony with Gregory's genuine works. Testimony in favor of authenticity is a rather

links the New Eve with the New Adam:

> Through man [came] death, and through man salvation. The first man fell into sin; the second raised up the fallen. Woman has spoken in behalf of woman. The first woman gave entrance to sin; this woman helped justice enter in. The former followed the serpent's counsel; the latter presented the serpent's destroyer and brought forth the author of light. The former introduced sin through the wood; through the wood the latter introduced blessing instead. By the wood I mean the cross; and the fruit of this wood becomes life ever green and imperishable for those who taste of it.[19]

The same line of thought is suggested by Amphilochius, Bishop of Iconium, who was linked to the three Cappadocians by personal and theological ties: "The world has been set free through a virgin — the world that of old fell subject to sin through that other virgin. It is through a virginal birth that so many and such horrible herds of demons have been hurled into hell."[20] And, in a passage designed to demonstrate that the instruments of our condemnation have become the instruments of our glory, Chrysostom remarked pithily from Antioch: "A virgin cast us from paradise; through a virgin we have found life eternal."[21]

---

lengthy citation, in a letter of Severus of Antioch, from "Gregory ... the brother of Basil the great, and bishop of Nyssa"; *Patrologia Orientalis*, Vol. 14, 82-85.

[19] *In diem natalem Christi; PG*, 46, 1148.

[20] Amphilochius, *Oratio 1: In Christi natalem*, n. 4; PG, 39, 40-41.

[21] John Chrysostom, *Expositio in ps. 44*, n. 7; PG, 55, 193. In a homily on the birthday of Christ (*In Christi nativitatem oratio; PG*, 56, 392-393: among the works of Chrysostom), the author says: "Of old the devil deceived Eve, who was a virgin; for this reason Gabriel brought good tidings to Mary, who was a virgin. But when Eve was deceived, she brought forth a word that was cause (αἴτιον) of death; when the glad tidings were brought to Mary, she gave birth in flesh to the Word, the author (πρόξενον) for us of life eternal. Eve's word made known the wood, through which it cast Adam from paradise; but the Word from the Virgin made known the cross, through which He brought the robber into paradise in place of Adam." The homily was published in 1883, under the name of *Gregory the Wonder-Worker*, by J. P. Martin in Pitra's *Analecta sacra*, Vol. 4, 134-144 (Armenian), 386-396 (Latin). As known in the Armenian version, Gregory's authorship was rejected by Harnack, upheld by Loofs, Neubert, and Jugie; cf. *Analecta Bollandiana*, Vol. 43, 1925, p. 94. In *Revue d'Histoire Ecclésiastique*, Vol. 24/1, 1928, pp. 364-373, Ch. Martin pointed out that the Greek text could be read

It is justifiable to conclude that in the fourth century the concept of Our Lady as the counterpart of Eve had been incorporated into the soteriology of the Syrian Church and had become a commonplace in the theology of the Greek-speaking world.

It was the fifth century, however, that witnessed the proliferation of the Eve-Mary parallelism in the Greek Church. Here the significant documents are homilies, particularly on the Annunciation, the Incarnation, and the divine motherhood. The primary influences on these homilies are the primitive Marian feast and the Nestorian controversy. And in the homilies impressive segments of the Greek Church make their voices heard: Egypt through Cyril of Alexandria, Thrace through Proclus of Constantinople, Galatia through Theodotus of Ancyra, Arabia through Antipater of Bostra, and Palestine through Hesychius and Chrysippus of Jerusalem.[22]

Cyril of Alexandria remarks that the Son of God was born of a woman to destroy the curse leveled at the first woman: "in sorrow shalt thou bear children." In consequence of the fact that Mary gave birth to Emmanuel in flesh, to Him who is Life, the power of the curse was destroyed: "woman no longer gives birth unto death, no

---

in *PG*, 56, 385-394, and that from the beginning of the fifth century it passed for an authentic work of Chrysostom. He insisted that, in view of the Greek MS tradition, the clarity and preciseness of its theological formulations, the Antiochene tendency of its Christology, and the absence of anti-Sabellian preoccupation in its trinitarian theology, the homily cannot be attributed to Gregory. Martin placed it in Antiochene circles of the fourth century and was impressed by Cyril of Alexandria's citations of it as from Gregory. In 1940 B. Marx assigned the homily to Proclus of Constantinople. A year later Martin showed that we are justified in regarding it as an authentic work of Chrysostom; cf. *Le Muséon*, Vol. 54, 1941, pp. 30-33.

[22] In an important article, *Le omelie mariane nei Padri Greci del V secolo*, in *Marianum*, Vol. 8, 1946, pp. 201-234, Dino del Fabbro has synthesized the results of contemporary research on the authenticity of the Marian homilies emanating from the fifth-century Greek Church. He concludes that a solid, sufficient basis for the Mariological doctrine of that century is provided by five strictly Marian sermons, fourteen on Christ's birth or the Incarnation, one on the Hypapante, and one on the birth of the Baptist.

longer in sorrow."[23] Proclus, who became second successor to Nestorius as Patriarch of Constantinople, and with his celebrated Marian sermon of 429 was one of the first to oppose Nestorius' errors, concentrates rather on the theme of sin and salvation, disobedience and obedience. In His birth Christ "made gate of salvation her who of old was door of sin."[24] Theodotus of Ancyra in Asia Minor, closely linked to Cyril by his anti-Nestorian activity, and to Proclus by his Mariology, compares "the virgin of old" with "the second virgin."[25] And in his Homily 6, which ranks with the better productions of Greek homiletics, he speaks beautifully of the Eve-Mary parallelism in terms of death and life, sorrow and joy, condemnation and redemption:

> In place of the virgin Eve, who had ministered to death, a virgin was graced by God and chosen to minister life. ... This woman, worthy of her Creator, divine providence has given us as procurer of blessings, not provoking to disobedience but showing the way to obedience ... not holding out death-bringing fruit but offering life-giving bread. ... It is not [Gabriel says] conception in iniquities or conception in sins that I shall announce to you; it is rather joy that I shall expound to you, joy that softens the sorrow which stems from Eve. It is not a painful pregnancy or a mournful birth that I announce; it is rather a consoling, gladdening birth that I foretell. ... I proclaim

---

[23] Cyril of Alexandria, *Comm. in Lucam, hom. 2*; ed. I. B. Chabot, *C.S.C.O.*, Vol. 70, *Scriptores syri 27* (Louvain, 1954), 11-12 (Syriac); Latin tr., R. M. Tonneau, *C.S.C.O.*, Vol. 140, Scriptores syri 70 (Louvain, 1953), 3.

[24] Proclus, *Oratio 1: Laudatio in sanctissimam Dei genitricem Mariam*, n. 1; ed. E. Schwartz, *Acta conciliorum oecumenicorum*, Tom. 1, Vol. 1, Part 1 (Berolini et Lipsiae, 1927-1930), 103; *PG*, 65, 681. Cf. also *Oratio 5: Laudatio in sanctam virginem ac Dei genitricem Mariam*, n. 3; *PG*, 65, 720: We greet Mary as blessed among women because she alone has "healed Eve's sorrow," wiped away her tears, carried the world's ransom, given birth to Emmanuel without suffering. J. Lebon sees in *Oratio 5* a sermon of Atticus of Constantinople, with the collaboration of Proclus; cf. *Le Muséon*, Vol. 46, 1933, p. 174. Ortiz de Urbina suggests that in the Syriac version we have two homilies, the first by Proclus, the second by Atticus; cf. *Orientalia Christiana Periodica*, Vol. 6, 1940, p. 64, note 1. Along the same lines, cf. the solution of del Fabbro, *art. cit.*, p. 215: the first homily, which corresponds to the Greek *Oratio 5*, has Proclus for author; the second, which comprises the remaining section *De nativitate*, has Atticus for author, in collaboration with Proclus.

[25] Theodotus, Hom. 4: *In sanctam deiparam et in Simeonem*, n. 5; *PG*, 77, 1396. For the authenticity of this homily, cf. del Fabbro, *art. cit.*, p. 220.

the rising of the light that illumines the world. For through you the horrid sorrows of Eve have ceased; through you the shabby and the paltry have perished; through you error is vanished; through you sorrow is set at nought; through you the condemnation is cancelled. Eve has been redeemed through you.[26]

Antipater, Metropolitan of Bostra in Arabia, continues the tradition when he reflects that Gabriel's greeting to Mary, "Hail, full of grace," is the counterpart of God's declaration to Eve, "In sorrow shalt thou bear children." Eve's sorrow in childbearing is destroyed by Mary's joy.[27] More importantly, God's object in the Incarnation was "that he who in the beginning was overthrown through Eve might himself be saved through the conception of the Virgin."[28] Hesychius, a priest of Jerusalem in the first half of the fifth century, likewise insists that the "second virgin" drove away at the Annunciation the oppressive sorrow which surrounded childbearing in consequence of the sentence passed on the "first virgin."[29] Mary is "our nature's noble ornament, the boast of our clay, who set Eve free from her shame, Adam from the threat, and cut off the devil's boldness. ..."[30] From Jerusalem too, Chrysippus, a rather remarkable writer, pictures the devil faced with the realization that through a woman we have been called to the adoptive sonship that was primitively ours:

> How can it be [Satan asks himself] that the vessel which was originally my accomplice is now my adversary? A woman helped make me despot of the human race, and a woman deposed me from my despotic rule. The ancient Eve raised me up; the new Eve cast me down. For the current Eve is indeed Eve by nature, though not Eve in

---

[26] Theodotus, *In sanctam Mariam Dei genitricem et in sanctam Christi nativitatem*, nn. 11-12; *Patrologia Orientalis*, Vol. 19, 329-331. Its editor, M. Jugie, considers the authenticity of this homily unimpeachable; cf. pp. 292-293. Cf. also Nilus of Ancyra, *Epistolae*, lib. 1, ep. 267; PG, 79, 180-181; the inspiration here derives from Epiphanius.

[27] Antipater, *In sanctissimam deiparae annuntiationem*, n. 3; *PG*, 85, 1777. Despite the attribution of passages of this homily to other authors (Origen, Eudoxius the Arian), del Fabbro believes it a genuine work of Antipater; cf. *art. cit.*, pp. 221-225.

[28] Antipater, *op. cit.*, n. 10; *PG*, 85, 1781.

[29] Hesychius, *Sermo 4: De sancta Maria deipara*; PG, 93, 1453.

[30] Hesychius, Sermo 5: De sancta Maria deipara; PG, 93, 1465.

engendering. ... As is fitting ... through her have I been taken captive through whom I took captives; through her have I been conquered through whom I conquered. ... Of all these [miracles performed by Christ, the cross, resurrection of Christ and of the dead] who is the cause ($\alpha\grave{\iota}\tau\acute{\iota}\alpha$)? Who else save her who gave birth to Him who performed these wonders? It were better for me, after all, had I not deceived her through the serpent.[31]

The insights of Irenaeus, Ephraem, and the fifth-century homilists will be continued, without being significandy furthered, in the period of patristic decline: in Anastasius I, Patriarch of Antioch in the latter half of the sixth century;[32] in three Greek homilies on the Annunciation falsely ascribed to Gregory the Wonder-Worker;[33] in a seventh-century homiletic masterpiece on the Mother of God that has traveled illegally under the protection of Epiphanius;[34] in the anti-Monothelite Patriarch of Jerusalem, Sophronius;[35] and, at the setting of the patristic age, in a passage of John Damascene which supplies a splendid epitome of the past:

Dear daughter worthy of God, human nature's beauty, our first

---

[31] Chrysippus, *In sanctam Mariam deiparam*, n. 3; *Patrologia Orientalis*, Vol. 19, 340-341. Its editor, M. Jugie, sees no reason for doubting the authenticity of this homily; cf. p. 295.

[32] Cf. Anastasius I, *Sermo 3: In laudatissimae Dei genitricis annuntiationem*, n. 2; PG, 89, 1388. Anastasius looks on Mary as the origin ($\grave{\alpha}\rho\chi\acute{\eta}$) of woman's joy.

[33] Cf. *PG*, 10, 1145-1178. *Sermo 1*, a potpourri of an author later than the fifth century (cf. Jugie, in *Analecta Bollandiana*, Vol. 43, 1925, p. 90), insists that "in the holy Virgin alone has Eve's fall been healed"; col. 1148. In Sermo 2, another potpourri, the author, who apparently lived after the middle of the sixth century (cf. Jugie, pp. 90-91), declares that the Word took flesh of Mary "in order that through the same flesh through which sin entered the world, through that same flesh sin might be condemned in the flesh ... and life eternal live in the world"; col. 1156; cf. col. 1157. Sermo 3 was written probably in the second half of the fifth century — in any event, before the introduction of the March 25 feast (cf. Jugie, p. 91); it preaches that "life contrived its entrance where death had made its exit"; col. 1177.

[34] Cf. Ps.-Epiphanius, *De laudibus sanctae deiparae*; PG, 43, 501. Despite points of contact with Basil of Seleucia, Proclus, and Cyril of Alexandria, del Fabbro finds the general development of the homily more akin to the Marian homilies of the seventh and succeeding centuries; cf. art. cit., p. 228.

[35] Cf. Sophronius, *Oratio 2: In sanctissimae deiparae annuntiationem*, n. 22; PG, 87c, 3241.

mother Eve's reparation! For by your childbearing she who had fallen has been lifted up again. Dear daughter most consecrate, splendor of women! For though the first Eve offended and, through her, death entered in as she served the serpent against our first father, Mary for her part, in total subjection to God's will, herself deceived the deceiver serpent and brought immortality to the world.[36]

For the historian of dogma the problem and the pertinence of all this evidence is the theological significance which the Fathers themselves attached to the Eve-Mary parallelism. On this score I submit, first, that the Christian writers of the patristic age in the East found in the analogy fresh insights primarily, if not exclusively, into the role played by Our Lady in the redemptive activity of her Son. The contrasts are constantly disobedience and obedience, sorrow and joy, woman cursed and woman blessed, a despot devil and a captive devil, darkness and light, sin and salvation, fall and restoration, condemnation and redemption, death and life, paradise lost and paradise regained.

Second, Our Lady is, in some genuine sense, responsible for the redemptive effects achieved by her Son; she co-operated in the objective Redemption. In the tradition of the patristic East the Second Eve is "cause of salvation,"[37] "gate of salvation";[38] she paid Eve's debt to sin,[39] "helped justice enter in."[40] She is "cause of life";[41] she "brought immortality to the world."[42] Through her "Eve has been redeemed";[43] through her "the world has been set free."[44] She has deposed the devil from his despotic rule;[45] she trampled Satan

---

[36] John Damascene, *Hom. 1 in nativitatem Mariae*, n. 7; *PG*, 96, 772. For a more detailed treatment of Damascene's Eve-Mary doctrine, cf. C. Chevalier, *La mariologie de saint Jean Damascene* (Rome, 1936), pp. 150-156.

[37] Irenaeus, note 7 above; cf. Antipater, note 28 above.

[38] Proclus, note 24 above.

[39] Cf. Ephraem, note 12 above.

[40] Gregory of Nyssa (?), note 19 above.

[41] Ephraem, note 11 above; Epiphanius, note 17 above; cf. Chrysostom, note 21 above; Theodotus, note 26 above.

[42] John Damascene, note 36 above.

[43] Theodotus, note 26 above.

[44] Amphilochius, note 20 above.

[45] Cf. Chrysippus, note 31 above.

underfoot;[46] through her the "demons have been hurled into hell."[47]

Third, the redemptive co-operation of the New Eve, when clarified or explicated by the Fathers themselves, is regularly reduced to the divine motherhood, to the fact that Mary gave birth to the Redeemer, that she lent consent, open-eyed and free, to an Incarnation integral to salvation.[48] Ephraem, for example, time and again assigns to Our Lady a certain causality in the task of Redemption: through her has been paid the debt signed and sealed by the serpent against all generations. How? Because of the treasure to which she has given birth; because in her the Light has arisen that scatters the darkness.[49] For Epiphanius, Our Lady is cause of life in the sense that she gave birth to Him who is Life and gives life.[50] In Amphilochius' eyes, Mary peoples hell with demons — through the Virgin Birth.[51] Cyril of Alexandria, Theodotus, Ps.-Gregory the Wonder-Worker, and others find pregnancy's sorrow transmuted into joy precisely because Mary gave birth to Emmanuel in flesh, to Life Incarnate.[52] Chrysippus stresses Mary's contrast to Eve "in engendering."[53] To Ps.-Epiphanius, it is at the Nativity that angels extol Our Lady for raising up fallen Eve and opening barred paradise.[54] The vision of the Fathers is epitomized by Sophronius: "through you your ancestors are saved; for you are to give birth to the Savior, who effects divine salvation for them."[55]

---

[46] Cf. Ephraem, note 14 above.

[47] Amphilochius, note 20 above.

[48] For the viewpoint of Irenaeus, cf. *Mary in Western Patristic Thought*, pp. 129-130.

[49] Cf. Ephraem, *Hymni de beata Maria*, 9, n. 4; Lamy, Vol. 2, 549. Cf. *Hymni de nativitate Christi in carne*, 2, n. 31; Vol. 2, 457: "Mary's foot crushed him who had struck Eve with his heel." Note what Ephraem adds immediately: "Blessed is He who by His birth laid him prostrate."

[50] Cf. Epiphanius, *Panarion*, haer. 78, 18; G.C.S., 37, 468-469.

[51] Cf. Amphilochius, note 20 above.

[52] Cf. Cyril, note 23 above; Theodotus, note 26 above; Ps.-Gregory, *In annuntiationem sermo 3*; *PG*, 10, 1177: "Hail, you who have sunk in your womb the death of your mother."

[53] Chrysippus, note 31 above.

[54] Cf. Ps.-Epiphanius, *De laudibus sanctae deiparae*; *PG*, 43, 501.

[55] Sophronius, Oratio 2: *In sanctissimae deiparae annuntiationem*, n. 22; *PG*, 87c, 3241.

Fourth, this is not to imply that indications of a more proximate co-operation of Our Lady in the objective Redemption are utterly absent from Eastern patristic thought. Hesychius, for example, preaches that at the presentation of Christ in the Temple Mary made her offering "not for herself but for the whole race."[56] Gregory of Nyssa (?) remarks that the New Eve introduced blessing to men in place of sin through the vivifying wood of the cross.[57] Cyril of Alexandria tells the Fathers of Ephesus that it is Mary through whom "the tempter-devil fell from heaven, the fallen creature is taken up into heaven, all creation ... has come to the knowledge of the truth, holy baptism has come to believers. ..."[58] Proclus calls her "God's only bridge to men."[59] For Anastasius I, she is "the ladder hung to heaven, the gate of paradise, the entrance to immortality, the union and link of men with God."[60] But it must be emphasized that genuine expressions of an immediate co-operation in the Redemption are relatively few; their underlying import is never clarified by the writers themselves; and the effort to interpret them in harmony with the contemporary doctrine of Coredemption runs frequently afoul of obstacles like the strange patristic vision of Mary's mentality beneath the cross.[61] The principle of redemptive co-operation as understood today may well be unassailable; but to find more than a germ of it, more than a basis for it, in the patristic East is to do violence to the evidence.[62]

---

[56] Hesychius, Sermo 6: *In praesentatione Christi*; *PG*, 93, 1469.

[57] Cf. note 19 above.

[58] Cyril of Alexandria, *Hom. div. 4*; ed. E. Schwartz, *A.C.O.*, Tom. 1, Vol. 1, Part 2, 102; PG, 77, 992.

[59] Proclus, Oratio 1: *Laudatio in sanctissimam Dei genitricem Mariam*, n. 1; ed. E. Schwartz, *A.C.O.*, Tom. 1, Vol. 1, Part 1, 103; *PG*, 65, 681.

[60] Anastasius I, *Sermo 3: In laudatissimae Dei genitricis annuntiationem*, n. 4; PG, 89, 1389.

[61] Cf. Part IV of this chapter, on Our Lady's sanctity.

[62] Mary's co-operation in the objective Redemption is not the only aspect of Marian theology which scholars have tried to trace to the Eve-Mary analogy of the Fathers, nor is this parallelism the sole patristic basis on which theologians rest their theses. A fruitful field of patristic investigation has been Our Lady's role in subjective Redemption, i.e., the part she plays not in the acquisition but in the distribution of grace. For a good summary, with bibliographical indications, of both aspects of Marian mediation in Eastern

II. PERPETUAL VIRGINITY

If the Eve-Mary parallelism furnished the Fathers with an initial penetration into the redemptive significance of Our Lady, Mary's virginity provided the patristic age with its first vexing problem in her regard. Historically, the investigation of her virginity has focused on three phases of Our Lady's life: the years before Bethlehem, the moment of childbearing in the cave, and the period subsequent to the birth of Jesus.

The crux of the first phase may be epitomized in two questions: Was Mary a virgin physically at the hour of the Annunciation? Was the conception of Christ a virginal conception, effected independently of intercourse with man? On neither count did Eastern Christianity hesitate; the scriptural evidence was all too clear. That is why the virginity of Mary and the virginal conception of Jesus are categorically affirmed as early as Ignatius of Antioch (ca. 110) in language which recalls the primitive kerygma and in accents which suggest that proof would be superfluous.[63] Not many years later, in the earliest extant Christian apology (ca. 125), the philosopher Aristides of Athens informs the Emperor Hadrian that Jesus' birth of a virgin, without human seed, is part and parcel of a Christian's creed, confessed in the same breath with the divinity of Christ, His redemptive crucifixion, and His resurrection.[64] In similar fashion, Justin's exegesis a quarter century later, to the effect that Isa. 7:14 means that "the virgin shall conceive without

---

theology, cf. M. Gordillo, *Mariologia orientalis* (Roma, 1954), pp. 58-87; cf. also his article, *La mediazione di Maria Vergine nella teologia bizantina*, in *Mélanges Martin Jugie* (Paris, 1953), pp. 120-128. Worth recording is Gordillo's evaluation (*Mariologia orientalis*, p. 74) of the striking texts so often adduced from Damascene: these passages have reference to Mary's mediatorial activity in conceiving Christ, at the outset of our deification. If our problem concerns her co-operation in the Redemption effected on the cross, "we must by all means confess that on this score Damascene is silent."

[63] Cf. Ignatius, *Ad Ephesios*, n. 19, 1; ed. Funk-Bihlmeyer (Tübingen, 1924), p. 87; id., *Ad Smyrnaeos*, n. 1, 1; Funk-Bihlmeyer, p. 106. What Ignatius finds it imperative to stress, against the Docetists, is not the virginal but the real conception of Christ.

[64] Cf. Aristides, *Apologia*, n. 2; ed. E. Hennecke, *Texte und Untersuchungen*, Vol. 4, Part 3, p. 9.

intercourse,"[65] is echoed by Irenaeus (ca. 177),[66] who insists moreover that "the birth from a virgin" is a belief which, like the belief in God the Creator, in the Word made flesh, in the Holy Spirit, in the passion, resurrection, and ascension, the universal Church "has received from the apostles and their disciples."[67]

There are discordant notes. We know that the pagan philosopher Celsus (ca. 178) peddled in the East a story, supposedly of Jewish inspiration, that Mary was convicted of adultery with a soldier named Panthera, was turned out in hatred by her carpenter husband, wandered about in disgrace, and gave birth to Jesus in secret.[68] What we do not know at firsthand is the reaction of the second-century Christian; but Origen's retort to Celsus sixty years later may well sum it up: this sort of thing is "street-corner abuse."[69]

In contrast, a genuine problem begins to take shape with the question: Did Our Lady remain a virgin while giving birth to Jesus? On this score the historical tradition is less clear and slower to

---

[65] Justin, *Apologia* 1, cap. 33; PG, 6, 381; cf. *Dialogus cum Tryphone*, cap. 84 and 100; PG, 6, 673-676, 709-712. Justin is evidence that by the middle of the second century Our Lady was commonly referred to as simply "the Virgin."

[66] Cf. Irenaeus, *Adversus haereses*, lib. 3, cap. 26, 2 (Massuet, 3, 21, 6); Harvey, 2, 118; *PG*, 7, 953. The theological significance which Irenaeus attaches to Jesus' birth of a virgin emerges impressively from the role which he assigns to Mary's virginity in his Second Eve doctrine.

[67] Irenaeus, *Adversus haereses*, lib. 1, cap. 2 (Massuet, 1, 10, 1); Harvey, 1, 90-91; *PG*, 7, 549.

[68] Cf. Origen, *Contra Celsum*, lib. 1, cap. 28-39; *G.C.S.*, 2, 79-90. A. Deissmann, *Der Name Panthera*, in *Orientalische Studien T. Nöldeke gewidmet* (Giessen, 1906), p. 871 ff., has shown that the name was common at this period, especially as a surname of Roman soldiers. L. Patterson, *Origin of the Name Panthera*, in *Journal of Theological Studies*, Vol. 19, 1917-1918, pp. 79-80, thinks that some Jewish controversialist pounced on the name because of its similarity to παρθένος. "Then the legend of the Roman soldier grew up and found its way into the Talmud with the purpose of discrediting and vilifying the Christian tradition, as soon as the gospel story became known to the general public."

[69] Origen, *Contra Celsum*, lib. 1, cap. 39; *G.C.S.*, 2, 90. Cf. the text of Origen conserved by Pamphilus, *Apologia pro Origene*, cap. 1; PG, 17, 554: Some, like the Ebionites and Valentinians, say that Jesus "was born of Joseph and Mary." Cf. also Origen, *Hom. 17 in Lucam*; *G.C.S.*, 35, 115.

solidify.[70] To recapture the Eastern belief before Nicaea we have at our disposal several imaginative apocrypha and a handful of perplexing patristic testimonies.

The apocryphal witnesses are primarily three.[71] In the Ascension of Isaias, a fusion piece whose Jewish and Christian components were united about the year 150, the Christian section testifies that Mary has conceived her Child as a virgin, has borne Him through a period of gestation as a virgin, and has given Him birth as a virgin: "her womb was found as formerly before she had conceived."[72] With respect to this evidence it may be said that (*a*) the section in which it appears can be persuasively dated in the last decade of the first century;[73] (*b*) there is no apodictic justification for the widespread assumption that the author of the pertinent passage inclined to Docetism;[74] (*c*) whether orthodox or Docetic, he affirms unequivocally Mary's virginity in childbearing.

Equally unmistakable are tbe Odes of Solomon, a remarkable example of ancient Christian hymnody which may date back to 120 or earlier.[75] *Ode 19* represents the Holy Spirit as opening the Father's

---

[70] Several reasons for this sluggish development are suggested in Mary in Western Patristic Thought, p. 120.

[71] A splendid analysis and evaluation of this evidence is presented by J. C. Plumpe, *Some Little-Known Witnesses to Mary's Virginitas in partu*, in *Theological Studies*, Vol. 9, 1948, pp. 567-577.

[72] Cf. *Ascensio Isaiae*, cap. 11, nn. 2-11; English translation from R. H. Charles, *The Ascension of Isaiah* (London, 1900), pp. 74-76.

[73] Cf. Charles, *op. cit.*, pp. xxii ff., xxxvii f., xliv f.; E. Tisserant, *Ascension d'Isaie* (Paris, 1909), p. 60.

[74] Cf. Plumpe, *art. cit.*, pp. 573-574. In fact, Charles, *op. cit.*, pp. xxii-xxiii, 77, has tried to show that the *Ascensio* is the source of the celebrated sentence in the anti-Docetic Ignatius, Ad *Eph.*, n. 19, 1: "And the prince of this world was in ignorance of the virginity of Mary and her childbearing. ..."

[75] Cf. Plumpe, *art. cit.*, pp. 576-577. The Odes were probably written originally in Greek. The striking similarities between the language of the odist and that of Ignatius (even on the Virgin Birth) has led J. Rendel Harris and A. Mingana to the conclusion that the Bishop of Antioch knew the Odes, even quoted them; they are convinced that the home of the collection is Antioch, its origin before the end of the first century; cf. The Odes and Psalms of Solomon (Manchester, 1916-1920), Vol. 2, pp. 42-49, 67. J. H. Bernard prefers a date between 150 and 200; cf. The Odes of Solomon, in Texts and Studies, Vol. 8, n. 3 (Cambridge, 1912), p. 42.

bosom and mingling the milk of the Father in a cup which is the Son; then the odist continues:

> The womb of the Virgin took (it)
> and she received conception and brought forth:
> And the Virgin became a mother with great mercy;
> And she travailed and brought forth a son without incurring pain;
> And it did not happen without purpose;
> And she had not required a midwife,
> For He delivered her,
> And she brought forth, as a man, of her own will. ...[76]

More significantly still, the Protoevangelium of James, composed between 150 and 180 by a Judeo-Christian living somewhere outside Palestine, perhaps in Egypt,[77] has for its idée capitale the thesis that Mary, virgin in conceiving Christ, did not forfeit virginity in giving Him birth. The proof offered is visual and tactual: a midwife present at the Nativity, and a woman named Salome who "made trial" of Mary's virginity soon after Jesus' birth.[78] This graphic argument from sight and touch is relevant here, not for any factual information on the first Christmas, but because (*a*) it suggests that at the mid-point of the second century Mary's virginity in childbearing constituted an area of disagreement, if not among orthodox Christians, then between certain orthodox and certain Gnostics; (*b*) it is not likely that Ps.-James the Less was the first to defend Our Lady's virginity with so indelicate a weapon; and (*c*) this Infancy narrative exercised an influence difficult to exaggerate.[79]

---

[76] *Odae Salomonis*, 19, vv. 6-10; tr. Harris-Mingana, *op.* cit., Vol. 2, 299, save for the alternative "of her own will" in preference to "by (God's) will." Harnack's pithy interpretation is splendid: "der Geburtsact sich bei ihr so selbständig vollzog, wie der Zeugungsact beim Manne"; in *Texte und Untersuchungen*, Vol. 35, Part 4 (Leipzig, 1910), p. 50.

[77] Cf. E. Amann, *Le Protévangile de Jacques et ses remaniements latins* (Paris, 1910), pp. 99-100; J. Quasten, *Patrology*, Vol. 1 (Westminster, Md., 1950), pp. 119, 121.

[78] Cf. *Protevangelium Iacobi*, 18-20; ed. Amann, *op.* cit., pp. 246-256.

[79] Cf. Plumpe, *art. cit.*, pp. 570, 572. Amann concludes that nothing is less certain than the alleged Docetism of the Protevangelium Iacobi, or a Docetic origin of the Virgin Birth doctrine; cf. *op.* cit., p. 36. — The virginal conception of Christ and Mary's virginal childbearing are clearly indicated in a Christian section of the *Sibylline Oracles*, lib. 8, vv. 456-479; ed. J.

If nothing else, the evidence of the apocrypha reveals a strong current of popular opinion in the second-century East, among apparently orthodox Christians, to the effect that Our Lady did not cease to be a virgin in giving birth to Our Lord, and that this aspect of her virginity was a sheerly physical thing, consisting precisely in the preservation unimpaired of her generative structure.[80]

The theologians of the pre-Nicene period are not as dogmatic, not as unequivocal, not as much in evidence. Three merit mention: Irenaeus, Clement of Alexandria, and Origen. With respect to Irenaeus, it can still be convincingly argued, despite the research and reasoning of H. Koch, that there is no passage from his pen — including the adhuc virgo texts — which clearly contradicts the virginity of Mary in Bethlehem.[81] On the other hand, there is an inescapable allusion to this prerogative in his Demonstration of the Apostolic Preaching, written about 190. Irenaeus takes Isa. 66:7, where the prophet foretells a remarkable repopulation of Jerusalem through Mother Sion, and interprets it as spoken of the Virgin Mary who gave birth to a man child in unique fashion, without birth pangs. "Also, concerning His birth, the same prophet [Isaias] says in another place: 'Before she who was in labour brought forth, and before the pains of labour came, there came forth delivered a man child'; he proclaimed His unlooked-for and extraordinary birth of

---

Geffcken, G.C.S., 8, 171-172. I have thought it prudent, however, not to stress this testimony, because more probably the section of Book 8 which contains these verses does not antedate the third century; cf. A. Rzach, *Sibyllinische Orakel,* in Pauly-Wissowa-Kroll-Witte, *Real-Encyclopädie der classischen Altertumswissenschaft,* 2. Reihe, 4. Halbband (1923), col. 2146; this, despite the belief of Geffcken that Book 8 should be dated before 180; cf. *Texte und Untersuchungen,* Vol. 23, Part 1 (Leipzig, 1902), pp. 38-46.

[80] Plumpe believes, with good reason, that they do more; cf. *art. cit.,* p. 577. They offer, he concludes, a full commentary and illustration of Ignatius' claim that Jesus was "really born of a virgin"; they remove all doubt that "of a virgin" meant in partu as well as ante partum; for the time between Ignatius and Origen they are a formidable chain of witnesses to this permanent virginity; they lend certitude to indications in Justin and Irenaeus that they too regarded Mary as ἀειπάρθενος.

[81] Cf. *Mary in Western Patristic Thought,* pp. 121-122. Koch's pertinent works are *Adhuc virgo* (Tübingen, 1929), and *Virgo Eva — Virgo Maria* (Berlin und Leipzig, 1937).

the Virgin."[82] If his language is not limpid and his mind not manifest, it may simply be that Irenaeus never found occasion to confront this rather nuanced, delicate theological theme.

Clement is jejune but instructive. We are informed that toward the close of the second century the virginity of Mary in Bethlehem was matter of dispute in Egypt, denied by an impressive number, if not a majority, of Christians: "many (τοις πολλοις: most?) even down to our own day think that Mary is a woman who was in labor owing to the birth of her Son." Clement himself does not agree: "actually she was not in labor." The sole obvious source of his opinion is the apocryphal tradition we have already met in the *Protoevangelium of James*: "for some say that, after she bore her Child, a midwife examined her and found her a virgin." However, he does glimpse in this prerogative an analogy with the Scriptures: "they give birth to the truth and continue virgin."[83]

For Origen's thought, a passage from *Homily 14 on Luke*, composed perhaps in 233 or 234,[84] is indispensable:

> Male children, which were holy because they had opened their mother's womb, were offered before the altar of the Lord: "every male child that opens the womb," it says (Ex. 34:23), signifies something sacred. In point of fact, whatever male you may mention as having come forth from the womb, he does not open the womb of his mother in the way the Lord Jesus did, seeing that it is not childbirth but intercourse that unlocks the womb of all women. But the womb of the Lord's mother was unlocked at the time of her childbearing; for before the birth of Christ no male touched in the slightest that holy womb, worthy of all esteem and veneration.[85]

---

[82] Irenaeus, Demonstratio apostolicae praedicationis, cap. 54; Patrologia Orientalis, 12, 701; tr. J. P. Smith, op. cit., p. 83.

[83] Clement of Alexandria, Stromata, lib. 7, cap. 16; G.C.S., 17, 66. E. Neubert, Marie dans l'église anténicéenne (Paris, 1908), pp. 177-178, believes it deceiving to claim that, according to Clement, the majority of Christians rejected the belief. The question did not occur to the masses. For them, Mary was a virgin and she had borne God. How reconcile these affirmations was not their preoccupation; such, too, is the attitude of the faithful in general today.

[84] So R. P. C. Hanson, Origen's Doctrine of Tradition (London, 1954), pp. 20-22, 26.

[85] Origen, Hom. *17 in Lucam*; G.C.S., 35, 100.

Two pertinent beliefs of Origen emerge from the text. Before the birth of Jesus, Mary was a virgin; in giving birth to Jesus, Mary did not preserve her physical integrity. If we are not to misconstrue the latter thesis, which may be due to the direct influence of Tertullian[86] and certainly stems from a paradoxically slavish interpretation of Scripture,[87] a passage from the Commentary on Matthew, composed probably in 246,[88] cannot be overlooked:

A certain tradition has come to us to this effect. There is a place in the Temple where virgins may pause and pray (adore?) God; but those who had experienced intercourse were not allowed to stand there. Now Mary, after giving birth to the Saviour, went in to adore and stood in that place for virgins. Those who knew that she had borne a son tried to keep her away, but Zachary ... said to them: "She is worthy of the place for virgins; for she is still a virgin."[89]

Two conclusions seem justified by the text. First, the passage does not constitute an implicit retractation of Origen's earlier statement that Our Lady forfeited physical integrity in Bethlehem. In the text, "virgins" are opposed to those who have "experienced intercourse." Mary has not experienced intercourse, and therefore is "still a virgin." Second, the passage strongly suggests that, for Origen, loss of physical integrity in childbearing is not incompatible with perfect, perpetual virginity. This suggestion finds a twofold confirmation. In the Homilies on Luke Origen calls Mary virgin even though he is speaking of her after childbearing;[90] and in the Commentary on Matthew he refers to her as the first-fruits of virginity with respect to women, as Jesus was in regard of men.[91] In a word, Origen apparently understands physical virginity only in terms of marital intercourse. In giving birth to Jesus, Our Lady surrendered her bodily integrity; she did not relinquish her

---

[86] Vagaggini finds this influence difficult to deny; cf. op. cit., pp. 89-91.

[87] Cf. Ortiz de Urbina, *Lo sviluppo*, p. 54.

[88] So Hanson, *op. cit.*, pp. 16-17, 27.

[89] Origen, *Comm. in Matthaeum*, ser. 25; G.C.S., 38, 42-43.

[90] Cf. Origen, *Hom. 17 in Lucam*; G.C.S., 35, 115.

[91] Cf. Origen, *Comm. in Matthaeum*, Tom. 10, cap. 17; G.C.S., 40, 21-22.

virginity. In Bethlehem virginity was not an issue.[92]

From the evidence available, therefore, it would seem that at the end of the second century and during the first half of the third century, the Christians of Egypt, of Palestine, and perhaps of Asia Minor generally, were not conscious of an obligation to represent Our Lady as virgin in her act of childbearing.[93]

Such is the state of the evidence before Nicaea. Strangely enough, the testimony of the century that follows is not strikingly more extensive. It is difficult to decide, for example, whether a genuinely virginal childbearing was admitted, denied, ignored, or overlooked by such impressive churchmen and influential writers as Athanasius of Alexandria, Cyril of Jerusalem, and Epiphanius of

---

[92] For a more detailed treatment of Origen on *virginitas in partu*, cf. Vagaggini, *op. cit.*, pp. 80-97. The concept of virginity in parturition does not seem to have been totally unfamiliar to Origen, but for polemical reasons he seems to take "virginem peperisse" as opposed to "vere peperisse"; cf. In *epist. ad Titum*; the pertinent text has been preserved by Pamphilus in *Apologia pro Origene*, lib. 1, cap. 1; *PG*, 17, 554 (reproduced in *PG*, 14, 1304), where he rejects the idea. Of some pertinence here is Origen's understanding of Mary's purification after childbearing. In *Hom. 14 in Lucam*, stemming from about 233, Origen says: Mary required purification because she contracted a sordes not merely legal but real. He does not specify its nature, save to affirm that it is not to be identified with sin; *G.C.S.*, 35, 96. In 244, *Hom. 8 in Leviticum*, Origen states that Mary by exception is not unclean by reason of her childbearing, because Lev. 12:2 refers to women who have given birth after normal conception, i.e., of human seed; *G.C.S.*, 29, 394-396. Here the sordes of the infant and the immunditia of the mother are understood of sin. Why does Scripture call a woman who gives birth unclean sinfully, and that by reason of childbearing itself? Origen confesses that he is face to face with mystery. In neither homily is he able to explain clearly in what the sordes consisted and therefore the purification therefrom. But Origen recognizes that, because Mary conceived virginally of the Spirit, (*a*) Jesus born of her entered this world pure, (*b*) she remained immune from the sinful contamination of childbearing, and (*c*) she had no need to fulfill the law of purification.

[93] Cf. G. Jouassard, *Marie à travers la patristique: Maternité divine, virginité, sainteté*, in *Marie, Etudes sur la Sainte Vierge*, ed. H. du Manoir, Vol. 1 (Paris, 1949), p. 81. It is no longer legitimate, with Neubert, op. cit., pp. 185-190, to use the homily, *In natalem Christi diem*, as a pre-Nicene witness, and specifically as a work of Gregory the Wonder-Worker; cf. note 21 above.

Salamis.[94]

The contributions of the three Cappadocians on this issue are startlingly unequal. Gregory of Nazianzus does no more than suggest virginity in Bethlehem.[95] Basil the Great is somewhat more satisfying but hardly perlucid. Insisting that Mary never ceased to be a virgin, he stresses the fact that "the selfsame woman is virgin and mother: she abides in the holiness that is virginity, and she is blessed with the birth of a child."[96] It is with Gregory of Nyssa that

---

[94] Cf., e.g., Athanasius, De incarnatione Verbi, n. 17; *PG*, 25, 125; id., Epistola ad Epictetum, n. 7; PG, 26, 1061; note the realistic language in the latter work, n. 5; *PG*, 26, 1057. It is true that the term, ἀειπάρθενος, "ever virgin," begins to be applied to Our Lady in the second half of the fourth century (cf. J. A. de Aldama, in Estudios Eclesiásticos, Vol. 21, 1947, pp. 487-489), specifically by Athanasius (Fragmenta in Lucam; PG, 27, 1393), by Epiphanius (*Ancoratus, n. 119; G.C.S., 25, 148; Panarion, haer. 78, 10; G.C.S., 37, 461; Expositio fidei, n. 15; G.C.S., 37, 515), and by Didymus (De trinitate, lib. 1, cap. 27; PG, 39, 404). It may be argued, however, that the sheer use of the word,* ἀειπάρθενος, is not an apodictic proof that the authors who employ it consider Our Lady virgin in childbearing. What is needed, over and above, is evidence that the author in question, as general practice or at least in a particular context, does not understand virginity merely quantum a viro (to use Tertullian's expressive phrase) but extends the concept to cover the issue of parturition. Thus, Didymus does say that it is beyond human comprehension "how the Virgin gave birth without flux (afterbirth?), remaining a virgin"; De trinitate, lib. 3, cap. 2, n. 20; *PG*, 39, 793. — If Peter of Alexandria († 311) is cited as the first to have employed the term, ἀειπάρθενος (so Ortiz de Urbina, Lo sviluppo, p. 54, and Die Marienkunde in der Patristik des Ostens, p. 99), it should be pointed out that the text (Frag. 1, n. 7; PG, 18, 517) is not certainly authentic; cf. de Aldama, p. 488. Likewise, the lovely antiphon, Sub tuum praesidium (cf. Part III of this chapter), which in the original Greek may go back to the third century, should not be cited as witness to ἀειπάρθενος; in none of the Greek recensions is there any mention of virginity, while the Latin version, "libera nos semper virgo gloriosa et benedicta," is ambiguous.

[95] Cf. Gregory of Nazianzus, *Oratio 40: In sanctum baptisma*, n. 45; *PG*, 36, 424.

[96] Basil the Great, *Homilia in sanctam Christi generationem*, n. 4; *PG*, 31, 1465-1468. The authenticity of this homily, denied by Dom Garnier, is admitted — justifiably, it seems — by H. Usener, *Religionsgeschichtliche Untersuchungen*, Vol. 1 (2nd ed.; Bonn, 1911), p. 249 ff.; Söll, art. cit., pp. 178-185; Ortiz de Urbina, *Lo sviluppo*, pp. 54-55; Jouassard, *art. cit.*, p. 89, note 14, and p. 90. Many patristic texts (e.g., that of Basil above; cf. also Gregory of Nyssa, note 97 below) are deceptive if read superficially and are difficult to

a genuine clarity begins to emerge. Not that Gregory is consistently unambiguous; he is not.[97] But, like Irenaeus, he applies Isa. 66:7 to Our Lady: as no sensual pleasure was prelude to parturition, so no labor was its consequence.[98] Like the bramble (Ex. 3:2) aflame but not consumed, Mary brings the Light to birth and is not corrupted;[99] for the Light "kept the kindled bush incorrupt; the sprout of her virginity was not withered by her childbearing."[100] More pithily still, "her pregnancy was without coition, her childbed undefiled, her travail free from pain. ... His birth alone was without labor, just as His formation was without union." It is a misuse of language, he remarks, to speak of labor with respect to her who was unwed and incorrupt, because virginity and labor are irreconcilable in the same person. The Eve-Mary analogy demands "that the mother of Life begin pregnancy with joy and finish childbearing through joy."[101] In sum, the Bishop of Nyssa attaches the concept of virginity not simply to coition but to parturition as well; and he affirms flatly that Mary's virginity was not affected by her parturition.

In this matter a genuine importance attaches to Amphilochius

---

interpret, because "childbearing" may and often does refer not to the specific act which is parturition but to the general condition which is pregnancy.

[97] Thus, Gregory seems to include the act of childbearing, parturition, when he writes: "The Virgin becomes a mother, and remains virgin. With other women, while a woman is a virgin, she is not a mother; when she becomes a mother, she does not have virginity. But here the two titles coincide; for the same woman is both mother and virgin. Virginity was no hindrance to childbearing, and childbearing did not destroy virginity." But he goes on to say: "it was fitting that He who became man to give all men incorruption should begin human life of an incorrupt mother; for men are accustomed to call her incorrupt who is unwed." In diem natalem Christi; PG, 46, 1136. His preoccupation, therefore, is with virginity ante partum. The same may be said of a passage where Gregory interprets Lc. 11:27: the Evangelist felicitates Mary's womb, because it ministered to an immaculate, undefiled childbearing, "inasmuch as childbearing did not destroy virginity, nor did virginity prove an obstacle to her pregnancy." De virginitate, cap. 19; ed. J. P. Cavarnos, in Gregorii Nysseni opera, ed. W. Jaeger, Vol. 8, Part 1 (Leiden, 1952), p. 324.

[98] Gregory of Nyssa, In Christi resurrectionem, orat. 1; PG, 46, 604.

[99] 99 Cf. In diem natalem Christi; PG, 46, 1136.

[100] Gregory of Nyssa, De vita Moysis; PG, 44, 332.

[101] Gregory of Nyssa, In Cantica canticorum, hom. 13; PG, 44, 1053.

of Iconium, disciple of the Cappadocians. Much that he has to say on Our Lady's virginity is vexingly vague;[102] but his merit is that he has faced up to *Lc.* 2:23 (based on Ex. 13:2), stumbling block for many an early exegete: "whatever male offspring opens the womb is to be reckoned sacred to the Lord." Amphilochius makes three points, records an objection, and answers it. His first point: it is to Our Lord alone that Scripture here refers; only He is, as Gabriel put it (*Lc.* 1:35), the Holy One, "sacred to the Lord." His second point: it is regularly by intercourse that a woman's womb is first opened. His third point: this did not happen in the case of Our Lady; the Saviour opened her womb without intercourse. There is an obvious objection. If the biblical text refers to Our Lord, then "the Virgin did not remain a virgin"; Mary's womb was opened. The answer is a distinction. If we focus on Mary and her virginity, "the virginal gates were not opened at all"; for this is Ezechiel's "gate of the Lord," where He goes in and out, and still the gate is closed (cf. Ez. 44:2). If we focus on the Incarnate Lord and His power, "nothing has ever been closed to Him; all things are open to Him."[103] In a word, "He opened the Virgin's womb without intercourse; He came forth in a fashion inexpressible."[104] Amphilochius' language has not crystallized, but his basic idea is sufficiently clear: in parturition as in conception, Our Lady's virginity was maintained inviolate.

The sermon, *On the Birthday of Christ*, which seems to stem from Chrysostom, is unequivocal. Mary gave birth "without experiencing corruption." After her childbearing, "pure and holy" as it was, she is virgin still, a "supernatural" thing. The Son's inexpressible birth of a virgin parallels His unutterable generation from the Father. In being born of her, God "preserves her womb unchanged, and maintains her virginity unharmed"; "the seal of her virginity" is "unblemished."[105]

---

[102] Cf. Amphilochius, Oratio 1: *In Christi natalem*, nn. 1-2; *PG*, 39, 37; ibid., n. 4; *PG*, 39, 40-41; Oratio 2: *In occursum domini*, n. 1; *PG*, 39, 44-45.

[103] Amphilochius, *Oratio 2: In occursum domini*, nn. 2-3; *PG*, 39, 48-49. Cf. Söll, art. cit., pp. 301-303.

[104] Amphilochius, *Oratio 2: In occursum domini*, n. 2; *PG*, 39, 48.

[105] *In natalem Christi diem; PG*, 56, 387-393. For the authenticity of this work, cf. note 21 above. Cf. also Chrysostom's moving presentation of the virginal conception, Hom. *49 in Genesim*, n. 2; *PG, 54, 445-446.*

In Ephraem's Hymns on Blessed Mary, Our Lady's virginity in childbearing is a constantly recurring theme. She gives birth without pain; her body abides intact; she gives of her milk without loss of virginity; she is the "closed gate" of Ezechiel; the seals of her virginity are as inviolate as the seals of Christ's sepulcher, inviolate even in death.[106] It is true that in the Commentary on the Diatessaron Ephraem seems unwittingly ensnared by Ex. 13:2 and *Lc.* 2:23: "By His birth He opened the closed womb; by His resurrection He opened the enclosed ... tomb."[107] But this bald statement, so pregnant with implications, finds its necessary complement in another passage of the same work: "just as [the Lord] made His entrance when the doors were closed, in the same way did He come forth from the Virgin's womb, because this virgin really and truly gave birth without pain."[108] Unlike Amphilochius, Ephraem makes no effort to reconcile the two ideas. It is legitimate to conclude, however, that in his eyes the Incarnate God could somehow "open the womb" of Mary without violating her virginity; for, when she gave birth to Him, "her virginity remained safe and sound."[109]

It is with the Council of Ephesus (431), and probably in consequence of the Council, that the last lingering doubts on Our Lady's virginity in parturition disappear from orthodox circles. Around the beginning of the Nestorian controversy (428) Nilus of Ancyra bears witness to the existence of a belief, even in high

---

[106] *Cf. Ephraem, Hymni de beata Maria,* 1, 2; 2, 3; 4, 7; 4, 10; 5, 1-2; 6, 2; 7, 6; 8, 3; 10, 2; 11, 4; 11, 6; 12, 1; 15, 2; 15, 5; 18, 20; ed. Lamy, Vol. 2, 519, 523-525, 532, 533, 540, 545, 547, 553, 567, 569, 573, 583, 611.

[107] *Ephraem, Explanatio evangelii concordantis,* cap. 21, n. 2; C.S.C.O., Vol. 137, 312 (Arm.); Vol. 145, 223 (Latin). Although the *Explanatio* is doubtless Ephraem's work, the researches of Zahn, Euringer, and C. Peters indicate that the Armenian translators have not always rendered the original Syriac faultlessly; cf. Ortiz de Urbina, *Lo sviluppo,* p. 61.

[108] Ephraem, *Explanatio ...,* cap. 2, n. 6; *C.S.C.O.,* Vol. 137, 26-27 (Arm.); Vol. 145, 20 (Latin).

[109] Ephraem, *Explanatio ...,* cap. 2, n. 8; *C.S.C.O.,* Vol. 137, 28 (Arm.); Vol. 145, 20 (Latin). Cf. also *Explanatio ...,* cap. 21, n. 21; C.S.C.O., Vol. 137, 326 (Arm.); Vol. 145, 232 (Latin): The sealed tomb was a witness to the sealed womb; its virginity was sealed up, yet the Son of God went forth from its midst. Cf., however, the reservations of Jouassard, *art. cit.,* p. 88, note 10.

places, that Mary's virginity was not perfect and perpetual, and responds in part: "In His birth Our Lord Christ opened the undefiled womb; after His birth He sealed the womb by His own wisdom, power, and wondrous activity. He did not break the seals of her virginity at all."[110] But during the Council itself there is no evidence of uncertainty.[111] In fact, before the Council convened, Theodoret of Cyrus, destined to be one of the leaders of the Oriental, anti-Cyrillan faction, had pronounced clearly and unmistakably in favor of the privilege.[112] The belief of the theological era that dawned with Ephesus, so evident in celebrated preachers like Hesychius of Jerusalem[113] and Proclus of Constantinople,[114] is epitomized in Cyril of Alexandria, for whom Exodus' burning bush, kindled but not consumed, prefigures Our Lady, who "gives birth to the Light and is not corrupted."[115] In Cyril's expressive word, Mary is "Virgin-Mother."[116]

A third phase of Our Lady's virginity concerns her life after Bethlehem. Did Mary have conjugal relations after the birth of Jesus? To point up the problem: Did Mary have any children besides

---

[110] Nilus, *Epistolae*, lib. 1, ep. 270; *PG*, 79, 181.

[111] From a line of argument launched against Cyril's first Anathematism by Andrew of Samosata (cf. Schwartz, A.C.O., Tom. 1, Vol. 1, Part 7, 34; PG, 76, 317-320), some have concluded that uncertainty did obtain just before the Council; cf. A. Eberle, Die Mariologie des heiligen Cyrillus von Alexandrien (Freiburg im Breisgau, 1921), p. 115; H. du Manoir de Juaye, Dogme et spiritualité chez saint Cyrille d'Alexandrie (Paris, 1944), p. 273. In reality, as Jouassard has pointed out (*art.* cit., p. 138, note 7), Andrew is concerned with the virginal conception alone. Cyril's reply, however, touches the virginal parturition as well.

[112] Cf. Theodoret, *De incarnatione domini*, n. 23; *PG*, 75, 1460-1461. Though edited under the name of Cyril of Alexandria (*PG*, 75, 1420-1477), the work is certainly Theodoret's; cf. J. Lebon, in *Revue d'Histoire Ecclésiastique*, Vol. 26/1, 1930, pp. 524-536.

[113] Cf. Hesychius, Sermo 4: *De sancta Maria deipara; PG*, 93, 1460; id., Sermo 5: *De sancta Maria deipara; PG*, 93, 1461-1464.

[114] Cf. Proclus, Oratio 1: *Laudatio in sanctissimam Dei genitricem Mariam*, n. 10; ed. Schwartz, A.C.O., Tom. 1, Vol. 1, Part 1, 107; *PG*, 65, 692.

[115] Cyril, *Adversus anthropomorphitas*, cap. 26; *PG*, 76, 1128-1129.

[116] The Greek word is παρθενομήτωρ: Cyril, *Adversus nolentes confiteri sanctam virginem esse deiparam*, n. 4; *PG*, 76, 260. For a brief synthesis of Cyril's doctrine on virginity in parturition, cf. Eberle, *op. cit.*, pp. 114-116; also du Manoir, *op. cit.*, pp. 272-274, obviously dependent on Eberle.

Jesus? It is the age-old problem of "the brethren of the Lord."[117] What relationship to Christ did early Christianity see in these "brothers and sisters"? Were they perhaps children which Joseph had by Mary after her "first-born" Son? Or were they offspring of Joseph by a previous marriage? Or is the kinship a more distant thing?

If the extant evidence is typical, the Christian East was as slow as the West to face the problem.[118] The silence is broken in the third quarter of the second century by the apocryphal Protoevangelium of James: Joseph is a widower, with children by his former wife, and too advanced in years to have conjugal relations.[119] The Protoevangelium solution to the problem of "the Lord's brethren" found an incredibly warm welcome; in fact, it became the classical explanation in the East.[120] It is discoverable, for example, in a fragment from Clement of Alexandria: the Jude who wrote the Catholic Epistle was "a brother of Joseph's children," and so "the brother of James."[121] It came to the knowledge of Origen; but Origen's thinking on Mary's perpetual virginity is not enfeoffed to apocrypha.

On the essential fact Origen's position is clear: "no one whose mind on Mary is sound would claim that she had any child save Jesus."[122] More than that, the allegation of a heretic that Mary was wed to Joseph after the birth of Jesus (and for that reason was repudiated by her Son) does not rest on evidence: "for the so-called sons of Joseph were not born of Mary, and there is no mention of it in Scripture."[123] Who, then, were these "brethren" of Christ? ... some say that the brethren of Jesus are children [sons?] of Joseph by a

---

[117] Cf. Mt. 13:55-56; Mk. 6:3; Jn. 2:12; 7:3, 10; Acts 1:14; *1 Cor.* 9:5; Gal. 1:19.

[118] For the Western development, cf. *Mary in Western Patristic Thought*, pp. 140-147.

[119] Cf. *Protevangelium Iacobi*, 9, 2; ed. Amann, *op.* cit., p. 216.

[120] For the history of the *Protevangelium Iacobi* in Christian Greek literature, cf. Amann, *op.* cit., pp. 109-137.

[121] Clement of Alexandria, *Adumbrationes in epistolam Iudae; PG*, 9, 731.

[122] Origen, *Comm. in Ioannem,* lib. 1, n. 4 (6); *G.C.S.*, 10, 8.

[123] Origen, Hom. *7 in Lucam*; *G.C.S.*, 35, 49. It does not appear that Origen is classifying as heretical the opinion itself (denial of virginity after childbirth) of the heretic, name unknown, whom he is denouncing; cf. Vagaggini, *op. cit.*, pp. 131-133.

former wife, who had lived with him before Mary. They are motivated by a tradition of the so-called Gospel according to Peter, or the Book of James. Now those who say this wish to preserve the dignity of Mary in virginity to the end, that the body chosen to minister to the Word ... might not know intercourse after the Holy Spirit had come upon her and the power from on high had overshadowed her. And I think it reasonable that Jesus was, in regard of men, the first-fruits of the purity that resides in chastity, and Mary in regard of women; for piety forbids us to ascribe to someone else besides her the first-fruits of virginity.[124]

Origen was convinced, therefore, with at least a segment of the Christian people, that Our Lady preserved her virginity from the birth of Jesus to the end. He found this belief so utterly congenial to the Christian sense that he censured its denial not as heretical but as senseless. The dominant influence motivating his conviction was not his ascetical ideas and ideals (which were rather rigorous in the matter of marriage), much as these may have played the role of contributory factors;[125] not apocryphal literature like the Protoevangelium of James, much as this may have provided a plausible exegesis of the "brethren";[126] not even the silence of Scripture on a wedding of Joseph and Mary after Bethlehem. The basic inspiration for the conviction of Origen and many contemporary Christians that Mary remained a virgin to the end was theological: a deep-rooted persuasion that by the Incarnation the body of Our Lady had been irrevocably consecrated to the Holy Spirit and to the Word.

Such is the evidence before Nicaea. It is confessedly scanty, but it touches Egypt, Palestine, and Asia Minor generally. If the authors in question show themselves consistently favorable to the thesis of

---

[124] Origen, *Comm. in Matthaeum*, Tom. 10, cap. 17; *G.C.S.*, 40, 21-22.

[125] For the pertinent ascetical ideas of Origen, and their influence in the present context, cf. Jouassard, *art. cit.*, pp. 80-81, and Vagaggini, pp. 122-127.

[126] Cf. Vagaggini, *op. cit.*, pp. 128-130. In the passage quoted from *Comm. in Matthaeum*, Origen neither accepts nor rejects the solution supplied by the apocrypha. According to a fragment taken from catenae on Jn., Origen did commit himself to it; cf. *G.C.S.*, 10, 506-507. Regrettably, the passage is found among the fragments (1-105) whose authenticity is strongly suspect; cf. R. Devreesse, *Chaînes exégétiques grecques*, in *Supplément au Dictionnaire de la Bible*, Vol. 1, cols. 1198-1199.

Mary's abiding virginity, the philological data at hand do not reveal that the Christian East in 325 was conscious of a peremptory obligation to represent Our Lady as virgin save for the years before Bethlehem.[127]

The precise state of the question between Nicaea and Ephesus is hardly easier to reconstruct. Eusebius, Bishop of Caesarea in Palestine, simply asserts that the Lord's "brethren" were not children of Mary.[128] The Catechetical Lectures of Cyril cast no light on the belief of Jerusalem.[129] Athanasius in Alexandria is astonishingly noncommittal, to judge from the works which have survived in Greek; but the little treatise, *On Virginity*, transmitted in Coptic, attests the existence in Egypt of individuals who claimed that Our Lady had other children besides Jesus, and reveals Athanasius as defender of Mary's virginity after Bethlehem, though it gives no inkling that a point of faith was felt to be involved.[130]

More importantly, a discourse of the famous Arian, Eunomius of Cyzicus, in which he declared that Joseph and Mary had marital relations after the birth of Jesus, provoked a reply from an orthodox theologian who is almost certainly Basil the Great, Bishop of Caesarea in Cappadocia.[131] Basil rejects the thesis of Eunomius, but it is his reasoning that is significant. He confesses that Christian doctrine, faith, is not at stake: virginity was necessary for the Incarnation alone. Why, then, the retort to Eunomius? Because "lovers of Christ refuse to lend ear to the idea that the Mother of God ever ceased to be a virgin."[132] In the second half of the fourth century, therefore, in part of the Greek world the perpetual virginity of Mary was regarded by orthodox believers as not part and parcel

---

[127] Cf. Jouassard, *art. cit.*, pp. 83-84.

[128] Eusebius, *Comm. in psalmos*, Ps. 68, 9; *PG*, 23, 737-740.

[129] The virginal conception is proposed by Cyril with a clarity that leaves no room for doubt; cf. *Catecheses*, 12, 29-34; *PG*, 33, 761-768.

[130] The treatise was discovered and edited by L. Th. Lefort, *S. Athanase: Sur la virginité*, in *Le Muséon*, Vol. 42, 1929, pp. 197-275. There are good reasons for believing it an authentic work of Athanasius.

[131] On the discourse of Eunomius, cf. Photius' summary in Philostorgius, *Hist. eccl.*, lib. 6, n. 2; G.C.S., 21, 71. For confirmation, cf. *PG*, 56, 635. On Basil's authorship, cf. note 96 above.

[132] Basil, *Homilia in sanctam Christi generationem*, n. 5; PG, 31, 1468.

of Christian dogma.

This attitude is quite compatible with the convictions of Ephraem and Chrysostom. Ephraem knows of "some who dare to say that Mary was Joseph's wife after the Saviour's birth." His answer reminds us of Origen: "How could this be, that she who was the home where the Spirit dwelt, she whom God's power overshadowed, should become wife of mortal man? ... As she conceived in purity, so did she abide in sanctity."[133] About 390 Chrysostom preaches in Antioch that Mary remained virgin her whole life long — though he presents her virginity after Bethlehem, unlike the virginal conception, rather as a deduction from Scripture than a truth taught explicitly therein.[134]

Before Chrysostom, however, a current of thought is discernible which is utterly uncompromising, a movement more dogmatic in tone. In 374 Epiphanius records the belief of the Antidicomarianites that Mary had intercourse with Joseph after the birth of Jesus.[135] In 377 he replies by reproducing a letter addressed some years before to Christians in Arabia. The letter castigates the opinion as novelty, audacity, madness. Of all depravity it is the most ungodly. Mary has always been known as Virgin; it is her cognomen of honor. The "brethren" of Jesus were children of Joseph by a former marriage. Joseph was over eighty when Mary was espoused to him. Our Lady never had carnal intercourse; "perish the thought!" Jesus was her only Child, she was "ever virgin."[136] More impressive however, than Epiphanius' vehement language are two suggestive facts: (*a*) in the

---

[133] Ephraem, *Explanatio evangelii concordantis*, cap. 2, n. 6; *C.S.C.O.*, Vol. 137, 26-27 (Arm.); Vol. 145, 19-20 (Latin). Mary had no other child: cf. Explanatio ..., cap. 5, n. 7; *C.S.C.O.*, Vol. 137, 62 (Arm.); Vol. 145, 46 (Latin). The very fact that Jesus gave Mary to John on Calvary proves that the "brethren" were not her children, Joseph not her husband: cf. Explanatio ..., cap. 2, n. 11; *C.S.C.O.*, Vol. 137, 29 (Arm.); Vol. 145, 22 (Latin).

[134] Cf. John Chrysostom, Hom. *5 in Matthaeum*, n. 3; *PG*, 57, 58. Cf. also Didymus, De trinitate, lib. 3, cap. 4; *PG*, 39, 832: "... neither did ... Mary wed anyone nor did she ever become mother of another; but she remained even after pregnancy ever and always virgin immaculate. ..."

[135] Cf. Epiphanius, *Ancoratus*, n. 13; *G.C.S.*, 25, 22.

[136] Cf. Epiphanius, *Panarion*, haer. 78, nn. 5-24; *G.C.S.*, 37, 455-475. Epiphanius finds it hard to believe the rumor that Apollinaris or his disciples held this opinion; cf. *Panarion*, haer. 77, n. 36; *G.C.S.*, 37, 448.

second creed of Epiphanius Our Lady is denominated "ever virgin";[137] and (b) the opinion of his adversaries is catalogued as a heresy. It is true, the word "heresy" was quite imprecise at the time. In our context, however, the minimal exegesis is that Epiphanius was denouncing the thesis of the Antidicomarianites as in some genuine sense alien to orthodoxy.

As the Nestorian controversy dawned (428), was the orthodox East universally persuaded of Mary's permanent virginity? The question is not impertinent if we recall that Nilus of Ancyra was even then taking sharp issue with an individual who claimed the contrary;[138] and, though he borrows his arguments from Epiphanius, unlike Epiphanius he does not tax his adversary with heresy. Jouassard may well be correct in concluding that Nilus is dealing with theological laggards, with people behind the times; for at this critical juncture of Christian history there is no evidence of any community whose bishop subscribes to the theory that Our Lady sacrificed her virginity after Bethlehem.[139]

However that may be, one is left with the impression that the Council of Ephesus definitively consecrated in the Oriental Churches the belief not merely in Mary's divine maternity but in her perpetual virginity as well.[140] It is not simply that the prerogative was preached by orthodox churchmen of the time, such as Cyril of Alexandria,[141] Proclus of Constantinople,[142] and

---

[137] Cf. Epiphanius, *Ancoratus*, n. 119; *G.C.S.*, 25, 148. Cf. J. N. D. Kelly, *Early Christian Creeds* (London, New York, Toronto, 1950), pp. 335-337 and passim.

[138] Cf. Nilus, *Epistolae*, lib. 1, epp. 269 and 271; *PG*, 79, 181.

[139] Cf. Jouassard, *art. cit.*, p. 100.

[140] Cf. *ibid.*, pp. 138-139.

[141] Mary is "ever virgin" and "crown of virginity": Cyril, *Hom. div. 4*; Schwartz, A.C.O., Tom. 1, Vol. 1, Part 2, 102 and 104; *PG*, 77, 992, 996. She had only one son, and remained thereafter virgin: cf. *Oratio ad dominas*, n. 190; A.C.O., Tom. 1, Vol. 1, Part 5, 111; *PG*, 76, 1317. The "brethren" were sons and daughters of Joseph by a former marriage: cf. Comm. in Ioannis evangelium, lib. 4, cap. 5; ed. P. E. Pusey, *Cyrilli in d. Ioannis evangelium*, Vol. 1 (Oxonii, 1872), p. 584; *PG*, 73, 637; also *Glaph. in Genesim*, lib. 7; *PG*, 69, 352. Cf. Eberle, *op. cit.*, pp. 116-118.

[142] Cf. Proclus, Oratio 2: *De incarnatione domini*, n. 6; *PG*, 65, 700.

Theodotus of Ancyra.[143] What is more striking still, the same belief (including virginity in parturition) was soon to be the common, though not unanimous, conviction of the dissidents as well.[144] Little wonder that the Greeks experienced little, if any, difficulty in accepting the third canon of the Lateran Council in 649, and confessing (*a*) that the ever-virgin Mary conceived God the Word "without seed," (*b*) that she brought Him to birth "without corruption," and (*c*) that after childbearing her virginity remained "indissoluble."[145]

III. MARY'S MOTHERHOOD

A third problem in patristic Mariology is Mary's Maternity. Strangely enough — as I have pointed out elsewhere[146] — what was first denied to Our Lady was not the prerogative, Mother of God, but what her contemporaries never dreamed of denying, that she was Mother of Jesus (cf. Mk. 6:1-3). The early crisis was Docetic — the affirmation that the Saviour did not have a genuinely human body, or at any rate simply passed through the Virgin without being fashioned of her substance. But there was a complementary denial. Where the Gnostics introduced a distinction between Jesus born of Mary and the Christ who descended into Jesus at baptism, they denied implicitly that the Child of Mary was God.

The Christian reaction in the first three centuries is expressive. Not that Our Lady is categorically denominated Mother of God; there is no indisputable evidence for any such title before the fourth

---

[143] Cf. Theodotus, *Hom. 4: In sanctam deiparam et in Simeonem*, n. 3; PG, 77, 1412.

[144] Cf. the survey of the Eastern tradition, orthodox and dissident, in Gordillo, *Mariologia orientalis*, pp. 168-184

[145] Cf. J. D. Mansi, *Sacrorum conciliorum nova et amplissima collectio*, Vol. 10 (Florentiae, 1764), col. 1151. As Jouassard points out, op. cit., p. 139, note 15, this canon simply expresses in more explicit fashion a doctrine which the Greeks had already accepted in the Second Council of Constantinople, when they declared Mary "ever virgin."

[146] Cf. *Mary in Western Patristic Thought*, p. 147.

century.[147] But the orthodox East had a two-edged answer for the Gnostic position. On the one hand, it employed expressions tantamount to an affirmation of divine Maternity. On the other, it propounded the twin premises for its conclusion: (*a*) Jesus was genuinely born of Mary; and (*b*) Jesus born of Mary is God.

Ignatius, as always, is unceremonious. At odds with the heretics who refused Our Lord a true humanity, he states flatly that Jesus Christ is "David's scion and Mary's Son"; He "was really born and ate and drank. ..."[148] More than that, He is "sprung both from Mary

---

[147] The texts adduced to prove a third-century usage of Theotókos in East or West have all been challenged. (a) *In the Greek text of Hippolytus' De benedictionibus Iacob,* cap. 1, we read: "... Joseph betroths Mary to himself and becomes a trustworthy witness to the Mother of God (θεοτόκου)"; *Texte und Untersuchungen,* Vol. 38, Part 1, p. 13. Unfortunately, there is nothing in the Georgian translation (*Texte und Untersuchungen,* Vol. 26, Part 1, p. 3) to correspond to it; only the Greek has it. Bardenhewer branded it an interpolation; cf. *Geschichte der altkirchlichen Literatur,* Vol. 2 (2nd ed.; Freiburg, 1914), p. 608, note 1. H. Rahner, however, made a laudable effort to accredit the Greek text and concluded that Hippolytus, about 220, attests the title; cf. *Hippolyt von Rom als Zeuge für den Ausdruck θεοτόκος,* in *Zeitschrift für katholische Theologie,* Vol. 59, 1935, pp. 73-81. Dom. B. Reynders, however, pointed out that the Armenian text, which is the intermediary whereby the Georgian reaches the original Greek, had been edited by L. Mariès (Paris, 1935), that it does not give the passage in question (cf. pp. 46-47), and that therefore the hypothesis of an interpolation must stand; cf. *Bulletin de Théologie Ancienne et Médiévale,* Vol. 2, 1933-1936, n. 1153; so, too, J. Lebreton, in *Recherches de Science Religieuse,* Vol. 26, 1936, p. 204, note 25. (*b*) The historian Socrates claims that Origen, in the first volume of his commentary on Romans, treated the question, how Mary is θεοτόκος; cf. Hist. eccl., lib. 7, cap. 32; *PG,* 67, 812. Rahner, *art. cit.,* p. 73, thought it a moot point whether Socrates meant that Origen was defending merely Mary's maternal dignity or the actual title. Vagaggini, *op. cit.,* p. 106, note 37, sees no reason to doubt that, in Socrates' context, it is the title itself that is primarily in view. In any event, none of the extant works of Origen contains the word indisputably; for unreliable readings, cf. Vagaggini, p. 107, note 40. (*c*) The title of a homily, περι της θεοτόκου, attributed to Pierius, Bishop of Alexandria at the beginning of the fourth century, by Philip of Side (cf. Texte und Untersuchungen, Vol. 5, Part 2, p. 171), may well be due to a copyist; cf. Bardenhewer, *op. cit.,* Vol. 2, pp. 237-238, and p. 238, note 1. (*d*) On the antiphon, *Sub tuum praesidium,* cf. note 176 below.

[148] Ignatius, *Ad Trallianos,* n. 9, 1; ed. Funk-Bihlmeyer, p. 95; tr. J. Kleist, in *Ancient Christian Writers,* Vol. 1 (Westminster, Md., 1946), 77.

and from God."[149] If the latter expression tempts us to conceive two individuals, one human (from Mary), the other divine (from God), living somehow side by side in Christ, Ignatius leaves no room for any such illusion: "The fact is, our God Jesus Christ was conceived by Mary according to God's dispensation, 'of the seed of David,' it is true, but also of the Holy Spirit."[150] Mary conceived God. That, in brief, is the message hurled across the second century by Aristides, for whom a Christian's confession is that Christ "is the Son of the most high God, that He ... was born of a holy virgin ... and so took flesh";[151] by Justin, who insists that it was God who became man by Mary;[152] by Irenaeus, whose insight is that, if God's birth from Mary is unreal, our Redemption is equally unreal.[153]

The early Alexandrians are no less insistent. Whatever traces of Docetism may lurk in Clement, they are not in evidence when he calls Mary "the Mother of the Lord,"[154] or when he observes that "the Son of God ... took flesh and was carried in a virgin's womb."[155] More impressive still, Origen takes issue openly with the Gnostic enemy. He knows the thesis of Valentinus that Christ was "born through Mary and not of Mary."[156] He recognizes not simply the bald doctrine of Marcion: Jesus did not have a human soul or an earthly body, was not born of Mary, appeared suddenly in Judaea with imaginary flesh at the age of thirty. He has uncovered Marcion's motivation: "the pretext of giving greater glory to the Lord Jesus" by divesting Him of matter.[157] He is aware that Apelles conceded genuine flesh to Christ, but from the heavens, not from

---

[149] Ignatius, *Ad Ephesios*, n. 7, 2; Funk-Bihlmeyer, p. 84; tr. Kleist, p. 63.

[150] *Ad Ephesios*, n. 18, 2; Funk-Bihlmeyer, p. 87; tr. Kleist, p. 67.

[151] Aristides, *Apologia*, n. 2; *Texte und Untersuchungen*, Vol. 4, Part 3, p. 9.

[152] Cf. Justin, *Apologia* 1, cap. 63; *PG*, 6, 425; Apologia 2, cap. 6; *PG*, 6, 453.

[153] Cf. Irenaeus, *Adversus haereses*, lib. 3, cap. 31, 1 (Massuet, 3, 22, 1); Harvey, 2, 121; *PG*, 7, 956. I have treated Irenaeus more at length in *Mary in Western Patristic Thought*, pp. 148-149.

[154] Clement of Alexandria, *Stromata*, lib. 1, cap. 21; G.C.S., 15, 91.

[155] *Stromata*, lib. 6, cap. 15; G.C.S., 15, 496.

[156] Origen, *In epistolam ad Galatas; PG, 14,* 1298; cf. *In epistolam ad Titum; PG,* 14, 1304.

[157] Origen, *In epistolam ad Titum; PG,* 14, 1304.

Mary.[158] His refutation is simple but unwavering: Scripture calls Christ "Son of Man"; He had human passions, human emotions; His birth is less a scandal than His death.[159] Origen's retort to Marcion is in the tradition of Irenaeus: no human nature, no salvation.[160]

Moreover, Origen realizes that Christ is not sheer Man: in Him humanity has been uniquely united to divinity. Origen's insight into the intimate nature of this union is necessarily imperfect; but his grasp of the essential fact of the Incarnation, his understanding of its implications, is so clear that the divine Maternity emerges unmistakably from his writings.[161] He declares that it was not a mere man but the Son of God who was present in Mary's womb;[162] and he comes remarkably close to the actual expression, *Mother of God*, when he says: "... as soon as Mary spoke the word which the Son of God had prompted in His Mother's womb, [John] leaped for joy. ..."[163]

With the fourth century the title *Theotókos* is quite common and its theological basis comes into view rather clearly. The development down to Ephesus is especially dramatic in the East, not least because at its beginning, middle, and end the story touches, respectively, Arius, Julian the Apostate, and Nestorius.

Of its very nature, the speculation of Arius on the Word could not but have repercussions on Mariology; for, if the Logos is not God, then Mary is hardly the Mother of God. Did Arius draw the conclusion? There exists no positive proof that he did. But, as Jouassard has pointed out, it is significant that even before the Council of Nicaea, in one of the first documents relative to the controversy — the circular letter by which Alexander, Bishop of Alexandria, announced to his colleagues the deposition of Arius (*ca.*

---

[158] Cf. Origen, *Hom. 14 in Lucam*; G.C.S., 35, 97; *Hom. 17 in Lucam*; G.C.S., 35, 115.

[159] Cf. Origen, *Hom. 1 in Ezechielem*, n. 4; G.C.S., 33, 327-328.

[160] Cf. Origen, *Comm. in Ioannem*, lib. 10, n. 6 (4); G.C.S., 10, 176.

[161] On Origen's grasp of the Incarnation, cf. Vagaggini, *op. cit.*, pp. 101-104.

[162] Cf. Origen, *Hom. 7 in Lucam*; G.C.S., 35, 51-52; *Hom. 8 in Lucam*; G.C.S., 35-58; *Hom. 7 in Lucam*; G.C.S., 35, 48.

[163] Origen, *Hom. 7 in Lucam*; G.C.S., 35, 45.

319) — Alexander gives Mary the title *Theotókos.*[164] But even then the word flows from his pen so naturally, his use of it is so nonchalant, that it leaves an impression of everyday usage, long established and uncontroverted.

However that may be, much of the Christian East soon echoes with it. In Alexandria, Alexander's disciple and successor, Athanasius, uses the term a number of times,[165] and, in insisting that "the Saviour ... was always God," he indicates inchoatively the theological principle which legitimates the title.[166] In Caesarea of Palestine, the historian Eusebius takes the term for granted when he records that Helena honored the childbearing of "the Mother of God" by decorating Bethlehem's cave in every possible way.[167] Cyril of Jerusalem preaches "the Virgin Mother of God" to his catechumens,[168] and declares that it is the Son of God Himself who was born of the Virgin Mary.[169] Basil the Great uses the expression once, in the Christmas homily which assures his flock that "lovers of Christ refuse to lend ear to the idea that the Theotókos ever ceased to be a virgin";[170] his younger brother, Gregory of Nyssa, employs it five times.[171] The term occurs in Epiphanius of Salamis[172] and in Didymus of Alexandria.[173] So welcome is the word that Gregory of Nazianzus not merely makes casual use of it against

---

[164] Cf. Alexander of Alexandria, *Epist. ad Alexandrum Constant.*, n. 12; PG, 18, 568. Cf. Jouassard, *art. cit.*, p. 85.

[165] Cf. Athanasius, *Oratio 3 contra Arianos,* nn. 14, 29, 33; PG, 26, 349, 385, 393; id., *Vita s. Antonii,* n. 36; *PG,* 26, 897.

[166] Cf. Athanasius, *Oratio 3 contra Arianos,* n. 29; *PG,* 26, 385.

[167] Cf. Eusebius, *De vita Constantini,* lib. 3, n. 43; G.C.S., 7, 95. On Constantine's alleged use of θεο μήτηρ κόρη, originally in Latin according to Eusebius, cf. *PG,* 20, 1265; also P. Clément (cited below, note 177), pp. 603-604.

[168] Cyril, *Catecheses,* 10, 19; PG, 33, 685.

[169] Cf. *Catecheses,* 12, 4; *PG,* 33, 729.

[170] Basil, *Homilia in sanctam Christi generationem,* n. 5; PG, 31, 1468.

[171] Cf. Gregory of Nyssa, *De virginitate,* cap. 14 (13) and 19; ed. Cavarnos, *op. cit.,* pp. 306, 323; id., *In diem natalem Christi; PG,* 46, 1136; id., *In Christi resurrectionem, orat.* 5; *PG,* 46, 688.

[172] Cf. Epiphanius, *Ancoratus,* n. 75; G.C.S., 25, 95.

[173] Cf. Didymus, *De trinitate,* lib. 2, cap. 4; PG, 39, 484.

Eunomius[174] but finds in it a tessera of orthodoxy and can hurl anathema at Apollinaris:

If anyone does not admit that holy Mary is Theotókos, he is separated from the divinity. If anyone should say that [Christ] passed through the Virgin as through a channel, but was not fashioned in her divinely and humanly — divinely because without the help of man, humanly because by the law of conception — he too is godless. If anyone should say that the man was fashioned and then God stole in, he is condemned; for this is not a generation of God but an escape from generation. If anyone introduces two sons, one from God the Father, the other from the mother, but not one and the same, let him fall from the adoption promised to orthodox believers.[175]

It is the theologian who speaks through Gregory. But while the theologian wielded the word as a weapon, the layman whispered it in accents of love; for from the same fourth century comes a precious papyrus leaf, from which we can reconstruct the original Greek of our lovely prayer, "We fly to thy patronage, O holy Mother of God" — and the word that stands out clearly is *Theotóke*,[176] Little wonder that, in this atmosphere where theology and piety are one, we hear Julian the Apostate's cry of frustration: "You Christians

---

[174] Cf. Gregory of Nazianzus, *Oratio 29*, n. 4; *PG*, 36, 80.

[175] Gregory of Nazianzus, *Epistola 101*; *PG*, 37, 177-180.

[176] Cf. C. H. Roberts, ed., *Catalogue of the Greek and Latin Papyri in the John Rylands Library*, Vol. 3 (Cambridge, 1939), n. 470; F. Mercenier, *L'antienne mariale grecque la plus ancienne*, in *Le Muséon*, Vol. 52, 1939, pp. 229-233; id., *La plus ancienne prière à la sainte Vierge*, in *Questions Liturgiques et Paroissiales*, Vol. 25, 1940, pp. 33-36. The conservative dating of Roberts, not before the second half of the fourth century, has been disputed by G. Vannucci, who prefers the opinion of Lobel, based on sheerly paleographic grounds, that the document is not later than the third century; cf. *La più antica preghiera alla Madre di Dio*, in *Marianum*, Vol. 3, 1941, pp. 97-101. More recently, O. Stegmüller has objected to Mercenier's restoration and submitted his own; paleographic, liturgical, patristic, and apocryphal data persuade him that the prayer ought not to be dated before the end of the fourth century; cf. *Sub tuum praesidium: Bemerkungen zur ältesten Überlieferung*, in *Zeitschrift für katholische Theologie*, Vol. 74, 1952, pp. 76-82. Gordillo considers Stegmüller's dating less probable and assigns the prayer to the third century; cf. *Mariologia orientalis*, p. 7, and note 56, *ibid.*

never stop calling Mary Mother of God (*Theotókos*)."[177] It is an intriguing fact that, while Theotókos was used without scruple by the Alexandrians and by the Cappadocians who were theologically kin to them, the word is conspicuously absent from Antiochene literature.[178] Not that the word was unfamiliar to fourth-century Antiochenes; they did, however, shy away from it. Two reasons may be suggested. First, Arian misuse of the term may have engendered reservations with respect to its propriety, and a consequent disinclination to employ it.[179] Second, if it be true that fifth-century Nestorianism had its historical and logical roots in fourth-century Antioch, then we may surmise that a word with the implications of *Theotókos* sat as uncomfortably in the Christology of a Diodore as it was later to do in the theology of Theodore,

---

[177] Quoted by Cyril of Alexandria, *Contra Iulianum*, lib. 8; PG, 76, 901. P. Clément has concluded, from the literature, monuments, liturgy, and Collyridian heresy, that at the end of the fourth century not only the ecclesiastical writers but even the generality of the faithful felt a profound attachment to this Marian prerogative; cf. *Le sens chrétien et la maternité divine de Marie avant le conflit Nestorien*, in *Ephemerides Theologicae Lovanienses*, Vol. 5, 1928, 599-613.

[178] Two exceptions may be authentic. The first stems from the Synod of Antioch at the beginning of 325; for the text, cf. H.-G. Opitz, *Athanasius Werke*, Vol. 3/1, 1-2, Urkunde 18, p. 39. Historians tend more and more to accept the existence of this Council; cf. G. Bardy, in J. R. Palanque, et al., The Church in the Christian Roman Empire, Vol. 1, The Church and the Arian Crisis, tr. E. C. Messenger (New York, 1953), pp. 85-86. The other text stems from Eustathius, Bishop of Antioch 324-330; cf. *Frag. 68;* ed. M. Spanneut, Recherches sur les écrits d'Eustathe d'Antioche (Lille, 1948), p. 116. Its authenticity is doubted by Sellers and Zoepfl, upheld by Cavallera, Bardenhewer, and Spanneut; cf. A. Grillmeier, Die theologische und sprachliche Vorbereitung der christologischen Formel von Chalkedon, in Das Konzil von Chalkedon: Geschichte und Gegenwart, edd. Grillmeier-Bacht, Vol. 1 (Würzburg, 1951), p. 125 and note 14, ibid. Ephraem does not use the Greek word, Theotókos, nor any Syriac word which could be so translated, although he affirms the divine Maternity clearly; cf. Ortiz de Urbina, La mariologia nei Padri siriaci, p. 104; Gordillo, Mariologia orientalis, pp. 8, 29. With respect to Chrysostom, the homilies where the word occurs are not his, but are probably the work of Severian of Gabala; cf. B. Marx, Severiana unter den Spuria Chrysostomi bei Montfaucon-Migne, in Orientalia Christiana Periodica, Vol. 5, 1939, pp. 281-367.

[179] Cf. Grillmeier, *art. cit.*, p. 126, note 14.

Theodoret, and Nestorius.[180]

Much of the Nestorian controversy is clouded in uncertainty. We do know that, from 428 on, a rising reluctance to call Mary *Theotókos* provoked violent reactions. We know that, when Nestorius of Constantinople gave his blessing to a bishop who preached, "If anyone says that holy Mary is *Theotókos*, let him be anathema," Cyril of Alexandria retorted, "If anyone does not confess that ... the holy Virgin is Theotókos ... let him be anathema."[181] We know that, when the Council of Ephesus convened in 431, Cyril wrote of that first session to his flock in Alexandria:

> Know, then, that on the [22nd of June] the holy Synod met at Ephesus in the great church ... of Mary, Mother of God. We spent the whole day there, and finally ... we deposed ... Nestorius and removed him from the episcopal office. Now there were about 200 (more or less) of us bishops gathered together. And the whole populace of [Ephesus] was waiting tensely, waiting from dawn to dusk for the decision of the holy Synod. When they heard that the unfortunate fellow had been deposed, with one voice all started to shout in praise of the holy Synod, with one voice all began to glorify God, because the enemy of the faith had fallen. When we left the church, they escorted us to our lodging with torches; for it was evening. Gladness was in the air; lamps dotted the city; even women went before us with censers and led the way.[182]

---

[180] Neither the content of *Theotókos* among the Alexandrians nor the Antiochene reluctance to employ the term can be appreciated without some understanding of Alexandrian and Antiochene Christology. Cf., e.g., Grillmeier, *art. cit.*, pp. 5-202; E. Weigl, *Christologie vom Tode des Athanasius bis zum Ausbruch des nestorianischen Streites* (373-429) (München, 1925); R. V. Sellers, *Two Ancient Christologies* (London, 1940); F. Loofs, *Leitfaden zum Studium der Dogmengeschichte*, Part 1 (ed. K. Aland; Halle, 1950), p. 205 ff.; Söll, art. cit., pp. 310-317. — It is worth noting that a man like Chrysostom, whose orthodoxy is beyond suspicion, avoids Theotókos not so much from deep-rooted theological prepossessions as (*a*) because his master, Diodore, refuses to use it, and (*b*) because he is primarily a preacher, who prefers the more common, more indeterminate, less loaded terminology.

[181] Cyril of Alexandria, Epistola *17*, n. 12; A.C.O., Tom. 1, Vol. 1, Part 1, 40; *PG*, 77, 120. It is interesting that before 428 Theotókos appears in Cyril very infrequently, perhaps not at all; cf. Jouassard, art. cit., p. 99, note 59.

[182] Cyril, *Epistola 24;* A.C.O., Tom. 1, Vol. 1, Part 1, 117-118; *PG*, 77, 137. For the background of Ephesus and subsequent events, cf. Jouassard, p. 122 ff. In a recent attempt to determine the precise theological value of Ephesus'

That is the fact of Ephesus, and on the surface it is simple enough. A bishop had questioned Mary's most precious prerogative, and his brother bishops had banned him from their fellowship. But that is not quite the significance of Ephesus. Nestorius' concept of Mary stemmed from his concept of Christ. Similarly, what Ephesus determined with respect to Mary's Motherhood was rooted in what Ephesus believed with respect to Christ's Sonship. That is why Nestorius, for all his reluctance, could say to Cyril in all honesty: "It is not on the ground of a [mere] name that I part from you; it is on the essence of God the Word and on the essence of the Man."[183] What was at stake was the Incarnation itself. In what sense can we say with St. John, "the Word was made flesh"?

The solution of Nestorius is shrouded in obscurity. How he conceived that incredible union of God and human nature in the womb of a virgin is not at all clear; somehow God dwelt in flesh as in a temple. What is clear is the set of conclusions he drew therefrom. "Does God have a mother? [He does not.]" "I say it is the flesh that was born of the Virgin Mary, not God the Word. ..." "It is not right to say that God is two or three months old." "A born God, a dead God, a buried God I cannot adore."[184]

The answer of Ephesus was unequivocal. It canonized the letter to Nestorius in which Cyril declared:

> We must not ... sever into two sons the one Lord Jesus Christ. Such severance will be no help at all to the correct expression of the faith, even if one allege unity of persons. Scripture, you see, has not said that the Word united to Himself the person of a man, but that He has been made flesh. Now the Word's being made flesh is nothing else than that He partook of flesh and blood in like manner with us, and

---

first session, Ortiz de Urbina has concluded that the divine Maternity was expressly and directly defined; cf. *Il dogma di Efeso*, in Mélanges Martin Jugie (Paris, 1953), pp. 233-240; but cf. Jouassard, p. 135, for a more conservative opinion.

[183] Nestorius, Liber Heraclidis, 2, 1; tr. based on French version by F. Nau, *et al.*, *Le Livre d'Héraclide de Damas* (Paris, 1910), p. 171.

[184] *Nestorii sermo; A.C.O.*, Tom. 1, Vol. 5, Part 1, 30; *Liber Heraclidis*, 2, 1; tr. Nau, p. 176; *Nestorii tractatus; A.C.O.*, Tom. 1, Vol. 5, Part 1, 38; J. P. Bethune-Baker, *Nestorius and His Teaching* (Cambridge, 1908), p. 71. Cf. also Nilus a S. B., *De maternitate divina b. Mariae semper virginis Nestorii Constantinopolitani et Cyrilli Alexandrini sententia* (Romae, 1944), pp. 1-19.

made our body His own, and proceeded Man of a woman, without having cast away His divinity. ... This is what the expression of the exact faith everywhere preaches; this is the mind we shall find in the holy Fathers. In this sense they did not hesitate to call the holy Virgin God's Mother (Theotókos) — not as though the nature of the Word or His divinity took beginning of being from the holy Virgin, but that of her was begotten the holy body animated with a rational soul; to this body the Word was united personally, and so He is said to have been born according to the flesh.[185]

Briefly, then, Mary is Mother of God. She is Mother, because the flesh which God took, He took from her flesh; and because Mary gave to her Son everything any mother gives to her child in its fashioning. She was pregnant with Christ. And she is Mother of God, simply because the human being who came forth from her womb was and is God.

It is understandable, then, why Ephesus was so exercised over a single word, *Theotókos*. True, in the minds of some reputable historians Ephesus is synonymous with imprudence, intrigue, ecclesiastical politics. But, to its credit, Ephesus recognized that the denial or even the abandonment of *Theotókos* was equivalent to a disavowal of Nicaea. Not that the Council of Nicaea had called Mary "Mother of God"; but that, unless Mary is God's Mother, the Christian cannot confess, with the Fathers of Nicaea, "I believe in ... Jesus Christ, God's Son ... who for us men and for our salvation came down, was made flesh, became Man. ..."[186]

Call Ephesus, if you will, a war of words; there is no need to blush. A word is the incarnation of an idea. A century before, in the Arian crisis, the Christian world had been ruptured by a word. With that word, *homooúsios*, "consubstantial," Athanasius summed up orthodox belief on the Eternal Word, the Son of God. In the Nestorian controversy the Christian East was sundered once more by a word. With that Word, *Theotókos*, "Mother of God," Cyril summed up orthodox belief on the Word Incarnate, the Son of God made flesh. That is why Cyril could thunder: "To confess our faith

---

[185] Cyril, Epistola 4, n. 6; A.C.O., Tom. 1, Vol. 1, Part 1, 28; PG, 77, 48.

[186] Cf. Cyril, *Epistola 1*, nn. 5-6; *A.C.O.*, Tom. 1, Vol. 1, Part 1, 12-13; *PG*, 77, 16. For the text of the Symbol of Nicaea, cf. I. Ortiz de Urbina, *El Símbolo Niceno* (Madrid, 1947), p. 21.

in orthodox fashion ... it is enough to ... confess that the holy Virgin is *Theotókos.*"[187] And three centuries later St. John Damascene, whose glory it is to have summed up in himself the theology of the Greek Fathers, wrote so simply: "This name contains the whole mystery of the Incarnation."[188]

IV. OUR LADY'S HOLINESS

As with her divine Maternity and her abiding virginity, so too with respect to Our Lady's holiness, the year 431 marks a turning point for Eastern patristic thought. Before Ephesus, Oriental theology is apparently unaware of a problem in this regard. Where the literature touches the sanctity of Mary, it does so for the most part obliquely, in passing, with a disinterest which is disconcerting and at times a familiarity which borders on discourtesy. The pre-Ephesus portrait of Mary is paradoxical. For that reason it seems advisable to present separately the two ingredients of which the paradox is compounded: (*a*) the evidence which indicates an awareness of Our Lady's sanctity; and (*b*) the texts which seem to limit, minimize, or contradict such a consciousness.[189]

Even before Nicaea several facts suggest that the Christian East was not insensitive to Mary's sanctity. In the first place, the second-century calumny — actually a flanking attack on Christ — that the Mother of Jesus was an adulteress, perhaps a prostitute, must have been met with scorn by any Christian who confessed with Ignatius and Aristides, with Justin and Irenaeus and the universal Church, that the Saviour Christ was born of a virgin.[190] The Marian vision of the early East may well have been myopic; it did not, however, see in Mary a woman of questionable morality.

---

[187] Cyril, *Hom. div. 15,* n. 4; *PG;* 1093. For a more comprehensive picture, cf. Eberle, *op. cit.,* pp. 21-104.

[188] John Damascene, *De fide orthodoxa,* lib. 3, cap. 12; *PG,* 94, 1029. A synthetic view of Damascene's doctrine on the divine Maternity may be found in Chevalier, *op. cit.,* pp. 94-129.

[189] The Oriental tradition for the first five centuries, specifically on Mary's "original sanctity," has been set forth with customary scholarliness and acumen by M. Jugie, *L'Immaculée Conception dans l'Écriture sainte et dans la tradition orientale* (Romae, 1952), pp. 55-94.

[190] Cf. notes 64-67 above.

Second, the Eve-Mary parallelism is not impertinent here. Eastern Christianity saw in Our Lady a cause of salvation, at least in the sense that she gave birth to the Saviour: source of life because Mother of Life. Her consent to an Incarnation recognized as redemptive was not simply an act of singular felicity, undoing the devastation achieved by Eve. It had exceptional moral value; it was an act of uncommon obedience.[191] From this premise, Mary's uncompelled and unparalleled role in the Redemption, did the Fathers conclude to a rare sanctity, either after her fiat or before? The pre-Ephesus evidence does not warrant the affirmation that they did.[192] But the germ of later development is already there.

Third, the adjective "holy" is prefixed to "Virgin" even in ante-Nicene times. Thus, Hippolytus (who, for all his Roman activity, was Greek in origin, mentality, and language)[193] states, without explanation, that "God the Word descended into the holy Virgin Mary."[194] On this score, however, what I have emphasized elsewhere with reference to the West is equally germane to the East:

> The difficulty is, such a usage is ill-defined. The word sanctus or ἅγιος has not always been able to boast of a clearly delimited meaning in ecclesiastical use. Does Hippolytus use ἅγιος as a rather vague laudatory epithet, or as a title of dignity, or to imply moral excellence, or to signify the respect reserved for one who is segregated from profane things and belongs to God by some sort of consecration? The answer must, in the state of the evidence, be a confession of ignorance.[195]

Similar difficulties arise with respect to kindred adjectives. The Inscription of Abercius (before 216) mentions that "faith ... set before [him] for food the fish from the spring, mighty and pure,

---

[191] Cf. notes 5 and 7 above.

[192] Jugie argues that Irenaeus' concept of Mary's sublime role at the side of Christ (i.e., it is to Jesus and Mary that humanity owes its return to primitive incorruption) removes from her ipso facto any such thing as original corruption; cf. *L'Immaculée Conception*, p. 67. The conclusion may be theologically valid; it is nevertheless obvious that Irenaeus did not grasp the implications of his premise.

[193] Cf. J. Quasten, *Patrology*, Vol. 2 (Westminster, Md., 1953), 163.

[194] Hippolytus, Contra Noetum, cap. 17; PG, 10, 825.

[195] *Mary in Western Patristic Thought*, pp. 138-139. Cf. also H. Delehaye, *Sanctus*, in *Analecta Bollandiana*, Vol. 28, 1909, pp. 145-200.

whom a spotless (ἀγνή) virgin caught."[196] A passage attributed with scant reason to Origen speaks of "the all-holy (πανaγίaς) Mother of God."[197] About 300, the anonymous ("Adamantius") author of a dialogue on orthodox belief says that the Word "took man to Himself of the immaculate (ἀχράντου) Virgin Mary."[198] In all these instances holiness is predicated of Mary, but its intimate nature is indeterminate.

Fourth, there is testimony which suggests that here again popular piety may have anticipated scientific theology. The witness is the apocryphal but influential Protoevangelium of James (150-180). The pertinent ideas discoverable therein concern Our Lady's virginal purity, the unusual circumstances of her conception, and the description of Mary as "a fruit of justice."

To begin with, an insistent theme in the Protoevangelium is Mary's virginal purity. The author will not abide anything which, from her infancy on, could be construed as contamination or defilement.[199] True, the contamination directly envisaged is physical and legal; but it may be argued with some justification that in the context purity of body demands purity of soul, especially in her who was destined to be Mother of the Saviour.[200]

More significant, however, is the possibility that the Protoevangelium suggests a virginal, and therefore implicitly an immaculate, conception of Mary. Joachim has retired to the desert

---

[196] *Epitaphium Abercii,* vv. 12-14; ed. J. Quasten, in *Florilegium patristicum,* Vol. 7 (Bonnae, 1935), 22-24. For the view that the "virgin" is Our Lady, cf. F. J. Dölger. ΙΧΘΥΣ, Vol. 2 (Münster, 1922), 487-488; J. Quasten, *Flor. patr.,* Vol. 7, 24, note 2; J. C. Plumpe, Mater ecclesia (Washington, D. C., 1943), p. 28, note 32. For the conviction that the Church is intended, cf. A. Greiff, *Zum Verständnis der Aberkiosinschrift,* in *Theologie und Glaube,* Vol. 18, 1926, pp. 78-88; G. Bardy, *La théologie de l'église de s. Clément de Rome à s. Irénée* (Paris, 1945), pp. 123-124; and, tending in the same direction, A. Müller, *Ecclesia-Maria: Die Einheit Marias und der Kirche* (2nd ed., Freiburg i. d. Schweiz, 1955), pp. 43-44 and note 58, ibid. — Cf. also *Ascensio Isaiae,* cap. 11, n. 5: Joseph keeps Mary as "a holy virgin"; Charles, *Ascensio d'Isaie,* p. 204.

[197] Hom. *7 in Lucam;* G.C.S., 35, 50. Cf. Vagaggini, *op. cit.,* pp. 25 and 107, note 40.

[198] Adamantius, *De recta in Deum fide; G.C.S.,* 4, 190, 191. Cf. also *Oracula Sibyllina,* lib. 8, v. 461: ἀχράντοισι ... κόλποις; *G.C.S., 8, 171.*

[199] Cf. *Protevangelium Iacobi,* 7-16; ed. Amann, *op. cit.,* pp. 204-242.

[200] Cf. Jugie, *L'Immaculée Conception,* p. 57.

to lament Anne's sterility, to fast, and to pray.[201] After a lengthy absence Joachim is greeted, first by an angel and then by Anne, with the news of a conception.[202] At this point our problem turns textual and grammatical. Some scholars are persuaded that, according to the primitive text, the angel said, "Your wife has conceived," and Anne said, "I have conceived."[203] In the context (so runs the argument at its most cogent) a verb in the perfect argues a conception that is virginal, and a virginal conception implies an immaculate conception. On the other hand, several objections deserve recording. (a) Though the perfect-tense reading is relatively ancient and enjoyed wide diffusion at an early date, other (perhaps most) manuscripts have the future, and the future was adopted by Tischendorf as the textus receptus.[204] (b) Even the perfect tense does not necessarily involve a virginal conception. For one thing, Joachim's separation from Anne may have begun no more than forty days before. Besides, Epiphanius' fourth-century interpretation is not implausible: by the use of the perfect the angel "foretold what was to be, to forestall any uncertainty."[205] (c) Though some Christians did take the perfect tense literally and concluded to a virginal conception, Epiphanius indicates that this way of thinking did not represent the mind of the Church.[206] In a word, Mary's conception emerges as confessedly miraculous, but not convincingly immaculate.

A bit later the *Protoevangelium* lays a canticle on the lips of Anne after the birth of Mary: "... the Lord has given me a fruit of [His] righteousness, single and manifold before Him."[207] The text is uncertain; its meaning is problematical. Still, a not unlikely exegesis interprets the fruit as Mary; she is worthy of the holiness of the God who gave her to Anne; she is unique of her kind; she contains all

---

[201] Cf. *Protevangelium Iacobi*, 1, 4; Amann, pp. 182-184.

[202] Cf. *Protevangelium Iacobi*, 4, 2 and 4, 4; Amann, pp. 192-194.

[203] So Jugie, *L'Immaculée Conception*, p. 60.

[204] For a discussion of the textual problem, cf. Amann, *op. cit.*, pp. 17-21; Jugie, *L'Immaculée Conception*, pp. 58-62.

[205] Cf. Epiphanius, *Panarion*, haer. 79, n. 5; *G.C.S.*, 37, 480.

[206] Cf. Epiphanius, *Panarion*, haer. 79, n. 5; also haer. 78, n. 23; *G.C.S.*, 37, 474: her body "was conceived of a man and a woman."

[207] *Protevangelium Iacobi*, 6, 3; Amann, p. 202.

manner of admirable, God-given qualities.[208]

Fifth, the early Alexandrians insinuate Mary's sanctity, but they do little more. There is a fugitive allusion to it when Clement compares the Church to Our Lady. Each is a virgin and consequently undefiled; each is a mother and therefore lovingly affectionate.[209] Origen is somewhat more detailed. He claims that before the Annunciation Mary was "holy," that she meditated daily on Scripture.[210] Gabriel's greeting, "Hail, full of grace," Origen sees as a hapax legomenon in Scripture, reserved exclusively for Mary; but he fails to clarify its significance.[211] Our Lady's journey "into the hill country with haste" strikes him as deeply meaningful: it indicates a significant stage in her efforts to scale the heights of perfection.[212] The Visitation was a source of remarkable "progress" for Elizabeth and John the Baptist, "from the nearness of the Lord's Mother and the presence of the Saviour Himself."[213] Mary can sing, "My soul magnifies the Lord," not that the Lord is capable of increase, but because her soul's likeness to its Lord is increasing.[214] The "humility of His handmaid" Origen interprets as her righteousness, moderation, courage, and wisdom.[215] Briefly, Origen's portrait of Mary corresponds to his general conception of a soul that is making progress in the spiritual life — and her progress reflects her own good dispositions and the special protection of the Holy Spirit.[216]

The extant evidence, therefore, if meager, indicates sufficiently that for some of the ante-Nicene writers in the East a certain sanctity did attach to the person of Mary. For the most part its essence is unsuspected, though Origen reveals that it involves the practice of virtue, the intervention of God, and an ascent toward perfection. The evidence does not justify us in concluding that the

---

[208] Cf. Jugie, *L'Immaculée Conception*, pp. 62-63.

[209] Cf. Clement, *Paedagogus*, lib. 1, cap. 6; G.C.S., 12, 115.

[210] Cf. Origen, *Hom. 6 in Lucam*; G.C.S., 35, 40.

[211] Cf. *Hom. 6 in Lucam*; G.C.S., 35, 39-40.

[212] Cf. Origen, *Hom. 7 in Lucam*; G.C.S., 35, 46.

[213] Origen, *Hom. 9 in Lucam*; G.C.S., 35, 62.

[214] Cf. Origen, *Hom. 8 in Lucam*; G.C.S., 35, 55-57.

[215] Cf. *Hom. 8 in Lucam*; G.C.S., 35, 58.

[216] Cf. Vagaggini, *op.* cit., pp. 136-156, 168-170.

pre-Nicene East envisioned a rare or singular sanctity in the Mother of God, or believed formally that her conception was sinless. If it be insisted that the Immaculate Conception is a legitimate deduction from the patristic doctrine of the Second Eve, let it be remembered that it is deduction and that the deduction was not made before Nicaea.

Between Nicaea and Ephesus, Marian theology makes scant progress in the East. It is Arianism that preoccupies the Fathers; mention of Our Lady is mostly casual and incidental. In the fourth century the two patristic authors who lend fresh insight into Mary's sanctity are Epiphanius among the Greeks and Ephraem in the Syriac speaking Church.[217]

Epiphanius, we have seen, recognizes that Mary is "mother of the living" in a sense far more profound than was Eve: she is cause of life because she gave birth to Life.[218] Does this involve an uncommon holiness? Epiphanius seems to take it for granted:

To pass on to the New Testament: If women were appointed by God to be priests or to perform any ministerial function in the Church, it was Mary herself who should have discharged the office of priest in the New Testament. She was thought worthy to welcome in her own womb the absolute Monarch and heaven's God, God's Son; her womb was prepared, in God's love for man and by an astounding mystery, as a temple and dwelling-place for the Lord's Incarnation.[219]

But there is more. Not merely is Our Lady properly prepared to receive the Word in her womb; she is "graced in every way."[220] Does this imply that she was conceived free from sin? As Epiphanius failed to deduce from his Second Eve doctrine Mary's resemblance to Eve in original sinlessness, so here he makes no inference from

---

[217] If the treatise, *On Virginity*, transmitted in Coptic, is authentic (cf. note 130), Athanasius should he added to Epiphanius and Ephraem. It describes in highly laudatory terms the life of Mary as a young girl. Incidental reservations suggest that the author may have glimpsed in her some trifling, momentary failings; but on the whole the picture is striking. The treatise presents Our Lady as a unique model for Christian virgins.

[218] Cf. note 17.

[219] Epiphanius, *Panarion*, haer. 79, n. 3; *G.C.S.*, 37, 477.

[220] *Panarion*, haer. 78, n. 24; *G.C.S.*, 37, 474.

Mary's fullness of grace. Nevertheless, his "graced in every way" is not to be taken lightly; for with reference to Our Lady, Epiphanius is aware that he must keep a careful eye on his language and his theology.[221] That is why he reproves the Collyridians who make a goddess of Mary by offering sacrifice to her, and rejects the thesis of the Protoevangelium of James that Our Lady was conceived virginally.[222] And still he can speak of her as "graced in every way." The phrase need not involve sinless conception, but it does suggest high holiness.

Further conjectures on the implications of Epiphanius' thought would be sterile. Perhaps the sentence that best epitomizes his explicit theology on Mary's sanctity is this: "though Mary is remarkably good, though she is holy, though she is to be held in honor, still she is not to be adored."[223]

The witness of Ephraem is more striking still. Despite the chaotic condition of the so-called Ephraemite literature, the essence of Ephraem's authentic thought on Mary's sanctity may be recaptured in a single idea: Our Lady is singularly sinless. First, he insists that the Cherubim are not her equal in holiness, the Seraphim must yield to her in loveliness, the legions of angels are inferior in purity.[224] Second, he links Mary and Eve in their "innocence and simplicity," despite the fact that one was principle of salvation, the other of death.[225] Third, in what is perhaps his most suggestive Mariological insight, Ephraem addresses Our Lord as follows: "In very truth, you and your Mother are alone perfectly beautiful in every respect; for in you, Lord, there is no stain at all, and in your Mother there is no spot. Among my children there is no one like these two beautiful ones."[226]

The implications of the last-cited text have been drawn out

---

[221] Cf. X. Le Bachelet, *Immaculée Conception*, in *D.T.C.*, Vol. 7, 879.

[222] Cf. Epiphanius, *Panarion*, haer. 78, n. 23, and haer. 79, n. 5; *G.C.S.*, 37, 474, 480.

[223] *Panarion*, haer. 79, n. 7; *G.C.S.*, 37, 482.

[224] Cf. Ephraem, *Hymni de beata Maria*, 13, nn. 5-6; Lamy, Vol. 2, 577. Cf. *Hymni ...*, 14, n. 1; Lamy, Vol. 2, 577: heaven is not loftier than Mary.

[225] Cf. Ephraem, *Sermones exegetici; Opera omnia syriace et latine*, Vol. 2 (Romae, 1740), 327.

[226] Ephraem, *Carmina Nisibena*, 27; ed. G. Bickell (Lipsiae, 1866), p. 40.

briefly but persuasively by Ortiz de Urbina.[227] Ephraem likens the spotlessness of Mary to the stainlessness of Jesus. In this respect they are unique in humankind; the privilege is exclusively theirs. Moreover, in the context the beauty in question is a spiritual thing; for with this loveliness the Church of Nisibis contrasts its own unsightliness. This spiritual beauty is not limited to virginity; for in the loveliness which is virginity many human beings share. The stain, therefore, is sin, and stainlessness is sinlessness; and so the text excludes from the Mother of God and from her Son all taint of sin, whatever it be — consequently, even original sin.

If it be objected that the passage cannot be cited in favor of the Immaculate Conception unless Ephraem had a clear, acceptable concept of original sin,[228] and if it be added that such a concept is wanting in the writings which are authentically his,[229] Ortiz de Urbina has a two-edged answer. The former objection, he holds, is a little illogical; for a negative and absolute proposition like Ephraem's excludes everything that is genuinely sin, whatever be the author's inability to understand sin comprehensively. The latter objection, he maintains, is not quite true; for Ephraem did realize that our inheritance from Adam is properly sin.

In this instance the problem of interpretation is confessedly complex. Without challenging the right of Ephraem to be listed as witness to the Immaculate Conception, I would simply submit (a) that it is not at all clear from the texts quoted by Ortiz de Urbina that Ephraem recognized original sin for what it is; and (b) that it is dangerous precedent to hold a patristic author to all the logical implications of his negative and absolute propositions.

Such, in brief compass, is the evidence for one side of the paradox. It indicates that before Ephesus Eastern Christianity was not unaware of Our Lady's holiness, recognized it at times as an uncommon thing, and may even have caught a fleeting glimpse of a conception that rivaled Christ's in its sheer sinlessness. The other side of the paradox comprises a set of patristic affirmations which suggest that Mary's life was not free of actual sin and imply

---

[227] Cf. Ortiz de Urbina, *La mariologia nei Padri siriaci,* pp. 107-108; *Lo sviluppo,* pp. 59-60.

[228] Cf. L. Hammersberger, *op. cit.,* p. 57 ff.

[229] Cf. B. Altaner, *Patrologie* (2nd ed.; Freiburg, 1950), p. 301.

concomitantly that her conception was not exempt from original sin. In their more positive form the affirmations attribute specific faults to Our Lady; in a more negative form they relate a purification or sanctification of Mary, commonly on the day of the Annunciation.[230]

In the first place, some of the Fathers and early ecclesiastical writers allege specific faults. The root of these allegations may well be a general principle enunciated by Clement of Alexandria: "only the *Logos* Himself is sinless." He goes on to quote Menander: "for to sin is natural to all and common, but to make amends for sin is not the part of any and every man, but [only] of a remarkable man."[231] Cyril of Alexandria recalls the principle before 423: Aaron had to offer sacrifice for his own sins. "The reason is that, being a man, he should not be looked upon as superior to sin. But for Christ anything of this sort simply will not do; far from it. As God, you see, He enjoyed sinlessness by His very nature."[232] In a word, among human beings the Incarnate Word alone is without sin.

The imputation or insinuation of specific faults centers around four episodes in Mary's life: the Annunciation, Cana, the "mother and brethren" scene (Mt. 12:46 ff.), and Calvary. With reference to Gabriel, Chrysostom asks why the angel did not act toward Mary as he did toward Joseph, i.e., why he did not wait until conception had taken place before telling her the truth about her maternity. His answer? "To keep her from being much confused and troubled; for it was likely that, not knowing the clear truth, she would reach some absurd decision in her regard and, unable to endure the shame, hang or stab herself."[233]

The marriage at Cana is a proverbial trouble-area for exegetes: "What is that to me and to you?" (*Jn.* 2:4.) Irenaeus believes that with these words Our Lord "checked [Mary's] untimely haste," her

---

[230] Cf. X. Le Bachelet, *art. cit.*, cols. 885-893.

[231] Clement, *Paedagogus*, lib. 3, cap. 12; G.C.S., 12, 287.

[232] Cyril of Alexandria, *Glaph. in Leviticum*; PG, 69, 584. For the date (before 423), cf. G. Jouassard, *L'activité littéraire de saint Cyrille jusqu'à 428. Essai de chronologie et de synthèse*, in *Mélanges E. Podechard* (Lyon, 1945), p. 170.

[233] John Chrysostom, *Hom. 4* in Matthaeum, n. 5; PG, 57, 45. Chrysostom's answer is the more surprising as in the same context he recognizes Mary's reaction to Gabriel's greeting as admirable and virtuous.

yearning to quicken the miracle of the water made wine.[234] Severian, Bishop of Gabala in Syria, finds that Jesus "reproves His Mother for a useless and unsuitable suggestion."[235] Chrysostom does not hesitate to say that with her appeal, "They have no wine," Mary "wanted to store up favor with [the disciples] too, and make herself still more illustrious through the medium of her Son."[236]

Mt. 12:46 ff. pictures the Mother and brethren of Jesus on the outskirts of a crowd, eager to speak with Him. Chrysostom finds the attitude of the brethren (and presumably Mary too) all too human: "their desire was not to hear anything useful, but to show that they were related to Him and so to indulge some vainglory. ..."[237] In another passage he deals with Our Lady specifically: "What she tried to do sprang from excessive ambition; for she wanted to display herself to the people as having full authority over her Son. As yet she had no extraordinary idea of Him; that is why her approach was so ill-timed."[238] It is worth noting that this is not ivory-tower exegesis; the Homilies on John and the Homilies on Matthew were preached to the Christians of Antioch about the years 389 and 390.[239]

Calvary and Simeon's "sword of sorrow" pose perhaps the most troublesome problem of all, if seen through the eyes of Origen, Basil the Great, and Cyril of Alexandria. For Origen, the sword is the scandal — concretely, uncertainty and unbelief — experienced by Mary during the passion of her Son. What is more significant, Origen proceeds to defend his exegesis on theological grounds: "Shall we think that, when the apostles were scandalized, the Lord's Mother was exempt from scandal? If she did not experience scandal at the Lord's passion, Jesus did not die for her sins. But if 'all have

---

[234] Irenaeus, *Adversus haereses*, lib. 3, cap. 17, 7 (Massuet, 3, 16, 7); Harvey, 2, 88; *PG*, 7, 926. Ephraem too sees Mary rebuked at Cana for excessive haste; cf. *Expositio evangelii concordantis*, cap. 5, n. 5; *C.S.C.O.*, Vol. 137, 61 (Arm.); Vol. 145, 45 (Latin).

[235] Severian, *In sanctum martyrem Acacium*; ed. J. B. Aucher, *Severiani ... homiliae* (Venetiis, 1827), p. 317.

[236] John Chrysostom, *Hom. 21 in Ioannem*, n. 2; *PG*, 59, 130.

[237] *Id., Hom. 27 in Matthaeum*, n. 3; *PG*, 57, 347.

[238] *Id., Hom. 44 in Matthaeum*, n. 1; *PG*, 57, 464-465.

[239] Cf. Bardenhewer, *op. cit.*, Vol. 3 (Freiburg, 1912), 337-338.

sinned and need the glory of God' (*Rom.* 3:23), then undoubtedly Mary was scandalized at that time."[240] Origen's influence is evident in Basil, who interprets the sword of "a certain unsteadiness," "some sort of doubt," in Mary's soul as she stood by the cross. Why this exegesis? Because "it was imperative for the Lord to taste death for all. ..."[241] In a vivid passage Cyril portrays Our Lady beneath the cross and makes three points. First, there is the fact: "in all likelihood, even the Lord's Mother was scandalized by the unexpected passion, and the intensely bitter death on the cross all but deprived her of right reason." Her train of thought is partly this: "He may well have made a mistake when He said, 'I am the Life.'" Second, Mary's way of thinking is due to "her ignorance of the mystery" and has roots in Cyril's typically Oriental view of woman: "No wonder that a woman fell like this," seeing that Peter himself was once scandalized. Third, Cyril insists that "these are not just idle guesses, as someone might suppose, but derive from what has been written of the Lord's Mother"; for Simeon's sword is "the sharp assault of the passion, cutting the woman's mind to strange thoughts."[242]

So much for specific faults. A second major objection on the score of Mary's holiness stems from a set of patristic propositions which lead us to believe that Our Lady was not definitively delivered from sin until the day of the Annunciation. Cyril of Jerusalem asserts that "the Holy Spirit coming upon her sanctified her so as to enable her to receive Him through whom all things were made."[243] Gregory of Nazianzus remarks that the Word was "conceived of the Virgin, who was purified in advance by the Spirit in soul and in flesh; for honor had to be paid to her maternity, and

---

[240] Origen, *Hom. 17 in Lucam*; G.C.S., 35, 116-118. The Homilies on Luke, which were preached in some form to the Christians of Caesarea in Palestine, are difficult to date; Hanson inclines to place them at 233-234; cf. *op. cit.,* pp. 20-22, 26.

[241] Basil, *Epistola 260*, n. 9; *PG,* 32, 965-968. For a dating in 377, cf. *PG,* 32, 954.

[242] Cyril of Alexandria, *Comm. in Ioannis evangelium,* lib. 12; ed. Pusey, *op. cit.,* Vol. 3, 90-91; PG, 74, 661-664. The time of composition of the Commentary on John may have run from ca. 425-428; cf. Jouassard, *L'activité littéraire de saint Cyrille,* p. 172.

[243] Cyril of Jerusalem, *Catecheses,* 17, 6; *PG,* 33, 976.

preference given to her virginity."[244] Ephraem speaks of a prior purification through the Holy Spirit;[245] he mentions a purification of Mary's mind, imagination, thoughts, and virginity through the Life that dwelt in her;[246] he even declares that the Son regenerated His Mother through baptism.[247]

Can the paradox be resolved? To begin with, the area of conflict can be reduced if we cut away the accumulated undergrowth. The sanctification and purification of Mary described by Cyril of Jerusalem, Gregory of Nazianzus, and Ephraem need have no immediate connection with sin, whether original or actual. In each case the context is satisfied by an increase in holiness, in what the Catholic calls grace, given by God with a view to the divine Maternity. Such sanctification would have for its object not forgiveness but more intimate union.[248]

The general proposition, "Only Christ is without sin," is not fatal to the thesis of Mary's sinlessness. There is a sinlessness which is the fruit of nature; such sinlessness has always been, in orthodox Christian thinking, the exclusive prerogative of God. And there is a sinlessness which is the fruit of grace; it is theoretically compatible with human living. Did the Alexandrians, Clement and Cyril, deny such God-given sinlessness in the concrete order of

---

[244] Gregory of Nazianzus, *Oratio 38*, n. 13; *PG*, 36, 325; same passage in *Oratio 45*, n. 9; *PG*, 36, 633.

[245] Cf. Ephraem, *Sermo adversus haereticos (= De margarita); Opera omnia graece et latine*, Vol. 2 (Romae, 1743), 270.

[246] Cf. Ephraem, *Sermones exegetici; Opera omnia syriace et latine*, Vol. 2 (Romae, 1740), 328.

[247] Cf. Ephraem, *Sermo 11 in natalem domini; Opera omnia syriace et latine*, Vol. 2, 429-430.

[248] Mary's baptism as envisaged by Ephraem is difficult to reconcile with his thesis that Our Lady is loftier than heaven, superior to angels. On this score I simply note (*a*) that the context gives no inkling of the purpose and effect of Mary's baptism, save that it is a rebirth; (*b*) that sin does not enter the picture he is painting; and (*c*) that we may be face to face here with an early Christian intuition that Our Lady is prototype of the Church. If this intuition has place in the passage under discussion, then the words placed on Our Lady's lips, "You [my Son] will regenerate me with your baptism," may well be uttered in the name of the Church, Cf. Müller, *Ecclesia-Maria*, p. 150 and note 57, *ibid.*

things? An affirmative answer is not justified by the texts alleged.[249] For Clement and Cyril, Christ is natively sinless, because He is God; man is natively sinful, because he is man. There is middle ground which neither text invades: the possibility of sinlessness through grace.

Some of the specific faults imputed to Mary, such as Irenaeus' "untimely haste" and Severian's "useless and unsuitable suggestion," are not necessarily sins.[250] In at least one instance, Chrysostom's interpretation of the Annunciation, there is question not of actual fact but of unverifiable hypothesis: "she would have ..."[251] Again, it is not evident that the doubts which Cyril lays on Our Lady's lips were deliberate and therefore formally sinful.[252] But the residue is rather formidable: not merely Chrysostom's "vainglory" and "ambition," but especially Origen's "unbelief" and Basil's "doubt," because based on a dogmatic premise, the universality of Redemption.[253]

How resolve our original paradox? It would seem that before Ephesus some prominent churchmen and some of the laity in Alexandria and Caesarea of Cappadocia, in Antioch and Caesarea of Palestine, (a) were not aware of an obligation to represent the Mother of God as utterly sinless; and (b) did not regard the presence of sin, perhaps even serious sin, as incompatible with her singular sanctity. Did they espy a connection between such faults and original sin, so that in alleging the former they would eo ipso admit the latter? Any answer would be conjecture; Origen, Basil, and Chrysostom never posited the problem in these terms. It is evident, however, that they did not attribute to Mary the perfect holiness which would be an implicit proof of the Immaculate Conception.[254]

The Nestorian controversy and the Council of Ephesus focused attention on Mary's virginal Maternity. Concomitantly preachers were inspired to speak of her sanctity. On this head, however, progress is surprisingly sluggish. In the fifth century startling

---

[249] Cf. notes 231 and 232 above.

[250] Cf. notes 234 and 235.

[251] Cf. note 233.

[252] Cf. note 242.

[253] Cf. notes 237, 238, 240, and 241.

[254] Cf. Le Bachelet, *art. cit.*, cols. 888-889.

eulogies of Mary go hand in hand with apparent rejection of her primordial holiness; even where logic demands a sinless conception, a patristic pen is not always logical.[255]

Cyril of Alexandria sees Our Lady as uncommonly holy[256] and ascribes to her many of the redemptive effects achieved by her Son;[257] but, in the realm of original sin, seemingly it has never occurred to him to make an exception of Mary.[258] Proclus of Constantinople claims that no creature in the universe is comparable to God's Mother, but he fails to draw out the implications of his insight with a view to her personal holiness.[259] Theodotus of Ancyra is startlingly inconsistent. In one homily he can speak of the Second Eve as "virgin with woman's nature but without woman's malice; virgin innocent, unspotted, all-blameless, untainted, undefiled, holy in soul and in body, having sprouted like a lily amid thorns, uninstructed in the vices of Eve. ..."[260] And yet in another homily he can lament that the adversaries of the divine Maternity "have had no desire to understand what we teach with respect to the Virgin's transformation to holiness." He draws a

---

[255] Cf. Jugie, *L'Immaculée Conception*, pp. 77-94.

[256] Cf. Cyril, *Adversus Nestorii blasphemias*, lib. 1, cap. 1; A.C.O., Tom. 1, Vol. 1, Part 6, 16; *PG*, 76, 17.

[257] Cf. Cyril, *Hom. div. 4*; A.C.O., Tom. 1, Vol. 1, Part 2, 102-103; *PG*, 77, 992.

[258] Cf., e.g., Cyril, *Adversus anthropomorphitas*, cap. 26; *PG*, 76, 1129. The problem of Mary's sinlessness is complicated by Cyril's concept of original sin. His casual statements leave the impression that human nature shares in Adam's sin; but, when he confronts the problem specifically, he emphasizes the element of concupiscence. Cf. Jugie, *L'Immaculée Conception*, pp. 32-33, 78; du Manoir, *op. cit.*, pp. 282-283. — It is interesting that Nestorius comes fairly close to affirming the Immaculate Conception by his concept of Mary's "flesh without sin" and because he exempts her from dolorous parturition, the penalty of original sin which is proper to women. For the texts, cf. F. Loofs, *Nestoriana* (Halle, 1905), pp. 324-326, 349.

[259] Cf. Proclus, *Oratio 5: Laudatio in sanctam virginem ac Dei genitricem Mariam*, n. 2; *PG*, 65, 717-720. On the authorship of this homily, cf. note 24 above. Cf. also *Oratio 6: Laudatio sanctae Dei genitricis Mariae*, n. 8: Mary was "fashioned of pure (good?) clay"; *PG*, 65, 733. She is "the sacred innermost shrine of sinlessness"; Oratio 6 ... n. 17; *PG*, 65, 753. However, the authenticity of Homily 6 is suspect; cf. Jugie, *L'Immaculée Conception*, p. 80; del Fabbro, *art. cit.*, pp. 212-214, 219.

[260] Theodotus, *In sanctam Mariam Dei genitricem et in sanctam Christi nativitatem*, n. 11; *Patrologia Orientalis*, Vol. 19, 329.

comparison from a scrap of iron, black and dross-laden, which is purified by fire. If this is possible in the material order, "why be astonished if the all-immaculate Virgin was fired to a perfect purity by her contact with the divine, immaterial fire; if she was purified from all that was material and foreign to her nature, and radiantly constituted in her native beauty, so as to be thereafter impervious to, unsusceptible to, beyond the reach of all carnal degeneration?"[261] It may be that the comparison swept the preacher beyond his authentic theology.[262] It seems more likely that Theodotus and his contemporaries were not aware of an anomaly here; what we recognize as contradictory they simply took for granted.[263] That is perhaps why Hesychius can attribute to Mary privileges like incorruptibility, immortality, triumph over Satan, immunity from concupiscence,[264] and still interpret Simeon's sword as contradictory thoughts on Calvary; "for, though she was a virgin, she was a woman; though she was Mother of God, she was of our compound."[265] Perhaps it explains why Chrysippus, even more disconcertingly, remarks that Mary's kinship with Eve has established her in Eve's fall, and in almost the next breath calls her "by nature the blameless offshoot" of a wicked people; "it is a thorn-bearing field that produces your rose."[266]

In the three centuries that followed Chalcedon, Mariology escaped the general decadence that enveloped theology. This anomalous situation was due in great measure to the institution of a cycle of feasts covering the principal mysteries of Our Lady's life: the Annunciation (March 25), her Nativity (September 8), her Dormition (August 15), the Conception of Anne (December 9).

---

[261] Theodotus, *Hom. 4: In sanctam deiparam et in Simeonem*, n. 6; PG, 77, 1397.

[262] So Jugie, *L'Immaculée Conception*, pp. 82-83.

[263] So Jouassard, *Marie à travers la patristique*, pp. 140, 141.

[264] Cf. Hesychius, *Sermo 5: De sancta Maria deipara; PG*, 93, 1464-1465.

[265] Hesychius, *Sermo 6: In occursum domini; PG*, 93, 1476. Hesychius does not imply that Mary's doubts were sinful.

[266] Chrysippus, *In sanctam Mariam deiparam*, n. 2; *Patrologia Orientalis*, Vol. 19, 338-339. Jugie inclines to interpret this involvement of Mary in Eve's fall as *debitum remotum* or *proximum*. — For the pertinent ideas of Basil of Seleucia and Antipater of Bostra, cf. Jugie, *L'Immaculée Conception*, pp. 92-93.

These feasts provided orators and poets with the opportunity of singing the praises of the Virgin, with emphasis on her dignity as Mother of God and her role in the Redemption. Nevertheless, as Jugie has pointed out, even during these centuries theologians do not frame explicitly the question of the Immaculate Conception. They run the gamut of implicit testimonies, the major premises which logically demand the privilege in question; but it is only incidentally, almost accidentally, that a few theologians, such as Andrew of Crete and Sophronius of Jerusalem, formulate the prerogative in explicit or equivalent terms. The emphasis is on Our Lady's perpetual holiness rather than on her exemption from original sin.[267] As the patristic age draws to a close, Eastern Christianity can say with one voice to Our Lady: "You are all-fair ... and there is nothing to blame in you."[268]

V. DEATH AND ASSUMPTION

With respect to the Assumption the significant literature in the patristic East comprises (*a*) two passages from Epiphanius, (*b*) the apocryphal accounts called *Transitus Mariae*, and (*c*) the Greek homilies on the Dormition stemming from the seventh and eighth centuries.

As the evidence stands, the first explicit reference to a genuine Assumption of Our Lady occurs ca. 377.[269] In a digression typical of his *Medicine Chest* against eighty heresies, Epiphanius is concerned to forestall a perilous accommodation of Jn. 19:27 ("From that day the disciple took [Mary] into his home"). He is afraid that in the

---

[267] Cf. Jugie, *op. cit.*, pp. 95-146. With respect to this period some fine insights may be found in Jouassard, *Marie à travers la patristique*, pp. 139-147.

[268] Andrew of Crete, *Oratio 4: In nativitatem b. Mariae; PG*, 97, 872.

[269] Before Nicaea the only overt reference to the close of Our Lady's earthly life is a phrase attributed to Origen: "With respect to the brethren of Jesus (*Jn.* 2:12), there are many who ask how He had them, seeing that Mary remained a virgin until her death"; *G.C.S.*, 10, 506. The passage, whose authenticity is suspect (cf. note 126 above), is more significant as testimony to Mary's permanent virginity than as evidence for her death. True, her death is mentioned obliquely, as though it were self-evident; but this manner of speaking need not reflect a tradition; it may stem from lack of reflection on the dignity of God's Mother. In a word, we may conclude no more than that the author took Our Lady's death for granted.

John-Mary relationship clerics may find a pseudo-justification for retaining in their homes the much-discussed virgines subintroductae. He insists that the case of Mary was guided by a wise providence, that this procedure is to be regarded as an exception to the common conduct obligatory in the way of God, and that once John had taken Mary into his home she did not remain with him any longer. And he continues:

> But if some think us mistaken, let them search the Scriptures. They will not find Mary's death; they will not find whether she died or did not die; they will not find whether she was buried or was not buried. More than that: John journeyed to Asia, yet nowhere do we read that he took the holy Virgin with him. Rather, Scripture is absolutely silent [on the end of Mary] because of the extraordinary nature of the prodigy, in order not to shock the minds of men.
>
> For my own part, I do not dare to speak, but I keep my own thoughts and I practice silence. For it may be that somewhere we have found hints that it is impossible to discover the death of the holy, blessed one. On the one hand, you see, Simeon says of her, "And your own soul a sword shall pierce, that the thoughts of many hearts may be revealed" (*Lc.* 2:35). On the other hand, when the Apocalypse of John says, "And the dragon hastened against the woman who had brought forth the male child, and there were given to her an eagle's wings, and she was carried off into the wilderness, that the dragon might not seize her" (*Apoc.* 12:13-14), it may be that this is fulfilled in her.
>
> However, I do not assert this absolutely, and I do not say that she remained immortal; but neither do I maintain stoutly that she died. The fact is, Scripture has outstripped the human mind and left [this matter] uncertain, for the sake of that valued vessel without compare, to prevent anyone from harboring carnal thoughts in her regard. Did she die? We do not know. At all events, if she was buried, she had had no carnal intercourse. ...[270]

Twelve chapters later Epiphanius returns briefly to the problem of Mary's end:

> ... either the holy Virgin died and was buried; then her falling asleep was with honor, her death chaste, her crown that of virginity. Or she was killed, as it is written: "And your own soul a sword shall pierce"; then her glory is among the martyrs and her holy body amid blessings, she through whom light rose over the world. Or she

---

[270] Epiphanius, *Panarion*, haer. 78, nn. 10-11; *G.C.S.*, 37, 461-462.

remained alive, since nothing is impossible with God and He can do whatever He desires; for her end no one knows. ...[271]

The testimony of Epiphanius is crucial for two reasons. Before Ephesus he alone deals expressly with the problem at issue; and he knows the Holy City and its traditions as few others of his time. It is the more regrettable, therefore, that his witness is so vague that several interpretations of his thought are possible. As a defensible exegesis I submit three points, (a) How did Mary end her life? Epiphanius does not know. There are three possibilities: natural death, bloody martyrdom, deathless immortality. Of these, it is illegitimate to exclude any, illegitimate to impose any. (b) In any event, the end of Mary's life on earth was worthy of God and in harmony with her dignity and holiness, (c) Epiphanius' importance lies in this, that he has posed the problem and allowed us to glimpse the possible solutions.[272] It is not difficult to see in him the first

---

[271] *Panarion*, n. 23; *G.C.S.*, 37, 474.

[272] This is essentially the middle-of-the-road solution of M. Jugie, *La mort et l'Assomption de la sainte Vierge* (Città del Vaticano, 1944), pp. 77-81. A more benign interpretation is offered by O. Faller, *De priorum saeculorum silentio circa Assumptionem b. Mariae virginis* (Romae, 1946), pp. 33-43. As he sees it, (a) Epiphanius has no doubt that the passage of Mary from this life was miracle-laden; this miraculous element explains the silence of Scripture on her death. (b) In fact, this miracle is so remarkable that it is possible to admit an immediate passage of her body and soul into life immortal. (c) Epiphanius does not doubt Mary's glorification, even in the body. His one unresolved problem concerns the manner of her passing: did she die or not? (d) The third hypothesis means a translation to glory without the prelude of death; this is the hypothesis favored by Epiphanius. Faller's exegesis is followed by F. de P. Solá, *La Asunción de María en la tradición patrística*, in *Estudios Marianos*, Vol. 6, 1947, pp. 121-123. A more conservative conclusion is reached by B. Altaner, *Zur Frage der Definibilität der Assumptio B.M.V.*, in *Theologische Revue*, Vol. 44, 1948, cols. 131-134. From a more extensive collection of texts Altaner finds (a) that in the two passages under discussion Mary's end is veiled for Epiphanius in a mysterious obscurity. What is "astonishing and amazing" is simply this, that we must reckon with the possibility that Mary died a martyr, or that she was carried off to some unknown place on earth, where she continues in life. (b) The third hypothesis cannot be interpreted of an Assumption thesis; it means that Mary may have been transferred elsewhere on earth. (c) This evaluation of Epiphanius is supported by the silence of Jerome, Origen, Athanasius, Ambrose, and Augustine. — The problem is soberly treated by E. R. Smothers, *Saint Epiphanius and the Assumption*, in *The American*

theologian of the Assumption, in the sense that he had an intuition of the mystery and was fascinated by it.[273]

This rather conservative interpretation of Epiphanius, which emphasizes the absence of a fixed historical tradition on the final lot of Mary, is not shaken by other extant pre-Ephesus evidence, specifically that of Ephraem, Gregory of Nyssa, Severian of Gabala, and the so-called Timothy of Jerusalem. It is true, Ephraem sees Our Lady lifted on the wings of Christ and carried through the air; she has received a garment of glory sufficient to cover the nakedness of all men; Christ has clothed her with a new garment; she has put on His grandeur and magnificence; He who is of heaven has introduced her to heaven.[274] Ephraem has her say: "I shall enter, in a moment, the verdant gardens of paradise, and there I shall praise God, where Eve fell so ingloriously."[275] Regrettably, Ephraem's language is too general to find in it a bodily glorification. He believes that Mary died;[276] he maintains that she lives in glory. More than that he does not specify.[277]

In an unusual passage Gregory of Nyssa compares the Virgin with other virgins, to illustrate the victory of virginity over bodily death. Ordinary virgins destroy death's power by refusing to give it new victims. "With reference to Mary, God's Mother, the death which held sway from Adam to her (for it was near her too) first stumbled on the fruit of her virginity as on some rock, and was

---

Ecclesiastical Review, Vol. 125, 1951, pp. 355-372.

[273] So F. Cayré, L'Assomption aux quatre premiers siècles: État embryonnaire de la doctrine, in Studia Mariana, Vol. 4: Vers le dogme de l'Assomption (Montréal, 1948), pp. 144-145. Epiphanius' discovery, Cayré believes, was that Mary can be the woman of Apoc. 12, miraculously withdrawn from the fury of the dragon who ravages God's kingdom on earth. This insight motivated his hesitation as to her death and resurrection.

[274] Cf. Ephraem, *De nativitate domini sermo 12*, sermo 11, sermo 4; Opera omnia syriace et latine, Vol. 2, 415.

[275] Ephraem, *Sermo 1 de diversis; Opera omnia syriace et latine*, Vol. 3, 600. Jugie finds this sentence reminiscent of an early patristic idea which located the temporary abode of just souls in an earthly paradise; cf. *La mort et l'Assomption*, p. 60.

[276] Cf. Ephraem, *Hymni de beata Maria*, 15, n. 2; Lamy, Vol. 2, 583.

[277] In Ephraem's works there is no express declaration of Our Lady's glorious resurrection; on this point his remarks are consistently vague. Cf. Ephraem, *Sedra de probis et iustis*; Lamy, Vol. 3, 231-237.

crushed in regard of her. ..."[278] The passage is not perlucid. What Gregory has in view, however, is the triumph of Mary's Son over death. Death has approached Mary by attacking the fruit of her womb. In the assault death has been smashed, because Christ rose from the dead, escaped the tomb's corruption. Gregory neither affirms nor denies Our Lady's death or her share in her Son's triumph by a glorious resurrection.[279]

Severian of Gabala pictures Eve hearing herself constantly called a sorry, pitiful thing, while Mary each day hears herself called blessed:

> But you say, what good is it to her [i.e., Mary], since she does not hear it? Indeed she does hear, seeing that she is in the place of brightness, in the land of the living, she who is the mother of salvation, the source of the Light perceptible to sense — yes, perceptible to sense by reason of [His] flesh, accessible to mind by reason of [His] divinity. Thus, then, in every way is she called blessed. In fact, while she was yet living in the flesh she was called blessed, for she heard felicitation while still in flesh. ...[280]

Severian's thought is obscure. It may be argued that "the mother of salvation" ought herself to be utterly saved, that "the source of sensible Light" should be in the land of the living in her sensible frame, that she who is "in every way pronounced blessed" hears the felicitations with ears as well as mind, that "life in the flesh" means simply life here on earth. But Severian does not say so. He seems to assume that Mary died; he has not confronted the problem of her glorious resurrection.[281]

A passage frequently adduced to bolster the testimony of Epiphanius derives from a homily on Simeon by a certain Timothy, who is styled by the best manuscripts "a priest of Jerusalem" and on internal evidence was located by Jugie toward the end of the fourth century or at the beginning of the fifth.[282] From the text as reconstituted by Faller we gather that

---

[278] Gregory of Nyssa, De virginitate, cap. 14 (13); ed. Cavarnos, op. cit., p. 306.

[279] Cf. Jugie, *La mort et l'Assomption*, p. 63.

[280] Severian of Gabala, In mundi creationem oratio 6, n. 10; *PG*, 56, 498.

[281] Cf. Jugie, *La mort et l'Assomption*, pp. 64-65.

[282] Cf. *ibid.*, pp. 73-74.

some have supposed that the Mother of the Lord was put to death with a sword and won for herself a martyr's end. Their reason lies in the words of Simeon, "And your own soul a sword shall pierce." But such is not the case. A metal sword, you see, cleaves the body; it does not cut the soul in two. Therefore the Virgin is immortal to this day, seeing that He who had dwelt in her transported her to the regions of her assumption [OR: to the places of His ascension; OR: into the regions high above].[283]

Despite the unsatisfactory state of the text, and the ambiguities inherent in the significant adjective ἀναλήψιμος, the conclusion seems justified that the author holds for a translation of Mary, body and soul, to a supraterrestrial region. Scholars cannot agree, however, whether the phrase, "immortal to this day," (*a*) implies that Mary did not die, and (*b*) presents her immortality as a provisory, temporary thing.[284] The text and its problems have lost some of their pertinence and fascination ever since Capelle argued so convincingly that "Timothy of Jerusalem" is an unknown author of the Byzantine world who wrote between the sixth and eighth centuries.[285]

To sum up: Before Ephesus the scant evidence suggests strongly (*a*) that a widespread ignorance prevailed relative to Our Lady's destiny, and (*b*) that, save for isolated instances, Eastern Christianity had not yet confronted the problem.

An intriguing corpus of literature on the final lot of Mary is formed by the apocryphal *Transitus Mariae*.[286] The genesis of these accounts is shrouded in history's mist. They apparently originated before the close of the fifth century, perhaps in Egypt, perhaps in Syria, in consequence of the stimulus given Marian devotion by the

---

[283] *In prophetam Simeonem*; ed. Faller, op. cit., p. 26; cf. PG, 86, 245.

[284] For two well-reasoned interpretations, cf. Jugie, *La mort et l'Assomption*, pp. 74-76, and Faller, *op. cit.*, pp. 30-31.

[285] Cf. B. Capelle, *Les homélies liturgiques du prétendu Timothée de Jérusalem*, in *Ephemerides Liturgicae*, Vol. 63, 1949, pp. 5-26. Jugie was not impressed by Capelle's argumentation; cf. *L'Immaculée Conception*, p. 74 and note 3, *ibid.*; he continues to consider Timothy a contemporary of Epiphanius.

[286] Cf. Jugie, *La mort et l'Assomption*, pp. 101-171; A. C. Rush, *The Assumption in the Apocrypha*, in *The American Ecclesiastical Review*, Vol. 116, 1947, pp. 5-31; id., *Assumption Theology in the Transitus Mariae*, *ibid.*, Vol. 123, 1950, 93-110.

definition of the divine Maternity at Ephesus. The period of proliferation is the sixth century. At least a score of *Transitus* accounts are extant, in Coptic, Greek, Latin, Syriac, Arabic, Ethiopic, and Armenian. Not all are prototypes, for many are simply variations on more ancient models.

What do the *Transitus Mariae* stories say? In point of fact, the divergences are so pronounced that the accounts cannot be reduced to a genuine unity. A first common feature is that all recount the death of Mary; this is their theme, their primary concern, the event which invests them with a specious homogeneity. Around this central event several characteristic, legendary details are grouped: the miraculous arrival of all or some of the Apostles; the tidings brought to Mary of her approaching death; Mary's experience of fear; some hostile Jewish intervention on the occasion of her burial. A second common feature is that all postulate in connection with Mary's death a divine intervention unique on such an occasion. It is on the nature, the time, and the locale of this intervention that disagreement arises. Some accounts speak of a translation of Mary's body to a presumably earthly paradise, where it is preserved incorrupt under the tree of life; still others describe a genuine assumption, a reunion of soul and body which entails Our Lady's entrance into heaven. The interval between death and prodigy varies from some moments to seven months. The locale is now the Mount of Olives, now the Valley of Josaphat, now Gethsemane.

A splendid example of this literary genus lies in the fragments of a Syriac account entitled *Obsequies of the Holy Virgin*, which may well be the oldest of the *Transitus* narratives. In this account the Apostles are keeping a three-day vigil at Mary's tomb when Christ descends from heaven with Michael and sits among them:

> ... Our Lord made a sign to Michael, and Michael began to speak with the voice of a mighty angel. And angels descended on three clouds; and the number of angels on each cloud was a thousand angels, uttering praises before Jesus. And the Lord said to Michael: "Let them bring the body of Mary into the clouds." And when the body of Mary had been brought into the clouds, Our Lord said to the Apostles that they should draw near to the clouds. And when they came to the clouds they were singing with the voice of angels. And Our Lord told the clouds to go to the gate of paradise. And when they had entered

paradise, the body of Mary went to the tree of life; and they brought her soul and made it enter her body. And straightway the Lord dismissed the angels to their places.[287]

In the second half of the fifth century, therefore, an original Syrian apocryphon, emanating perhaps from Jacobite circles, teaches explicitly the anticipated resurrection of Mary — the oldest unmistakable affirmation.[288]

What is the value of these witnesses? As historical accounts of an actual event — Mary's death, her translation, her Assumption — by individuals who were personally present, or else were in contact with the event through unimpeachable sources, the Transitus literature is valueless.[289] But theologically the tales are priceless. They reveal the reaction of early Christian piety when confronted with the apparent fact of Our Lady's death; they evidence the first

---

[287] *Obsequies of the Holy Virgin;* W. Wright, *Contributions to the Apocryphal Literature of the New Testament* (London, 1865), p. 46 f. On the probable date, cf. Jugie, *La mort et l'Assomption,* pp. 107-109.

[288] A pertinent but controverted document is the *Euthymiaca historia,* lib. 3, cap. 40, found in John Damascene's *Hom. 2 in dormitionem Mariae,* n. 18; PG, 96, 748-752. The unknown author has Juvenal, Archbishop of Jerusalem, narrated at the time of Chalcedon what he has learned about Mary's passing "from an ancient and utterly unerring tradition." This embraces her death, the arrival of the Apostles, the vision of angels, the commitment of Mary's soul to God's hands, the burial in Gethsemane, the discovery after three days of a coffin empty save for burial shrouds, the Apostles' conclusion that Christ wanted to honor His Mother's immaculate body "with incorruption and transposition before the common, universal resurrection." The *Historia* of which this is an extract has not been recovered. Many scholars consider the extract an interpolation in Damascene's homily. Jugie, e.g., insists that it should not be dated much before 890; cf. *La mort et l'Assomption,* pp. 160-164. He calls the Juvenal narration sheer legend (cf. *ibid.,* pp. 164-167), while Gordillo follows Kekelidze, Abel, and Baldi in admitting its historicity, pointing to the temperate narrative and its similarity to Epiphanius' approach; cf. *Mariologia orientalis* (Roma, 1954), p. 222 and note 45, ibid. A. Wenger asserts that Jugie has convincingly demonstrated the apocryphal character of the Juvenal story, but he observes justly that the *MS Sinait.* gr. 491, the oldest witness of the *Historia,* forbids us to date the legend later than 750; cf. *L'Assomption de la T. S. Vierge dans la tradition byzantine du VIe au Xe siècle: Études et documents* (Paris, 1955), p. 137.

[289] In this sense Altaner was surely justified when he insisted that "no tradition underlies the *Transitus* which is to be taken seriously from a historical point of view"; *art. cit.,* col. 135.

unequivocal solutions to the problem of Mary's destiny. The solutions, though divergent, disclose a genuinely Christian insight: it was not fitting that the body of Mary should see corruption. More importantly, the solution is given, incorruption is postulated, on theological lines: the principles of solution are the divine Maternity, Mary's unimpaired virginity, her unrivaled holiness. Finally, the more ancient of these apocrypha exercised a perceptible influence on the establishment of the Eastern feast of the Dormition or of the Migration of the Mother of God.[290] The feast, once established, gave

---

[290] The influence of the apocrypha is evident in a pastoral letter, The Dormition of Our Lady (*ca.* 620), in which John, Archbishop of Thessalonica, introduced the Dormition feast into his diocese shortly after Emperor Maurice prescribed it for the Empire; cf. Jugie's edition, *Patrologia Orientalis,* Vol. 19, 1926, pp. 344-438. John's purpose was to disengage from numerous interpolated versions the genuine eyewitness story of Mary's last hours. But, despite its sobriety, piety, and influence, John's account is legendary. Capelle has concluded that, save for a personal prologue and peroration, John has (with superficial exceptions) simply transcribed an earlier Greek apocryphon which is itself the source of the Latin Transitus (ed. Wilmart, Studi e testi, Vol. 59, 1933, pp. 323-357) on which Ps.-Melito depended; cf. Les anciens récits de l'Assomption et Jean de Thessalonique, in Recherches de Théologie Ancienne et Médiévale, Vol. 12, 1940, pp. 209-235. Capelle's conclusion found independent confirmation from L. Carli, Le fonti del Racconto della Dormizione de Maria di Giovanni Tessalonicese, in Marianum, Vol. 2, 1940, pp. 307-313. Subsequently Capelle returned to the problem, compared the two recensions of John with the Latin accounts of Ps.-Melito, Wilmart's Transitus, and the previously unedited Transitus Colbertinus, and concluded that John's pastoral letter gives us in the original language the whole apocryphon (going back to at least the sixth century) of which the other witnesses are but résumés or rather free adaptations; cf. Vestiges grecs et latins d'un antique 'Transitus' de la Vierge, in Analecta Bollandiana, Vol. 67, 1949, pp. 21-48. — Especially disappointing is John's epilogue; of fifteen manuscripts consulted by Jugie, only three speak clearly of a glorious resurrection. Capelle believes that John deliberately omitted mention of the bodily Assumption, because it was not certainly genuine. J. M. Bover, however, believes he has established that the authentic epilogue contained the Assumption account, and that consequently John is probably the first Greek author who testifies explicitly to the Assumption; cf. *La Asunción de María en el 'Transitus W' y en Juan de Tesalónica*, in *Estudios Eclesiásticos,* Vol. 20, 1946, pp. 415-433. Cf. the Epitome of John's account published by F. Halkin, *Une légende byzantine de la Dormition: L'Epitomé du récit de Jean de Thessalonique,* in *Mélanges Martin Jugie* (Paris, 1953), pp. 156-164. It confirms two of Jugie's theses: the attribution of the original work to John, and the

rise to new *Transitus* accounts and occasioned the Greek homiletic literature which blossomed from the seventh to the ninth centuries — the fairest flowering of patristic thought on the final lot of Mary.[291]

The earliest extant Byzantine discourse on the August 15th feast, the first monument of genuine Greek theology affirming the Assumption in categorical terms, is dated by Jugie at the end of the seventh century or the beginning of the eighth. This *Panegyric on the Falling Asleep of the Mother of God*, long attributed to Modestus, Patriarch of Jerusalem († 634), is remarkable for its doctrinal content, its independence of the apocrypha (which it does use), its reasonable conjectures, and its repeated, unhesitating affirmation of the Assumption.[292] Mary died, yes: "ever anguished by a mother's

extent of its influence. The epilogue, perhaps added by the scribe, includes the reunion of Mary's soul and body.

[291] According to Jugie, the first traces of a special solemnity that makes express mention of Mary's death and Assumption do not go back beyond the second half of the sixth century. In many churches, however, this feast of the Dormition was an outgrowth of the primitive Marian feast, the Commemoration of Blessed Mary, which celebrated in general fashion Mary's entry into the Church Triumphant. In the absence of indisputable scriptural or traditional data on the way in which this entrance was effected, the feast emphasized the Virgin-Mother idea and Mary's role as New Eve. After the Transitus tales had won popularity, the Commemoration tended to be transformed into the feast of the Dormition and Assumption. The institution of this feast, Jugie claims, does not constitute an apodictic proof in favor of a genuine Assumption doctrine. In East and West the liturgy reflected the actual state of theology: a perceptible inclination for the radical solution of the future, but unquestionable traces of the incomplete solution, bodily incorruption till the Last Judgment. Cf. Jugie, *La mort et l'Assomption*, pp. 172-212. Faller finds in the fifth-century Commemoration a proper feast of Mary's death and Assumption; cf. *op.* cit., p. 26. Altaner considers Faller's evidence unacceptable; cf. *Theologische Revue*, Vol. 45, 1949, p. 136. Cf. the summary of the development of the feast in W. O'Shea, *The History of the Feast of the Assumption*, in *Thomist*, Vol. 14, 1951, pp. 118-132.

[292] Cf. *Encomium in dormitionem sanctissimae dominae nostrae semperque virginis Mariae; PG*, 86, 3277-3312. The long-accepted paternity of Modestus († 634) is quite problematical; cf. Jugie, *La mort et l'Assomption*, pp. 215-218. L. Carli, however, sees no reason for questioning its authenticity; cf. *Marianum*, Vol. 2, 1940, p. 387. In any event, it remains the best production of patristic Greek homiletics on the Assumption. I have not been able to make proper use of the recently published discourse of Theoteknos, Bishop

yearning for her Son divine, she quit her holy body with her eyes upon Him, and into His hands she commended her all-blessed, all-holy soul."[293] Why did she die? "As His Mother all-holy, she followed Him. ..."[294] What happened to her body in the tomb? The Mother of God, "after childbirth ever virgin, in the grave suffered not corruption of the body that held Life, preserved by the omnipotent Saviour Christ who came forth from her."[295] A genuine Assumption, preceded by a glorious resurrection and postulated by the divine Maternity, is reiterated again and again: "... as Mother all-glorious of the Giver of life and of immortality, Christ our Saviour and God, she was given life by Him, concorporate with Him in incorruption for eternity, with Him who raised her from the tomb and took her to Himself, in the way that He alone knows. ..."[296] The same idea is summed up in a strikingly lovely sentence:

> Christ, God, who took ... flesh from her who was ever virgin, summoned her and clothed her in the incorruption of His own body [in concorporate incorruption], and glorified her with incomparable glory, so as to be His heir, she who was His all-holy Mother, in harmony with the Psalmist's song: "At your right hand stands the queen in a vesture of gold, all hung about with embroidery" (Ps. 44:10).[297]

It has been asserted — and I incline to agree — that Modestus' affirmation of Mary's incorruption, resurrection, and Assumption,

---

of Livias (about thirty-five kilometers east of Jerusalem), for the Marian feast of August 15, which he calls ἀνάληψις. Written between 550 and 650, this homily may be the first genuinely Catholic affirmation of the glorious Assumption; cf. discussion, text, and French translation in Wegner, *op. cit.*, pp. 96-110, 271-291.

[293] *Encomium*, n. 11; *PG*, 86, 3308.

[294] *Encomium*, n. 12; *PG*, 86, 3308.

[295] *Encomium*, n. 7; *PG*, 86, 3293.

[296] *Encomium*, n. 14; PG, 86, 3312. The expression, "concorporate in incorruption," is peculiar to Modestus, is repeated several times, and means that, as the bodies of Jesus and Mary were similar on earth in passibility and mortality, so He wanted His Mother's body to resemble His in her risen state; cf. Jugie, *La mort et l'Assomption*, p. 222.

[297] *Encomium*, n. 5; PG, 86, 3289. Modestus likewise insists on Mary's mediatorial role in glory — a common possession of Byzantine Mariology in this period. She intercedes with her Son and makes Him propitious to us; cf. *Encomium*, n. 6; PG, 86, 3292-3293.

so serene, categorical, free from all hesitation and any palliation, gives the impression that the author is not defending a disputable thesis but expounding an admitted truth.[298]

Germanus, Patriarch of Constantinople in the early eighth century, is as categorical as Modestus with reference to the Assumption.[299] In a rather fictitious historical framework he affirms the fact of Mary's death:

> Give to the earth without distress [Our Lord says to Mary] what is the earth's. ... Trust your body to me, seeing that I myself entrusted to your womb my divinity. ... Death will not vaunt itself over you, for you have conceived Life. ... Lie down in the tomb of Gethsemane, and that for appearance alone. I will not leave you long an orphan therein. I will come to you, as soon as you have been laid to rest in the grave, not to be conceived by you anew ... but rather to take you to myself to dwell with me. Lay your body with great confidence in Gethsemane, there where I before my passion bent my knees to pray the prayer of a man; for, prefiguring your dormition, I bent in that place the knees of the body I took from you. Therefore, just as I, after bending my knees there, went forth willingly to the lifegiving death of the cross, so you, after depositing your remains, will pass to life without delay.[300]

Mary died (*a*) because her Son Himself willed to die, (*b*) because her nature is no different from our own, and (*c*) because her death was intended as confirmation of the reality of the Incarnation. She rose from the dead, was taken up to her Son, in the integrity of her human nature, because it was impossible for the vessel that had held God to be dissolved in dust. "For since He who had emptied Himself in you was God from the beginning and Life from eternity, it could not but be that the Mother of Life should live with Life, that she should entertain death as if it were sleep, and as Mother of Life submit to migration as if it were a waking."[301] This, Germanus implies, is what the Christian sense imperiously demands. The bodily Assumption is a consequence of the divine Maternity.

---

[298] Cf. Jugie, *La mort et l'Assomption*, p. 223.

[299] The three homilies as edited in *PG*, 98, 340-372, are actually but two; the first two (cols. 340-357) are two parts of one homily.

[300] Germanus, *Hom. 3 in dormitionem*; *PG*, 98, 368.

[301] Germanus, *Hom. 1 in dormitionem*; PG, 98, 348.

Andrew, contemporary of Germanus and Metropolitan of Gortyna on the Island of Crete, consecrated a trilogy of sermons to the Dormition. He tells the Cretans that the object of the feast is the Dormition of God's Mother, a mystery "celebrated hitherto by a few, but now lovingly honored by all."[302] His basic ideas on the final lot of Mary include her death, the reunion of her soul and body, her glorious entrance into heaven, and the premises which postulate such a destiny, i.e., holiness, virginity, Maternity:

> She who has introduced into heaven that which is dust, strips off the dust and lays aside the veil she has carried from her birth, and restores to the earth what is kin to earth. She who gave life to Life migrates up to a new life, makes her home in a place where life originates and life is indestructible. ... And, last of all phenomena, that which appears to our eyes rises up and in a spiritual way goes along with that which is spiritual in the manner known to Him who of old linked the two together, and after dissolving them united them anew. ... See if a more astounding miracle can be discovered than the marvel that was accomplished so incredibly in her. ... A spectacle truly new it was, and beyond human thinking: the woman who surpassed the heavens in her purity, crossed the threshold of heaven's sanctuary; the virgin who surpassed the Seraphim by the marvel of her divine Maternity, drew close to the primal nature, God the Creator of all things; the mother who had given birth to Life itself, crowned her life by an end that rivaled her childbearing. ... For, as the womb of the mother knew not corruption, so too the flesh of the dead did not perish.[303]

---

[302] Andrew of Crete, *Hom. 2 in dormitionem*; *PG*, 97, 1072. The order of the first two homilies should be reversed.

[303] Andrew of Crete, Hom. *1 in dormitionem*; *PG*, 97, 1080-1081. Andrew's mind would be clear enough, were it not for three hypotheses which he subjoins immediately. In Jugie's interpretation (*La mort* et l'Assomption, pp. 239-240), the hypotheses are: (*a*) a glorious Assumption in body and soul; (*b*) assumption of soul to heaven, transfer of incorrupt body to an unknown spot in this world; (*c*) some other exceptional and marvelous condition, not specified. Andrew favors the first hypothesis, but it remains a hypothesis. Faller has essayed a refutation of Jugie; cf. *op*. cit., pp. 9-18. For him there is no question of the place to which soul and body went, but of their state or condition relative to each other. The three hypotheses are: (*a*) soul and body simply united to form the same living organism as before; (b) soul rapt in some divine ecstasy, body sharing in spiritual qualities, while remaining a true body; (*c*) whole speculation left to God. Faller's interpretation has the

Another trilogy of sermons for the feast of the Dormition was delivered by John Damascene, very probably at Gethsemane on August 14th and 15th, about the year 740. Like Germanus, but with greater discretion, he makes use of apocrypha, especially John of Thessalonica. With the candor of Andrew he confesses that the circumstances surrounding his account of Mary's end are conjecture or rhetoric.

As Damascene sees it, Mary dies because she is human; moreover, it is through death's crucible that mortality gives place to immortality.[304] More accurately still, "she yields to the law of her own Son." Though she gave life to all, as daughter of Adam she is subject to the hereditary debt; for even her Son, Life itself, did not refuse to die.[305] Though *Homily 3* contains Damascene's clearest affirmations of Mary's glorification in soul and body, it is in *Homily 2* that he enumerates, in one of the most moving of patristic texts, Our Lady's titles to the Assumption:

> For there was need that this dwelling meet for God, this undug well of remission's waters, this unploughed field of heaven's bread, this unwatered vineyard of immortality's wine, this olive-tree of the Father's compassion, ever green and fair and fruitful, be not imprisoned in the hollows of the earth. Rather, just as the holy and incorrupt body that had been born of her, the body that was united hypostatically to God the Word, rose from the tomb on the third day, so was there need that she too be snatched from the grave and the Mother restored to her Son; and, as He had descended to her, so she had to be carried up ... to heaven itself. There was need that she, who had entertained God the Word in the guest-chamber of her womb, be brought home to the dwelling of her Son; and, just as the Lord said that He must be in the place that belongs to His Father, so the Mother had to take up her abode in the palace of her Son, in the house of the Lord, in the courts of the house of our God. There was need that the body of her who in childbirth had preserved her virginity without stain, be preserved incorrupt even after death. There was need that she who had carried her Creator as a babe on her bosom, linger

---

merit of solving an otherwise insoluble problem: how could Andrew have written so paradoxical a passage?

[304] Cf. John Damascene, Hom. *3 in dormitionem Mariae*, nn. 2-3; PG, 96, 753-757.

[305] Cf. John Damascene, Hom. 2 in dormitionem Mariae, n. 2; PG, 96, 725.

lovingly in the dwelling of her God. There was need that the bride whom the Father had betrothed to Himself, live in the bridal-chamber of heaven. There was need that she who had looked so closely on her very own Son on the cross, she who there felt in her heart the sword-pangs of sorrow which in bearing Him she had escaped, there was need that she look upon Him seated with His Father. There was need that the Mother of God enter into the possessions of her Son and, as Mother of God and handmaid, be reverenced by all creation. ... For the Son has enslaved all creation to His Mother.[306]

Two remarks are in order. First, Damascene's ἔδει ("there was need") seems to be more than sheer appropriateness; there is in this a certain exigence. Second, Damascene's arguments for the Assumption are derived not primarily from Scripture (which serves him rather for illustration),[307] and only in general from tradition.[308] They are drawn principally from the analogy of faith; he plays the theologian, not the exegete or historian. The Assumption is for him a postulate of Mary's other prerogatives: to some extent her virginity and holiness, but more than all else her divine Motherhood.[309]

At the end of the patristic period in the East the doctrine of the Assumption has reached the level of theological elaboration. It is not

---

[306] John Damascene, *Hom. 2 in dormitionem Mariae*, n. 14; *PG*, 96, 740-741.

[307] Cf. John Damascene, *Hom. 1 in dormitionem Mariae*, nn. 8 and 12; *PG*, 96, 712, 720; Hom. 2, n. 2; *PG*, 96, 724.

[308] Cf. John Damascene, *Hom. 2 in dormitionem Mariae*, n. 4; *PG*, 96, 729.

[309] Mention should he made of Cosmas Vestitor, an orator of moderate ability, who apparently lived in Constantinople toward the middle of the eighth century. His four discourses on the Dormition reveal not simply a number of improbable legends but an Assumption theology remarkably sound in its principle and applications. He sees the mystery of Mary's earthly end and bodily glorification as analogous to the mystery of Jesus' death and resurrection, because the flesh of the Son and the flesh of the Mother are one same flesh. Mary died and her body remained incorrupt in the tomb for three days. On the morning of the third day Christ came to raise her up; from that moment she is in heaven in body and soul, hard by her Son. For an analysis of these significant homilies, and a persuasive effort to situate Cosmas in his age and milieu, cf. A. Wenger, *Les homélies inédites de Cosmas Vestitor sur la Dormition, in Mélanges Martin Jugie*, pp. 284-300. Wenger finds that Cosmas has drawn on the apocrypha, Ps.-Dionysius, the *Euthymiaca historia*, John of Thessalonica, and probably Germanus of Constantinople.

simply that the basic truth, Our Lady's glorification in soul and body, is accepted as indisputable by the outstanding orators of the Dormition feast, and apparently by the main body of the faithful as well. Still more significant is the fact that the Assumption is postulated on theological premises.[310] Not that the whole structure of Assumption theology, as expounded in early Byzantine homiletic literature, will be recognized as solid by succeeding centuries; modern doubts on Mary's death are a case in point. But the heart of the matter has been touched; the task of the future will be to sift

---

[310] In his *Early Christian Interpretations of History* (Bampton Lectures, 1952.; New York, 1954), R. L. P. Milburn has devoted an Appendix (pp. 161-192) and part of a chapter (pp. 134-141) to the historical background of the Assumption doctrine. His reconstruction of the extant evidence (patristic, liturgical, apocryphal) of early Christian thought on Mary's final lot is, on the whole, sober historical fact. And Mr. Milburn admits, quite honestly, that there is "no means of disproving the doctrine of the Assumption, for, in the absence of historical data, it is not given to mankind lightly to confine the power of a God 'whose judgements are unsearchable and whose ways are past finding out'" (p. 139). But Mr. Milburn is playing the theologian rather than the historian when he states baldly and badly that "to elevate the doctrine of the Assumption to equality with the fundamental truths of the Christian creeds is to abandon the ancient claim of the Church to declare, as its Gospel, the mighty works of God manifested in history" (p. 141). Moreover, Mr. Milburn reveals little awareness of the concept or role of doctrinal development in Christian belief — an awareness essential, not indeed for reconstructing an era's explicit belief, but surely for evaluating the link (or lack of it) between a particular doctrine and Christ's own revelation. He is less than fair as a historian to Modestus, Germanus, Andrew, and Damascene when he does not reveal that their primary reasons for asserting an Assumption of Mary are not pseudo-historical but theological, and so leads us to believe that the only significant influences which "operated in favour of the doctrine of the Assumption" were (*a*) a medieval love of the miraculous, (*b*) impatience with the silence of Scripture and the Fathers, (*c*) desire for parallelism between Jesus and Mary, (*d*) rivalry between Jerusalem and Ephesus for an empty tomb, (*e*) misunderstandings of authors' and artists' meanings, (*f*) eagerness to convert metaphor or reverie into concrete fact, (*g*) influence or miraculous translations in Graeco-Roman and Jewish tradition. Underlying the whole treatment is, I fear, an unspoken principle: if history does not declare an event, neither should the Church. If history traces a doctrine's primitive life to unfounded legend, the Church had best beware of it. "But the grave difficulty ... is that ... something has been solemnly stated as assured historical fact that has no other strictly historical basis ... than a Coptic romance" (p. 140).

incontestable Christian doctrine from probable opinion and illegitimate speculation.[311]

---

[311] Cf. the splendid brief survey of the patristic period by G. Jouassard, *L'Assomption corporelle de la sainte Vierge et la patristique*, in *Assomption de Marie: Bulletin de la Société Française d'Études Mariales*, 1948 (Paris, 1949), pp. 99-117.

Mary in the Apocrypha of the New Testament

By Alfred C. Rush, C.SS.R., S.T.D.

N THIS section on Mary in the Apocrypha of the New Testament no attempt will be made to mention every single reference to Mary; rather, sufficient references will be gathered that indicate a trend. These trends in Mariology will be high-lighted. It is with the Mariology of the Apocrypha that these pages are primarily concerned. In other words, no attempt will be made to reconstruct the series of events of Mary's life as given in these documents. Only those events will be given that are necessary background for understanding the Mariological principles and truths stressed in these works.

The Mariology of the Apocrypha is a most fitting theme, especially when one considers the nature of the Apocrypha. The Apocrypha of the New Testament are works which attempt to supply added information regarding the lives of Christ, Mary, and the Apostles. To enlarge on the information contained in the canonical Scriptures, to supply information not given there, and to edify their readers, the authors of these works give free play to their imaginations. These writings abound in accounts of the miraculous that are frequently fantastic. At times, these works were used by heretics, especially the Gnostics, as vehicles for their tenets. To lend weight to their accounts, the writers pose as Apostles or as people closely associated with the Apostles. Thus, side by side with the canonical writings, there grew up apocryphal Gospels, Acts, Epistles, Apocalypses.

Although, generally speaking, these works are of little historical value, in the sense of being reliable accounts of the historical events narrated, they are of tremendous value along other lines. They furnish a deep insight into the mentality of the times in which they were written. They show the tendencies and customs, and attest to the beliefs of early Christian times. Hence, they are of importance for the theologian and the historian of dogma. Specifically, they are of great value for the study of Mariology. With this information, we can now proceed to the subject of the Mariology in the Apocrypha.[1]

EXCEPTIONAL BIRTH AND EARLY YEARS OF MARY

Any mention of Mary and the Apocrypha will have to begin with the Protoevangelium of James, a work that purports to be written by James the Less, the first bishop of Jerusalem. In its original form it dates from about the middle of the second century and was probably written by a Christian of Jewish origin who lived outside of Palestine.[2] This work shows the great part that Mary occupied in popular piety at this early date. The aim of the author is the glorification of Mary, Virgin and Mother, and this is the first in a long line of works down through the ages that have set out to proclaim the glories of Mary.[3]

Already in the second century, attacks were made against Christ by attacking His Mother. Christ, it was charged, was born of a poor country girl who obtained her livelihood by spinning. Sent away by her spouse who was a carpenter on the charge of adultery, she gave birth to Jesus, the son of a soldier by the name of Pantherus.[4] Living in a milieu where such charges were made, Pseudo-James shows his indignation. In the Bible he saw that there were exceptional and extraordinary circumstances in the birth of people whom God destined for great work. To cite one, mention can be made of the extraordinary events surrounding the conception and birth of St. John the Baptist.[5] Mary, who was to be the Mother of Christ, was

---

[1] For information on the Apocrypha, cf. J. Quasten, *Patrology*, Vol. 1 (Westminster, Md., 1950), pp. 106-157; A. Robert and A. Tricot, *Guide to the Bible*, English translation prepared under the direction of E. Arbez and M. McGuire, Vol. 1 (Westminster, Md., 1951), pp. 61-69; B. Altaner, *Patrologie* (Freiburg i/Br., 1950), pp. 45-67; E. Amann, *Apocryphes du nouveau testament, in Dictionnaire de la bible, supplément*, Vol. 1 (1928), cols. 460-533.

[2] J, Quasten, *op. cit.*, pp. 119-121. The term Protoevangelium is the usual designation for this Gospel of James. This is the name given to the work by Postel in 1552.

[3] E. Amann, *Le protoévangile de Jacques et ses remaniements latins* (Paris, 1910), pp. vii, 10.

[4] Origen, *Contra Celsum*, 1. 32 (G.C.S., Vol. 1, 1899, p. 83, ed. Koetachau; *PL*, 11, 720 f.).

[5] Lk. 1:5-25, 57-80.

not less favored. She received not only the same favors as John and other saints of the Old Testament, but she received these blessings in a more excellent manner.

Pseudo-James then states that Mary was the child of Joachim and Anna, a child who was given by God to this elderly couple who had prayed to Him to remove the curse of sterility and bless them with offspring.[6] The exceptional element in the birth of Mary is that she was a child obtained by prayer, that she was born of a woman advanced in years and sterile. The author, however, obviously thought that the conception of Mary took place by the normal union of husband and wife, and was not a miraculous virginal conception. Thus, he writes of Joachim: "The angel of the Lord came down to him saying: Joachim, Joachim, the Lord God has heard your prayer. Go down from here for your wife Anna will conceive in her womb." When Joachim came, Anna ran up to meet him and exclaimed: "Now I know that the Lord my God has blessed me exceedingly. For behold the widow is no longer a widow. I who was without child shall conceive."[7] In all probability the original text uses the future, that is, "your wife will conceive" and "I shall conceive." Some versions and recensions use the past tense and postulate that Mary was conceived by a virginal conception.[8]

When Mary was three years old she was presented in the Temple.[9] There she lived as a model of purity until the time came when she was presented to Joseph. This part will be taken up under the Virginity of Mary.

THE VIRGINITY OF MARY

If the Protoevangelium set out to glorify Mary by reason of her birth, it aimed to glorify her all the more by proclaiming and

---

[6] *Protoevangelium Jacobi*, 1-6 (Amann, pp. 178-198). The text can also be found in C. Tischendorf, *Evangelia apocrypha* (Leipzig, 1876), pp. 1-50; C. Michel, *Evangiles apocryphes*, Vol. 1 (Paris, 1911), pp. 2-50.

[7] *Protoevangelium*, 4. 2-4 (Amann, pp. 192-194).

[8] E. Amann, *op. cit.*, pp. 17-22; X. *Le Bachelet, Immaculée Conception*, in *Dictionnaire de théologie catholique*, Vol. 7, 1927, cols. 875-877.

[9] On the feast of the Presentation of Mary, cf. Sr. M. J. Kishpaugh, *The Feast of the Presentation of the Virgin Mary in the Temple. An Historical and Literary Study* (Washington, D. C., 1941).

defending her absolute and perpetual virginity. The author aims to leave no doubt that Mary was a virgin ante partum, in partu, and post partum.[10]

The Gospel proclaims the exceptional birth of Christ from Mary.[11] From early times the virginity of Mary was part of Catholic belief, and the expression, *natus ex Maria virgine*, was part of the Christian catechesis and contained in the various symbols of faith.[12] In Catholic thought it was taken for granted that the word "virgin" when applied to Mary meant absolute and perpetual virginity. There was no need of going into specific details. However, the second century saw attacks on the virginity of Mary. The general attitude is summed up in the charge that Jesus invented the story of His virgin birth, that he was born of fornication.[13] It is against such a background that the author of the Protoevangelium rallied to the defense of Mary's perpetual virginity.[14]

According to the Protoevangelium, Mary was consecrated to God by the vow of her mother who exclaimed: "As the Lord my God lives, if I bring forth either a boy or a girl, I will bring it as a gift to the Lord my God, and it shall be ministering to Him all the days of its life."[15] By this act Mary was vowed to the service of God by perpetual virginity. In this account, however, Mary is regarded almost as a purely physical agent in the work of the Redemption. The author accentuates a purity in Mary that can be described as a legal or exterior purity, and he overlooks the freedom of will on Mary's part in all this work. Hence, when the general theme of the Protoevangelium appeared in the Western aprocryphon of Pseudo-Matthew there was a reaction against such an attitude. In this we see that it is Mary who, of her own free will, resolves to remain a virgin. Pseudo-Matthew relates that the priest Abiathar wanted to

---

[10] J. Quasten, *op. cit.*, p. 121.

[11] Mt. 1:18-25; Lk. 1:26-38; Jn. 1:13.

[12] E. Dublanchy, S.M., Marie: *Enseignement néo-testamentaire sur la virginité de Marie*, in *Dictionnaire de théologie catholique*, Vol. 9, 1927, cols. 2341-2349; *Enseignement traditionnel concernant la virginité de la Mère de Dieu*, ibid., cols. 2369-2373.

[13] Origen, *Contra Celsum*, 1. 32; Acta Pilati, 2. 3 (Tischendorf, p. 224).

[14] E. Amann, *Le protoévangile de Jacques*, pp. 10-15.

[15] *Protoevangelium Jacobi*, 4. 1 (Amann, p. 192).

take Mary as a wife for his son, and then he goes on with the following account: "Mary forbade them to do this and said: It cannot happen that I know a man or that a man knows me. Then the priests and all her relatives said to her: God is honored by children and He is adored by descendants. It has always been such in Israel. Mary answering them said: God is honored first of all by chastity. ... This is what I have learned in the temple of God since my youth, namely, that a virgin can be dear to God. This is why I have resolved in my heart never to know man."[16] Interpreting the Protoevangelium in this way, Pseudo-Matthew, who wrote in the sixth century, is merely reflecting the thought of previous writers who saw in Mary a model of virginity and one who consecrated herself to God by a vow of virginity.[17]

In the Protoevangelium, then, Mary is vowed to God as a virgin to whom marriage was excluded. This poses an acute problem for the author of the Protoevangelium with regard to the relationship between Mary and Joseph. On the one hand he must admit a conjugal bond because of the testimony of the New Testament; on the other hand he must hold to the virginity of Mary. It is because of this that his language and his descriptions of the relationship between the two is somewhat obscure and vacillating. Stressing the virginity of Mary *ante partum*, he concentrates more on the fact that Mary was given to Joseph as a charge; she was given to Joseph who, by reason of his age, could guard her intact.[18]

Going on to give further proof that Mary was a virgin *ante partum*, the Protoevangelium insists, in the language of the New Testament, that Mary conceived of the Holy Spirit. Furthermore, he represents both Joseph and Mary as submitting to the trial of drinking the bitter waters to show their complete innocence of all

---

[16] *Pseudo-Matthew, Liber de ortu Beatae Mariae et infantia Salvatoris*, 7 (Amann, pp. 300-304). The text is also found in C. Tischendorf, *Evangelia apocrypha*, pp. 51-112; C. Michel, *Evangiles apocryphes*, Vol. 1, pp. 54-158.

[17] E. Dublanchy, Marie: *Le voue de virginité émis par Marie*, in *Dictionnaire de théologie catholique*, Vol. 9, 1927, col. 2386.

[18] On this problem, cf. E. Amann, *op. cit.*, pp. 24-27.

guilt in the matter of Mary's pregnancy.[19]

Mary was not only a virgin *ante partum*, but also a virgin *in partu*. The virginity of Mary *in partu* is really the *"idée capitale"* of the Protoevangelium. To give proof of his belief in this aspect of Mary's virginity, the author of the account has the condition of Mary attested to by a midwife. By these minute physical details the author emphasizes not only the virginity of Mary but also the actuality and reality of Christ who took flesh *ex Maria*.[20]

In the Protoevangelium Mary was not only a virgin *ante partum* and *in partu*; she also remained a virgin *post partum*. Her consecration and dedication to God demanded this. However, to leave no room for doubt in this matter and to show his belief in this fact, the author portrays St. Joseph as an old man, as a widower, who had children by his first wife and not by Mary.[21] Incidentally, it is in this way that he solves the problem of the brethren of Jesus.[22]

There are ever so many documents in which the events described in the Protoevangelium are utilized and recalled, and which emphasize the above-mentioned virtues of Mary. It would take us too far afield to go into them, but at least some of the main ones can be mentioned. There are, of course, the various versions of the Protoevangelium in Syriac,[23] Ethiopic,[24] and Armenian.[25] There are no direct Latin translations, but there are Latin elaboration as

---

[19] Protoevangelium, 13-17 (Amann, pp. 230-242). The author accommodates here to suit his own purpose the trial of drinking the bitter water mentioned in Num. 5:12 ff.

[20] *Protoevangelium*, 19-20 (Amann, pp. 250-256). The virginity of Mary *in partu* is also mentioned in such early apocrypha as the *Ascension of Isaias*, 11: 2-11; *Odes of Solomon*, 19: 6-10. On these documents, cf. J. Plumpe, *Some Little-known Early Witnesses to Mary's Virginitas in Partu*, in *Theological Studies*, Vol. 9, 1948, pp. 567-577. For the testimony of the *Epistola Apostolorum*, 3, cf. J. Quasten, *Patrology*, Vol. 1, p. 151.

[21] Protoevangelium, 9: 2-3 (Amann, pp. 216-218).

[22] E. Amann, *op. cit.*, pp. 36-39.

[23] A. Lewis, *Apocrypha syriaca: Protoevangelium*, in *Studia sinaitica*, Vol. 11, 1902, pp. 1-12.

[24] M. Chaine, *Apocrypha de B. Maria Virgine: Liber nativitatis Mariae*, in *Corpus scriptorum christianorum orientalium*, ser. 1, Vol. 7, 1909, pp. 1-16.

[25] F. Conybeare, *Protoevangelium Mariae*, in *American Journal of Theology*, Vol. 1, 1897, pp. 424-442.

seen in the Gospel of Pseudo-Matthew from the sixth century[26] and the work on the infancy of Mary from the Carolingian period.[27] Additional matter is found in the Coptic lives of the Virgin[28] and the history of St. Joseph.[29] To these may be added the various Infancy Gospels.[30]

Once the virginity of Mary had been so vigorously defended and emphasized in the Protoevangelium and its allied documents, we find that later Apocrypha speak of Mary's virginity in the celebrated phrase "ever-Virgin." This is very noticeable in the literature known as the *Transitus Mariae.*[31] To the Latin writer, Pseudo-Melito, Mary is *beata semper virgo Maria.*[32] The Greek writer, Pseudo-John, speaks of Mary as one who was ever a virgin. To him she is ἀειπάρθενος.[33]

Mary, who was always a virgin, was a virgin both in body and soul. The Coptic account of Theodosius, speaking of the reunion of the body and soul of Mary in heavenly glory, refers to Ps. 44:15, which speaks of the virgins who will be brought to the King. With this as his background he goes on to say: "Then we understood that today there were brought to the King virgins, even the soul and

---

[26] *Pseudo-Matthew, Liber de ortu Beatae Mariae et infantia Salvatoris* (Amann, pp. 272-339).

[27] *De nativitate Mariae* (Amann, pp. 340-365). The text can also be found in C. Tischendorf, *Evangelia apocrypha*, pp. 113-121. Dom Lambert (*Revue Bénédictine*, Vol. 46, 1934, pp. 275-282) argues that this is a work of Paschasius Radbertus.

[28] F. Robinson, *Coptic Apocryphal Gospels: Sahidic Fragments of the Life of the Virgin*, in *Texts and Studies*, Vol. 4, No. 2, 1896, pp. 1-41.

[29] F. Robinson, Coptic *Apocryphal Gospels: Bohairic Accounts of the Death of Joseph, with Sahidic Fragments*, ibid., pp. 130-185; P. Peeters, *Histoire de Joseph le charpentier*, in *Evangiles apocryphes*, Vol. 1, pp. 193-245. Cf. S. Morenz, *Die Geschichte von Joseph dem Zimmerman, übersetzt, erläutert und untersucht* (*Texte und Untersuchungen*, Vol. 56) (Berlin, 1951).

[30] P. Peeters, *Evangiles apocryphes*, Vol. 2, *L'évangile de l'enfance* (Paris, 1914).

[31] Pertinent data on the *Transitus Mariae* literature will be given below when they are studied in connection with the death and Assumption of Mary.

[32] Pseudo-Melito, *Transitus Beatae Mariae*, prolog. (C. Tischendorf, Apocalypses apocryphae [Leipzig, 1866], p. 124, note). In the edition of Tischendorf this prologue is given as a note; in other editions it is given as Chapter 1. This accounts for the difference in the number of chapters.

[33] Pseudo-John, *Liber de dormitione Mariae*, 1 (Tischendorf, p. 95).

body which were united."[34]

In this literature the virginity of Mary is regarded as a postulate for her Assumption and for the privilege of not undergoing the corruption of the grave. Thus, in the work of Pseudo-Melito, when Christ came to raise Mary from the dead, He is pictured as saying: "Arise, my love and my kinswoman, thou who didst not suffer corruption by carnal intercourse, thou shalt not suffer corruption in the sepulchre."[35]

MARY'S DIVINE MATERNITY

With regard to Mary's divine Maternity there is a parallel between the presentation of this doctrine in the Apocrypha and in the patristic tradition. Although this truth is not explicitly affirmed in the New Testament, it is manifestly contained in the truth that Mary conceived and brought forth Jesus, that Mary is the Mother of Jesus who is the Verbum, the Second Person of the Blessed Trinity, and that everything that concerns Jesus must be attributed to the Person of the Word who is true God.[36] Furthermore, the period up to the fourth century is characterized by an evident affirmation of the fact of the divine Maternity, even though the expression "Mother of God" was not formally employed. In the second and third centuries the traditional teaching was directed against the erroneous tenet that attributed to Jesus an apparent body or a body that was not material like ours. To combat this, it was asserted that Jesus was born *ex Maria*, and that Jesus, *natus ex Maria*, is God.[37] In this early period, also, the doctrine of the divine Maternity is found in the formulas of the creed, such as, "born of the Virgin," "born of Mary," and "born of the Holy Spirit and of the Virgin Mary." In the fourth and fifth centuries we have the use of the explicit term *Theotokos*, and an investigation of the theological principle on

---

[34] Theodosius, *The Falling Asleep of Mary*, 9. 14 (Robinson, *Coptic Apocryphal Gospels*, p. 127).

[35] Pseudo-Melito, *Transitus Beatae Mariae*, 16. 1 (Tischendorf, p. 135).

[36] E. Dublanchy, *Marie: Enseignement néo-testamentaire sur la maternité divine*, in *Dictionnaire de théologie catholique*. Vol. 9, 1927, col. 2340.

[37] G. Bareille, *Docétisme, in Dictionnaire de théologie catholique*, Vol. 4 (1939), cols. 1484-1501.

which this truth rests.[38] With the Council of Ephesus and the definition of Mary's divine Maternity, this doctrine is the focal point in Mariology. Prior to this time there was more emphasis on the virginity of Mary, and on the concept of Mary as the New Eve; now she is pre-eminently the Theotokos and there is a constant emphasis on the *Mater Dei* theme.

The early apocryphal literature, e.g., the Protoevangelium and its allied documents, stressed, as was seen, the virginity of Mary. In keeping with the parallel literature of the patristic tradition, there is no explicit emphasis on the divine Maternity. Here the divine Maternity is expressed merely by repeating the expressions in the Gospels on which this truth is based. Here it should be noted that the emphasis on the virginity of Mary in these documents is at the same time a recognition of her divine Maternity. In the phrase, *natus ex Virgine*, they stressed the virgo element; the recognition of motherhood, as is evident, is found in the first part of the phrase "*natus ex.*"

In some of these documents that appeared after the *Theotokos* theme became current, there is an emphasis on the divine Maternity. This is especially noticeable in the Coptic lives of the Virgin.[39] The second Sahidic fragment, after stating that the angel was sent to give the good tidings to the Virgin, goes out of its way to repeat the same idea by saying that the angel was sent to the Mother of God to proclaim to her the great good tidings.[40] In these documents there are many expressions describing the divine Maternity. The one that merits special attention is the phrase "the holy God-bearer." It is as succinct and emphatic as "*Sancta Dei Genetrix*," or our English phrase "Holy Mother of God."[41]

It is especially in the *Transitus Mariae* literature that we find

---

[38] E. Dublanchy, Marie: *Enseignement patristique ou théologique concernant la maternité divine*, in *Dictionnaire de théologie catholique*, Vol. 9, 1927, cols. 2349-2351; V. Schweitzer, *Alter des Titels Theotokos*, in *Katholik*, ser. 3, Vol. 17, 1903, pp. 97-113; G. Jouassard, *Marie à travers la patristique: Maternité divine, virginité, sainteté*, in *Maria. Etudes sur la Sainte Vierge*, Vol. 1 (Paris, 1949), pp. 71-157.

[39] F. Robinson, *Coptic Apocryphal Gospels*, pp. 1-41.

[40] *Sahidic Fragment* 2, B (Robinson, p. 17).

[41] *Sahidic Fragment*, 4 (Robinson, p. 39).

constant emphasis on the theme of the divine Maternity. This is only normal in literature that developed after the definition of this doctrine, when the divine Maternity became the focal point of Mariology. Just as in the patristic literature, so also in this literature, Mary is predominantly the *Theotokos*. The *Transitus Mariae* literature high-lights Mary's divine Maternity in a threefold manner: it constantly calls her the Mother of God; it contains scenes in which an act of explicit belief is made in Mary's divine Maternity, and it exalts Mary's divine Maternity by proclaiming her Assumption as postulated by this extraordinary privilege.

It would be tedious and repetitious to cite every passage in which Mary is called the Mother of God. One from the more important early accounts must suffice. In the complete Syriac version, the angel appears to Mary and announces: "Hail to thee, Mother of God! Thy prayer has been accepted in heaven before thy Son, our Lord Jesus Christ."[42] The sixth-century Coptic account of Theodosius is written in honor of the "Lady of us all, the holy God-bearer Mary."[43] The account of Pseudo-Melito speaks of the departure of the "Blessed Mary ever-Virgin, the Mother of God."[44] To Pseudo-John, Mary is the "all-holy glorious Mother of God."[45] The constant repetition of this title is like a growing crescendo. Actually, one would have to read these documents personally to see how they are pervaded with the theme of Mary's divine Maternity. A faint idea can be had of this when it is realized that in the account of Pseudo-John, which takes up about nine pages of actual text in the edition of Tischendorf, there are at least fifty references stating outrightly or equivalently that Mary is the Mother of God.

These documents also high-light Mary's divine Maternity by portraying scenes in which individuals make an express profession of faith in Mary as the Mother of God. In the Greek account of Pseudo-John, as in many others, there is the story of Jephonias who tried to harm the body of Mary as it was being brought to burial. As

---

[42] *Transitus Mariae*, 1 (Lewis, Apocrypha syriaca, p. 21).

[43] Theodosius, *The Falling Asleep of Mary* (Robinson, Coptic Apocryphal Gospels, p. 91).

[44] Pseudo-Melito, *Transitus Beatae Mariae*, Prolog (Tischendorf, Apocalypses apocryphae, p. 124, note).

[45] Pseudo-John, *Liber de dormitione Mariae*, 1 (Tischendorf, p. 95).

he did this an angel cut his two hands from off his body and left them hanging in the air about the bed. When the people saw this they cried out: "Truly, He is the true God who was born of thee, Mary, Mother of God, ever-Virgin." Jephonias himself exclaimed: "Holy Mary, thou didst bear Christ who is God, have mercy on me."[46] The complete Syriac account pictures the same person, who is here called Yuphanya, as setting out to proclaim Mary among the Jews. When the Jews were astonished at his message he explained how he had been cured and then he goes on to say: "I have become a disciple of Jesus the Son of the glorious God, and of Mary His Mother who bore him. ... And I believe in her that she is the Mother of God."[47]

It must be recalled that the *Transitus Mariae* is a type of popular literature. In literature of this kind, such cases in which people were won over and made explicit professions of faith in Mary as the Mother of God was the type of proof that would have a natural appeal to the popular mind. This is the closest that this literature comes to the tendency in patristic literature of pointing out the theological principle that justifies the use of the expression *Theotokos.*[48]

Finally, these documents stress the divine Maternity of Mary by postulating a special glorification for her after her death, precisely because she is the Mother of God. Thus, in the Latin account of Pseudo-Melito, Peter and the Apostles say to Christ: "If therefore it might be brought about by the power of Thy grace it has seemed right to us Thy servants that as Thou, having overcome death, reignest in glory, so Thou shouldst raise up the body of Thy Mother and take her with Thee rejoicing in heaven."[49]

The Coptic account of Theodosius has a similar emphasis. When Christ came to raise up the body of Mary and glorify her in body and soul, He is portrayed as standing over the coffin and saying:

---

[46] Pseudo-John, *Liber de dormitione Mariae*, 47 (Tischendorf, p. 110).

[47] *Transitus Mariae*, 3 (Lewis, p. 51).

[48] E. Dublanchy, *Marie: Enseignement patristique au IV et au commencement du V siècle*, in *Dictionnaire de théologie catholique*, Vol. 9, 1927, cols. 2351-2355.

[49] Pseudo-Melito, *Transitus Beatae Mariae*, 15. 3 (Tischendorf, p. 135).

"Arise from thy sleep, O thou holy body, which was to Me a temple. ... Arise. Why sleepest thou yet in the earth? Array thyself with thy soul, and come to the heavens with Me, unto My good Father and the Holy Spirit; for they long for thee. Arise, O thou holy body, from which I built Me My flesh in a manner incomprehensible; wear thy soul which was to Me a dwelling place. ... Arise, O thou holy body; be joined to the blessed soul. Receive from Me thy resurrection before the whole creation."[50]

THE DEATH OF MARY

The death of Mary, together with her final lot after death, is treated in the apocryphal literature known as the *Transitus Mariae*. The *Transitus* attempts to give information on these matters and thus supply for the silence of the canonical Scripture on these points. There is a great deal of controversy with regard to the locality and the time in which this literature developed. It seems that this type of literature developed in Syria in the fifth century after the definition of the divine Maternity at Ephesus had given a great impetus to the development of Mariology.[51] The Transitus was an extremely popular type of literature as seen from the accounts in Syriac, Latin, Greek, Coptic, and other languages.[52]

Before discussing the treatment of Mary's death, something must be said about the nature of these documents and Mary's outlook on death. With regard to the nature of these documents, it can be said that the authors of these works, with their attention riveted on the glories of Mary, the *Theotokos*, began to write about the marvels and miracles that were associated with Mary's last days on earth and with her passing from this earth. The writers surcharge their accounts with descriptions of the miraculous that are utterly fantastic, and which manifest bad taste not only theologically but artistically. With regard to this specific aspect of

---

[50] Theodosius, *The Falling Asleep of Mary*, 8. 10 ff. (Robinson, pp. 121-123).

[51] M. Jugie, A.A., *La mort et l'Assomption de la Sainte Vierge* (*Studi e testi*, Vol. 114) (Vatican City, 1924), pp. 108, 169.

[52] C. Balić, O.F.M., *Testimonia de Assumptione Beatae Mariae Virginis*. Pars prior (Rome, 1948), pp. 14-65, 137-153; M. Jugie, *op. cit.*, pp. 103-171; A. C. Rush, *The Assumption in the Apocrypha*, in *The American Ecclesiastical Review*, Vol. 116, 1947, pp. 5-31.

the nature and style of these works, B. Altaner offers a valid explanation. There is a certain parallel between the *Transitus* literature and the legendary Acts of the Martyrs insofar as fictitious episodes are introduced and extraordinary miracles are multiplied. There was a keen disappointment in Christian circles over the fact that the genuine data on so many outstanding personages of the early centuries was unknown. Consequently, writers gave free rein to their imagination in writing up the acts of the martyrs and lives of the saints; the period from the fourth to the sixth century was noted for such legendary works and it is within the limits of this period that the Transitus developed, furnishing fictionalized episodes of Mary's last days on earth and multiplying miracles at will.[53]

Regarding Mary's outlook on death, it can be said that these documents are notorious for playing up the horrors of the *exitus animae,* that is, the horror of the devil at death and the many foes that the soul encounters in its journey to eternity.[54] Some

---

[53] B. Altaner, *Zur Frage der Definibilität der Assumptio* in *Theologische Revue,* Vol. 44, 1948, p. 136. In this and the corresponding articles in the Theologische Revue, Vol. 45, 1949, pp. 129-142, and Vol. 46, 1950, pp. 5-20, Altaner placed too much emphasis on historical tradition; he tried to discover the teaching of the Church's dogmatic tradition by a sheerly historical method. Cf. W. Burghardt, S.J., The Catholic Concept of Tradition in the Light of Modern Theological Thought, in The Catholic Theological Society of America, Proceedings of the Sixth Annual Convention (1951), p. 73; J. Ternus, *Zur historisch-theologischen Tradition der Himmelfahrt Mariens,* in *Scholastik,* Vol. 25, 1950, pp. 321-360.

[54] For the *exitus animae* theme in ancient Christian writers, cf. J. Quasten, *Die Grabinschrift des Beratius Nikatoras,* in *Mitteilungen des deutschen archäologischen Instituts,* Römische Abteilung, Vol. 53, 1938, pp. 50-69; A. C. Rush, C.SS.R., *Death and Burial in Christian Antiquity* (Studies in Christian Antiquity, Vol. 1, Washington, D. C., 1941), 32-35. In the *Transitus Mariae* literature the terror of the *exitus animae* is portrayed very graphically in the Coptic accounts. Incidentally, this was a favorite theme with such early Egyptian writers as Origen, *Homilia 23 in Lucam* (G.C.S., Vol. 9, p. 154, ed. Rauer); Athanasius, *Vita S. Antonii,* 65 (PG, 26, 933); Cyril of Alexandria, *Homilia 14: De exitu animi* (PG, 77, 1073). When a Latin version of the *Transitus* mentions (even though more moderately) a description of the exitus animae, it does this not simply as something borrowed from and patterned on the Eastern *Transitus* theme, but as something that played a part in Western culture as well. Cf. A. C. Rush, *An Echo of Christian*

documents have the bad taste to submit Mary to such a mentality of fear, and this is very probably one of the reasons why the *Transitus* literature met with disfavor and was rejected by the decree known as the *Decretum Gelasianum.*[55] Actually, what these authors are doing is projecting a very popular eschatological mentality into Mary. It is impossible for them to write about death without stressing the ever popular theme, the *exitus animae.* As versions of the *Transitus* multiplied and were written more in keeping with true Catholic sense, this aspect was decidedly toned down, e.g., in the account of Pseudo-Melito. Even in documents where this mentality is highly pronounced, there are indications that Mary was not entirely dominated by it.[56]

Turning now to the question of Mary's death, the *Transitus* literature portrays Mary's departure from this world as a departure by death, the common lot of mankind. It excludes both martyrdom and immortality. To these authors the most obvious solution was that she died a natural death. The Greek account of Pseudo-John is actually a discourse on the Falling Asleep of Mary, κοίμησις being an accepted Christian expression to designate the sleep of death.[57] Pseudo-Melito speaks of Mary's death as the departure of the Blessed Mary ever Virgin, the Mother of God. This departure took place by the ordinary process of the soul being taken out of the body.[58] Mary was to be subject to death, the universal law for man; she, however, would meet it in victory. Thus, when Mary prayed to

---

Antiquity in *St. Gregory the Great: Death a Struggle with the Devil* in *Traditio,* Vol. 3, 1945, pp. 369-380.

[55] On the *Decretum Gelasianum,* cf. B. Altaner, Patrologie, p. 414; G. Bardy, *Gelase, decret de,* in *Dictionnaire de la bible, Supplément,* Vol. 3, 1938, cols. 579-590.

[56] A. C. Rush, *Scriptural Texts and the Assumption in the Transitus Mariae,* in *Catholic Biblical Quarterly,* Vol. 12, 1950, p. 373.

[57] Pseudo-John, *Liber de dormitione Mariae (Tischendorf, Apocalypses apocryphae,* pp. 95-112). Jugie (*La mort et l'Assomption,* p. 117) believes that this dates from the sixth century in the period between 550 and 580. On the Christian concept of death as a sleep, cf. A. C. Rush, *Death and Burial in Christian Antiquity,* pp. 1-22.

[58] Pseudo-Melito, *Transitus Beatae Mariae,* 2. 1 (Tischendorf, p. 125). Jugie (op. cit., p. 111) believes that this is a Catholic adaptation of the work rejected by the *Decretum Gelasianum* and that it is to be dated about 550.

Christ to be delivered from the power of darkness, and asked that she see not the ugly spirits coming to meet her, Christ says to her: "When I was sent by My Father for the salvation of the world and was hung on the Cross, the prince of darkness came to Me. But because he was unable to find any vestige of his work in Me, he departed conquered and crushed. When thou shalt see him, thou shalt see him in virtue of the common law of mankind, whereby death is allotted to thee. However, he cannot harm thee, because I am with thee to help thee. Come, without fear, for the heavenly hosts await thee to bring thee into the joys of paradise."[59]

It is not necessary to use all these documents that mention the fact that Mary died a natural death. Greater attention, however, will be given to some of the Coptic accounts because it is especially in these that there is a more detailed theological speculation on the death of Mary. In the sixth-century sermon, written by Theodosius, the Monophysite Patriarch of Alexandria,[60] when the Apostles were grieved on hearing that Mary was going to die, she said to them: "My sons, wherefore do you weep and grieve my spirit? Is it not written that all flesh must needs taste death? I also must needs return to the earth, as all the inhabitants of the earth."[61] Theodosius again repeats the fact of Mary's death by pointing to the universal law of death and by showing that her death makes her conformable to Christ. This is seen in the words of Christ addressed to Mary: "O My beautiful mother, when Adam transgressed My commandment I passed upon him a sentence, saying, Adam, thou art earth and thou shalt return unto the earth again. For also I, the Life of all men, tasted death in the flesh which I took from thee, in the flesh of Adam, thy forefather. Yet since My Godhead was one with it,

---

[59] Pseudo-Melito, *Transitus Beatae Mariae*, 7. 2 (Tischendorf, p. 129).

[60] E. Amann, *Théodose d'Alexandrie*, in *Dictionnaire de théologie catholique*, Vol. 15, 1946, pp. 325-328. The text is given by F. Robinson, *Coptic Apocryphal Gospels: Bohairic Accounts of the Falling Asleep of Mary*, in *Texts and Studies*, Vol. 4, Part 2, 1896, pp. 90-126, and also by M. Chaine, *Sermon de Théodose, patriarche d'Alexandrie, sur la dormition et l'Assomption de la Vierge*, in *Revue de l'Orient Chrétien*, Vol. 29, 1933-1934, pp. 272-314. Chaine gives the long introduction and the conclusion which Robinson omits.

[61] Theodosius, *The Falling Asleep of Mary*, 5. 4-5 (Robinson, p. 107).

therefore I raised it from the dead."[62] In the foregoing words emphasis is placed on the fact that Christ took flesh from Mary. This is to prove the reality of Christ and is at the same time a refutation of Docetism. On the same score, Mary's death is necessary to show that she was truly human, and consequently to show that Christ and His work were actualities. Thus, after Christ told Mary that He raised up His flesh because of the Godhead that was in it, He goes on to say: "I did not wish to suffer thee to taste death, but to translate thee up to the heavens as Enoch and Elias. But these also, even they must needs taste death at last. And if this happens to thee, wicked men will think concerning thee, that thou art a power (angelic spirit) which came down from heaven; and that this dispensation took place in appearance. I know the heart of all men, and understand their thoughts."[63]

The account of Pseudo-Evodius, who represents himself as a disciple of St. Peter and his successor at Rome, is very similar to that of Theodosius in the treatment of Mary's death.[64] When Peter and the rest of the disciples asked Christ if it were not possible that Mary should never die, this answer is given: "I wonder at you, O My holy apostles, for this word which you have spoken now. Can the word which I spoke from the first prove a lie? Nay, God forbid. But I pronounced a sentence of death from the first upon all flesh, that they must needs taste death. Because of the flesh which I took, I also tasted death, I who am the Lord of all men, that I might loose the pangs of death."[65] When this answer was given on the certainty of Mary's death, Peter asked Christ if it were not possible that Mary be allowed to remain with them a while longer. To this Christ answered: "O My chosen Peter, knowest thou not that there is an appointed time laid down for each man to accomplish in the world;

---

[62] *The Falling Asleep of Mary*, 5. 15-18 (Robinson, p. 107 f.).

[63] *The Falling Asleep of Mary*, 5. 18-21 (Robinson, p. 109).

[64] There is an Evodius who is mentioned as the successor of St. Peter at Antioch. Cf. R. Devresse, *Le patriarcat d'Antioche* (Paris, 1945), p. 115; F. Robinson, *Coptic Apocryphal Gospels*, p. 207. On the problem of the episcopal succession at Antioch, cf. C. Karalevskij, *Antioche: Les origines chrétiennes jusqu'au concile de Nicéa*, in *Dictionnaire d'histoire et de géographie ecclésiastiques*, Vol. 3, 1924, col. 567.

[65] Pseudo-Evodius, *The Falling Asleep of Mary*, 8. 10-13 (Robinson, p. 55).

and when it is fulfilled, it is not possible for him to stay for a single hour. Now therefore the appointed time of My mother is fulfilled today. Therefore she must needs lay down her body, and I will take her up to the heavens with Me in glory."[66] The *Transitus Mariae* literature, then, takes for granted that Mary died. It also adduces reasons for her death. Among these reasons we find the universality of death, the conformity of Mary to Christ, and the reality of Mary with the consequent reality of the redemptive work of Christ.

THE ASSUMPTION OF MARY

The Assumption of Mary is a theme that is found in the *Transitus Mariae*. Important as are the statements on the glorification of Mary as contained in these documents, it must be kept in mind that the Transitus is concerned primarily with the death of Mary and with the miraculous happenings surrounding it. Then, in a somewhat brief manner, it treats of the final lot of Mary after death.[67] As was noted, this literature developed after the definition of Ephesus had resulted in an intense awareness of the *Theotokos*. Accounts were written of her death and then writers speculated on the lot of Mary after death. Once there was an actual confrontation of the death of Mary, this latter problem had to be faced also. When this took place, the Christian sense of the writers of these accounts revolted against the idea that one so glorious as Mary suffered the corruption of the grave; hence, they postulate a glorification of Mary. She who was extraordinary in life, they claim, was extraordinary in death.

Except for the account which states that the body of Mary will be hidden in the earth and preserved incorruptible,[68] these accounts postulate a glorification for Mary in body and soul. It is not easy to pass a definitive judgment on the nature of this glorification due, in part, to the very involved eschatology of these documents. At any

---

[66] *The Falling Asleep of Mary*, 8. 16 (Robinson, p. 55).

[67] H. Jürgens, *Die kirchliche Ueberlieferung von der leiblichen Aufnahme der seligsten Gottesmutter in den Himmel*, in *Zeitschrift für katholische Theologie*, Vol. 4, 1890, p. 602.

[68] *Sahidic Fragment of the Life of the Virgin*, 4. 82-82 (Robinson, *Coptic Apocryphal Gospels*, p. 35). Cf. M. Jugie, *La mort et l'Assomption de la Sainte Vierge*, p. 126; C. Balić, *Testimonia de assumptione*, p. 39.

event, there is no doubt that, in some versions, this glorification is a genuine assumption, comprising death, the glorification of the soul, the resurrection of the body, and the reunion of soul and body in everlasting glory. Others, e.g., the Greek account of Pseudo-John and derived documents, seem to draw a distinction between the glorification of the soul and that of the body. According to this, Mary's soul is in the heavens, in the treasuries of the Father; her body is transplanted to an earthly paradise where it is preserved incorrupt.[69]

The Syriac fragment from the end of the fifth century, which Jugie regards as the oldest *Transitus*,[70] in simple language describes the resurrection of Mary and the reunion of the body and soul in paradise. While the Apostles were gathered before the sepulcher of Mary, Christ appeared with Michael and a host of angels. At the bidding of Christ, the body of Mary was placed upon the clouds which then went to the gates of paradise. On entering paradise, the body of Mary was set down by the tree of life; then her soul was brought and placed in her body.[71]

In the Latin account of Pseudo-Melito, which was a quasi-official version in the Latin Church,[72] Christ appeared to the Apostles who were gathered at the sepulcher after burying Mary. Christ said to them: "Before I ascended to My Father, I promised you saying, that you who have followed Me, in the regeneration when the Son of Man shall sit on the throne of His majesty, you also shall sit on the twelve thrones, judging the twelve tribes of Israel. I have chosen this woman out of the tribes of Israel by the command of My Father to be My dwelling place. What, then, do you wish that I should do

---

[69] Pseudo-John, *Liber de dormitione Mariae*, 39 (Tischendorf, *Apocalypses apocryphae*, p. 107 f.). On this point, cf. M. Jugie, *op. cit.*, pp. 117-126, and the argumentation of C. Balić, op. cit., pp. 15-23.

[70] M. Jugie, *op. cit.*, p. 108.

[71] W. Wright, *Contributions to the Apocryphal Literature of the New Testament* (London, 1865), p. 46. This fragment is entitled: *Obsequies of the Holy Virgin*.

[72] A. Wilmart, *L'ancien récit latin de l'Assomption*, in *Studi e testi*, Vol. 59, 1933, p. 323. In the light of the text here edited by Wilmart, J. Rivière brought forth a study, entitled *Le plus vieux Transitus latin et son dérivé grec*, in *Recherches de théologie ancienne et médiévale*, Vol. 8, 1936, pp. 5-23. Jugie (*op. cit.*, pp. 110, n. 1, 150-154) argues that this is an abbreviated Latin version of the Greek account by John of Thessalonica.

with her." On hearing this, Peter and the Apostles immediately answered: "Lord, Thou hast chosen this Thy handmaid to become Thy immaculate chamber, and us Thy Apostles for the ministry. Before the ages Thou hast foreknown all things with the Father, with Whom to Thee and the Holy Spirit there is one equal divinity and infinite power. If, therefore, it might be brought about by the power of Thy grace, it has seemed right to us Thy servants that as Thou, having overcome death, reignest in glory, so Thou shouldst raise up the body of Thy mother and take her with Thee rejoicing in heaven."[73] At once Christ commanded Michael to bring on the soul of Mary to have it ready to re-enter her body. In the words of Pseudo-Melito, the resurrection is described as follows: "The Lord said: Arise, My love and My kinswoman, thou who didst not suffer corruption by carnal intercourse, thou shalt not suffer corruption in the sepulcher. And at once Mary rose from the tomb, blessed the Lord, and threw herself at the Lord's feet, adoring Him and saying: I am not able to offer Thee fitting thanks, O Lord, for Thy immense benefits, which Thou hast deigned to confer upon me, Thy handmaid. May Thy name, O Redeemer of the world, and God of Israel be blessed for ever."[74] After the Lord had kissed her, Mary was taken up to the paradise of God together with Christ and the angels.[75]

The theme of a genuine Assumption is equally clear and emphatic in the Coptic account of Theodosius. The mind of Theodosius on the extraordinary glorification of Mary after death is seen in the threefold announcement of what is going to happen to Mary. Addressing words of consolation to Peter and John who were grieving over the news of Mary's departure, Christ said: "Be of good cheer, My friends and Apostles. I will not suffer her to be long away from you, but she shall appear to you quickly. There are two hundred and six days from her death until her holy assumption. I will bring her unto you arrayed in this body again, even as this body also, as you see her now, whilst she is with you. And I will translate her up to the heavens to be with My Father and the Holy

---

[73] Pseudo-Melito, *Transitus Beatae Mariae*, 15. 2-3 (Tischendorf, p. 134).

[74] *Transitus Beatae Mariae*, 16 (Tischendorf, p. 135).

[75] *Transitus Beatae Mariae*, 17 (Tischendorf, p. 135 f.).

Spirit, that she may continue praying for you all."[76] The same promise is made as soon as Mary died.[77] As the body of Mary was being brought to burial, Theodosius pictures a Galilean as saying under the inspiration of the Holy Spirit: "This corpse that is borne, this is the body of Mary, the daughter of Joachim and Anne, who bore the Messias, who is Christ. He it was who healed your sick, and gave light to your eyes, and raised your dead. We believe that as He raised your dead, He will raise His Mother also, and will take her to the heavens with Him."[78]

When the time for the actual Assumption arrived, Christ came down from heaven and ordered the body to rise. This is the beautiful passage "Arise from thy sleep, O thou holy body" which has already been quoted in the section on the divine Maternity of Mary. Describing what then took place, Theodosius goes on to relate: "When the Lord had said these things over the coffin of stone, straightway it opened; for it was shut even as the ark of Noah aforetime, which no man could open save God, who shut it aforetime. Forthwith the body of the honorable Virgin arose, and embraced its own soul, even as two brothers who are come from a strange country, and they were united one with another."[79] Giving us a final glimpse of Mary, Theodosius states: "She also, at once Our Lady and our Succorer, blessed us; and we saw them no more. But the voice of the powers that sang hymns before them was sounding in our ears, saying: Alleluia. Bring to the Lord glory and honor; bring to the Lord honor to His holy name. Alleluia. Bring to the Lord the sons of God, and sing glory in His holy temple. Alleluia. Then we understood that today there were brought unto he King virgins, even the soul and the body which were united."[80]

These are but a few of the many testimonies to Mary's

---

[76] Theodosius, *The Falling Asleep of Mary*, 5. 23-28 (Robinson, *Coptic Apocryphal Gospels*, p. 109). For a study of the belief in the Assumption among the Copts, cf. A. van Lantschoot, *L'Assomption de la Sainte Vierge chez les Coptes*, in *Gregorianum*, Vol. 27, 1946, pp. 493-526.

[77] Theodosius, *The Falling Asleep of Mary*, 6. 13 (Robinson, p. 113).

[78] *The Falling Asleep of Mary*, 7. 7-10 (Robinson, p. 117).

[79] *The Falling Asleep of Mary*, 9. 1-3 (Robinson, p. 125).

[80] *The Falling Asleep of Mary*, 9. 10-15 (Robinson, p. 127).

Assumption in the Apocrypha.[81] These apocryphal accounts are extremely important and interesting, because it is in them that we have the first testimonies in writing to Mary's Assumption. This poses a very weighty and involved problem, namely, the origin of this belief. This problem is seen to be all the more acute when it is borne in mind that there is no explicit statement in Scripture regarding Mary's Assumption, and that, prior to the *Transitus Mariae* literature, there is no patristic tradition on this matter. These facts argue to the nonexistence of an oral tradition of apostolic origin on the final lot of Mary.[82]

The glorification of Mary after death and the Assumption theme in the *Transitus Mariae*, then, demand an explanation. It isimpossible to regard these accounts as reliable historical reports of the events described. On the other hand, they are not merely the product of imaginations allowed to run wild. Altaner's explanation for the bizarre style of these documents, as noted above,[83] is a very valid explanation. However, this does not explain the Assumption theme introduced into these documents. For the explanation of this, other factors were at work.

These are accounts that proclaim the glories of Mary. Although previous to these writings there were no testimonies to Mary's Assumption, there was in Sacred Scripture and tradition a definite *corpus Marianum*. Mary was revered as the Mother of God, as the *Virgin ante*, in, and *post partum*; she was the New Eve associated with Christ, the New Adam, in the work of the Redemption. She was hailed as a creature of unique holiness. Consequently, when these authors consciously confronted the problem of Mary's final lot, their Christian piety revolted against the idea that one so exceptional underwent the corruption of the grave; they postulated for her a glorification in body and soul. To them, this glorification was based on and flowed from the above-mentioned Mariological

---

[81] For other accounts of the Assumption, cf. M. Jugie, *La mort et l'Assomption*, pp. 103-171; C. Balić, *Testimonia de Assumptione*, pp. 14-65, 137-153; A. C. Rush, *The Assumption in the Apocrypha*, in *The American Ecclesiastical Review*, Vol. 116, 1947, pp. 5-31.

[82] M. Jugie, *op. cit.*, pp. 168-171, 585-589, 609-612.

[83] B. Altaner, *Zur Frage der Definibilität der Assumptio B. M. V.*, in *Theologische Revue*, Vol. 44, 1948, p. 136.

truths and principles. Hence, in these Apocrypha we have the origin of the movement to approach the Assumption of Mary from a theological viewpoint.[84] This trend gained tempo with the passing of the ages. Under the guidance of the Holy Spirit and the protection of Christ, the Church came to a greater insight into the deposit of revelation; the Assumption of Mary was a truth believed and taught by the ordinary and universal *magisterium*, and was solemnly declared a dogma of faith by Pope Pius XII on the first of November, 1950.[85]

THE QUEENSHIP OF MARY

Explicit testimonies to the Queenship of Mary did not appear before the fifth century.[86] Prior to this time, however, there were implicit manifestations of this belief.[87] The *Mater Domini* of the New Testament, where the word *Dominus* definitely connotes royalty and sovereignty,[88] led to the use of the word *Domina*.[89] Similarly, there was the evolution from the concept "Mother of Christ who is King" to "Mother of the King" and then the explicit use of the word "Queen."[90]

It would not advance the proof in any noticeable way to quote the passages from the Protoevangelium of James and its allied documents that repeat the Gospel scenes of the Annunciation, Nativity, and the Visitation which form the basis of this truth. In the

---

[84] A. C. Rush, *Assumption Theology in the Transitus Mariae,* in *The American Ecclesiastical Review,* Vol. 123, 1950, pp. 93-110. J. M. Bover, S.J., *Los apócrifos y la tradición asuncionista,* in *Estudios Marianos,* Vol. 6, 1947, pp. 99-118.

[85] Pius XII, *Munificentissimus Deus,* in *Acta Apostolocae Sedis,* Vol. 42, 1950, pp. 753-777.

[86] H. Barré, *La royauté de Marie pendant les neuf premiers siècles,* in *Recherches de science religieuse,* Vol. 29, 1939, p. 145.

[87] A. Luis, C.SS.R., *La realeza de Maria,* (Madrid, 1942), p. 34.

[88] L. Cerfaux, *Le titre Kyrios et la dignité royale de Jésus,* in *Revue de sciences philosophiques et théologiques,* Vol. 11, 1922, pp. 40-71.

[89] A good brief summary of the history and theology of Mary's Queenship is given by A. Santonicola, C.SS.R., *La royauté de Marie* (Nicolet, Quebec, Canada, 1951).

[90] M. Donnelly, S.J., *The Queenship of Mary during the Patristic Period,* in *Marian Studies,* Vol. 4, 1953, pp. 86-91. This entire issue of Marian Studies is given over to articles on the Queenship of Mary.

Protoevangelium of James, however, there is a passage that should be noted. The priests of the Temple decided to have a veil spun for the temple from various kinds of thread. To make this veil, young girls were chosen who were virgins and of the tribe of David. Lots were cast to determine who would weave the gold, linen, etc. It fell to Mary's lot to weave the true purple and scarlet.[91] Purple, the color of royalty, was allotted to Mary, to one who was the offspring of a royal line and who was destined for a royalty higher than all the dignities of earth.[92] The author does no more than state that the purple was allotted to Mary. In the Latin version of Pseudo-Matthew, Mary likewise received the purple. When this happened, the other virgins were jealous and explained it by saying that she received the purple because she was the youngest. Then in a sarcastic manner they began to call her, "Queen of virgins." No sooner had they referred to Mary as the Queen of virgins, when an angel of the Lord appeared in their midst and said to them: "This word will not be a word spoken in sarcasm, but it will be a true prophecy."[93]

Referring to this designation of Mary in Pseudo-Matthew, Amann remarks that the author has understood perfectly the thought of the Protoevangelium when this document assigned to Mary the task of weaving the purple.[94] In connection with the appellation of Mary as Queen in Pseudo-Matthew, it is interesting to note that the author makes a very significant change in the Annunciation scene. In this document, the angel is represented as saying to Mary: "Fear not, Mary, thou hast found favor with God. Behold thou shalt conceive in thy womb and bear a King who will rule not only on earth but also in heaven, and He shall reign for ever and ever."[95]

The explicit title of "Queen" in Pseudo-Matthew is a far advance

---

[91] *Protoevangelium Jacobi*, 10 (Amann, *Le Protoévangile*, pp. 218-220).

[92] E. Amann, *op. cit.*, p. 220, note.

[93] Pseudo-Matthew, *Liber de ortu Beatae Mariae et infantia Salvatoris*, 8. 5 (Amann, p. 310).

[94] E. Amann, *op. cit.*, p. 311, note.

[95] Pseudo-Matthew, *Liber de ortu Mariae*, 9. 2 (Amann, p. 312). Amann sees in this change the dependence of Pseudo-Matthew on Sedulius who writes in his well-known hymn: *Salve sancta parens, enixa puerpera regem.*

on the Protoevangelium. This, however, is not surprising in a work that comes from the sixth century. It is a good illustration showing how later recensions of a specific theme, such as that of the Protoevangelium, can mirror explicit and developed viewpoints current in their own time.

In a similar way, late Infancy Gospels clearly portray Mary as Queen. This is particularly noticeable in the Arabic Gospel of the Infancy, where Mary has a very predominant role.[96] Here Mary is constantly referred to as "Queen." The title *Domina*, applied to Mary, is always linked with the title Dominus, applied to Christ. Christ is Herus, Dominus; Mary is Hera, Domina. Mary is *Domina nostra*, the Mother of Christ the King. Because of this, she is *Domina nostra*.[97]

Since explicit testimonies to Mary as Queen date from the fifth century and are linked so closely with her divine Maternity, the richest source of this doctrine is the Transitus Mariae literature. In proclaiming the glories of the Mother of God and in describing her triumphant entrance into paradise, they hail her as a glorious queen. The testimonies to this doctrine are somewhat subdued in the early Greek accounts and very effusive in the Syriac and Coptic versions.

In Pseudo-Melito there is no direct statement that Mary is a queen. Two points, however, are stressed, namely, the Kingship of Christ and Mary's divine Maternity. Mary, therefore, is the Mother of the King of Glory. It is to Christ as the King of glory that Mary addresses her prayers.[98] This is as much as can be drawn from Pseudo-Melito on the royalty of Mary. Mary is the Mother of the King; and this phrase represents a fact, and also one of the stages of development or evolution of the Queenship of Mary.

The Greek discourse by Pseudo-John frequently refers to Mary

---

[96] E. Amann, *Apocryphes du nouveau testament*, in *Dictionnaire de la bible, Supplément*, Vol. 1, col. 485.

[97] *Evangelium infantiae Salvatoris arabicum*, 3, 6, 11, 16, 21 (Tischendorf, Evangelia apocrypha, pp. 182, 183, 185, 188, 191). In studying the Mariology in the Apocrypha and in the Christian tradition, we must not overlook the part that Mary plays in Islamic thought which was greatly influenced by the Apocrypha. A good survey on Mary in Islamic culture is given by J-M. Abd-el-Jalil, Marie et l'Islam (Etudes sur l'histoire des religions) (Paris, 1951).

[98] Pseudo-Melito, *Transitus Beatae Mariae*, 2, 3; 7. 1 (Tischendorf, *Apocalypses apocryphae*, pp. 126, 129).

as the "Mother of the Lord." The Lord is both God and King. The Mother of the Lord, then, is both Mother of God and Mother of one who is King. In this term, Mother of the Lord, there is conveyed the idea of royalty and sovereignty. Pseudo-John, moreover, explicitly proclaims the Queenship of Mary when he uses δέσποινα, a word that conveys the meaning of "Sovereign Lady" or "Queen."[99] This is seen when he states: "The Apostles, therefore, rose up immediately and went from the house carrying the bed of the Sovereign Lady, the Mother of God."[100]

In the Syriac *Transitus Mariae*[101] Mary is referred to again and again as "Lady Mary."[102] She is "Lady Mary, the Mistress of the world." This Lady Mary is the one who bore Him who is the Governor of the heaven and of the world.[103] This Governor of the world is Christ the King who came down from heaven to be beside the Lady Mary in death.[104] Throughout, the royalty of Mary is linked with the Kingship of Christ, the Son of God whom she bore. Not only does He proclaim her Queenship, but He proclaims her as a very special queen, for she is the Mistress of the world.

The Coptic account of Theodosius is a panegyric on the "Lady of us all, the holy God-bearer Mary."[105] Mary is the Lady of us all because she brought forth Him who bears the universe.[106] The concept of the royalty of Mary is brought out in the words which Christ addressed to the Father when He took the soul of Mary to heaven after she died. To Him He says: "Receive from Me, O My good Father, the bush which received the fire of the Godhead and

---

[99] H. Liddel and R. Scott, *Greek-English Lexicon* (New York, 1929), Vol. 1, p. 334.

[100] Pseudo-John, Liber de dormitione Mariae, 32 (Tischendorf, p. 105).

[101] A. Lewis, *Apocrypha syriaca: Transitus Mariae*, in *Studia sinaitica*, Vol. 11, pp. 12-69. An edition of this from a slightly later manuscript is given by W. Wright, *The Departure of my Lady Mary from the World*, in *Journal of Sacred Literature and Biblical Record*, fourth ser., Vol. 6, January, 1865, pp. 417-449; Vol. 7, April, 1865, pp. 110-160.

[102] *Transitus Mariae*, 1, 3 (Lewis, pp. 14, 18, 38, 39).

[103] *Transitus Mariae*, 2, 3 (Lewis, pp. 24, 32, 34).

[104] *Transitus Mariae*, 4 (Lewis, p. 55).

[105] Theodosius, *The Falling Asleep of Mary*, prolog. (Robinson, *Coptic Apocryphal Gospels*, p. 92).

[106] *The Falling Asleep of Mary*, 3. 13 (Robinson, p. 101).

was not burnt. I offer Thee, O My Father, a royal gift today, even the soul of My virgin mother."[107] Mary, in truth, is a royal gift because she is the Queen whom Christ called from the grief, trouble, and groaning of this life that she might receive everlasting joy and gladness.[108]

Even more enthusiastic are the testimonies to the Queenship of Mary in the account of Pseudo-Evodius. Like Theodosius, he also sets out to proclaim the glory of the "Lady of us all, the holy God-bearer Mary."[109] For him the day on which Mary died was the day on which "the Queen of all women, Mary the Virgin, the Mother of the King of kings was to go unto her beloved Son, our Lord, Jesus Christ."[110] Mary the Queen, the Mother of the King of kings is the heavenly Queen who takes her stand at the right hand of her Son. Thus, when Christ came to call Mary in death and take her to heaven, He said to the Apostles: "O My glorious members, whom I chose out of all the world, this is the day that the prophecy of My father David has been fulfilled, 'The Queen stood at thy right hand.'"[111] David himself is portrayed as a witness to Mary's Queenship. When Mary died "David the holy singer struck his spiritual harp, and cried out, saying: Precious before the Lord is the death of His holy ones. Be glad, O Mary, thou mother of Christ, the King of kings. This is the day that the prophecies are fulfilled which I spoke concerning thee, thou true Queen."[112]

The foregoing testimonies are sufficient to show the thought and trend of these documents on the Queenship of Mary. They clearly show that the Mother of the Lord is *Domina,* and that the Mother of Christ the King is *Regina.* These documents glory in hailing and proclaiming Mary as a queen. In popular and homiletical literature of this type, however, there is little theological speculation on the nature and basis of this Queenship. There are, it is true, many indications of why Mary is a queen, and it is with deep regret that these, due to lack of space, cannot be handled here at the

---

[107] *The Falling Asleep of Mary,* 6. 18 (Robinson, p. 113).

[108] *The Falling Asleep of Mary,* 5. 30 (Robinson, p. 111).

[109] Pseudo-Evodius, *The Falling Asleep of Mary,* prolog. (Robinson, p. 44).

[110] *The Falling Asleep of Mary,* 10. 1 (Robinson, p. 56).

[111] *The Falling Asleep of Mary,* 7. 6 (Robinson, p. 53).

[112] *The Falling Asleep of Mary,* 12. 15 (Robinson, p. 60).

present time. One obvious conclusion, however, stands out most clearly, namely, that the divine Maternity of Mary and her Queenship are always linked together.

THE INTERCESSION OF MARY

In the New Testament we see Mary as the means by which Christ, the Source of all blessings, came to man. We also see Mary using her power of intercession with her Son in favor of the married couple at Cana.[113]

Regarding the invocation of Mary and her intercession, there is not a word in the Protoevangelium of James. On the other hand, in Pseudo-Matthew, the sixth-century Latin elaboration of this work, there are scenes in which people have recourse to Mary. Describing Mary's life in the Temple, he says that if any sick people touched her they were immediately cured of their malady.[114] When the virgins who sarcastically referred to Mary as queen were rebuked by the angel, they at once asked Mary to pardon them and pray for them.[115] When the people made rash judgments about Mary's pregnant condition, and Mary proved them to be wrong, they implored her to have compassion on them and to pardon them.[116]

Such a theme, introduced into this sixth-century version of the Protoevangelium, is not at all surprising, for this work is the product of an age where Mary was hailed as the Dispensatrix of all graces, the Hope of the sick, the Help of the afflicted, and the Refuge of sinners.[117] This same mentality is especially pronounced in the Arabic Gospel of the Infancy where Mary plays a very

---

[113] On the mediation and intercession of Mary, cf. E. Dublanchy, *Marie: Médiation universelle de Marie en vertu de sa maternité divine*, in *Dictionnaire de théologie catholique*, Vol. 9, 1927, cols. 2389-2405; *Marie: Toute-puissance d'intercéssion de Marie au ciel*, cols. 2435-2439; J. Bittremieux, *De mediatione universali B. Mariae quoad gratias* (Bruges, 1926); J. Carol, O.F.M., *The Theological Concept of Mediation and Co-redemption*, in *Ephemerides theologicae lovanienses*, Vol. 14, 1937, pp. 642-650.

[114] Pseudo-Matthew, *Liber de ortu Mariae et infantia Salvatoris*, 6. 3 (Amann, *Le Protoévangile*, p. 300).

[115] *Liber de ortu Mariae*, 8. 5 (Amann, p. 310).

[116] *Liber de ortu Mariae*, 12. 5 (Amann, p. 322).

[117] E. Amann, *Le Protoévangile*, p. 40.

dominant role and is the Mediatrix of all blessings bestowed by the Infant.[118] This document is replete with scenes in which people come to Mary in their needs and are then helped by Mary and the Child whom she bore.[119]

The *Transitus Mariae* literature which proclaims the glories of Mary and which proclaims Mary's Assumption and Queenship because she is the Mother of God also high-lights the invocation and intercession of one who, as the Mother of God, can obtain all graces and blessings from her Son. To show the trend of these documents on this point, these few following testimonies must suffice.

In the Syriac *Transitus*, many people came to Mary in their needs with pleas for help on their lips. Describing one of these scenes, the *Transitus* states: "And persons without number went forth and went to Bethlehem; and they knocked at the door of the Blessed one's upper chamber. And the Apostles did not open the door to them. And when they did not open the door to them, they implored, saying: O Lady Mary, Mother of God, have mercy on us. And the Lady Mary heard the voice of the persons who were crying to her, and she prayed and said: My Master the Christ, whom I have in heaven, hearken to the voice of these afflicted souls. And straightway great strength and help went forth from the Blessed one to all these sick people, and they were cured."[120] From the lips of the Governor who was won over to Mary's cause, we hear these beautiful words: "The earth on which thou walkest becomes heaven. The heaven that beholds thee gives a blessing to the creatures who believe in thee. The healthy who behold thee receive gladness. To the sick who come unto thee thou givest health. I worship thee, Lady Mary. Stretch out thy right hand and bless me, and this my only child."[121] The angel who came to Mary to announce to her that she was to leave the world hails her with this greeting: "Hail to thee, Mother of God! Thy prayer hath been accepted in heaven before thy Son, our Lord Jesus Christ. And therefore thou shalt

---

[118] E. Amann, *Apocryphes du nouveau testament*, in *Dictionnaire de la bible*, Supplément, Vol. 1, col. 485.

[119] For two such illustrations, cf. *Evangelium infantiae arabicum*, 14, 27 (Tischendorf, Evangelia apocrypha, pp. 187, 194).

[120] *Transitus Mariae*, 3 (Lewis, Apocrypha syriaca, p. 35).

[121] *Transitus Mariae*, 3 (Lewis, p. 46).

depart from this world unto life everlasting. For thus I have been sent to tell thee and to cause thee to know that at the time when thou didst pray on earth, at once thou wast answered in heaven; and whatsoever thou dost seek from the Christ, thy Son who is in heaven on the right hand of God, thou shalt have both in earth and in heaven, and thy will is done."[122]

The power of Mary to help those in need is brought out very graphically by Pseudo-Melito when he tells the story of the Jewish priest who tried to overturn the body of Mary and whose arms were cut off from his shoulders and clung to the bier. It is at this point that the author goes on to say: "Then Peter made the bier stand still and said to him: If thou wilt believe with thy whole heart in the Lord Jesus Christ, thy hands will be loosed from the bier. And when he had said this, immediately his hands were loosed from the bier and he began to stand on his feet; his arms, however, were still withered and the pain did not leave him. Then Peter said to him: Go up to the body, kiss the bed and say: I believe in God, and in the Son of God, Jesus Christ, whom this woman bore, and I believe all things whatever Peter, the Apostle of God, has told me. Then coming near he kissed the bed, and at once all pain left him and his hands were healed."[123]

Pseudo-John gives the name of Jephonias to the person who tried to overturn the body of Mary. When Jephonias was punished for this rash act and was in excruciating pain, he cried out: "Holy Mary, thou didst bear Christ, who is God, have mercy on me."[124] This calling upon Mary is most helpful because her power of intercession is so great. This idea is brought out very graphically in these words which Christ addresses to Mary: "Let thy heart be glad and rejoice, for every grace and every gift has been given thee of My Father who is in heaven and of Me and of the Holy Spirit. Every soul that calls upon thee shall not be put to shame, but shall find mercy and consolation and help and confidence both in this world and in the world to come before My Father who is in heaven."[125] The

---

[122] *Transitus Mariae*, 2 (Lewis, p. 21).

[123] Pseudo-Melito, *Transitus Beatae Mariae*, 13. 2 (Tischendorf, Apocalypses apocryphae, p. 133).

[124] Pseudo-John, *Liber de dormitione Mariae*, 47 (Tischendorf, p. 110).

[125] *Liber de dormitione Mariae*, 43 (Tischendorf, p. 109).

power of Mary to obtain for us not only the needs of the present life, but also the help necessary to attain eternal life is also stressed by the author when he says: "By the prayer and intercession of Mary may we all be accounted worthy to come under her protection and help and guardianship both in this world and in the world to come."[126]

In these writings it is brought out that the intercession of Mary was great while she was living here on earth and also equally great when she was taken to heaven. Mary the Queen, assumed into heaven, is there beside her Son to intercede for us. In the sermon of Theodosius, this role of Mary, the Queen of heaven, receives great prominence. When Christ came to call Mary to heaven, Theodosius portrays Christ as saying to Peter and John: "And I will translate her up to the heavens to be with My Father and the Holy Spirit, that she may continue praying for you all."[127]

CONCLUSION

The foregoing pages show that there are ample testimonies to Mary in the Apocrypha of the New Testament. Ample as these testimonies are, it must not be forgotten that the testimonies mentioned are selective. At the same time, the testimonies selected are representative of the Marian trends in these writings.

Aside from individual works like the Ascension of Isaias, the Odes of Solomon, and the like, there are two main Marian sources in the Apocrypha. For the earlier period (second century on) there is the Protoevangelium of James, together with its various versions and allied documents. For the later period (fifth century on) there is the *Transitus Mariae* literature. The Protoevangelium literature is concerned primarily with the exceptional birth and the virginity of Mary; the *Transitus Mariae* literature is a glorification of Mary as the *Theotokos* and is a witness to her death and Assumption. It must not be imagined that these two Marian sources are parallel sources in the sense that they run parallel and never meet. Thus, later versions of the Protoevangelium and later allied documents can and

---

[126] *Liber de dormitione Mariae*, 50 (Tischendorf, p. 112).

[127] Theodosius, *The Falling Asleep of Mary*, 5. 27 (Robinson, *Coptic Apocryphal Gospels*, p. 109).

do reflect teachings current in their own age, teachings which are normally given greater emphasis in the *Transitus Mariae* literature. To illustrate, the Latin account of Pseudo-Matthew and the Arabic Gospel of the Infancy witness to the Queenship of Mary and the power of her intercession, themes normally found in the *Transitus Mariae* as a glorification of the *Theotokos*. Conversely, accounts of the *Transitus Mariae* (e.g., that by Pseudo-Evodius) utilize the theme of the Protoevangelium.

The various testimonies adduced in these pages show that there is a very definite and sublime corpus of Mariology in these documents. Four observations are called for regarding this Mariology. Sublime as the Mariology of these documents is, it is hoped that this has not given a one-sided view of these documents and portrayed them in too favorable a light. This Mariology is often given against a bizarre and fantastic background of fabricated legends and miracles. The wheat of these documents, that is, their teaching on Mary, has been gathered and used; the chaff, that is, the fantastic background has been rejected except when absolutely necessary for continuity. Second, with regard to the Mariology of the Apocrypha, the writer was very happy to find so many and clear testimonies. The texts were clear and spoke for themselves; they did not have to be read into or twisted to form a corpus of Mariology. Third, the sublime Mariology in these works is a priceless witness to the fundamentally sound Christian feeling of the faithful for Mary. This points up the basic importance of these accounts for the theologian and the historian of dogma; as witnesses to tradition they are of great value. Finally, as witnesses to tradition, it should be remarked that very often there is a close parallel between the development and the explicitation of a doctrine in the apocryphal teaching and the patristic *praedicatio*.

By Very Rev. Cuthbert Gumbinger, O.F.M.Cap., S.T.D.

INTRODUCTION

HE cult of the Mother of God began in the East with the early Church. Christ confided His Mother to the care of St. John, the beloved disciple. She was the joy and consolation of the Apostles and the other early followers of Christ. With her they received the Holy Spirit on Pentecost Sunday. From her they learned many facts of Christ's early history, which were then incorporated into the Gospels of Matthew and Luke. Some of the Apostles, or at least John, knew of her glorious Assumption into heaven.

From these facts we can understand how the early Church revered the Mother of God. But the persecutions and strenuous missionary work of the early times prevented the Church from insisting on Mary's glories and privileges as she would have liked to do. Nonetheless, Mary had a place in the liturgy even before the Council of Ephesus.[1] But it is difficult, if not impossible, to say just when devotion to the Mother of God found a place in the liturgical cult of the Church. We know that some of the Apostolic Fathers wrote about Mary's Virginal Conception of Christ and her divine

---

[1] Cf. Otto Menzinger, *Mariologisches aus der vorephesinischen Liturgie* (Regensburg, 1932), p. 181. In the West there was no liturgical cult of Mary until the fifth century. Cf. B. Capelle, O.S.B., *La liturgie mariale en Occident,* in *Maria. Études sur la Sainte Vierge* (ed. H. du Manoir, S.J.), Vol. 1 (Paris, 1949), pp. 217-245; M. Jugie, A.A., *La première fête mariale en Orient,* in *Echos d'Orient,* Vol. 22, 1923, pp. 129-153. The first feast was celebrated on December 26 and was called the *Commemoration of St. Mary.* It honored especially her divine Maternity and her Virginal Conception of Christ. Cf. M. Doumith, *Marie dans la liturgie syro-maronite,* in *Maria. Études sur la Sainte Vierge* (ed. H. du Manoir), Vol. 1, pp. 329-351. The Assumption was celebrated in Jerusalem from about the year 450. Cf. S. Salaville, *Marie dans la liturgie byzantine ou grec-slav,* in H. du Manoir's set, Vol. 1, pp. 249-326. For the origin of the Marian cult in Ethiopia, cf. Samuel A. B. Mercer, *The Ethiopic Liturgy* (1915).

Maternity.[2] Thus, SS. Ignatius of Antioch, Irenaeus, Justin, and Aristides affirm the Virginal Conception of Christ.[3] Justin and Irenaeus compare Mary to Eve.[4] From the year 190 until the year 325 various ecclesiastical writers treat of Mary, especially Tertullian, Origen, and Clement of Alexandria.[5] After the Council of Nice (325) there are more references to Mary not only in the East but also in the West, due to the Christological controversies and heresies.[6] It was precisely the defense of Catholic doctrine regarding the divinity of Christ that brought out the glory of Mary in her divine Maternity. This increased love and devotion to both Christ and His Blessed Mother and gave her a more prominent place in the liturgy especially after the Council of Ephesus (431).[7]

Christ and Mary are of the East. Their cult arose in the East. We do well to study the Eastern liturgies, therefore, to see in what manner the Christian devotion of the East honors Christ and His immaculate Virgin Mother. The wealth and beauty of the Eastern hymns, odes, and prayers to Our Lady are truly amazing. This is especially seen in the Byzantine, Ethiopian, and Syrian liturgies.[8] The Byzantines have hundreds of kontaks and thousands of canons in varied forms and in the eight tones in honor of Mary. These verses fill some twenty huge volumes, while those inedited and lost would fill many more.[9] Three fourths of the Byzantine Office consists of hymns, and perhaps the best and greater part of them is in honor of Mary's privileges and offices.[10] It is somewhat similar in the Ethiopian and Syrian liturgies. But in all the Eastern liturgies

---

[2] Cf. Jouassard, *Marie à travers la patristique*, in H. du Manoir's set, Vol. 1, pp. 71-157.

[3] *Ibid.*, pp. 72-77. Cf. P. R. Botz, *Die Jungfrauschaft Mariens* in *N. T. und in der nachapostolischen Zeit. Eine dogmatisch-biblische Studie* (Bottrop in Westphalen, 1935).

[4] Jouassard, *art. cit.*, p. 73.

[5] *Ibid.*, pp. 73-85.

[6] *Ibid.*, pp. 85-100.

[7] Cf. Salaville, *art. cit.*, p. 249.

[8] Cf. G. Giovanelli, *Il culto della Madre di Dio nell'iconografia bizantina*, in *Alma Socia Christi*, Vol. 5, fasc. 2 (Romae, 1952), pp. 16-28. On the various Eastern liturgies, see the subsequent sections of our paper.

[9] *Ibid.*, p. 24.

[10] *Ibid.*

Mary has a prominent place.

The theological foundation of Eastern devotion to Mary is her divine Maternity. Although the term *hyperdulia* is generally not used among the Eastern writers, yet the entire body of Eastern Christians actually give her this special cult, for they agree (except the Nestorians) that Mary has a dignity above that of every other creature and above all other creatures, because she is the Mother of God.[11] Thus, the cult of Mary in the East is identical with that in the West, which we call *hyperdulia*, even though the East, for lack of theological analysis in this matter, does not use this term. In fact, an Orthodox theologian, Mihalcescu, calls Mariology "Papist theology."[12]

In the following pages we attempt to review briefly the place that Mary has in the Eastern liturgies; but it is impossible here to give a full idea of the beauty and wealth of doctrine that they contain. The true Church both in the East and the West will never cease to praise the all-holy and immaculate Virgin Mother of God, to multiply hymns, feasts, and practices in her honor; for in doing so the Church glorifies God with Mary and begs her, who is all-powerful with her divine Son, to grant us mercy, peace, and grace. This is well expressed in the following prayer of the Byzantine liturgy:

> Whilst we sing the glories of thy Son, we praise thee, too, O Mother of God, living Temple of the Godhead. ... O purest One, do not despise the petitions of the sinner; for He who deigned to suffer for us will also be merciful towards us and save us. O Christ, behold Thy Mother, she who conceived Thee in her womb, without the loss of her virginity, and who after she had given Thee birth remained a stainless Virgin. We present her to Thee that she may be our Advocate, O Thou who art all mercy, Thou who dost grant pardon to those who say to Thee from their hearts: Be mindful of me, O Lord, when Thou art come into Thy kingdom.[13]

---

[11] Cf. M. Gordillo, S.J., *Fondamento teologico del culto della Vergine Madre di Dio presso gli orientali*, in *Alma Socia Christi*, Vol. 5, fasc. 2, pp. 1-16, esp. pp. 13 and 15.

[12] Gordillo, *art. cit.*, p. 15.

[13] Cf. I. Card. Schuster, O.S.B., *The Sacramentary* (trans. by A. Levelis-Marke), 5 vols. (London, 1927), Parts 5 and 6, *Euchological Appendix*, p. 442.

In fine, it is devotion to the Mother of God even among the Dissident Eastern Christians that gives us hope for the reunion of Churches. She, the Mother of the Good Shepherd, we hope, will lead back to the true flock those countless souls who for so long have been without a shepherd. By knowing the Eastern liturgies better we can grow in love for the East, and thus hasten the day when there will be a united Christendom ruled by the Vicar of Christ.

I. MARY IN THE BYZANTINE LITURGY

The richest of all the Eastern rites in Marian praises is that of Byzantium, or Constantinople. Even before the Council of Ephesus in 431 Our Lady had a noble place in the Eastern rites.[14] From that time on there was a marvelous development.[15] The Byzantine rite glories in its liturgical devotion to the all-holy Mother of God.

The Byzantine rite is used by Catholics and Orthodox who hold Constantinople as their liturgical mother. They are the most numerous of the Eastern Christians and can be found from Poland to Japan, and from the Sudan to the White Sea. There are numerous colonies of them in western Europe especially since World War II, as well as in North and South America and even in Australia.[16] Various nations follow this rite and it uses various languages (more among the Orthodox than among the Catholics). The rite is used by Greeks, Slavs of Russia and the Balkans, Italo-Greeks of Sicily and Calabria, Melkites of Syria and Egypt, Ukrainians, Podcarpatho-Rusins, some Hungarians and Rumanians.[17]

There are some minor differences in the liturgical books of these various nations and languages, but essentially the rite is the same. The same is true of the vestments used. The chant differs quite a bit among the various nations.

The Marian cult among the Byzantines is rich and profound in doctrine. They seem to have no end in praising her, who is above all praise. They use an enormous number of titles and figures for her

---

[14] Cf. Menzinger, *op. cit.*, p. 181.

[15] Cf. Salaville, *art. cit.*, p. 249; Jugie, *art. cit.*, pp. 129-153.

[16] *Sacra Congregazione Orientale, Statistica con cenni storici della gerarchia e dei fedeli di rito orientale* (Tip. Pol. Vaticana, 1932), p. 93.

[17] Cf. Salaville, *art. cit.*, p. 249.

taken from Sacred Scripture, and from her various offices and privileges. Then, too, they give her names taken from the animals, plants, flowers, stars, and other material things. Archbishop Assaf of Petra, Philadelphia, and the Transjordan has counted up no less than 197 titles of Mary in the Byzantine liturgical books.[18] Here we shall treat first of the Marian Year, then of Mary in the Divine Office, and finally of Mary in the Divine Liturgy.

1. MARY IN THE BYZANTINE CALENDAR

During the liturgical year which begins with the first of September, there are various feasts of Mary embellished with beautiful antiphons, tropars, and kondiaks in her honor. Of old the civil year in Byzantium began with the first of September and the faithful of the Byzantine rite have ever kept this for the liturgical year as well.

Among the twelve greater feasts in this rite eight are in honor of Christ (two of them partly in honor of Mary, namely Christmas and the Purification of Mary) and four are in honor of Mary, namely her Nativity, her Presentation in the Temple, the Annunciation, and the Falling Asleep (Assumption) of Mary. From October 1 to 14 there is commemorated the Protection (Intercession) of Mary.[19]

September: On the first of this month there is the Commemoration (Synaxis) of Our Lady of Miasenes in honor of her manifestation at the monastery of that place in 864. In the Office for that day we read:

> Hail, Mother of God, Virgin full of grace, Refuge and Protection of the human race; for it is from thee that the Redeemer of the world has taken flesh. Thou alone art at one and the same time Mother and Virgin, blessed and glorified forever. Pray to Christ, Our God, to grant

---

[18] Cf. M. Assaf, *Culte de la Vierge Marie dans le rite byzantin*, in *Marie*, Sept.-Oct., 1953, pp. 20-29.

[19] For Slavs and Rumanians, cf. Salaville, *art. cit.*, pp. 251, 252. Isabel Florence Hapgood, *Service Book of the Holy Orthodox-Catholic Apostolic Church*, revised edition (New York: Association Press, 1922), pp. xv, xvi. Cf. F. E. Brightman, *Liturgies, Eastern and Western* (Oxford: Clarendon Press, 1896), pp. lxxxi-xcvi, 309-411. D. C. McPherson, *The Divine Office in the Byzantine Rite*, in *Eastern Churches Quarterly* (St. Augustine's Abbey, Ramsgate), Vol. 7, Nos. 3, 5, 7.

peace to the world.[20]

This is the type of prayer used so often in the Byzantine rite. Mary's intercession with her divine Son is stressed in many forms in the Office and the Divine Liturgy. In Byzantine art this theme is called the *Deisis* (intercession) and Christ is represented between Our Lady and St. John the Baptist, who are interceding with Him.[21] The vigil of Our Lady's Nativity has this prayer in the Office:

> ... The Daughter of God, Mary, is sent into the world. Heaven and earth rejoice. ... Hail, O Virgin, glory of Christians.[22]

The feast of Our Lady's Nativity, September 8: This is a great feast, which has lost some of its solemnity in the West, and which is still held as a day of obligation in many parts of the East. The following prayer is used even in the Latin Liturgy:

> Thy Nativity, O Mother of God, has announced joy to the whole world; for from thee there has risen the Sun of Justice, Christ, our God, who breaking the curse, has given blessing, and confounding death, has given us life everlasting.[23]

Some other prayers for this feast are:

> Today the barren gates are opened, and the Divine Virginal Gate advances. Today is devoted to Fruit-bearing, its grace manifesting the Mother of God to the world; by her the earthly is united to the heavenly, for the salvation of our souls.

> Today the joy of the whole world has its beginnings; today the breezes blow messengers of salvation; the barrenness of our nature is destroyed; for the Virgin Mother is manifested, who was a Virgin after the Birth of the Creator, by whom that which was estranged, was reconciled to the Nature of God, and salvation was accomplished for the wanderers in the flesh, Christ, the Lover of man and Redeemer of our souls.

> Today the barren Anna bringeth forth a blessed Child, the foreordained from all generations to be the dwelling of the King and Creator, Christ our God, for the working of the divine Plan, through which we, the earth-born, are re-established and renewed from

---

[20] Salaville, *art. cit.*, p. 250.

[21] *Ibid.* Cf. Ch. Diehl, *Manuel d'art byzantin*, 2 ed. (Paris, 1926), 2 vols.

[22] Salaville, *art. cit.*, p. 251.

[23] *Ibid.*

corruption to the eternal life.[24]

At Thy Nativity, O Immaculate, Joachim and Anna were delivered from the opprobrium of sterility; Adam and Eve from corruption and death. Thy people also celebrate this Nativity, for they are freed from the bondage of sin and cry out: She who was sterile gave birth to the Mother of God, who nourishes our spiritual life.[25]

October: The Slavs and Rumanians have the commemoration of the Protection of the Virgin from the first to the fourteenth of this month. This is taken from the feast of the Mantle of the Virgin, still celebrated on July 2 in the Church of Constantinople. Among the Greeks this feast honored first the mantle itself and then Mary's protection, as seen in the Office (similar to that of Our Lady's Cincture on August 31). Among the Slavs the feast is that of Mary's protection, even though icons of the *Prokov* (covering) show either Mary or the angels spreading her mantle over the faithful.[26]

The Slavic and Rumanian Offices have this prayer:

Today, we the faithful people ... contemplating thy pure image, cry out in all humility: Cover us with thy precious patronage and deliver us from all evil, praying thy Son, Christ our God, to save our souls.[27]

Today the Virgin intercedes in the Church, and with the invincible armies of saints, prays to God for us; angels and pontiffs prostrate themselves; apostles and prophets rejoice, for the Mother of God prays the eternal God for us.[28]

On the Sunday Between October 11 and 17 there is the feast of the Second Council of Nice (787) but it really commemorates the first seven General Councils. In the liturgy for this feast we have the following prayer:

---

[24] *The Office for the Lord's Day as Prescribed by the Orthodox Greek Church* (London: Hayes, 1880), p. 161.

[25] Salaville, *loc. cit.*

[26] *Ibid.*, pp. 251, 252, 277, 278. Cf. *Alma Socia Christi, Acta Congressus Mariologici-Mariani*, Romae Anno Sancto MCML celebrati, Vol. 5, fasc. 2, De B. V. *Maria penes Ecclesias Orientis* (Romae: Officium Libri Catholici, 1952); David Lathaud, A.A., *Le thème iconographique du Prokov de la Mère de Dieu; Origene, Variantes*, pp. 54-68.

[27] Salaville, art. cit., p. 252.

[28] *Ibid.*

O Lord of all goodness, by the intercession of Thy Mother, and of the Fathers assembled in the seven Councils, strengthen Thy Church, fortify the faith, and grant us a part in the Kingdom of Heaven, when Thou comest on earth to judge every creature.[29]

November: On November 15 the Slavs celebrate the feast of Our Lady of Compassion. This title responds to the Greek *Theotokos Eleousa,* given to many Byzantine icons of Mary.[30]

On the vigil of Our Lady's Presentation in the Temple we read:

[She is] truly the Temple of the Divine Word. The whole world, filled with joy, cries out: The Virgin is a heavenly Tabernacle.[31]

The feast of Our Lady's Presentation in the Temple on November 21 is one of the twelve principal feasts of the year, and ranks higher in the East than in the West.

Today we, the faithful, rejoice in psalms and hymns, singing unto the Lord, honoring also His sanctified Tabernacle, the living Ark, the Container of the Uncontainable Word; for she, being marvellously brought forth in the flesh, is offered to God; and the great High Priest Zachary receives her, gladdened, as the Dwelling Place of God.

Today the living Temple of the holy glory of Christ our God, the only-blessed Undefiled One among women, is offered in the legal Temple, to dwell in the holy places; and Joachim and Anna rejoice in spirit, and virginal choirs sing unto the Lord in melodious psalms, and honor His Mother.

O Virgin Mother of God, thou art the Proclamation of the Prophets, the Glory of the Apostles, and Boast of the Martyrs, the Renewal of the earth-born; by thee we are reconciled to God. Wherefore we honor thy entrance into the Temple of the Lord, and with the Angels we cry aloud in psalms: Hail to thee, the all-august, being saved by Thy intercession.[32]

Today is the prelude of the blessing of God, and the announcement of the salvation of men. The Virgin is presented in the Temple of the Lord, and she announces Christ beforehand to all. Let us also cry to her with a loud voice: Hail, thou who art the fulfillment of the plan of

---

[29] Ibid.

[30] Cf. J. Martinov, *Annus ecclesiasticus graeco-slavicus,* in *Acta Sanctorum of the Bollandists,* October, Vol. 77 (Paris, 1870), p. 281.

[31] Salaville, *art. cit.,* p. 252.

[32] *The Office of the Lord's Day,* p. 163

the Creator.

She who is the most pure Temple of the Saviour, She who is at one and the same time a Virgin and a nuptial chamber of great price, the true Treasure of the Glory of God, enters today into the house of the Lord, bringing with her the grace of the Divine Spirit. The Angels of God sing hymns to her. She is the heavenly Tabernacle.[33]

December: The Immaculate Conception is considered in an active sense, namely the conception of Mary by Anna. This is the title for the feast found in modern liturgical books, "Feast of the Conception of Anna." But in the Middle Ages the other title was frequendy used, "Feast of the Conception of the Mother of God." The hymnographers have ever celebrated the fact of Mary's conception, and paid little attention to the miraculous or legendary circumstances surrounding it. These writers treat of the special intervention of the Blessed Trinity in preparing the palace of the Word made Flesh. This gives the hymnographers an occasion to honor the perpetual sanctity of Our Lady. The feast of the Immaculate Conception was not developed in the East under the influence of theological controversies as in the West. The feast expressed the initial holiness of Our Lady, whom God prepared in a special way to be the Mother of His Son. A *kontakion* reads:

Today the whole world celebrates the Conception of Anna, which is the work of God; for she has brought forth into the world her, who, in an ineffable manner, has begotten the Word made Flesh.[34]

Again:

Today are burst the bonds of barrenness, for God, hearing the desire of Joachim and Anna for children, clearly promised them a holy Daughter, from whom shall be born He, who is Uncontainable, who shall become a Mortal by the summons of the Angel crying aloud to her: Hail, O full of grace, the Lord is with thee.[35]

From December 18 to 24 the following antiphons are read:

O Virgin, the living Palace of God, He, whom the Heavens cannot contain, found place in Thee: who in the cave was brought forth above thought, taking part in poverty and flesh, that He might deify

---

[33] Salaville, *art. cit.,* p. 254.
[34] *Ibid.*
[35] *The Office of the Lord's Day,* p. 191.

me, and enrich poverty, weakness and bitter hunger.

The All-Holy and Blameless One, perceiving the ordinances of nature renovated by the incomprehensible Birth cried out to the Son: O much desired Child, I am amazed at the great mystery, how, remaining a Virgin, I also brought forth by Thy Power, who madest all things by Thy Will.[36]

> Today the Virgin begets the Supersubstantial One,
> The earth offers the shelter of the cave to the Inaccessible One,
> The Angels chant the Glory of God with the shepherds,
> The Magi walk with the star,
> For there is born for us,
> The new Infant, God before all ages.[37]

On Christmas Day Mary is honored with these prayers:

... For He, the unchangeable Image of the Father, the Impress of His eternity, hath taken the form of a servant, coming forth from His virginal Mother, but unchanged; for what He was, that He still remained, True God; and what He was not, He assumed, through Love for men becoming Man. To Him we cry aloud: O God, who wast born of a Virgin, have mercy upon us.[38]

From the Hymn of Anatolius:

When Jesus the Lord was born of the Holy Virgin, all things were enlightened. ... O God who art, and wast before, and shinest forth from the Virgin, have mercy upon us.

From the Hymn of Casia:

When Augustus reigned alone upon the earth, the many rulers of men ceased; and when Thou becamest Man of the Pure One, the many godheads of the idols fell.[39]

After the Consecration in the Divine Liturgy, Mary is praised with this hymn:

It is easy, O Virgin, to love thee in silence, without having anything to fear; but it is difficult to chant hymns to thee as we would like, well suited to thy love. At least, O Mother, grant us to do so according to

---

[36] *Ibid.*, p. 164.

[37] Salaville, *art. cit.*, p. 255.

[38] *The Office of the Lord's Day*, p. 164.

[39] *Ibid.*, p. 265.

our desire.[40]

On December 26 there is celebrated the Synaxis or Commemoration of Mary, which is really the feast of her divine Maternity and was the first feast in honor of Mary. A kontakion for this day reads:

He, who before the dawn was begotten of the Father without having a Mother, took flesh today in thy womb without having a father. Therefore the star announces His Birth to the Magi and the Angels sing of thy virginal childbearing with the shepherds, O thou full of grace.[41]

On the Sunday after Christmas there is a commemoration of St. Joseph, Spouse of Mary, of David the Prophet, and of James the Lord's cousin, to show the messianic descent of Joseph and the relationship of James. The tropar at Vespers declares:

O Joseph, announce to David that thou hast seen a Virgin with child, and that, informed by the angel, thou hast glorified God with the shepherds, whom thou hast adored with the Magi. Beg Christ our God to save our souls.[42]

In the Christmas Office there are many tropars and kondiaks in honor of Mary, e.g.:

The dew-shedding fiery furnace imaged forth the type of a marvellous wonder: for its flames scorched not the Holy Children whom it had received, even as the fire of the Godhead scorched not the Virgin when it entered into her womb.[43]

Magnify, O my soul, the Virgin, the all-pure Birth-giver of God, more honorable and more glorious than the hosts on high.

A mystery strange and most glorious I behold. The cavern, Heaven; the Cherubic Throne a Virgin; the manger, the receptacle wherein lieth Christ, our God, whom nothing can contain. Him, therefore, do we magnify, praising Him in song.[44]

January: Although there is no special Marian feast in this month, the Office of the Circumcision is filled with the idea of the

---

[40] Salaville, *art. cit.*, p. 255.

[41] *Ibid.*, p. 256.

[42] *Ibid.*

[43] Hapgood, *op. cit.*, p. 179.

[44] *Ibid.*

divine Maternity of Mary. So, too, in the Latin Office for this feast the antiphons for Vespers and Lauds are obviously taken from the Byzantine Office (*O admirabile commercium*, etc.). A Byzantine theotokion reads:

> Who could worthily celebrate the supernatural mystery of the conception wrought in thy womb? For thou hast begotten in the flesh, O All-Holy One, God who has manifested Himself to us the Saviour of men.

> The bush of Sinai, in contact with the fire without being consumed, prefigured thee, O Mother ever Virgin, Mary, O most chaste Mother of God.[45]

Although the feast of Epiphany is mainly to honor the Lord's Baptism, it does not forget His Mother. These strophes of Matins are in her honor:

> Every tongue finds it hard to praise Thee worthily. The heavenly spirits themselves exult to praise thee, O Mother of God. Nonetheless in thy goodness, accept our faith, for thou knowest our desire. Thou art the Protectress of Christians; we glorify thee.

> O incomprehensible wonder of Thy child-bearing! Virgin all-pure, blessed Mother, by whom we have received complete salvation. O thou, our Benefactress, we present to thee the worthy homage of our gratitude.[46]

This latter prayer is used also during the Divine Liturgy.

February: On the vigil of Mary's Purification we find this strophe:

> The heavenly choir of the angels of God, prostrate on the earth, sees arriving at the Temple a tiny Infant carried in the arms of a Virginal Mother, the First-born of all creation. In their joy mixed with fear, the angels sing with us the hymn of preparation for the feast.[47]

The Presentation of Christ in the Temple, or Purification of Mary, is one of the twelve great feasts of the Byzantine rite and is generally a holyday of obligation. In the Office we find the following tropars:

> Hail, O virgin Birth-giver of God; for from thee hath shone forth the

---

[45] Salaville, *art. cit.*, pp. 256, 257.

[46] *Ibid.*, p. 257.

[47] *Ibid.*

Sun of Righteousness, Christ our God, who giveth light to those who are in darkness. ...

We magnify Thee, O life-giving Christ, and we do homage to Thy Mother most pure, by whom Thou hast now been brought into the Temple of the Lord, according to the Law.

O Virgin Birth-giver of God, the Hope of Christians, protect, guard and save thou those who put their trust in thee.

Incomprehensible unto Angels and unto men is that which is wrought with thee, O Virgin Mother Pure.

A pure Dove, a spotless Lamb bringeth into the Church the Lamb and the Shepherd.[48]

The response *"Adorna thalamum tuum Sion,"* used in the Latin chants for the procession on this feast, is a translation of a Byzantine tropar for Vespers on this feast. The Latin version is a bit changed. The Byzantine reads:

Adorn thy nuptial chamber, O Sion, and receive Christ thy King. Receive Mary with love, who is the heavenly Gate; she has been made the Cherubic Throne and the Gate of the King of Glory. The Virgin is the luminous Cloud, who bears in her arms her Son begotten before the dawn. Simeon, receiving Him in his arms, has proclaimed to the peoples that He is the Master of life and death and the Saviour of the world.[49]

March-April: For the vigil of the feast of the Annunciation there is this kontakion:

Today, let us celebrate with joy the prelude of universal exultation. Behold, Gabriel approaches, bringing to the Virgin with admiration and respect the glad tidings: Hail, O Full of Grace, the Lord is with thee.[50]

The feast of the Annunciation is one of the twelve great feasts of the Byzantine rite, and is generally a holyday of obligation. The divine message of the feast and its importance are repeated in various ways in the Divine Office for this feast, together with praise of Mary and prayers to her.

---

[48] Hapgood, *op. cit.*, pp. 198-200.

[49] Salaville, *art. cit.*, p. 258.

[50] *Ibid.*, p. 259.

> Today is the beginning of our salvation, and the manifestation of that mystery which is from everlasting; the Son of God becometh the Son of a Virgin, and Gabriel announceth the glad tidings of grace. Wherefore, let us also cry aloud with him unto the Birth-giver of God; Hail, thou that art full of grace, the Lord is with thee.

> O Birth-giver of God, Fountain living and inexhaustible! Spiritually establish thou those who hymn thee, convoked in a choir, and vouchsafe unto them crowns in thy heavenly glory.

The Akathistos Hymn: This long hymn in honor of the Annunciation is very old, but it is uncertain just when it was composed.[51] Its name means the "not seated," for it is sung standing as a sign of joy in praise of the Virgin for her victories in favor of the people. This hymn is sung in its entirety on the fifth Saturday of Lent in Byzantine churches, i.e., it is anticipated on Friday evenings. It is in such favor that a fourth of it is sung on the four preceding Friday evenings.[52] The hymn has 24 *oikoi* or strophes, each beginning with a letter of the Greek alphabet. There are also an introductory strophe and a concluding invocation. The hymn fills about thirty pages in the Greek version of Grottaferrata (1949) in ordinary pamphlet size. After speaking of the Archangel Gabriel announcing the glad tidings to Mary the hymn breaks forth in jubilation which sets the tone for the whole hymn:

> I will open my mouth and it shall be filled with the Spirit; I will break forth into a hymn to the Queen Mother and with joy I will present myself to honor her and I will sing her privileges with exultation.[53]

The hymn then goes on to salute and praise the Mother of God under the most diverse titles in true Eastern style and with a rare sense of fitness. It is a rich and magnificent hymn breathing forth love and admiration for the Immaculate Virgin Mother of God and Dawn of Salvation. Some of the titles given to her are:

> Hail, O Virgin Divine Spouse, Rehabilitation of Adam, Destruction of Hell!
> Hail, Brilliant Throne of the Almighty, who hast brought forth the

---

[51] *Ibid.* Cf. McPherson, *art. cit.*, April-June, 1949, pp. 128, 129. — *Officio del Inno Akathistos in onore della SS. Madre di Dio* (Grottaferrata, 1949).

[52] Salaville, *art. cit.*, p. 259.

[53] *Officio del Inno Akathistos*, p. 10.

incorruptible Rose!

Hail, O Perfume of the Universal King, purest Virgin, Salvation of the World!

Hail, O Lady, fragrant Lily, that perfumes the faithful, sweet-smelling Thyme, precious Ointment!

Hail, O Mother of God, living and copious Fountain, confirm thy devoted ones!

Hail, O Splendid Dawn, that has brought us the Sun who is Christ! Hail, O unique Gate, through which only the Word passed!

Hail, O inaccessible Height of human intelligences, O inscrutable Profundity even to the eyes of the Angels!

Hail, thou Throne of the King! Hail, who carriest Him who sustains all! Hail, O heavenly Ladder whereby God came down to earth!

Hail, O Bridge that brings mortals from earth to Heaven!

Hail, thou pleasing Incense of intercession!

During the singing of this hymn the celebrant incenses the icon of Mary several times and kisses it. At last he prostrates himself before the icon, incenses it again, and kisses it. He then goes to the sanctuary to finish the Office of the day.[54]

The Compassion of Mary: Although the general Byzantine rite has no special feast of Our Lady of Sorrows, there are special tropars in honor of her compassion in every Lenten Office. These tropars are called *Stavrotheotokia,* because addressed to Our Lady at the foot of the cross, and are used especially on Lenten Sundays, Wednesdays, and Fridays. The following are some of these tropars:

In contemplating Thee, Divine Lamb, crucified on the Wood with two thieves, O generous Logos, and on seeing Thy Side pierced with a lance, Mary uttered these maternal lamentations: What is this strange and awful mystery, O my Jesus? How canst Thou go to be covered by the tomb, Thou who art the infinite God? O unspeakable spectacle! Do not leave me alone, Thou whom I have begotten, O my sweetest Son.[55]

The purest Virgin Mother contemplating Him on the Cross cried out with sighs: Alas, my Son! What hast Thou done? Thou, the most beautiful of the children of men, Thou appearest without breath and without beauty. ... Alas! O my Light, I cannot bear to see Thee sleep; I am wounded to the core of my being, and a cruel sword transfixes my heart. I glorify Thy Passion, I adore Thy Compassion and Thy

---

[54] Salaville, *art. cit.,* pp. 262-265.
[55] *Ibid.,* p. 266.

Mercy, O magnanimous Saviour, glory be to Thee![56]

On Good Friday at Matins the following antiphons are read:

In seeing Thee suspended on the Cross, O Christ, she who begot Thee cried out: What a strange mystery do I see, O my Son? How dost Thou die on the Cross, Thou who art the Head and the Dispenser of life.[57]

With dramatic insistence the following antiphon cries out:

Mary, with the other women, followed Him consumed with sorrow and crying out: Whither goest Thou, my Son! Why dost Thou hasten Thy step! Is there another marriage at Cana, where Thou wouldst undertake to change water into wine for them! Would that I could come with Thee, my Son! Or rather that I could remain with Thee! Give me a word, O Logos; do not pass me up in silence, Thou who hast preserved me a Virgin. For Thou art my Son and my God.[58]

Again:

Today the Virgin undefiled, beholding Thee, the Word, uplifted upon the Cross, weeping with the tender love of a mother, was sore wounded in heart, and moaned grievously from the depths of her soul, wiping her face with her hair. Wherefore also beating her hands, she cried piteously: Woe is me, O my Son divine! Woe is me, O Light of the World! Why hast Thou departed from mine eyes, O Lamb of God? For which cause also the host of bodiless Powers were seized with trembling, and said: O Lord ineffable, glory to Thee![59]

On Holy Saturday there is this antiphon:

... When she beheld Him hanging on the Cross, she cried with weeping, and with maternal feeling exclaimed: Woe is me, my Son! Woe is me, my Light, and the Beloved of my bosom! that which was foretold in the Temple by Simeon today hath come to pass! A sword shall pierce my heart, but into the joy of the Resurrection lament shall be changed. ...[60]

Again:

Lament not for me, O Mother, when Thou beholdest in the tomb the

---

⁵⁶ *Ibid.*

⁵⁷ *Ibid.*

⁵⁸ *Ibid.*

⁵⁹ Hapgood, *op. cit.*, p. 218.

⁶⁰ *Ibid.*, p. 223.

Son whom, without seed, Thou didst conceive in Thy womb; for I will rise again and glorify Myself; and in that I am God, I will raise in glory that hath no ending those who with faith and love magnify Thee.[61]

Mary and the Resurrection of Christ: The Byzantine rite is similar to the others in joining Mary to the joy of Christ's Resurrection. Romanos the hymnographer sang: "Have confidence, O Mother, for Thou shalt be the first to see me rise from the tomb."[62] At Matins an ode reads:

The angel cried addressing the One Full of grace: Rejoice, O Virgin, again I say, rejoice! Thy Son is risen from the tomb the third day.[63]

At every hour of the Office during Paschal week there is read this antiphon in honor of Mary, the Cause of our joy:

Rejoice thou, who art the divine Tabernacle of the Most High; for it is through thee, O Mother of God, that there has been given the joy to repeat to thee: Thou art blessed among women, O Immaculate Queen.[64]

On Easter there is this tropar in the Divine Office:

O Christ, who did not break the Virgin's gate by Thy birth, Thou didst rise from the dead, having kept intact the seals; and Thou hast opened unto us the gates of Paradise.[65]

Again:

Rejoice thou, O pure Birth-giver of God, in the rising again of Him whom thou didst bear.[66]

Rejoice, O Virgin! Rejoice, O Blessed One! Rejoice O greatly Glorified One! For thy Son is risen from His three days' sojourn in the tomb.[67]

May: On May 11 there is the feast of the dedication of the City of Constantinople, which the Byzantine rite considers an act of

---

[61] *Ibid.*, p. 224.

[62] Salaville, *art. cit.*, p. 271.

[63] *Ibid.*

[64] *Ibid.*

[65] Hapgood, *op. cit.*, p. 230.

[66] *Ibid.*, p. 232.

[67] *Ibid.*, p. 233. For "Our Lady of the Living Source," on Friday after Easter, see Salaville, *art. cit.*, pp. 272-275.

homage to Mary. Even the Slavs, the Melchites, and the Rumanians have this feast. The very first tropar at Vespers shows the Marian character of this feast:

> The Queen of Cities dedicated her foundation to the Queen of creation; for it is in her that she finds her support. Hence she cries out: It is thou, O Virgin, who art the support of the crown, the scepter and the rulers.[68]

July-August-October: On July 2 there is the feast of the Mantle of the Mother of God at Blakhernes, on August 31 the feast of the Cincture of the Mother of God, and on October 1 that of the Protection or Patronage of the Mother of God. On all of these feasts we see the doctrine of Mary's intercession clearly expressed, as stated previously for the feast of October 1.[69]

August 15: The feast of the Falling Asleep of the Holy Virgin, or the Assumption. This is the most solemn Marian feast in the Byzantine rite. It is preceded by a small fast of two weeks and a vigil. The feast is a holyday of obligation.

There are three kinds of texts in the Byzantine liturgy for this great feast. The first is quite explicit regarding the Resurrection and Assumption of Mary. The second speaks only of the Assumption of her soul and the incorruption of her body. The third category is ambiguous in the sense that the texts speak either of the Assumption of her soul or of her departure without defining just how.[70] The clearest texts telling of Mary's Assumption to heaven body and soul are generally those of St. John Damascene, St. Cosmas, Bishop of Maiouma (both of the eighth century) and St. Theophane Graptos, Bishop of Nice (in the ninth century).

> The heavenly tabernacles, O all-Pure One, have received thee worthily as a living Heaven; thou hast presented thyself to our King and God in all the splendor of beauty, as a Spouse entirely immaculate.

> It was a marvel to contemplate the living Heaven of the King of the Universe, elevated above the earthly places. How admirable are Thy works! Glory to Thy Power, O Lord!

---

[68] Salaville, *art. cit.*, p. 276.

[69] *Ibid.*, pp. 277-281.

[70] M. Jugie, *La Mort et l'Assomption de la Sainte Vierge, Étude historico-doctrinale* (Rome, 1944), p. 188.

In bringing forth God, O Immaculate One, thou hast gained the palm of victory over nature. Nonetheless, after the example of thy Creator, who is also thy Son, thou hast yielded supernaturally to the laws of nature; therefore dying with thy Son, thou hast arisen for eternity.

The tomb and death could not retain in their power the Mother of God, whose intercession never ceases, and whose protection constitutes our firm hope; her title Mother of Life has entitled her to pass to life by the power of Him, who has dwelt in her virginal womb.[71]

Others read as follows:

O marvel wonderful! The Source of life is laid in a grave, and the tomb becometh the ladder unto Heaven. Rejoice, O Gethsemane, thou holy abode of the Mother of God.

Sing, O ye people, sing to the Mother of our God; for today she doth yield up her all-radiant soul into the hands most pure of Him, who, without seed, was incarnate of her; whom, also, she doth unceasingly entreat that He will give unto the world peace and great mercy.

In giving birth, thou didst preserve thy virginity; in thy Falling-asleep thou hast not forsaken the world, O Mother of God. Thou hast passed into life, thou who art the Mother of God, and through thine intercession dost deliver our souls from death.

When the holy Angels beheld thine Assumption, they marvelled how a Virgin should ascend from earth to Heaven.

The laws of nature were conquered in thee, O Virgin pure; for in giving birth was virginity preserved, and with death is life conjoined. Thou who, after giving birth didst remain a Virgin, though dead, art yet alive, Birth-giver of God, and savest always thine inheritance.[72]

August is Mary's month with the Byzantines. The first half is devoted to the fast in preparation for the feast of the Assumption. Then there is the feast itself, and then its prolongation until August 23. It was Emperor Andronicus II Paleologus of Constantinople who issued the decree in 1297 that the entire month of August be dedicated to the Mother of God. Until the city fell to the Turks in 1453 the month of August was celebrated with solemnity in honor of Mary. The festivities began at the Church of Our Lady of

---

[71] Salaville, *art. cit.*, pp. 281-285.
[72] Hapgood, *op. cit.*, pp. 263-265.

Hodeges and was continued at the different churches throughout the month. On the fifteenth the services were held at Santa Sophia and on the thirty-first at Blakhernes, the Byzantine Lourdes, "Our Lady of the Living Source."[73] The custom spread in the lands of the Byzantine rite with some variations. Today every evening during the first two weeks of August they sing the votive office of Our Lady known as the *Paraklisis*.[74]

2. MARY IN THE DIVINE OFFICE

The praises of Mary occur every day in the Divine Office. The following are examples taken from various parts of the Office:

> O most Glorious and Blessed Mother of God, ever Virgin, present our prayer to thy Son, our God, and beg Him to save our souls through Thee.

> ... I place all my hope in thee, O Mother of God, protect me in thy care.

On Sundays:

> O purest Virgin, in seeing thy Son divinely risen again from the dead, the whole world was filled with ineffable joy, in glorifying Him and in venerating thee.

> Hail, O Venerable One, thou who hast brought forth God in the flesh, thou through whom the human race has found salvation. For through thee we shall find Paradise, O Virgin pure and blessed.

> O Christ, who art the Light, enlighten me with Thyself, by the intercession of the Mother of God, O Saviour, and save me.

On Wednesdays and Saturdays we find this tropar:

---

[73] Salaville, *art. cit.*, pp. 285, 286. Archdale A. King, *The Assumption of Our Lady in the Oriental Liturgies*, in *Eastern Churches Quarterly*, Vol. 8, Nos. 3 and 4; for Byzantine rite, No. 4, October-December, 1949, pp. 228, 229. See also Vol. 9, No. 2, Summer, 1951, Michael Gavrilof, *The Dormition and Assumption of the Blessed Virgin in Slav Iconography*, pp. 113-119, with 14 illustrations; Dom Edmund M. Jones, O.S.B., *The Iconography of the Falling Asleep of the Mother of God* in *Byzantine Tradition*, pp. 101-112; Atanasio G. Welykyj, O.S.B.M., *L'Assunzione della B. V. Maria Deipara nella Liturgia Bizantina*, in *Alma Socia Christi*, Vol. 5, fasc. 2, pp. 36-53; M. Jugie, A.A., *La fête Byzantine de la Conception de Sainte Anne*, in *Alma Socia Christi*, Vol. 5, fasc. 2, pp. 29-35.

[74] Salaville, *art. cit.*, p. 287.

Standing at the foot of the Cross, she, who brought Thee forth virginally, sighed and said: Alas! O my sweetest Son, how hast Thou passed from my eyes, how hast Thou been counted among the dead?

On Thursdays there is this prayer, in which we see a fine declaration of Mary's relation to the three Divine Persons:

Mary, the purest Golden Censer, has become the Tabernacle of the Trinity, whom nothing can contain. With this Tabernacle, the Father is pleased, the Son has dwelt therein, and the Holy Spirit, O Virgin, covering thee with His shadow, has made thee Mother of God.

On Saturdays:

We glory in thee, O Mother of God, and we have thee for Protectress before God; extend thine invincible arm and destroy our enemies; send down to thy servants aid from on high.

On Sundays:

Thou art blessed above all, O Virgin Mother of God; for it is through Him, who took flesh of thee, that hell has been made captive, that Adam has been freed, that the curse was destroyed, that Eve has been delivered, that death has been sent to death, and that life has been restored to ourselves. Therefore we sing: Blessed be Christ our God.

At the Little Hours these tropars occur:

Let us glorify without respite, with heart and mouth, the most glorious Mother of God, holier than the angels, and proclaim her Birth-giver of God, for she has really brought forth God Incarnate, and that she should intercede for our souls.

At Prime and before the Divine Liturgy:

Open to us the door of mercy, Blessed Mother of God. Hoping in thee, may we not be confounded. Through thee may we be delivered from all dangers, for thou art the Hope of Christians.

At Tierce:

O Birth-Giver of God, thou art the true Vine that has produced the Fruit of life. We beg of thee, intercede, O Queen, with the Apostles and all the saints, so that our souls will receive mercy.

At Sext:

Thou art the Source of mercy, deign to show us thy compassion, O Birth-giver of God; cast an eye on this sinful people, show it, as ever, thy power. Filled with hope in thee, we repeat to thee the salutation, which the Archangel Gabriel brought to thee of old.[75]

It is monastic custom to have the midday meal between Sext and None. During the meal, in monasteries and in many Christian families, an icon of Mary, hung in a prominent place, receives special honor. This ceremony is called the Exaltation of the *Panagia* (All-Holy). Some bread in the form of a triangle is placed before her icon. At the end of the meal, one of the community or family incenses this bread and raising it before all says: "Great is the Name of the Trinity! Most Holy Mother of God, protect us." The others answer: "In virtue of her prayers, O God, have mercy on us, and save us." Then the bread is cut and all present take a piece which is called the panagia. This ceremony is explained in the following manner in the *Horologion*:

After Christ's Resurrection and the descent of the Holy Spirit Our Lady and the Apostles lived together. At meals there was a vacant place at table where a piece of bread was placed in honor of Christ. After the meal the diners recited praise to the three Persons of the Blessed Trinity. On the third day after the burial of Our Lady the Apostles came together to dine, and when they began the prayer in honor of the Blessed Trinity, Our Lady appeared to them and told them to rejoice, for she would be ever with them. The Apostles begged her aid. Then they went to her tomb and found it empty, and they understood that she had arisen like her Son on the third day after her death. Hence in this custom of raising an icon of Mary at table and of blessing the bread and praising the Blessed Trinity we find the belief in Mary's Assumption.[76]

At None:

Come, let us all praise Him who has been crucified for us. Mary saw Him on the wood of the Cross and said: Although Thou sufferest the Cross, Thou art my Son and my God.

At Vespers:

Often during Lent, and on certain other ferial days, there are two tropars in honor of Mary:

O Virgin Birth-giver of God, Hail Mary, full of grace, the Lord is with

---

[75] *Ibid.*, pp. 289-293.
[76] *Ibid.*, pp. 293, 294.

thee, blessed art thou amongst women and blessed is the Fruit of thy womb; for thou hast brought forth the Saviour of our souls.

We have recourse to thy mercy, O Birth-giver of God, do not thou disdain our supplications in our necessities, but deliver us from dangers, O thou who art alone pure and alone blessed.

The evening table prayers have these words:

Thy womb, O Mother of God, has become the sacred table bearing the heavenly Bread, Christ our God, who promises immortality to whomsoever eats it, according to the word of Him who is the universal Provider.

O Virgin Birth-giver of God, make us worthy of thy gifts, forget our sins, and give us the spiritual remedies, we who receive thy blessing with faith, O Immaculate One.

At Compline:

Having confidence in thee that will never be confounded, I shall be saved. Assured of thy protection, O Immaculate One, I shall fear nothing; I shall pursue my enemies and destroy them, having thy help as my only shield. So, too, imploring thy assistance, I cry to thee: O Queen, save me by thy intercession and make me to come forth from dark sleep to sing thy praises, by the power of God, thy Son, who took flesh from thee.[77]

This part of the Office ends with an unusually long prayer attributed to the monk Paul († 1054), founder of the Monastery of Our Lady of Evergate.[78] These tropars, antiphons, and odes are only some examples of the rich *Theotokia* in the Byzantine Office. Many more are used especially on certain feasts at Matins and Vespers. Besides that, the Byzantine rite also has some Votive Offices. The *Akathistos Hymn* is often used that way. Others are called the *Small Canon of Supplication* and the *Great Canon of Supplication to the All-Holy Birth-Giver of God.*[79]

3. MARY IN THE DIVINE LITURGY

The icons of Christ and the all-holy Mother of God are present at every Divine Liturgy. They are incensed at various times by the

---

[77] *Ibid.*, pp. 295-298.

[78] *Ibid.*, pp. 297, 298.

[79] *Ibid.*, pp. 312-324.

celebrant or deacon. On opening the royal door, the celebrant recites the prayer given above beginning with the words: "Open to us the door of mercy." Before Mary's icon he says:

Thou art the Font of mercy, O Mother of God, vouchsafe us thy compassion. Look down upon a sinful people, show thy power as always. Hoping in thee, we cry to thee: Hail, as did once Gabriel, the Captain of the angels.[80]

Placing a piece of bread on the paten in honor of Mary the celebrant says:

In honor and in memory of our most blessed and glorious Lady, Mother of God, and ever-Virgin Mary, through whose intercession do Thou, O Lord, receive this sacrifice on Thy heavenly altar. The Queen stood at Thy right hand, clothed in a robe of gold and many colors.[81]

During the Divine Liturgy the Mother of God is invoked various times, e.g.:

By the intercession of the Mother of God, O Saviour, save us.

May Christ our God, by the prayers of His Immaculate Mother ... and of all the saints, have mercy on us and save us, for He is the gracious Lover of men.[82]

Remembering our all-holy, immaculate, most blessed and glorious Lady, the Mother of God, and ever-Virgin Mary, and all the saints, let us commend ourselves, each other, and all our life to Christ our God.[83]

O only-begotten Son and Word of God, who being immortal didst vouchsafe to take flesh for our salvation of the Holy Birth-giver of God, and ever Virgin Mary; Thou who without change didst become man and wast crucified, O Christ our God, by death trampling down death; Thou who wast Thyself one of the Holy Trinity, who art glorified with the Father and the Holy Spirit, save us.[84]

---

[80] *Ibid.*, p. 303. Cf. Cuthbert Gumbinger, O.F.M.Cap., *The Cult of the Mother of God in Byzantine Liturgy*, in *Franciscan Studies* (St. Bonaventure, N. Y.), Vol. 22; New Series, Vol. 1, No. 3, September, 1941, pp. 49-61.

[81] Dom Placid De Meester, O.S.B., *The Divine Liturgy of our Father among the Saints, John Chrysostom* (Greek text witb Introduction and Notes) (London: Burns, Oates and Washbourne, 1926), p. 13.

[82] *Ibid.*, p. 27.

[83] *Ibid.*, p. 29.

[84] *Ibid.*, p. 31.

In this prayer we hear the echoes of the early Councils of the Church crying down the ages that Christ is true God and true Man, and Mary is truly the Mother of God. The great Eastern Doctors of those ages speak to us in this prayer, and in others of this rite, they who proclaimed these doctrines with such force and clarity. Mary is commemorated several times in shorter prayers. Then after the Consecration, the priest incenses the Sacred Species and praises Mary, immaculate, all-holy, and ever Virgin. The choir sings the *megalynarion* (which varies on certain feasts):

> Meet indeed it is to bless thee, Mother of God, ever blessed and most sinless Mother of our God. Honored above the Cherubim, infinitely more glorious than the Seraphim, who didst bear God the Word without stain. Mother of God in truth, we magnify thee.[85]

On Mary's feasts the tropars and antiphons multiply in her honor, e.g.:

> Thy mysteries are above understanding and most glorious, O Mother of God, for, spotless and a virgin, thou art acknowledged a true Mother, who hast borne the true God; pray to Him that He save our souls.
>
> Hail, thou Gate of the Lord! Hail, Bulwark and Protection of those who fly to thee! Hail, untroubled Haven and Virgin, who hast borne in flesh thy Creator and God! Do not cease to pray for those who laud and reverence thy child-bearing.
>
> As the treasure of our resurrection, do thou, O universally celebrated Virgin, raise up those hoping in thee from the pit and depth of sin; for thou hast saved the repentent from sin, having borne our Salvation, and wast a Virgin before bearing child, a Virgin in bearing, and after bearing hast ever remained a Virgin.[86]

From these excerpts of the Byzantine liturgical texts we see how profound and how tender is the Marian doctrine of the Byzantines. They are justly proud of it. We do well to study these prayers to increase our own devotion to the all-holy and immaculate Virgin Mother of God. When we consider that the Orthodox use these same prayers, we are consoled to think that Mary, in her merciful

---

[85] *Ibid.*, p. 69.

[86] Theophile A. Zatkovich, *The Bread of Life, Prayer Book for Catholics of the Old Slavonic Rite* (Homestead, Pa., 1935), pp. 100, 101, 106, 110. Cf. Salaville, art. cit., pp. 302-304.

goodness, will eventually lead them back to the one true Church of Christ, over whom He had appointed Peter and his successors to rule and teach infallibly for all ages. With all the Byzantines we ask the Mediatrix of All Graces:

> For the peace of the whole world, for the good estate of all the holy churches of God, and for the union of all.[87]

SELECTED BIBLIOGRAPHY

Attwater, Donald, *The Christian Churches of the East*, 2 vols. (Milwaukee: Bruce, 1946, 1947).

– *Prayers from the Eastern Liturgies* (London: Burns, Oates and Washbourne, 1931).

Brian-Chaninov, Nicolas, *The Russian Church*, translated from the French by Warre B. Wells (New York: Macmillan, 1930).

Fortescue, Adrian, *The Uniate Eastern Churches, The Byzantine Rite in Italy, Sicily, Syria and Egypt* (London: Burns, Oates and Washbourne, 1923).

Gordillo, Mauritius, S.I., *Compendium Theologiae Orientalis* (Romae: Pont. Institutum Studiorum Orientalium, 1950).

King, Archdale A., *The Rites of Eastern Christendom*, 2 vols. (Rome: Catholic Book Agency, 1948), Vol. 2, *Byzantine Rite with Variants*, pp. 1-250.

Kirsch, Johann Peter, *Die Kirche in der Griechisch-Roemischen Kulturwelt* (Kirchengeschichte 1) (Freiburg im Breisgau: Herder, 1930).

Larsson, Raymond, E. F., *Saints at Prayer* (New York, Coward-McCann, 1942). Many Eastern prayers to Mary are here given.

Raes, Alphonsus, S.I., *Introductio in Liturgiam Orientalem* (Romae: Pont. Institutum Studiorum Orientalium, 1947).

For Byzantine anaphoras see Aleksyei Maltzev, *Die Goettlichen Liturgien unserer heiligen Vaeter Johannes Chrysostomus, Basilios des Grossen und Gregorios Diologos* (Berlin, 1890). Also Migne, Patrologia Graeca, Vol. 63, col. 90 et seq.

---

[87] De Meester, *op. cit.*, p. 25.

II. MARY IN THE ALEXANDRIAN AND ETHIOPIAN LITURGIES

1. THE ALEXANDRIAN LITURGY

The Church of St. Mark at Alexandria and its faithful use the Alexandrian liturgy. After the Council of Chalcedon Egypt fell into Monophysism, when the Patriarch Dioscoros of Alexandria was deposed by the Council. Nearly all the clergy and faithful of Egypt, and many also in Syria, refused to accept the definitions of this Council. Politics, too, played a part in this, and for the next century Alexandria had sometimes Catholic, sometimes Monophysite, patriarchs. By 567 two lines of patriarchs were established, one Catholic and one Monophysite. The Catholics were in a minority. Both Catholic and Monophysite Egyptians are called Copts. This condition remains to the present day. Various attempts at reunion have taken place in recent centuries, but with little effect. In 1899 Pope Leo XIII granted the Catholic Copts a patriarch in the person of Cyril Makarios. Since then they have increased in numbers and power. Yet even Makarios went into schism for a time. The present patriarch is Mark II Khouzam, appointed by Pope Pius XII, August 10, 1947.[1]

The splendid Alexandrian liturgy gives great praise to Mary and is used by both the Catholic and the Monophysite Copts. This liturgy is a form of the early Greek liturgy of Alexandria and it has three anaphoras, namely of St. Basil for Sundays and ordinary days; of St. Mark and St. Cyril, used on the feasts of these saints and at the consecration of a bishop; and of St. Gregory Nazianzen for great feasts. This last anaphora is addressed to Our Lord. The language used is Coptic, a language derived from the old Egyptian and mixed with some Greek.[2]

---

[1] D. Attwater, *The Christian Churches of the East*, Vol. 1 (Milwaukee, 1946), pp. 132-141, 132, 134. *Ibid.*, Vol. II, for Dissidents (Milwaukee, 1947), pp. 199-211. *Annuario Pontificio* (Città del Vaticano, 1953), p. 90.

[2] Attwater, *op. cit.*, Vol. 1, p. 137. A. A. King, *The Rites of Eastern Christendom* Vol. I (Rome, 1947), pp. 387, 393. S. Congregazione Orientale, *Statistica con cenni storici della gerarchia e dei fedeli di rito orientale* (Roma, 1932), pp. 33-40. O. H. E. Hadji-Burmester, *The Rites and Ceremonies of the Coptic Church*, in *Eastern Churches Quarterly* (Ramsgate), Vol. 7, April-June, 1948, pp. 373-

The *Ethiopian liturgy* is derived from the Alexandrian, translated from the Coptic and Arabic in the course of centuries, without much order. It is being re-edited at present.[3] The Alexandrian liturgy manifests a tender and abiding devotion to the Mother of God. It was this devotion of the Egyptians, as well as that of the Syrians and Persians that so impressed the Mohammedan conquerors that even they honor Mary as full of grace, as the noblest of women and the chosen one of God.[4]

A. The Mass

Mary is honored in the Alexandrian liturgy at Mass by being named first among the saints, and before the Lord's Prayer at the breaking of the Host. At the Commemoration Mary is named as "she who is full of glory, that is a virgin unto all time, holy Mary, the holy Mother of God."[5] A little later the intercession of Mary is asked: "Exalt the horn of the orthodox Christians through the power of the life-giving cross ... through the prayers and supplications which our Lady, the Lady of us all, the holy Mother of God, holy Mary, doth at all times make for us all."[6]

At the incensation of Mary's icon the priest says:

Hail to thee, the faithful Dove, which hath borne for us God the Word.

403; Vol. 8, January-March, 1949, pp. 1-39; Spring, 1950, pp. 291-316; Vol. 9, Spring, 1951, pp. 1-27.

[3] S. Congregazione Orientale, *op. cit.*, pp. 41-47. King, *op. cit.*, pp. 337-495. A. J. Butler, *The Ancient Coptic Churches of Egypt* (Oxford, 1884), 2 vols. R. M. Woolley (translator), *The Coptic Offices* (New York, 1930). D. Attwater, *The Liturgy of the Copts, in Orate Fratres* (Collegeville), April-May, 1942. Anonymous, *Some Notes on the Egyptian Christians, in Eastern Churches Quarterly*, Vol. 7, April-June, 1948, pp. 412-425.

For Ethiopian rite see: King, *op. cit.*, pp. 497-658; G. Nicollet, *Le Culte de Marie en Ethiopie* in H. du Manoir, S.J., *Maria. Études sur la Sainte Vierge*, Vol. 1 (Paris, 1949), pp. 365-413; A. A. King, *The New Ethiopic Missal, in Eastern Churches Quarterly*, Vol. 6, October-December, 1946, pp. 496-501.

[4] Amba Alexander, *Devotion to Our Lady* in the *Coptic Rite, in Eastern Churches Quarterly*, Vol. 7, April-June, 1948, pp. 404-408. H. Belloc, *The Great Heresies* (New York, 1938), p. 79. A. Arce, O.F.M., *Culte islamique au tombeau de la Vierge, in Atti dei Congresso Assunzionistico Orientale* (Gerusalemme, 1951), pp. 175-194.

[5] King, *op. cit.*, p. 464.

[6] *Ibid.*, p. 466.

We give thee salutation with the Angel Gabriel, saying, Hail, thou art full of grace; the Lord is with thee.

Hail to thee, O Virgin, the very and true Queen; hail, glory of our race. Thou hast borne for us Emmanuel.

We pray thee, remember us, O thou our faithful Advocate with our Lord Jesus Christ, that he may forgive us our sins.[7]

During the incensation the faithful sing these touching words:

The golden thurible of Aaron, the priest, is the Virgin; the sweet fragrance which it exhales is the Saviour. She bore Him and He saved us. O Mary, thou art the pure censer containing the blessed and Holy fire.[8]

When the priest unveils the oblation at the Preface the people chant:

By the intercession of the Blessed Virgin Mary who bore for us the Saviour of the world, grant us, O Lord, pardon for our sins.[9]

On Marian feasts there are special praises in her honor.

B. The Divine Office

It is in the Divine Office that we find rich and precious doctrine about the glory and privileges and power of the Mother of God. According to this liturgy, Mary must be commemorated and invoked at every ceremony, at every Office. Hence we cannot give all these texts. Mary is honored in a special way as the Queen and Mother of the priest. She is invoked as such at every canonical hour:

Hail Mary! We beseech thee, holy one, full of glory, ever Mother of God, Mother of Christ, lift up our prayers to thy beloved Son, that He may forgive us our sins. Hail, holy Virgin, who didst mother the true Light, Christ our God. Intercede for us with the Lord, that he may show pity on our souls and pardon us our sins. O Virgin Mary! Mother of God, faithful Advocate of the human race, supplicate for us Christ whom thou didst mother, that we may obtain forgiveness of our sins. Hail to thee, O Virgin Queen, truly righteous! Hail, the honor of our race, who didst give birth to Emmanuel; be mindful of us we implore thee, O faithful Advocate with Our Lord Jesus Christ, that he

---

[7] *Ibid.*, pp. 438, 439.

[8] Amba Alexander, *op. cit.*, p. 407.

[9] *Ibid.*, p. 408.

may pardon us our sins.[10]

In the prayer before the Creed at Matins and Compline Mary is thus honored:

We glorify thee, O Mother of the true Light; we venerate thee, O Holy Mother of God, for thou didst give birth to the Redeemer of the world.[11] ...

The following prayer is recited at the end of Tierce:

O Mother of God, thou art the true vine bearing the Grape of Life. In union with the Apostles we beseech thee, O full of grace, obtain for us the salvation of our souls. Blessed be the Lord our God. May the God of our salvation prepare our way before us. O Mother of God, thou Portal of heaven, open to us the gates of mercy.[12]

At None:

When the Mother of the Lamb and Good Shepherd saw the world's Redeemer hanging on the Cross, she said through her tears: "The world rejoices because it has received salvation; but my heart is broken at witnessing this crucifixion which Thou dost suffer for all mankind, O my Son and my God."[13]

At Vespers:

Hail, thou who hast found grace, Holy Mary, Mother of God; blessed be thou among women and blessed be the fruit of thy womb; because thou didst give birth to the Saviour of our souls.[14]

During Holy Week the following invocation is used morning and night: "Hail to thee, O spotless Dove, Spouse of the Holy Spirit, we pray thee to be mindful of us before thy Son." All blessings and favors are asked of God in all the ceremonies through the intercession of the Mother of God.[15]

As among other rites of the Christian East Mary's image or icon has special honor in the church and is incensed during the sacred functions. The Alexandrian Church always portrays Mary with the

---

[10] *Ibid.*, pp. 406, 407.

[11] *Ibid.*, p. 407.

[12] *Ibid.*

[13] *Ibid.*

[14] *Ibid.*

[15] *Ibid.*, p. 408.

divine Child. Pictures of her alone are not in favor, for she is ever honored as the *Theotokos*, the Mother of God. The Alexandrians learned this love for God's all-holy Mother from the Council of Ephesus and from St. Cyril of Alexandria, its hero. Therefore Mary is almost always present in the Alexandrian liturgy, despite age-long schism and heresy, even among the Monophysites. Her light shines upon all who use this liturgy. The Catholics pray that some day this light of Mary and love for her will bring the dissidents back to the true Church.[16]

C. Marian Feasts and Privileges

The Marian feasts in this liturgy are thirty-two and in this the Ethiopians imitate them. But not all these feasts are observed everywhere. The three major Marian feasts are her Nativity, her Presentation in the Temple, and her Assumption. As the Alexandrians honor Mary's divine Maternity, so, too, they honor her Assumption as her greatest feast. This is celebrated on August 22 and is preceded by a strict abstinence for a fortnight, when the diet consists of fruit and uncooked food. It is a little Lent, when the solemnization of marriage is forbidden, and it is a time of prayer.[17]

Some feasts of Christ are also feasts of Mary, e.g., the Annunciation, Christmas, the Presentation of Christ in the Temple, and the Entry Into Egypt.[18] Besides these, other Marian feasts are, e.g., that of the Holy Family, the Immaculate Conception (two feasts, July 31 and December 9), Death of Mary (January 16) — but among the Catholics this day commemorates the consecration of the first church dedicated to Our Lady — the Divine Motherhood, the Commemoration of the Council of Ephesus, and the days of the dedication of Marian churches at Atrib, Heliopolis, Philipponis, and Itib.[19]

Mary's privileges and power of intercession are clearly stated in the liturgy and hymns of the faithful. Egypt glories in the Mother of God, so much so that even the Mohammedans had been influenced

---

[16] *Ibid.*

[17] King, *op. cit.*, p. 398; Amba Alexander, *op. cit.*, p. 406.

[18] King, *op. cit.*, pp. 397, 398.

[19] *Ibid.*, pp. 398, 399; Amba Alexander, *loc. cit.*

by this devotion. Mary's purity is unsullied; she is compared to the burning bush that was not consumed. Her Immaculate Conception, her perpetual virginity, her plenitude of grace, her painless childbearing, her power of intercession, and her heavenly glory in body and soul — all these privileges and graces of Mary are stated explicitly many times in this rich and splendid liturgy.[20] Father Gabriel Giamberardini, O.F.M., gives excellent testimony to the Marian devotion of the Coptic Church in his fine work on the assumptionist theology of that church.[21] From this we see that Coptic love and devotion to the Mother of God, handed on to them from St. Cyril of Alexandria and the Council of Ephesus, has never grown weak, but has continued strong and glorious through the centuries.

Honorable titles and attributes generously applied to Our Lady prove this devotion of the Alexandrian liturgy. Some of these titles and attributes are:

David's Daughter, Ark of the Covenant robed in purest gold, Flower of Jesse, who draws down the Saviour, Garden enclosed where dwells the Godhead, the Father's Chariot radiant with divine light, Ladder to heaven seen by the Patriarch Jacob, having the Spirit of God at its summit, Silver Censer enclosing burning coals, Lantern resplendent, Light of Paradise, Strength of Samson, Rod of Aaron blossoming unwatered, Bush of myrrh which Moses saw crowned with flame on Mount Tor, Vase of alabaster, Precious Treasure, Tower of Ivory, Dome of Moses, Fruitful Vineyard, Throne of God which Daniel the Prophet saw above the Seraphim, Sacred Altar which God inhabits, and Immaculate Virgin betrothed to the Spouse.[22]

2. THE ETHIOPIC LITURGY

In modern times revisions of the Ethiopic liturgy have taken place. In 1945 the Vatican Press completed the printing of the revised missal, called the Book of the Oblation. This missal is based

---

[20] A. Van Lantschoot, O.Praem., *Le culte de la Sainte Vierge chez les coptes*, in *Alma Socia Christi*, Acta Congressus Mariologici-Mariani Romae Anno Sancto MCML celebrati, Vol. 5, fasc. 11 (Romae, 1952), *De B. V. Maria penes Ecclesias Orientis*, pp. 103-108.

[21] G. Giamberardini, *La teologia assunzionistica nella Chiesa Egiziana*, in *Atti dei Congresso Assunzionistico Orientale* (Gerusalemme, 1951), pp. 41-174.

[22] Amba Alexander, *loc. cit.*

on old manuscripts and on that of Diredawa in Ethiopia. The book contains the Ordinary of the Mass, the Anaphora of the Apostles and seventeen others. The liturgical language is Ge'ez, a Semitic language used in Ethiopia until the seventeenth century.[23]

A. The Mass

Mary is mentioned at the beginning of the liturgy of the Catechumens:

Blessed be the only Son our Lord Jesus Christ, who was made man of Mary, the holy Virgin, for our salvation.[24]

While incensing the image of Mary the priest says:

Thou art the golden censer which didst bear the live Coal of fire. Blessed is he who receiveth out of the sanctuary him that forgiveth sin and blotteth out error, who is God's Word, who was made man of thee, who offered himself to his Father for incense and an acceptable offering. We worship thee, Christ, with thy good heavenly Father and thine Holy Spirit, the life-giver, for thou didst come and save us.[25]

After the incensation of the altar the priest recites the Hail Mary alternately with the people.[26] After the epistle there is another incensation of the altar when the priest prays:

Hail, O thou of whom we ask salvation, O holy praiseful ever-virgin Parent of God, Mother of Christ: offer up our prayer on high to thy beloved Son that He forgive us our sins. Hail, O thou who barest for us the very Light of Righteousness, even Christ our God. O Virgin pure, plead for us unto the Lord, that he show mercy unto our souls and forgive us our sins. Hail, O Virgin pure, Mary, holy Parent of God, very pleader for the race of mankind, plead for us before Christ thy Son, that he vouchsafe us remission of our sins. Hail, O Virgin pure, very Queen; hail, O Pride of our kind. Hail, O thou that barest for us Emmanuel. We pray thee that thou remember us, O very Mediatrix, before our Lord, Jesus Christ, that He forgive us our sins.[27]

Going outside the veil the priest says:

---

[23] King, *op. cit.*, pp. 562-566; cf. note 3 of this paper.

[24] *Ibid.*, p. 591.

[25] *Ibid.*, p. 594.

[26] *Ibid.*, pp. 596, 597.

[27] *Ibid.*, p. 600.

This is the time of blessing, this is the time of choice incense, the time of the praise of our Saviour, lover of men, Christ. The censer is Mary; the incense is He who was in her womb which is fragrant; the incense is He whom she bare; He came and saved us, the fragrant ointment, Jesus Christ. ... To Michael was given mercy, and glad tidings to Gabriel and a heavenly gift to Mary, the Virgin. ... The fragrant ointment is Mary: for He that was in her womb, who is more fragrant than all incense, came and was made flesh of her. In Mary Virgin pure the Father was well pleased and He decked her for a tabernacle for the habitation of His well-beloved Son. ...[28]

At the Trisagion the priest says: "Holy God, holy mighty, holy living immortal, who was born of Mary the holy Virgin, have mercy on us, O Lord."[29] The Catholics leave out the interpolation.

After the Preface the deacon recites a litany wherein Mary is named first among the saints.[30] A little later the priest says:

Thou who sendest Thy Son from heaven into the bosom of the Virgin, He was carried in the womb, was made flesh, and His birth was revealed of the Holy Ghost.[31]

Mary is mentioned again shortly before the words of Consecration.[32] She is named again, in a prayer before Communion.[33] She is again mentioned at the end of a prayer when the priest puts a particle of the Host into the chalice.[34] Toward the end of the liturgy there is a long prayer, wherein Mary is named as the Mother of God and immaculate.[35] After that she is mentioned in another prayer as "immaculate in virginity, pure for ever and ever."[36] Among the many anaphoras of this rite there is one entitled "Of our Lady, Mary the Virgin." The first part of it praises Our Lady, who is typified in the lives of Old Testament characters, and who is

---

[28] *Ibid.*, p. 601.
[29] *Ibid.*, p. 602.
[30] *Ibid.*, p. 616.
[31] *Ibid.*, p. 619.
[32] *Ibid.*, p. 620.
[33] *Ibid.*, p. 632.
[34] *Ibid.*, p. 633.
[35] *Ibid.*, p. 643.
[36] *Ibid.*, p. 645.

the source of all Christian graces.[37]

B. *The Divine Office and Marian Hymns*

The Divine Office in this rite needed revision as did the other liturgical books. The psalter, lessons, and office of Our Lady were published for the Catholics in 1926.[38] The definitive Ethiopic breviary will soon appear in its revised edition. The Ethiopic hymnology and prayers to Mary are rich and numerous. Mary is given many splendid titles, many feasts honor her, and in all the liturgical texts we see the wealth of oriental imagery used to glorify her, who is above all praise. Genevieve Nicollet states that it is well-nigh impossible to gather all the Marian hymns. They have a plain chant all their own and go back to early centuries.[39] There was a renaissance of Marian hymnography in the fifteenth century during the reigns of the Ethiopian kings Zara-Yaqob, his son Baeda-Maryam, and Naod. These kings also ordered the ancient hymns to be collected. At this time many new ones were composed as well.[40]

The Marian hymns are a study in themselves, for in them we see so many influences both native and foreign, that they are a literary problem. Above all, they prove the ceaseless ardor of the Ethiopians to praise the all-holy Mother of God, to enrich the treasure of her hymns, and to multiply her glorious praises. There are so many of these hymns for every feast, even for every day of the week, that it seems the authors must have vied with one another in composing them. And even if all the hymns are not original and native to the land, yet their superabundance manifests the profoundly Ethiopian sentiment of absolute confidence in Mary.[41]

Many of these Marian hymns are in the liturgical collections, others are for popular use. In the *Deggua*, a book of plain chant for the days of the year, there are several Marian hymns. For example, one hymn glorifies the birth of Christ, another compares Our Lady

---

[37] *Ibid.*, pp. 646-648; Nicollet, *op. cit.*, pp. 376-379.

[38] King, *op. cit.*, p. 566.

[39] Nicollet, *op. cit.*, p. 395; A Grohmann, *Aethiopische Marienhymnen* (Leipzig, 1919). Three great Marian hymns are here translated with a rich philological commentary.

[40] Nicollet, *loc. cit.*

[41] *Ibid.*, p. 396.

to the golden candlestick seen by the Prophet Zachary in a vision (Zach. 4:2). This latter hymn is filled with scriptural allusions to Mary from the Old Testament. Another hymn compares Mary to the burning bush seen by Moses (Exod. 3:4). Still another one likens her to a dove, or to the Tabernacle of the Chosen People.[42]

In the *Meeraf*, a book composed probably in the second half of the fifteenth century, we find other Marian hymns. This book is really a guide for the chanted offices. Here one hymn calls Mary the "golden table," while there are other hymns in honor of Mary's Nativity, the Annunciation, and one where she is styled "Mother of God and the Saviour," and another where she has the names of "Vine and Vase filled with manna." Finally there is a hymn in honor of her Assumption.[43] Other liturgical books containing Marian hymns are *Mawaseet* (an antiphonary); *Zemmare* (hymns for Easter, Pentecost, and Epiphany); *Matshafa Kidana Mehrat* (Book of the Pact of Mercy); *Weddase Maryam* (Praises of Mary); *Argonona Dengel* by George the Armenian; *Enzira Sebhat* (Harp of Glory); *Weddase wa-genay la-emma Adonay* (Praises and humble thanks to the Mother of Adonai); *Weddase em-qala nabiyat* (Praises taken from the words of the Prophets); and the *Laha Maryam* (Lamentations of Mary). The *Mazmura Dengel* (Psalter of Mary) has 105 strophes of four verses each. The religious sentiment is predominant in all these works. There we see the profound and childlike love of the Ethiopians for the Mother of God.[44] A good number of other Marian hymns are used occasionally also in the liturgy.[45]

C. Marian Feasts and Privileges

From the important place Mary has in the Ethiopian liturgy we see that even though the Ethiopians, as well as the Egyptians and Syrians, have erred in the past in regard to the dogmatic explanation of the mystery of the Incarnation, they have, nevertheless, retained intact the privilege of the divine Maternity of

---

[42] *Ibid.*

[43] *Ibid.*, pp. 396, 397.

[44] *Ibid.*, pp. 397, 398, 405; translations into French.

[45] *Ibid.*, pp. 406-413.

Mary — and this despite all their trials and persecutions through the centuries.[46] Echoes of the Council of Ephesus, proclaiming Mary's divine Maternity are heard in all the liturgies, and in a special way in those of Alexandria and Ethiopia. Even the Dissidents retain this great devotion to Mary and manifest it in their liturgy and devotions.

In the Chronicles of King Zara-Yaqob (1431-1468) of Ethiopia we read that after he had conquered and killed with his own hand the terrible Mohammedan chief Arwe Badlay, an order was given that the "thirty-two feasts of Our Lady should be celebrated like Sundays with the greatest punctuality ... under pain of excommunication."[47] Later he commanded that every church should have a *tabot* (altar) dedicated to the holy Virgin. These customs are still in use and the Ethiopians have never failed in their love and devotion to the Mother of God.[48] Even Job Ludolf, a German Protestant scholar of the seventeenth century, famous for his works on Ethiopia, had to admit that the Ethiopians honor Mary much more than all the other saints.[49] It is impossible to give an exact list of the Marian feasts celebrated in the Dissident Ethiopian liturgy today, because their number differs in various places. Some Ethiopian Marian feasts celebrate some famous Marian sanctuary, others some miracle wrought at Mary's intercession. Nearly one third of the year, the Ethiopian calendar has feasts on which work is forbidden.[50] The Coptic calendar is the foundation for that of Ethiopia. Often the same feast is celebrated many times in the year. For example, Christmas is commemorated on the twenty-fourth or twenty-fifth of every month except March.[51]

The principal Catholic Marian feasts are the Immaculate Conception (December 9), the Death of Mary (January 16), the Assumption (August 22), the Nativity of Mary (September 8). Other feasts are the Presentation of Mary in the Temple (November 29), and the Annunciation (December 18 and every twenty-second day

---

[46] Van Lantschoot, *op. cit.*, p. 103.

[47] Nicollet, *op. cit.*, p. 379.

[48] *Ibid.*, p. 380.

[49] Ibid.; I. Ludolf, *Commentarius ad historiam aethiopicam*, 1691, p. 361.

[50] King, *op. cit.*, p. 546. Nicollet, *op. cit.*, pp. 379-395.

[51] King, *op. cit.*, pp. 546, 547.

of other months and March 25 which is also the feast of the Incarnation).[52]

From these feasts we see that the Ethiopians admit Mary's great graces and privileges, as well as her power of intercession with her divine Son. The Assumption is the greatest Marian feast. It is commemorated every month. Some texts for the feast are:

> I salute the Assumption of thy Body which the human heart can never conceive. Doubly surrounded with grace and clothed in a like glory, O Mary, thy flesh was like to a pearl, and death itself was shamed when with wonder it saw thee ascending resplendent through the clouds to heaven.[53]

> I salute the Assumption of thy Body truly worthy to be praised, which outshines in beauty the splendor of the sun and the glory of the moon. Except thee, O Virgin, and thy first-born Son of Joy, there is no one who has loosened the bonds of death and has awakened the dead from Sheol.[54]

> I salute the resurrection of thy flesh, twin of the resurrection of Christ, who hid himself alive in thee. Clothe me, O Mary, Dove of Ephrate, and shelter me under thy wings in the day of judgment, when the earth will give back those whom she had taken into her keeping.[55]

D. Mary in Popular Ethiopian Devotion

It is true the Ethiopians have mixed a bit of superstition with their devotion to Mary. This is a souvenir of ancient African beliefs, such as all races have, but the fact remains that the Ethiopian faith in Mary is strong and sound, and that they have a tender love for her and an absolute trust in her all-powerful intercession.[56] Ethiopia received the Faith from Alexandria and with it a great love and devotion to the Mother of God. With Alexandria, Ethiopia, too, fell into Monophysism, probably without fully realizing what this

---

[52] Nicollet, *op. cit.*, pp. 384-395.

[53] King, *op. cit.*, p. 542.

[54] *Ibid.*

[55] *Ibid.*, D. Attwater, *Eastern Catholic Worship* (New York, 1945); H. Engberding, *Maria in der Froemmigkeit der Oestlichen Liturgien*, in P. Straeter, *Maria in der Offenbarung* (Paderborn, 1947), pp. 119-136; De Lacy, O'Leary, *The Daily Office and Theotokia of the Coptic Church* (London, 1911); id., *The Coptic Theotokia* (London, 1923).

[56] Nicollet, *op. cit.*, pp. 366, 367; King, *op. cit.*, p. 541.

doctrine implied. But Ethiopia has no body of doctrine in the true theological sense as we have in the West. Hence they have no full body of doctrine regarding the Mother of God, except that they follow the Fathers of Alexandria. *Haymanota Abaw*, the Faith of the *Fathers*, is what they call the collection of truths which forms their belief. St. Cyril of Alexandria plays a great part in this doctrine, as well as other Fathers of the East and the decrees of the Council of Ephesus. Hence with this Council and St. Cyril of Alexandria the Ethiopians believe in the Mother of God, the *Waladita Malak*, the *Theotokos*. Even the Dissidents appeal to St. Cyril of Alexandria, and consider him one of their Doctors.[57] In their liturgy and hymns the Ethiopians have expressed the true faith in Mary as Mother of God, and they echo the words of St. Cyril of Alexandria and the definition of the Council of Ephesus. The Dissident Ethiopians still honor Alexandria as their spiritual mother, receive their spiritual directives from Alexandria, and until lately received their *Abuna* or metropolitan from there. The Catholic Ethiopians are united to Alexandria spiritually and historically, but their bishops are appointed by the Pope.[58]

The Ethiopians speak of heretics as "Enemies of Mary." The great Ethiopian devotion to Our Lady can explain to a certain degree why some historians wanted to see nothing in the Ethiopian liturgy but a confusion between the cult due to God and that due to Mary.[59] The truth, however, is that the Ethiopians, both Catholic and Dissident, have correct doctrine regarding Mary, her privileges and power, and this they manifest in their practices and hymns as well as in their liturgy.

In conclusion it is well to see some of the titles the Ethiopians give Mary, and thus prove their sound doctrine about her:

> Permanent Temple, Sacerdotal Vestibule, Chosen Column, Verdant Tree, Garden of the Heavenly Son, Lamp of the Universe, Light of the Stars, Unbreakable Wall, Extension of Heaven, Veil of Fine Linen, City of Jewels, Spouse of Heaven, Golden Censer of the Seraphs, Harvest of Prophecies, Mother of Justice, Doctrine of Peace, Vine of Sweet Grapes, Mother of the Glorious Sun, Book of Life, Vessel of Our

---

[57] Nicollet, *op. cit.*, pp. 369, 370.

[58] *Ibid.*, pp. 368, 369.

[59] *Ibid.*, p. 396, note 63.

Riches, Superabundance of the time of Fruit and Compensation for the Years of Famine, Satiety of Those Who Hunger, Queen of Love, Gate of Paradise, and Help of Sinners.[60]

Conclusion

Egyptian devotion to Mary as Mother of God is deep-rooted in all the faithful. Their love for Mary prompts them to abstain for two weeks before the feast of her Assumption. This practice is so ancient that even the Mohammedans of the country observe it in great numbers down to the present day.[61] Another sign of this Egyptian devotion to Mary is seen in the many temples dedicated to her throughout Egypt. In the eighth century there were twenty-two Marian shrines in Upper Egypt and seven in Lower Egypt. Two of these are still dedicated to Mary's Assumption. They are centers of pilgrimage and great Marian festivities are held there by the Dissidents on the feast of the Assumption.[62]

Egypt was sanctified by the presence of the Holy Family. The Egyptians are proud of this great honor and wish to be second to none in their love for Christ and His all-holy Mother. May she lead the Dissident back to the true Church of her divine Son and may she protect all the faithful of the Alexandrian and Ethiopian rites who are so devoted to her who is the Mother of God, ever Virgin Immaculate, and all-powerful with her divine Son.

SELECTED BIBLIOGRAPHY

Black, G. F., *Aethiopica and Amharica*, A List of Works in the New York Public Library, 1928.

Budge, E. A. Wallis, *The Miracles of the Blessed Virgin and the Life of Hanna*, 1910.

De Vries, G., S.I., *Oriente Cristiano Ieri e Oggi* (Roma, 1949).

Etiopia in Vol. 14 of the *Enciclopedia Italiana* (Milano, 1935).

Fortescue, A., *The Lesser Eastern Churches* (London, 1913).

Grebaut, S., and Tisserant, E., *Bibliothecae Apostolicae Vaticanae*

---

[60] *Ibid.*, p. 365 et passim.

[61] Amba Alexander, *The Assumption of Mary in the Liturgy of the Church of Alexandria*, in *Eastern Churches Quarterly*, Vol. 9, Summer, 1951, pp. 93-101, p. 95. (He mentions two traditions in regard to Mary's Assumption.)

[62] *Ibid.*, p. 99. The places are Haret Zouela and Deir Dronka or Adronka.

codices aethiopici, Vaticani et Borgiani, 1936.

Harden, J. M., *The Anaphoras of the Ethiopic Liturgy*, 1928.

Jones and Monroe, *Abyssinia* (Oxford, 1935).

Macaire, *Histoire de l'Eglise d'Alexandrie* (Cairo, 1894).

Matshafa Qeddasê (Ethiopian missal) (Città del Vaticano: Tipografia Poliglotta Vaticana, 1945).

Mercer, S. A. B., *The Ethiopic Liturgy*, 1915.

O'Leary, *The Saints of Egypt* (London, 1938).

Pollera, A., *Lo Stato etiopico e la sua Chiesa*, 1926.

Rossini, C. Conti, *Liber Axumae*, 1910.

Strothman, *Die Koptische Kirche in der Neuzeit* (Tübingen, 1932).

III. MARY IN THE ANTIOCHENE LITURGY

The liturgy of Antioch is one of the most ancient liturgies. It was modified for use in Jerusalem and then this form supplanted the older form at Antioch itself. This liturgy is the source of the Armenian, Byzantine, and Maronite liturgies, and perhaps also of that used by the Chaldeans. After the Council of Chalcedon (a.d. 451) many of the Syrians followed the Monophysites and refused to accept the decrees of that Council, mostly for political reasons. The Monophysite Syrians are called Jacobites from their organizer in the sixth century, Jacob al-Baradai. The Syrians who remained Catholics formed that branch of the Byzantine rite known as the Melkites. In the course of centuries a goodly number of the Jacobites have returned to the true Church. At various times these Catholics have had bishops confirmed by Rome, and in 1801 Michael Jarweh became the first patriarch of Antioch of the Catholic Syrians. These faithful are mostly in the old Turkish Empire and Egypt, but there are also several thousands in the United States, the Argentine, Chile, Australia, and Paris.[1]

1. The Mass

The Antiochene liturgy is the richest of all because it has so many anaphoras. The Catholics ordinarily use that of St. James. They also use at times the anaphoras of St. John the Evangelist, of St. Eustace of Antioch, of St. Basil of Caesarea, and of St. Cyril of Jerusalem. There are sixty-four Syrian anaphoras, of which the Catholics use only seven. Brightman gives the list of those used by the Jacobites.[2] He also gives the translations of those of the Apostolic Constitutions and of St. James[3]

The liturgical texts are very ancient. Those used by the Catholics received their definitive form in the eighth century under

---

[1] D. Attwater, *The Christian Churches of the East,* Vol. I (Milwaukee, 1946), pp. 104, 152-164. Attwater, *Eastern Catholic Worship* (New York, 1945).

[2] F. E. Brightman, *Liturgies Eastern and Western* (Oxford, 1896), pp. xlviii-lxiii.

[3] *Ibid.,* pp. 1-109.

James of Edessa.[4] In the liturgy of St. James, Mary is commemorated in the preparation of the gifts, and in the beginning of the liturgy of the Catechumens followed by an incensation with the words: "With the smoke of spices be there a remembrance to the Virgin Mary, Mother of God." Again incensing the gifts: "Let Mary who brought thee forth, and John who baptized thee be suppliants unto thee in our behalf." Mary is again named before the Trisagion, and in the beginning of the Gospel reading. After the Consecration and prayers for various classes of persons, the commemoration of the saints begins with that of the Mother of God by the deacon:

> Again then we commemorate her who is to be called blessed and glorified of all generations of the earth, holy and blessed, and ever Virgin, blessed Mother of God, Mary.

After the priest breaks the Host and recites a silent prayer, the deacon prays:

> My blessed Lady Mary, beseech with thine only Begotten that he be appeased through thy prayers and perform mercy on us all.[5]

The Maronite liturgy is merely the ordinary part of the Syrian liturgy of St. James and at times some other anaphora is inserted.[6] After the Anamnesis the Maronites have these prayers to Mary:

> Especially then and firstly we remember the holy and glorious and ever Virgin Mother of God, Mary, Mother of our Lord Jesus Christ; intercede for me with the only begotten Son who was born of thee that he forgive me my offenses and sins and receive from my vile and sinful hands this sacrifice which my abjectness offereth upon this altar, by thine intercessions for me, O holy Mother.

The deacon says:

> Remember her, O Lord God, and by her pure and holy prayers be

---

[4] E. Rahal, *L'Assomption de la T. Ste. Vierge au ciel selon le rite syrien d'Antioche*, in *Atti del Congresso Assunzionistico Orientale* (Gerusalemme, 1951), pp. 225-237.

[5] Brightman, *op. cit.*, pp. 73-76, 92, 93, 98. *Missale Syriacum iuxta ritum Ecclesiae Antiochenae syrorum* (Romae, 1843).

[6] D. Attwater, *The Christian Churches of the East*, Vol. I, pp. 174, 175; G. Gorayet, *The Maronite Liturgy* (Buffalo, 1915); P. Sfeir, *The Maronite Liturgy*, (Detroit, 1936); Attwater, *Eastern Catholic Worship* (New York, 1945).

propitious and have mercy and hear us.[7]

After Communion the priest says:

May the prayer of the blessed one be a wall to us, Halleluia, her prayer be with us. Bless, O my Lord. The ladder which Jacob saw was a figure of thee, O Virgin Mother of God, for on thee God, the hope of all of us, came down to afford hope to the hopeless.[8]

When the Malabar Jacobites of India began to enter the Church in 1930 with Bishop Mar Ivanios and his suffragan Bishop Mar Theophilus, Pope Pius XI permitted them to keep their Antiochene liturgy and customs. More bishops, priests, and lay people have since returned to the true Church.[9] Their liturgy is the West Syrian rite (Antiochene) without most of the modifications which the Syrian Catholics have introduced. This Malabar liturgy, and the faithful who follow it, are called *Malankarese*. Most of the prayers are in the vernacular Malayalam; the priest's secret prayers are in Syriac.[10]

2. The Divine Office

The Antiochene Office is rich and complicated. Mary is honored with prayers and hymns, especially on her feast days. At Sunday Sext we find this prayer:

By the prayer of Thy Mother and of all the saints, pardon us, O our Lord, and rest the departed. The memorial of Mary be for our blessing and her prayer be a wall to our souls. ... Glory to Him who hath magnified the memorial of His Mother, and may He make the saints resplendent and rest the departed. By the prayer of Thy Mother and of all Thy saints, pardon us, O our Lord, and rest the departed.[11]

One of the ordinary anthems to Mary reads:

---

[7] H. W. Codrington, *The Maronite Liturgy* in *Eastern Churches Quarterly*, Vol. II (Ramsgate), January, 1937, pp. 27-37. Sacra Congregazione Orientale, *Statistica con Cenni Storici della Gerarchia e dei Fedeli di Rito Orientale* (Romae, 1932), pp. 54-63.

[8] Codrington, *op. cit.*, p. 36.

[9] Attwater, *The Christian Churches of the East*, Vol. I, p. 179.

[10] *Ibid.*, p. 180.

[11] H. W. Codrington, *The Syrian Liturgy*, in *Eastern Churches Quarterly*, Vol. I, January-October, 1936, pp. 135-148.

O holy virgin Mother of God, Mary, pray thine only Son to make His tranquillity to dwell in His creation. Watchers and angels, lo! they rejoice on the day of the memorial of the Virgin Mary who bore the Son of God.[12]

Wednesday is dedicated to Mary in this liturgy. A prayer to her at Matins reads:

Peace to thee, who didst bear in the flesh the Word most high, Virgin Mother, maiden pure and holy, Mary Mother of Christ, full of mercies and grace. Peace to thee, who wast a second heaven to the eternal Word of the Father. Peace to thee, who wast the small cloud to the Creator of all creation. But, O holy one, we implore of thee, pray thine only Son, God above all, to grant tranquillity to the creation for the sake of the abundance of His mercifulness.[13]

Regarding devotion to Mary in the Antiochene liturgy, Chorepiscopos Paul Hindo writes:

Besides the solemn proclamation in the liturgy the Syrian Church commemorates the Mother of God at the Offertory, at the ceremony of incensation, at the breaking of bread, at the distribution of Communion, and at the end of Mass. The canonical Office, both ferial and festive, contains a great number of chants and hymns in honor of the Virgin, notably 1) at Vespers, Lauds and Prime every day; 2) at Matins, and precisely at the first nocturn, with the exception of Fridays, from Easter to Advent; Fridays are consecrated to the Holy Cross; 3) at the end of Matins, the Magnificat is recited daily with special Marian praises called Mawerbe, that is of the Magnificat; 4) the Wednesday Office is specially consecrated to the Holy Virgin, above all at Vespers, Lauds, Prime and Tierce. According to Syrian tradition, Wednesday is the day of Mary's birth and death.[14]

In the liturgy of the Maronites, Mary is also frequently invoked. Before Mass every day a prayer in the form of a litany is addressed to Christ through the intercession of Mary. Praises, after the manner of St. Ephrem, are dedicated to her on Wednesdays and on her feasts. She is also commemorated at other times with hymns,

---

[12] *Ibid.*

[13] *Ibid..*, pp. 138, 139.

[14] P. Hindo, *Disciplina Antiochena Antica — Siri IV* (Roma, 1943), p. 307, n. 1, in *Codificazione Canonica Orientale* — Fonti, serie 11, Fasciculo XXVIII, *Sacra Congregazione per la Chiesa Orientale.*

especially at the Gospel procession. All the anaphoras mention Mary between the Anamnesis and the Epiclesis. On her feast days she has hymns in her honor, especially when the gifts are brought to the altar.[15]

3. Marian Feasts and Privileges

The Marian feasts in the Antiochene liturgy are of two kinds, movable and fixed. The movable Marian feasts are in preparation for Christmas. In ancient times this liturgy celebrated two feasts during Advent, that of St. John the Baptist and that of the Virgin (divine Maternity and Immaculate Conception). The feast of the Virgin goes back to the year 428. The Nestorians who separated from the true Church in the fifth century have the same tradition as the Catholics of this liturgy and call Advent *Subara* or Annunciation. At the time of their separation the feast of the Virgin was called the Salutation of the All-Holy Mother of God. James of Saroug (451-521) has left us homilies for the time of Advent, on the Annunciation of Zachary, the Annunciation of Mary, the Visitation of Mary to Elizabeth, and the Nativity of our Lord. By the seventh century the five Sundays before Christmas were dedicated to the Annunciation of the birth of the Precursor, the Annunciation of Mary, the Visitation of Mary to Elizabeth, the Revelation of the conception of Christ to St. Joseph, and finally the Genealogy of Christ. The Nestorians have the same feasts as the Syrians and Maronites to this day.[16]

The fixed feasts of Mary in this rite are the Immaculate Conception, the Nativity of Mary, the Presentation of Mary in the Temple, the Annunciation (second feast), the Praises or Felicitations to the Mother of God (December 26), the Presentation of Christ in the Temple, and the Assumption of Mary. For the latter feast there is a preparation of a fast lasting two weeks. Besides these feasts both the Syrians and Maronites have added others of a more local character. Thus the Syrians have added the Marian feasts of January 15, May 15, and June 15. The Maronites also have that of May 15 to bless the harvest. The Maronites have also added a fixed feast of the

---

[15] M. Doumith, *Marie dans la liturgie syro-maronite*, in H. du Manoir, S.J., *Maria. Études sur la Sainte Vierge* (Paris, 1949), pp. 329-340.

[16] Doumith, *op. cit.*, pp. 331, 332.

Visitation (besides the one in Advent) on July 2, the feasts of Our Lady of Mt. Carmel on July 16, the Marriage of Mary and Joseph on September 30; and a movable feast of Our Lady of the Rosary on the first Sunday of October.[17]

On September 9, after the feast of Mary's Nativity, the Antiochene liturgy celebrates the commemoration of her parents, Joachim and Anna. Such commemorations are made also after the feasts of Christ to honor certain persons connected with the mystery of Christ's life just celebrated.[18]

Except for the feast in the cycle of Christmas and the Nativity, the feast of the Assumption is the only Marian feast celebrated in every Eastern rite. This shows the universality of the belief of these ancient churches. The Dissidents have the same belief in Mary's Assumption.[19]

The faithful of the Antiochene rite have ever had definite doctrine in regard to Mary's death and burial, her corporal incorruptibility, her bodily Assumption into heaven, and her universal Queenship over heaven and earth.[20] St. Ephrem, the Syrian, Doctor of Mary's Immaculate Conception and other glories, is also the Doctor of her Assumption.[21] The Antiochene Office testifies to Mary's death and burial:

> The Lord has chosen thee for his Mother and has glorified the day of thy memorial. He has caused thee to pass from life through the portal of death, so that thou mayest rejoice in the heavenly kingdom.[22]

> This tomb was the ladder that brought thee to heaven, next to thy Lord, thy Son and thy God.[23]

---

[17] *Ibid.*, p. 332.

[18] *Ibid.*

[19] A. A. King, *The Assumption of Our Lady in the Oriental Liturgies*, in *Eastern Churches Quarterly*, Vol. 8, October-December, 1949, pp. 225-231.

[20] Rahal, *op. cit.*, p. 226. M. Maklouf, *La doctrine de l'Assomption dans la rite maronite*, in *Atti del Congresso Assunzionistico Orientale* (Gerusalemme, 1951), pp. 197-212.

[21] Rahal, *op. cit.*, p. 226; Lamy, *Sancti Ephremi Syri Hymni et Sermones* (Mechliniae, 1882-1902), Vol. 2, col. 584.

[22] Rahal, *op. cit.*, p. 227; G. Shelhot and J. David, Fenqitho (*Bréviaire festival*), 7 vols. (Mosul, 1886-1896), Vol. 7, col. 379a.

[23] Rahal, *op. cit.*, p. 227; Shelhot and David, *op. cit.*, Vol. 7, col. 405b.

The Office gives testimony to Mary's corporal incorruptibility after death: "The [burning] bush is a symbol of thy holy Body."[24] Her body is compared to the Ark of the Covenant, made of incorruptible wood.[25]

Mary's corporal Assumption is clearly and firmly stated in this liturgy:

Although thy Body was placed in a tomb according to the law of mortals, nonetheless it is not like the body of Moses ... which was hidden from the Hebrews by God. ... For thy immaculate Body was taken to heaven by the Lord, and there he placed it in the blessed dwellings. There thou standest next to the throne of thy Son. Pray for us to thy Son Jesus.[26]

Mary's bodily Assumption is a consequence of her Immaculate Conception and the divine Maternity:

By the Holy Spirit she was freed from the curse of the first mother, for she never opened the door to sin. So her passing is the admiration of the whole world.[27]

Blessed be thou, O Justice, who wast never contaminated, O Eve who hast brought forth Emmanuel.[28]

Mary rules as Queen of heaven and earth:

As thou, O Lord, hast rejoiced the heavenly armies, on this day, whereon thou hast raised up Mary, thy Mother, to heaven in body and soul, and where thou hast made her to sit on a throne elevated over all the choirs of angels, and where thou hast made her Queen of the heavenly spirits and of those who dwell on earth, we likewise rejoice, with spiritual joy, free from all human passion; grant us to feel at every moment the effect of the prayers which she makes for us and help her that she will favor us, so that we will be protected and can imitate her pure and divine life and merit to rejoice, after her example, on the day of our parting from this world, through thy grace and that

---

[24] Rahal, *op. cit.*, p. 231; Rahmani, Shihimo (*Bréviaire ferial*) (Charfet, 1902),p. 118.

[25] Rahal, *op. cit.*, p. 231; Rahmani, *op. cit.*, pp. 77, 244, 245.

[26] Rahal, *op. cit.*, p. 232.

[27] *Ibid.*, p. 233.

[28] *Ibid.*, p. 234.

of thy Father and thy Spirit, Amen.[29]

It was the Emperor Maurice (582-603) who extended the feast of the Assumption to the whole Byzantine Empire. This feast on August 15 is the most popular feast of the Mother of God in all the Eastern rites.[30] At an incensation the priest prays:

O Messias, our God ... Thou who hast glorified the memory of the Assumption of thy Mother, the Immaculate Virgin, accept the perfume of our incense. ... Grant that this may be in honor of thy Mother, Queen of Angels and Empress of Saints.[31]

Mary's Immaculate Conception, her utter sinlessness, her perpetual virginity, her suffering with Christ, her power of universal intercession are also celebrated in the various prayers of the Antiochene rite.

The Maronite liturgy has this hymn to Mary:

Hail, Mary, ever Virgin, Mother of the Almighty who fills both the heavens and the earth.

Hail, Mary, ever virgin, Mother of the Ancient of Days whose name was before the sun was created. Hail, Mary, ever virgin, Mother of Him who made Adam from the mold of the earth.

Hail, Mary, ever virgin, Mother of Him who formed Eve and gave her to Adam.

Blessed art thou, Mary, the Mother of Him who gave righteousness and virtue to the sons of Levi.

Blessed art thou, Mary, for within thee dwelt the Only-Begotten, the Light of the Father, the Child of the Godhead.

Blessed art thou, Mary, for thou hast nourished Him who giveth to all creatures to eat.

Blessed art thou, Mary, who hast carried in thy lap and arms the Son of the Most High whom the powers of heaven acclaim.

All generations bless thy maidenhood, for He who is born of thee hath driven the curse of fear from the earth. We too bless thee, O holy Virgin, here kneeling before thee. Intercede with the Lord who was born of thee that He may bestow His graces on all people and ever have pity on us. Praise to Thee, O Lord, born of a Virgin, who became man, uniting two natures and two wills in one person. Glory be to

---

[29] *Ibid.*, pp. 234, 235.

[30] *Ibid.*, p. 235.

[31] *Ibid.*, p. 236.

Thee, to Thy Father, and to Thine Holy Spirit, three persons in one undivided God. Amen.[32]

A Syrian prayer to Mary:

How can I praise thee duly, O most chaste Virgin? For thou alone among men art all holy, and thou givest to all the help and grace they need. All we who are on earth put our hope in thee: strengthen our faith, shine through the dimness of this world, while we, children of the Church, sing thy praise. Throne of the cherubim art thou and Gate of Heaven; pray without ceasing for us, that we may be saved in the day of dread. Amen.[33]

A Maronite prayer to Mary:

Let thine intercession be with us, O Mother most pure, and come to us in our need as is thy wont. We are exiles on this earth, with our end before our eyes, and even now many of us perish; help us by thy prayers, O merciful Maiden, and be always our Advocate lest we be lost through our own ill will. Blessed and most holy one, plead for us before God, who was carried in thy womb, that He may be pitiful to us through thine asking. Amen.[34]

Both the Antiochene and Chaldean liturgies glory in the splendid writings of their illustrious Doctor, St. Ephrem of Edessa and Nisibis. It is especially in his poems and sermons on the glories and power of the Mother of God that he is famous in the whole Church. One of his prayers to Mary is used on the feast of Mary, Mediatress of All Graces in the Roman Seraphic Breviary:

O my Queen, most holy Mother of God, full of grace, endless sea of divine and secret gifts and graces ... Queen of all after the Trinity, another Consoler after the Paraclete, and Mediatress of the whole world after the Mediator, see my faith and my desire divinely given. ... Mother of God ... Thou hast taken away all tears from the face of the earth, thou hast filled creation with every kind of benefice, thou hast brought joy to those in heaven, thou hast saved those on earth. Through thee we hold a most certain guarantee of our resurrection; through thee we hope to gain the heavenly kingdom; through thee all glory, honor and holiness, O only immaculate one, has been derived, are derived and will be derived from Adam to the consummation of

---

[32] D. Attwater, *Prayers from the Eastern Liturgies* (London, 1931), pp. 17, 18.
[33] *Ibid.*, p. 20.
[34] *Ibid.*

the world for the Apostles, Prophets, the just and humble of heart; and every creature rejoices in thee, O thou full of grace.[35]

A prayer of St. Ephrem to Mary Immaculate:

O pure and immaculate and likewise blessed Virgin, who art the sinless Mother of thy Son, the Mighty Lord of the universe, thou who art inviolate and altogether holy, we sing thy praises. We bless thee, as full of grace, thou who didst bear the God-man; we all bow low before thee; we invoke thee and implore thine aid. Rescue us, O holy and inviolate Virgin, from every necessity that presses upon us and from all the temptations of the devil. Be our intercessor and advocate at the hour of death and judgment: deliver us from the fire that is not extinguished and from the outer darkness; make us worthy of the glory of thy Son, O dearest and most clement Virgin Mother. Thou indeed art our only hope most sure and sacred in God's sight, to whom be honor and glory, majesty and dominion for ever and ever world without end. Amen.[36]

Thus the Antiochene liturgy in its various forms and parts gives magnificent testimony to the faith of the Syrians, Maronites, and Malankarese in all the glories, privileges and power of the all-holy and immaculate Virgin Mary, Mother of God.

IV. MARY IN THE ARMENIAN LITURGY

The Armenian liturgy is used by the Armenians alone. These people formerly lived between the Caucasus and Taurus Mountains, the Black Sea and the Caspian Sea. Greater Armenia was to the east of the Euphrates, and Lesser Armenia to the west. In later times the Armenians also lived in Cilicia. They are an Indo-Germanic people and so their language is of the same origin. In 294 they received their first bishop in the person of St. Gregory the Illuminator, who baptized King Tiridates. The Armenians glory in being the first nation to embrace the true Faith officially and in a body. The Armenian Church went into schism about the year 500, repudiating

---

[35] *Breviarium Romano-Seraphicum* (Romae, 1943), Pars Verna, 31 Maii, II Noct.

[36] *The Raccolta of Prayers and Devotions* (edited by J. P. Christopher and C. E. Spence: New York, 1944), No. 339, pp. 252, 253. Cf. G. *De Vries, S.I., Oriente Cristiano Ieri e Oggi* (Roma, 1949), pp. 339-356. A. A. King, *The Rites of Eastern Christendom*, Vol. 1, pp. 61-336.

for political reasons the Council of Chalcedon (a.d. 451). Toward the end of the twelfth century Armenians who had fled from the Mohammedans founded the Kingdom of Little Armenia in Cilicia and were reunited to Rome. More and more have entered the Church through the centuries. Both Catholic and Dissident Armenians use the same rite.

1. The Mass

The Armenian liturgy is basically the Greek liturgy of St. Basil, translated into classical Armenian, and then modified in the course of time by Syrian, Constantinopolitan, and finally Latin influences. Thus it is unique among all the liturgies. It is a rich and splendid liturgy and is marked by constantly uniting Christ and Mary in the divine cult. The first invocation to Mary is at the beginning of Mass. There is another on her feasts. After the Trisagion her intercession is again invoked. In the Preface she is called the "Instrument of the Divine Economy." In the context the Incarnation is recalled and Mary is named the "Mother of God and the Holy Virgin Mary." She is again invoked shortly after the Consecration.[1]

2. The Ritual

Mary is constantly invoked in the administration of both the sacraments and sacramentals. She is the companion of all human joys and sorrows. In the blessing of a betrothal we read:

Today the ineffable mystery, hidden to the nations and to the tepid, has been revealed by the Annunciation of the Archangel to the Virgin Mary, our Advocate with the Lord.

For Holy Viaticum:

By the intercession of the ever Virgin Mother of God, save me from the snare of the invisible enemy.

For Benediction:

Thou who wert inflamed by the sun like the bush, and wert not consumed, but hast given to men the Bread of Life, intercede with Christ that He blot out our sins.

---

[1] 1 V. Tekeyan, *La Mère de Dieu dans la liturgie arménienne* in H. du Manoir, S.J., *Maria. Études sur la Sainte Vierge*, Vol. 1 (Paris, 1949), pp. 355-361.

In the blessing for grapes, on the feast of the Assumption, Mary is again honored.

> When Thou hast willed finally to manifest Thy paternal love for men, Thou hast sent Thy only Son, making a branch come forth from the root of Jesse and an admirable and perfumed Flower to come forth from the Immaculate Virgin Mary.[2]

3. Divine Office

At Matins, Mary is invoked daily. On Sundays she is named ten times at Matins and still oftener on her feasts. She is also named on feasts of saints and on days of abstinence. An example:

> O Lord, who lovest men, by the intercession of Thy Holy and Immaculate Virgin Mother and by Thy precious Cross, hear our prayers and save us.

After the Magnificat there are three strophes in honor of Mary. She is called "Holy Mother of Admirable Light." One strophe reads:

> Pray for us to God, who took flesh of thee so that He would unite His Holy Church built on the foundation of the Apostles and the Prophets, and that He would preserve it immaculate to the day of His second coming, we beg thee, Holy Mother, intercede for us.

After the Trisagion there is another prayer to Mary beginning with the words: "Holy Mary, Mother of Christ, our God" attributed to St. Thomas the Apostle. On Wednesday, dedicated to the Annunciation, the final hymn is dedicated to Mary:

> O Spouse offered by earth to heaven, we raise our hearts to thee. Pray that on the day on which thou hast received the annunciation of the Incarnation, we may be worthy to hear from thy only Son this other message, Come ye blessed of my Father.

The final hymn of None is dedicated to Mary. At Compline:

> We prostrate before thee, Mother of God, and we beg thee unchangeable Virgin, to intercede for us and pray thy only Son that He would save us from temptation, and from all dangers.[3]

4. Marian Feasts

In the hymns used for Marian feasts we see the great love and

---

[2] *Ibid.*, pp. 355, 356.

[3] *Ibid.*, pp. 356-357.

devotion of the Armenians to the Mother of God. There are six classical Marian feasts, Christmas, Epiphany, Purification, Annunciation, Assumption, and Immaculate Conception. The names and invocations used for these feasts are similar to those found in the Litany of Loreto, or those used by other Eastern liturgies. Thus Mary is called "Throne of Salvation," "Dawn of Peace," "Orient of the Sun of Justice," "Daughter of Light," "Altar of the Holy Spirit," "Tree of Life for the Fruit of Immortality," "Peace of the Afflicted," "Foundation of the Church," "Mediatress Between God and the Human Race," "Joy of the World."[4]

The Armenian liturgy does not go far in the development of Marian doctrine. But it insists on the great dignity of Mary in various offices and titles. Some examples will suffice:

Divine Maternity and Perpetual Virginity

Mary is styled "Holy Mother of Admirable Light"; "Mother of the Only Begotten"; "She who brought forth the Word"; "Mother of Life"; "Mother of the Spouse of the Church"; "Abode of the Incarnation." On the Assumption she is addressed thus:

More sublime than the Seraphs and the Cherubs with multiple eyes, O Mother of the Saviour, Holy Virgin, Ark of the Covenant, Vessel of Gold, Mysterious Altar of the Word of the Father, the Churches of the world today keep festive day with hymn of benediction for the solemnity of thy birth [entrance into heaven].

On the third day of the octave of Epiphany:

O Mother and Virgin, Servant of Christ, who art ever the Advocate of the world, all nations bless Thee. Pure dove, heavenly Spouse, Mary, Temple and Throne of God the Word, all nations bless thee.

Mother and Virgin — these two grand privileges of Mary are ever united in the liturgical prayers:

Three tremendous mysteries are manifested in thee, O Mother of God: Virginal Conception, immaculate childbirth, and virginity after childbirth.

Mary is called: "Delight of the Word"; "Mother of Virgins";

---

[4] *Ibid.*, pp. 357-358.

"Unconsumed Bush"; "Lily of the Valleys"; "Rock cut without the aid of human hands"; "Sealed Fountain"; "Fleece of Gedeon"; "Sealed Door"; "Incorruptible Treasure."

The divine Maternity is always the grand theme in these liturgical prayers. Mary is the final preparation for Christ, as the branch bears the fruit. She is the "Rising of the Sun of Justice" (Assumption); the "Spiritual Orient"; the "Tree of life planted in the Garden of Eden, who has given its fruit to men, namely the Son" (Epiphany). "Joachim and Anna have given us the Fleece that contains the heavenly Rose" (Nativity of Mary). She is the "Temple of the Creator" (Octave of the Assumption); the "Temple of the King of the Heavens" (*ibid.*); the "Abode of the Holy Spirit" (Assumption); the "House and Temple of the Spirit" (Octave of the Assumption).

The holiness of Mary is not much developed in this liturgy. At times it is affirmed in strong terms: Mary has received the sevenfold grace; she is entirely blessed. Her holiness is understood in connection with her divine Maternity.[5]

Mary, Our Mediatrix

The Armenian liturgy often treats of the advantages we have from God through the intercession of Mary. She is our Mediatrix, the Patroness of the Church, the Queen of the World, the Hope and Refuge of Christians. Owing to the many persecutions of the Armenians, they learned to hope and trust in the Mother of God to help them, and deliver them from all their enemies. Mary is "She who has born Him who delivers us from the bonds of death"; Mary is the "Salvation of the human race"; Mary is the "Tree of life, who has given the fruit of immortality to the first mother Eve, delivering her from the sorrows of death"; "Thou art the Glory of human Virginity, the Joy of Angels, thou, the one who liberates from malediction." Through Mary we have access to the Tree of Life. "Rejoice, O Mother of God, Throne of salvation and Hope of the human race, Mediatrix of Law and of Grace."[6]

---

[5] *Ibid.*, pp. 358-359.

[6] *Ibid.*, p. 359.

Mary, Patroness of the Church

This title is dear to the Armenian people and has been in their liturgy for ages. "May Christ protect His Church, by the intercession of the Mother of God." Mary is the "Foundation of the Church and the Altar of the Holy Spirit." "By the intercession of the all-holy Virgin, fortify the foundations of Thy Church, for Thou art the unique Sovereign Lord of the World." "The Church of thy Son acknowledges thee, Mother of God." "The Church confesses the Holy Virgin Immaculate." "Today the Spouse, Holy Church, celebrates with joy, in company with the heavenly spirits, the solemnity of the Immaculate Virgin, Mother of God."[7]

Mary, Queen of the Universe

Mary is the Queen of the Universe. She "carried in her arms Him before whom the celestial spirits tremble." "Before her the Powers are prostrate." "The Legions of Heavens exalt the Immaculate Temple of the Word of God." "We, the human race, we glorify thee, Mother of God, whom the angelic powers honor." "Mother of God, when thou takest thy place, radiant Light, at the right hand of thy Son, call upon Him then, that He save us from the horrible flame."[8]

Mary, Hope and Refuge of Christians

There are many invocations that show the confidence of the faithful in Mary's power as the Hope and Refuge of Christians. "Mother of God, our Refuge and our Hope, pray to thy only Son, that He save us from the fire of hell and grant us the Kingdom of Heaven." "Never cease to pray for us, O Blessed among all women." "We have placed our hope in thee; thou, who art brighter than the sun, do not cease to intercede for us, Mother of Christ, our God." "We take refuge in thee, O most Holy One, Sublime, Admirable One, and distributor of graces; thou art a fountain for the thirsty, rest for the afflicted, thou who hast born the Word Divine."[9]

---

[7] *Ibid.*, pp. 359, 360.

[8] *Ibid.*, p. 360.

[9] *Ibid.*

The Immaculate Conception and the Assumption of Mary

Although the Armenian liturgy has no theological formula of the Immaculate Conception, the terms it uses for Mary's sinlessness must be understood in the most absolute sense. Mary "alone is blessed among all women"; she is the "Daughter of Light"; she has "lifted the curse"; she is "The one who frees from the sin of Eve."

The feast of Mary's Assumption is the greatest Marian feast among the Armenians. It is preceded by a week of abstinence and celebrated with an octave. This feast is rooted in the most ancient traditions of the Armenian Church. The liturgical prayers are explicit in regard to the bodily Assumption of Mary:

Today the heavenly spirits bring to heaven the Abode of the Holy Spirit, making her enter into the heavenly Jerusalem, to the immaculate tabernacle, to us inaccessible, close to the Holy Trinity.

Today the celestial spirits have carried to heaven the immaculate body of the Virgin Mother of God, placing it among the angels to share in delights beyond our telling. Therefore Holy Church sings to thee exultingly a new hymn of praise.

Having lived in this body an immaculate life, thou art brought by the Divine Will to the Kingdom of thy Son, our God; pray for us.[10]

An Armenian hymn to Mary:

Mother of God, gateway of Heaven to men, with a divine voice the angel declared: Hail, full of grace, the Lord is with thee. He who sitteth with the Father above the cherubim, was pleased to dwell within thy maiden body; Hail, full of grace, the Lord is with thee.

He who dwelt amid the flaming seraphim was seen among men in a woman's arms; Hail, full of grace, the Lord is with thee.[11]

The many prayers to Mary and the titles the Armenians give her prove their ancient and ardent devotion to the Mother of God. They honor her with a sublime cult, and ask her to bring the Dissident back to the true Church.

---

[10]   *Ibid.*, pp. 360-361. *Ritual, Mashdotz* (Vienna, 1902). *Hymnodium* (Charagnotz, Venezia, 1898).

[11] D. Attwater, *Prayers from the Eastern Liturgies* (London, 1931), pp. 16, 17.

SELECTED BIBLIOGRAPHY

Attwater, D., *Eastern Catholic Worship* (New York, 1945).

Brightman, F. E., *Liturgies Eastern and Western* (Oxford, 1896), pp. 412-457.

Isserverdentz, *The Armenian Ritual* (Venice, 1876).

– *Armenia and the Armenians* (Venice, 1886).

King, A. A., *The Rites of Eastern Christendom*, Vol. 11 (Rome, 1948), pp. 521-646.

Talatinian, B., O.F.M., *L'Assunta nella liturgia e teologia della Chiesa Armena*, in *Atti del Congresso Assunzionisiico Orientale* (Gerusalemme, 1951), pp. 17-30.

Weber, *Die Katholische Kirche in Armenien* (Freiburg i/Br., 1903).

V. MARY IN THE CHALDEAN LITURGY

This liturgy is used by the Christians of Mesopotamia, Persia, and Malabar, and derives from the primitive liturgy in an East Syrian form. In ancient times Edessa was its center. In the fifth century this portion of the Church lapsed into Nestorianism. Many members of this rite are still Nestorians. Others, since 1551, have become Catholics and are known as Chaldeans in Mesopotamia and Persia, and as Malabarese on the Malabar coast of India. Both Catholics and Dissidents of this rite use the liturgy of SS. Addai and Mari. All, except the Malabarese, use also two other anaphoras on Sundays and feasts from Advent until Palm Sunday and five other days of the year.

1. The Mass

Mary is honored in the Holy Sacrifice in the litany before the Offertory:

> For the memorial of the blessed Lady Mary the holy Virgin, Mother of Christ our Saviour and Lifegiver, let us pray. Amen. That the Holy Ghost who dwelt in her, sanctify us by His grace and perfect His will in us and seal in us His truth all the days of our life.

She is mentioned again by the deacon at the Offertory:

> Glory be to the Father and to the Son and to the Holy Ghost. On the holy altar let there be a memorial of the Virgin Mother of Christ. From everlasting to everlasting world without end.[1]

2. The Divine Office

In the Office Mary is given a great place. In the hymns three times a week, Mary is invoked after the invocation to God or to Christ. She it is "who gave birth to the Remedy which vivifies the children of Adam." She is "the holy Virgin, the Mother of Jesus, the Saviour." She is "the Mother of the King of Kings." She is invoked for "mercy for sinners, peace for the whole world, protection for the Church from the wicked; for the end of wars and for blessing on the seasons of the year; and (finally) for entrance into the Kingdom."

---

[1] F. E. Brightman, *Liturgies, Eastern and Western* (Oxford, 1896), pp. 264, 268.

Wednesday is dedicated to her. She is honored with a special couplet twice that day, and at evening the priest prays:

> O Lord, our God, defend us with solid and invincible arms, by the prayers of the holy Mother, the blessed Virgin Mary, and give us with her a portion of heavenly glory.

Another Wednesday prayer has this splendid praise of Mary:

> Mary has glorified the Word, the Son, with a great glory in her bosom, and she has become the Mother and Servant of Jesus, the Saviour of all. Therefore all creatures rejoice on her feast and are invited to the luminous reunion for the joy that will have no end; and all of us, with all generations, we call her blessed, and we give glory to Him, who has chosen her for the habitation of His glorious Image.

The following prayer is similar to the Latin "Sub tuum praesidium" in affirming Mary's universal intercession:

> We take refuge at every hour, chaste Mary, under the protection of thy prayers; they defend us at all times, and through them we shall find mercy and pity on the day of judgment.

Every day in the Office, morning and evening, in the hymns for the martyrs, there is a strophe in honor of Mary, just before the doxology. Thus, e.g., on Thursday evening:

> Blessed art thou, holy Virgin; blessed art thou, Mother of God; blessed art thou, for all generations call thee blessed. Blessed art thou, for the Father has been in thee, the First-Born has dwelt in thee, and the Holy Spirit has glorified thy name in the world.[2]

3. Feasts in Honor of Mary

Mary is not invoked especially on Sundays, but she has various special feasts in the course of the year. First there are three ancient feasts that testify to the devotion of the Chaldeans to Mary. They have a peculiar Eastern charm.

The Feast of the Congratulation of the Holy Virgin. This is celebrated the day after Christmas. Its purpose is to felicitate Mary on the birth of Christ. It is known in the whole East as a Marian feast, but the Chaldeans have beautiful hymns for the day. These were composed by George Warda in the thirteenth century, and

---

[2] A. M. Massonat, O.P., *Marie dans la Liturgie Chaldéenne*, in H. du Manoir, S.J., *Maria. Études sur la Sainte Vierge* (Paris, 1949), Vol. 1, pp. 343-351.

apply figures of the Old Testament to the Mother of God. The Chaldeans delight in these hymns. These thoughts occur in one of them:

> The Church says to Mary: Come and we will go together to pray the Son of the Lord for the sins of the world. Pray thou to Him because thou hast nourished Him; I shall pray to Him for He has mingled His blood with my nuptials. Pray thou to Him as a Mother, and I as a spouse; He will hear His Mother, He will answer His bride.

The Feast of Our Lady, Guardian of the Harvest is a popular local feast in Mesopotamia, and is celebrated on May 15, to ask Mary's blessing on the harvest, which begins at that time. There is no mention of this special intention in the Office, but the powerful intercession of Our Lady is brought out in the prayers:

> O Christ, who has heard the prayers of Thy Mother while she was on earth, and who now hears and helps at all times those who have recourse to her and call upon Thee for her mediation, have mercy on us.

> Mary is the source of help and the refuge of the afflicted in all creation. And he who celebrates the feasts of Mary will be helped by her prayers. Glory to Thee, O Lord, Son of God, who hast honored Mary, Thy Mother.

The Assumption of Mary, August 15, is the greatest Marian feast for the Chaldeans. They fast for five days before it; the Nestorians for seven days. The traditional Chaldean idea is that the Apostles, the Prophets, and the angels were present with Our Lady on the day of her death. This is based on the Eastern custom of people coming together when a person is dying. Some of the Apostles rose from the dead for this occasion; so, too, did the Prophets and Patriarchs, says this liturgy.

> We thank Thee and glorify Thee, O Christ, our Saviour, that it pleased Thy majesty to transfer the Mother of life from the terrestrial world to places full of joy, so that she can rejoice eternally with the legions of spirits and the heavenly powers. In Thy mercy, O Lord, render us worthy of rejoicing with her in life that will have no end.[3]

---

[3] *Ibid.*, pp. 344-346. H. W. Codrington, *The Chaldaean Liturgy*, in *Eastern Churches Quarterly* (Ramsgate), Vol. 11, April, July, October, 1937. M. Kyriakos, *L'Assomption chez les Chaldéens, in Atti del Congresso*

Since the Chaldeans have returned to the Catholic Church, four other Marian feasts have been added to their calendar, namely the Annunciation, the Visitation, the Nativity of Our Lady, and the Immaculate Conception. For the Annunciation the liturgy has merely prayers composed by the Patriarch Joseph Audo at the time of Pius IX, and certain texts of the Advent liturgy from the Gospels. For the feast of the Visitation (June 21) there are also prayers of the Patriarch Audo and commentaries on the Gospel narrative of the Visitation. The feast of the Nativity of Our Lady has prayers likewise of the Patriarch Audo and a hymn from the works of George Warda.

The prayers for the feast of the Immaculate Conception contain excellent doctrine. They are the work of Damian, a priest of the monastery of Alkosh.

> Glory to the Highest, who has done great things in Mary the Virgin, for from the bosom of His Mother, He has brought it to pass that she has none like to her among the angels.

> O Christ, who hast freed Mary from the sin of Adam by the merits of Thy blood, and hast effected her redemption in a manner far superior to that of all the children of Adam, by not allowing her, for even a second, to be under the rule of the Evil One, have mercy on us.

> A beautiful flower, without equal, has appeared this day on the barren earth, full of thorns and thistles: Mary, of the race of the unfortunate Adam and daughter of Eve, who killed the serpent, was conceived by the power of the Lord without original sin. It is an astonishing and incomprehensible thing which no words can describe. Glory to the power divine!

> O Queen of Queens, all rich, enrich with benefits thy servants, O Mother of the Most High! For He has made thee the Dispensatrix of His treasures, and universal Queen, for it has pleased the King of Kings to place Thee over all. By thy goodness, pour out on all the gifts they need, so that the whole world can prepare for thee a crown of thanks.

> How beautiful art thou, O Virgin Spouse, for the glorious Spouse, the Divine Word! It is in thy bosom that He has placed His treasures, and in thee He has gathered together graces as in a sea, and He has made

---

Assunzionistico Orientale (Gerusalemme, 1951), pp. 33-37. O. Mensinger, *Mariologisches aus der vorephesinischen Liturgie* (Regensburg, 1932).

thee the source of life for mortals. ... O Merciful One in needs, come to the help of all the children of the Church, now and at the hour of death.[4]

4. Mary in Popular Chaldean Devotion

When we recall the important role the liturgy played in the daily life of the Chaldean people, and how its texts and hymns strengthened and developed their spiritual life, we can well understand the great love and devotion they have ever had for the Mother of God, who is so highly praised in their liturgy. Some of their important churches are dedicated to her. Thus at Mosul, the city of the Patriarch, there is the Church of The Pure, where the liturgy was developed. Nearby is the Monastery of the Virgin, the largest monastery of the Chaldean monks of the Congregation of Rabban Hormez. Our Lady of the Harvest extends her maternal care to the young priests, who are generally ordained on that feast day, May 15. Many of the faithful bear the name of Mary or of Our Lady of the Assumption. A frequent exclamation in time of danger, or after long work, is "la Mariam," "O Mary." Many persons make a vow to fast on Saturday in honor of Our Lady; or to celebrate the months of May and October by reading lectures on Mary added to the Marian Offices, or by reciting the Rosary publicly. In many churches in Mesopotamia some women take turns reciting the Rosary during the day. This they do in the language of Christ and Mary.

Thus the liturgy of the Chaldeans agrees with the other Catholic liturgies in praising the Mother of God and asking her all-powerful intercession. The Catholics of this rite were once very numerous and their liturgy is very ancient. In fact it is claimed that their Office is the most ancient public prayer of the Church.[5] The Chaldeans brought the true Faith to the East as far as China, Mongolia, and India. They glory in many saints and martyrs, but especially in St. Ephrem the Deacon, Doctor of the Church, who is called the Lyre

---

[4] Massonat, *op. cit.*, pp. 348-350.

[5] Kyriakos, *op. cit.*, p. 34. Tfinkji, *L'Eglise chaldéene* (Paris, 1913). Rabban, *La Messa caldea detta "Degli Apostoli"* (Roma, 1935). D. Attwater, *The Christian Churches of the East*, Vol. I, pp. 198-209; ibid., Vol. II, pp. 185-198. D. Attwater, *Eastern Catholic Worship* (New York, 1945). A. A. King, *The Rites of Eastern Christendom*, Vol. 11, pp. 251-520.

of the Holy Spirit. He is justly famous for his great poems on the Mother of God, and his defense of her Immaculate Conception. Chaldean devotion to the Blessed Virgin impresses the heretics and even the Mohammedans, and it should help them to enter the true Church of Christ.

MARY IN THE WESTERN LITURGY

By Simeon Daly, O.S.B.

INTRODUCTION

F ANYONE is tempted to feel that devotion to Mary is a prerogative of our own age, he need only look to the sacred liturgy to realize that this devotion is a part of the very structure of Catholic worship. Mary's life and privileges are completely summarized in the cycle of the Church year.[1]

Among the feasts honoring the memory of her early life are the Immaculate Conception, the Nativity, and the Presentation. The hallowed activities of her adult life are recalled in such feasts as the Annunciation, the Espousals with St. Joseph, the Visitation, the Maternity, the Holy Family, the Seven Sorrows, and the Assumption. In the temporal cycle of the liturgical year she frequently holds a place of veneration in the feasts of Our Lord, such as Christmas, Epiphany, and the Presentation. Hence, to be ignorant of her place of honor in Catholic life is to miss not only an essential doctrine but the very key to the area of Catholic worship which is so thoroughly permeated with veneration of her.

This study is concerned with Mary's place in the Western liturgy. Specifically, the main objective will be to find reflected in the Western liturgy evidence of the dogmatic truths we profess concerning Our Lady. One should find here the answer to the question: How does the worship of the Christian society, which is the Church, reflect a vital realization of the dogmas concerning the Blessed Mother?

Our field of investigation is limited to the Western liturgies and even here limited primarily to the Roman liturgy. This is not a

---

[1] Henry Lawrence Janssens, O.S.B., *De cyclo liturgico mariali*, in *Ephemerides Liturgicae*, Vol. 38, 1924, pp. 157-161. Cf. P. Oppenhcim, O.S.B., *Maria nella liturgia cattolica* (Roma, 1944); *Maria in der lateinischen Liturgie*, in *Katholische Marienkunde*, ed. P. Sträter, Vol. 1 (Paderborn, 1947), pp. 183-267.

structural or an historical study of the individual feasts, but rather a factual investigation of the relation between dogma and prayer in Mariology.

The method of procedure briefly will be as follows: a few remarks on the liturgy in relation to faith; a résumé of the facts concerning the initial traces of honor paid to Mary in the liturgy; a study of the main doctrines of Mariology: Maternity, Sanctity, Virginity, Queenship, and Mediation, as reflected in the Marian feasts; the presentation of a few feasts and devotions not included in the above; and, finally, a brief conclusion to the whole study.

The term *liturgy* may be taken in its primary meaning, which is the active work of redemption that Christ continues to carry on and to apply through the Church in the Holy Sacrifice and the Sacraments, or it may apply to the concrete records of the Church's tradition which form the basic guide or norm for current practice, such as the texts themselves of the official books of the liturgy. It is the latter meaning of the word that we shall use in this paper.[2]

The sacred liturgy is the life of the Church. Through it she continues the divine mysteries of the life of Christ and applies their saving graces to men. Through it she offers worthy praise and thanksgiving night and day throughout the world; through it she offers expiation and satisfaction for sin and pleads with God for all the individual needs of this society; through it she reconsecrates to God persons and things, as it were, lost to Him by Adam's sin. By means of the liturgy, then, we are drawn into bonds of closest union with the saints in heaven.

Our study of the texts of this liturgy will take us to the Missal, the Breviary, the Pontifical, and the Ritual, which are the official source books in the Roman Church for sacrifice, prayer, and blessings.

Getting closer to the heart of our study, we must first see the important relationship between faith and worship, between our believing and our praying, between dogma and cult.

LITURGY IN RELATION TO FAITH

---

[2] For the other meaning cf. C. Howell, S.J., *The Blessed Virgin in the liturgy,* in *Orate Fratres,* Vol. 24, 1949, pp. 1-8. Also published as *Marian Reprint,* No. 17 (Dayton, Ohio, Marian Library, 1953).

There are two fundamental principles that must be considered in this regard, namely, that what is to be found in the liturgy must have its foundation in the canons of the Faith, and that not all the doctrines of faith are necessarily reflected in the liturgy. The latter is important in the discussion of our particular paper because we know that at least in the Western liturgy, there is no trace of Marian cult before the fifth century, yet we know that devotion and doctrine concerning Our Blessed Lady did exist right from the time of the Apostles. There is no necessary demand that what be of faith be also in the liturgy. The other principle, however, namely, that what is in the liturgy must have its foundation in faith, will concern us more directly in this study.

Our Holy Father, Pope Pius XII, in his encyclical letter, *Mediator Dei*, points up the importance of the interrelationship between faith and prayer, and specifically liturgical prayer. He quotes the time-honored maxim or principle, *Legem credendi lex statuat supplicandi*[3] (let the law of prayer determine the rule for belief). He stresses the importance of this statement and yet warns against its false interpretation. He says:

> On this subject We judge it Our duty to rectify an attitude with which you are doubtless familiar, Venerable Brethren. We refer to the error and fallacious reasoning of those who have claimed that the sacred liturgy is a kind of proving ground for the truths to be held of faith, meaning by this that the Church is obliged to declare such a doctrine sound when it is found to have produced fruits of piety and sanctity through the sacred rites of the liturgy and to reject it otherwise. ... But this is not what the Church teaches and enjoins. The worship she offers to God, all good and great, is a continuous profession of Catholic faith and a continuous exercise of hope and charity. ... The entire liturgy, therefore, has the Catholic Faith for its content, inasmuch as it bears public witnesss to the faith of the Church. ...

> The sacred liturgy, consequently, does not decide or determine independently and of itself what is of Catholic faith. More properly, since the liturgy is also a profession of eternal truths and subject as such to the Supreme Teaching Authority of the Church, it can supply

---

[3] Denzinger, 139. *De gratia Dei "Indiculus"* until recently attributed to Pope St. Celestine I. It was probably written by St. Prosper of Aquitaine. Cf. M. Cappuyns, O.S.B., *Revue Bénédictine*, Vol. 41, 1929, p. 156 ff.

proofs and testimony, quite clearly of no little value, towards the determination of a particular point of Christian doctrine.[4]

We see here that there is an interrelationship or interdependence one upon another, so that if we find something in the liturgy, it should also have its foundation in Catholic faith. This formula, *Legem credendi lex statuat supplicandi*, was originally used only in a specific instance, against the Pelagian heresy, pointing out that the sacraments and prayers of the liturgy as expressed in the liturgy were an argument for the true doctrine of grace. Though originally applied only to a specific problem, it was gradually taken up as a formula of universal extent until by the time of St. Thomas it was accepted as a general axiom or law. St. Thomas himself considered the liturgy as a prime source for doctrine, practically equating it at times with Scripture.[5]

It follows then that if we find reflected in the liturgy these doctrines regarding Mary's life and prerogatives, we have a very definite witness to their having been clearly the belief of the Church throughout the ages.

MATERNITY

Devotion to Mary must be reduced to the practical application of the doctrine of the Communion of Saints. Because this doctrine is not contained explicitly in the Apostles' Creed, there is no ground for surprise if we do not find any clear traces of the cult of the Blessed Virgin in the first Christian centuries.[6] In fact, at present it is impossible to determine the first manifestation of cult shown to the Virgin before the peace of the Church in the year 312. Catacomb monuments, frescoes, and the like, picture her with Our Lord, but

---

[4] Pius XII, *Encyclical Letter of His Holiness Pius XII, on Sacred Liturgy* (Vatican library translation) (Washington, D. C.: N.C.W.C. [n.d.]), pp. 20-21. The official text of the encyclical, *Mediator Dei,* will be found in A.A.S., Vol. 39, 1947, pp. 521-595.

[5] P. Oppenheim, O.S.B., *Institutiones systematico-historicae in sacram liturgiam,* Vol. 7, *Principia theologiae liturgicae* (Torino, Marietti, 1947), pp. 98-106. Oppenheim cites forty passages where St. Thomas appealed to liturgical usage or liturgical texts to establish his doctrine.

[6] H. Thurston, S.J., *Virgin Mary, Devotion to the Blessed,* in the *Catholic Encyclopedia,* Vol. 15, p. 459.

without particularly indicating that homage was offered to her.[7] However, one might justly suppose that, granting the fact of the universal recognition of her prerogatives,[8] men would extend to her a place of veneration at least equivalent to that of the martyrs.

By the second half of the fourth century, however, we have definite indication of the recognition of the legitimacy, even the urgency of this cult in Epiphanius.[9]

The real turning point for this veneration comes with the Council of Ephesus in 431. The history of this third ecumenical council of the Church reads like the pages of a novel, not only because of its complications, but also because of the great concern of the people for the accurate definition of Mary's motherhood.[10] From this time on, honor toward Mary was expressed in one way or another — through the dedication of churches, through the composition of prayers to her, and eventually in the seventh century (in the West) through the introduction of definite feasts.

That Marian cult developed from or was a sequel to the cult of angels is an opinion held among scholars, but without implying that it is anything more than a theory[11] and likewise without implying that there were insufficient doctrinal grounds for the cult to give rise to itself. It is a fact that in many of the ancient litanies the Archangels Michael and Gabriel are invoked after the Persons of the

---

[7] H. Leclercq, O.S.B., *Marie, Mère de Dieu; culte liturgique*, in *DACL*, Vol. 102, c. 2035. Cf.: M. Armellini, *Notizie storiche intorno all'antichità del culto di Maria Vergine* (Roma, 1888).

[8] Primum factum [cultus venerationis] est Christianorum fides relate ad principales praerogativas et praecipue privilegia B. M. Virginis, videlicet: Eius divina maternitas, eius virginitas, eius universalis mediatio prout clare apparet ex frequenti antithesi inter Evam et Mariam. In symbolo (saltem inde a saeculo II in Occidente) habebantur verba: "natus ex Maria Virgine"; ex quo apparet B. Virginis privilegia nedum Patribus et Doctoribus sed etiam fidelibus a quibus symbolum recitabatur, et quibus antequam baptizarentur exponebatur, habitualiter nota esse. G. Roschini, O.S.M., *Compendium Mariologiae* (Romae: Scientia Catholica, 1946), pp. 487-488.

[9] *Haeres*, 79. *PG*, 41, 749-751.

[10] Cf. M. Barret, O.S.B., *Our Lady in the liturgy, considerations on certain feasts of the Mother of God* (London: Sands & Co.; St. Louis, Mo.: B. Herder, 1912), pp. 11-15. For the history of the Council see C. Hefele, *Histoire des Conciles* ... (Paris: Letouzey et Ané, 1907 —), Vol. 21, 1908, pp. 219-422.

[11] H. Thurston, *Virgin Mary*, p. 459.

Trinity and immediately before the Blessed Virgin.[12]

At any rate the devotion to and veneration of Mary took root in the period of a few centuries following the Council of Ephesus and expressed itself by liturgical prayer and liturgical feasts. While it is difficult to give precise dates for the introduction of the various feasts, it can be said with certainty that the feasts of the Assumption, the Annunciation, the Nativity, and the Purification can be traced to this period.[13]

The first prerogative of Mary that we turn to is her Maternity because it seems to be the final cause of all her other privileges.[14]

We look to the liturgy for a living, practical, poetical expression of the doctrine that Mary is truly the Mother of Christ, the God-Man, and further that she exercises spiritual motherhood over all men, especially over the Christians.

The first place that we naturally go to for reflections of the doctrine of the Maternity in the liturgy is the feast of the divine Maternity itself (October 11). Only in 1931 was this feast raised to the rank of a double of the second class for the universal Church by Pope Pius XI at the time of the fifteenth centenary of the Council of Ephesus.[15] Before that time, this doctrine which is reflected in all the Marian feasts was especially emphasized in the Advent and Christmas seasons, as I shall try to indicate later. The privilege of observing the feast of the Maternity was first granted to the King of

---

[12] M. Hasset, *Angels*, in the *Catholic Encyclopedia*, Vol. 1, p. 486a.

[13] H. Thurston, *Virgin Mary*, p. 462.

[14] A theory recently proposed merits consideration, namely, that the fullness of grace is the basic principle of Mariology. Alois Müller, *The basic principles of Mariology*, in *Theology Digest*, Vol. 1, 1953, pp. 139-144. This article is a condensation of one that appeared in *Divus Thomas* (Freiburg), Vol. 29, 1951, pp. 385-401, which in turn was the summary of the results of his patristic study as a doctoral thesis: *Ecclesia-Maria: Die Einheit Marias und der Kirche* (Freibourg, 1951).

[15] Pius XI, *Lux veritatis*, in *A.A.S.*, Vol. 23, 1931, pp. 493-517. In this encyclical Pope Pius XI ordered that a new Office and Mass be prepared, p. 517. They did not officially appear until the following year: *A.A.S.*, Vol. 24, 1932, pp. 151-159.

Portugal in 1751 and was assigned to the first Sunday in May.[16] In the Mass for this feast we find the following passages:

"Behold a Virgin shall conceive and bear a son" (Introit).

"O God who didst will that thy Word should take flesh at the message of an angel in the womb of the blessed Virgin Mary, grant unto us thy suppliants that we who believe her to be indeed the Mother of God may be aided by her intercession with thee" (Collect).

"There shall come forth a rod out of the root of Jesse: and a flower shall rise up out of his root" (Gradual).

"Virgin Mother of God, He whom the whole world cannot hold, enclosed Himself in thy womb, being made man" (Alleluia).

The Gospel speaks of "his parents."

"When his Mother Mary was espoused to Joseph, she was found with child of the Holy Ghost" (Offertory).

"Through thy mercy, O Lord, and by the intercession of the Blessed Mary ever Virgin, Mother of Thy Only-begotten Son, may this oblation secure for us present and perpetual prosperity and peace" (Secret).

"Blessed is the womb of the Virgin Mary, which bore the Son of the Eternal Father" (Communion).

"May this communion, O Lord, cleanse us from guilt, and by the intercession of the Blessed Virgin Mary, Mother of God, make us partakers of the heavenly remedy" (Postcommunion).

These passages give an opportunity to point out once for all the sources for the texts applied to Mary in the liturgical books.[17] Primarily, Sacred Scripture is the fount. Some passages of the Old Testament have their literal[18] fulfillment in Mary, e.g., "A virgin

---

[16] F. Holweck, *Calendarium liturgicum festorum Dei et Matris Mariae* (Philadelphia: *The American Ecclesiastical Review*, The Dolphin Press, 1925), p. 148 and passim. Cf. also his article on the Maternity in the *Catholic Encyclopedia*, Vol. 10, p. 40d.

[17] B. Capelle, O.S.B., *La liturgie Mariale en occident*, in *Maria. Études sur la Sainte Vierge*, edited by Hubert du Manoir, S.J. (Paris, Beauchesne, 1949), Vol. 1, pp. 236-237.

[18] For the full signification of the literal sense cf. M.-D. Philippe, O.P., *Remarques sur les signes divins, in Laval théologique et philosophique*, Vol. 5, 1949, pp. 111-118.

shall conceive." Some of the prophetic, messianic psalms, such as Psalm 44, seem to have direct application to her. Some texts are used in an accommodated sense, as, for example, the *Canticle of Canticles, Wisdom* literature, and the *Book of Judith*. In each of these the literal sense is some other more obvious fact, but for some extrinsic reasons they are applied to Mary. This gives rise to the mystical aura that pervades some of her feasts. The interpretation of the applied texts comes only from a knowledge of the Scripture background, knowledge of the Marian doctrines, and quiet contemplation.

Besides Scripture, texts from the Fathers are used, or even texts composed specifically for some feast or occasion. Thus, the beautiful Communion verse above is of ecclesiastical origin and is used quite frequently throughout the Missal and Breviary. It might be well to point out that many of these passages quoted in this paper for one or the other feast or doctrine frequently occur in other parts of the Breviary or Missal.

I remarked previously that this doctrine of the Maternity was clearly expressed and even emphasized in the liturgy long before Pope Pius XI promulgated the feast for the universal Church. The season of Advent, in fact, very dramatically and delicately makes constant reference to the Maternity of Our Lady[19] though always in reference to her future Maternity. Hence on days of temporal office in Advent, the doxology *Jesu, tibi sit gloria, Qui natus es de Virgine* in the Breviary must be omitted because of its reference to an already completed Maternity. The second Collect for ferial Masses in this season is the proper oration of the Blessed Virgin, which is identical with the one quoted above for the feast of the Maternity. While the words definitely affirm the Maternity of Mary as completed, there is also the "message of the angel" to give it an "annunciation" tone.[20]

The prophecy, "Behold a Virgin shall conceive and bear a son"

---

[19] Cf. Joseph Alvarez, *De Beata Maria Virgine in liturgia Adventus,* in *Ephemerides Mariologicae,* Vol. 1, 1951, pp. 531-533, and I. Schuster, O.S.B., *The Sacramentary,* translated from the Italian by Arthur Levelis-Marke (New York: Benziger Bros., 1930), Vol. 1, Advent, *passim.*

[20] This oration is also the same as the one for the feast of the Annunciation (March 25).

(Isa. 7:14), which comes in the Scripture lesson of the Saturday within the first week of Advent, the seventh responsory of the first Sunday of Advent, and the Communion antiphon of Ember Wednesday, keeps this privilege of Mary before our minds.

Gabriel's message to Mary threads its way in and out of the Divine Office and the Mass in the fourth week. Ember Wednesday and Friday, in fact, seem to be Marian feasts, always, however, maintaining the prophetic tone.[21]

The first Sunday of Advent, the vigil of Christmas, and the first Mass of Christmas are celebrated at the stational church of St. Mary Major. This particular church was chosen for these occasions in honor of Mary, who gave us Christ.[22]

The beautiful feast of Christmas and its octave particularly highlight Mary's Maternity. January 1 had been celebrated in Rome as a Marian feast, the first and only one of the early Marian feasts that originated in the West.[23] However, by the beginning of the ninth century, it was considered to be a feast of Our Lord, the Circumcision.

In whatever way the historians of the liturgy may solve the origins, the fact remains that Christmas and its octave are replete with striking references to the Maternity — Mary and Jesus cannot be separated here if the fullness of the mystery is to be preserved.[24]

---

[21] For an explanation of the origin of the Ave Maria as an Offertory verse for the fourth Sunday of Advent, cf. René-Jean Hesbert, O.S.B., *Antiphonale missarum sextuplex* (Bruxelles: Vromant & Co., 1935), pp. xxxviii-xxxix, xliv.

[22] Cf. *St. Andrew's Missal* for the first Sunday of Advent.

[23] F. Holweck, *Calendarium*, p. 1. Although the title definitely appears in manuscripts of calendars and missals, Hesbert seriously questions whether the feast was ever intended to be anything other than the octave of Christmas or possibly a misreading of *Natalis Sanctae Martinae*, who was honored on this day. R.-J. Hesbert, *Antiphonale missarum sextuplex*, p. lxxxi. Bernard Botte, O.S.B., argued the other view in *La première fête de la liturgie romaine* in *Ephemerides Liturgicae*, Vol. 47, 1933, pp. 425-430; holding that the feast of St. Martina did not appear in the calendars before the end of the seventh century and claiming that January 1 was celebrated as a Marian feast before it was celebrated as the octave of Christmas.

[24] For passages from the Breviary, translations will be taken, when possible, from: *The Roman Breviary* ... translated out of Latin into English by John, Marquess of Bute, K.T., a new edition (Edinburgh and London: W. Blackwood and Sons, 1908).

"This is the day whereon the King of Heaven was pleased to be born of a Virgin" (1st Responsory at Matins).

"How great is this mystery, how wonderful is the teaching of the faith! The beasts saw the new-born Lord lying in a manger. Blessed is that Virgin whose womb was made meet to bear our Lord Christ" (4th Responsory).

"Blessed is God's Holy Mother, Mary, maiden undefiled. This day hath she brought forth the Saviour of the world" (5th Responsory).

This last prayer is particularly beautiful, expressing so succinctly Mary's Maternity, sanctity, and virginity. The next responsories are equally beautiful, but these will suffice to show our point.

It would seem that the psalms of the first of the two Christmas offices are the source for the psalms of the Office of the Blessed Virgin. January 1 — the octave of Christmas (and probably a Marian feast) — uses the psalms of the first office; February 2 and other Marian feasts have the same psalms with only two modifications. The Office of Virgins then gets its series of psalms from these.[25]

In considering the Maternity, we cannot fail to look at the feast of the Annunciation of March 25 which was for centuries, liturgically speaking, a feast of the Maternity.[26] Both the Mass and the Office are replete with references to Our Lady's Maternity:

"O God, Who hast willed that ..." (Collect — same as for Maternity, see

---

[25] Georges Frénaud, O.S.B., *Le culte liturgique de Notre-Dame* in *Revue Grégorienne*, Vol. 31, 1952, p. 107. This is a section from a review of the first volume of Maria, edited by Du Manoir, with special attention to Abbot Capelle's contribution on Mary in the Western liturgy. This opinion counters that of Capelle who feels that the Office of Virgins is the source for the psalms of the Marian office. Cf. B. Capelle, *La liturgie Mariale en occident*, p. 236. Psalms for the feast of the Assumption, see his: *La fête de l'Assomption dans l'histoire liturgique*, in *Ephemerides Theologicae Lovanienses*, Vol. 3, 1926, pp. 39-41.

[26] One of the four earliest Marian feasts celebrated in the Roman Church. It probably dates from the middle of the seventh century. It is one of the four feasts for the celebration of which Sergius I (687-701) prescribed a procession in the *Liber Pontificalis*. The other three were: the Purification (February 2), the Assumption (August 15), and the Nativity (September 8). L. Duchesne, *Origines du culte chrétien, étude sur la liturgie latine avant Charlemagne*, 2. édition (Paris: A. Fontemoing, 1898), pp. 118, 261. (There is a fifth edition, 1925.) For the record of the spread of the feast of the Annunciation, cf. Holweck, *Calendarium*, pp. 60-61.

above).

"Receive, O Virgin Mary, receive the word of the Lord, which is sent thee by His angel. Thou shalt conceive and shalt bring forth God and Man together. And thou shalt be called blessed among all women" (3rd Responsory at Matins).

This is sufficient to show that the concept of Mary's Maternity is clearly expressed in the sacred liturgy. We do not find here the precision of expression that one expects in a theology textbook, but rather the living, pulsing expression of a praying Church animated with love and devotion.

It is interesting to note that the privileges of Mary are frequently mentioned in the Pontifical and the Ritual. A few expressions honoring her Maternity are: Sweet Mother; Dwelling Place of God; Dwelling Place of the Son of God; Mother of Christ; Mother of Our Lord Jesus Christ; The Word took flesh from her womb; She who bore Him and she who nourished Him at the breast.[27]

One ancient and beautiful prayer that is found in the Breviary, the Ritual, and the Pontifical honoring Mary's Maternity is the *Sub tuum praesidium* (Compline of Little Office; Versicle at 3rd Nocturn of Maternity and Mediatrix of all Grace).

> We take refuge under thy protection, O holy Mother of God. Despise not our supplications in our need, but deliver us from all dangers, O Ever Virgin, glorious and blessed.[28]

SANCTITY

The second concept or privilege of Mary we want to consider is her eminent sanctity. Rooted in the Scripture — "Hail, full of grace" — this doctrine has ever been evident in the teaching of the Church. The doctrine is implicitly contained in almost every feast honoring Mary, though there is no specific feast honoring her under this general title.

When we refer to Mary's sanctity we include all her privileges insofar as each, *de facto*, did increase her holiness, either actually, such as her Immaculate Conception, or, at least, by providing a

---

[27] A. Onofrio, *De B. V. Maria in precibus Ritualis et Pontificalis Romani*, in *Ephemerides Liturgicae*, Vol. 61, 1947, p. 104.

[28] This prayer will be discussed more at length later.

means for sanctity, such as her virginity.

Mary was not only free from any stain of original or actual sin, but her soul — more than any other except that of her own divine Son — was steeped in divine grace. The sacred liturgy expresses this in different ways.

From the feast of the Annunciation (March 25) we have the words of Scripture: "Hail Mary, full of grace, the Lord is with thee, blessed art thou among women" (Alleluia, Gospel, and Offertory). "Thou hast found grace with God" (Gospel). These phrases from the holy Gospel interlace the whole framework of this feast and keep returning like a theme in most of the feasts in which she is honored. In the Common Office of the Blessed Virgin, the fifth lesson taken from St. John Chrysostom has this magnificent passage:

> Verily, dearly beloved brethren, the Blessed Virgin Mary was a great wonder. What thing greater or more famous than she hath ever at any time been found or can be found? She alone is greater than heaven and earth. What thing holier than she hath been or can be found? Neither Prophets, nor Apostles, nor Martyrs, nor Patriarchs, nor Angels, nor Thrones, nor Lordships, nor Seraphim, nor Cherubim, nor any other creature visible or invisible can be found that is greater or more excellent than she. She is at once the handmaid and the parent of God, at once Virgin and Mother.

This passage certainly high-lights Mary's eminent holiness. Another passage from the Common Office expresses her sanctity very beautifully but less obviously:

> "I am black but comely, O ye daughters of Jerusalem. Therefore the king has loved me and brought me into his chambers" (3rd Antiphon of Lauds).

Perhaps the feast most intimately connected with the concept of sanctity is that of the Immaculate Conception, which honors Mary's singular prerogative of having been conceived from the very first moment free of any stain of sin. It is her triumph over Satan. She is mankind's one unspotted soul.

The doctrinal emphasis of this feast was implied in the feast of the Annunciation where Mary's fullness of grace and spotlessness of soul are stressed. A special feast seems to have developed from the parallel feast of the Conception of St. John the Baptist (September 24). The step from one to the other is not hard to recognize. The Eastern rite here too was ahead of the West. Already in the ninth century, in the Marble Calendar of Naples, there is a feast of the Conception of St. Ann. Although Naples is in the West, it was at that time under the Byzantine rule and this calendar entry represents a Byzantine feast.

Even so, the origin of the feast in the West seems to have been independent of this and cannot be placed much — if at all — before 1060. It seems to have been England's privilege to have introduced this feast to the West.[29] The question of Ireland's role as the first to have the feast seems to have been conclusively discounted, especially since it has been shown that the entries in the early Irish calendars were insertions of a later date.[30]

Pius IX defined the doctrine of the Immaculate Conception in 1854 (*Ineffabilis Deus*). In the document of the definition he refers to the presence of the feast in the liturgy as a sign and a reflection of the faith of the Church in the doctrine.[31] Sixtus IV had in 1477 extended the feast to the universal Church. The Mass and Office

---

[29] E. Bishop hinted that the extensive traffic between Rome and England in this period may well have influenced the passage of the feast from Italy to England: Liturgica historica (Oxford: Clarendon Press, 1918), p. 258. Cf. B. del Marmol, O.S.B., Quelques précisions sur le culte de la Vierge au XIIe siècle, in Mémoires et Rapports du Congrès Marial tenu à Bruxelles, 1921, Vol. 1 (Bruxelles, 1922), pp. 231-241.

[30] For a discussion of the whole problem of the origin of this feast, cf. Andrea M. Cecchin, O.S.M., *L'lmmacolata nella liturgia occidentale anteriore al secolo XIII* (Rome: Edizioni Marianum, 1943), pp. 15-27. Edmund Bishop has two studies in his Liturgica historica, pp. 239-259. The first is a reprint of an article in the Downside Review, April, 1886. The second (pp. 250-259) is an essay on "Irish Origins" of the feast which was written thirty years after the first essay. While his study is interesting and his methods commendable, the force of his argument has been lost now that Fr. Grosjean has pointed out that the entries in the Martyrology of Tallaght (end of the eighth century) and the Martyrology of Oengus (end of the eighth or beginning of the ninth century) relative to this feast (May 3, Conception of the Blessed Virgin Mary) are later insertions: Analecta Bollandiana, Vol. 61, 1943. pp. 91-95.

[31] "By which illustrious act she pointed out the conception Iof the Virgin as singular, wonderful, and very far removed from the origin of the rest of mankind and to be venerated as entirely holy, since the Church celebrates festival days only of what is holy." Pius IX, *Official documents connected with the definition of the dogma of the Immaculate Conception of the Blessed Virgin Mary* (in Latin and English) (Baltimore: J. Murphy, 1855), p. 62.

that he had approved on that occasion were replaced in 1863 by Pius IX with the Mass formula we have today. Leo XIII, on November 30, 1879, raised the feast from the rank of a double of the second class to that of a double of the first class with a common octave.

As is usually the case, the Oration for the feast captures the particular aspect or phase of doctrine the Church is stressing in her celebration.

> O God, who by the Immaculate Conception of the Virgin didst make her a worthy habitation for Thy Son, and didst by His foreseen death, preserve her from all stain of sin; grant we beseech Thee, that through her intercession we may be cleansed from sin and come with pure hearts to Thee.

We may notice here even the important theological distinction concerning the merits of Christ. It was precisely this distinction that cleared the theological atmosphere around this doctrine. Until it was made, there had been some hesitancy concerning the doctrine from fear of encroaching on the teaching of mankind's universal need of Christ's redeeming grace.

Of even richer poetic beauty is the Introit of the Mass — taken from the prophecy of Isaias:

> I will greatly rejoice in the Lord and my soul shall be joyful in my God, for He hath clothed me with garments of salvation and with the robe of justice He hath covered me, as a bride adorned with her jewels.

The use of passages of Holy Scripture referring to "the uncreated Wisdom" (Epistle) and His eternal origin are here applied to the origin of Mary, which was preordained by one and the same decree with the Incarnation of the Divine Wisdom.[32]

The Gradual and the Alleluia verse for the feast are:

> Blessed art thou, O Virgin Mary, by the Lord the most high God above all women upon earth. Thou art the glory of Jerusalem, thou art the joy of Israel, thou art the honor of our people.

> Thou art all fair, O Mary, and there is in thee no stain of original sin.

This latter phrase — original sin — is distinctive in the liturgical texts of the Mass. Editions of the Missal prior to 1863, and even in

---

[32] Pius IX, *Official documents*, p. 83.

the ancient calendars,[33] entitled the feast *In conceptione B. Mariae Virginis.*[34]

The Sarum Missal of the early sixteenth century had a special Alleluia verse that mentioned the glorious conception of the Virgin Mary. It also had a sequence: "Let this day be celebrated in which the Conception of Mary is piously recalled."[35]

The Invitatory of Matins says: "Let us keep the feast of the stainless conception of the Virgin Mary; let us worship Christ, her Son and her Lord and ours." This passage is interesting for the explicitness of its dogmatic reference to Mary's conception as well as for the theological balance it portrays by reflecting Mary's honors to Christ. This is a pattern that goes through the whole structure of the liturgical texts on Mary.

There follow some further passages pertaining to this concept — all from the Breviary for the feast of the Immaculate Conception.

"O Lord, how excellent is Thy Name in all the earth, Who has made Thee a worthy tabernacle in the Virgin Mary" (1st Antiphon at Matins).

"Grace is poured into her Conception and she is fairer than the daughters of men" (4th Antiphon of Matins).

"By this I know that thou favorest me, because mine enemy can not triumph over me" (Versicle of 2nd Nocturn).

"For the Lord hath created me in righteousness and hath held mine hand and hath kept me" (4th Responsory).

And finally the first Antiphon of Lauds and Vespers:

"Thou art all fair, O Mary; there is no spot of original sin in thee."

In a fourteenth-century manuscript of the Sarum Missal the feast of the Conception is in the calendar (December 8) but it does not have a special Mass formula or Office; it is celebrated with the

---

[33] Cf. F. Wormald, *English Kalendars before A.D. 1100* (London: Henry Bradshaw Society, 1934), Vol. 1.

[34] A Roman Missal printed in 1858 (four years after the definition) still has this simple title. However, a Breviary printed in 1856 has Immaculatae inserted in the title for this feast.

[35] *Missale ad usum insignis et praeclarae Ecclesiae Sarum. Labore ac studio Francisci* H. Dickinson (Burntisland, 1861-1883), p. 130.

feast of the Nativity.[36] The Mass on that day makes no explicit reference to Mary's conception which would seem to indicate that the latter feast was only tacked on. Even in the later Roman Missals the two Masses are very similar, being identical from the Introit through the Gospel except for the change of the word "Nativity" to "Conception." The feast of the Nativity is one of the earliest Marian feasts in the Western liturgy, celebrated in Rome during the pontificate of Sergius I (687-701) and probably some years before. Like the feast of the Immaculate Conception, it owes its origin probably to the Gospel narration and the early feast of the birth of John the Baptist. The feast had its origin in the East, probably in Syria or Palestine. The object of the feast, namely, the birth of Mary, lacks historical details and is based somewhat on apocryphal writings, which abounded after the Council of Ephesus. Evidence is wanting to show why September was chosen,[37] though it is certainly because of that date that the feast of the Conception was celebrated on December 8, nine months earlier. Because of this lack of historical foundation, the feast was slow in being accepted universally.[38]

A person might ask why the birth of Mary is particularly set aside for honor, since in the case of the saints the Church "celebrateth only the day of their being made perfect at death" (6th Lesson, December 9). The answer will be found in this that in the case of Our Blessed Mother as in the case of St. John the Baptist, the Church venerates even their birth since they were sanctified in the womb. Hence every phase of her life is worthy of honor who even at her birth was a singularly perfect and holy creature.

There follow some pertinent passages from the Office of the feast of the Nativity:

> "Today is the Nativity of the Holy Virgin Mary, whose glorious life is the ornament of all the churches" (Versicle and Responsory at Vespers).

---

[36] In nativitate et in conceptione Sancte Marie. *The Sarum Missal*, edited from three early manuscripts by J. Wickham Legg (Oxford: Clarendon Press, 1916), p. 318.

[37] F. Holweck, *Nativity of the Blessed Virgin Mary*, in the *Catholic Encyclopedia*, Vol. 10, p. 712.

[38] Holweck, *Calendarium*, p. 312.

"Let us tell again of the right worthy Birth of the glorious Virgin Mary who gained the honor of Motherhood without losing the guilelessness of a Maiden" (Antiphon at the Magnificat, 1st Vespers).

"Thy birth, O Virgin Mother of God, was a message of joy to the whole world, for out of thee rose the Sun of righteousness ..." (6th Responsory of Matins).

"Let us keep with rejoicing the Birthday of the Blessed Virgin Mary that she may pray for us to our Lord Jesus Christ" (5th Antiphon at Lauds).

"Let us this day keep solemnly the Birthday of Mary, Mother but still Maiden, her Birth a step toward the loftiness of her throne" (Antiphon at the Benedictus').

One might remark the obvious supernatural mentality reflected in all these prayers. The perfectly natural event of Mary's birth is seen in the light of the beauty of her soul and the height of her calling to be Virgin Mother and Queen.

Since holiness means attachment to the supreme good (God) and distance from evil (sin), Mary is certainly most holy. We have seen how the sacred liturgy expresses these concepts in a concrete way, especially in the two feasts of the Annunciation and the Immaculate Conception.

VIRGINITY

We pass now to the mystery of Mary's life closely associated with her sanctity, namely, her virginity. Our Lord himself tells us that virginity is not a necessary sign of sanctity,[39] but we know that Mary's virginity is very intimately connected with the holiness of her life and flows from it. Before she ever realized the height of her calling, she had consecrated herself body and soul, to almighty God. Her "How can this be done?" is universally interpreted by exegetes as a reference to her vow of virginity.[40] The angel's assurance was all she needed: "Be it done unto me according to thy word."

With regard to giving the full doctrine of Mary's virginity (before, in, and after the birth of Christ) the expressions of the

---

[39] Mt. 19:12.

[40] M. Scheeben, *Mariology*, translated by Rev. T. L. M. J. Geukers (St. Louis, Mo.: B. Herder, 1946), Vol. 1, p. 116.

liturgy are general and all-inclusive, using the simple term "virgin" to include all its implications. In some passages, however, more of the fullness of her virginity is expressed, for example:

"Mother of God, when Moses saw the bush unconsumed, we own that it was a figure of the preservation of thy most wonderful virginity. Pray for us" (3rd Antiphon at Lauds, feast of Circumcision).

"The joy of a Mother was hers, remaining a Virgin unsullied" (from the 2nd Antiphon of Lauds on Christmas).

"Long ago Ezechiel prophesied: I saw the gate shut; behold God went forth from it before the ages for the salvation of the world. And it was shut again, showing forth the Virgin, because after child-birth she remained a virgin. The gate which thou sawest, the Lord only shall enter by it" (2nd Responsory of Matins on Wednesday in the 1st Week in Advent).

Although there is no feast today in the Roman calendar honoring Mary in her virginity, there have been, in certain places, days set aside to honor her through this privilege: fourth Sunday in July — her Virginity; third Sunday in May — Queen of Virgins; first Sunday in August — Faithful Virgin, etc.[41] In the Roman Missal there is a feast of the Purity of the Blessed Virgin Mary assigned to October 16.[42] We pray in the Oration of that Mass:

Grant, we beseech thee, Almighty and eternal God, that we who venerate with festive celebration the most perfect virginity of the most pure virgin Mary, may by her intercession attain to purity of mind and body.

The feast of the Immaculate Heart of Mary, which our Holy Father, Pope Pius XII, extended to the universal Church after consecrating the world to her Immaculate Heart on December 8, 1942, might also be considered here. The new Office and Mass were promulgated on May 4, 1944.[43] It is fixed on August 22, the octave of the Assumption.

It is not possible or necessary to cite the countless references in the Missal and Breviary referring to Mary's virginity. But that the liturgy incorporates in full the dogmatic teaching concerning it,

---

[41] Cf. Holweck, *Calendarium.*

[42] *Missae pro aliquibus locis.*

[43] *A.A.S.*, Vol. 37, 1945, pp. 44-52.

there can be no doubt. Mary's name is seldom mentioned without affixing to it this her glorious privilege.

> "O Mary, how holy and how spotless is thy virginity. I am too dull to praise, for thou hast borne in thy womb Him whom the heavens can not contain" (6th Responsory of Christmas Matins).

ASSUMPTION

We shall consider Mary's role as Coredemptrix, which would logically come here, in connection with her mediatory powers.

We pass now to that privilege of Mary so recently exalted by the solemn definition of Pope Pius XII —the Assumption.[44] This privilege — one of the first honored in both the Roman and Gallican liturgies — is the one which in our day has received the most attention. Study, research, and prayer prepared the way for the definition, and the definition has evoked more study, research, and prayer.[45]

The doctrine defined is Mary's glorious bodily assumption into heaven and her glorification in heaven. The definition does not extend to the death of Mary — a point considered by some to be forever undefinable, because of the lack of historical evidence. However, the sacred liturgy does refer to Mary's death. Doctrinally, the Assumption is the climax, the glorious completion of the most holy life of Mary. It involves not only her victory over death, but also her glorification in heaven above all the saints and angels.

We shall try to see how the Church is able to incorporate both aspects of this doctrine into her prayer life — her liturgy. But first let us consider the feast itself.

---

[44] Ibid., Vol. 42, 1950, pp. 753-771. Cf. C. Morin, *The Assumption and the Liturgy,* in *Vers le dogme de l'Assomption* (Montréal, 1948), pp. 391-397; G. Giamberardini, O.F.M., *Il valore dommatico della liturgia assunzionistica,* in *Atti del Congresso Mariano dei Frati Minori d'Italia* (Roma, 1948), pp. 511-557; F. Antonelli, O.F.M., *La festa dell'Assunzione nella liturgia romana,* ibid., pp. 223-239; G. Brasso, O.S.B., *Contenido doctrinal de las fórmulas asuncionistas de la liturgia romana,* in *Estudios Marianos,* Vol. 6 (Madrid, 1947), pp. 147-154.

[45] J. Carol, O.F.M., *A Bibliography of the Assumption,* in *The Thomist,* Vol. 14, 1951, pp. 133-160; *Recent Literature on Mary's Assumption,* in *The American Ecclesiastical Review,* Vol. 120, 1949, pp. 376-387; *The Mariological Movement in the World Today,* in *Marian Studies,* Vol. 1, 1950, pp. 37-42.

The Gallican feast of Our Lady, celebrated on January 18, most probably came West from the Coptic liturgy with Cassian around the year 550.[46] This was the only Marian feast of the Gallican liturgy prior to the influence brought about by the dissemination of the Roman liturgical books.[47]

Around the turn of the eighth century the date was changed under Roman influence from January 18 to August 15.[48]

The Mozarabic liturgy seems to have depended on Roman influence for its feast of the Assumption and at a late date.[49]

The object of the Roman feast at first seemed to have been only the death of Mary with no reference to the Assumption until the end of the seventh century.

As mentioned above, there was a procession in Rome on this day, inaugurated by Pope Sergius I. From the seventh to the sixteenth century, the papal cortège, including members of the Senate and representatives of the people, passed from the Church of Adrian on the Forum to St. Mary Major.[50] When the people had assembled for the procession, the following formula was read:

> It is our duty to honor the solemnity of the day, O Lord, in which the Holy Mother of God did indeed suffer temporal death, although the bonds of this death could not hold back her whose flesh formed the body of Thy Son, Our Lord.[51]

This is truly a remarkable passage in that it is not just a prayer but rather a declaration of the fact of Mary's victory over death and

---

[46] A. King, *The Assumption of Our Lady in the Oriental Liturgies*, in *Eastern Churches Quarterly*, Vol. 8, 1949-1950, p. 204. Cf. B. Capelle, *La fête de l'Assomption*, p. 35; and *La Messe gallicane de l'Assomption: son rayonnement, ses sources*, in *Miscellanea liturgica in honorem* L. Cuniberti Mohlberg (Rome: Edizioni Liturgiche, 1949, Vol. 2, pp. 33-59.

[47] For an excellent treatment of the problem of introducing uniform liturgical books, cf. M. Andrieu, *Les Ordines Romani du Haut Moyen Age* (Louvain, 1948), Vol. 2, pp. xvii-xlix.

[48] B. Capelle, *La fête de l'Assomption*, pp. 35-36.

[49] B. Capelle, *La liturgie Mariale en Occident*, p. 233.

[50] I. Schuster, O.S.B., *The festival of the Assumption into heaven of the Blessed Virgin Mary in the ancient Roman liturgy*, in *The Sacramentary*, translated from the Italian by Arthur Levelis-Marke (New York: Benziger Bros., 1930), Vol. 5, pp. 32-35.

[51] From the *Gregorian Sacramentary. PL*, 39, 133.

an explicit avowal of her bodily assumption. It is remarkable also, because the Mass formula (i.e., before the new one) is rather noncommittal — one which was derived from the Common of Virgins.[52] In fact, the oration makes no mention of the Assumption. The Introit is adapted for the Assumption, but the formula — Gaudeamus — really belongs to the Mass of St. Agatha (February 5) and occurs eight times in the Missal. The Alleluia verse and the Offertory are the same. They repeat the first Antiphon of Vespers and Lauds: "Mary hath been taken to heaven; the angels rejoice; they praise and bless the Lord." This verse is retained as the Alleluia verse in the new Mass which our Holy Father approved for the universal Church for the feast of the Assumption.[53]

The Introit of this new Mass is from the Apocalypse. The text is that of the woman (Apoc. 12:1):

A great sign has appeared in the heavens: a woman clothed with the sun, with the moon under her feet and on her head a crown of twelve stars. Ps. 97, v. 1. Let us sing a new song to the Lord, for he has done great things!

The Oration is classic in its structure:[54]

Almighty and eternal God, Who hast assumed the Immaculate Virgin Mary, the Mother of Thy Son, body and soul into heavenly glory, grant, we beseech Thee, that always intent on higher things, we may merit to be sharers of her glory.

This has a happy suggestion of the essential relation of the Assumption to the Immaculate Conception. It likewise puts the verb in the active voice, showing God's immediate action. God has

---

[52] Cf. B. Capelle, *La fête de l'Assomption*, pp. 38-40, where he discusses the Mass at length, and the following two references where he analyzes the prayer, *Veneranda*, just quoted: *L'oraison 'Veneranda' à la messe de l'Assomption*, in *Ephemerides Theologicae Lovaniensis*, Vol. 26, 1950, pp. 354-364; *La témoignage de la liturgie*, in *Études Mariales*, 1949. *Assomption de Marie*, Part 2 (Paris: Vrin, 1950), pp. 49-52.

[53] *A.A.S.*, Vol. 42, 1950, pp. 793-795.

[54] Cf. Sister Mary Gonzaga Haessly, O.S.U., *Rhetoric in the Sunday Collects of the Roman Missal* (Cleveland: Ursuline College, 1938), passim; C. Egger, *De quibusdam Ecclesiae precibus latinis*, in *Latinitas*, Vol. 1, 1953, pp. 141-147; J. M. Bover, S.J., *Uso liturgico de los textos biblicos en la nueva Misa de la Asunción*, in *Estudios Marianos*, Vol. 12 (Madrid, 1952), pp. 97-110.

assumed Mary to Himself. Mary is in glory, body and soul. The whole doctrine is here.

The Epistle accommodates the passage from *Judith*. This same Epistle is used for the feast of the Seven Sorrows. The scriptural passages referring to that valiant woman are here applied to Mary. I include only three pertinent passages: "Blessed art thou, O daughter, by the Lord the most high God, above all women upon the earth." "Blessed be the Lord who made heaven and earth, who hath directed thee to the cutting off the head of the prince of our enemies." "Thou art the glory of Jerusalem, thou art the joy of Israel, thou art the honor of our people." The middle passage is most expressive in reference to Mary's victory over Satan. This idea is brought up again shortly after in the Offertory verse, which is the *Protoevangelium:* "I will put enmity between thee and the woman, between thy seed and her seed."

The Gospel is that of the Visitation. Elizabeth's words of praise and Mary's *Magnificat* are the pertinent passages.

This should suffice to show that the new Mass formula clearly transposes dogma to prayer. Without question it is a superior formula when compared to the former *Gaudeamus* Mass.

The new Office of the Assumption[55] makes changes for the most part by offering new texts in places where the old Office was of the Common. However, the really characteristic passages remain.

> "The Virgin Mary hath been taken into the (bridal) chamber on high where the King of kings sitteth on the throne amid the stars" (2nd Antiphon of Lauds).

> "This is the day whereon Mary went up into heaven. Rejoice for she reigneth forever with Christ" (Magnificat Antiphon for 2nd Vespers).

These passages, as well as the antiphon quoted earlier ("Mary hath been taken to heaven, etc.") may well have been incorporated into the liturgy from an epistle-sermon Cogitis me by Paschasius Radbert.[56]

---

[55] *A.A.S.*, Vol. 43, 1951, pp. 385-399; cf. M. Gordillo, S.J., *Las lecciones del II nocturno de la Asunción en la historia del Breviario Romano,* in *Estudios Marianos,* Vol. 12 (Madrid, 1952), pp. 111-123.

[56] This is the opinion of Capelle, *La liturgie Mariale en Occident,* pp. 224-225. Dom Frénaud in his review of Capelle (*Revue Grégorienne,* Vol. 31, 1952, p. 106) holds the *Cogitis* me to be rather a witness and commentary on the

Another very beautiful passage is the first responsory of Matins. It is a delicate interweaving of six different passages from the *Canticle of Canticles* and of one from *Sirach*.[57] This Responsory, too, is retained in the new Office:

I saw her, when fair like a dove, she winged her flight above the rivers of waters. The priceless savor of her perfumes hung heavy in her garments. And about her it was as the flower of roses in the spring of the year, and lilies of the valley. . Who is this that cometh out of the wilderness like a pillar of smoke, perfumed with myrrh and frankincense?

We see, then, all the important facts relative to the doctrine of Our Lady's Assumption expressed in the sacred liturgy. Sometimes, indeed, expressed in most simple and direct terms, sometimes in figure, sometimes in the ecstatic prayer of the mystic, but always in a manner and with an accuracy befitting the Spouse of Christ.

QUEENSHIP

Immediately following on Mary's Assumption and implied in it is her Queenship. She is the Queen of Heaven. Yet in reality her Queenship is simultaneous with her Maternity. For from the first moment of her conception of the God-Man she was Mother of a King. Not just Queen-Mother as understood in kingdoms today, but truly Queen. The fact is implied in Holy Scripture and has been attested to by one pope after another.[58] The nature of her Queenship is more than metaphorical; it is queenship in the proper sense. She enjoys that power of intercession proper to a mother and a spouse of the king and enjoys personal dignity attendant on her position. She is Queen of queens because she is Mother and Spouse of the

---

already existing texts. In his own review of this (his own) article, which came a full year after Frénaud had made these observations, Capelle makes no reference to them as involving a problem: Bulletin de théologie ancienne et médiévale, Vol. 4, No. 2066.

[57] Cant. 2:3; 5:12; 4:11; 2:1; Ecclus. 50:8; Cant. 3:6; 5:6.

[58] Cf. E. Carroll, O.Carm., *Our Lady's Queenship in the magisterium of the Church*, in *Marian Studies*, Vol. 4, 1953, pp. 29-81; or, more briefly, G. M. Roschini, O.S.M., *Royauté de Marie*, in *Maria. Études sur la Sainte Vierge* (ed. H. du Manoir, S.J.) (Paris: Beauchesne, 1949), Vol. 1, pp. 601-606. Cf. also K. B. Moore, O.Carm., *The Queenship of the Blessed Virgin in the Liturgy of the Church*, in *Marian Studies*, Vol. 3, 1952, pp. 218-227.

King of kings and because by her life she helped to attain victory for the kingdom.

The sacred liturgy takes explicit recognition of both her intercessory powers and her dignity. There has been an active effort of late to have a feast introduced in honor of Mary's Queenship — to correspond to the new feast of Christ the King. Until such time, the feast of the Assumption can certainly be considered to honor her Queenship since her glorification in heaven (which is one of the objects of that feast) is but the King's royal welcome and rewarding of His Queen into their kingdom.

In the Oration of the Mass we speak of her as having glory in heaven: "Almighty and eternal God, Who hast gathered to Thyself the Immaculate Virgin Mary, Mother of Thy Son, body and soul to *heavenly glory* ..." The Epistle speaks of her eminent dignity; she is blessed by God above all women — and then: "Thou art the glory of Jerusalem, thou art the joy of Israel, thou art the honor of thy people." The Gradual is a verse from Ps. 44, which is the prophetic psalm of the new kingdom: "Hear, O Daughter, and see and incline thy ear and the king will desire thy beauty. The daughter of the King enters with all beauty; golden are her garments."

The Postcommunion appeals to God through the merits and intercession of Mary, thus bringing out the other aspect of her Queenship — power before the throne.

Mary's pre-eminence even over angels is attested in the Versicle and Responsory — "The Holy Mother of God is exalted above the choirs of angels to the heavenly kingdom." Since the fifth century, Mary's name has appeared after God and before the angels in the litanies, giving recognition to this dignity.

Mary's Queenship is hers by a natural law — not just of inheritance as a descendant of David, but in the very nature of her motherhood of a King. "He shall be King over the house of Jacob forever; and of his kingdom there shall be no end."[59]

She has some acquired rights as queen, i.e., as a consequence of her co-operation in the work of the kingdom, the redemption of men. Her first "Be it done unto me according to thy word" implicitly expressed this total co-operation. The feast of the Annunciation

---

[59] Lk. 1:33.

honors her for this, while the feasts of the Purification and Seven Sorrows expand on the actual role she played in the struggle for victory.

From the Office common to the Blessed Virgin, the following passages give further evidence of the notion of queenship:

"Upon thy right hand did stand the queen in a vesture of gold wrought about with divers colors, and when the daughters of Sion saw her, they cried out that she was most blessed" (Verse and Response, 6th Responsory of Matins).

"I am black but comely, O ye daughters of Jerusalem. Therefore the king hath loved me and brought me into his chamber" (3rd Antiphon of Lauds).

"In thy comeliness and in thy beauty, ride on triumphant and reign" (Short Resp., Lauds).

The King's reign is eternal — so too shall be the queen's.

The beautiful antiphons, *Salve Regina, Ave Regina coelorum, Regina coeli* should be mentioned here since they thread through the Divine Office day by day throughout the year keeping Mary's Queenship before our minds.

These few examples taken from the Missal and the Breviary should be adequate to show clearly Mother Church's desire to place on the lips and in the hearts of her children prayers that express her understanding of the doctrine of Mary's Queenship.

MEDIATION

We come now to the final doctrines which integrate all the above under the practical aspect of Mary's role in the whole plan of redemption — her role as Coredemptrix and Dispenser of graces. They are treated here under one topic because her work as Dispenser of graces flows from her share in the work of redemption.

Her perfect union with her divine Son from the first moment of His mission down to the tortuous way of Calvary merited for her a unique role in the redemptive actions of our divine Saviour. Her every act was unique in that its perfection and its purity rendered it most pleasing and consequently meritorious before God. Her sorrows and her deep compassion with every suffering step of our Redeemer in the course of the Passion were such that she has merited the title of Coredemptrix.

Taking this into account and then considering her other glorious prerogatives, Mother, Saint, Virgin, and Queen, it is not hard to understand the unique role she plays in heaven as the Mediatrix and the Dispensatrix of all graces.

We need not here proceed any further than this into the theological aspects of these doctrines, especially since there are variations of opinion among theologians on the extent of her role in the plan of salvation. Next to the doctrine of the Assumption no other problem has been more fully treated in recent literature.[60] Whatever the theological solution might be, the texts of the liturgy of the Church will hardly exert more force in the final proof than to imply the unique intercessory powers of Mary in heaven and some mode of co-redemption during her life here on earth.[61]

Mary's "Behold the handmaid of the Lord; be it done unto me according to thy word" is her complete acceptance of God's plan for her. This consent celebrated on the feast of the Annunciation (March 25) is the foundation for her office of Mediatrix. Words do not convey the degree of dedication contained in this consent, but there could be no halfway measures for this soul whose intellect was unclouded by ignorance and whose will was undivided by concupiscence or selfish consideration. This was the turning point in history, and Mary consented to provide herself body and soul to the cause.

Later she was called upon to carry out in deed this consent of her spirit, especially when she followed her divine Son to the cross.

---

[60] J. Carol, O.F.M., *Mariological Movement* in the World Today, Section E — "Mary's Co-redemption," in *Marian Studies*, Vol. 1, 1950, pp. 34-37 for the beginnings of a bibliography from both points of view.

[61] Cf. G. Cozien, O.S.B., *La Maternité de grâce dans la liturgie, in Quatrième Congrès Marial bréton tenu à Folgoat ... 1913* (Quimper, 1915), pp. 244-249; P. Charles, S.J., *L'hymnologie mariale et la Médiation de la T. S. Vierge, in Mémoires et Rapports du Congrès Marial tenu à Bruxelles*, 1921 (Bruxelles, 1922), Vol. 2, pp. 475-494; I. Van Houtryve, O.S.B., *La Médiation de Marie dans la liturgie, in La Vie Diocésaine*, Vol. 11, 1922, pp. 349-360; Serapio de Iragui, O.F.M.Cap., *La Mediación de la Virgen en la himnografía latina de la edad media* (Buenos Aires, 1939); D. Baier, O.F.M., *The Franciscan Office of St. Mary of the Angels and the Mediation of Grace*, in *Orate Fratres*, Vol. 10, 1936, pp. 399-402.

Her oneness with Him especially here and her glorious merits consequent on the anguish of soul she endured, give her a unique relationship with the Redeemer, a relationship theologians have not hesitated to include under a special name — Coredemptrix. It is the feast of the Seven Sorrows, especially the one in Passion Week, that brings to mind this mystery.

"There stood by the cross of Jesus, His Mother" (Introit). She would not be separated from Him now. By this fidelity and co-operation at the foot of the cross "an ineffable union is made to exist between the two offerings, that of the Incarnate Word and that of Mary; the Blood of the Divine Victim and the tears of the Mother, flow together for the redemption of mankind."[62]

> "O God, at whose passion according to the prophecy of Simeon, a sword of sorrow pierced the most sweet soul of the glorious virgin and mother, Mary, grant in Thy mercy that we who call to mind with veneration her soul transfixed with sorrow through the merits and prayers of all the saints faithfully standing by Thy cross, may obtain the blessed result of Thy Passion" (Oration).

As Collects go, this one is a rather poor composition, and it is also exceptional in this that it is prayed directly to Christ. The Oration for the feast of the Seven Dolors (September 15) omits the reference to the other saints and simply reads: "... mercifully grant that we who reverently meditate on her sorrows may reap the happy fruit of Thy Passion."

"Holy Mary, the Queen of heaven and Mistress of the world, stood by the cross of Our Lord Jesus Christ, full of grief" (Alleluia, September 15). There is in this verse a hint of the teaching of Pope Pius XII: that Mary is "Queen" by right of conquest.[63] Her Queenship is here stressed, and her endurance even to the point of spiritual martyrdom merits the victory. In connection with our thought — the Queen has shared the victory with the King.

"Happy the senses of the Blessed Virgin Mary which without dying earned the palm of martyrdom beneath the cross of our Lord" (Communion). This is the great paradox of Christianity! There is

---

[62] P. Guéranger, O.S.B., *The Liturgical Year*, translated from the French by Dom Laurence Shephard, O.S.B. (Westminster, Md.: Newman, 1952), Vol. 6, Passiontide and Holy Week, p. 175.

[63] *A.A.S.*, Vol. 38, 1946, p. 266.

victory in death and victory in martyrdom without death, and both of these seeming contradictions took place at the same time on Calvary in Jesus and Mary.

No one with even the most elementary contact with liturgical books would question that they reflect the belief in Mary's intercessory powers. The Offertory of the Mass we were just considering is in itself a sufficient witness. "Be mindful, O Virgin Mother of God, when thou standest in the sight of the Lord to speak good things for us and to turn away His anger from us" (Offertory). Mary's word on our behalf at the throne of God is what we seek, confident of the power of her intercession on our behalf.

After the Salve Regina which is recited at least once a day from Pentecost to Advent, there is this versicle, response, and prayer:

> *V.* Pray for us, O holy Mother of God.
> *R.* That we may be made worthy of the promises of Christ.
> Let us pray. O almighty and everlasting God who by the cooperation of the Holy Ghost, didst prepare the body and soul of Mary, glorious Virgin and Mother to become the worthy habitation of Thy Son, grant that by the gracious intercession of her at whose memory we rejoice, we may be delivered from present evils and everlasting death.

We pray to her to intercede for us for those things most essential to us (our prayer is really to God, but with an absolute confidence that Mary is simultaneously making our prayer her own on our behalf): (1) that we be made worthy of the promises of Christ (final perseverance); (2) grace to avoid the occasions of sin; and (3) grace to avoid sin itself with its eternal consequences (everlasting death).

There are two prayers that can be added here because of their intercessory contents. The first is the Magnificat Antiphon of the first Vespers of the Common Office of the Blessed Virgin:

> O holy Mary, be thou a help to the helpless,
> a strength to the fearful,
> a comfort to the sorrowful.
> Pray for the people, plead for the clergy,
> make intercession for all women vowed to God.
> May all that are keeping this thy holy feast day feel the might of thine assistance.

Certainly this beautiful antiphon embodies in full the idea of intercession. We pray to Mary, confident of her competence to help all with the might of her assistance. This antiphon has been taken from a sermon attributed to St. Augustine.[64] It breathes a deep confidence in Mary and in her intercessory powers.

The second prayer worthy of note is a very short antiphon that only recently has been discussed as being a third-century witness of a prayer of intercession to Our Lady.[65] This prayer is a translation from the Greek original. Today its place in the Breviary is in the Little Office, the antiphon at the Nunc Dimittis; it occurs once in the Pontifical and twice in the Ritual. "We take refuge under thy protection, O holy Mother of God. Despise not our petitions in our necessity, but deliver us from all dangers, ever Virgin glorious and blessed."[66] We find in this prayer, especially interesting because of its early date, an assertion of Mary's role as Mother and Virgin as well as Intercessor. To have placed our trouble in the hands of Mary is to be assured that she will handle "our case" with God.

We have seen, then, that the liturgy does reflect the faith of the Church regarding Mary's Coredemption and intercessory powers. While the doctrines are never fully expressed in just those words, they are contained there in substance.

Having covered the main doctrines concerning Our Lady that find expression in the liturgy, it is not out of place at this time to consider Mary's cult in general as it exists in the Roman liturgy and to treat of a few special feasts and prayers that are pointed to her honor.

IN GENERAL

In the daily life of the Church we find Mary invoked over and over again. The Divine Office never begins without a Hail Mary and never ends without a Marian antiphon. In the Office and at Mass the *Confiteor* seeks her intercession. Low Masses are always concluded

---

[64] *PL*, 39, 2104.

[65] F. Mercenier, O.S.B., *La plus ancienne prière à la Sainte Vierge*, in *Questions liturgiques et paroissiales*, Vol. 25, 1940, pp. 33-36.

[66] For the placement of the comma before or after semper (ever) which would change the meaning from "ever Virgin" to "ever deliver us," cf. A. Paladini, C.M., in *Ephemerides Liturgicae*, Vol. 61, 1947, pp. 109-110.

with the three *Hail Marys* and the *Hail, Holy Queen* prescribed by Pope Leo XIII for the conversion of Russia. The oration A cunctis prescribed for most seasons of the year and prayed on ferial days and on days of simple feasts invokes the special intercession of Mary.

The daily use of the *Magnificat* has a significance both in the way of honoring Mary who first prayed it, and in urging us to pray in joyful gratitude at the beginning of each liturgical day of grace (at Vespers) for the mystery of God's loving mercy, our salvation. Not infrequently the *Magnificat* antiphon locks up in a few words the whole mystery of the feast being celebrated.

While no one of these prayers alone is particularly convincing, taken together they converge to focus the Church's consciousness of the role of Mary in our daily spiritual life.

The weekly Mass and Office for Saturday are celebrated in her honor whenever they are not hindered by some higher-ranking feast. Further, there are five different forms of this Mass that give variations corresponding to the temporal cycle in which they fall. It is noteworthy that this Mass and Office are of very ancient origin, probably dating as far back as Alcuin († 804).

Throughout the year at different times the Litany of Loreto is prescribed (May and October in parishes), and the Litany of All Saints, prayed especially on Rogation Days and at ordinations, gives Mary the place of honor after the Divine Trinity.

FEAST OF THE PURIFICATION

The feast of the Purification (double of second class) but briefly mentioned above is worthy of attention because it is one of the four feasts that go back to the middle of the seventh century. The procession prescribed for that day is still extant in a modified form. Both the feast and the procession have their origin in the East. There, however, the date was usually February 14 in place of February 2, since the Nativity of Our Lord was celebrated on January 6 instead of December 25. The twelve days' difference accounts for the different dates of this feast which is based on the historical fact of Mary's bringing the Child to the Temple forty days

after His birth.[67] The feast originally was a feast of Our Lord —
YPAPANTI Domini (the meeting of the Lord, i.e., the meeting of
Jesus and His parents with Simeon and Anna), which title the feast
frequently had even in Western calendars.[68] It was only some time
after the tenth century that the blessing of candles was introduced.
The Presentation of Jesus and not the Purification is the principal
object of the feast even though it is definitely Marian in tone.

SEVEN DOLORS

This meeting of Mary with Simeon, who prophesied her
sorrows, directs us to another feast of Mary — the Seven Dolors.
This feast is celebrated in the Temporal Cycle on Friday of Passion
Week and in the Sanctoral Cycle on September 15. Both feasts have
the same object, i.e., the martyrdom of the Mother of God and her
compassion in the sufferings of her Son,[69] although the former's
original object was more precisely the compassion of Mary at the
foot of the cross, while the object of the latter is the Seven Dolors.
For all practical purposes the Masses are identical. St. Bernard's
lessons in the second Nocturn on the Compassion of Mary at the
foot of the cross are common to both Offices.

> The martyrdom of the Virgin is set before us, not only by the
> prophecy of Simeon, but also in the story itself of the Lord's Passion.
> ... the sword did, indeed, pierce through thy soul! for nought could
> pierce the Body of thy Son, without piercing thy soul likewise. Yea,
> and when this Jesus of thine had given up the ghost, and the bloody
> spear could torture him no more, thy soul winced as it pierced His
> dead side. His own soul might leave Him, but thine could not.
>
> The sword of sorrow pierced through thy soul so that we may truly
> call thee more than Martyr in whom the love that made thee suffer
> along with thy son wrung thy heart more bitterly than any pang of
> bodily pain could do. ... Marvel not, my brethren, that Mary should be

---

[67] M. Higgins, *Note on the Purification and Date of Nativity in Constantinople
in 602*, in *Traditio*, Vol. 1, 1943, pp. 409-410. Also published more recently in
Archiv für Liturgiewissenschaft, Vol. 2, 1952, pp. 81-83.

[68] Of the twenty calendars edited by Wormald (English calendars before A.D.
1100) fifteen have Purificatio Beatae Mariae, but there are five that have
YPAPANTI Domini — and some of these represent calendars as late as 1000.

[69] F. G. Holweck, *Sorrows of the Blessed Virgin Mary*, in *The Catholic
Encyclopedia*, Vol. 14, p. 151.

called a martyr in spirit.

The Office of the feast in Passion Week is notable for its lack of specific reference to the number of Mary's sorrows. It is more centered on the Passion. The counting of the individual sorrows was a later development — a natural development of affective piety. The responsories at Matins in the Office for the September feast enumerate these seven sorrows. In both feasts though, there is an emotional tenderness and affective element quite rare in most of the liturgical texts.

Both feasts are late in the calendar, the former in 1423, the latter in 1668 (not for the universal Church until 1814). The September feast was celebrated on the third Sunday in September until Pope Pius X's reform in 1913 assigned it to September 15.[70]

Characteristic of the Mass of September and the Office of the Friday of Passion Week is the poignant Stabat Mater of Jacoponi da Todi, O.F.M. (†1306),[71] or perhaps of St. Bonaventure († 1274).[72] The hymn is very personal in expression, giving pointed evidence to the more personalized asceticism beginning around this period. It is based on the following passages of Holy Scripture: John 19:25; Luke 2:35; Ezechiel 13:6; 2 Corinthians 4:10; and Galatians 4:17.

Because they both have the same object, these two feasts are somewhat of an anomaly in the sacred liturgy which has a governing principle of never doing the same thing twice (*Numquam bis de eodem*).

VISITATION

The visit of Mary to Elizabeth was honored in the late Middle Ages on Friday of Ember Week in Advent when the Gospel of the Visitation is read. The Franciscans were the first to celebrate this as a special feast in 1263. It was extended to the universal Church in 1389 and confirmed again in 1441.[73] Because of its close affinity to

---

[70] Holweck, *Calendarium*, pp. 76, 320, 342.

[71] G. M. Dreves, *Ein Jahrtausend Lateinischer Hymnendichtung ... Nach des Verfassers Ableben revidiert von Clemens Blume, S.J.* (Leipzig: O. R. Reisland, 1909), Vol. 1, pp. 390-391. Cf. J. Julian, *A Dictionary of Hymnology ...*, revised edition (London: John Murray, 1915), pp. 1081-1084, 1706.

[72] A. Manser, *Stabat mater*, in *Lexikon für Theologie und Kirche*, Vol. 9, p. 760.

[73] Holweck, *Calendarium*, pp. 213-214.

the feast of St. John the Baptist, our feast is celebrated on July 2, which is the first free day after the octave of St. John. The Mass, except for the Epistle and Gospel, is taken from the feast of the Nativity (September 8). The doctrinal implication of the Gospel is perhaps Mary as Mediatrix. Origen did not hesitate to attribute St. John's sanctification to her Mediation.[74] The feast is celebrated in the Church today as a double of the second class.

HOLY NAME

The feast of the Holy Name of Mary (September 12) is closely connected with the feast of her Nativity (September 8) just as the feast of the Circumcision and the naming of Our Lord follows after Christmas. However, the origin of this feast may well have developed as a consequence of the simple and tender love of the faithful. St. Bernard's grandiloquent words on the name of Mary may well have fostered that devotion:

It is said: "And the virgin's name was Mary." Let us speak a few words upon this name, which signifieth, being interpreted, "Star of the sea," and suiteth very well the Maiden Mother, who may very meetly be likened unto a star. A star giveth forth her rays without any harm to herself, and the virgin brought forth her Son without any hurt to her virginity. ... She, I say, is a clear and shining star, twinkling with excellencies, and resplendent with example, needfully set to look down upon the surface of this great and wide sea.

O thou, whosoever thou art, that knowest thyself to be here not so much walking upon firm ground as battered to and fro by the gales and storms of this life's ocean, if thou wouldst not be overwhelmed by the tempest, keep thine eyes fixed upon this star's clear shining. If the hurricanes of temptation rise against thee or thou art running upon the rocks of trouble, look to the star, call on Mary. If the waves of pride, or ambition, or slander, or envy toss thee, look to the star, call on Mary. If the billows of anger, or avarice, or the enticements of the flesh beat against thy soul's bark, look to Mary. If the enormity of thy sins trouble thee, if the foulness of thy conscience confound thee, if the dread of judgment appall thee, if thou begin to slip into the deep of despondency, into the pit of despair, think of Mary. ... If thou keep her in mind, thou wilt never wander. If she hold thee, thou wilt never

---

[74] *In Lucam homiliae,* n. 7. PG, 9, 1817-1819.

fall. If she lead thee, thou wilt never be weary. If she help thee thou wilt reach home at last — and so thou wilt prove in thyself how meetly it is said: "And the Virgin's name was Mary" (2nd Nocturn).

The feast, first celebrated in Spain in 1513, was dropped twice, once by Pius V and once by Benedict XIV, but was reintroduced by Innocent XI in 1683 after the deliverance of Vienna from the Turks.[75]

PRESENTATION

The feast of the Presentation of Our Lady (November 21) is a feast honoring the coming of Mary to the Temple at the age of three years. The only evidence for this event is taken from an apocryphal source. And for this reason, probably, the feast was very slow in coming from the East. It was not celebrated in the West until after the Crusades, even though it had been celebrated at Jerusalem since the sixth century.

Despite this flimsy historical foundation, the feast cannot fail to attract one to the inspirational realization that Mary —free from all stain or fault — had consecrated herself even from her infancy to God. No doubt, it is in emulation of that dedication that some religious communities pronounce their vows on that day and celebrate the feast with solemnity.

It was probably because of its weak historical foundation that Pius V dropped it from the calendar. Then Benedict XIV did the same thing after it had been in the meantime reintroduced into the liturgy. The present feast, a greater double, dates from the reign of Clement VIII.[76] The formula is very discreetly silent about Mary's presentation except in the Oration and in the Lesson where St. John Damascene refers to the legend.

The *Magnificat* antiphon is particularly beautiful and interesting in that it shifts the idea of Temple to Mary herself and expresses pithily her major prerogatives. "O Blessed Mary, Mother of God, Virgin forever, Temple of the Lord, sanctuary of the Holy Ghost, thou without any example (before thee) didst make thyself well-pleasing to our Lord Jesus Christ."

---

[75] Holweck, *Calendarium*, p. 317.

[76] *Ibid.*, p. 386.

*   *   *

These certainly do not represent all the Marian feasts (Holweck lists around 940), but they do give a good cross section of them, reflecting how the knowledge of Mary's life and her spiritual prerogatives pass over into the prayer life of the Church. In honoring Mary or some phase of her life we are honoring Christ and, through Christ, God.

LITTLE OFFICE

A word should be said about the so-called Little Office of the Blessed Virgin. Seemingly a development from the Common, it is, on the contrary, the most ancient of the Marian Offices appended to the Common Offices of the saints in the Breviary. From it the Office of the Blessed Mother on Saturday was developed as something special. Even before that the Little Office had come to be the Common of the Blessed Mother. Pius V inserted three nocturns into the Office to be used on greater feasts, but the rest of the framework was the Little Office. It was only as late as the pontificate of Pius IX that a separate Common was drawn up relegating this ancient form into somewhat of an appendix.

It was in the monasteries undoubtedly that this Office began to be recited as a devotional accretion to the Divine Office,[77] but it soon passed over to the laity so that it became their preferred devotion down to the end of the Middle Ages. The interesting and beautiful little volume so often represented in manuscript holdings and known as the "Book of the Hours" was nothing more than the Little Office of the Blessed Virgin.

Characteristic of the Office is its one nocturn of three psalms and a lesson each day. The psalms were taken from Matins of the feast of the Assumption, three each day repeated twice in the course of the week. At Lauds the antiphons are taken from the feast of the Assumption except in Advent when they are taken from the feast of the Annunciation (March 25), and after the Nativity when they are taken from the feast of the Purification (February 2). Thus we

---

[77] H. Thurston, S.J., *Virgin Mary, Devotion to the Blessed*, in *The Catholic Encyclopedia*, Vol. 15, p. 463c.

see how the principal Marian feasts celebrated at that time were interwoven into this Office.

It would be impossible to estimate the extension of the use of this Little Office, but it is safe to say that thousands upon thousands have consecrated their day-by-day existence through praying it. Even to this day, it is the prayer of many religious communities of women and lay Brothers.

MARIAN ANTIPHONS

There remains for us to examine the four Marian antiphons, gems of doctrinal and devotional content that have always been close to the hearts of the lay people as well as of the clergy and religious.

These antiphons, each in its proper season, are prescribed to be recited after Lauds and after Compline. The *Alma Redemptoris Mater* is recited from the first Sunday in Advent until the feast of the Purification; *Ave Regina Coelorum* until Easter; the *Regina Coeli* during Paschaltide; and finally the *Salve Regina* throughout the rest of the year. In many religious communities the antiphon after Compline is sung. Thus, the last official use of the voice before the great night silence is a quiet, tender prayer to Our Lady.

The *Alma Redemptoris*[78] is considered the most literary composition of the group. It was probably written by Hermanus Contractus († 1054), a monk of Reichenau, who seems to have gotten his inspiration from the already extant hymn, Ave Maris Stella.[79] At least the phraseology is strikingly similar.

---

[78] Cf. H. T. Henry, *Alma Redemptoris Mater*, in *The Catholic Encyclopedia*, Vol. 1, p. 326; J. Julian, *A Dictionary of Hymnology*, pp. 51-52.

[79] This hymn is found in three ninth-century manuscripts, but is probably not older than that. The lines of the first verse high-light the ideas to be developed in the subsequent verses, e.g., *Ave, Mater, Virgo*. Cf. H. T. Henry, *Ave Maris Stella*, in *The Catholic Encyclopedia*, Vol. 2, p. 149a; G. M. Dreves, *Ein Jahrtausend Lateinischer Hymnendichtung*..., Vol. 2, pp. 238-239; J. Julian, A *Dictionary of Hymnology*, p. 99.

ALMA REDEMPTORIS MATER	AVE MARIS STELLA
Alma Mater Sweet Mother	*Alma Mater*
Coeli Porta Gate of Heaven	*Coeli Porta*
Stella maris Star of the Sea	*Maris stella*
Virgo prius et posterius Virgin before and after	*Semper Virgo* Always Virgin
Gabrielis ab ore From the mouth of Gabriel	*Grabielis Ore*
Sumens illud Ave Accepting that greeting (of Gabriel) *Ave*	*Sumens illud Ave*

Just a glance at this grouping gives evidence of the similarity, but it also forcefully shows the wealth of vigorous phrases used to express in delicate poetic language the key doctrines concerning Our Lady.

The versicle, response, and oration following the *Alma Redemptoris Mater* change at Christmas, adapting themselves to the character of the season. Before Christmas: "The Angel of the Lord declared unto Mary and she conceived by the Holy Ghost"; after Christmas: "After Childbirth thou didst remain a pure Virgin. Intercede for us, O Mother of God."

The second antiphon, the *Ave Regina Coelorum*, was introduced into the Office by Clement VI (1342-1352), who felt he perceived in it noble accents and aspirations of many doctors, such as St. Athanasius, St. Ephrem, and St. Ildephonse.[80] The date of its origin

---

[80] H. T. Henry, *Ave Regina*, in *The Catholic Encyclopedia*, Vol. 2, p. 149b.

is uncertain, though it is found in a twelfth-century manuscript.[81] It has been an antiphon for the feast of the Assumption, which helps to explain its motif: Queen of Heaven, Queen of Angels, Glorious Virgin, rejoice, Good-bye (*Vale*). Farewell is made to the Virgin who is proceeding to heaven where she will reign as Queen, even of the angels, and will make intercession with Christ for us.[82]

The *Regina Coeli* is most obviously proper to the Paschal season. The date of origin and author are unknown, but in an antiphonary of the twelfth century for St. Peter's in Rome it was assigned to Easter Vespers. It honors Mary as Queen of Heaven, who merited to bear Him who has arisen from the dead. Queenship, Maternity, sanctity, and intercession are all briefly but certainly expressed.

Finally, we come to the *Salve Regina*. It was probably written by Hermanus Contractus (✝ 1054) or perhaps by Adhemar du Puy (✝ 1098), but was definitely written before St. Bernard's time, and all to the contrary notwithstanding, neither is he the author of the three final invocations, "O Clement, O Pious, O Sweet Virgin Mary."[83]

This is an antiphon almost every Catholic knows by heart because it is recited in the vernacular after every Low Mass for the conversion of Russia. It is a beautiful prayer pleading for the intercession of the Mother of Mercy in behalf of her distressed children. The emphasis on our distress is certainly pointed: "*We, banished children of Eve, cry unto thee, we send up our sighs, mourning and weeping in a vale of tears.*" Our prayer is for the beatific vision in heaven — man's most legitimate prayer.

The melodies for these four antiphons are among the most beautiful in the whole Gregorian repertory. Deeply religious in spirit, this music lends itself as an efficient means of revealing the

---

[81] J. Julian, *A Dictionary of Hymnology*, p. 99.

[82] J. Otten, *Antiphon*, in *The Catholic Encyclopedia*, Vol. 1, p. 575c.

[83] Capelle, *La liturgie Mariale en Occident*, p. 244. Cf. *Le culte de Marie et les bénédictins*, in *Revue liturgique et monastique*, Vol. 7, 1921-1922, p. 247; E. Carretón, *La Salve en la liturgia*, in *Liturgia* (Burgos), Vol. 6, 1951, pp. 141-146; J. Julian, *A Dictionary of Hymnology*, pp. 991-992; cf. also J. Maier, *Studien zur Geschichte der Marienantiphon "Salve Regina"* (Regensburg, 1939); S. Navarro, C.M.F., *El autor de la Salve*, in *Estudios Marianos*, Vol. 7 (Madrid, 1948), pp. 425-442; C. Boyer, S.J., *Le "Salve Regina,"* in *Marianum*, Vol. 14, 1952, pp. 270-275.

mystical contents of the texts.[84]

Let, then, the concluding climax of the day's sacred liturgy itself conclude our considerations about the sacred liturgy as an accurate and full reflection of the dogmatic truths concerning Our Blessed Mother. The many areas of investigation completely untouched here should only tend to make the position stronger. The Church believes; the Church prays, and her prayer unfolds her belief. We have tried to present only this much: that what the Church believes about Mary is adequately and beautifully expressed in the sacred liturgy.

---

[84] J. Otten, *Antiphon*, p. 575c.

Outline History of Mariology in the Middle Ages and Modern Times

By George W. Shea, S.T.D.

 ARIOLOGY is that part of the science of theology which treats of Mary, Mother of God and of the sons of God. Essential to all theology, and therefore also to Mariology, are two elements, steadfastness in tradition, and yet progress.[1]

Steadfastness in tradition, that is, unswerving fidelity to the truths of public revelation, to the Word of God both "written and handed down," according as it has been preserved inviolate and faithfully expounded by the Catholic Church.[2] The data of public revelation, which was concluded with the death of the Apostles, are immutable, admitting neither addition to their number nor alteration of their meaning.[3]

And yet there is room for progress, without which theology would not be a science; subjective progress, progress in our recognition, understanding, elaboration, and formulation of the immutable truths of revelation, of their further implications and their interrelations.[4] Two factors make such advance possible and inevitable. One is the intrinsic richness of revealed truth.[5] The other is the manner in which these profound verities were originally

---

[1] Hence theology is both positive and speculative, which is to say, with the Scholastics, that both *auctoritas* and *ratio* must come into play; cf. J. Quasten, *Patrology*, Vol. 2 (Westminster, Md., 1953), p. 59; J. Bilz, *Einfuehrung in die Theologie* (Freiburg im Br., 1935), pp. 101-102.

[2] Cf. D.B. (Denzinger-Bannwart-Umberg, *Enchiridion Symbolorum*, Freiburg im Br., ed. 21-23, 1937), nn. 783, 1781, 1787, 1792, 1800, 1836.

[3] Cf. *Ibid.*, nn. 1800, 1818, 2058-2064, 2080.

[4] Cf. Bilz, *op. cit.*, pp. 67-72.

[5] Cf. Pius XII, Litt. Encycl. *Humani generis* (August 12, 1950) : "Accedit quod uterque doctrinae divinitus revelatae fons tot tantosque continet thesauros veritatis ut numquam reapse exhauriatur"; *A.A.S.*, Vol. 42 (September 2, 1950), p. 568.

transmitted to us via Scripture and the Apostles — in rudimentary form, so to speak; somewhat as unorganized data waiting to be worked up, or as raw materials with which to construct a harmonious whole.[6]

To illustrate the first factor, eminently appropriate is Mary's dignity as the Mother of God, a prerogative freighted with tremendous consequences.[7] "Because she is the Mother of God," says Aquinas, "the Blessed Virgin has a kind of infinite dignity from the infinite good which is God."[8] This single revealed truth alone, Mary's divine Maternity, would insure the forward march of theology, specifically, of Mariology, as John Henry Newman recognized in a passage which is almost a commentary on the statement of St. Thomas just quoted:

> When once we have mastered the idea, that Mary bore, suckled, and handled the Eternal in the form of a child, what limit is conceivable to the rush and flood of thoughts which such a doctrine involves? What awe and surprise must attend upon the knowledge, that a creature has been brought so close to the Divine Essence?[9]

As to the second factor, Origen noted it thus in his "First Principles":

> The holy apostles, in preaching the faith of Christ, delivered themselves with the utmost clearness on certain points which they believed to be necessary to everyone ... leaving, however, the grounds of their statements to be examined into by those who should deserve the excellent gifts of the Spirit ... while on other subjects they merely stated the fact that things were so, keeping silence as to the manner or origin of their existence; clearly in order that the more zealous of their successors, who should be lovers of wisdom, might have a subject of exercise on which to display the fruit of their talents. ...[10]

---

[6] Cf. G. Roschini, O.S.M., *La Madonna secondo la Fede e la Teologia*, Vol. 1 (Roma, 1953), p. 6.

[7] Cf. Pius XI, Litt. *Encycl. Lux veritatis* (December 25, 1931), *A.A.S.*, Vol. 23 (December 26, 1931), p. 513; Pius XII, Litt. *Encycl. Fulgens corona* (September 8, 1953), *A.A.S.*, Vol. 45 (October 8, 1953), p. 580.

[8] S. Th., I, q. 25, a. 6, ad 4um.

[9] J. H. Newman, *Difficulties of Anglicans*, Vol. 2 (London, 1914), pp. 82-83.

[10] *De principiis*, lib. 1, praef., n. 3; PG, 11, 116-117; Engl. transl., *The Ante-Nicene Fathers*, Vol. 4 (New York, 1925), p. 239. Cf. J. Quasten, *op. cit.*, Vol. 2, p. 59.

Whence, after indicating "the particular points clearly delivered in the teaching of the apostles," the Alexandrian came to dwell on theology's office of progress and development:

> Every one, therefore, must make use of elements and foundations of this sort ... if he would desire to form a connected series and body of truths agreeable to the reason of all these things, that by clear and necessary statements he may ascertain the truth regarding each individual topic, and form ... one body of doctrine, by means of illustrations and arguments — either those which he has discovered in Holy Scripture, or which he has deduced by closely tracing out the consequences and following a correct method.[11]

The Church's "lovers of wisdom" have ever given themselves to the glorious task of intellectual conquest so well described by Origen, and in due course they undertook to enlarge and to solidify the realm of our knowledge of Mary.

Here, as in other areas, the onward march of theology acquired but slowly momentum, direction, discipline, and co-ordination; nor has it proceeded always at a steady pace, always inexorably forward, always unerringly, always with even deployment along the entire front. A variety of circumstances now accelerated the general advance, now retarded it; now made for successful thrusts and salients here, for hesitation there, for temporary withdrawals or evasive tactics elsewhere, in the face of phantom foes or supposedly impassable obstacles.

Yet the over-all gain down the centuries has been prodigious, especially in our age, as the modern treatises of Mariology eloquently attest. But, even so, one may still repeat Frederick William Faber's dictum that "no province of theology will have to widen itself as much as that which speaks" of Our Lady.[12] "How many Marian truths," exclaims Roschini, "still implicit in the sources, await a robust and penetrating mind which will render them explicit and present them in a more effulgent light! In this field, so vast and so delicate, many things remain to be done, some

---

[11] *De principiis*, lib. 1, praef., n. 10; PG, 11, 121; *The Ante-Nicene Fathers*, Vol. 4, p. 241. Cf. Quasten, *op. cit.*, Vol. 2, pp. 59-60.

[12] F. Faber, *Bethlehem*, 25th Amer. ed. (Baltimore-New York: J. Murphy Co.), p. 395. Faber had in mind the enlargement of theology even here below, not only that which comes with the beatific vision.

things to be done over."[13]

For those who would participate in this endeavor to consolidate and to extend the precious conquests of the centuries, almost indispensable is some familiarity with the history of Mariology.[14] It is not otherwise than with a new commander on a field of battle; to cement his grip on the terrain already won, to plan and effect additional gains, he must first orient himself, striving to understand the position and disposition of his forces by diligent study of the campaign's history.

Earlier chapters in this volume have reported the progress and development of Marian dogma and theology during the patristic era. It is the scope of the present chapter to continue that history, from the Middle Ages down to modern times. Within the allotted space, no more than a bare outline may be attempted.[15] Hence it will be impossible to record all the notable contributors and contributions to Marian thought during these centuries, or to trace closely the movement and evolution of that thought. But one may hope that what does come to be said will show how grossly Otten underestimated the room for progress when, about to devote a few

---

[13] G. Roschini, *op. cit.*, p. 6.

[14] Cf. *ibid.*, p. 135; H. Rondet, S.J., preface to J.-B. Terrien, S.J., *Le Mère des hommes*, Vol. 1, ed. 8 (Paris, 1950), pp. 6-7.

[15] The Mariological literature and developments of our century alone are immense, while the magnitude of earlier materials can he estimated from the huge collections made (somewhat indiscriminately and uncritically, to be sure) by: H. Marracci, *Bibliotheca Mariana*, 2 vols. (Romae, 1648); *idem*, Appendix ad *Bibliothecam Marianam* (Coloniae, 1683); J. Bourassé, *Summa aurea de laudibus B. M. V.*, 13 vols. (Parisiis, 1862); A. Roskovany, *B. Virgo Maria in suo Conceptu Immaculata, ex monumentis omnium saeculorum demonstrata*, 9 vols. (Nitriae, 1873-1881), covering some 25,000 Marian writings from the first century down to a.d. 1880. The contents of the above collections are indicated in G. Roschini, *Mariologia*, ed. 2, Vol. 1 (Romae, 1947), pp. 290-291, 301-302, 304-305.

Our outline will owe much to Roschini, op. cit., Vol. 1, pp. 217-305, 390-399; *idem, La Madonna secondo la Fede e la Teologia*, Vol. 1 (Roma, 1953), pp. 88-95, 148-166; to various articles in *Marian Studies*, Vol. 1-4 (Washington, D. C., 1950-1953), and in the symposia edited by P. Sträter, S.J., *Katholische Marienkunde*, Vol. 1 (Paderborn, 1947), and by H. du Manoir, S.J., *Maria*, Vols. 1-2 (Paris, 1949, 1952). For a rapid survey, still useful, despite need for revision, is M. Scheeben, *Handbuch der katholischen Dogmatik*, Vol. 3 (Freiburg im Br., 1882), pp. 476-479.

pages to the Mariology of the Middle Ages, he wrote:

> With the exception of a few subordinate points, dogmatic Mariology was fully developed during Patristic times. ... All this was a matter of Catholic belief before the Scholastics began to systematize the teaching of the Fathers. Hence there was little room for development in the Mariological teaching of the Church, except by way of setting forth certain details which had been only lightly touched upon by Patristic writers.[16]

Inaugurating as he did the scientific treatment of Marian doctrines, St. Anselm of Canterbury is the logical point of departure for our outline.[17] The nine centuries to be traversed can be divided into three main periods which embrace, roughly, medieval, modern, and contemporary Mariology: I. the twelfth to the sixteenth century, from St. Anselm to Protestantism; II. the late sixteenth to the nineteenth century, from Protestantism to the dogmatic definition of the Immaculate Conception; III. the nineteenth and twentieth centuries, from 1854 to the present.

I. MEDIEVAL MARIOLOGY
(TWELFTH TO SIXTEENTH CENTURIES)

Scientific Mariology, in the strict sense of the word,[18] is of comparatively recent origin. This rigorously scientific discipline, enjoying the status of a distinct and quasi-autonomous tract within theology,[19] with its several theses systematically organized and connected under the control of one master principle and various

---

[16] B. Otten, S.J., *A Manual of the History of Dogmas*, Vol. 2 (St. Louis, 1918), p. 397.

[17] For the period from the eighth century down to St. Anselm, cf. Roschini, *Mariologia*, Vol. 1, pp. 211-217, 390.

[18] Cf. *ibid.*, pp. 325, 396.

[19] Roschini, art. *Mariologia*, in *Enciclopedia Cattolica*, Vol. 8 (Città del Vaticano, 1952), s.v. Maria, col. 85: "In modern times, consequent upon many positive and speculative studies conducted with a rigorously scientific method, Mariology has received a development which confers upon it a certain autonomy." That is, while remaining an integral part of theology, Mariology is no longer treated as a kind of appendix to the tract *de Verbo Incarnato*; cf. idem, *Mariologia*, Vol. 1, pp. 324-325.

secondary principles,[20] did not exist in the Middle Ages.[21] The Scholastics expressed their thought on the prerogatives of Our Blessed Lady now in sermons and other discourses, now in devotional and ascetical writings, now in commentaries on Scripture, in letters sometimes amounting to veritable theological opuscula, and on other occasions, especially in the course of their tracts on the Incarnation. Not until the fifteenth century, with the *Tractatus de B. Virgine* of St. Bernardine of Siena, did there appear more or less systematic Marian treatises, which, however, were still far removed from the organic perfection and comprehensiveness of today's Mariological tract.[22]

But let us hasten to add that, if the medieval "lovers of wisdom" did not themselves achieve the well-rounded, highly developed, and scientifically refined Marian disquisitions which grace modern dogmatic theology, they did make distinguished contributions to the evolution of such treatises. For the Scholastics were not at all content simply to transmit, without further ado, the deposit of revealed Marian verities and the patristic elaborations thereof. Here, as elsewhere, the doctors and other theologians of the Middle Ages struggled, with no little — if incomplete — success, to win deeper insight into the data of revelation, to clarify and to formulate the data more precisely, to lay bare their ramifications and interrelations, to harmonize and reconcile them, to recognize, state, and solve new problems. Briefly, the mystery of Mary, too, was an object of the Scholastics' "fides quaerens intellectum."[23] And

---

[20] Cf. *ibid.*, pp. 323-326, 338.

[21] Cf. J. Carol, O.F.M., *The Mariological Movement* in the *World Today*, in *Marian Studies*, Vol. 1, 1950, pp. 25-26; F. Connell, C.SS.R., *Toward a Systematic Treatment of Mariology*, in *Marian Studies*, Vol. 1, p. 56; E. Burke, C.S.P., *The Beginnings of Scientific Mariology*, in *Marian Studies*, Vol. 1, pp. 117-118; J. A. de Aldama, S.J., *Mariologia*, in *Sacrae Theologiae Summa*, Vol. 3 (Matriti, 1950), p. 289.

[22] Cf. Roschini, *La Madonna secondo la Fede e la Teologia*, Vol. 1, p. 151.

[23] It could not have been otherwise — the mystery of Mary is, after all, inseparable from that of Christ; cf. M. Mueller, O.F.M., Maria. *Ihre geistige Gestalt und Persoenlichkeit* in *der Theologie des Mittelalters*, in P. Straeter, S.J. (ed.), *Katholische Marienkunde*, Vol. 1 (Paderborn, 1947), pp. 269-271, developing the point that in the religious life and thought of the Middle Ages "Jesus and Mary are a single concept."

therewith were had at least the beginnings of scientific Mariology.

The initial impetus was delivered by St. Anselm of Canterbury († 1109), not only through the beneficent influence exercised on all subsequent theology by the "Father of Scholasticism,"[24] but also through his specifically Marian writings.[25] To be sure, these, when spurious and doubtful works have been eliminated,[26] are but few and, at first glance, theologically unpromising; a few passages in *Cur Deus homo* and *De conceptu virginali et de originali peccato* aside, they are of a devotional character, Anselm's three celebrated prayers to Our Blessed Lady.[27]

Yet one should not on that account underestimate the saint's value as a Mariologist. His contribution at the level of positive theology is indisputable.[28] But, what is more, if we probe more deeply, a great speculative theologian may be seen in the midst of

---

[24] Cf. F. Cayré, A.A., *A Manual of Patrology and History of Theology*, transl. by H. Howitt, Vol. 2 (Paris, 1940), pp. 404-407; J. Bainvel, Anselme, in DTC (Dictionnaire de Théologie Catholique), Vol. 1, cols. 1343-1348.

[25] Cf. R. Jones, *Sancti Anselmi Mariologia* (Mundelein, 1937); E. Burke, C.S.P., *The Beginnings of a Scientific Mariology*, in *Marian Studies*, Vol. 1, 1950, pp. 117-137; Roschini, *Mariologia*, Vol. 1, pp. 217-224. Anselm's Mariology is touched on in many places in the *DTC*; cf. the *Tables générales, s.v. Anselme*, col. 176, for references.

[26] For a convenient, not necessarily definitive, catalogue of the authentic works of Anselm and other medieval Mariologists, cf. Roschini, *op. cit.*, p. 217 ff.; *idem, La Madonna seconda la Fede e la Teologia*, Vol. 1, pp. 88-92.

[27] *Orationes* 50, 51, 52 (in PL, 158); these are now designated as *Orationes* 5, 6, 7 in the critical edition of *S. Anselmi Opera Omnia*, ed. F. Schmitt, O.S.B., Vol. 3 (Edinburgi, 1946), pp. 13-14, 15-17, 18-25. Cf. A. Wilmart, *Les propres corrections de S. Anselme dans sa grande prière à la Vierge Marie*, in *Recherches de Théologie ancienne et médiévale*, Vol. 2, 1930, pp. 189-204.

[28] R. Jones, *op. cit.*, p. 84: "Vocari potest S. Anselmus magnus doctor marianus, non quidem quia de B. Virgine multa scripsit opera theologica sed quia tanta claritate tantaque vi traditionem de ea protulit. Omnes veritates quas hodie de Maria docet *magisterium* ecclesiasticum ipsi fuerunt non tam notiones explicandae quam facta laudanda atque adhibenda. Traditionem sibi a Patribus traditam accepit et quasi ex re mortua vel dormiente fecit rem vivam et apertam; et deinde ex hac doctrina viva, facilius potuerunt theologi post eum varios illius deducere theologicos aspectus." Not that one may expect to find reference to all Marian doctrines; thus no direct testimony to the Assumption is available apart from Homilia 9 (PL, 158, 644), which is commonly regarded as spurious.

prayer; Father Eugene Burke's sensitive study has emphasized of Anselm's Marian corpus "the close relation between doctrine and devotion and how the whole emanates from an essentially theological approach."[29] Thus one can discover there in germ the basic Mariological principle which theologians have used ever since, the principle that her divine Maternity is the very wellspring of Mary's dignity and prerogatives; from the divine Maternity Anselm infers Our Lady's purity, virginity, sanctity, and intercessory power.[30]

As to Mary's spiritual Maternity, so clear and explicit was Anselm's doctrine on this, as well as her role in the distribution of all graces, that he surpassed all previous and paved the way for all future efforts to express Our Lady's mediatorial functions.[31]

For all his realization that the Blessed Virgin's purity and sanctity must be proportioned to her dignity as the Mother of God, Anselm failed, as some no less able minds were to fail after him, to perceive the implications of this principle for the Immaculate Conception. Texts which would place him among the defenders of the latter doctrine are not his; whereas statements surely his logically exclude that glorious Marian prerogative, while conceding a special sanctification of Our Lady in the womb.[32] Nevertheless, it

---

[29] E. Burke, *art. cit.*, p. 136, where the author also points out that similar studies would be rewarding for a better understanding and appreciation of such other earlier medieval writers as Hugh of St. Victor and St. Bernard.

[30] Cf. *ibid.*, pp. 121-136. Anselm extols the divine Maternity thus in De conceptu virginali et de originali peccato: "Nempe decens erat ut ea puritate, qua maior sub Deo nequit intelligi, Virgo illa niteret, cui Deus Pater unicum Filium ... ita dare disponebat"; c. 18 in *Opera omnia*, ed. Schmitt, Vol. 2, p. 150; c. 17 in PL, 158, 451. Again: "Nihil aequale Mariae, nihil nisi Deus maius Maria. Deus Filium suum ... dedit Mariae"; *Orat.* 7 in ed. Schmitt, Vol. 3, pp. 21-22; Orat. 52 in *PL*, 158, 956.

[31] So Roschini, *Mariologia*, Vol. 1, p. 219, who includes in this judgment Anselm's teaching on Mary's part in our Redemption. However, that teaching would not seem to go beyond indirect, remote, mediate co-operation of Mary in the objective Redemption; cf. J. Carol, O.F.M., *De Corredemptione Beatae Mariae Virginis* (Civitas Vaticana, 1950), p. 153, nota 87.

[32] Cf. Roschini, *op. cit.*, pp. 222-223. Anselm's rejection of the Immaculate Conception is not admitted by all; e.g., F. Spedalieri, S.J., Anselmus per Eadmerum, in Marianum, 5, 1943, pp. 205-219, considers it significant that

is a great merit of Anselm that he furthered mightily the final solution of the medieval controversy on the Immaculate Conception, through his speculations in *Cur Deus homo* and in *De conceptu virginali et de originali peccato*,[33] particularly by his criticism of the Augustinian theses on the transmission of original sin.[34]

Still under the influence of that Augustinian doctrine, St. Bernard of Clairvaux (✝ 1153), likewise failed to extend Mary's sanctity, admittedly incomparable in all other respects, to her conception.[35] His famous letter to the Canons of Lyons, while avowing a special sanctification of Our Lady in the womb, denied, but with submission given in advance to any contrary

the above privilege was upheld by the saint's three most intimate disciples, among them Eadmer of Canterbury (✝ 1124?), his friend and biographer. The latter's *Tractatus de Conceptione sanctae Mariae* (*PL*, 159, 301-318), long attributed to Anselm, is the first monograph on the Immaculate Conception. Another work wrongly ascribed to Anselm is Eadmer's *De excellentia Virginis Mariae* (*PL*, 159, 557-580), notable for its doctrine on Mary's Queenship and its testimony to her corporeal Assumption. On Eadmer, cf. Roschini, *op. cit.*, p. 224 (with bibliography); for some other Benedictine writers of the eleventh and twelfth centuries, cf. J. Leclercq, *O.S.B., Dévotion et théologie mariales dans le monachisme bénédictin, in Maria*, ed. H. du Manoir, Vol. 2, pp. 555-562.

[33] Cf. E. Burke, *art. cit.*, pp. 122-128; A. Gaudel, *Péché originel*, in *DTC*, Vol. 12, cols. 438-439.

[34] Cf. Gaudel, *loc. cit.*; X. Le Bachelet, *Immaculée Conception*, in *DTC*, Vol. 7, cols. 995-1001. According to the teaching attributed to St. Augustine, original sin is indivisibly constituted by concupiscence and the privation of sanctifying grace, and is transmitted by the fact that generation is linked with concupiscence, which excludes any sanctifying activity on the part of the Holy Spirit; cf. J. Leclercq, *art. cit.*, p. 573. Although he criticized that teaching, Anselm's own doctrine on original sin led to the same conclusion: only one born of a virgin is immune from original sin.

[35] Cf. C. Clemencet, *La Mariologie de S. Bernard* (Brignais, 1909); B. Haensler, O. Cist., *Die Marienlehre des hl. Bernhard* (Regensburg, 1917); D. Nogues, O.C.R., *Mariologie de S. Bernard* (Paris, 1935); A. Raugel, *La doctrine mariale de S. Bernard* (Paris, 1935); P. Aubron, S.J., *L'oeuvre mariale de S. Bernard* (Paris, 1935); Roschini, *op. cit.*, Vol. 1, pp. 225-235; J. Leclercq, *art. cit.*, pp. 568-574; Dom J.-B. Auniord, *Cîteaux et Notre Dame*, in *Maria*, ed. H. du Manoir, Vol. 2, pp. 583-613. Bernard's Mariology is discussed frequently in the *Dictionnaire de Théologie Catholique*; cf. the *Tables générales*, s.v. Bernard (Saint), col. 428.

pronouncement the Church might make in the future, that Mary was conceived free from original sin.[36]

This error is the sole blemish marring Bernard's reputation as the most illustrious Doctor of Mary. The influence exercised by the Abbot of Clairvaux down through the ages, not only on Marian piety, but also on the theologians of Our Blessed Mother, is unparalleled in the annals of the Marian movement.[37]

Surprisingly enough, the Abbot of Clairvaux did not write much of the Blessed Virgin.[38] His letter to the Canons of Lyons is his only Marian work of an explicitly theological character; for the rest, Bernard's doctrine on Our Lady is expressed in a dozen sermons delivered on various feasts of the Blessed Mother, in the four homilies (collected under the title *De laudibus V. Matris*) on the Gospel Missus est of Ember Wednesday in Advent, and here and there in a few other sermons.[39]

Hence, to account for St. Bernard's tremendous influence one must look to factors other than the quantity of his Marian writings. Certainly the charm of their style, their fervor and unction, help explain that influence — never was their author more deserving of the title *Doctor mellifluus* than when he addressed himself to the subject of Mary. For Dom J. Leclercq that is the whole secret of St. Bernard's success, and the only rightful basis for his reputation as "the Marian Doctor"; according to the Benedictine scholar, the

---

[36] Epist. 174; *PL*, 182, 332-336; Engl. transl. in *The Life and Works of St. Bernard*, ed. by J. Mabillon (transl. and additional notes by S. Eales), Vol. 2 (London, 1889), pp. 512-518. Attempts to interpret Bernard benignly, as a defender of the Immaculate Conception (cf. Roschini, *Mariologia*, Vol. 1, p. 232), are curtly rejected by J. Leclercq, *art. cit.*, p. 573, with whom J.-B. Auniord, *art. cit.*, pp. 588, 591, would agree; cf. also X. Le Bachelet, *Immaculée Conception*, in *DTC*, Vol. 7, cols. 1010-1015.

[37] Cf. Roschini, *op. cit.*, Vol. 1, pp. 227, 390-391.

[38] Cf. J.-B. Auniord, *art. cit.*, pp. 587-590; also J. Leclercq, *art. cit.*, pp. 568- 569, who points out that the very paucity of Bernard's Marian writings refutes those who would reduce his religion to *Mariolatry*, his theology to Mariology; the saint, Leclercq further observes in this connection, always considered the Blessed Mother in relation and in due subordination to her divine Son.

[39] *Epist. 174* excepted, all are found in *PL*, 183; for references, cf. Auniord, art. cit., pp. 587-590, and Roschini, *op. cit.*, Vol. 1, pp. 226-235, cf. p. 226 for the many spurious and doubtfully authentic works ascribed to Bernard.

Abbot of Clairvaux is overrated as a theologian of Mary — "Bernard expressed (save for his denial of the Immaculate Conception) the traditional doctrine common to his epoch, contributing hardly any new precisions or great doctrinal originality."[40]

In the opinion of most, however, and theirs would seem the more equitable judgment, the science of Mary was considerably enriched by her greatest troubadour. If Bernard had no penchant for speculation, this was not for want of power of mind or of sound theological instinct.[41] That his Mariology is concrete in form and character is understandable from its pulpit origins, and from the saint's close adherence — born of his strict orthodoxy and wariness of innovations, to the Bible and to the Fathers.[42] Yet if, as with Anselm, one delves beneath the surface, a competent and even creative theologian may be seen in action. Bernard's Marian doctrine surpasses that of his predecessors by the richness and range of its synthesis, nor is it lacking in explicitations, new precisions, original argumentation.[43]

To document this judgment somewhat, we may remark the fact that Bernard's Mariology was evolved under the control of certain

---

[40] J. Leclercq, *art. cit.*, in *Maria*, ed. H. du Manoir, Vol. 2, p. 574; cf. also pp. 568-569, and idem, Bernard de Clairvaux, in *Catholicisme, hier, aujourd'hui, demain*, Vol. 1, col. 1478. Compare G. Dumeige, *Une session d'études théologiques sur saint Bernard*, in *Études*, Vol. 279, 1953, p. 249: Bernard "est davantage l'admirable Docteur de la dévotion mariale qu'à proprement parler le théologien de la Vierge;" "non," the same writer conceded earlier, "qu'il manque de sens théologique ou de force de pensée — on s'en rend compte en etudiant sa doctrine si solide, sur le Christ, et l'auteur du traité sur la Grâce et le libre arbitre a montré ce dont il était capable."

[41] As was just conceded by Dumeige, in note 40; cf. also F. Cayré, *Manual of Patrology* and *History of Theology*, Vol. 2, pp. 430-432.

[42] Especially St. Ambrose and St. Augustine; for other patristic and later sources used by Bernard, cf. Leclercq, *art, cit.*, in *Maria*, Vol. 2, p. 578. Such zeal for orthodoxy is a guarantee that the troubadour of Mary did not allow his ardor to carry him beyond the bounds of assured dogma; cf. P. Régamey, O.P., *Les plus beaux textes sur la Vierge Marie*, nouvelle éd. (Paris, copyright 1946), p. 125. On the other hand, mistakenly applied, it betrayed Bernard into his denial of the Immaculate Conception; cf. Régamey, *op. cit.*, p. 125; Leclercq, art. cit., *in Maria*, Vol. 2, p. 574.

[43] Cf. Auniord, *art. cit.*, in *Maria*, Vol. 2, pp. 587, 612; Régamey, *op. cit.*, pp. 125-126.

principles, especially the composite one of the grandeur of Mary's divine Maternity and her exalted role as Mediatrix between God and men, her association with the supreme Mediator in the work of our Redemption; with these prerogatives he links up the purity of the Mother and Associate of the divine Redeemer, her sanctity, virginity, her other virtues and privileges.[44] Or we may note that the Abbot of Clairvaux was not content to be one of the stanchest witnesses to the fact of Mary's Assumption and glorification: he went on to assign intrinsic reasons for this privilege, arguing it, e.g., from her integrity, from the fact that heaven is our true home, whither she has preceded us in order to act as our advocate and to summon us there.[45]

Finally and above all, one must mention, as St. Bernard's foremost contribution to Mariology, his development of the doctrine of Mary's Mediation, which earned for him the title of "Doctor of Mediation," *par excellence*. To refer to but one aspect of that rich and complex teaching,[46] the Abbot of Clairvaux affirmed in unprecedented fashion the role of Our Lady in the distribution of all graces, e.g., in the well-known texts, oft quoted by the Sovereign Pontiffs: Mary is "the aqueduct" through whom all graces come to us;[47] God "willed that we have all through Mary";[48] "God willed that

---

[44] Cf. Roschini, *Mariologia*, Vol. 1, pp. 226-234.

[45] Cf., *e.g.*, *In Assumptione B. V. Mariae, Sermo* 1; *PL*, 183, 415-417. In connection with the Assumption St. Bernard quite naturally also enlarged on Mary's Queenship; thus in the sermon just cited and elsewhere, e.g., *PL*, 183, 425, 431, 436, 438.

[46] Cf. Auniord, *art. cit.*, pp. 601-608; Roschini, *Mariologia*, Vol. 1, 229-232. According to J. Carol, *De Corredemptione B. V.* Mariae, pp. 155-156, it is questionable that Bernard upheld Mary's immediate co-operation in the objective Redemption. And although he teaches in effect the spiritual Maternity of the Blessed Virgin, Bernard never actually refers to her as "our mother," despite St. Anselm's use of this term and its equivalents; doubtless the Abbot of Clairvaux avoided such expressions because he did not find them in St. Ambrose or St. Augustine (another instance of his concern for orthodoxy); cf. P. Morineau, S.M.M., *Comment la doctrine de la Maternité spirituelle de Marie s'installe dans la théologie mystique de Saint Bernard*, in *Bulletin de la Société Française d'Études Mariales*, 1935, pp. 121-148; Régamey, *op. cit.*, p. 125.

[47] *Sermo in Nativitate B. V. Mariae*, nn. 3-5; PL, 183, 439-440.

[48] *Sermo in Nativitate B. V. Mariae*, n. 7; PL, 183, 441.

we have nothing that does not pass through Mary's hands."[49]

Dom J. Leclercq believes that, when the teaching of Bernard on Mary's Mediation is compared with that of earlier writers, it is distinguished more by its vigor than by its precision.[50] But may we justly expect to find in that doctrine, and in that of other twelfth-century authors who were inspired by Bernard,[51] doctrine expressed, moreover, in sermons rather than in professedly theological works, all the explicit distinctions and precisions of twentieth-century theologians?[52] It is enough that, in progressing beyond the formulas of St. Anselm and of other predecessors, St. Bernard paved the way for those later distinctions and precisions; therewith Mariology took a great stride forward.[53]

The next medieval Mariologist of major importance[54] is St. Anthony of Padua († 1231).[55] His other attainments long

---

[49] *In Vigilia Nativitatis Domini, Sermo 3*, n. 10; PL, 183, 100.

[50] J. Leclercq, *Bernard de Clairvaux (Saint)*, in *Catholicisme, hier, aujourd'hui, demain*, Vol. 1, col. 1478.

[51] Other Cistercians contemporary with Bernard were likewise strong proponents of Mary's Mediation and spiritual Maternity; among them we may mention (cf. Auniord, *art. cit.*, pp. 614-617; Roschini, *Mariologia*, Vol. 1, pp. 225, 236-237; *DTC*, Tables générales): Blessed Guerric, Abbot of Igny († 1151 or 1155), whose sermons are rated almost on a par with Bernard's; St. Amadeus of Lausanne († 1159), noted also for his strong testimony to Our Lady's corporeal Assumption, which was commemorated by Pius XII in the Apost. Const., *Munificentissimus Deus*; Arnold of Chartres, Abbot of Bonneval († 1160), regarded as the "Corredemptionis marialis primus adsertor" (cf. J. Carol, *op. cit.*, p. 156); and Blessed Ailred, Abbot of Rievaulx († 1166).

[52] Cf. Roschini, *op. cit.*, p. 237, on Blessed Ailred.

[53] Cf. Auniord, *art. cit.*, pp. 605; 603, note 78; E. Druwé, S.J., *La médiation universelle de Marie, in Maria*, ed. H. du Manoir, Vol. 1, pp. 547-549.

[54] Among lesser figures we may mention Alexander Neckam († 1217), of some significance in the controversy on the Immaculate Conception; cf. X. Le Bachelet, *Immaculée Conception*, in *DTC*, Vol. 7, cols. 1037-1041, 1068-1069.

[55] Cf. R. Huber, O.F.M.Conv., *The Mariology of St. Anthony of Padua*, in *Proceedings of First Franciscan National Marian Congress (Studia Mariana, cura Commisionis Marialis Franciscanae editae, VII)* (Burlington, Wis., 1952), pp. 188-268; G. Roschini, *La Mariologia di Sant' Antonio da Padova*, in *Marianum*, Vol. 8, 1946, pp. 16-67; L. Di Fonzo, O.F.M.Conv., *La Mariologia di Sant' Antonio*, in *the symposium S. Antonio Dottore della Chiesa* (Città del

overshadowed the fact that the celebrated thaumaturgist and preacher was, in addition, "a remarkable theologian in dogmatic investigations," until Pope Pius XII reminded us of this in pronouncing the Franciscan Saint a Doctor of the Church Universal.[56] The "Evangelical Doctor" might also be styled another "Marian Doctor," side by side with St. Bernard.

For, although St. Anthony was heavily indebted to the latter, his Marian teachings "are not only an echo of the past, they are also a torch which sheds its light far into the future" — besides embracing all the then accepted tenets, they also anticipated doctrines which only centuries later were either defined as dogmas (the Assumption, perhaps the Immaculate Conception) or established as common doctrine.[57]

In St. Anthony we again have one whose Mariology must be gleaned mainly from sermons.[58] Those discourses, however, treat of the Blessed Mother with such admirable theological precision and such fullness that one can construct from them a veritable and complete Marian theology.[59]

The master principle in that Mariology would be Mary's divine Maternity and the virginal birth of our Saviour, around which St. Anthony makes everything else revolve, either as prerogatives preliminary to the divine and virginal Maternity, or as prerogatives subsequent to it. Among the former he numbers Mary's plenitude of graces, her perpetual virginity, and (possibly) her Immaculate Conception; among the others, the prerogatives consequent upon

---

Vaticano, 1947), pp. 85-122; B. Costa, O.F.M.Conv., *La Mariologia di S. Antonio da Padova* (Padova, 1950); additional literature cited in Huber, *art. cit.*, pp. 266-268.

[56] Cf. Pius XII, Litt. Apost., *Exulta, Lusitania felix* (January 16, 1946); *A.A.S.*, 38 (1 Iunii 1946), pp. 200-204; Eng. transl. in *The National Catholic Almanac* (Paterson, N. J., 1947), pp. 203-206.

[57] Cf. Huber, *art. cit.*, pp. 189, 206.

[58] Eight sermons on the Blessed Virgin, with much relevant material in many other sermons, especially those for the Sundays and for the feasts of Our Lord; cf. Huber, art. cit., pp. 189-190. Cf. A. Locatelli, *S. Antonii Patavini Thaumaturgi Incliti Sermones Dominicales et in Solemnitatibus* (Patavii, 1895); representative selections in L. Guidaldi, O.F.M.Conv., *Il Pensiero Mariano di S. Antonio di Padua* (Padova, 1938).

[59] Cf. Huber, *art. cit.*, pp. 190, 206, 207.

the divine Maternity, St. Anthony emphasizes Mary's bodily Assumption into heaven and glorification as Queen of angels and saints, her cooperation in the redemption of mankind, her intermediary position in the distribution of graces, and others.[60]

Whether the Evangelical Doctor actually taught the Immaculate Conception is much debated; certainly he never denied it and was, at the least, favorably disposed toward this doctrine.[61] As to the Assumption, we may recall the declaration of Pius XII, in the Apostolic Constitution, *Munificentissimus Deus*, that St. Anthony "holds a special place" among witnesses to that truth. Noteworthy, too, is the caliber of his teaching on Mary as Coredemptrix and spiritual Mother of men, as Mediatrix in the distribution of all graces, matters in which St. Anthony is judged to have been quite ahead of his time.[62]

Thus far in our résumé of medieval Mariology we have had to study it as reflected in the ascetical writings and sermons of an Anselm, a Bernard, an Anthony, where Marian thought mingles with devotion in a kind of symbiosis.[63] Rewarding though such study is, our major interest centers on formally theological treatment of the Blessed Mother and her prerogatives. Such treatment, theological discussion *ex professo*, makes its appearance with the great luminaries of Scholasticism, among them St.

---

[60] Cf. *ibid.*, p. 206.

[61] Cf. *ibid.*, pp. 215-225. For the opposite opinion see the scholarly book by C. M. Romeri, O.F.M., *De Immaculata Conceptione B. M. Virginis apud S. Antonium Patavinum* (Romae, 1939).

[62] Cf. Huber, *art. cit.*, pp. 241-246, 264.

[63] For information on many other authors whose devotional writings illustrate the Marian thought of the twelfth and early thirteenth century, cf. Roschini, Mariologia, Vol. 1, pp. 237-241; and the several articles on devotion to Mary in various religious orders and congregations, in Maria, ed. H. du Manoir, Vol. 2, pp. 547-906; e.g., pp. 617-622, 686-693, 718-720. As a representative of the secular clergy we may mention Richard of St. Lawrence († c. 1245), whose *Mariale* or *Tractatus de Laudibus beatae Mariae Virginis*, which for centuries was mistakenly attributed to St. Albert the Great, sheds light on the state of the question as it then obtained regarding Our Lady and her prerogatives; cf. Roschini, *op. cit.*, Vol. 1, pp. 240-241; J. Carol, *De Corredemptione B. V. Mariae*, p. 161, nota 106.

Bonaventure († 1274).[64]

The Seraphic Doctor expressed his Marian thought not only in oratorical works, his 27 sermons on the Blessed Virgin, sermons for the feasts of the Epiphany and of Christ's Nativity, the *Collatio VI de donis Spiritus Sancti,* but also in his Commentary on the Gospel according to St. Luke, in the Commentary on the Sentences of Peter Lombard, and in the *Breviloquium.*[65]

Characteristic of the saint's Marian writings is their caution; in glowing love for Our Lady, Bonaventure yielded to none, yet at the same time he was deeply concerned not to heap unfounded honors on her who has no need of questionable praise.[66]

The dominant principle in the Seraphic Doctor's Mariology is a composite one, the divine Maternity of Our Lady and her association with Christ in the work of our redemption; from this twofold source flow, for Bonaventure, all Mary's other prerogatives and privileges, e.g., her plenitude of grace and of virtue; her freedom from all personal sin, even venial; her Assumption into heaven.[67]

Unfortunately, influenced by the authority of St. Bernard (his chief Mariological mentor, whom he cites some 400 times) and by his own native caution, the Seraphic Doctor was among those who failed to realize that Mary's transcendent role as Mother of the divine Redeemer also called for her complete preservation from original sin, rather than for a mere prenatal sanctification. But if he sided with opponents of the Immaculate Conception, holding theirs "the more common, more reasonable, and safer" view,[68] [69]

---

[64] Cf. E. Chiettini, O.F.M., *Mariologia S. Bonaventurae* (Sibenici-Romae, 1942); L. Di Fonzo, O.F.M.Conv., *Doctrina S. Bonaventurae de universali Mediatione B. Virginis Mariae* (Romae, 1938); Roschini, *Mariologia,* Vol. 1, pp. 241-245; additional literature, p. 241, nota 1, and in J. Carol, *De Corredemptione Beatae Virginis Mariae,* p. 162, nota 110.

[65] Cf. Roschini, *op. cit.,* Vol. 1, p. 242, for these main repositories of Bonaventure's Marian teachings, also for a list of the spurious works once ascribed to him.

[66] Cf. *Sent.* 3, d. 3, p. 1, a. 1, q. 2, ad 3, and d. 4, a. 3, q. 3; in Opera omnia, ed. *Ad Claras Aquas* (1882-1902), Vol. 3, 68 and 115.

[67] Cf. Roschini, *op. cit.,* Vol. 1, pp. 242-243.

[68] Cf. *Sent.* 3, d. 3, p. 1, a. 1, q. 2.

[69] Cf. Balić, *De regula fundamentali Theologiae Marianae Scotisticae* (Sibenici, 1938), p. 6, quoted in Roschini, op. cit., Vol. 1, p. 243.

nevertheless he refused to reprehend the other school of thought.69 Indeed, St. Bonaventure may even be said to have helped the doctrine of the Immaculate Conception toward ultimate victory, in that he admitted Mary's soul could have come under the influence of the Redemption from the first moment of its creation.[70]

As we have already intimated, the Seraphic Doctor exalted Our Lady's association with Christ in the redemption of mankind, whence he has come to share in St. Bernard's title, "Doctor of Mediation."[71] "The Blessed Virgin is Mediatrix between us and Christ, as Christ is Mediator between us and God."[72] St. Bonaventure insists on Mary's personal participation in the sacrifice of her divine Son and in its consequences, although the precise nature of his teaching regarding the extent of her co-operation in the objective redemption is disputed.[73] Be that as it may, the spiritual Maternity of Our Lady is inculcated in a variety of ways, as when the Seraphic Doctor explicitly declares that Mary "is not only the physical mother of God, but also the spiritual mother of men."[74] Varied, too, and emphatic, are the expressions by which he unfolds Mary's part in the subjective redemption, her role of intercession,[75] her association with Christ in the actual distribution of all graces.[76] Truly, St. Bonaventure is a *Doctor Mediationis.*[77]

---

[70] Cf. *Sent. 3*, d. 3, p. 1, a. 1, q. 2; cf. X. Le Bachelet, *Immaculée Conception*, in *DTC*, Vol. 7, cols. 1047-1048; J. de Dieu, O.F.M.Cap., *Le culte marial chez les Fils de Saint François d'Assise*, in *Maria*, ed. H. du Manoir, Vol. 2, pp. 788-789; Roschini, *Mariologia*, Vol. 2, Pars 2 (Romae, 1948), p. 56.

[71] Cf. Roschini, *Mariologia*, Vol. 1, pp. 243-244.

[72] *Sent. 3*, d. 3, p. 1, a. 1; *Opera omnia*, Vol. 3, p. 67.

[73] Cf. J. de Dieu, *art. cit.*, in *Maria*, Vol. 2, pp. 789-791; J. Carol, *De Corredemptione Beatae Mariae Virginis*, pp. 162-164.

[74] Sermo 2, In Pentec., n. 4.

[75] "We have three Advocates, Christ, the Holy Ghost, and the Virgin. The first contends for us, the second speaks for us, the third intercedes for us"; *In Joan.*, c. 14; *Opera omnia*, Vol. 6, p. 303.

[76] E.g., repeating St. Bernard's "all graces pass through Mary's hands"; Serm. 4, *De Annuntiatione B. M. V.*; Opera omnia, Vol. 9, p. 673.

[77] St. Bonaventure's reputation in this regard remains established even though he is not the author of the *Speculum B. M. V. (seu Expositio salutationis angelicae)*, which belongs rather to a colleague in religion, Conrad of Saxony, O.F.M. († 1279). This charming and profound little work, a commentary on the "Hail Mary" (as then recited, i.e., down to "Holy

At least equally deserving of that title, already shared by Bernard and Bonaventure, is another, St. Albert the Great († 1280).[78] "Mediatrix" and its equivalents recur habitually in his Marian writings.[79] On no subject, other than the Eucharist, did the Universal Doctor dwell more often, more at length, or with greater predilection, than Our Lady, particularly with an eye to her role in the economy of salvation.[80] He enlarged on the Blessed Mother not only in his encyclopedic *Mariale super Missus est*,[81] in the *Compendium super Ave Maria*, in a dozen and more Marian sermons, but also in the course of scriptural commentaries (especially that on the Gospel according to St. Luke), and of theological works such as the Commentary on the Sentences, the *Summa de Incarnatione*, and the treatise *De natura boni*.[82] In a word, St. Albert seized every

---

Mary"), is a compendium of Mariological questions, with emphasis on Our Lady's mediatorial functions; cf. Roschini, *Mariologia*, Vol. 1, pp. 251-252; J. de Dieu, *art. cit.*, in *Maria*, ed. H. du Manoir, Vol. 2, p. 790. The opusculum, along with another spurious work, has been published in English under St. Bonaventure's name: *The Mirror of the Blessed Virgin and the Psalter of Our Lady* (St. Louis, 1932).

[78] Cf. M.-A. Genevois, O.P., *Bible mariale et mariologie de S. Albert le Grand* (Saint-Maximin, 1934); M.-M. Desmarais, O.P., *S. Albert le Grand, docteur de la médiation mariale* (Paris-Ottawa, 1935); J. Bittremieux, *S. Albertus Magnus Ecclesiae doctor, praestantissimus Mariologus*, in *Ephemerides Theologicae Lovanienses*, Vol. 10, 1933, pp. 217-231; M. Cordovani, O.P., *La Mariologia di S. Alberto Magno*, in *Angelicum*, Vol. 9, 1932, pp. 203-212; Roschini, *Mariologia*, Vol. 1, pp. 252-261; for additional literature, cf. Roschini, p. 252, nota 1, and *DTC*, Tables générales, s.v. Albert le Grand, cols. 67-68.

[79] Cf. Desmarais, *op. cit.*, p. 135.

[80] Cf. H. Wilms, O.P., *Albert der Grosse* (Muenchen: Verlag J. Koesel & F. Pustet, n.d.), pp. 178-180.

[81] This work (in *Alberti magni opera omnia*, edit. Borgnet, Vol. 37, 1-362) is not to be confused with the Mariale of Richard of St. Lawrence (cf. supra, note 63; this spurious work is also in Borgnet, Vol. 36). (Editor's Note. As this volume goes to press, reliable information reaches us from Europe concerning the recent discovery to the effect that the *Mariale* [ed. Borgnet, Vol. 37] long attributed to St. Albert, was not actually written by him. Cf. R. Laurentin, *Court traité de théologie mariale* [Paris: 1953], p. 52, note 48a.)

[82] On the authentic Mariological writings of St. Albert, cf. Roschini, *op. cit.*, Vol. 1, pp. 252-253; Desmarais, *op. cit.*, pp. 148-167; P. Meersseman, O.P., *Introductio in opera omnia B. Alberti Magni*, O.P. (Brugis: apud C. Beyaert, n.d.), 118-121; M.-A. Genevois, O.P., *La Mariologie de Saint Albert-le-Grand*, in *Bulletin de la Société Française d'Études Mariales*, 1935, pp. 27-51. Excerpts

occasion to express his love and devotion for the Mother of God and of men; he wrote more in the sphere of Mariology than any other theologian of his era.[83]

No less admirable is the quality of these extensive writings. Always clear, almost always doctrinally solid, often profound, they are further distinguished by the range of Marian questions dealt with, and by some tendency toward synthesis, systematization, and yet other functions proper to scientific Mariology.[84] In this connection we may note that St. Albert's argumentation in behalf of Mary's bodily Assumption into heaven is singled out for special praise in the Apostolic Constitution, *Munificentissimus Deus*.

Flaws there are, of course; among them, the exaggeration of Our Lady's knowledge.[85] Then, too, although with St. Augustine, St. Anselm, and Scholastics all, St. Albert acknowledged in Mary a plenitude of grace, of purity, and of virtue second only to Christ's,[86]

---

are given in French translation in A. Garreau, *Saint Albert le Grand* (Paris: Aubier, n.d.).

[83] Thus M. Grabmann, in Wilms, *op. cit.*, p. 178.

[84] Cf. Genevois, *art. cit.*, in *Bull. de la Soc. Franç. d'Ét. Mar.*, 1935, p. 47, note 1, and pp. 50-51, regarding St. Albert's contribution to the evolution of theological method; cf. also E. Lajeunie, O.P., *Quelques aspects de la Théologie mariale actuelle*, in *Bull. de la Soc. Franç. d'Ét. Mar.*, 1935, pp. 55-59; Cordovani, *art. cit.*, in Angelicum, Vol. 9, 1932, pp. 210-212; Bittremieux, *art. cit.*, in *Eph. Theol. Lov.*, Vol. 10, 1933, pp. 218-219, 229-231.

[85] Cf. *Mariale*, qq. 96-111; Roschini, *op. cit.*, Vol. 1, p. 261.

[86] *De bono*, tract. 3, q. 3, a. 9, sol. (*Alberti Magni Opera Omnia*, cura B. Geyer, Vol. 28 [hujus editionis numerus currens 1], Monasterii Westfalorum, 1951, n. 302): "Impium est non credere virginitatem et munditiam gloriosae et sanctae theotocos omnem creaturae munditiam excellere in quattuor. ... Primum est liberatio ab immundante, quod est peccatum, de quo dicit Augustinus (*De nat. et gratia*, c. 36, n. 42; *P.L.* 44, 267), quod cum de peccatis agitur, nullam de beata virgine vult haberi quaestionem propter honorem Filii eius, domini nostri Iesu Christi. Aliud est quantum ad immunitatem fomitis et incentivi ad libidinem, quia fomes penitus fuit in ea exstinctus. Et haec duo plenius notata sunt in quaestione *De sanctificatis in utero*. Tertium est puritas virgineae mentis in omni cogitatu, verbo et opere ipsius. ... Quartum autem est sacramentum perpetuae gratiae in corde et in corpore. ..." *Mariale*, q. 32 (*Opera omnia*, ed. Borgnet, Vol. 37, Parisiis, 1908, p. 69): "Nulla alia creatura plena est gratia susceptive praeter beatam Virginem, quae sola tantum accepit, quod pura creatura recipere plus non potuit." Cf. Bittremieux, *art. cit.*, in *Eph. Theol. Lov.*, Vol. 10, 1933, pp. 220-222.

he also was among those who failed to perceive that, consistently with her singular mission and dignity, the Mother of God must have been preserved from original sin.[87] Moved by the authority of Bernard of Clairvaux, and by the Augustinian view on the transmission of original sin, the Universal Doctor admitted only a prenatal sanctification of the Blessed Mother.[88]

Such shortcomings are, however, offset by the excellence of St. Albert's doctrine on Mary's part in the work of our salvation. The "secretary and scribe of the Mother of God" stands as an incomparable witness to her mediatorial role, even if, as M.-A. Genevois holds, that role occupies only a secondary place in St. Albert's Mariology.[89] Dispersed throughout his writings are the essentials "of all the later theological elaborations" of Mary's Mediation.[90] Albert the Great would seem to have surpassed all his predecessors and contemporaries in expounding Our Lady's formal and intimate co-operation in the objective redemption.[91] Emphasized, too, is her spiritual Maternity, her Mediation in the spiritual regeneration of mankind.[92] No less explicit is the teaching

---

[87] *Postilla super Isaiam*, c. 11, 1 (*Opera omnia*, cura B. Geyer, Vol. 19 [huius editionis numerus currens 2], Monasterii Westfalorum, 1952, p. 162, lin. 76-78): "Mater (Maria) enim, quamvis in originali peccato concepta sit, tamen ante nativitatem mundata ad rectitudinem deducta est." Cf. also In *3 Sent.*, d. 3, a. 5; a. 8; Mariale, q. 163, 3.

[88] Cf. Genevois, *art. cit.*, in Bull. de la *Soc.* Franç. d'Ét. Mar., 1935, pp., 37-38, 47-48; Lajeunie, *art. cit.*, in Bull. de la Soc. Franç. d'Ét. Mar., 1935, pp. 59-61; X. Le Bachelet, *Immaculée Conception*, in *DTC*, Vol. 7, cols. 1044-1045.

[89] Cf. Genevois, *art. cit.*, pp. 45-46.

[90] Desmarais, *op. cit.*, p. 146; for a summary of Albert's doctrine on *Marian Mediation*, cf. ibid., pp. 135-147; Bittremieux, *art. cit.*, in *Eph. Theol. Lov.*, Vol. 10, 1933, pp. 222-227; Roschini, *Mariologia*, Vol. 1, pp. 255-259.

[91] Cf. Bittremieux, *art. cit.*, p. 223; Cordovani, *art. cit.*, in Angelicum, Vol. 9, 1932, pp. 207-208; J. Carol, *De Corredemptione Beatae Virginis Mariae*, pp. 164-167, 198.

[92] *Postilla super Isaiam*, c. 11, 1 (*Opera omnia*, cura B. Geyer, Vol. 19, p. 163, lin. 22-24): "Mater (Maria) enim figura est ecclesiae castis visceribus concipiens et pariens, natus autem figura regeneratorum." Mary is the "mother of regeneration," the "spiritual mother of the whole human race," the "mother of all Christians," etc.; cf. *Mariale*, qq. 11, 29, 36, 43, 145, 148, 150, 166; cf. Desmarais, *op. cit.*, pp. 128-132; W. O'Connor, *The Spiritual Maternity of Our Lady in Tradition*, in *Marian Studies*, Vol. 3, 1952, pp. 161-163.

of this Doctor of the Church that Mary is Mediatrix also by her part in the actual distribution of all graces.[93]

From St. Albert we turn to his illustrious disciple, St. Thomas Aquinas (✝ 1274).[94] Neither the exuberance of his teacher nor the warm effusions of his friend, St. Bonaventure, are to be found in the Marian writings of the Doctor communis; one is struck by their economy and their sober restraint.[95]

For, despite his great personal devotion to Our Lady,[96] to her whose quasi-infinite dignity as the Mother of God lifts her above all angels and entitles her to the special veneration called hyperdulia,[97] Aquinas would seem to have written more profusely of the angels than of their Queen.[98] Not only did he forego the many minor questions which fill a large part of St. Albert's Mariology but, what is more, St. Thomas has given us no ex professo treatment of such major themes as those which bear on Mary's role of Mediatrix.[99]

---

[93] See, e.g., *Mariale*, qq. 29, 51, 146, 147, 164; cf. Roschini, *op. cit.*, Vol. 1, pp. 257-258; Bittremieux, *art. cit.*, in *Eph. Theol. Lov.*, Vol. 10, 1933, pp. 225-227; Desmarais, *op. cit.*, pp. 80-114; H. Wilms, *Albert der Grosse*, p. 179.

[94] Cf. F. Morgott, *Die Mariologie des hl. Thomas von Aquin* (Freiburg im Br., 1878); G. Roschini, *Mariologia*, Vol. 1, pp. 245-251; idem, *La Mariologia di S. Tommaso* (Roma, 1950), cf. pp. 25-33 for a complete bibliography.

[95] Cf. A. Duval, O.P., *La dévotion mariale dans l'Ordre des Frères prêcheurs*, in *Maria*, ed. H. du Manoir, Vol. 2, pp. 753-754; Morgott, *op. cit.*, pp. 3-4; Roschini, *La Mariologia di S. Tommaso*, pp. 34-35.

[96] Cf. Duval, *art. cit.*, pp. 753–754; Roschini, *op. cit.*, pp. 14–15; Morgott, *op. cit.*, p. 3.

[97] Cf. S. Th., I, q. 25, a. 6, ad 4; III, q. 30, a. 2, ad 1; III, q. 25, a. 5, c; II-II. q. 103, a. 4, ad 2.

[98] St. Thomas discussed the angels ex professo in a special treatise, De substantiis separatis, and in S. Th., I, qq. 50-64, 106-114; S. c. Gentiles, lib. 2, cc. 91-101; lib. 3, cc. 80, 103, 105-110. It has been surmised that this wealth of teaching earned St. Thomas his title of "Angelic Doctor"; cf. F. Cayré, Manual of Patrology and History of Theology, Vol. 2, p. 594. Revealing are the entries in the "Index tertius" to the Summa Theologica: 356 under Angelus, 39 under Maria. Suarez was to note and to correct the disproportion in Scholastic treatment of angels and of their Queen; cf. De mysteriis vitae Christi, praefatio, n. 2 (Opera omnia, ed. Vivès, Vol. 19, Parisiis, 1860, pp. 1-2).

[99] Cf. Roschini, *La Mariologia di S. Tommaso*, pp. 164-191; idem, Mariologia, Vol. 1, pp. 248-249; R. Bernard, O.P., *La Maternité spirituelle de Maria et la pensée de Saint Thomas*, in *Bull. de la Soc. Franç. d'Ét. Mariales*, 1935, pp. 89-

What he did say of the Blessed Mother is found mainly in the following: S. Th., III, qq. 27-35; In III Sent., dd. 3-4; *S. c. Gentiles*, lib. 4, q. 45; *Compendium Theologiae*, p. 1, cc. 221-225; Expositio salutationis angelicae; and in a half-dozen Marian sermons.[100]

As to style and presentation, the *Adoro te* (or rather, Oro te devote) and the *Pange lingua* sufficiently demonstrate his powers of exalted and poetic expression; and yet, when St. Thomas spoke of Our Lady, even in his sermons, he eschewed the ardent language, the rich imagery, the forceful utterances of a Bernard, an Anthony, a Bonaventure, an Albert.[101]

Nevertheless, the Angelic Doctor is also a Marian Doctor, ranked with the foremost, and deservedly so.[102] He who gave to theology its *statut véritablement scientifique*[103] laid the firm foundations for the construction of a stringently scientific

---

90: "Je ne vais pas essayer de dire comment saint Thomas a traité de la maternité spirituelle de Marie, pour la bonne raison qu'il n'en a pas traité, si ce n'est par quelques réflexions incidentes, pas très nombreuses." Cf. also J. Carol, *De Corredemptione Beatae Virginis Mariae*, pp. 168-169. Further, Aquinas barely touched on Mary's Queenship; cf. Roschini, *La Mariologia di S. Tommaso*, p. 192. The corporeal Assumption of Our Lady is another topic with which St. Thomas never dealt directly, although, as Pius XII noted in *Munificentissimus Deus*, he did find occasions to uphold that truth: S. Th., III, q. 27, a. 1; q. 83, a. 5, ad 8; *Expositio salutationis angelicae*; In Symb. Apostolorum expositio, a. 5; In *IV Sent.*, d. 12, q. 1, a. 3, sol. 3; d. 43, a. 1, a. 3, sol. 1, 2.

[100] There is, of course, much incidental treatment of Marian matters throughout the *Summa Theologica* and the commentary on the Sentences; moreover, St. Thomas adverted to the Blessed Mother some 21 times in his commentaries on ten books of the Old and New Testament; for a detailed inventory of Marian passages in St. Thomas, cf. Roschini, *La Mariologia di S. Tommaso*, pp. 15-22; cf. pp. 23-24 for vindication of the authenticity of the *Expositio salutationis angelicae*.

[101] Cf. Roschini, *La Mariologia di S. Tommaso*, p. 34.

[102] Cf. *ibid.*, pp. 13-14, 34-35; Morgott, *op. cit.*, pp. 2-5; Duval, *art. cit.*, in Maria, ed. H. du Manoir, Vol. 2, p. 754; E. Hugon, O.P., *S. Thomae doctrina de B. M. V. Mediatrice omnium gratiarum*, in *Xenia Thomistica*, Vol. 2, 1925, p. 540: "Concludimus Angelicum, licet non singula explicite expenderit, statuisse firma ac solida Mariologiae fundamenta. ..."

[103] Cf. M.-A. Genevois, *art. cit.*, in *Bull. de la Soc. Franç. de l'Ét. Mar.*, 1935, p. 50.

Mariology, both positive and speculative.[104] Depth, if not breadth, solidity rather than élan, and clear, precise concepts in preference to dazzling images and ambiguous metaphors, are the invaluable contributions of St. Thomas to the science of Mary.

The disciplined form which he imparted to the traditional teaching on the Blessed Mother, his constant effort to relate that teaching to the whole of revelation, made for accurate orientation of subsequent theological reflection and opened up new perspectives. His method, principles, and insights have guided and inspired the labors of Mariologists ever since. Despite the omissions in S. Th., III, qq. 27-35, omissions admitting of satisfactory explanation,[105] the doctrine there contained stands as the primitive nucleus of a special tract "De B. Virgine"; the later elaboration of that nucleus by Suarez was to constitute one of the major advances of Mariology.[106]

St. Thomas, the Mariologist, is especially renowned as the Doctor of the divine Maternity. His scientific and exhaustive treatment of this dogma is unrivaled.[107] The divine motherhood is, moreover, the central point of his Mariology, from which all else radiates, the incomparable dignity of the Blessed Mother, her fullness of grace, and whatever other Marian privileges and prerogatives St. Thomas came to discuss.[108]

---

[104] The reputation of St. Thomas as a speculative theologian should not be allowed to obscure his concern for positive theology, in Mariology and elsewhere; cf. Roschini, *La Mariologia di S.* Tommaso, pp. 37-39; R. Bernard, *art. cit.,* in *Bull. de la Soc. Franç. de l'Ét. Mar.,* 1935, pp. 91-92.

[105] Cf. Roschini, *op. cit.,* pp. 167-168.

[106] Cf. J. A. de Aldama, *Mariologia,* in *Sacrae Theologiae Summa,* Vol. 3 (Matriti, 1950), p. 289.

[107] Cf. Roschini, *op. cit.,* pp. 117-162.

[108] Cf. Morgott, *op. cit.,* p. 5. In effect, then, the divine Maternity operated as the primary principle of the Angelic Doctor's Mariology, although he never explicitly discussed such a principle (John Gerson would be the first to do so). According to Roschini, *La Mariologia di S. Tommaso,* pp. 35-36, the primary Marian principle of St. Thomas was the divine Maternity considered in the concrete, that is, as historically verified, which would include not only Mary's physical motherhood of Christ but also her spiritual motherhood, as regards men; briefly, the principle of Mary's "universal maternity"; this position presupposes, of course, Roschini's attempt, *op.* cit., pp. 164-191, to interpret the Angelic Doctor's mind on the questions of Mary's Mediation,

Regrettably, Aquinas thought it necessary to exclude from among those privileges the singular one of the Immaculate Conception.[109] "The Blessed Virgin did indeed contract original sin, but was cleansed therefrom before her birth."[110] The Angelic Doctor based his view ultimately on a point which St. Albert had raised without, however, having particularly insisted on it, the universality of the Redemption.[111] "If Mary had been conceived without original sin," wrote St. Thomas, "she would not have had to be redeemed by Christ, and so Christ would not be the universal Redeemer of men, which detracts from His dignity."[112]

Thus the genius of the Angelic Doctor did not rise to the idea of a redemption which is able not only to liberate from sin already contracted but also to preserve from contracting the guilt of original sin at all — a more sublime mode of redemption which heightens rather than derogates from the dignity of Christ as universal Redeemer.[113] On the other hand, one must acknowledge that St. Thomas contributed in no small measure to the final solution of the controversy, by purging the idea of the Immaculate Conception from certain false elements, by further clarifying the issues in marshaling the strongest possible objections against the doctrine,

---

insofar as his views can be gleaned from incidental utterances or are implicit in other statements.

[109] Roschini, *op. cit.*, pp. 193-237, refutes those who try to show that St. Thomas was not an adversary of the Immaculate Conception.

[110] *S. Th.*, III, q. 27, a. 2, ad 2; cf. q. 27, aa. 1-2; *Comp. Theologiae*, p. 1, c. 224; etc. St. Thomas held with the opinion that Mary's sanctification in the womb was wrought "cito post conceptionem, et animae infusionem," Quodl., 6, q. 5, a. 7; cf. Roschini, *op. cit.*, pp. 228-229.

[111] Cf. M.-A. Genevois, *art. cit.*, in *Bull. de la Soc. Franç. de l'Ét. Mar.*, 1935, p. 48.

[112] *Comp. Theologiae*, p. 1, c. 224; Engl. transl., C. Vollert, S.J., *Compendium of Theology by St. Thomas Aquinas* (St. Louis, 1947), pp. 263-264.

[113] Pope Pius IX, Litt. Apost., *Ineffabilis Deus* (December 8, 1854): "Omnes pariter norunt quantopere solliciti fuerint sacrorum antistites ... profiteri, sanctissimam Dei Genetricem Virginem Mariam, ob praevisa Christi Domini Redemptoris merita numquam originali subiacuisse peccato, sed praeservatam omnino fuisse ab originis labe, et idcirco sublimiori modo redemptam." Quoted from *Le Encicliche Mariane*, ed. A. Tondini (Roma, 1950), p. 40.

and by developing powerful arguments for at least a special sanctification of Mary in the womb — arguments which can easily be adapted to the Immaculate Conception.[114]

No history of Mariology, however brief, could fail to give special notice also to John Duns Scotus († 1308).[115] Few will deny to him the title of Doctor Marianus, although it rests not on any wide contribution to the science of Mary but rather on the great Franciscan's unique role in the development of the dogma of the Immaculate Conception.[116]

To be sure, as we shall learn, other theologians before Scotus had defended that glorious privilege of the Blessed Mother, even at Paris — stronghold of the "maculists." But the Subtle Doctor is generally credited with having turned the tide, by his brilliant solution of the theological difficulties which then prevailed against the doctrine.[117]

---

[114] Cf. E. Dander, S.J., *Mariologia*, in L. Lercher, S.J., *Institutiones Theol. Dogm.*, Vol. 3, ed. 3 retractata (Oeniponte, 1942), n. 305; Roschini, *op. cit.*, pp. 236-237; F. Cayré, *Manual of Patrology and History of Theology*, Vol. 2, p. 627. Cf. X. Le Bachelet, *Immaculée Conception*, in *Dict. de Théologie Catholique*, Vol. 7, cols. 1050-1060.

[115] Cf. Roschini, *Mariologia*, Vol. 1, pp. 263-265; Vol. 2/2, ed. 2 (Roma, 1948), pp. 65-69; P. Raymond, O.F.M.Cap., *Duns Scot*, in *Dict. de Théol. Cath.*, Vol. 4, cols. 1896-1898; X. La Bachelet, *Immaculée Conception*, in *Dict. de Théol. Cath.*, Vol. 7, cols. 1073-1078; J. de Dieu, *art. cit.*, in *Maria*, ed. H. du Manoir, Vol. 2, pp. 794-797; additional literature is cited in Roschini, *op. cit.*, Vol. 1, p. 263, nota 1. The Marian teachings of Scotus are contained in his commentary on the Sentences, begun at Oxford (*Opus* Oxoniense), resumed and completed at Paris (*Reportata Parisiensia*); a critical edition of the relevant passages has been furnished by C. Balić, O.F.M.; *Ioannis Duns Scoti ... Theologiae Marianae Elementa* (Sibenici, 1933).

[116] The Marian questions which Scotus treated *ex professo* are these: Mary's Immaculate Conception; her marriage with St. Joseph (perpetual virginity); the divine Maternity, treated with depth and originality; the question of a real filiation of Christ in relation to Mary. Cf. Raymond, *art. cit.*, cols. 1896-1898; B. Merkelbach, O.P., review of Balić, op. cit., in Angelicum, Vol. 12, 1935, pp. 408-409; Balić, *La prédestination de la Très-Sainte Vierge dans la doctrine de Jean Duns Scot*, in *La France Franciscaine*, Vol. 19, 1936, pp. 114-158; Carol, *De Corredemptione Beatae Virginis Mariae ...*, p. 170.

[117] Cf. X. Le Bachelet, *art. cit.*, cols. 1073-1078, 1078-1083; F. Cayré, *Manual of Patrology*, etc., Vol. 2, pp. 657-658; Merkelbach, *art. cit.*, p. 409, accords Scotus the title Doctor immaculatae conceptionis. Roschini, *op. cit.*, Vol. 1,

Decisive, above all, was his insistence at Oxford and then at Paris (c. 1307) on the distinction between what came to be called the "liberative" and, in Mary's case, the "preservative" redemption, together with Scotus' insight that such preservation of Mary from original sin was a more sublime mode of redemption, thus heightening rather than lessening the dignity of Christ as Redeemer.[118] At Oxford Scotus had asserted not only the speculative possibility but also the factuality of the Immaculate Conception.[119] If at Paris he wrote more cautiously on the latter point, this may be attributed to deference on his part toward opponents of the doctrine, so numerous then in Paris and backed by such great authorities as Anselm, Bernard, Bonaventure, and Aquinas.[120] The story that the Subtle Doctor defended the Immaculate Conception victoriously in a public disputation before the University of Paris would seem to have a kernel of truth beneath the accretions of legend.[121]

After this necessary tribute to the towering figures of medieval Mariology there is room only for brief mention of other noteworthy contributors in this period to the science of Our Lady.[122] One may

---

pp. 264-265, and Vol. 2/2, pp. 68-69, contends that the Subtle Doctor's role in regard to the clarification of the doctrine has been highly exaggerated.

[118] Cf. *In 4 Sent.*, lib. 3, d. 3, q. 1; in Balić, op. cit., pp. 20-43 (Opus *Oxon.*), 45-54 (Report. *Par.*).

[119] Cf. X. Le Bachelet, *art. cit.*, col. 1075.

[120] Cf. *ibid.*, col. 1076. Roschini, op. cit., Vol. 1, p. 265, nota 1, spurns this explanation. He further remarks (p. 265) that the opusculum known as the Theoremata denies the Immaculate Conception, and that this work "certainly belongs to Scotus — as Father Balić has apodictically demonstrated"; Merkelbach, art. cit., p. 408, likewise represents Balić as regarding the Theoremata to be certainly authentic; actually, Balić, op. cit., p. cxlv, is content to say that the question is not yet settled, and that in the meanwhile the traditional view on the authenticity of the work remains in possession.

[121] Cf. Balić, *op. cit.*, pp. xcvii-cxiv; X. Le Bachelet, *art. cit.*, cols. 1076-1077.

[122] On these and other medieval Mariologists, cf. Roschini, *Mariologia*, Vol. 1, pp. 262-276; M. Mueller, O.F.M., *Maria. Ihre geistige Gestalt und Persoenlichkeit* in *der Theologie des Mittelalters, in Katholische Marienkunde,* ed. P. Sträter, S.J. (Paderborn, 1947), Vol. 1, pp. 268-316; also the several articles on devotion to Mary in various religious orders and congregations, in *Maria,* ed. H. du Manoir, Vol. 2, pp. 547-906.

not, of course, forget other scholars of the University of Oxford whose early support of the doctrine of the Immaculate Conception paved the way for Duns Scotus. Among these we may account the Cistercian, Alexander Neckam (✝ 1217), and Robert Grosseteste, of the secular clergy (✝ 1253, as Bishop of Lincoln).[123] The latter's university lectures to sons of St. Francis of Assisi are credited by some with having laid the primary foundation of the traditional teaching of the Franciscan theologians on the Immaculate Conception.[124] Then there is also William of Ware, O.F.M. (✝ c. 1300), who lectured at Oxford, thereafter at Paris.[125] Reputedly the teacher of Duns Scotus, he is considered by some to have supplied his disciple with essentially all that the Subtle Doctor was to say in defense of the Immaculate Conception.[126] Others, however, attribute his teaching on the subject to the influence of his celebrated pupil.[127]

Famed chiefly as the compiler of the popular Golden Legend, James of Voragine (rather, Varagine), O.P. (✝ 1298, as the Archbishop of Genoa), deserves also to be remembered as the author of the Mariale aureum and of many other Marian sermons,

---

[123] On both theologians, cf. F. Mildner, O.S.M., *The Oxford Theologians of the Thirteenth Century and the Immaculate Conception*, in *Marianum*, Vol. 2, 1940, pp. 284-299; on Neckam, cf. also supra, footnote 54.

[124] Cf. Mildner, *art. cit.*, in *Marianum*, Vol. 2, 1940, p. 299.

[125] Cf. Gulielmi Guarrae, J. D. Scoti, Petri Aureoli, *Quaestiones disputatae de Immaculata Conceptione B. M. V.* (Ad Claras Aquas, 1904). Cf. X. Le Bachelet, *Immaculée Conception*, in *DTC*, Vol. 7, cols. 1060-1062.

[126] Cf. Roschini, *Mariologia*, Vol. 1, pp. 264-265, and Vol. 2/2, pp. 68-69; X. Le Bachelet, *Immaculée Conception*, in *DTC*, Vol. 7, col. 1075; M. Grabmann, *Die Geschichte der katholischen Theologie seit dem Ausgang der Vaeterzeit* (Freiburg im Br.), p. 89. Roschini and Le Bachelet acknowledge Scotus' superiority in this respect, that, unlike William of Ware, he rejected the old theory of concupiscence infecting the flesh and transmitting original sin, in favor of St. Anselm's position (already adopted by Aquinas) which placed the essence of original sin in the privation of sanctifying grace.

[127] Cf. J. de Dieu, *art. cit.*, in *Maria*, ed. H. du Manoir, Vol. 2, p. 794. On the interdependence between Ware and Scotus relative to the Immaculate Conception, see the interesting and well-documented paper by L. Siekaniec, O.F.M., *William of Ware*, in *The Scotist*, 1941, pp. 38-40; likewise M. Müller, O.F.M., *Johannes Duns Scotus* (Gladbach, 1934), p. 12; F. Pelster, S.J., *Duns Scotus nach englischen Handschriften*, in *Zeitschrift für katholische Theologie*, Vol. 51, 1927, p. 68; J. Lechner, *Wilhelm von Ware*, in *Lexikon für Theologie und Kirche*, Vol. 10, col. 910.

Scholastic in cast, which exercised great influence in the Middle Ages.[128]

Remarkable on many other grounds, the Spanish theologian, Bl. Raymond Lull († 1316), a member of the Third Order of St. Francis, merits attention for his Mariology as well.[129] The latter is found mainly in his Disputatio Eremitae et Raymundi super aliquibus dubiis quaestionibus sententiarum Petri Lombardi, the *Liber de Sancta Maria*, and the poems, *Plant de Nostra Dona Santa Maria* and *Horas de Nostra Dona Santa Maria.* The Doctor Illuminatus was perhaps the first to uphold the doctrine of the Immaculate Conception at Paris, in his *Disputatio Eremitae* ... (a.d. 1298); however, his explanations were not without flaw, and their importance has been exaggerated at the expense of William of Ware and of Duns Scotus. Outstanding, on the other hand, were the Spaniard's teachings on the spiritual Maternity of Mary.

That Mariology came to win a special place in theology is due in no small degree to the efforts of Peter Auriol, O.F.M. († 1322 as Bishop of Aix).[130] He is renowned especially for his defense of the Immaculate Conception, in a special treatise, *Tractatus de Conceptione B. M. V.*, and in a vindication of the latter work, *Repercussorium editum contra adversarium innocentiae Matris Dei.* Among the reasons for believing that God preserved the Blessed Virgin from original sin, Peter cited Mary's Assumption and the conviction that her body had been spared from all corruption. The same author was the first to discuss explicitly the question, destined to be long controverted: Was Mary exempted from original sin not

---

[128] Cf. P. Lorenzin, O.F.M., *Mariologia Iacobi a Varagine, O.P.* (Romae, 1951).

[129] Cf. Roschini, *Mariologia,* Vol. 1, pp. 265-266; E. Longpré, O.F.M., *Lulle, Raymond,* in *DTC,* Vol. 9, cols. 1127-1128; X. Le Bachelet, *Immaculée Conception,* in *DTC,* Vol. 7, cols. 1062-1064.

[130] Cf. Roschini, *Mariologia,* Vol. 1, pp. 267-269; A. Teetaert, O.F.M.Cap., *Pierre Auriol,* in *DTC,* Vol. 12, cols. 1821-1826, 1873-1875; idem, *Un grand Docteur marial franciscain: Pierre d'Auriol,* in *Études Franciscaines,* Vol. 39, 1927, pp. 352-375; Vol. 40, 1928, pp. 124-152; J. de Dieu, *art. cit.,* in Maria, ed. H. du Manoir, Vol. 2, p. 802. Cf. Gulielmi Guarrae, J. D. *Scoti, Petri Aureoli quaestiones disputatae de Immaculata Conceptione B. M. V.* (Ad Claras Aquas, 1904).

only *de facto* but also *de jure*?[131]

Among others who enriched medieval Mariology we may mention the Franciscans, Francis of Meyronnes († 1325)[132] and William of Nottingham († 1336);[133] Engelbert, Benedictine abbot of Admont († 1331), author of an extensive dogmatic monograph, De gratiis et virtutibus B.V.M., and of a doctrinally interesting Marian psalter;[134] John Bacon or Baconthorp, the great Carmelite theologian († 1348), who, after initial opposition, became one of the stanchest defenders of Mary's Immaculate Conception, thus bringing about the triumph of that doctrine among the Carmelites;[135] the Viennese theologian, Henry of Langenstein, also known as Henry de Hassia, Sr. († 1397);[136] John Gerson († 1429), renowned as the first to treat, ex professo, Marian principles and to lay down sage directives for Mariologists.[137]

So superbly and completely are Marian themes elaborated in the sermons of St. Bernardine of Siena († 1444), that the Franciscan deserves to be ranked among the great medieval Doctors of Mary.[138]

---

[131] Cf. J. de Dieu, *art. cit.*, in Maria, ed. H. du Manoir, Vol. 2, p. 802; Teetaert, *art. cit.*, in DTC, Vol. 12, cols. 1873-1874. For the later history of this controversy, cf. J. Schwane, Dogmengeschichte, Vol. 4 (Dogmengesch. der neueren Zeit) (Freiburg im Br., 1890), pp. 179-183.

[132] Cf. J. de Dieu, *art. cit.*, in *Maria*, ed. H. du Manoir, Vol. 2, p. 803; M. Mueller, *Maria. Ihre geistige Gestalt und Persoenlichkeit in der Theologie des Mittelalters*, in *Katholische Marienkunde*, ed. P. Straeter, Vol. 1, pp. 270, 294, 298 f., 301, 310, 313 f.

[133] Cf. A. Emmen, O.F.M., Immaculata Deiparae Conceptio secundum Guillelmum de Nottingham, in Marianum, Vol. 5, 1943, pp. 220-244.

[134] Cf. G. Fowler, Intellectual Interests of Engelbert of Admont (New York, 1947), pp. 43-44; S. Beissel, S.J., Geschichte der Verehrung Marias in Deutschland waehrend des Mittelalters (Freiburg im Br., 1909), pp. 246-248.

[135] Cf. X. Le Bachelet, art. *Immaculée Conception*, in DTC, Vol. 7, col. 1082; and DTC, *Tables générales*, s.v. Baconthorp, col. 349.

[136] Cf. M. Grabmann, *Die Geschichte der katholischen Theologie seit dem Ausgang der Vaeterzeit* (Freiburg im Br., 1933), p. 115 f.

[137] Cf. Roschini, *Mariologia*, Vol. 1, pp. 270-271, 323, note 3. The Marian contributions of this somewhat neglected theologian have been appreciated by A. Combes, *La doctrine mariale du chancelier Jean Gerson*, in *Maria*, ed. H. du Manoir, Vol. 2, pp. 865-882.

[138] Cf. Roschini, *Mariologia*, Vol. 1, pp. 271-273; G. Folgarait, *La teologia mariana di San Bernardino da Siena* (Milano, 1939); P. Emm. ab Izegem, O.F.M.Cap., *De doctrina mariologica S. B. Senensis*, in *Collectanea Francescana*,

Acclaimed as "the echo of St. Bernard," he is regarded as the greatest theologian of the universal Mediation of Our Lady; and his doctrine on her Assumption, applauded by Pope Pius XII in *Munificentissimus Deus,* has moved some to salute him as "the Doctor of the Assumption."[139]

Other medieval preachers and theologians to whom Marian science is indebted include Alphonsus Tostatus, Bishop of Ávila († 1455);[140] Ambrose Spiera, O.S.M. († 1455);[141] St. Antoninus, O.P., Archbishop of Florence († 1459);[142] Cardinal John Torquemada, O.P. († 1468);[143] the Carthusian, Denis of Ryckel († 1471);[144] and Bl. Bernardine of Busti, O.F.M. († 1515), with whom the period came to a not inglorious close.[145]

During that four-century span from St. Anselm to Bl. Bernardine, Mariology registered many substantial gains. Some of them may be briefly noted. The dogma of the Divine Motherhood, defined at Ephesus, achieved theological deepening, especially at the hands of St. Thomas Aquinas and Duns Scotus. With St. Anselm, the Scholastics emphasized that Mary's exalted office as the Mother of God required in her the greatest purity, sanctity, and fullness of grace after Christ. Implicit in such teaching is the doctrine of the Immaculate Conception. If St. Bernard and many subsequent theologians of great name failed to recognize this and even denied Mary's immunity from original sin at her conception, some excuse

---

Vol. 10, 1940, pp. 383-394; L. di Fonzo, O.F.M.Conv., *La mariologia di S. B. da Siena,* in *Miscellanea Francescana,* Vol. 47, 1947, pp. 3-102; D. Scaramuzzi, O.F.M., *La dottrina del B. G. Duns Scoto nella predicazione di S. Bernardino da Siena* (Firenze, 1930), pp. 135-141.

[139] Cf. E. Longpré, *Bernardin de Sienne (Saint),* in *Catholicisme, hier, aujourd'hui, demain,* Vol. 1, col. 1488.

[140] Cf. Grabmann, *op. cit.,* p. 122.

[141] Cf. Roschini, *Mariologia,* Vol. 1, p. 273.

[142] Cf. *ibid.,* p. 273.

[143] Cf. *ibid.,* p. 273; Grabmann, *op. cit.,* p. 100.

[144] Cf. Roschini, *Mariologia,* Vol. 1, p. 274; J. De Wit, *Dionysius de Karthuijser over onze lieve Vrouw,* in *Handelingen van het vlaamsch Maria-Congres te Brussel,* Vol. 1 (Brussel, 1922), pp. 345-351.

[145] Cf. Roschini, *op. cit.,* p. 275; J. de Dieu, *art. cit.,* p. 806; F. Cucchi, O.F.M.Conv., *La Mediazione universale della Santissima Vergine negli scritti di Bernardino de'Bustis* (Milano, 1942).

can be found in the confused state of the question in the twelfth and thirteenth centuries,[146] and in the seemingly insoluble difficulties, especially on the score of the universality of the Redemption. The ensuing controversy gradually brought about the clarification of the true issues; the solution, by Duns Scotus and others, of the formidable objections; and the development of positive arguments favorable to the thesis of the Immaculate Conception.[147]

Therewith the opposition, which had never been universal,[148] dwindled rapidly. By the end of the fourteenth century the original sanctity of Mary's soul was common doctrine among the Franciscans, who were joined in the latter half of the century by the Carmelites, Augustinians, Premonstratensians, Trinitarians, Servites, and by many Benedictines, Cistercians, and Carthusians.[149] In the fifteenth century the great majority of theologians upheld this glorious privilege of the Blessed Mother.[150] In the meanwhile, however, they continued to debate the manner of Mary's preservation from original sin.[151]

Another significant development in medieval Mariology was the triumph of the doctrine of Our Blessed Mother's Corporeal Assumption into heaven. This Marian prerogative had been controverted from the ninth to the twelfth centuries, but thereafter

---

[146] Cf. X. Le Bachelet, art. *Immaculée Conception*, in *DTC*, Vol. 7, cols. 1041-1042.

[147] Cf. *ibid.*, cols. 1089-1093; A. Teetaert, art. *Pierre Auriol*, in *DTC*, Vol. 12, cols. 1823-1824.

[148] X. Le Bachelet, *art. cit.*, *DTC*, Vol. 7, col. 1058, observes that "the opposition was not universal, but particular and, in a certain sense, local. Alexander of Hales, Albert the Great, St. Bonaventure, St. Thomas Aquinas, and their disciples, all pertained to the same literary milieu, the university of Paris." Cf. idem, art. *Marie — Immaculée Conception*, in *Dictionnaire Apologétique de la Foi Catholique*, Vol. 3 (Paris, 1926), col. 263.

[149] Cf. X. Le Bachelet, *art. cit.*, in *DTC*, Vol. 7, cols. 1078-1089.

[150] Cf. *ibid.*, cols. 1108-1132; J. Schwane, *Dogmengeschichte*, Vol. 3 (*Dogmengesch. der mittleren Zeit*) (Freiburg im Br., 1882), pp. 426-428; Vol. 4 (Dogmengesch. der neueren Zeit) (Freiburg im Br., 1890), pp. 178-179. M. Mueller mistakenly declares that most medieval theologians rejected the Immaculate Conception; cf. *art. cit.*, in *Katholische Marienkunde*, Vol. 2, p. 295.

[151] Cf. X. Le Bachelet, art. *Immaculée Conception*, in *DTC*, Vol. 7, cols. 1093-1094; cf., *supra* note 131.

it became the common teaching, vindicated by arguments upon which subsequent centuries would find it difficult to improve.[152] The contributions of the great Scholastics in this sphere are admirably summarized by Pope Pius XII in *Munificentissimus Deus.*[153]

As our references to the great Doctors of Marian Mediation have already suggested, another central preoccupation of medieval theologians was the role of the Blessed Mother in the redemptive work of Christ, and, by the same token, her relations with the Church,[154] and with all men, her spiritual children.[155] Fruitfully discussed in this period was not only Mary's part in the distribution of all graces, but also the fact of and the mode of her co-operation in the acquisition of those graces, i.e., her part in the objective Redemption.[156] The elucidation of the latter aspect of Marian Mediation was facilitated to some extent by the theological deepening of the dogma of the divine Maternity, and by the gradual acceptance of Our Lady's Immaculate Conception.[157] In its turn, the growing appreciation of the Blessed Mother's coredemptive role contributed to a heightened understanding of her Queenship.[158]

These major accomplishments of medieval Mariologists suffice to refute B. Otten's contention that the Church Fathers had left the

---

[152] Cf. G. Roschini, *Il Dogma dell'Assunzione* (*Studi Mariani*, 3), ed. 2 (Roma, 1951), pp. 81-83; C. Balić, O.F.M., *Testimonia de Assumptione B. V. M. ex omnibus saeculis. Pars prior: Ex aetate ante Concilium Tridentinum* (Romae, 1948), pp. 222-387. C. Piana, O.F.M., *Assumptio B. V. M. apud scriptores saec. XIII* (*Bibliotheca Mariana Medii Aevi*, fasc. 4) (Sibenici-Romae, 1942).

[153] 133 Cf. *A.A.S.*, Vol. 42 (4 nov. 1950), pp. 762-766; Engl. transl., *Catholic Mind*, January, 1951, pp. 72-74.

[154] Cf. H. Barré, C.S.Sp., *Marie et l'Église; du Vénérable Bede à Saint Albert le Grand*, in *Marie et l'Église. Bull. de la Soc. Franç. d'Ét. Mar.*, 1951 (Paris, 1952), pp. 59-143.

[155] Cf. W. O'Connor, *The Spiritual Maternity of Our Lady in Tradition*, in *Marian Studies*, Vol. 3, 1952, pp. 153-168.

[156] Cf. J. Carol, O.F.M., *De Corredemptione B. M. V.* (Civitas Vaticana, 1950), pp. 151-198; L. Riley, *Historical Conspectus of the Doctrine of Mary's Co-Redemption*, in *Marian Studies*, Vol. 2, 1951, pp. 47-54; Roschini, *La Madonna seconda la Fede e la Teologia*, Vol. 1 (Roma, 1953), pp. 149-150.

[157] Cf. M. Mueller, *art. cit.*, in *Katholische Marienkunde*, ed. Sträter, Vol. 1, pp. 282-286, 286-295.

[158] Cf. W. Hill, S.S., *Our Lady's Queenship in the Middle Ages and Modern Times*, in *Marian Studies*, Vol. 4, 1953, pp. 135-153, 154-155 (summary).

Scholastics little room for further development of Marian doctrines.[159] At the same time, they validate the judgment of G. Philips, that, if the theological treatise *De Beata* be of recent origin, its constitutive elements have an ancient and thoroughly respectable history.[160]

MODERN MARIOLOGY
(SIXTEENTH TO NINETEENTH CENTURIES)

This period extends from the Council of Trent, which expressly excluded "the blessed and immaculate Virgin Mary, Mother of God" from its decree on original sin,[161] and thus paved the way for the dogmatic definition of her Immaculate Conception, to the definition itself on December 8, 1854.

The intervening centuries witnessed notable advances in the science of Our Lady. Tremendous impetus to such progress was given by the violent attacks on Marian cult and doctrines, which were mounted first by the Protestant "Reformers,"[162] then by the Jansenists and kindred spirits,[163] especially Adam Widenfeld, in his notorious brochure of 1673, *Monita salutaria B. Mariae Virginis ad cultores suos indiscretos*.[164]

In meeting these onslaughts the defenders of Catholic orthodoxy produced a huge volume of polemical and dogmatic literature,

---

[159] Cf. *supra*, note 16.

[160] G. Philips, in *Ephemerides Theologicae Lovanienses*, Vol. 19, 1953, p. 460, reviewing the *Marie et l'Église* volume of the *Société Française d'Études Mariales*.

[161] Sess. 5, cap. 6 (June 17, 1546); D.B., n. 792. Cf. M. Tognetti, *L'Immacolata al Conc. Tridentino*, in *Marianum*, Vol. 15, 1953, pp. 304-374.

[162] Cf. C. Dillenschneider, C.SS.R., *La Mariologie de S. Alphonse de Liguori*, Vol. I (Fribourg, Suisse, 1931), pp. 1-32; Roschini, Mariologia, Vol. 1, pp. 391-393; S. Beissel, S.J., Geschichte der Verehrung Marias im 16. u. 17. Jahrhundert (Freiburg im Br., 1910), pp. 100-111.

[163] Cf. Dillenschneider, *op. cit.*, Vol. 1, pp. 33-104; Roschini, *op. cit.*, Vol. 1, pp. 393-395.

[164] Attempts at a partial rehabilitation of Widenfeld have been undertaken by P. Hoffer, S.M., *La dévotion à Marie au déclin du XVIIe siècle autour du Jansénisme et des 'Avis salutaires de la B. Vierge Marie à ses dévots indiscrets'* (Paris, 1938); G. Cacciatore, S. Alfonso de Liguori e il Giansenismo (Firenze, 1942). Roschini rejects these efforts in his *La Madonna secondo la Fede e la Teologia*, Vol. 1, pp. 156-157.

which, if uneven in quality, nevertheless grounded more thoroughly and illumined more clearly the perfection of the Mother of God; her unrivaled sanctity; her immunity from all sin, both original and actual; her universal Mediation in the acquisition and the distribution of all graces; and the special veneration which is her due.[165]

Dozens of authors belonging to this period merit special mention, but these pages can notice only some of the more eminent champions of Mary's glories.[166] The first German Doctor of the universal Church, St. Peter Canisius, S.J. († 1597), unquestionably falls into this category, thanks to his masterful refutation of Protestant errors, the *De Maria Virgine incomparabili et Dei Genetrice sacrosancta libri quinque.*[167] This apologetical classic may be termed the first complete exposition of Catholic doctrine on the Mother of God.

As such, it assures its author a high place in the historical evolution of the science of Mary. However, the honor of having created the first modern Mariology, rigorously scientific and scholastic, belongs not to Canisius but to his confrere in religion,

---

[165] Cf. Roschini, *op. cit.,* Vol. 1, p. 153; Dillenschneider, op. cit., Vol. 1, pp. 150-151, 194-195, 226-227, 250-251; Beissel, op. cit., pp. 112-117; H. Rondet, S.J., preface to J.-B. Terrien, S.J., La Mère des hommes, Vol. 1, ed. 8 (Paris, 1950), pp. 13-44. For details on the Mariological progress in this era, confer: E. Dublanchy, art. *Marie,* in *DTC,* Vol. 9 (Paris, 1926), passim, especially cols. 2355-2369, 2392-2394, 2400-2403; 2436-2453; X. Le Bachelet, art. *Immaculée Conception,* in *DTC,* Vol. 7, cols. 1150-1209; J. Carol, *De Corredemptione B. V. M.,* pp. 198-480; L. Riley, *Historical Conspectus of the Doctrine of Mary's Co-Redemption,* in *Marian Studies,* Vol. 2, 1951, pp. 64-92; W. O'Connor, *The Spiritual Maternity of Our Lady in Tradition,* in *Marian Studies,* Vol. 3, 1952, pp. 168-172; W. Hill, S.S., *Our Lady's Queenship in the Middle Ages and Modern Times,* in *Marian Studies,* Vol. 4, 1953, pp. 155-169; C. Balić, O.F.M., *Testimonia de Assumptione B. V. M. ex omnibus saeculis. Pars altera: Ex aetate post Concilium Tridentinum* (Romae, 1950); P. Renaudin, *Assumptio B. Mariae Virginis Matris Dei* (Taurini-Romae, 1933), pp. 69-92.

[166] For other Mariologists of the modern era, cf. Roschini, Mariologia, Vol. 1, pp. 276-301; Dillenschneider, *op. cit.,* Vol. 1, pp. 107-254; Grabmann, *op. cit.,* passim; and various articles in *Maria,* ed. H. du Manoir, Vol. 2, pp. 547-991.

[167] Cf. Dillenschneider, *op. cit.,* Vol. 1, pp. 109-113. The *De Maria Virgine incomparabili* is reproduced in Vols. 8-9 of J. Bourassé, *Summa aurea de laudibus B. M. V.* (Parisiis, 1862).

Francis Suárez (✝ 1617).[168] As we have already remarked, the doctrine of Aquinas in the *Summa Theologica*, III, qq. 27-35, stands as the primitive nucleus of a special tract "De B. Virgine"; the Spanish Jesuit's elaboration of that nucleus, in the first twenty-three disputations of his *De mysteriis vitae Christi*,[169] is justly celebrated as a monumental contribution both to the content and method of Mariology.

Among the foremost Mariologists of all time one must number the Capuchin preacher, St. Lawrence of Brindisi (✝ 1619). Original, yet always theologically sound, and often profound, his *Mariale*, consisting of 84 sermons, amounts to a complete, if informal, treatise *De Beata*, which is especially remarkable for its thorough and effective vindication of the Immaculate Conception.[170]

The latter doctrine, championed also by St. Peter Canisius and Suarez, found a further supporter in St. Robert Bellarmine, S.J. (✝ 1621), whose sermons and Disputationes *de controversiis* rendered yet other valuable services to Marian doctrine and piety, notably by their refutation of Protestant errors.[171]

Some other distinguished Jesuit Mariologists of the period may be noticed here. The science of Our Lady owes a good deal, on the positive side, to D. Petau (✝ 1652), whose Dogmata Theologica (lib. 14) assembled and subjected to critical scrutiny the ancient traditions on Mary's prerogatives.[172] Also deserving of express mention are the prolific Theophilus Raynaud (✝ 1663);[173] George de

---

[168] Cf. J. de Aldama, S.J., *Piété et système dans la Mariologie du 'Docteur Eximius,'* in *Maria*, ed. H. du Manoir, Vol. 2, pp. 975-990, esp. pp. 979-983; Dillenschneider, *op. cit.*, Vol. 1, pp. 153-154, 157-161; J. Bover, S.J., *Suarez, mariólogo*, in *Estudios Eclesiásticos*, Vol. 22, 1948, pp. 311-337.

[169] Opera omnia, ed. Vivès, Vol. 19, pp. 1-337.

[170] Cf. Roschini, *Mariologia*, Vol. 1, pp. 281-283; idem, *La Mariologia di S. Lorenzo da Brindisi* (Padova, 1951); Jérome de Paris, *La doctrine mariale de S. Laurent de Brindes* (Paris, 1933); Dillenschneider, *op. cit.*, Vol. 1, pp. 213-218.

[171] Cf. Dillenschneider, *op. cit.*, Vol. 1, pp. 113-118; S. Tromp, S.J., *S. Robertus Bellarminus et B. Virgo*, in *Gregorianum*, Vol. 21, 1940, pp. 162-182; J. A. Hardon, *Bellarmine and the Blessed Virgin*, in *Our Lady's Digest*, Vol. 8, October, 1953, pp. 175-183; idem, *Mary Mediatrix in the Theology of Bellarmine*, in *The Homiletic and Pastoral Review*, Vol. 48, 1947, pp. 91-97.

[172] Cf. Dillenschneider, *op. cit.*, Vol. 1, pp. 167-170.

[173] Cf. *ibid.*, pp. 170-176.

Rhodes (✝ 1661), who incorporated in his Disputationes theologicae scholasticae an excellent treatise *De Maria Deipara;*[174] and Paul Segneri (✝ 1694), author of the little classic, *Il devoto della Vergine.*[175]

Dillenschneider has rescued from obscurity one of the ablest Marian theologians of the seventeenth century, John Baptist Novati, O.S.Cam. (✝ 1648). His *De eminentia Deiparae Virginis* adopted and developed many Suarezian theses; of chief interest is the work's discussion of Mariological principles and axioms, and of various aspects of Marian Mediation, particularly the Blessed Mother's immediate co-operation in the objective Redemption, and her spiritual Maternity.[176] The latter themes also found admirable treatment in the De hierarchia Mariana of Bartholomew de Los Rios, O.E.S.A. (✝ 1652).[177]

The traditions of the Franciscan school, especially its advocacy of the Immaculate Conception, were ably continued in the writings of Peter de Alvay Astorga, O.F.M. (✝ 1667),[178] and the *Conférences ... sur les grandeurs de la très Sainte Vierge Marie Mère de Dieu* of Louis D'Argentan, O.F.M.Cap. (✝ 1680).[179] Important for the study of Scotist Mariological thought are the *De eminentissima Deiparae Virginis perfectione* libri tres by John M. Zamoro, O.F.M.Cap. (✝ 1649),[180] and the remarkable Fons illimis theologiae scoticae marianae by Charles del Moral, O.F.M. (✝1731).[181]

Among the sons of St. Dominic who advanced Marian science in this period we may name Justin Miechow (✝1689), renowned for

---

[174] Cf. *ibid.,* pp. 178-182.

[175] Cf. *ibid.,* pp. 222-225.

[176] Cf. *ibid.,* pp. 161-166; J. Carol, *De Corredemptione B. V. M.,* pp. 288-290.

[177] Cf. Roschini, *Mariologia,* Vol. 1, p. 286; Carol, *op. cit.,* pp. 271-273; A. Musters, *La Souveraineté de la Vierge d'après les écrits mariologiques de Barthélemy de los Rios* (Bruges, 1946).

[178] Cf. Roschini, *op. cit.,* Vol. 1, p. 289.

[179] Cf. Dillenschneider, *op. cit.,* Vol. 1, pp. 187-194.

[180] Cf. Archangelus a Roc, O.F.M.Cap., *Joannes M. Zamoro ab Udine, O.F.M.Cap., praeclarus mariologus (1579-1649)* (Roma, s.a.), *extractum ex Collectanea Franciscana,* Vol. 15-19, 1945-1949.

[181] Cf. Roschini, *op. cit.,* p. 295; I. de Guerra Lazpiur, O.F.M., *Integralis conceptus Maternitatis divinae juxta Carolum del Moral* (Romae, 1953); Carol, *op. cit.,* pp. 339-342.

his exhaustive and solid commentaries on the Litany of Loreto;[182] Vincent Contenson (†1674), whose celebrated Theologia mentis et cordis contains an extensive and pellucid dissertation on the Blessed Mother's prerogatives;[183] and John Van Ketwig (†1746), whose *Panoplia Mariana is a Mariology ad mentem S. Thomae.*[184]

As could be expected of the "Order of Mary," the Servites have contributed profoundly to the development of Marian dogma and piety.[185] A shining example is the Austrian theologian, Caesar Shguanin († 1769), remarkable for the quality as well as the quantity of his writings on all phases of Mariology.[186] The science of Our Lady has also been enriched by the Clerics Regular of the Mother of God, especially by Hippolytus Marracci († 1675), another amazingly prolific author.[187]

Jansenist rigorism and the *Monita salutaria* of Widenfeld were strenuously combated by many of the controversialists and theologians already named in these pages. But exceptional in this regard were the labors of John Crasset, SJ. († 1692),[188] and, above all, of Henry Boudon († 1702).[189] Several spiritual writers of the era also entered the lists, with telling effect. Their devotional works not only nourished Marian piety but, at the same time, broadened and deepened its doctrinal bases, particularly in connection with the mediatorial role of Our Blessed Mother, a crucial issue in the

---

[182] Cf. Roschini, *op. cit.*, p. 285; Dillenschneider, *op. cit.*, Vol. 1, pp. 218-220.

[183] Cf. Dillenschneider, *op. cit.*, Vol. 1, pp. 182-184.

[184] Cf. *ibid.*, pp. 145-150.

[185] Cf. G. Roschini, *L'Ordre des Servites de Marie*, in *Maria*, ed. H. du Manoir, Vol. 2, pp. 885-907.

[186] Cf. idem, *Mariologia*, Vol. 1, p. 296.

[187] Cf. F. Ferraironi, O.M.D., *Le culte marial dans l'Ordre des Clercs Réguliers de la Mère de Dieu*, in *Maria*, ed. H. du Manoir, Vol. 2, pp. 917-923; Roschini, Mariologia, Vol. 1, pp. 290-291; Roschini, *Un grande precursore dell'era mariana: il P. Ippolito Marracci, O.M.D.*, in *Alma Socia Christi*, Vol. 11, 1953, pp. 219-232.

[188] Cf. Dillenschneider, *op. cit.*, Vol. 1, pp. 118-124; H. Baron, S.J., *Jean Crasset (1618-1692), le Jansénisme et la dévotion à la Sainte Vierge*, in *Bull. de la Soc. Franç. d'Études Mariales* (Paris, 1938), 249-255.

[189] Cf. Dillenschneider, *op. cit.*, Vol. 1, pp. 124-128, 242-246.

Jansenist controversy.[190]

Of the above group the most famous representatives are Cardinal de Bérulle († 1629);[191] John Olier († 1657);[192] St. John Eudes († 1680);[193] St. Louis M. Grignion de Montfort († 1716), universally renowned for his Treatise on the True Devotion to the Bl. Virgin;[194] and the no less celebrated Redemptorist Doctor of the Universal Church, St. Alphonsus Liguori († 1787), whose tremendously successful Glories of Mary is both dogmatic and ascetical, harmonizing profound science and great erudition with ardent filial affection for the Mother of God and Mother of men.[195]

To these doctrinally significant spiritual writers, mostly of the Bérullian school, one must add the last disciple of that school, William Chaminade († 1850), founder of the Marianists, whose published and unpublished writings are now being increasingly explored and appreciated.[196]

If we assign the contributions of Cardinal John Henry

---

[190] Cf. E. Druwé, S.J., *La Médiation universelle de Marie*, in *Maria*, ed. H. du Manoir, Vol. 1, pp. 551-552; M.-A. Genevois, O.P., in *Bull. de la Soc. Franç. d'Ét. Mar.* (Paris, 1936), p. 50.

[191] Cf. Dillenschneider, *op. cit.*, Vol. 1, 230-234; Roschini, *Mariologia*, Vol. 1, p. 284; J. Nicolas, O.P., *La doctrine mariale du Card. de Bérulle*, in *Revue Thomiste*, Vol. 43, 1937, pp. 81-100.

[192] Cf. Dillenschneider, *op. cit.*, Vol. 1, pp. 234-238.

[193] Cf. *ibid.*, pp. 238-242; E. George, *Saint Jean Eudes, Modèle et Maitre de vie Mariale* (Paris, 1946).

[194] Cf. Dillenschneider, *op. cit.*, Vol. 1, pp. 246-250; Roschini, *Mariologia*, Vol. 1, pp. 293-295; F. Setzer, S.M.M., *The Spiritual Maternity and St. Louis M. de Montfort*, in *Marian Studies*, Vol. 3, 1952, pp. 197-207.

[195] Cf. J. Kannengieser, art. *Alphonse de Liguori*, in *DTC*, Vol. 1 (Paris, 1903), col. 917; Roschini, *op. cit.*, Vol. 1, 297-301; J. Dillenschneider, *La Mariologie de S. Alphonse de Liguori*, Vol. 2 (Fribourg, Suisse, 1934); see also Vol. 1, pp. 252-382.

[196] E. Neubert, S.M., *La doctrine mariale de Messier Chaminade* (Paris, 1938); T. Stanley, S.M., *The Mystical Body of Christ according to the Writings of Father William Joseph Chaminade: a Study of His Spiritual Writings* (Fribourg, Switzerland, 1952); excerpt from the same, Mary and the Mystical Body (The Marian Library, University of Dayton, Dayton, Ohio, 1953); F. Friedel, S.M., *Dogmatic Foundation of Father Chaminade's Doctrine of Filial Piety*, in *Marian Studies*, Vol. 3, 1952, pp. 208-217.

Newman[197] to the latter half of the nineteenth century, Chaminade is the sole Mariologist worthy of note in the preceding fifty years. For, despite the defeat of Jansenism, and notwithstanding the many gains registered in the Post-Tridentine era, Mariology was in low estate in the early decades of the nineteenth century. Jansenism, though overcome, had, along with rationalism, semirationalism, and Josephinism, left its mark on all theology,[198] and on the science of Mary in particular.[199] In this decadent epoch, the general works of theology tended to neglect the traditional place given to Our Lady, being content to treat only of her divine Maternity and perpetual virginity.[200] For their part, Mariologists were prone to exalt the Blessed Mother without reference to the whole of theology.[201] In short, the unhealthy gap between theology and Mariology, which Suárez had sought to close, had widened.[202]

However, the labors of earlier theologians of Our Lady were to be instrumental in bringing about a glorious renascence of Marian studies. Their painstaking discussions on the Immaculate Conception had ripened this doctrine for the solemn definition it came to receive from Pope Pius IX, in the Bull *Ineffabilis Deus*, December 8, 1854. One of the salutary effects of that Papal pronouncement was the gradual development of a rigorously scientific and adequate Mariology, as an organically structured treatise distinct from, yet integrated with, the rest of theology. A

---

[197] Cf. F. Friedel, S.M., *The Mariology of Cardinal Newman* (New York, 1928); John Henry Newman: Maria im Heilsplan, (eingeleitet u. uebertragen von Birgitta zu Muenster, O.S.B.) (Freiburg im Br., 1953); Most Rev. John J. Wright, Mariology in the English-speaking World, in Marian Studies, Vol. 2, 1951, pp. 11-26.

[198] Cf. M. Grabmann, *Die Geschichte der katholischen Theologie seit dem Ausgang der Vaeterzeit (Freiburg im Br., 1933)*, pp. 206-219; J. Bellamy, *La théologie catholique au XIXe siècle*, ed. 3 (Paris, 1904), pp. 1-20; E. Hocedez, S.J., *Histoire de la théologie au XIXe* siècle, Vol. 1 (Bruxelles, 1949), pp. 13-24.

[199] Cf. Bellamy, *op. cit.*, p. 267; P. Régamey, O.P., *Les plus beaux textes sur la Vierge Marie* (Paris, 1946), p. 295.

[200] Cf. Bellamy, *op. cit.*, p. 267.

[201] Cf. *Theology Digest*, 1 (1953), p. 145 (summary of article on Mary and the Church, by R. Laurentin, in *La Vie Spirituelle*, 86, 1952, pp. 295-304).

[202] Cf. J. A. de Aldama, S.J., *Mariologia*, in *Sacrae Theologiae Summa*, Vol. 3 (Matriti, 1950), p. 289.

résumé of this providential evolution is attempted in the next and last section of our brief history of Mariology.

III. CONTEMPORARY MARIOLOGY (1854-1954)

In the century which has elapsed since the dogmatic definition of the Immaculate Conception, many factors combined to produce the present flourishing state of Marian studies.[203] But chief among them has been the efficacious influence of the Papal *magisterium*. The initial impetus delivered by Ineffabilis Deus was sustained and augmented by a succession of other pontifical documents, from the ten Rosary Encyclicals of Leo XIII to the manifold Marian pronouncements of Pius XII.

To be sure, this Papal encouragement given to renewed serious studies of Our Lady bore fruit only gradually, although the harvest in the second half of the nineteenth century was not as lean as has been suggested.[204] Positive theology was the first to reap the benefit of the definition of the Immaculate Conception;[205] either in preparation for or as an aftermath of *Ineffabilis Deus*, there appeared

---

[203] On these factors, for example, Catholic reaction to attacks on Marian doctrine and cult (by Protestants, Old Catholics, Modernists, the Eastern Dissidents), the celebration of Marian Congresses, the publication of source materials, the foundation of Mariological Academies, Centers, and Societies, and the erection of university chairs of Mariology, etc., cf. Roschini, *Mariologia*, Vol. 1, pp. 396-399; idem, *La Madonna secondo la Fede a la Teologia*, Vol. 1, pp. 158-166. Mariological societies will be dealt with at length elsewhere in the present work.

[204] On the history of Mariology in the latter half of the nineteenth century, cf. Hocedez, op. cit., Vol. 3 (Bruxelles-Paris, 1947), pp. 313-316; Bellamy, op. cit., pp. 267-281. A. Noyon, S.J., art. Mariolatrie, in Dict. Apologétique de la Foi Catholique, Vol. 3 (Paris, 1926), col. 316, contends that few of the many works produced in this period possessed lasting significance; H. Rondet, S.J., in his preface to J.-B. Terrien, S.J., La Mère des hommes, Vol. 1, ed. 8 (Paris, 1950), pp. 46-47, believes that the Marian theology of the period concerned itself almost exclusively with the Immaculate Conception. Both judgments appear too sweeping; a glance at Hocedez, and at the nineteenth-century authors quoted in J. Carol, De Corredemptione B. V. M., pp. 382-480, suffices to suggest that, between 1854 and 1900, a goodly company of writers dealt ably with a wide variety of Mariological themes.

[205] Cf. Bellamy, *op. cit.*, pp. 270-273.

the works of Perrone, Guéranger, Passaglia, Ballerini, and Malou.[206] On the speculative side, the science of the Blessed Mother achieved precious growth with the Dogmatik of Matthias Joseph Scheeben († 1888), the century's greatest theologian and Mariologist, in whom speculative genius was wedded to a profound knowledge of the Church Fathers, and of medieval and Post-Tridentine Scholasticism.[207] Measured against the towering figure of Scheeben, of lesser importance are J. Petitalot,[208] August Nicholas,[209] Louis di

---

[206] J. Perrone, S.J., *De Immaculato B. V. Mariae Conceptu* (Romae, 1847); P. Guéranger, O.S.B., *Mémoire sur la question de l'Immaculée Conception de le très-sainte Vierge* (Paris, 1850); C. Passaglia, *De Immaculato Deiparae semper Virginis Conceptu Commentarius,* 3 vols. (Romae, 1854-1855); A. Ballerini, S.J., *Sylloge Monumentorum ad Mysterium Virginis Deiparae illustrandum,* 2 vols. (Romae, 1854-1856); J. Malou, *L'Immaculée Conception de la très-sainte Vierge Marie,* 2 vols. (Bruxelles, 1857). On the source collections of Bourassé and Roskovany, already mentioned (supra, note 15), and on that of R. de Fleury, likewise uncritical, see Roschini, *Mariologia,* Vol. 1, pp. 301, 302, 304-305.

[207] Cf. Grabmann, *op. cit.,* p. 231; C. Feckes, in Scheeben-Feckes, *Die Braeutliche Gottesmutter* (Freiburg im Br., 1936), pp. VIII-IX. Scbeeben's *Mariologie* is found in the third volume of his *Handbuch der katholischen Dogmatik* (Freiburg im Br., 1882), pp. 455-600 (§§ 274-282), as the fifth and final chapter of the treatise on Christology: "The virginal Mother of the Savior and her relation to the work of the Redemption." However, the divine Maternity and the virginal conception of Christ are treated in earlier chapters of the Christology. Feckes has gathered these separated materials together and adapted them for easier reading, in the above-mentioned *Die Braeutliche Gottesmutter.* A similar compilation is the Flemish translation by H. van Waes, S.J., *Systematische Mariologie,* ed. 2 (Bruxelles, 1943), with introduction and notes by E. Druwé, S.J. The foregoing has been rendered into English by T. Geukers, *Mariology,* 2 vols. (St. Louis, 1946-1947), with translator's preface, Vol. 1, pp. III-XXXIV. An article by Scheeben in the periodical *Das oekumenische Konzil vom Jahre 1869,* discussing the parallel between the definition of Papal infallibility and that of the Immaculate Conception, has been hailed as "a gem of Mariology" by J. Schmitz, who republished the article in *Maria, Schutzherrin der Kirche* (Paderborn, 1936). Of interest also are Scheeben's early work, *Marienbluethen* (Schaffhausen, 1860), and a few pages in *Die Herrlichkeiten der goettlichen Gnade,* ed. 15 (A. Weiss, O.P.) (Freiburg im Br., 1925), pp. 111-117, 580-582, 592, 651.

[208] *La Vierge Mère d'après la théologie,* 2 vols. (Paris, 1866).

[209] *La Vierge Marie dans le plan divin,* 4 vols. (Paris, 1869). This work of Nicolas, a lay theologian, was acclaimed in its day as the definitive treatise on Marian doctrine (an exaggeration, as Roschini notes, *Mariologia,* Vol. 1, p. 304). Scheeben knew it in one of its many translations, and praised its rich

Castelplanio,[210] and the Dominican, Van den Berg.[211]

To Scheeben goes the distinction of having labored more than any other modern theologian to change Mariology into a scientific whole, distinct from, yet tightly integrated with, the rest of theology (especially with the treatise on the Church), and given inner cohesion by a fundamental principle of its own.[212] His views on the place Mariology should hold in the over-all system of theology are best summed up in his own words:

> I came to the conclusion that Mariology can and must be considered a link connecting the doctrine on the Redeemer and His work with the doctrine on the grace of the Redeemer and its distribution by the Church, and that, thus conceived, Mariology is called to occupy a much more important place in the system of dogmatic theology than is usually accorded it. As I endeavored to treat Mariology from this point of view, it shaped itself as the development of the profound concept of the ancient Church, which ideally beholds Mary in the Church, and the Church in Mary (Apoc. 12, 1). Thus, in my conception of it, Mariology, as the doctrine on the personal bride of Christ and the personal spiritual mother of mankind, when conjoined with ... the doctrine on Christ as the head of a Mystical Body and as the priestly Mediator of the supernatural life of this Body, becomes a rich source of light for the doctrine on the Church, on her inner organism and supernatural essence.[213]

Intimated in the above passage is Scheeben's conception, original with him — at least in its formulation — of what should be the master principle of Mariology. The Cologne professor

---

theological content (*Die Mysterien des Christentums*, ed. J. Weiger [Mainz, 1931], note 266); in fact, he gave dogmatic foundation to many of its intuitions; cf. Geukers, *op. cit.*, Vol. 1, p. XVII.

[210] *Maria nel consiglio dell'Eterno*, 3 vols. (Neapoli, 1872). Scheeben applauded the Franciscan's work as "sehr geistreich"; *Handb. der kath. Dogmatik*, Vol. 3, p. 478.

[211] Author of *Beatissima Virgo Maria*, one of his several excellent monographs on Thomistic teaching; cf. Grabmann, *op. cit.*, p. 272.

[212] Cf. E. Druwé, S.J., *Position et structure du Traité Marial*, in *Bull. de la Soc. Franç. d'Études Mariales* (Juvisy, 1936), pp. 24-29; Geukers, *op. cit.*, Vol. 1, pp. XVIII-XXXIII; C. Feckes, *Die Stellung der Gottesmutter Maria in der Theologie M. J. Scheebens*, in M. J. Scheeben, *der Erneuerer katholischer Glaubenswissenschaft*, ed. by Katholischen Akademikerverband, 1935.

[213] Preface to *Handb. der kath. Dogmatik*, Vol. 3, p. VI.

considered it to be the most characteristic note of the Blessed Virgin that she is both the Mother of Christ according to the flesh and His supernatural spouse. Scheeben erected "this 'maternal-sponsal character,' as he calls it, into the fundamental principle of Mariology, thus fusing in most intimate fashion the divine maternity and Mary's freely willed association with Christ, in which others prefer to see a distinct principle."[214]

Druwé remarks that, whatever one may hold as regards this methodological question (the aforesaid fusion into the one fundamental principle of the "bridal motherhood"), "the perfect association of Mary with the Redeemer — *principium consortii* — is recognized today by all Mariologists as fundamental, in this double sense: that it pertains to the *donné chrétien originel* and that it constitutes, with the divine maternity, the foundation of all of Mary's prerogatives."[215]

Not the least among Scheeben's merits was his masterful vindication of Catholic devotion to Mary. "With the deep and synthetic view that marked him as one of the greatest religious thinkers of the past century, he incorporated the Catholic doctrine regarding Mary into the whole of Catholic dogmatic theology. In doing so, he showed in an unexcelled way how the veneration of Mary takes root in the deepest soil of Christian belief."[216] Invaluable is his insight into the root of Protestant antagonism toward the Marian doctrines and cult of the Catholic Church: it is the intimate

---

[214] E. Druwé, S.J., *La Médiation universelle de Marie*, in *Maria*, ed. H. du Manoir, Vol. 1, p. 565. Among those who espoused Scheeben's version of the supreme principle of Mariology we may mention F. Schueth, S.J., *Mediatrix* (Innsbruck, 1925); C. Feckes, *Das Fundamentalprinzip der Mariologie*, in *Scientia Sacra, Theologische Festgabe...* (Duesseldorf, 1935), pp. 252-276; idem, *Das Mysterium des goettlichen Mutterschaft* (Paderborn, 1937) — Engl. transl., *The Mystery of the Divine Motherhood* (London, 1941); E. Druwé, *art. cit.*, in Bull. *de la Soc. Franç. d'Etudes Mariales* (Juvisy, 1936), pp. 24-29. Cf. Roschini, *Mariologia*, Vol. 1, pp. 328-330.

[215] E. Druwé, *art. cit.*, in *Maria*, ed. H. du Manoir, Vol. 1, p. 565. On the importance of the principium consortii for the right of Mariology to exist as a distinct theological treatise, cf. Druwé, *art. cit.*, in *Bull. de la Soc. Franç. de l'Études Mariales*, (Juvisy, 1936), pp. 16-29.

[216] Geukers, *op. cit.*, Vol. 1, p. IV.

rapport between Mary and the Church.[217]

Scheeben's pioneering work was not heeded immediately.[218] It remained for the twentieth century to resume his efforts at organizing Marian doctrines into a complete and cohesive treatise, and, rediscovering the ancient and medieval appreciation of the relationship between Mary and the Church, to forge a strong bond between Mariology and Ecclesiology.[219] By and large, the late nineteenth-century Mariologists were more interested in particular questions.

Understandably enough, they devoted a great deal of attention to the Immaculate Conception, both in order to explain the new dogma to the faithful, and to defend it against the attacks of rationalists, Protestants, Old Catholics, and Eastern Dissidents.[220] However, as we have already indicated,[221] the Marian scholars of this era addressed themselves to other matters as well. With the proclamation of the Immaculate Conception, Mary's bodily Assumption into heaven shone forth with a new radiance, and the study of this prerogative became the order of the day, especially after many of the bishops present at the Vatican Council requested that the doctrine be dogmatically defined.[222]

---

[217] Cf. E. Druwé, *art. cit.*, in Maria, ed. H. du Manoir, Vol. 1, pp. 566-567; Geukers, *op. cit.*, Vol. 1, p. XXI.

[218] Strange to relate, Scheeben's enthusiasm for Marian dogma was shared by few German theologians until quite recent years; cf. K. Rahner, S.J., *Probleme heutiger Mariologie, in Aus der Theologie der Zeit*, ed. G. Soehngen (Regensburg, 1948), p. 85.

[219] Cf. *supra*, note 154; *Theology Digest*, 1, 1953, pp. 145-146, summary of the article on *Mary and the Church*, by R. Laurentin, in *La Vie Spirituelle*, Vol. 86, 1952, pp. 295-304. The link between Mary and the Church was also known to, and exploited by, the Bérullian school, before Scheeben came to give a more theological expression to this tradition; cf. H. Rondet, preface to Terrien, *La Mère des hommes*, Vol. 1, ed. 8, p. 39.

[220] Cf. X. Le Bachelet, art. Immaculée Conception, in DTC, Vol. 7, cols. 1209-1218.

[221] Cf. *supra*, note 204.

[222] Cf. C. Balić, O.F.M., *Testimonia de Assumptione B. V. M. ex omnibus saeculis. Pars altera: Ex aetate post Concilium Tridentinum* (Romae, 1950), pp. 281-464; Hocedez, op. cit., Vol. 3, pp. 314-315; J. Bellamy, art. *Assomption*, in *DTC*, Vol. I, cols. 2140-2141; E. Campana, *Maria nel dogma Cattolico*, ed. 6 (Torino, 1946), pp. 744-751.

Another consequence, at least indirect, of the momentum imparted to Marian theology by *Ineffabilis Deus* was a renewed interest in and a more penetrating study of questions bearing on Mary's role as universal Mediatrix.[223] Paving the way for the profound developments which the twentieth century brought to these themes, many late nineteenth-century Mariologists, especially after the appearance of the Rosary Encyclicals of Leo XIII, gave their attention to Our Lady's part in the acquisition and the distribution of all graces, and to the concomitant doctrine of her spiritual Maternity.[224]

Thus, among the many who discussed Mary's co-operation, even proximate, in the objective Redemption, one may cite Frederick William Faber, O. Van den Berghe, J. De Concilio, P. Jeanjacquot, S.J., and Francis Risi.[225]

Jeanjacquot also deserves a place of honor in the history of the discussion on Mary's intervention in the distribution of all graces, a discussion thereafter taken up and notably advanced by R. de la

---

[223] Cf. Bellamy, *La théologie catholique au XIXe siècle*, ed. 3 (Paris, 1904), pp. 274-275.

[224] Cf. J. Bainvel, S.J., art. *Marie, in Dict. Apologétique de la Foi Catholique*, Vol. 3 (Paris, 1926), cols. 285-302; E. Dublanchy, art. *Marie, in DTC*, Vol. 9, cols. 2389-2409; Hocedez, *op. cit.*, Vol. 3, pp. 315-316.

[225] F. Faber, *The Foot of the Cross* (London, 1857); O. Van den Berghe, *Marie et le Sacerdoce*, ed. 2 (Paris, 1875); J. De Concilio, *The Knowledge of Mary* (New York, 1878); P. Jeanjacquot, *Simples explications sur la coopération de la Très-Sainte Vierge à l'oeuvre de la Rédemption et sur sa qualité de Mère des Chrétiens*, ed. 3 (Paris, 1889); F. Risi, *Sul motivo primario dell'Incarnazione del Verbo* (Brescia, 1898). On these and other authors, cf. J. Carol, *De Corredemptione B. V. M.*, pp. 382-480; L. Riley, *Historical Conspectus of the Doctrine of Mary's Co-Redemption*, in *Marian Studies*, Vol. 2, 1951, pp. 81-92.

Broise, S.J.;[226] J.-B. Terrien, S.J.;[227] J.-V. Bainvel, S.J.;[228] and E. Hugon, O.P.[229] Furthered by the celebration of Marian Congresses dedicated to Mary's "maternity of grace,"[230] and by Cardinal Mercier's enthusiasm on the subject of Our Lady's universal Mediation,[231] this topic, along with that of the Coredemption, has remained the object of intense study down to the present.[232]

Intense, in fact, have been the labors of the past several decades to consolidate and to enlarge the whole realm of our knowledge of the Blessed Mother. In consequence, Marian science has now achieved truly marvelous development.

---

[226] R. de la Broise, *Sur cette proposition: Toutes les grâces nous viennent par la Sainte Vierge*, in *Études*, Vol. 68, 1896, pp. 5-31; reproduced in R. de la Broise and J. Bainvel, *Marie Mère de grâce* (Paris, 1921); R. de la Broise, *La sainte Vierge au XIXe siècle*, in *Études*, Vol. 83, 1900.

[227] J.-B. Terrien, *Marie, Mère de Dieu, 2 vols.* (Paris, 1896-1900), and Marie, *Mère des hommes*, 2 vols. (Paris, 1899-1902); on this influential work see H. Rondet's preface to the eighth edition of *La Mère des hommes*, Vol. 1, pp. 44-48.

[228] J.-V. Bainvel, *Le "Fiat" de l'Incarnation, in Quatrième Congrès marial breton tenu au Folgoät en l'honneur de Marie, Mère de grâce* (4-6 sept. 1913), *Compte rendu* (Quimper, 1915), pp. 139-146; *De la Broise and Bainvel, Marie, Mère de grâce* (Paris, 1921). Cf. also Hocedez, *op. cit.*, Vol. 3, p. 316, on Bainvel's paper read at the International Marian Congress at Fribourg, Switzerland, August, 18-21, 1902.

[229] E. Hugon, La Mère de grâce (Paris, 1904).

[230] At Fribourg, 1902; Folgoät, 1913; etc. For a chronological list of these and similar events which have spurred Marian studies in the past fifty years, see J. Besutti, O.S.M., Cinquante ans (1900—1950), in Marie (Nicolet, Quebec, ed. R. Brien), Vol. 7, No. 2, pp. 14-16. For data on the proceedings of the many Marian Congresses, cf. E. Campana, Maria nel culto Cattolico, Vol. 2, ed. 2, cura G. Roschini, (Torino, 1946), pp. 487-652.

[231] J. Coppens, art. *Belgique, in DTC, Tables générales* (Paris, 1953), col. 401: Mariology received a remarkable impetus from what one has called the "intuitions" of Cardinal Mercier, who wished the Church to proclaim the universal Mediation of Mary as a dogma; he obtained the co-operation of C. Van Crombrugghe, B. Merkelbach, J. Lebon, J. Bittremieux.

[232] Cf. Campana, *Maria nel dogma Cattolico*, ed. 6 (Torino, 1946), pp. 171-184, 250-252; E. Druwé, S.J., *La Médiation universelle de Marie*, ed. H. du Manoir, Vol. 1, pp. 417-572; T. Koehler, S.M., *Maternité spirituelle de Marie, in Maria*, ed. H. du Manoir, Vol. 1, pp. 573-600; extensive bibliographies are provided in and at the end of both articles; literature on the question of the Coredemption will be cited below.

Thus, excellent general treatises, adequate in content and scientifically organized and executed, now abound.[233] Symposia, such as those edited by Fathers du Manoir and Sträter, bring together the ripest fruits of Marian scholarship and make them available to a wide public.[234]

The specialized literature has reached mountainous proportions; countless are the monographs, and the studies and articles appearing in the annuals of the various Mariological societies,[235] in

---

[233] Certainly the most comprehensive treatise, and one indispensable to all theologians, is that of G. Roschini, O.S.M., *Mariologia*, 4 vols., ed. 2 (Romae, 1947-1948); an adaptation of this work, somewhat more up to date, is the same author's *La Madonna secondo la Fede e la Teologia*, 3 vols. (Roma, 1953); there is also Roschini's smaller manual, *Summula Mariologiae* (Romae, 1952). A select list of other established treatises would include: G. Alastruey, *Mariologia*, 2 vols. (Vallisoleti, 1934/1942); J. de Aldama, S.J., *Mariologia*, in *Sacrae Theologiae Summa*, Vol. 3 (Matriti, 1950), pp. 288-418; D. Bertetto, S.D.B., *Maria nel dogma cattolico* (Torino, 1950); C. Boyer, S.J., *Synopsis Praelectionum de B. M. Virgine* (Romae, 1952); F. Dander, S.J., *Summarium tractatus dogmatici de Matre-Socia Salvatoris* (Oeniponte, 1952); idem, *Mariologia*, in L. Lercher, *Institutiones Theologiae Dogmaticae*, ed. 3, Vol. 3 (Oeniponte, 1942), pp. 279-359; R. Garrigou-Lagrange, *The Mother of the Saviour*, Engl. transl. by B. Kelly, C.S.Sp. (Dublin, 1949); J. Keuppens, *Soc. Miss. Afr.*, *Mariologiae Compendium* (Antwerpiae, 1938); A. Janssens, *De Heilige Maagd en Moeder Gods Maria*, 4 vols. (Anvers, 1928-1932); H. Lennerz, S.J., *De B. Virgine*, ed. 3 (Romae, 1939); B. Merkelbach, O.P., Mariologia (Parisiis, 1939); E. Neubert, S.M., *Marie dans le dogme*, ed. 2 (Paris, 1946); A. Plessis, S.M.M., *Manuale Mariologiae dogmaticae* (Pontchateau, 1942); Pohle-Preuss, *Mariology* (St. Louis, 1926); Pohle-Gierens, *Lehrbuch der Dogmatik*, Vol. 2, ed. 9 (Paderborn, 1937), pp. 248-315; Scheeben-Geukers, *Mariology*, 2 vols. (St. Louis, 1946-1947); M. Schmaus, *Katholische Dogmatik*, Vol. 2, ed. 3-4 (Muenchen, 1949), pp. 609-638, 879-908. Nor may we overlook the classic works of E. Campana, *Maria nel dogma Cattolico*, ed. 6 (Torino, 1946), and *Maria nel culto Cattolico*, 2 vols., ed. 2, cura G. Roschini (Torino, 1946).

[234] *Maria. Études sur la Sainte Vierge*, sous la direction d'Hubert du Manoir, S.J., Vol. 1 (Paris, 1949); Vol. 2 (Paris, 1952); *Katholische Marienkunde*, ed. Paul Sträter, S.J., 3 vols. (Paderborn, 1947-1951).

[235] Cf. Roschini, *La Madonna secondo la Fede e la Teologia*, Vol. 1, pp. 161-164; J. Carol, *The Mariological Movement in the World Today*, in *Marian Studies*, Vol. 1, 1950, esp. pp. 27-29. Valuable materials are also contained in the published proceedings of Mariological Congresses.

the theological periodicals of general interest,[236] and in those exclusively devoted to the science of Our Lady.[237] So vast is this literary production that bibliographers are hard put to record it,[238] while Marian Centers are equally hard pressed to collect and to house it in special libraries.[239] If we may high-light some of the more important features of contemporary Mariology, the first to be noted is the growing preoccupation with the declarations of the ecclesiastical *magisterium*, the ordinary as well as the extraordinary.[240] This is a most fruitful development. For one thing,

---

[236] *Gregorianum, Ephemerides Theologicae Lovanienses, Nouvelle Revue Théologique, Theological Studies, The Thomist*, etc. *The American Ecclesiastical Review* has for years included an article on Our Lady in every issue; a select cross section of these articles was published as *Studies in Praise of Our Blessed Mother* (Washington, D. C., 1952).

[237] *Marianum*, edited by G. Roschini, O.S.M., published at Rome, since 1939; *Ephemerides Mariologicae*, published by the Claretian Fathers in Madrid, since 1951. Mention may also be made of Marie, edited by R. Brien at Nicolet, Quebec, since 1947; although this periodical is not primarily theological in character, it often contains short papers by theologians of note.

[238] Cf. Roschini, *La Madonna secondo la Fede e la Teologia*, Vol. 1, pp. 167-170. A critical and complete Marian bibliography does not yet exist, although one is in preparation by the Servites of the International College of St. Alexius Falconieri in Rome. Some idea of their task may be gotten from the prodigious literary output of just two of the century's leading Mariologists, the late J. Bittremieux and Roschini; the 175 distinct publications of the former are listed by J. Coppens, *L'enseignement et l'oeuvre théologique de M. le Chanoine J. Bittremieux*, in *Ephemerides Theologicae Lovanienses*, Vol. 23, 1947, pp. 367-377; a partial catalogue of Roschini's writings down to 1949 runs to nine pages in the compilation of J. Besutti, O.S.M., *Gli scritti del P. M.o Gabriele M. Roschini, O.S.M.*, in *Marianum*, Vol. 11, 1949, pp. 496-505. Abundant bibliographical information is available in the issues of *Marianum, Ephemerides Mariologicae, Ephemerides Theologicae Lovanienses*, etc.; and in the *Ragguaglio Mariano*, published annually by the International Marian Center, Rome. H. Rondet gives a select bibliography at the end of his preface to J.-B. Terrien, *La Mère des hommes*, Vol. 1, ed. 8, pp. 62-76.

[239] Cf. L. Monheim, S.M., Some Marian Collections in the *World*, in *Marian Studies*, Vol. 1, 1950, pp. 46-55. The 1949 Booklist of the Marian Library, University of Dayton, Ohio, contains 10,539 entries.

[240] As all know, it is not only in the solemn pronouncements of popes and of ecumenical councils but also in the exercise of her ordinary and universal teaching office that the Church sets forth things to be believed with divine and Catholic faith; cf. *Concilium Vaticanum*, sessio 3, cap. 3 (Denzinger-

such declarations furnish the supreme arguments in theology, and are an indispensable safeguard in interpreting the data of Sacred Scripture and Tradition.[241] Moreover, the ecclesiastical *magisterium* is not only the authentic interpreter of all doctrinal evolution in the Church: it is at the same time, under the guidance of the Holy Spirit, the principal agent of all such evolution — a spur to the further development of doctrine.[242] As J. Dillersberger remarks:

The teaching Church from time to time in its dogmatic decisions determines the definitive form of such progress. But long before this there came from the teaching Church the stimuli to new development — we experience this especially in those truths which revolve around Mary.[243]

As concrete evidence of the keen attention now being given to the *magisterium* by Our Lady's scholars, one may cite the collections of Papal documents on Mary,[244] various studies on the Marian doctrine of individual popes,[245] and other studies on particular

---

Bannwart-Umberg, *Enchiridion Symbolorum,* n. 1792). See the valuable article by P. Franquesa, C.M.F., *Magisterio Ordinario y Mariología,* in *Ephemerides Mariologicae,* Vol. 4, 1954, pp. 25-66.

[241] Cf. Pope Pius XII, ency., *Humani generis,* August 12, 1950; A.A.S., Vol. 42, 1950, p. 567; N.C.W.C. translation, nn. 18, 21.

[242] Cf. C. Dillenschneider, C.SS.R., *Marie au service de notre Rédemption* (Hagenau, Bas-Rhin, 1947), p. 45.

[243] J. Dillersberger, *Das neue Wort ueber Maria* (Salzburg, 1947), p. 10; C. Feckes, *The Mystery of the Divine Motherhood* (London, 1941), pp. 137-138: the popes "have indicated the way which the theologian must follow to complete the portrait of Mary."

[244] Cf. *Le Encicliche Mariane,* ed. A. Tondini (Roma, 1950); reproduces, in their original language and with Italian or Latin translations, 56 documents from February 2, 1849, to May 1, 1948, with a complete elenchus (pp. 579-626) of all documents from 1849 to July 16, 1949; R. Graber, *Die marianischen Weltrundschreiben der Paepste in den letzten hundert Jahren* (Wuerzburg, 1951) — includes several useful indexes; W. Doheny and J. Kelly, *Papal Documents on Mary* (Milwaukee, 1954) — 36 documents from 1849 to 1953.

[245] Cf., for example, G. Roschini, *I Papi e Maria,* in *Marianum,* Vol. 4, 1942, pp. 153-166; J. Bittremieux, *Doctrina Mariana Leonis XIII,* in *Ephemerides Theol. Lovanienses,* Vol. 4, 1927, pp. 359-383; idem, *Ex doctrina Mariana Pii XI,* in *Ephemerides Theol. Lovanienses,* Vol. 11, 1934, pp. 95-101; G. Roschini, *La Madonna nel pensiero e nell'insegnamento di Pio XI,* in *Marianum,* Vol. 1, 1939, pp. 121-172; idem, *La Madonna nell'Enciclica 'Mystici Corporis Christi,'* in *Marianum,* Vol. 6, 1944, p. 108-117; J. Dillersberger, *Das neue Wort ueber*

questions in the light of Papal teachings.[246] To date, these explorations have confined themselves pretty much to the Papal *magisterium*; rich and inviting vein though they be, quite unexploited as yet are the teachings of the universal episcopate.[247]

Another heartening feature of contemporary Marian studies is

Maria (Salzburg, 1947) — the entire book is a commentary on the Marian epilogue of the encyclical Mystici Corporis Christi; C. Balić, O.F.M., *De doctrina philosophica et theologica Pii Papae XII eiusque momento* (Ad Claras Aquas, 1949), pp. 91-98; D. Bertetto, S.D.B., *La dottrina Mariana di Pio XII*, in *Salesianum*, Vol. 11, 1949, pp. 1-24; J. Carol, O.F.M., *Mary's Co-Redemption in the Teaching of Pope Pius XII*, in *The American Ecclesiastical Review*, Vol. 121, 1949, pp. 353-361; and, of course, the innumerable commentaries on the Apostolic Constitution, *Munificentissimus Deus*, November 1, 1950, defining the bodily Assumption of Our Lady into heaven.

[246] To cite but a few, cf. H. Seiler, S.J., *Corredemptrix. Theologische Studie zur Lehre der letzten Paepste ueber die Miterloeserschaft Mariens* (Rom, 1939); J. Carol, O.F.M., *De Corredemptione B. V. M.* (Civitas Vaticana, 1950), pp. 509-539; A. Baumann, *Maria Mater nostra spiritualis. Eine theologische Untersuchung ueber die geistige Mutterschaft Mariens in den Aeusserungen der Paepste vom Tridentinum bis heute* (Brixen, 1948); G. Shea, *The Teaching of the magisterium on Mary's Spiritual Maternity*, in *Marian Studies*, Vol. 3, 1952, pp. 35-110; E. Carroll, O.Carm., *Our Lady's Queenship in the magisterium of the Church*, in *Marian Studies*, Vol. 4, 1953, pp. 29-108; A. Robichaud, S.M., *The Immaculate Conception in the magisterium of the Church before 1854*, in *Marian Studies*, Vol. 5, 1954, pp. 73-145; A. Wolter, O.F.M., *The Theology of the Immaculate Conception in the Light of 'Ineffabilis Deus,'* in *Marian Studies*, Vol. 5, 1954, pp. 19-72.

[247] J. Carol, O.F.M., has gathered and analyzed episcopal teaching on his favorite subject: *Episcoporum doctrina de Beata Virgine Corredemptrice*, in *Marianum*, Vol. 10, 1948, pp. 210-258; idem, *De Corredemptione B.V.M.*, pp. 539-619. The mind of Pope Pius IX's fellow bishops on the Immaculate Conception was expressed in their replies to his encyclical, *Ubi primum* (February 2, 1849), which were published in *Pareri dell'Episcopato Cattolico ... sulla definizione dogmatica dell'Immacolato Concepimento della Beata Vergine Maria*, 10 vols. (Roma, 1851-1854). The mind of many bishops on the doctrine of the Assumption, as indicated in petitions sent to the Holy See between 1869-1941, can be seen in the monumental work of W. Hentrich, S.J., and R. De Moos, S.J., *Petitiones de Assumptione Corporea B. V. Mariae in caelum definienda ad Sanctam Sedem delatae*, 2 vols. (Typis Polyglottis Vaticanis, 1942). The materials in this work, in the Pareri ..., in the *Collectio Lacensis* and similar collections, in pastoral letters, catechisms, etc., invite study insofar as they reflect the mind of the universal episcopate on many other Mariological topics, e.g., Mary's spiritual Maternity; cf. G. Shea, *art. cit.*, in *Marian Studies*, Vol. 3, 1952, pp. 39, 53-54.

the high level of biblical Mariology. Noteworthy is the conscientious effort of scholars to determine and apply the principles involved in the explanation of the Marian texts of Sacred Scripture.[248] On these many passages[249] countless new commentaries have appeared, geared to the great progress of modern biblical science. Invaluable, although at times ultraconservative, is the *Mariologia biblica* of Father Ceuppens, which endeavors to expound all the major Marian texts of the Bible.[250] Among the many other general works of lasting significance one must single out for express mention those of the Dominican, F.-M. Braun, and the Jesuit, Paul Gächter.[251] Illustrative of the numerous major studies of particular texts are the contributions of J.-F. Bonnefoy, O.F.M., T. Gallus, S.J., and B. Le Frois, S.V.D.[252]

Nor has that other branch of positive theology been neglected, study of the monuments of Tradition. The impetus which was given to such study by the dogmatic definition of the Immaculate Conception and by subsequent non-Catholic attacks on the newly

---

[248] Cf. D. Unger, O.F.M.Cap., *The Use of Sacred Scripture in Mariology*, in *Marian Studies*, Vol. 1, 1950, pp. 67-116; S. Alameda, O.S.B., *La Mariología y las fuentes de la revelatión*, in *Estudios Marianos*, Vol. 1, 1942, pp. 41-72.

[249] Cf. A. Robert, P.S.S., *La Sainte Vierge dans l'Ancien Testament*, in *Maria*, ed. H. du Manoir, Vol. 1, pp. 21-39; A. Bea, S.J., *Das Marienbild des Alten Bundes*, in *Katholische Marienkunde*, ed. Sträter, Vol. 1, pp. 23-43; G. Hilion, *La Sainte Vierge dans le Nouveau Testament*, in *Maria*, ed. H. du Manoir, Vol. 1, pp. 43-68; A. Merk, S.J., *Das Marienbild des Neuen Bundes*, in *Katholische Marienkunde*, ed. Sträter, Vol. 1, pp. 44-84; Scheeben-Geukers, *Mariology*, Vol. 1, pp. 9-41; Scheeben-Feckes, *Die Braeutliche Gottesmutter*, pp. 1-18.

[250] F. Ceuppens, O.P., *De Mariologia biblica* (Theologia biblica, 4), ed. 2 (Taurini, 1951).

[251] F.-M. Braun, O.P., *La Mère des fidèles. Essai de théologie johannique* (Paris, 1953); P. Gächter, S.J., *Maria im Erdenleben. Neutestamentliche Marienstudien* (Innsbruck, 1953).

[252] J.-F. Bonnefoy, O.F.M., *Le mystère de Marie selon le Protévangile et l'Apocalypse* (Paris, 1949); T. Gallus, S.J., *Interpretatio mariologica Protoevangelii* (Gen. 3, 15) tempore postpatristico usque ad Conc. Tridentinum (Romae, 1949); idem, Interpretatio mariologica Protoevangelii posttridentina usque ad definitionem dogmaticam Immaculatae Conceptionis. Pars prior: aetas aurea ... usque ad annum 1660 (Romae, 1953); B. Le Frois, S.V.D., The Woman Clothed With the Sun (Rome, 1954); D. J. Unger, O.F.M.Cap., The First-Gospel: Genesis 3, 15 (Saint Bonaventure, N. Y., 1954).

defined dogma was intensified by Modernist opposition to Marian doctrines (A. Loisy, J. Turmel, H. Koch, and others),[253] by the century-long movement culminating in the solemn definition of Our Lady's corporal Assumption, and by controversies among Catholic theologians on Mariological questions still open to debate. Under this stimulation scholars have produced a vast literature exhibiting and evaluating the Marian testimonies of the Church Fathers and of the ancient liturgies.[254] In addition, as our footnotes will have suggested, the Mariological teachings of earlier theologians have been the object of tireless research.[255]

Discussions on the systematic treatment of Mariology are another remarkable feature of the contemporary scene.[256] Involved here are several questions, intimately interrelated: the right of Mariology to exist as a distinct tract within the theological system, the proper location of that distinct treatise within the over-all system, the organization and structure of the treatise, and the existence and nature of a first principle which would preside over the structure of Mariology, giving the treatise organic unity and order.[257] The problem as to the nature of the fundamental principle of Mariology is complicated by various questions on the nexus between the different prerogatives of Our Lady,[258] and has, in

---

[253] Cf. E. Dublanchy, art. *Marie*, in *DTC*, Vol. 9, cols. 2345-2347; E. Campana, *Maria nel dogma Cattolico*, ed. 6, pp. 603-606, 625-652.

[254] For orientation in this field, cf. *Katholische Marienkunde*, ed. Straeter, Vol. 1, pp. 85-136 (articles on the Eastern Fathers and liturgies), pp. 137-267 (articles on the Latin Fathers and liturgies); G. Jouassard, *Marie à travers la Patristique*, in *Maria*, ed. H. du Manoir, Vol. 1, pp. 71-157; see also pp. 215-361, articles on Mary in the liturgies.

[255] Mention may he made here of the small hut useful anthology of P. Palmer, S.J., Mary in the Documents of the Church (Westminster, Md., 1952), containing annotated selections from the ecclesiastical *magisterium* , from Church Fathers and theologians.

[256] Cf. F. Connell, C.SS.R., *Toward a Systematic Treatment of Mariology*, in *Marian Studies*, Vol. 1, 1950, pp. 56-66.

[257] Cf. Connell, art. cit.; E. Druwé, S.J., *Position et structure du Traité Marial*, in *Bull. de la Soc. Franç. d'Études Mariales* (Juvisy, 1936), pp. 7-34; R. Laurentin, *Le problème initial de méthodologie mariale*, in *Maria*, ed. H. du Manoir, Vol. 1, pp. 695-706.

[258] Cf. L. Everett, C.SS.R., *The Nexus between Mary's Co-Redemption and her other Prerogatives*, in *Marian Studies*, Vol. 1, 1950, pp. 132-137.

consequence, given rise to a great number of opinions.[259]

Side by side with these general and methodological problems, many particular questions of Mariology have been the center of contemporary interest. Quite naturally, the Apostolic Constitution, *Munificentissimus Deus* (November 1, 1950), the first centenary of *Ineffabilis Deus* (December 8, 1854), and the exhortations of the encyclical Fulgens corona (September 8, 1953), have focused attention on the sublime and interconnected prerogatives of the Immaculate Conception of Our Blessed Mother and of her corporal Assumption into heaven. As to the many other topics currently of major interest,[260] limitations of space permit only the bare mention of two, Our Lady's role of Coredemptrix,[261] and her relationship

---

[259] Cf. for discussion and bibliography, G. Roschini, *La Madonna secondo la Fede e la Teologia*, Vol. 1, pp. 97-116; idem, *Mariologia*, Vol. 1, pp. 324-337; A. Mueller, *Um die Grundlage der Mariologie, in Divus Thomas* (Fribourg), Vol. 29, 1951, pp. 385-401 (summary in Theology Digest, Vol. 1, 1953, pp. 139-144); E. Ledvorowski, *Maternitas divina fundamentum Mariologiae*, in *Marianum*, Vol. 15, 1953, pp. 176-194.

[260] Cf. G. Philips, *Sommes-nous entrés dans une phase mariologique?*, in *Marianum*, Vol. 14, 1952, pp. 1-48; idem, *Les problèmes actuels de la théologie mariale*, in *Marianum*, Vol. 11, 1949, pp. 24-53; A. Michel, *Chronique de Théologie mariale, in L'Ami du Clergé*, Vol. 60, 1950, pp. 33-48, 97-112; J. Carol, *The Mariological Movement in the World Today*, in *Marian Studies*, Vol. 1, 1950, pp. 32-45.

[261] Cf. J. B. Carol, *art. cit.*, in *Marian Studies*, Vol. 1, 1950, pp. 34-37; idem, *De Corredemptione B. V. Mariae* (Civitas Vaticana, 1950), bibliography, pp. 9-42; idem, *The Problem of Our Lady's Coredemption*, in *The American Ecclesiastical Review*, Vol. 123, July, 1950, pp. 32-51; idem, *Our Lady's Coredemption in the Marian Literature of Nineteenth Century America*, in *Marianum*, Vol. 14, 1952, pp. 49-63; *Marian Studies*, Vol. 2, 1951 (the volume is devoted mainly to this question); C. Boyer, S.J., *Thoughts on Mary's Coredemption*, in *Studies in Praise of Our Blessed Mother*, ed. Fenton-Benard (Washington, D. C., 1952), pp. 147-161; *Alma Socia Christi* (Acta Congressus Mariologici-mariani Romae anno sancto 1950 celebrati), Vol. 2 (Romae, 1952), entirely devoted to this question; additional bibliography in L. Leloir, *La médiation mariale dans la théologie contemporaine* (Bruges-Paris, 1933), and in C. Dillenschneider, *Marie au service de notre Rédemption* (Haguenau, 1947); idem, *Pour une Corédemption mariale bien comprise* (Rome, 1949); idem, *Le mystère de la Corédemption mariale. Théories nouvelles* (Paris, 1951). Closely connected with Our Lady's Coredemption is the specific question of Mary's share in the priesthood of Christ. By far the best publications on this subject are those of René Laurentin, *Maria, Ecclesia, Sacerdotium; essai sur le*

with the Church.[262]

The theological deepening of these themes will, as has been the case with earlier Mariological developments, both reveal new facets in the gems adorning Our Lady's radiant crown of glory and, at the same time, yield precious new insights into the entire deposit of faith.

---

développement d'une idée religieuse (Paris, 1952); and *Marie, l'Eglise et le Sacerdoce; étude théologique* (Paris, 1953); cf. also the same author's important contribution *Rôle de Marie et de l'Eglise dans l'oeuvre salvifique du Christ*, in *Bulletin de la Société Français d'Études Mariales*, Vol. 10, 1952, pp. 43-62.

[262] Cf. G. Philips, *Perspectives mariologiques. Marie et l'Eglise. Essai bibliographique*, in *Marianum*, Vol. 15, 1953, pp. 436-511; H. Lennerz, S.J., *Maria-Ecclesia*, in *Gregorianum*, Vol. 35, 1954, pp. 90-98; *Études Mariales. Marie et l'Eglise, I* (Bull. de la Soc. Franç. d'Etudes Mariales, Paris, 1951); H. de Lubac, S.J., *Méditation sur l'Église* (Paris, 1953), pp. 273-329; K. Delahaye, *Maria: Typus der Kirche, in Wissenschaft und Wahrheit*, Vol. 5, 1949, pp. 79-92; Y. Congar, O.P., *Le Christ, Marie, et l'Église* (Bruges, 1952); additional bibliography in Theology Digest, Vol. 1, 1953, pp. 139-145, and particularly in R. Laurentin, *Bibliographie critique sur Marie et l'Eglise, in Bulletin de la Société Française d'Études Mariales* (Paris, 1953), pp. 145-152.

APPENDIX

THE HOLY NAME OF MARY

By Richard Kugelman, C.P, S.T.L., S.S.L.

HE etymology and meaning of Mary's name has fascinated her spiritual children since the days of the Fathers. Many titles of honor which Christian piety and the liturgy of the Church have bestowed on Mary had their origin in the ancient speculations on the meaning of her holy name. The history of the meaning of Mary's name supplies much valuable material for the history of Marian devotion.[1]

The study devoted to the meaning of Our Lady's name may seem to many moderns a useless, if pious, waste of time and talent. After all, names are only convenient tags to distinguish one person from another. The character and accomplishments of an individual, not the name which fond parents bestowed on their newborn infant, establish his or her place in history. Such a contemptuous appraisal of the study of the meaning of Mary's name would be justified, if it were not that, in the case of Our Lady, we are concerned with the victorious Woman of biblical prophecy, with the Mother of God our Saviour.

A cursory reading of the Bible will indicate the importance which the ancient Hebrews attached to the meaning of names. A close relation was presumed to exist between a name and the personality of its bearer. The Hebrew frequently used the name as almost an equivalent of the personality, or character, or nature of the person or thing named. When, for example, a prophet wished to express forcefully the character of a person or place, he said he will

---

[1] Cf. the "Vorwort" of O. Bardenhewer's monograph, *Der Name Maria, Biblische Studien*, Vol. 1, pp. 1-161 (Freiburg im Breisgau: Herder, 1896). With remarkable patience Bardenhewer collected and criticized all the etymologies proposed for the name Mary from Philo to the end of the nineteenth century. G. Roschini, O.S.M., *Mariologia*, Vol. 2, Pars Prima (Romae, 1947), p. 59, note 1, observes of Bardenhewer's work "ex quo auctores communiter hauriunt." The author of this article is no exception.

439

be called "so and so," or its name will be "such and such." Isaias indicates the personality and dignity of the future Messias by telling us he will be called "Emmanuel" (God with us) (Isa. 7:14; cf. also 9:6). The New Jerusalem, we are informed by Ezechiel, will bear the name "Yahweh Shamah" (God is there) (Ezech. 48:35).[2]

The contemporaries of Our Blessed Lady had inherited the Old Testament culture and concepts. It is not surprising, then, that the ancient Hebrew concept of the relation of name to person existed in the New Testament era. Faith in the mission and person of Jesus is expressed simply as faith "in his name" (e.g., Jn. 1:12; 2:23). In Acts 1:15 "names" (ὀνόματα) simply replaces "persons."

When speaking to mankind through men God accommodates Himself to the thought patterns of His spokesmen and their audience. In both Old and New Testaments God indicates the missions of the heroes of the history of salvation by the names which He imposes on them (For a few Old Testament examples cf. Gen. 17:5, 15; 35:10). The angel instructed Zachary that the child who was to be born to Elizabeth should be called John (Yahweh is gracious) (Lk. 1:13). Joseph is commanded to call Mary's Son, Jesus (Yahweh saves), "for he shall save his people from their sins" (Mt. 1:20-21). Our Blessed Lord presages the position of the Prince of the Apostles in His Church by changing his name to Peter (Cephas), "the Rock" (Jn. 1:42; Mt. 16:18). Therefore, as St. Lawrence of Brindisi observes, "it would be a mistake to think that this glorious name of Mary does not abound in mysteries, or that it was not divinely imposed, as was the name of Christ and John Baptist."[3]

It is not necessary, as St. Peter Canisius thought, to posit a special revelation of Mary's name to her parents, such as the

---

[2] Many examples could be cited. Cf. the article "Name" by G. B. Gray, *Hastings Dictionary of the Bible*, Vol. 3, pp. 478-481; also "Nom," H. Lesêtre, *Dictionnaire de la Bible*, Vigouroux, Vol. 4, cols. 1669-1677.

[3] The thesis expressed as follows by Roschini is common with mariologists: "Mariae nomen ab aeterno, ab ipso Deo, praefinitum fuit, tamquam expressivum dignitatis ad quam praedestinata fuit" (op. cit., p. 58). Cf. M. J. Scheeben, *Mariology*, transl. by T. Geukers, Vol. 1 (New York: B. Herder, 1948), p. 6; B. Merkelbach, O.P., *Mariologia* (Paris: Desclée, 1939), p. 103. Cf. S. Laurentius a Brundusio, *Mariale* (Patavii, 1928), p. 177.

revelation of Jesus' name to Joseph (Mt. 1:20).[4] It suffices that the parents of Our Lady, inspired by God (an influence of which very likely they were unconscious), called their child Mary.[5]

THE FORM OF THE NAME MARY

Mary is a proper feminine name borne by only one person in the Old Testament, the sister of Moses and Aaron (Exod. 15:20 f.; Num. 12:1-5, 10, 15; 20:1; Mich. 6:4).[6] In the Massorctic text the name is vocalized *Miryām*. The Septuagint renders it Mariám (Μαριάμ). The change of the first vowel probably represents the pronunciation current in Aramaic-speaking Palestine during the two centuries preceding Christ.[7] In the Vulgate the name becomes *Maria*.

When one considers the prominence of Mary the prophetess in the history of the Exodus, it seems strange that the Old Testament Hebrews did not honor her by conferring her name on their daughters. But the sister of Moses is not alone in her biblical isolation. The names of Abraham, Isaac, Jacob, Moses, and Aaron were also avoided, and, it seems, from pious reverence for the heroes of the Bible. A similar sentiment restrains Christians (Spanish-speaking Catholics are a singular exception) from giving the holy name of Jesus to their sons. And the early Christians would not call their daughters Mary.[8] The New Testament era saw a

---

[4] S. Petrus Canisius, *De Maria Virgine Incomparabili et Dei Genetrice Sacrosancta libri quinque* (Taurini, 1934), p. 1.

[5] Cf. Roschini, *op. cit.*, p. 58.

[6] The Massoretic text of 1 Par. 4:17 mentions a Miryām, apparently a male descendant of Ezra of Juda. The text is evidently corrupt. The LXX lists, in place of this Miryām, a son of Jether called Marôn according to most codices and preferred by Ralphs, or Maiôn according to Vaticanus and Alexandrinus and preferred by Swete, or Môeôr according to Colberto-Sarravianus and Purpureus Vindobonensis and preferred by Lagarde. Thus it is quite certain that the only bearer of the name Mary in the Old Testament is the sister of Moses.

[7] The Targum form of Mary's name was Maryām. Cf. Strack-Billerbeck, Kommentar zum Neuen Testament aus Talmud und Midrasch, Vol. 1, p. 36.

[8] There is no evidence that any Christian woman was named Mary in the early Christian centuries. Cf. Rohault de Fleury, *La Sainte Vierge. Études archéologiques et iconographiques*, Vol. 1 (Paris, 1878), p. 41; also F. Zorell, S.J., *Verbum Domini*, Vol. 7, 1927, p. 257.

reversal of the Old Testament practice. The contemporaries of Our Lady honored the great men and women of their history by calling their children after them. Perhaps there is also in this practice an indication of their keen expectation of the proximity of the Messianic Age. In the New Testament we meet, e.g., several individuals called Jacob (James) and a number of Marys.

In the Greek New Testament the form of Our Lady's name is the Septuagint rendition of the name of Moses' sister, *Mariám* (Mt. 13:55; Lk. 1:27, 30, 34, 38, 39, 46, 56; 2:5, 16, 34; Acts 1:14). There is only one exception. Most critical editions of the text (e.g., Tischendorf, Westcott-Hort, Merk, Bover) read, on the authority of Codex Vaticanus and Codex Bezae, Maria in Lk. 2:19. When it is not indeclinable Our Lady's name becomes in the oblique cases Μαρίας and Μαρία (once Μαρίαν in the accusative, Mt. 1:20). The form Maria is employed for the Magdalene and for Mary of James and of Clopas (Mt. 26:56; Mk. 15:47; 16:1, 9; Lk. 8:2; 24:10; Jn. 19:25; 20:1). The sister of Lazarus is called *Mariám* by both Luke and John (Lk. 10:39, 42; Jn. 11:2, 19, 20, etc.). Once John employs the form Mariám for the Magdalene (Jn. 20:16; perhaps also 20:18). Josephus uses the form Μαριάμμη, whether he refers to Moses' sister or to the women of the Herodian family who bore the name (Ant. Jud., II, 9, 4; III, 2, 4; IV, 4, 6).

W. Smith (*A Dictionary of the Bible*, Vol. 2 [London, 1853], p. 255) thinks that Maria is a distinct form, a shortened form of the more archaic Mariám, somewhat similar to Nathan, a shortened form of Jonathan. Authors generally, however, are agreed that Maria is merely a Hellenization of the Semitic *Maryām*. *Maria* gives a regular Greek feminine form of the first declension. The *Mariamme* of Josephus has been styled a "coquettish Hellenization."[9] It is possible that Matthew and Mark, in reserving the Semitic form *Mariám* exclusively for Our Lady, intend to distinguish her even in name from other women and to insinuate that she is the *Miryām* of the great liberation, which was prefigured and promised by the

---

[9] Cf. Deissmann, *Urgeschichte*, p. 22, cited by Moulton-Milligan, *The Vocabulary of the Greek New Testament Illustrated from the Papyri and Other Non-Literary Sources*, edition of W. Eerdmans Publishing Company (Grand Rapids, Mich., 1949), p. 388.

Exodus.[10] As in the Old Testament, so in the New, *Maria* is the only form of the name in the Vulgate.

THE ETYMOLOGY OF THE NAME MARY

No convincing argument has been adduced against the claim of the Massoretic *Miryām* to be the oldest and very likely the original form of the name Mary. While this is generally admitted, there is no agreement on the meaning of the name. More than seventy etymologies have been proposed (in 1885 Bardenhewer listed sixty-seven)!

This confusing variety is due to uncertainty concerning the derivation of the name, even uncertainty about the language to which it belongs, and to the pious avidity of preachers and writers to see Mary's prerogatives mirrored in her holy name. While some derive the name from ancient Egyptian, and a few from Syriac, the majority of exegetes have assumed that it is of Hebrew origin. Ancient and medieval authors generally took it to be a composite name, i.e., derived from two Hebrew roots. The moderns, who attach the name to the Hebrew, usually consider it a simple name.[11]

THE FIRST FOUR CENTURIES A.D.

The earliest extant writer to concern himself with the meaning of the name Mary was Philo (✝ a.d. 50), the learned Alexandrian Jew. The statement of Exod. 2:4 that the sister of Moses was "standing afar off, and taking notice what would be done" to her baby brother, lying in his basket in the sedges on the river's brink, leads Philo to observe that Mary's name means "hope." His comment on Num. 12:1-3, which records that "Mary and Aaron spoke against Moses because of his wife the Ethiopian," is that Mary signifies "brazen and bold sensuality."[12] As is evident, Philo is not giving the

---

[10] Cf. H. Lesêtre, "Marie," *Dict. de la Bible*, Vig., Vol. 4, col. 774.

[11] Bardenhewer, *op. cit.*, p. 16, points to the "echt hebräisches Gepräge" of Miryām: three radicals and the denominative termination Am, like Shephupham and Hupham sons of Benjamin, 'amram father of Moses. The root, he holds, is M R', Mārā'.

[12] Philo, *De somn.*, II, 20, cited by Bardenhewer, *op. cit.*, p. 17.

etymology of Mary's name. Rather he is assigning an allegorical and quite arbitrary meaning to her name because of her actions.

The ancient rabbis saw in Mary's name a symbol of Israel's bitter servitude in Egypt. Mary means "bitterness" (Hebrew, *Mērûr*). She was given this name, say the rabbis, because her birth coincided with the beginning of the Egyptians' hard treatment of the Jews.[13]

The ancient *Onomastica Sacra* have preserved the meanings ascribed to Mary's name by the early Christian writers and perpetuated by the Greek Fathers. "Bitter Sea," "Myrrh of the Sea," "The Light Giver," "The Enlightened One," "Lady," "Seal of the Lord," "Mother of the Lord" are the principal interpretations.[14]

Obviously influenced by the Septuagint *Mariám*, these etymologies suppose that the Hebrew form of the name is *Maryām*, not *Miryām*. "Bitter Sea" derives the name from Mar (bitter) and *Yām* (sea). Aside from the fact that such an etymology does not explain the first syllable of Our Lady's name (*Mir* could hardly be derived from *Mar*), this combination violates the usual Hebrew word order in which the noun precedes the adjective. "Myrrh of the Sea" supposes *Mor* (myrrh) and *Yām*. This also fails to account for the first syllable of Our Lady's name. And what is myrrh of the sea? Isn't myrrh a product of the vegetable kingdom, the resin of trees? "The Light Giver" (φωτίζουσα) regards Mary's name as a casuative (hiphil) participle of the verb 'ôr (to shine) or of the verb *rā'āh* (to see). But it is only with violence to the language that one can get *Miryām* from *Mē'îr* or *Mar'eh*. The interpretation "Lady" and "Our Lady" derives the name from the Aramaic word for Lord, *Mār'ē* (*Mār*). The feminine of this word, however, would be Mar'ā in the absolute state, Marth'ā in the emphatic state. In fact, this Aramaic word does occur as a feminine proper name in the New Testament.

---

[13] The loci of the rabbinical literature are given by J. Levy, *Neuhebräisches und chaldäisches Wörterbuch über die Talmudim und Midraschim* (Leipzig, 1876-1889), s.v. Mērûr.

[14] *Onomastica Sacra*, Paulus de Lagarde edidit (Gottingae, 1870), s.v. Μαρία, 176, 49; 179, 31; 183, 34; 195, 66 lists the meanings: κυριεύουσα, πικρὰ θάλασσα, κυρία ἡμων, ἀπὸ ἀοράτων, φωτίζουσα, s.v. Μαριάμ, 175, 22; 179, 32; 195, 66; 203, 17, φωτίζουσα, φωτιζομένη η φωτίζουσα ἀυτούς, η κύριος ἐκ γένους μου, η σμύρνα θαλλασία, κυρίου σφραγίς.

It is the name of the sister of Lazarus, Martha. Absolutely impossible is the meaning "Mother of the Lord" (*Deus ex genere meo*), which would derive the name from the Hebrew *Yāh* (God) and *Hārāh* (to conceive). "Seal of the Lord" supposes a bizarre combination of the Persian word muhur or muhr (seal) and the Hebrew *Yāh*. Among these interpretations of the *Onomastica* the Greek Fathers preferred "Myrrh of the Sea" and "Lady."[15]

ST. JEROME TO THE SIXTEENTH CENTURY A.D.

About the year a.d. 390 St. Jerome made available to Western Christendom the *Onomastica* of the Greeks. Jerome's *Liber Interpretationis hebraicorum Nominum* is a Latin translation and revision of a similar book of Origen, which in turn was based on a work of the Alexandrian Jew, Philo.[16] On the name Mary in Matthew's Gospel Jerome writes in the *Liber Interpretationis*: "Mariam plerique aestimant interpretari, illuminant me isti, vel illuminatrix, vel smyrna maris, sed mihi nequaquam videtur. Melius autem est, ut dicamus sonare eam stellam maris, sive amarum mare: sciendumque quod Maria, sermone Syro, domina nuncupetur."[17] With the exception of Stella Maris all these interpretations occur in the Greek *Onomastica*. Of course Stella Maris may have been in Jerome's copy of Origen's work, but more probably this is his personal contribution to the treasury of Marian etymologies. Jerome's indication of his preferences among the meanings he listed influenced all subsequent Latin writers. "Lady," "Bitter Sea," "The Light Giver," and especially "Star of the Sea" are the interpretations

---

[15] Cf. *PG*, 43, 488 f., (attributed to Epiphanius); *PG*, 94, 1157, John Damascene; also *PG*, 96, 689. J. Knabenbauer, S.J., *Evangelium secundum S. Matthaeum*, Pars Prior (Cursus Scrip. S.), 1892, p. 44, is one of the very few, if not the only modern, who prefers the meaning "myrrh": "Nomen myrrhae ex eo multum commendatur, quia puellarum nomina ex arboribus plantisque deprompta revera in usu erant."

[16] Cf. Jerome's Preface to this work, *PL*, 23, 771 f.; also A. Penna, *S. Girolamo* (Roma, 1949), p. 151 f.

[17] *Liber interpretationis Hebraicorum nominum*, PL, 23, 841-842; 789.

common in the West from Jerome until the sixteenth century.[18] *Stella Maris* was by far the favored interpretation.

The question has been raised whether Jerome wrote *Stilla* (drop) *Maris* rather than *Stella Maris*. The Hebrew language contains no word for star even remotely resembling Our Lady's name. There is, however, a Hebrew word *Mar*, meaning "drop" (cf. Isa. 40:15). When Jerome wrote the *Liber Interpretationis* he was already well versed in Hebrew. The conjunction *sive* in the text of Jerome suggests that he is offering alternative meanings for the word *Mar*, i.e., "drop" or "bitter" (*Melius autem est, ut dicamus sonare eam stellam maris, sive amarum mare*). The text of Jerome in the ninth-century Codex of Bamberg reads *Stilla*. The change to *Stella* is an understandable scribal error, especially when it is remembered that common speech confounded the vowels e and i. Countryfolk said *vea* for *via*, *vella* for *villa*, *speca* for *spica*, *leber* for *liber*.[19] St. Gregory the Great on the text of Job 36:27 "qui aufert stillas pluviae" gives a commentary that supposes stellas pluviae. The "stillas pluviarum" of Jer. 3:3 becomes in Gregory "stellae pluviarum."[20]

The "Star of the Sea" of Jerome's text is therefore very probably due to the lapse of one or several early copyists, who substituted *stella* for *stilla* because the two words were identical in pronunciation. Later copyists perpetuated the error because of the beautiful meaning *stella* gave to Our Lady's name. It would be unjust, however, to accuse the medieval scribes of deliberately changing Jerome's text in the interest of Marian devotion. Bardenhewer very wisely observes that had the medieval clients of Our Lady read *stilla maris* in their copies of Jerome, they would have found a symbolic relation between the drops of the sea and Our Lady as easily as they did for *stella maris*.[21] This unintentional

---

[18] Peter Chrysologus, *PL*, 52, 579; Isidore of Seville, 82, 289; Venerable Bede, 92, 316; Walafrid Strabo, 114, 859; Rabanus Maurus, 111, 75; Notker Balbulus, 131, 1005; Fulbert of Chartres, 151, 322; Herman Contractus, 143, 443; Peter Damian, 144, 508; Rupert of Deutz, 168, 361; Bernard of Clairvaux, 182, 1142 and 183, 70; Amadeus of Lausanne, 188, 1344; Innocent III, 217, 499.

[19] Cf. Quintillian, *Inst. Orat.*, Vol. 1, iv, 17; also Varron, *Rer. rustic.*, I, ii, 14, xlviii, 2, cited by Lesêtre, "Marie," *op. cit.*, col. 775.

[20] *PL*, 76, 405 and 76, 867.

[21] Bardenhewer, *op. cit.*, p. 73.

alteration of Jerome's text was really a *felix culpa*. To it we owe some of Christendom's most beautiful tributes to Our Lady. It suffices to mention the hymn *Ave Maris Stella* (ninth century) and St. Bernard's Second Homily on the words of Lk. 1:26, "Missus est."

The great Scholastic Doctors, Albertus Magnus, Thomas Aquinas, Bonaventure, accept without question the interpretations current in their day, which were derived from Jerome's work. Thus St. Thomas in his *Expositio super Angelica Salutatione* (cap. 6, 7, 8) explains Mary's name as "illuminatrix," "domina," "stella maris." St. Bonaventure gives the meanings "mare amarum," "stella," "domina" (e.g., *Comment. in Luc 1:17*).

THE MODERN PERIOD. SIXTEENTH AND SUBSEQUENT CENTURIES

The revival of Hebraic studies, which accompanied the Renaissance, led to a more critical appraisal of the meanings assigned to Our Lady's name. The author of the lexicon of proper names in the *Complutensis Polyglott* offered two new interpretations, "magistra sive doctrix maris" and "exaltata."[22] The first would derive Our Lady's name from *Môreh* (the hiphil participle of the verb *Yārāh*, which in the hiphil has the meaning "to teach") and *Yām*. Aside from the difficulty of explaining the origin of Mir from Môr, the meaning obtained seems meaningless. What is a "teacher of the sea"?

Angelus Caninius embraced enthusiastically the interpretation "exaltata." He regarded *Miryām* as a noun formed from the verb *Rwm* (to be high) and the very common preformant M.[23] Cornelius a Lapide accepts this interpretation in his commentary on Ecclus.

---

[22] In the appendix of the fifth volume, which contains "interpretationes ... nominum N.T." cited by Bardenhewer, *op. cit.*, p. 122, also by E. Vogt, S.J., *De nominis Mariae etymologia*, in *Verbum Domini*, Vol. 26 (1948), p. 164.

[23] *De locis S. Scripturae hebraicis, Angeli Caninii commentarius*, (Antverpiae, 1600), pp. 63-64. Roschini (*op. cit.*, p. 64), who, like the present author, probably depends on Bardenhewer for this citation, erroneously attributes this work to St. Peter Canisius.

43:7, and the great exegete Estius finds it "not displeasing."[24] But the exegetes and philologists generally rejected it on the grounds that a substantive formed from the root *Rwm* would be vocalized *Mārôm*, not *Miryām* or even *Maryām*, like *Mākôm* a quite frequent noun in the Old Testament derived from *Qwm*.[25] In fact *Mārôm* (height) is a common noun in the Old Testament. But in 1948 E. Vogt, S.J., the present rector of the Pontifical Biblical Institute, adduced some very telling arguments in favor of this etymology.[26] From the root *Dyn* (to judge) are derived two nouns meaning "strife," *Mādôn*, the usual form, and *Midyān*, a rare form. Philologically, therefore, the derivation of Miryām from Rwm is probable. Now the celebrated Ugaritic tablets, discovered at Ras Shamrah from 1929 through 1936, offer new and striking evidence in favor of this derivation. In this ancient Canaanite literature (mythological epics, religious poems, and sacrificial ritual in a language closely akin to Hebrew) there occurs a word MRYM used both as a noun and an adjective and identical in derivation and meaning with the Hebrew word *Mārôm*, "height." According to C. H. Gordon, who painstakingly worked out a grammar of this ancient Canaanite language, *MRYM* probably should be vocalized *Maryam(u)* or *Miraym(u)*.[27] The Ras Shamrah tablets date from the fourteenth century B.C. and so are contemporaneous with Moses and his sister Mary. Old Testament names like *Kelāl*, "perfection," "the perfect one" (1 Esdras 10:30) and Mib ār, "election," "the chosen one" (1 Par. 11:38), show that Hebrew parents did express their joy in their newborn children by conferring very flattering titles as names. Certainly "Highness" or "The Exalted One" is an appropriate name for Our Blessed Lady, who has been lifted by grace above all creatures, even the highest Seraphim.

St. Peter Canisius offers a number of meanings, e.g., "exaltata"

---

[24] *Annotationes in praecipua ac difficiliora S. Scripturae loca*, 1621, p. 479 b, in Lk. 1:27, cited by Vogt, *art. cit.*, p. 164.

[25] Bardenhewer, *op. cit.*, p. 125. Merkelbach, *op. cit.*, p. 104, observes that Van Hoonacker suggests a root Rûm with the meaning "to desire" like the Arabic Rama, as the source of Mary's name. In view of the silence of the lexicons it is pure conjecture to attribute such a meaning to the Hebrew root.

[26] Vogt, *art. cit.*, pp. 164-166.

[27] C. H. Gordon, *Ugaritic Grammar* (Romae, 1940), pp. 44, 103.

and "rebellio" (from the root *Mārāh*). But above all he endeavored to give the beloved *Stella Maris* a solid philological basis. He derives Mary's name from the verb *Heîr* and *Yām*. Apparently he has in mind the hiphil participle *Mē'îr* of the verb *'ôr*. This etymology is no more successful than the ancient φωτίζουσα.[28]

Cornelius a Lapide commenting on Exod. 15:20 rejects the Massoretic vocalization. *Maryām*, he thinks, is the original form of the name. It means either *"amaritudo maris"* (from Mar the construct of the noun *Mārāh* and *Yām*) or *"Magistra aut Domina maris."*

Christopher Vega, S.J., offered an original interpretation, *"domina diei"* or *"domina cribri,"* deriving the name from the Aramaic *Mar* (Lord) and *Yām (Yôm)* meaning "day," or *Yām* meaning "sieve."[29]

At the beginning of the eighteenth century Matthew Hiller proposed the interpretation "the rebellious" or "the contumacious," deriving Mary from *Merî* (rebellion) from the verb *Mārāh*.[30] The final Am of Our Lady's name he held to be simply a termination used in the formation of nouns. (*Mem intensivum* he called it.) Philologically there is no objection to this etymology. The meaning is also quite apt for the sister of Moses, who murmured against her brother in the desert. But such an interpretation could hardly be applied to Our Blessed Lady.[31]

Gesenius, the master of Hebrew lexicographers, in the first edition of his celebrated *Neues hebräisch-deutsches Handwörterbuch* identified the name Mary with the form *Miryām* (their rebellion) of Neh. 9:17. The name would be composed of the noun Merî and the third plural pronominal suffix am. In later editions Gesenius silently adopted Hiller's interpretation, explaining am as a substantive

---

[28] St. Peter Canisius, *op. cit.*, pp. 2-5.

[29] Christophorus de Vega, S.J., *Theologia Mariana*, Pars II (Lugduni, 1653), pp. 85-114.

[30] M. Hiller, *Onomasticum Sacrum* (Tübingen, 1706), pp. 173, 876, 886. As early as 1577 St. Peter Canisius had proposed Marah as the root of Mary's name. Cf. above, note 28.

[31] Roschini's attempt to apply this meaning to Our Lady seems very arbitrary and farfetched, op. cit., p. 64.

termination (*Ein Bildungszusatz*).[32]

In 1856 P. Schegg in his commentary on Matthew's Gospel proposed the verb *Mārā'* (to be fat) as the root of Our Lady's name. Arguing that to the Semitic eye a "well-developed," even a corpulent woman was beautiful, he gave as the meaning of Mary's name "the beautiful one." With Hiller and Gesenius he considers the final am of Mary's name a simple denominative termination.[33] Like Hiller's this etymology, from the viewpoint of philology, is probable. Normally, however, a noun formed from *Mārā'* with the aid of the termination am would be *Mir'ām*, not *Miryām*. While Aleph can be changed to Yod in certain cases, there is no proof that pronounced consonantal Aleph, following a consonant and preceding a vowel, can be changed to pronounced consonantal Yod.[34] Moreover, is it true that corpulency was associated with beauty in the Semitic mind? In Hebrew literature there is no example of the root *Mārā'* meaning "beauty." But quite a few authors have accepted Schegg's interpretation (e.g., Fürst, Gildmeister, Bardenhewer, Lesêtre, Janssens, Scheeben).[35] "The Beautiful" is certainly an appropriate name for her who was immaculately conceived and endowed with grace and holiness surpassing that of the highest angels, and who, in all probability, was also physically the most beautiful of the daughters of Eve. *Tota pulchra es, Maria!* In this interpretation the angel's greeting to Our Lady, Χαῖρε κεχαριτωμένη, *Ave gratia plena*, would express aptly the meaning of her holy name (Lk. 1:28).

Is Mary an Egyptian name? May not Mary, born in Egypt, have received an Egyptian name as did her brothers Moses and Aaron? Father Francis Zorell, S.J., proposed the hypothesis that the name *Miryām* is a composite word made up of the perfect passive

---

[32] Cf. Gesenius, *Neues hebräisch-deutsches Handwörterbuch*, also *Thesaurus philologicus criticus linguae hebreae et chaldaeae veteris Testamenti*, Editio Altera (Lipsiae, 1835-1839), Vol. 2, p. 819.

[33] P. Schegg, *Die heiligen Evangelien übersetzt and erklärt, Vol. 1, Evangelium nach Matthäus* (München, 1856), p. 419; also *Jacobus der Bruder des Herrn* (München, 1882), p. 56.

[34] Vogt, *art. cit.*, p. 167.

[35] C. Beckermann, O.S.A., *Et nomen Virginis Maria, Verbum Domini*, Vol. 1, (1921), pp. 130-136, gives arguments contra; Bardenhewer, *op. cit.*, pp. 147-151, gives the arguments pro, the association of beauty and corpulence.

participle of the Egyptian verb *mr* (to love), i.e., merî(t) and the Hebrew divine name *Yām* (i.e., *Yahweh*, as in *Abiam* for *Abi-yahu*). The holy name Mary would therefore have the most appropriate meaning, "The Beloved of God."[36]

Father Roschini, O.S.M., embraces Zorell's etymology as "most probable, not to say certain" (*probabilissima, ne dicamus certa*).[37] Moses is certainly an Egyptian name, and the name Aaron, which cannot be explained from the Hebrew, is probably also of Egyptian origin. It is possible that their sister also received an Egyptian name. But Roschini's argument that the name Mary would have occurred frequently in the Old Testament if it were of Hebrew origin is not at all convincing. Such a typically Hebrew name as Jacob is also unique in the Old Testament. Granted that Mary is an Egyptian name, the derivation from *Merî-Yām* is by no means established. Moses' sister presumably was named shortly after birth. Did the Hebrews in Egypt know then that God's name is Yahweh? Did not God reveal His name to men for the first time, when, many years after Mary's birth, He spoke to Moses out of the burning bush? (Exod. 6:2-3.) Zorell himself later called his hypothesis "doubtful." Since merî when transcribed in Assyrian (a Semitic language) becomes mai and in Greek appears as μι, the R being lost in transcription, the derivation of Miryam from this word is very questionable.[38]

Conclusion: The evidence available today is preponderantly in favor of the meaning "Highness" or "The Exalted One." *Miryām* has all the appearance of a genuine Hebrew name, and no solid reason has been adduced to warrant rejecting the Semitic origin of the word. Father Zorell turned to the Egyptian only because he despaired of finding a satisfactory explanation according to the known rules of Hebrew morphology. Had the grammarians and exegetes known the *Ras Shamrah* literature with its striking argument in favor of the derivation of *Miryām* from *Rwm*, there is no doubt that they would have embraced wholeheartedly this

---

[36] F. Zorell, S.J., *Was bedeutet der Name Maria? in Zeitschr. für Kathol. Theol.*, 30 (1906), pp. 356-360.

[37] Roschini, *op. cit.*, p. 65.

[38] F. Zorell, S.J., *Lexicon Graecum Novi Testamenti*, Editio Altera (Parisiis, 1931), col. 798.

etymology first proposed by Cardinal Ximenes' *Polyglott.*[39] Once again twentieth-century archaeology has supplied the key to a satisfactory solution of a centuries-old problem. The sweet name of Mary expresses fittingly the dignity and glory of the Mother of God and the Queen of all creation. She is "Highness," "The Exalted One."

Probably it were better, however, if Mariologists ceased searching exclusively for the reasons of God's choice of Our Lady's name in the etymology of the word, and looked for them rather in the relation of Mary (as antitype) to the sister of Moses. In view of the inferior position of women in ancient society the role of Moses' sister in the history of the Exodus is remarkable. She is a prophetess who supports the Liberator in his great work of freeing Israel from the Egyptian bondage. (Cf. the words of God in Mich. 6:4, "For I brought thee out of the land of Egypt, and delivered thee out of the house of slaves, and I sent before thy face Moses, and Aaron, and Mary.") The sister of Moses is an apt type of Mary, the *Alma Socia Redemptoris, the coadjutrix* of her divine Son in the liberation of mankind from the slavery of sin and the bondage of Satan.[40] May not God have inspired the parents of Our Lady to call their infant daughter after the sister of Moses, in order to indicate her mission in the Redemption of mankind?

LAUS DEO ET VIRGINI IMMACULATÆ EIUS.

---

[39] Cf. Vogt, *art. cit.,* p. 167.

[40] Mary's murmuring against Moses does not disqualify her as a type of Our Blessed Lady. The relation between type and antitype is never perfect. David and Solomon are types of Christ Our Lord and King, in spite of the adultery and murder of the one, and the profligacy of the other.